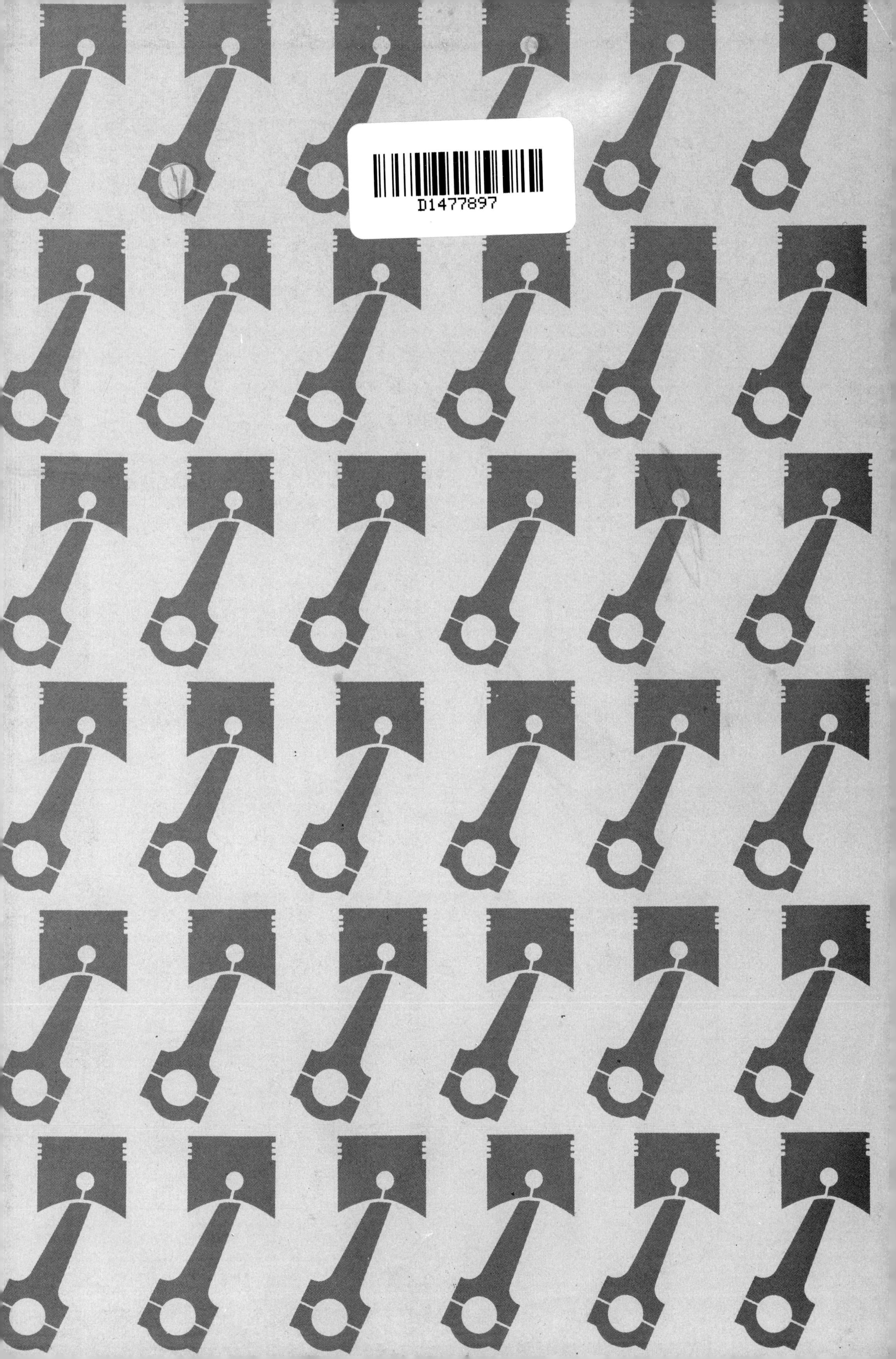

£3.50

The TOTAL book of CAR IMPROVEMENTS AND ACCESSORIES

The TOTAL book of

CAR IMPROVEMENTS AND ACCESSORIES

Marshall Cavendish
London & Sydney

Editor: Eden Phillips
Art Editor: Graham Beehag
Designers: Jonathan Alden
Jane Turton

Published by Marshall Cavendish Books Limited
58 Old Compton Street
London W1V 5PA

First published: 1980

Most of the material in this book was first published by Marshall Cavendish Limited in the partwork *On The Road*

Printed in Great Britain

ISBN 0 85685 764 5

Introduction

Apart from a house, a car is likely to be the most expensive single purchase of a lifetime. Why not care for it as you do for your home? *The Total Book of Car Improvements and Accessories* contains all the advice necessary to glamorize the car's exterior, make the interior comfortable and safe, and to uprate the engine and improve its performance.

A team of motoring writers, all experts in their fields, have combined to produce a book which encompasses a vast range of improvements – all of them explained by clear step-by-step procedures and full-colour photographs. Even the motorist who has never attempted any d-i-y work will find a wealth of easy to follow information to make his car look better, handle better and maintain its secondhand value. For the more experienced mechanic there are chapters on the subtleties of engine tuning, and fitting meters and gauges. The book is designed to stimulate the imagination of all car owners, presenting a scope of ideas from how to choose a hi-fi system to what to look for in a scrap yard.

For anyone who thinks that a car is more than just a means of getting from A to B, *The Total Book of Car Improvements and Accessories* points the way to running a vehicle that is fun to drive, stylish to look at, and above all, a valuable investment.

Contents

Part 1 Inside the car

Part 2 Outside the car

Part 3 Improving the engine

Part 1

Inside the car

Choosing a car radio

Long distance driving can become very tedious, especially if you are travelling alone, but one way to alleviate the monotony is to fit a radio into your car. On shorter, round-town journeys, a radio can be just as entertaining and can be a valuable source of advance warning of congestion on the roads ahead. There is a bewildering selection of radios on the accessory market but, with care, most car owners should be able to choose a unit to suit their particular requirements and their individual budget.

With cheaper radios you may find that sound reception becomes weaker as you travel further from the site of the transmitting station and that they are unable to reproduce the original sound without undesirable interference. The more expensive radios, however, can reproduce the original sound very clearly because they are equipped with powerful amplifiers and circuitry that is designed to cut out most interference. However, interference will remain a problem, even with expensive equipment, unless you also use a good aerial (see pages 18 to 22). These are all factors that you should bear in mind when you make your decision about which unit to buy (fig. 1).

Choosing a unit to suit your car

Most cars use a 12 volt electrical system though a few, such as the Volkswagen 1200, use a 6 volt system. Car radios are not generally interchangeable from one system to the other so check in your vehicle's handbook, if you do not already know, to find out which system is used on your car. As well as checking the voltage of the electrical system, check its polarity to see whether it has a positive or negative-earth. Looking at the battery will enable you to determine the polarity. If the positive terminal is connected to the car's body which acts as the earth, then your car has a positive earth and vice versa. The final point to consider is the amount of space available in your car to fit the radio.

Most radios are designed to the German DIN (see below) size of 180 mm ($7\frac{1}{8}$ins) wide by 44 mm ($1\frac{3}{4}$ins) high by 150 mm (6ins) deep and there is usually an opening behind a removable panel on the car's fascia that is of similar size into which the radio can be fitted. In a few isolated cases, however, radio manufacturers may vary the size of their designs, so check the measurements carefully to make sure that you actually have room to fit the unit of your choice. If you have a centre console fitted to your car (see pages 35 to 41) you may be able to fit a radio into it but the above conditions will still apply. If you are going to mount the radio under the fascia, the size will not be so important unless the unit interferes with any other components. Also, you should position it with safety in mind as in an accident severe injury can be caused by a badly sited radio.

Once you know the voltage and the polarity of your car (see page 23) and the amount of space you have in which the radio can be fitted, you can move on to investigate the basic features which will influence your choice of unit.

Waveband coverage

Most car radios are capable of receiving programmes broadcast on the Medium Waveband (MW) and the Long Waveband (LW), while a few, which are usually the more expensive models, can also receive broadcasts transmitted at Very High Frequency (VHF). Some of the cheaper radios can, in theory, receive VHF broadcasts though in

1 Offering varying qualities of signal reproduction, in either mono or stereo, and different types of tuning controls but all contained in the same size of casing, these radios exemplify the necessity of knowing just what to look, and listen for when buying in-car entertainment equipment. The radios in this small selection from the many units available bear, from top to bottom, the brand names of Clarion, Radiomobile (two units), National Panasonic, Sanyo, Blaupunkt (two units) and Hitachi (two units)

Peter Dazeley

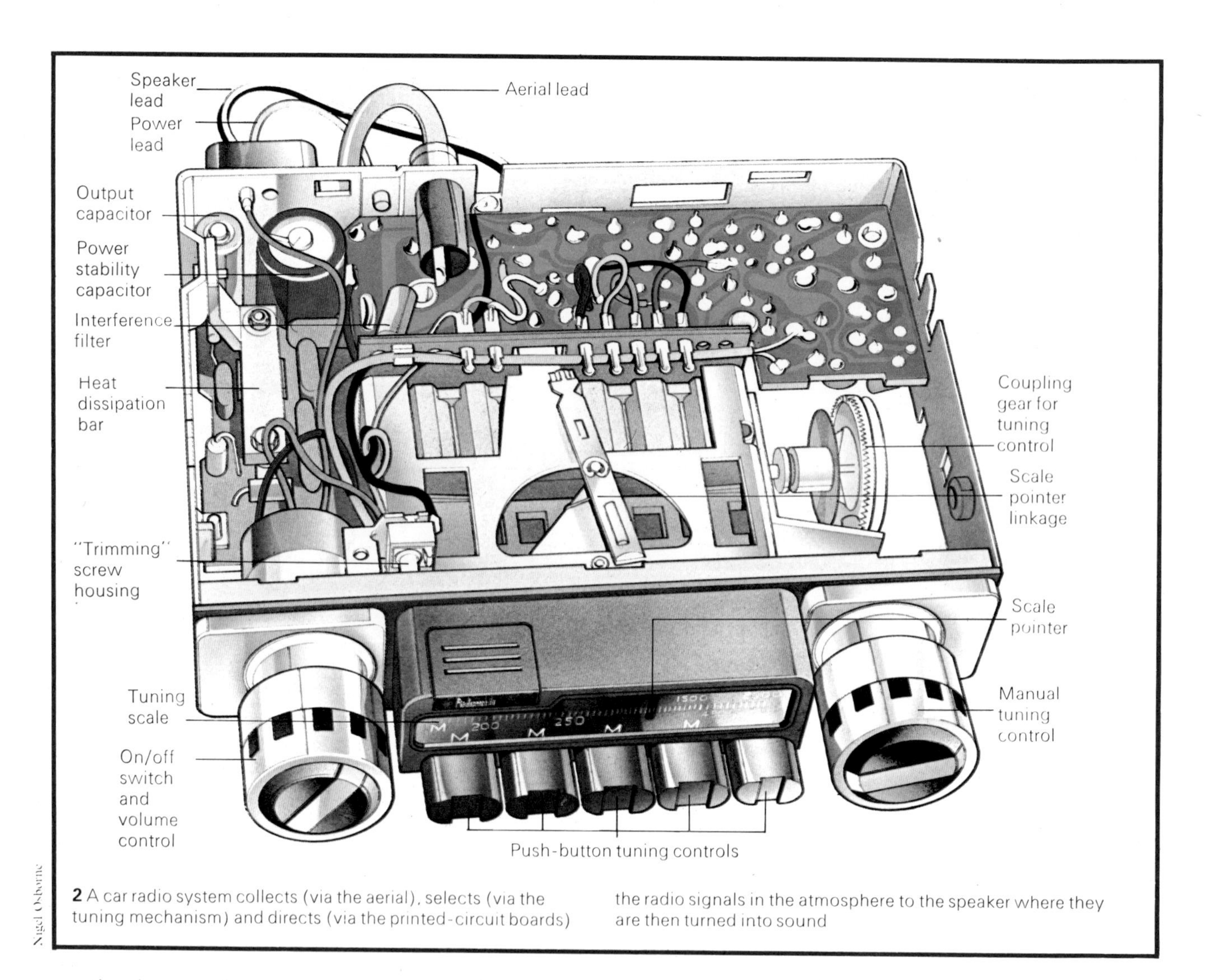

Nigel Osborne

2 A car radio system collects (via the aerial), selects (via the tuning mechanism) and directs (via the printed-circuit boards) the radio signals in the atmosphere to the speaker where they are then turned into sound

practice they are often unable to do so due to the shielding effects of buildings, trees and the terrain of the countryside. If you can afford one of the more expensive radios which does receive VHF, you will find that signal reproduction is much clearer than on the other wavebands.

Apart from being able to receive the various wavebands, most modern radios can be tuned or "trimmed" to suit the design of aerial used on the car. A radio should be able to reproduce the signals clearly. The cheaper radios, however, do not always do this as they often have poor selectivity as well as poor sensitivity. The *sensitivity* of a unit refers to the numbers of stations it can receive and the *selectivity* refers to whether a radio can separate one station from another when they broadcast on similar frequencies. Poor selectivity is particularly noticeable after dark because radio signals travel further then and the set will have more signals with which to cope. When selecting a radio, look to see if the specification mentions a tuned RF stage (see below) as this is a device that will help to eliminate both poor sensitivity and poor selectivity.

Power output

The power output of a radio unit refers to the power that is available through the loudspeaker(s) and is quoted in watts. A low rating will mean that a set will have to work close to its maximum volume level for most of the time, thereby risking the introduction of distortion into the reproduced signal. This is a failing that afflicts many car radios, particularly the lower-priced models. If you are to hear the set comfortably in a moving car then only radios with a minimum output of 5watts should be considered, a higher rating being advantageous. Problems of low output can be overcome by adding a booster amplifier and high-power speakers, which will also improve the quality of the sound, but this will increase the cost and you will probably be better off buying a more expensive radio to begin with.

Buying speakers

Apart from one or two units, when you buy most car radios you will have to buy the speakers separately. These should be chosen to match the radio in terms of power or you will ruin them the first time you use the radio on anything other than a low volume. The car radio dealer or the radio manufacturer should be able to tell you which speakers are recommended for which radios. See also pages 24 to 26 for additional information.

Tuning choice

The last major factor to influence your choice of radio is whether the unit can be tuned manually or by push-button selection of stations (figs. 2 and 3). Some inexpensive sets are offered in both formats with little other difference between them, except for the price. User convenience dictates that push-button tuning, as opposed to manual tuning only, should take preference as your most popular stations can then be selected simply by pressing the appropriate button. Most receivers have five buttons. Four for the medium waveband and one for the long waveband is the most common combination, although other permutations such as three medium and two long, or one medium, one long and three for FM on a VHF/FM set are other possibilities.

Push-button systems on car radios use mechanical

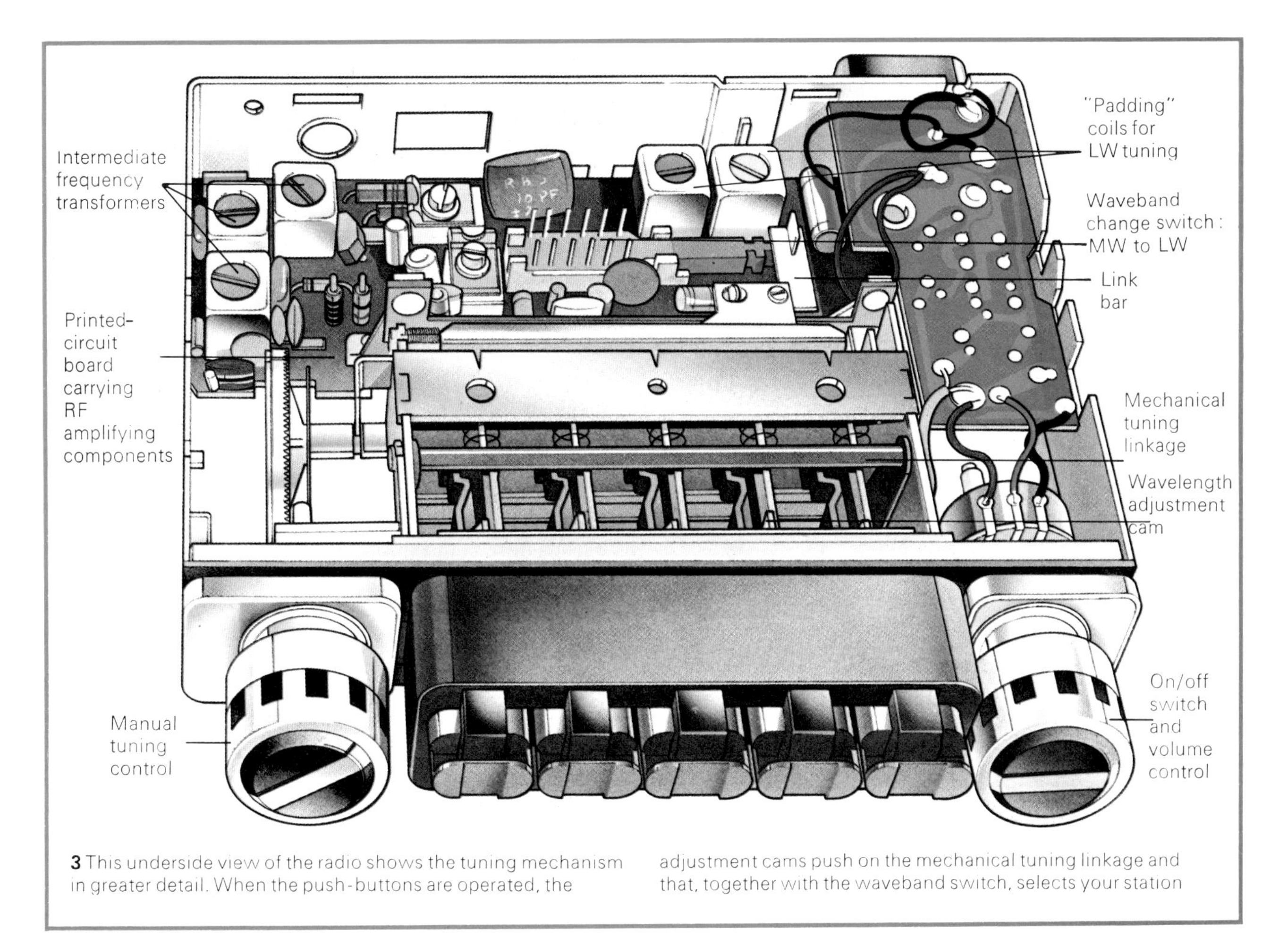

3 This underside view of the radio shows the tuning mechanism in greater detail. When the push-buttons are operated, the adjustment cams push on the mechanical tuning linkage and that, together with the waveband switch, selects your station

linkages to adjust the tuner and move the scale pointer and they are simple to set. The radio should first be tuned, using the manual knob, to a required station. Then one of the buttons appropriate to that waveband must be pulled outwards to release the linkage and then pushed fully home. The buttons also switch the wavebands. By pressing the long waveband button you automatically select that band and the station to which it has been set; pressing any one of the medium waveband buttons selects the relevant station on the medium waveband.

When you go to buy your radio, or if you read any of the manufacturers' literature beforehand, it is quite likely that you will be confronted with a mass of technical terms completely unfamiliar to you and therefore meaningless. Listed below are not only some of the more common terms but also some of those that you will encounter if you intend to buy a radio from the more expensive end of the market.

AM: This is an abbreviation of Amplitude Modulation and is used on medium, long and short wavebands. It is a signal imposed on the carrier wave used in radio broadcasting which varies the instantaneous amplitude of the carrier wave. The radio in your car then subtracts the carrier frequency from this signal which leaves the required signal free for amplification.

AFC: Standing for Automatic Frequency Control, this circuit is used on radios capable of receiving VHF signals in order to counteract "drift" and to hold the signal steady. This will usually be combined with ATC (Automatic Tuning Control) which helps to keep your radio tuned to the same station all of the time.

Balance Control: This is a variable potentiometer, or switch, fitted to stereo receivers to adjust the balance of the volume between the left and right-hand speakers.

Carrier: Audio signals are carried through space in the form of radio waves by a high-frequency oscillation known as a carrier wave.

DIN: Deutsche Industrie Norm. This is a German industrial standards board equivalent to the British Standards Institution.

ETC: Electronic Tuning Control achieves a similar result to ATC but uses a different method.

FM: Frequency Modulation of signals transmitted at VHF. This is between 88 MHz and 100 MHz for broadcasting purposes. In this particular case the imposed signal varies the carrier frequency.

IAC: Philips' patented Interference Absorption Circuit which effectively eliminates aerial-borne interference with FM reception. Basically the circuit constitutes an ultra high-speed electronic switching device which removes interference and prevents it being passed to the amplifying stages in the receiver. Other manufacturers using similar circuits employ their own terms, such as: ASU (automatic suppression unit); ISC (interference suppression circuit); AIR (automatic interference rejection); EIA (electronic interference absorption and PNL (Pioneer noise limiter) used by Pioneer. Several employ the Philips' design which is manufactured under licence.

IC: Integrated-Circuit. This is a semi-conductor assembly performing a number of electronic functions which would normally require many individual transistors and other components.

LW: Long Waveband.

MW: Medium Waveband.

SW: Short Waveband.

Note: In Australia, the Medium Waveband is termed AM and the Long Waveband FM. Most Australian-made and Japanese imported radios offer AM/FM.

Tuned RF Stage: RF is an abbreviation of Radio Frequency

and represents the broad spectrum of incoming radio signals. When tuned to the frequency of a required station, sensitivity and selectivity are improved.
Watt: A unit used to indicate the sound energy produced.

The market
Although there is a wide range of radios on the market, the following is a selection from the ranges of some of the better known manufacturers and importers. Unless it is stated to the contrary, you will have to purchase speakers separately (see page 16).
Audioline: Audioline offer a range of five sets including manual tuning and push-button MW/LW models and others adding FM in mono and stereo. The three models featuring FM also have push-button tuning and are equipped with "noise-killer" circuits. Audio output of the mono units is 6watts, with 6watts per channel for the FM stereo receivers. All models have fully-variable tone controls.
Binatone: This company market three inexpensive mono models at prices which include the cost of a speaker. The Thunderbird is a MW/LW set with manual tuning; the Pacific Mk. II is a push-button equivalent while the Lotus Mk. II also covers FM (mono) but does not include "noise-killer" circuitry. Output is on the low side at 2watts but the range may appeal to the budget conscious buyer.
Bird: Made in Poole, England, the Kestrel is a manual tuning MW/LW receiver with a simple top-cut tone control. The Merlin and Harrier models are similar but with push-button tuning and variable tone controls, the latter also has a power feed for an electric aerial. Output is 5watts in each case. The fourth unit, the Hawk, is a MW/LW/FM stereo push-button tuning model with provision for an electric aerial and an output of 5watts per channel.
Blaupunkt: In the UK you can purchase an imported range of five models made in France, Brazil and West Germany. The least expensive model is the Hildesheim which is a manual MW/LW receiver without tone control. The Hamburg is similar in specification but has push-button tuning and a variable tone control as do the remaining models in the range. The Santos, which comes from Brazil, is a manual set and covers the medium waveband plus seven short wave ranges. It is the only Blaupunkt radio without a connector for an electric aerial. The two remaining sets have push-button tuning, the Nurnberg catering for the MW, LW and FM bands in mono and the Frankfurt in stereo, with the addition of the short wave 49 metre band. All models have outputs of 5watts except the Frankfurt which has 5watts per channel. Both of the FM models have ASU "noise-killer" circuits.
Clarion: Clarion offer one model only. The RE378K is a MW/LW receiver with three push-buttons for the medium waveband and two for long wave. It has a variable tone control and a 5watts output.
Hitachi: This company markets three MW/LW receivers. One has manual tuning without a tone control and the other two are push-button units with variable tone. The difference between the latter two is that one has the additional facilities of dual polarity and provision for an electric aerial but both have tuned RF stages. Output is 5watts.
Lucas: Lucas make two identical sets that cover the medium and long wavebands. The sole difference is that one unit has manual tuning and the other is tuned by push-buttons. Each has a tuned RF stage, variable tone control, an output of 6watts and a connector for an electric aerial.
Motoradio: Motoradio offer three models. The only difference between two of the car units, both MW/LW, is that one has push-button tuning. The third model, the FM900S, is a MW/LW/FM stereo push-button receiver with a "noise-killer" circuit on FM and a top-cut tone control replaces the variable control used on the lower priced models. All three of the radios have a connector for an electric aerial. The output is 6watts on the basic models and 4.5watts per channel on the FM900S.
Motorola: British-made like the Bird, Lucas and Motoradio models, the Motorola series offers a range of five quality radios. Models 154 and 144 differ in that the 154 has manual tuning only and the 144 has push-buttons. They have variable tone controls and tuned RF stages. Model 142 is similar to the 144 but has a higher output of 8watts through two speakers. Models 145 and 146 are MW/LW/FM units, the former in mono FM with five push-buttons and the latter in stereo with six push-buttons. Both have "noise-killer" circuits on FM, variable tone controls and outputs of 5watts and 5watts per channel respectively.
National Panasonic: The CR462 is the only model in the car radio category from this company. It is a MW/LW push-button set with variable tone control, tuned RF stage, a connector for an electric aerial and an output of 5watts.
Philips: This company markets five car radios made in its own factories in Singapore and France. The least expensive, the AN162, is a manually tuned MW/LW unit without tone control while the similar AN361 has push-buttons and a variable tone control. The AN561 will appeal if you do not require long wave coverage as it provides only for medium waves and mono FM with manual tuning but without a tone control. Models AN783 and AN883 are push-button tuned MW/LW/FM receivers, the 783 being FM mono and the latter FM stereo. Naturally all Philips' FM sets incorporate their own IAC, the complete range having tuned RF circuits and 5watts output stages, except for the stereo model which has 5watts per channel.
Pioneer: Marketing only one car radio, Pioneer has a reputation for quality but the company's products are expensive. The GX3300 is a push-button unit covering the MW/LW frequencies with FM in stereo. Additional features of this radio are the PNS "noise-killer" circuit, variable tone control, tuned RF stage, an electric aerial connector and an output of 5watts per channel.
Radiomobile: One of the best known names in the UK in-car entertainment market, Radiomobile has a nine model range of interesting car radios. Between them they cover almost every permutation of waveband coverage with manual tuning and push-buttons. Most models have variable tone controls and all employ tuned RF stages. The two FM models, one mono and the other stereo, have "noise-killer" circuits and outputs across the range are 7.5watts and upwards and 7.5watts per channel for the 1190FM stereo model. An exception to the general run is the 1180, a push-button MW/LW unit having an input for a stereo cassette player and twin 7.5watts output stages to give stereo reproduction from tape.

Several car manufacturers have also entered the car radio field in one form or another. If you own a Ford, you can purchase a radio marketed through Ford dealers which has been designed and styled specifically for this company's products, though the units can easily be fitted to other car manufacturers' models. Similar marketing operations are carried out by Unipart (BL) and Chrysler.

Obviously, with the wide choice of radios that is open to you choosing any particular one and saying it is the best for your requirements is very difficult. However, if you visit one of the many car radio stockists which exhibits as wide a range as possible and listen to some of those on display, you should be able to make an informed decision.

Cassettes and speakers

A tape player, radio or combination of the two is one car accessory which really can make driving more pleasant. Some form of in-car entertainment (ICE) can also make an important contribution to driving safety—by keeping you awake on long, tiring journeys. The ideal set-up to have is a combined radio/tape stereo system which gives you a wide choice of listening. Understandably though, units like this are expensive and may not even be necessary if your car already has a radio fitted as standard.

This leaves you with a choice between a tape player and a radio (see pages 9 to 12). With the former you will get your own personal choice of listening and none of the problems traditionally associated with fitting a radio—buying the aerial (pages 18 to 22) and supressing the ignition. You may also be able to take advantage of the large discounts often given on tape playing equipment.

Another reason why many people choose a tape player rather than a combined tape/radio unit is ease of maintenance. Integrated car stereo systems are complicated machines and if one part of the unit fails the whole system must be taken out to be repaired, leaving you, temporarily at least, with no in-car entertainment at all. Bear in mind though that separate units are only practical if there is enough space in the car; on some smaller models space is often at a premium.

Although fitting a tape player is a relatively straightforward DIY job, buying one is by no means as simple. The last few years have seen a boom in the ICE industry with the result that the tape equipment market has become quite confusing for the potential buyer.

To begin with, there is the problem of price. The cost of tape players varies sharply and is not always a reflection of their quality and sophistication. The thing to do is to decide how much you want to pay before starting to look and then search for the best value. Stick to your decision and do not be talked into paying more than you have already decided to.

With your price limit fixed, you can now consider what kind of features you require in a tape player. To some extent price will restrict you, but you should not be tempted by an apparently cheap unit which does not fit your requirements exactly. Details of what to look for are outlined below.

When you have more or less decided on a suitable model you will come to the next problem—where to buy. Car tape equipment can be found in a variety of different places from the large discount store or mail order house, through the smaller electrical shop to the car accessory dealer. Unfortunately, there are no rules about where the best value is to be found. Tape players, like other electrical goods, are often heavily discounted; by how much depends on the retailer. Bargains can often be found in the most unlikely places so it is advisable to spend some time comparing prices before you commit yourself. Try all the different sources and do not hurry. Buying at Christmas time should be avoided.

One point worth bearing in mind is after-sales service. Tape players, like other machines, can often go wrong. You may consider it worth paying a bit more in order to get your equipment from a reputable dealer who can offer a full guarantee and back-up.

Another thing to remember when you actually come to

Nigel Messett

Rolls-Royce Motors Ltd./Peter Dazeley

1 Rolls-Royce fit separate tape players and radios as standard in their cars. The tape player shown here is a Blaupunkt Frankfurt and it is unusual because it has no amplifier of its own. Instead it makes use of the one in the compatible radio unit above

buy a tape player is that it will not perform without speakers. Make sure you know whether or not they are included in the price as they are costly items to buy separately.

Finally, do not forget to tell retailers if your car has a positive earth electrical system (see page 23). Otherwise you may irreparably damage your new machine and invalidate the guarantee.

Buying second-hand

You will always be able to find plenty of tape players on the second-hand market but the risks of buying a used unit generally outweigh the cheaper purchase price. For a start you have no means of redress if the machine goes wrong or does not work. Furthermore, if it is an obsolete model you may not be able to get spare parts to repair it and you will also miss the information and fitting instructions which accompany all brand-new products. Unless you are absolutely sure that you know what you are getting it always pays to buy new.

Cassettes and cartridges

When car tape players were first introduced there were two different systems available—the cassette and the cartridge. Nowadays, cartridge tape players have virtually disappeared from the market and the supply of cartridge tapes to suit them is rapidly dwindling. This leaves the cassette system as the only sensible choice to make.

The reason for this is that cartridges have several disadvantages although it has been said that manufacturers, realizing the fact, discontinued their cartridge systems at a time when they were still popular, thereby influencing public demand. Cassettes are less bulky and they can be produced with a longer playing time than cartridges—which rarely exceed a total playing time of sixty minutes.

Whereas cartridges once gave better sound quality, improvements in the design and manufacture of cassettes and cassette players have more than redressed the balance. Cartridge players were originally designed with in-car uses in mind and the fact that you simply push them into the machine for continuous play once made them ideal for a driver who needed to keep his hands on the wheel. Modern cassette players, however, incorporate these features and many of them have the additional benefit of a fast wind/rewind mechanism. This enables you to select a particular track or song without waiting for the tape to play right the way through. Some cassettes have an auto-reverse mechanism which means that you can play both sides without the need to change the cassette and without the risk of being annoyingly and dangerously distracted.

Perhaps the most important reason for the demise of the cartridge is the almost universal adoption of the cassette type of system in household stereo and portable tape recorders. This, coupled with the ability to record your own material, gives you more flexibility than a cartridge could ever offer.

Power output

A major feature to consider when you are buying a tape player is power output. Confusion often arises over this point because buying a powerful machine does not just mean having the ability to play it at a higher volume. The sound quality will probably be better too, providing you also have a good set of speakers (see page 16).

The power output of tape players is rated in watts. In-car systems usually have an output of between three and

Nigel Messett

2 This Roadstar tape player is a fairly simple unit but still has volume, tone and balance controls and a fast forward wind button

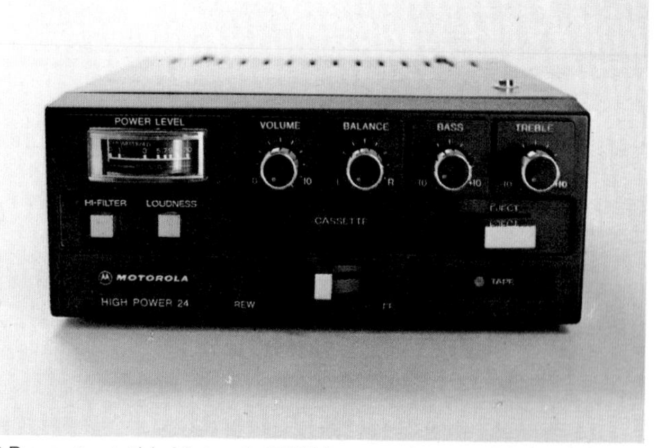

3 By contrast, this Motorola PS412 system is as sophisticated as many household cassette decks and includes a loudness switch

4 Hitachi's CS 320 cassette player is a good example of a high quality unit with button-type play and forward wind switches

5 The CS 370 unit is similar but has the added sophistication of a sliding forward/reverse switch and a programme control

seven watts per channel with the majority between the three to four level. Because the number of transistors in a machine normally dictates its wattage and because these components are expensive, it follows that powerful tape players are generally more costly. This is not always the case, but you should be wary of cheap models with more than five watts output per channel. The manufacturers may have saved money by cutting corners with other parts.

Technical specifications

Apart from the power output figures, a lot of other technical data is often to be found in tape player specifications. Most of it is useless to all but the audio expert, but sometimes it may help to give you some idea of the range and quality of a particular model.

The frequency response figure, which will be quoted in Herz (Hz), denotes the range of sound that the tape player can handle without distortion. On most tape players this is between 10,000 and 50,000 Hz but some stretch as low as 7,000 or as high as 125,000. Do not, however, set too much store by frequency response data because it will probably only be the claimed figure and not be actually guaranteed by the manufacturer.

"Wow" and "flutter" are two other terms which you might encounter in tape player brochures. They refer to the minute changes in speed which inevitably take place as the tape passes over the playback head. These cause momentary distortions in sound which can be quite noticeable. The modern tape player has been developed so that wow and flutter is kept to a minimum—normally in the region of 0.3 to 0.5 per cent—but be beware of older units where a much higher figure may be quoted.

Impedance (measured in ohms) refers to the electrical resistance of the amplifier circuit. If you are buying speakers separately, it is important that they match this figure (see below).

6 Sanyo's FT4020E cassette player comes complete with speakers and has push-button play, eject and fast forward wind controls

Winding mechanisms

With the most basic types of car tape players, you simply insert a cassette and leave it to play through to the end of one side. The majority of modern units, though, incorporate some form of winding mechanism to enable you to select individual tracks. In its simplest form this consists of a fast forward wind—by pressing a button or slide you run

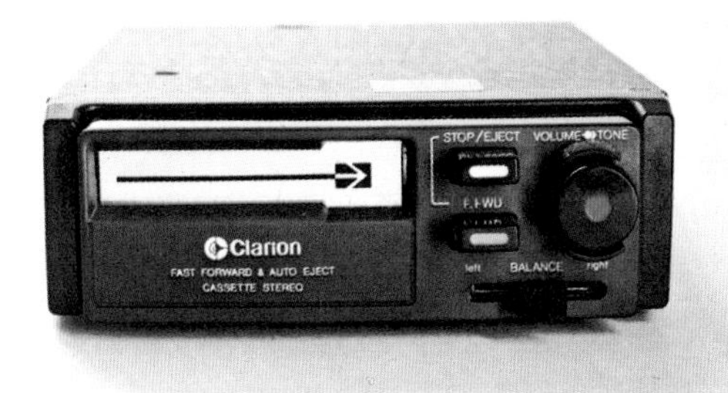

7 The Clarion PE 827A is another relatively unsophisticated tape player with simple controls. It plays and ejects automatically

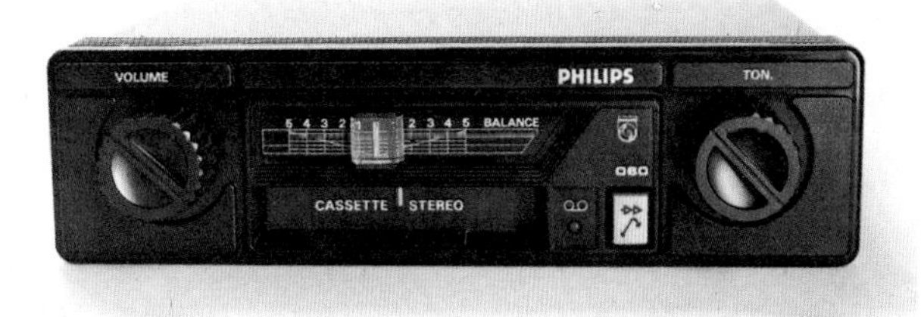

8 Simple but unusual, this Philips 22AC 060 cassette player has all the basic controls but could be mistaken for a car radio

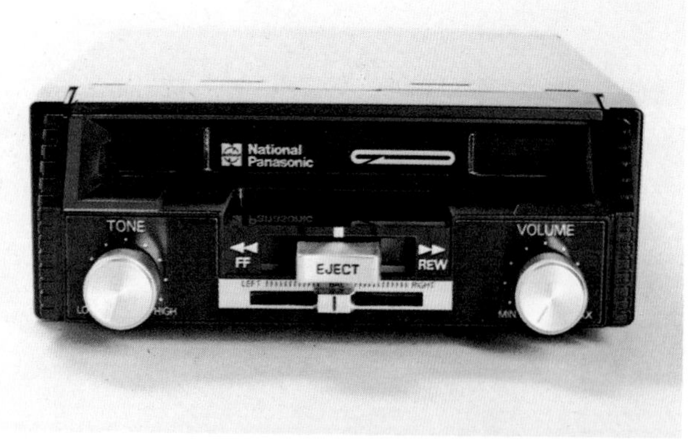

Nigel Messett

9 The National Panasonic CX 5000 tape player is a powerful unit with a 6 watts per channel output and an auto-eject mechanism

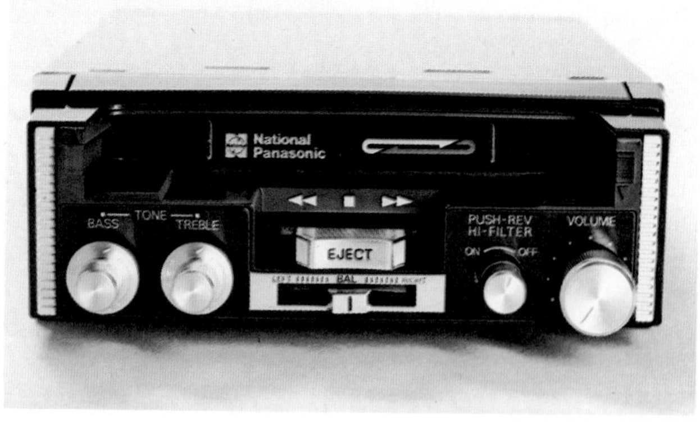

10 Panasonic's CX 7000 unit combines a similar output with extra features like a loudness filter and separate treble and bass controls

the tape on at many times its normal playing speed. The more complex units also include a rewind feature which gets rid of the need to turn the tape over in order to wind it back. The better players have locking devices so that you do not have to keep your finger on the button/slide.

Other features

Most tape players have some individual features to distinguish them from the rest, but these are only details—the controls rarely differ. A good tape player will have volume and tone controls, together with a balance control for the speakers. It should also have some form of cut-out to stop the motor when a cassette ends and many units disengage the cassette from the tape heads automatically.

Buying speakers

Speakers are among the most important components in any car tape system. The range available is growing year by year as more owners discover that a good set of speakers can make as much difference to sound quality as the tape player itself.

Some tape players are supplied with speakers and the cost of these is included in the price. With other models, a set of speakers specially designed for the player can usually be supplied separately. One advantage of buying speakers separately is that you have more freedom of choice and specification. High quality ones often offer a considerable improvement in sound over the more basic items and for that it is worth paying extra.

Your dealer should be able to give you specific advice but an important point to watch is that the player and speakers both have the same impedance. If, for instance, your tape player has an impedance of eight ohms, the total impedance of the speakers must not exceed this figure. So, if you decide to fit two speakers they should have an impedance of four ohms each.

Failure to match your tape player and speakers in this way can cause serious damage to your equipment, although some players do have alternative impedance levels.

How sophisticated you want your speakers to be really depends on how much money you want to spend on them. There are single and dual cone types, coaxial types, twin speakers with frequency cross-over control to expand their range (see above), and even triaxial models which are virtually three-in-one units. The co and triaxial speakers have separate speakers inside to reflect different parts of the sound (often referred to as "woofers" and "tweeters"). Speaker brochures always quote their maximum wattage and frequency range.

Apart from their technical composition, speakers come in all shapes and sizes to help you get round mounting problems. Some are designed specifically for mounting in doors while others are suitable for rear parcel shelf, side panel or fascia mounting.

Powerful speakers

Some car speakers are designed to take really powerful wattages—in the region of 20-30 watts—but for these you will need to add a booster to your cassette player. Boosters amplify the original current from the player and are available from several different manufacturers. About the size of a small electronic ignition unit, there are several places they can be fitted out of sight—under the fascia or in the boot, for instance.

The real benefit of such systems is not the increased volume, which is considerable, but the improvement in sound quality; more power generally takes you a step nearer the ultimate goal of perfect reproduction.

Mounting equipment

Tape players can be mounted in a variety of different places but you should bear in mind that a unit must be within easy reach of the driver. Dealers usually carry a comprehensive selection of mountings including pods to hold a player fitted into the fascia, brackets and panels for under-fascia mountings and special consoles. Consoles are made in many different shapes and sizes by accessory manufacturers and sometimes by the tape manufacturers themselves. They often include provision for storing cassettes and fitting a speaker.

Decide where your tape player is to be fitted before you buy one and you can then buy all the necessary bits and pieces at the same time.

Below is a selection of some of the more popular car tape players on the market, illustrating the variety of features and power outputs now available to car owners.

Academy: this Japanese firm offers the 808 and NA309 models. The 808 is fairly basic with a non-lockable, fast forward wind only. Output is three watts per channel with speakers available separately. The NA309 has non-lockable, fast forward wind and rewind. It is more powerful than the 808 with an output of seven watts per channel but speakers are separate.

Aiwa: this Japanese company offers the CT1050 which has non-lockable, fast forward and rewind and an output of four watts per channel. Speakers not included.

Amstrad: the Amstrad 9010 has lockable, fast forward and rewind plus an auto-reverse feature. This means that the

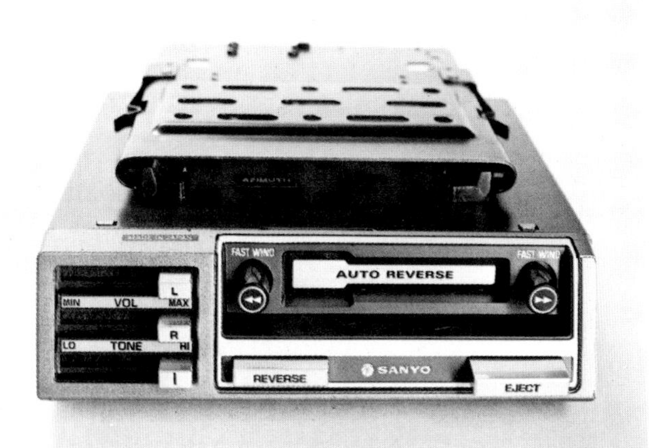

11 The Sanyo FT406E cassette player has separate forward wind and reverse buttons together with an automatic reverse feature

12 Because the FT406E slides into its special mounting bracket and plugs in at the back, it can be easily removed if necessary

unit plays side one, then side two, then side one again and so on until cancelled by the eject button. Output is five watts per channel and speakers are included with the set.
Astor: made in Hong Kong, the CP52 model is another fairly basic tape player. It has non-lockable, fast forward wind only and an output of four watts per channel. Speakers are included with the unit.
Audioline: this firm offers the 420, with non-lockable, fast forward and rewind and an auto-reverse feature similar to the Amstrad 9010. Output is five watts per channel and speakers are available separately.
Clarion: this firm offers two models, the PE 827A and the PE 828A. The 827A has non-lockable, fast forward wind only while the 828A has non-lockable, fast forward and rewind, plus an auto-reverse mechanism. Speakers are extra with both players.
Eagle: the MC 6100 model from this firm has non-lockable, fast forward wind only, an output of three watts per channel and speakers available separately.
Hanimex: also made in Japan, the HC 6012 tape player from this firm has non-locking, fast forward and rewind and an auto-reverse mechanism. Output is four watts per channel and speakers are extra.
Hitachi: this Japanese firm offers the CS320 and CS370 models. The CS320 has a lockable, fast forward wind only and an output of five watts per channel. The comprehensively-equipped CS370 has lockable, fast forward and rewind, an auto-reverse mechanism and a pause control to halt the tape temporarily. Output on the CS370 is seven watts per channel, speakers extra.
Lucas Audio: the LS210 model offered by this UK firm is made in Japan and includes non-lockable, fast forward and rewind and an auto-reverse feature. It also has a special control to boost the bass. Speakers are included.
Motoradio: the MC2000 tape player from this firm is made in the UK. It has non-lockable, fast forward wind only and an output of five watts per channel. Speakers are extra.
Motorola: the 401 model from this firm has non-lockable, fast forward and rewind and a five watts output per channel. Speakers are extra.
National Panasonic: this Japanese firm's CX 7000 model has separate bass and treble tone controls. Output is six watts per channel and speakers are available separately.
Philips: the Austrian-made AC 060 model has fast forward wind only and a five watt per channel output but speakers are included with the unit.
Pioneer: this firm offers the KP 292 model which has lockable, fast forward and rewind and an auto-reverse mechanism. It also incorporates a loudness switch. Output is five watts per channel and speakers are extra.
Pye: this firm offers the 2271 and 2273P models. The 2271 is fairly basic, with non-lockable, fast forward wind only, a three and a half watt output per channel and speakers available separately. The 2273P has non-lockable, fast forward and rewind and an auto reverse mechanism. Output is five watts per channel and speakers are included with the machine.
Radiomobile: this firm offers quite a wide selection of tape players of which the 321CS and the 354, both made in Japan, are typical. The 321CS is a simple unit with fast forward wind only, an output of four watts per channel and speakers available separately. The 354 has non-lockable, fast forward and rewind plus an auto-reverse mechanism. Output is six watts per channel and speakers are included with the player.
Roadstar: the Japanese-made RS 1000 and RS 4103 models are again representative of this firm's range of tape players. The RS 1000 has lockable, fast forward and rewind and an output of four and a half watts per channel. The RS 4103 has fast forward and rewind, an auto-reverse mechanism and an output of five watts per channel. Speakers extra.
Sanyo: among this well-known Japanese firm's products are the FT 402 tape player which comes complete with speakers and the more sophisticated FT 406E. This latter unit has no wiring connections but, instead, plugs into a special bracket which is mounted and wired up in the car.
Sharp: Japanese-made, this firm's RG 2700 tape player has non-lockable, fast forward and rewind, an auto-reverse mechanism and an output of four and a half watts per channel. Speakers are included with the unit.

Courtesy Jack Barclay Ltd/Peter Dazeley

13 An unusual site for a cassette player: in the back of a Rolls-Royce Phantom V1, for use only by the rear seat passengers

Buying car aerials

On the Long Wave (LW) and Medium Wave (MW) channels you may be lucky to get a vague signal, riddled with interference, if you disconnect your car aerial. On very high frequencies (VHF) you will get no reception at all. This demonstrates how totally dependent any car radio is on its aerial. A poor set will always be poor but a good one can be equally inadequate if it is not supplied with a strong signal, free from outside interference.

The car radio aerial serves two functions. It is there to pick up the broadcast signals as effectively as possible. A difficult task as the car is usually on the move and frequently surrounded by buildings or other artificial barriers which weaken the signal. The aerial's second function is to protect these signals until they reach the radio itself.

Inside every car there is a mass of electrical signals which are generated by the various components of the electrical system. It is the aerial lead connected to the radio which is chiefly responsible for keeping these signals at bay.

Screening

Screening is the term used to describe how an aerial lead keeps out unwanted signals. A "screened" lead has a layer of flexible wire-mesh surrounding the actual wire core and insulated from it by a further layer of plastic (fig. 8). The wire-mesh picks up the interference signals and feeds them through to the earths at the set end and at the aerial mounting. For this reason, aerial mountings must always make a good contact with the earth—a loose aerial or one fixed to a rusty wing will never be able to do its job properly.

Even the most sophisticated screened lead is unlikely to keep out the interference altogether, hence the need for suppressors on plug leads, generators and other electrical components. It will, however, make the job of suppressing interference a great deal easier and give better final reception.

When a cheap car aerial is found to give disappointing results it is often the screened lead rather than the metal aerial itself which is at fault. It is difficult to tell how good or bad a lead is when you buy it, but, generally speaking, cost is directly related to quality and, as in most cases, you get that for which you pay!

Positioning

Before you set out to buy a car aerial you should have some idea of where you are going to fit it. The optimum position on your particular car will greatly influence your eventual choice of aerial (fig. 1).

On front-engined cars, a site at the back has some advantages. It is away from the engine which is invariably

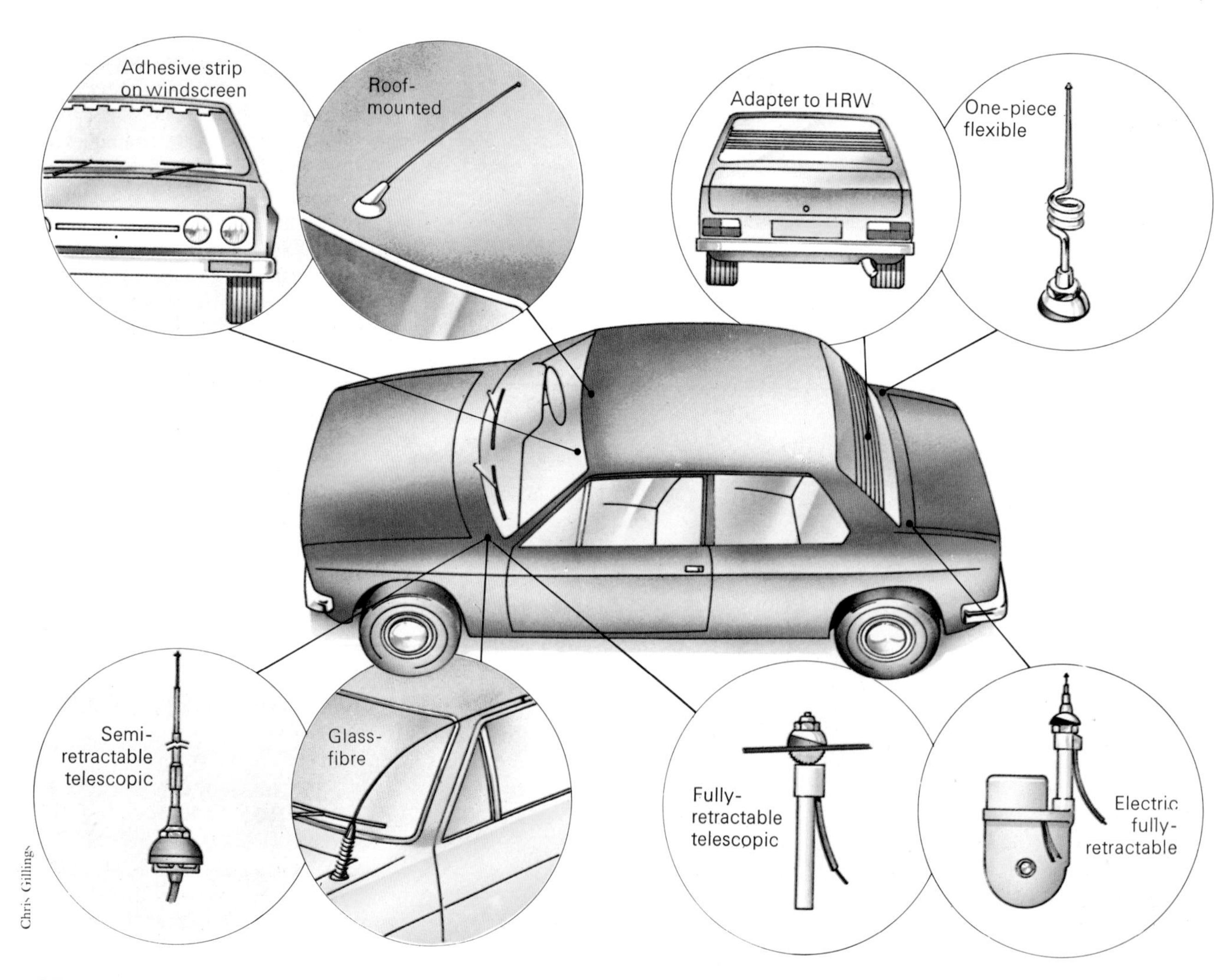

1 The wide range of car aerials available on the accessory market gives you plenty of different types and styles to choose from. Remember though, that your final choice will be influenced by the mounting position; check on your car to see which of the more popular sites shown above is the most convenient from a fitting point of view. You can then select an aerial accordingly

the biggest source of electrical interference. The aerial will also be sheltered behind the bulk of the passenger compartment, which means that it will not cause extra wind resistance or wind "roar".

The chief problem with a rear-mounted aerial, however, is its siting and installation. If your car is an estate or a hatchback, it may be impossible to find a suitable mounting point to enable you to work from underneath or inside the car. The screened lead can also pose problems. Unless the car is very small, a considerable length of lead will be needed to connect the aerial to a fascia-mounted radio. This extra length can make the radio more prone to interference. Hiding the lead behind trim, the rear seats and under the carpet can also prove difficult.

Ease of fitting usually encourages most car owners to fit the aerial at the front of the car. There is normally plenty of room underneath, which is especially important if you want to fit a retractable or electric aerial and the screened connection to the radio need only be short. With a front-mounted aerial though, you must expect to have more problems suppressing interference. On cars which have conventional engine layouts this can be minimized by placing the aerial on the opposite side to the main components of the ignition system: the generator, distributor and plugs. You must keep this in mind when selecting a site for the aerial.

With both front and rear locations, consider the amount of space available below the bodywork—if you want to fit a retractable or electric aerial, you will need plenty of room to accommodate the aerial holder and, in the latter case, the winding motor as well. If there is no room, you may be forced to choose a simple, semi-retractable aerial but these do have their drawbacks (see below).

One other alternative location is the roof. Roof-mounted aerials have the advantage of being high up on the car where they can pick up a strong signal and most can be lowered flat if, for instance, the car is going to be put through an automatic car wash.

Against this though, must be weighed the problems of fitting such aerials. The normal site for them is central, just above the windscreen. Depending on the make of aerial and the type of car, they are clipped to the guttering above the windscreen or bolted to the roof. The screened lead, however, must be passed into the passenger compartment and this is not always an easy task. Some cars, such as Renaults, Volvos and Citroens have channels in their windscreen pillars which happily accommodate the lead and from there it can be fed to the radio via the rear of the fascia panel. On other cars, the job can prove to be more difficult and you are advised to check on this.

If you are seriously considering buying a roof aerial, obtain some advice about your particular car from a dealer. He should be able to tell you if there is room for the lead and whether or not the car's headlining can be easily removed to hide the lead. Removing and replacing the headlining can be very difficult on certain cars so it is a good idea to check first.

Types of aerial

Car aerials are available in many shapes and sizes, but always bear in mind possible locations when you are making your choice. The telescopic rod type of aerial has always been the most popular because it is usually simple to fit and can be pushed down when not in use. One-piece flexible aerials for both body and roof mounting form another general category. Recent developments, however, suggest that the rod antenna type of aerial may one day be abandoned altogether in favour of more modern types.

Telescopic rod type (semi-retractable): These are often the cheapest aerials on the accessory market, mainly because they are simple in construction. This type of aerial clamps on to the car bodywork and can be folded down to a single section which is left protruding. The main disadvantage in this is that you cannot then take your car through an automatic car wash without removing the aerial. The aerial will also be prone to attack by vandals, even when folded to its limit. One good point with this type of aerial, however, is that there are less water-harbouring crevices than on the fully-retractable type with a recessed casing. Providing each telescopic section is occasionally polished and kept lightly coated with petroleum jelly there should be no corrosion problems to seize up the aerial. Semi-retractable aerials are also the natural choice if you select a mounting location on the body which has restricted space underneath for an aerial to retract into.

Telescopic rod type (fully-retractable): More expensive than the semi-retractable aerials, these are less vulnerable to vandalism because they retract into a casing underneath the body (fig. 8). They also get round the problem of car washes. Some fully-retractable aerials have a protruding tip which enables you to pull them up when fully retracted. Others retract completely and are raised by means of a special key. Whatever the method, statistics show that a vandal is unlikely to bother to raise a retracted aerial in order to break it. It is the fully extended ones that tend to get broken in this way.

Unfortunately, corrosion can sometimes be a problem with this type of aerial. Water seeps down the rod and into the casing where it gradually forms rust and eventually stops the aerial from extending at all. The problem can be avoided to some extent by regularly cleaning and polishing the rod but this is not always effective. When buying a fully-retractable aerial, look for one which has a substantial amount of sealing around the top of the casing.

Electrically-operated aerials: These are developments of the fully retractable type (fig. 8), and can be raised or lowered by remote control. In the past, electric aerials have had a poor reputation for reliability earned usually because either the rod seized up through corrosion or because the cable drive from the motor slipped its pulley and tangled. For this reason, aerial manufacturers have put a great deal of effort into producing water-tight and mechanically sound products. With careful maintenance as well, which only consists of regular cleaning and occasionally wiping the rod with a little petroleum jelly, today's electric aerials are a much better proposition.

Two types of electric aerial are available; manual and automatic. The manual type, which is usually cheaper, is operated by means of a separate switch and can be raised or lowered as necessary. The automatic aerials have a relay switch wired into the live supply to the radio. When the radio is switched on, the aerial goes up. It retracts automatically when the radio is switched off.

To cut down wind resistance and noise, it is a good idea to extend an aerial just enough to get a strong signal.

The advantage of manual aerials, therefore, is that they give you control over how much is extended. With automatic aerials, you do not get the choice; they are either fully up or fully down. Automatic aerials on the other hand, mean that you do not have to remember to lower them every time you park the car and their frequent use tends to prevent a build-up of damaging corrosion and dirt.

Whichever type you are considering, location is the most important factor and you should not commit yourself to

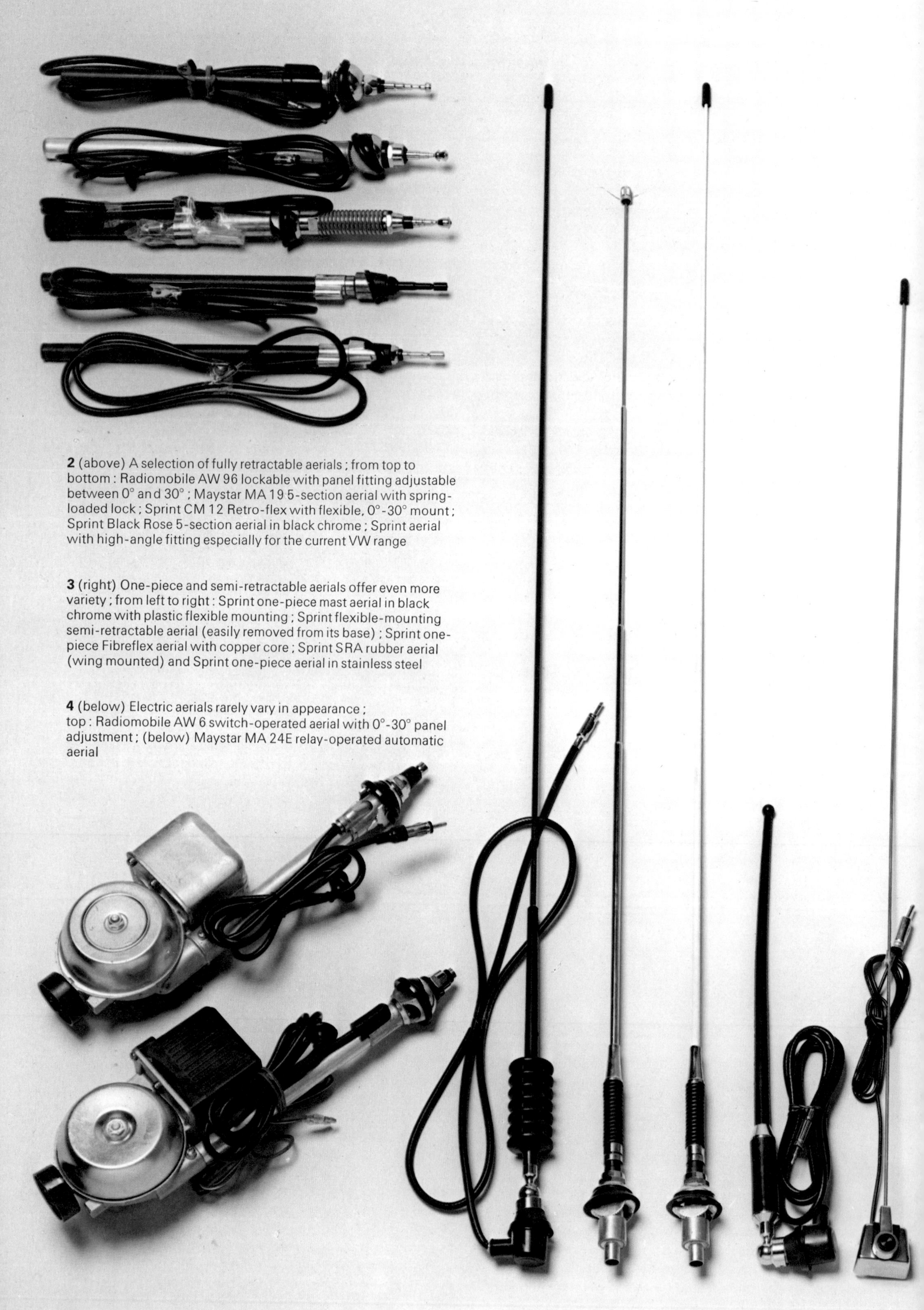

2 (above) A selection of fully retractable aerials; from top to bottom: Radiomobile AW 96 lockable with panel fitting adjustable between 0° and 30°; Maystar MA 19 5-section aerial with spring-loaded lock; Sprint CM 12 Retro-flex with flexible, 0°-30° mount; Sprint Black Rose 5-section aerial in black chrome; Sprint aerial with high-angle fitting especially for the current VW range

3 (right) One-piece and semi-retractable aerials offer even more variety; from left to right: Sprint one-piece mast aerial in black chrome with plastic flexible mounting; Sprint flexible-mounting semi-retractable aerial (easily removed from its base); Sprint one-piece Fibreflex aerial with copper core; Sprint SRA rubber aerial (wing mounted) and Sprint one-piece aerial in stainless steel

4 (below) Electric aerials rarely vary in appearance;
top: Radiomobile AW 6 switch-operated aerial with 0°-30° panel adjustment; (below) Maystar MA 24E relay-operated automatic aerial

5 (below) With these roof-mounted aerials the main differences are in the bases; from left to right: Maystar MA4 3-section aerial; Sprint Liteflex one-piece stainless steel aerial; Radiomobile 2-section chromed aerial; Sprint Teleflex 2-section roof aerial with spring base; Binatone High Gain roof aerial with 11-section plastic mast and a built-in signal amplifier for improved quality

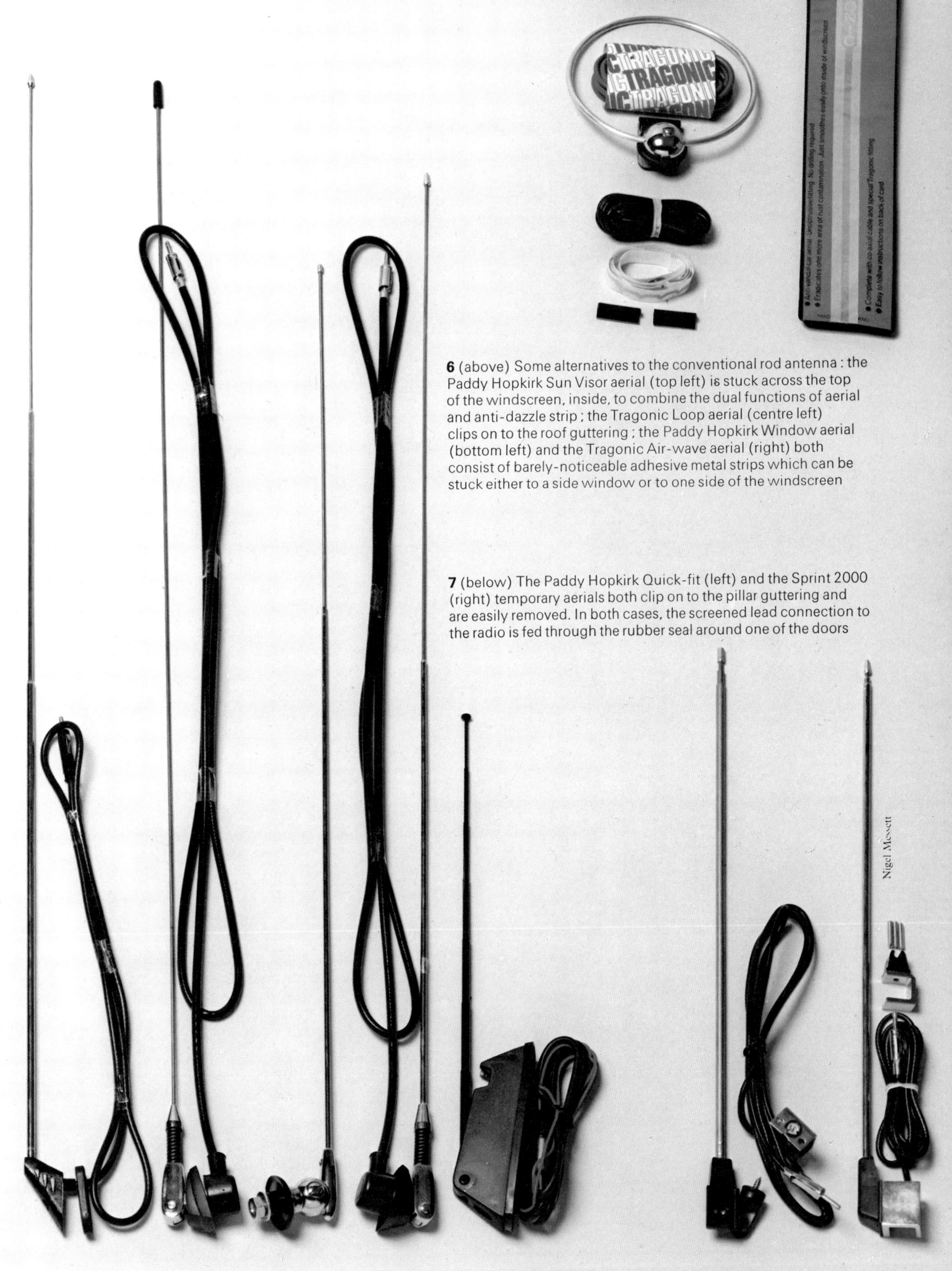

6 (above) Some alternatives to the conventional rod antenna: the Paddy Hopkirk Sun Visor aerial (top left) is stuck across the top of the windscreen, inside, to combine the dual functions of aerial and anti-dazzle strip; the Tragonic Loop aerial (centre left) clips on to the roof guttering; the Paddy Hopkirk Window aerial (bottom left) and the Tragonic Air-wave aerial (right) both consist of barely-noticeable adhesive metal strips which can be stuck either to a side window or to one side of the windscreen

7 (below) The Paddy Hopkirk Quick-fit (left) and the Sprint 2000 (right) temporary aerials both clip on to the pillar guttering and are easily removed. In both cases, the screened lead connection to the radio is fed through the rubber seal around one of the doors

Nigel Messett

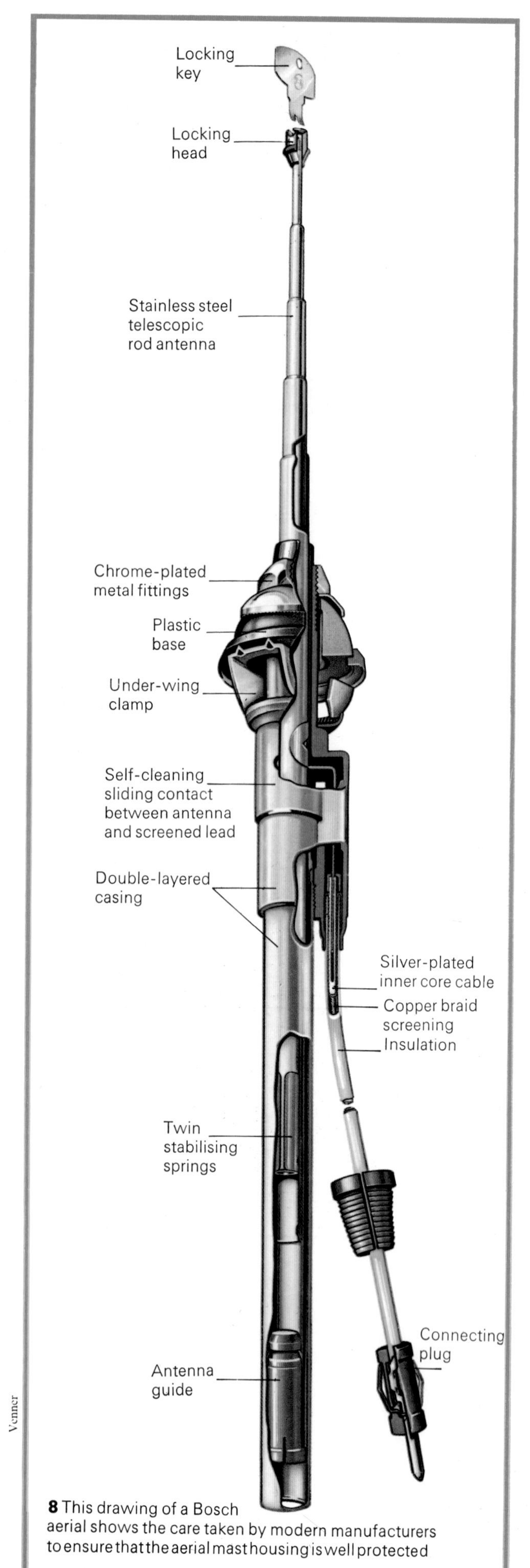

8 This drawing of a Bosch aerial shows the care taken by modern manufacturers to ensure that the aerial mast housing is well protected

buying an electric aerial unless you are sure that it can be properly installed in your car.

All electric aerials have a motor and winding mechanism attached to the lower casing and this needs more room than a conventional telescopic aerial. The mechanisms themselves must not be exposed to road dirt and spray which rules out mounting them in "open" front wings. The best place for an electric aerial is on a rear wing where the motor and winder are sheltered inside the luggage compartment, but this is not always practical on some modern hatchback designs. The rule therefore is: if you cannot find a suitable site, don't buy an electric aerial, find an alternative type.

One-piece aerials: These come in all shapes and sizes (fig. 3) and although not as discreet as the telescopic types, they do have the advantage of simple construction. One-piece aerials have to be flexible to guard against accidental knocks and the strain of wind resistance. The rods are usually made of stainless steel or, more commonly, glass fibre with a copper core. Bases invariably have a steel spring arrangement for even more flexibility and some have provision for the rod to be detached so that the car can be put through a car wash.

Extra-long glass-fibre aerials are popular with customizing enthusiasts and are certainly striking in appearance. Their flexibility and inherent strength enables them to be folded back in a loop and clipped down if required. Although they are efficient, they are no more so than conventional aerials and for this reason their growing appeal, particularly with the younger motorist, is entirely visual.

One-piece aerials in general, though, do have the advantage of being versatile. Because there is no casing below the bodywork, you are likely to have a far wider choice when it comes to finding a suitable location. Most are corrosion-proof as well.

Most roof aerials (fig. 5) fall into the one-piece category although there are telescopic ones available. The latter fold down into a single section. Both types have provision for folding flush with the roof should the need arise and, like the body-mounted aerials, they come with a variety of different bases and fixings.

Temporary aerials

Not everyone is able, or prepared, to drill a hole through the bodywork and fit a permanent aerial. If you have a company car or you have borrowed or hired a vehicle such modifications are probably not possible. Providing, though, that you have a portable radio capable of being used in a car, you can buy a temporary aerial to enhance its performance. A suitable radio will be one with an aerial input socket which, when connected, isolates the internal ferrite aerial in the radio itself.

The external type of temporary aerial (fig. 7) clips on to the roof guttering by means of a screw mounting. Its screened lead can then be passed into the passenger compartment via the rubber door seals and pushed into the radio. One disadvantage of this arrangement is that it usually causes wind noise at high speed around the area where the door seal has been "broken". However, this is not permanent and is eliminated when the aerial is removed.

An alternative is the window type of aerial. This has a simple slide arrangement which clips over the top of the window glass and the screened lead runs from the inside of the bracket. A disadvantage, however, is that the window cannot be opened with the aerial in place but if your car has rear-opening windows, this may not matter as the aerial can be fitted to one of these.

Step-by-step stereo

Why be content with plain old radio? Almost anything you have on a hi-fi set at home can now be duplicated in the car. A stereo receiver with cassette player, for example, can be a continual source of pleasure, especially on long journeys.

Before you choose your stereo equipment, there are three things to consider.

First, space. Most manufacturers now include a slot (sometimes covered with a metal plate) in the car's fascia for fitting a radio. This space may be a standard 18 cm by 5 cm (7in. by 2in.), but some slots are a centimetre or so less than this size—and some combined radio/cassette players a centimetre or two deeper. So if your car has one of these slots, measure all three dimensions —width, height and especially depth—so you can choose equipment to suit. It can be disheartening to spend money on a set, only to find that it protrudes from the fascia and cannot be fitted flush.

Should a dashboard-mounted radio or radio/tape player not be possible, an alternative is to fit the unit under the dashboard. A third method is to buy a centre console. These can be obtained for most popular cars and generally incorporate a gear-lever surround, oddments tray and ashtray, as well as a plain area in which a suitable slot for radio fitting can be cut.

Before you buy speakers, you will need to consider where they too will be fitted (see below).

The second point to consider is voltage. Only a few cars have 6-volt systems, and for those that do few 6-volt radios are made. To fit a 12-volt radio to a 6-volt system, you will need a transformer (it costs a few pounds), and this is fitted between the car battery and the line fuse (see below). Your car owner's manual should tell you whether the system is 6-volt or 12-volt. If in doubt, look at the battery; a 6-volt battery has three cells (and therefore six 'knobs' on top), whereas a 12-volt is twice as big.

The third point to consider is polarity. All cars' electrics work on the earth return system—that is, a single wire connects the battery with each of the various electrical fittings, while the return current to the battery is carried by the car body itself.

The current may 'flow' either way round, depending on how the car is wired. In a positive-earthed car, the body carries the positive current. A short length of wire connects the positive terminal of the battery, marked + or coloured red, to the chassis or body. In a negative-earthed car, the body carries the negative current, and the connection is between the negative terminal of the battery, marked —, and the chassis or body.

If your car is positive earthed, it will not accept a negative-earthed radio, and switching on could wreck the unit. Few positive-earthed radios are available, but there are dual-polarity radios which either change their polarity automatically or can be changed by means of a switch on the set itself. So check, before you go shopping, what kind of radio you will need.

Fitting sequence

The job of fitting the various units into the car will go more smoothly if they are tackled in the correct order.

Start by disconnecting either of the battery terminals. Then fit the radio—but temporarily, so that you can gain access later to the back of the set. Then fit the speakers, and finally the aerial. Lastly, you tackle the problem of reducing electrical interference noise.

With most radios, it is not a good idea to switch on without the speakers being connected. This can damage the set.

The radio/cassette player

Where the radio/cassette player is to be fitted in the car manufacturer's designed 18 cm by 5 cm aperture, the

1 A good fitting kit includes all wiring components, speakers, earthing straps (left of picture), and mounting brackets to suit the individual make and model of car. Before you start using a kit make sure the face plate and back plate fit your car; they are hard to cut neatly. This kit, from Radiomobile, is for the VW Golf

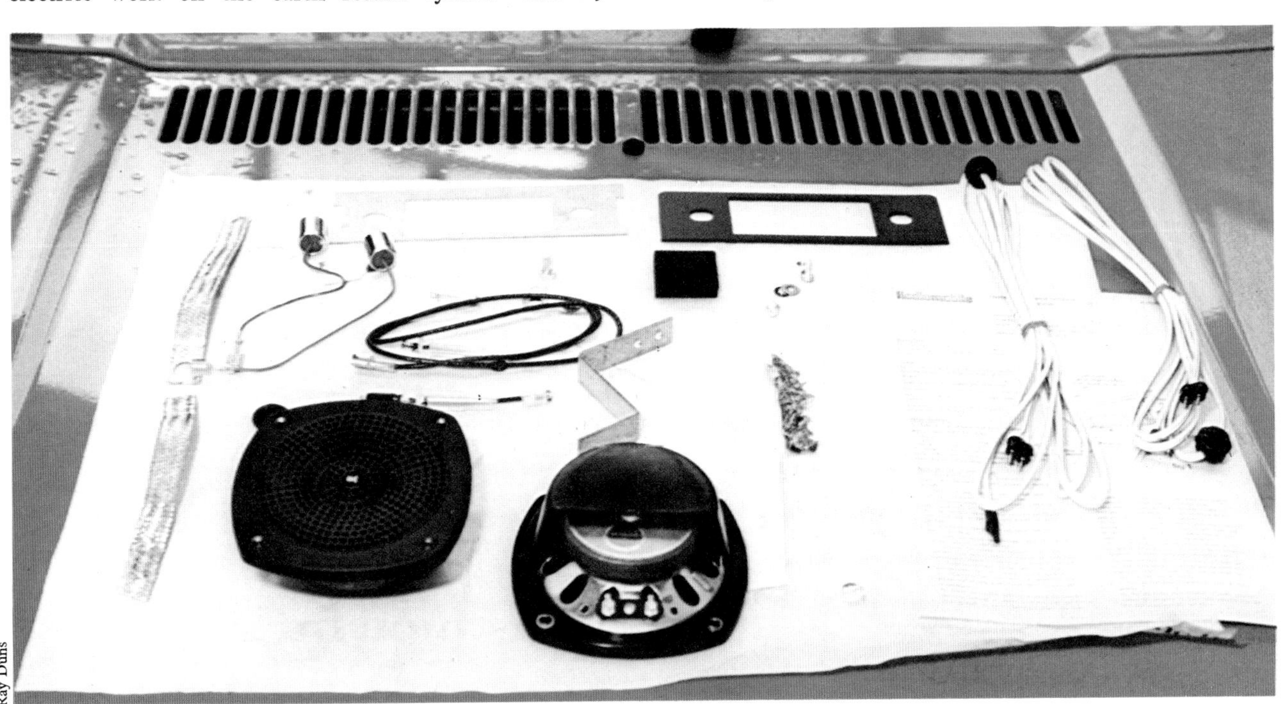

Ray Duns

actual fitting details will vary from car to car and on the fitting kit you buy with the set. Generally, the radio is supported at the front by nuts on the control spindles, usually taking in some kind of mounting plate or a pair of clamping plates.

Unless the radio is designed for front support only (refer to the instruction book) you will need further support at the rear of the set. Fitting kits usually give you a choice here. You can rest the back of the set on a foam pad mounted on some convenient part of the car's structure. Or you can use one or more of the metal strips supplied to make a mounting bracket. The strips are easily bent, and ready-drilled for bolting. If possible, fix one or both ends to an existing nut and bolt under the dashboard to save yourself drilling. If not, use self-tapping screws and spring washers rather than nuts and bolts.

If the set is to be mounted under the dashboard, fitting components will usually include either a saddle bracket or a pair of angle brackets. The set is fixed to the bracket(s) by drilled and tapped holes in the side of the set and screws which are provided. With the brackets fixed to the set, offer it up in the required position and mark through the holes with a centrepunch or pencil on to the underside of the dashboard. The holes are then drilled to suit either self-tapping screws or small nuts and bolts (usually provided with the fitting kit).

Normally, with a fitting of this kind, a fascia plate of moulded fibreboard or a similar material is provided to hide the unsightly brackets.

The set must be earthed and it is better if this is done by a separate earthing wire, even if the set is in direct contact with a metal fascia. The earth wire supplied should be connected to a 'known clean earth' (any clean, rust- and paint-free metal) on the car body. There is often such a point behind the dashboard for earthing instruments.

Connecting up

Connecting up is reasonably straightforward. There should be a line fuse holder (fig. 6) in the set's live wire. If none is supplied, the easiest kind to fit is the unsoldered type, which uses a clamp screw to hold each wire.

The live wire can be connected to a power source in several ways. It can be connected to the spare accessory terminal on the ignition switch, which means that the radio will automatically be switched off with the ignition to save drawing on the car battery. Often, it can be wired to a different position on the switch, which allows the radio to be used while the ignition is off. Your car owner's manual will tell you whether such a position is available.

Alternatively, the live wire can be taken to a 'constant live' point at the car's fuse box. An example is the 'live' side of the fuse for those accessories, such as the horn and courtesy lights, which can be operated with the ignition off. You can tell which fuse is which by using a

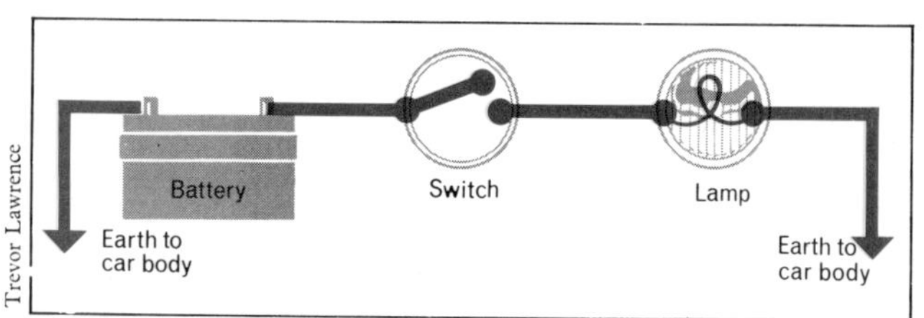

2 Simplified diagram of a typical car earth-return wiring system

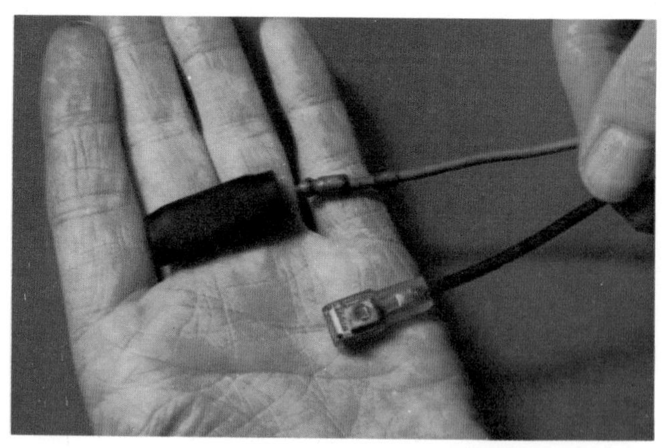
3 When wiring-in your radio you may find you have a mixture of wiring terminals. These are the bullet (above) and Lucar spade

4 Rather than remove terminals and solder on new ones, you can join wires with a connector such as this Scotchlok from 3M

circuit tester while the ignition is off, or by pulling fuses until you find the right one.

Yet another alternative, in some cars, is to take the lead to the spare accessory terminal in the car's fuse box.

If the radio is wired to any constantly live point you will need to be careful to switch it off when not in use, or a flat battery will result.

The terminals on all the wires from the radio will be of either the 'bullet' type or the Lucar spade type (fig. 3). Make sure that all terminals are of the right type to match those in the car; if not, replace them, or use the alternative method in figs. 3 to 5.

The final stage of wiring is to insert a fuse of the rating recommended by the radio manufacturer into the line fuse holder. However, the battery should be left disconnected until the speakers have been wired up.

The loudspeakers

It is important to decide where the speakers are to be fitted before buying them. First find out if there is a manufacturer-designed position for them, and if so whether the speakers you want will fit it. Likely places are at either end of the fascia, in the doors, or in the rear parcel shelf.

Pod-type speakers (not as good acoustically as the flush-mounted type, which make use of a baffle) can be fitted at the ends of the front parcel shelf or in the foot wells. Specially-shaped surface-mounted speakers are made for the rear parcel shelf. Flush-fitting speakers can go in manufacturers' provided positions and, sometimes, in the front foot wells or in the side trims in the back of a two-door car.

The rear parcel shelf is probably the easiest place to fit

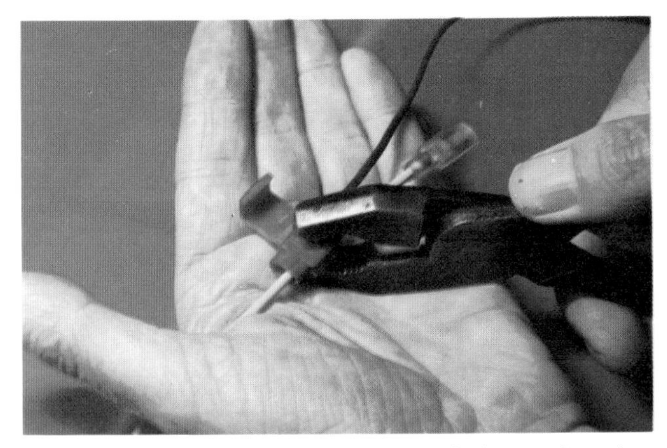

5 With one wire fed into each side of the terminal, press down the metal bridge so that it cuts through the plastic and links the wires

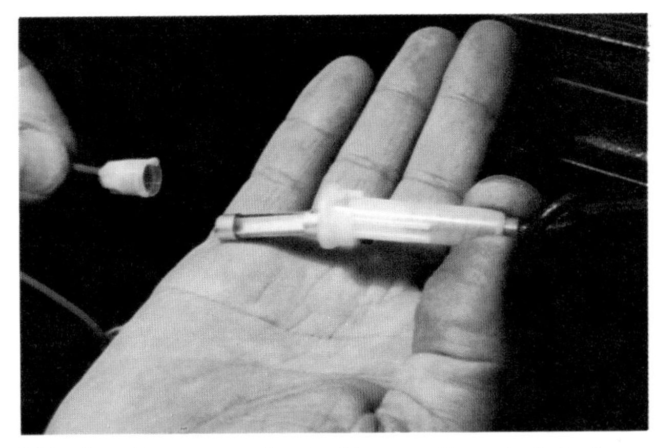

6 The live wire on your radio should come with one half of a line fuse carrier. Insert the fuse and join the two halves of the carrier

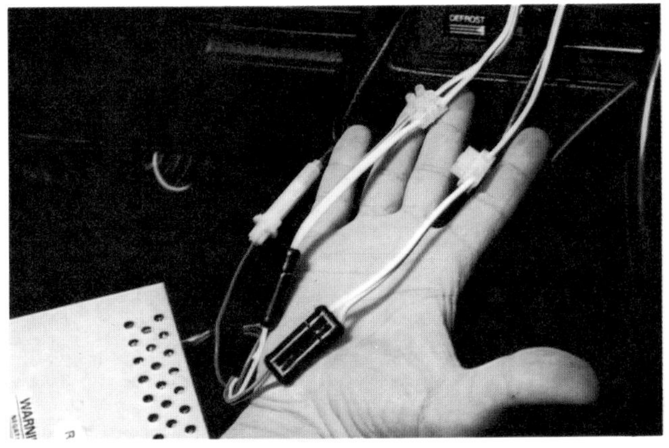

7 If wires are too long, do not leave too much slack where it might snag. Instead, shorten the wires with line connectors like these

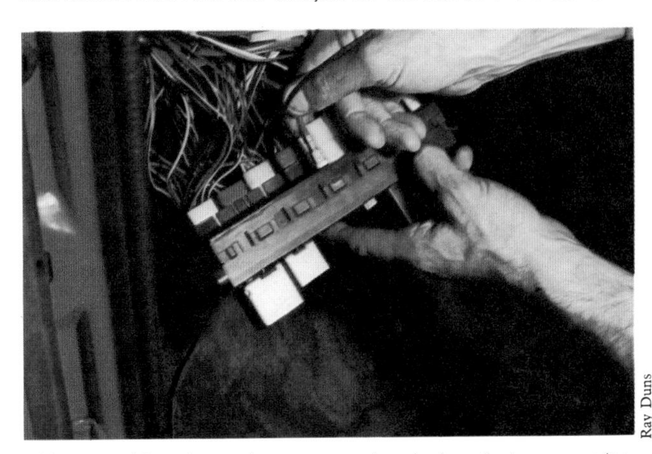

Ray Duns

8 Most cars' fuse boxes have a spare terminal so that accessories can be wired. This is the elaborate fuse box on a Volkswagen Golf

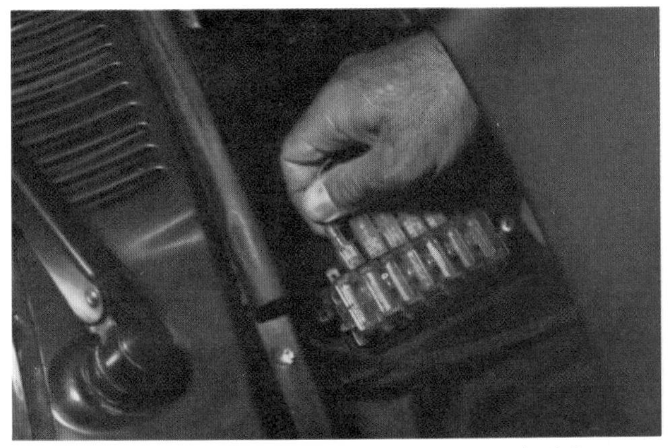

9 The simpler Ford fuse box, showing the spare terminal. Some cars have an alternative radio position on the ignition switch

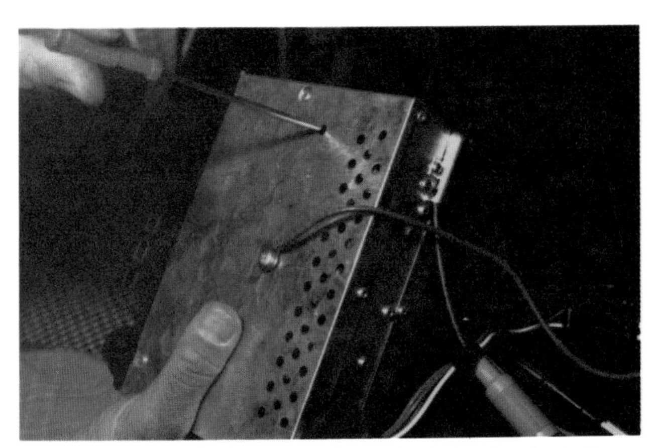

10 With the radio wired up according to the instruction book, it is matched to the aerial by turning a small adjusting screw

speakers, but it is not good acoustically, one problem being that the sounding-chamber effect of the boot produces over-prominent bass sounds. Neither is a position under the dashboard, where the sound will be poor—and aimed at the driver's and passenger's knees. The front foot wells and front kick panels are also dubious positions, and under the front seat (for obvious reasons) even worse.

In most four-door cars and many two-doors the best speaker position will be in the front door panels. Choice of position in the doors is likely to be somewhat restricted, since the window handles must revolve without touching the speakers. If the manufacturer has designated speaker positions or has pre-cut circles from the metal, use them; if not, place the speakers as high as possible in the door but not where the window can foul them when wound down.

In two-door cars, a good alternative position is in the trim panels under the rear side windows.

Installing the speakers

The first job is to remove the trim to see whether a pre-cut position is available and, if not, to cut one. Door trims are not usually hard to remove, but the operation is likely to involve taking off window-winding handles, door-latch fittings, armrests and perhaps ashtrays.

Speakers supplied in a radio-fitting kit are sometimes accompanied by a fitting template. Mark out the trim with a template and a ballpoint pen and cut it out with a Stanley knife with a sharp blade.

Next replace the trim temporarily while you mark the hole to be cut in the metal backing, if any. A professional installer would cut the hole with a sheet metal nibbler.

11 Loudspeakers come in a huge variety, including flush-mounted types and (right of picture) speakers for the rear parcel shelf

For the d-i-y man, the easiest way is to drill a series of small holes around the perimeter, knock out the metal disc and file smooth the edges of the hole.

The final problem is carrying the speaker wiring through to the dashboard panel and radio. If the speakers are in the doors, drill a 10 mm ($\frac{3}{8}$in.) hole in the leading edge of the door, and a higher one in the door pillar. Fit both holes with rubber grommets and feed the speaker lead through them, across behind the front kick trim and up behind the dashboard panel to the back of the set. Exposed parts of the wiring can be further protected by slipping a short length of rubber or plastic tubing over it.

If speakers are elsewhere, route the wires under the carpet. Follow the line of the wiring loom if possible; this makes a neater job.

Stereo speakers must be connected in phase. Usually the instruction book gives precise instructions, or there are marks on the terminals, to help you ensure that both speakers are wired-in in the same way. If in doubt, do not guess; ask the advice of your radio dealer.

Mono radio with two speakers

If a mono radio with two speakers is installed, a balance control is a good idea. This allows the volume of either speaker to be increased or decreased and so provides a balance of sound between the two.

The balance control is a compact device which will fit easily into a hole drilled in the dashboard (see above for drilling details). Wire it between the radio and the speakers, following the instructions supplied with the balance control itself.

The aerial

First make sure that the aerial you buy is a good one (see pages 18 to 22). It is unlikely that a bargain-price aerial will be as good as an expensive one from a well-known firm.

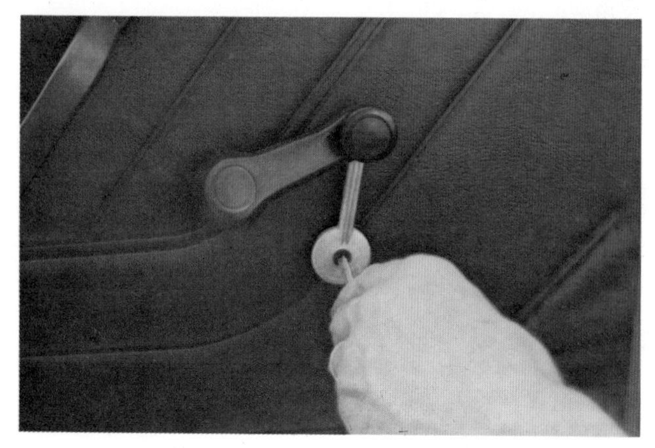

12 The first job in installing speakers is to remove the door trim. This window winder has a plastic cover which simply peels back

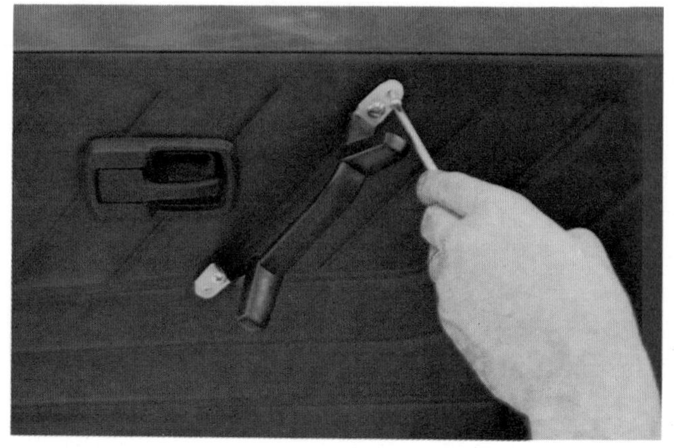

13 This door handle's cover also snaps back, exposing the retaining screws. A Phillips or Pozidriv screwdriver is needed to shift them

14 In some cases, plastic covers conceal the 'works' of a door latch. They have to be removed with a screwdriver or spike

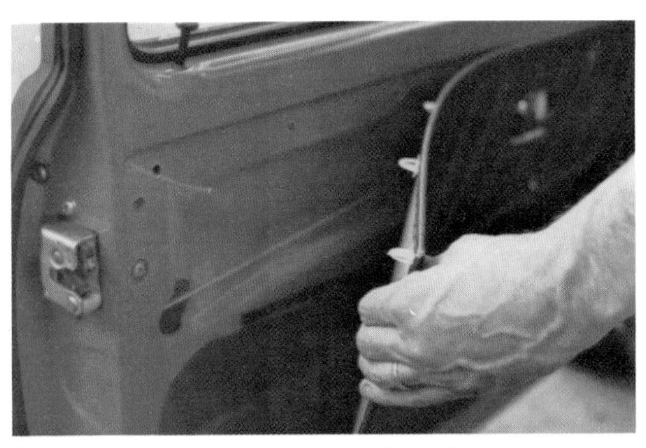

15 Now the door cover can be removed by pulling apart the plastic grips. Work carefully; most door trims are only flimsy hardboard

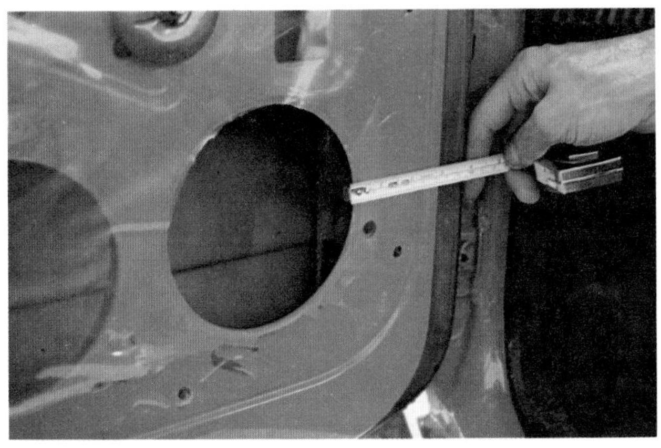

16 This car has a ready made speaker position. If none is available you will need to cut one, keeping it clear of the lowered window

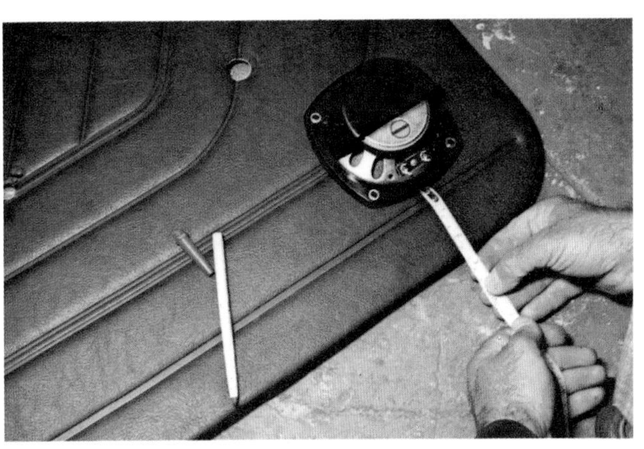

17 Transfer the speaker position measurements from the door to the trim. Remember the hole must be smaller than the speaker surround

18 A handyman's knife such as this Stanley will cut easily through the plastic — and, if you go carefully, through the hardboard too

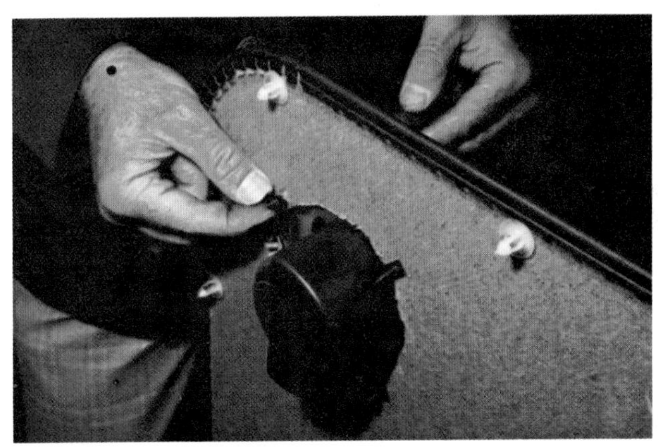

19 Fix the speaker to the trim with self-tapping screws and spire nuts. Replace the trim and re-check that the window will wind down

20 To carry the speaker wire, the hole in the door pillar should be about 5 cm (2in.) higher than that in the door, to avoid binding

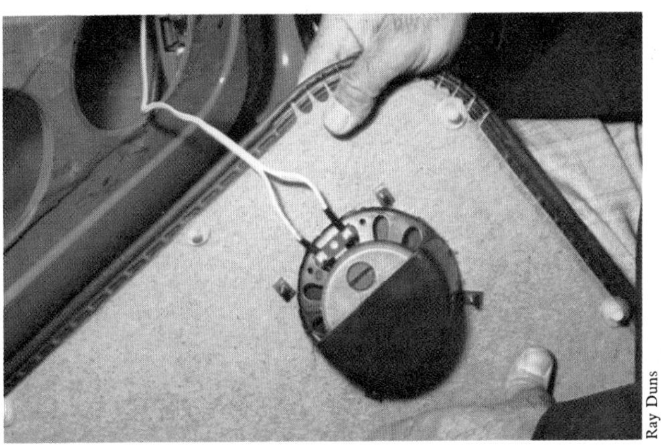

Ray Duns

21 When wiring the speaker, leave plenty of slack inside the door Be sure the speakers are wired in phase, as in the instructions

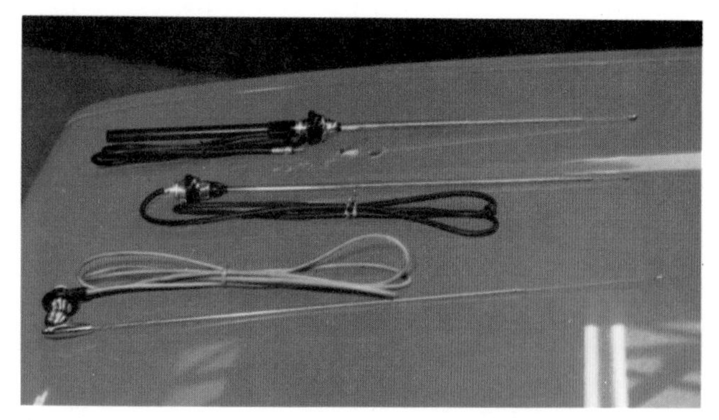

22 Three kinds of aerial: retractable (top), non-retractable and roof-mounted. Non-retractable aerials can be used where there is insufficient room for the base of the retractable type. But they can easily be broken, by vandals or in an automatic car wash

Inspect the aerial before you buy it to make sure that the collapsible stainless steel rod has some sort of device built in to maintain a good electrical contact between each of its segments.

The base should be metal lined with plastic, and there should be some provision for drainage at the bottom. Most important, the screening of the coaxial cable should be adequate. Because copper is expensive, this is where some manufacturers cut costs.

Make sure also that the capacitance of the aerial matches that of the set. British and European sets require an aerial of 65-75pF (picofarads). Japanese and American radios need a 95-110pF aerial. A signal loss of up to 25 per cent can result from a mis-match.

The position in which the aerial is fitted is important in minimizing interference. To find the best position,

23 Before installing the aerial, feel under the car to make sure there is only one thickness of metal where you propose to drill

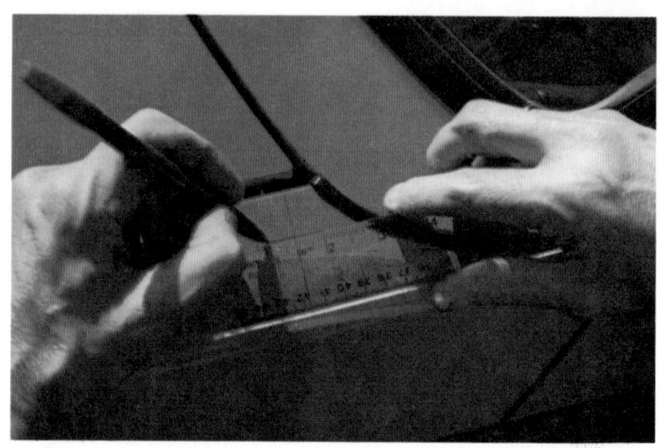

24 Mark the centre point of your proposed hole, using a felt-tipped pen so that it will rub off without damaging the paintwork

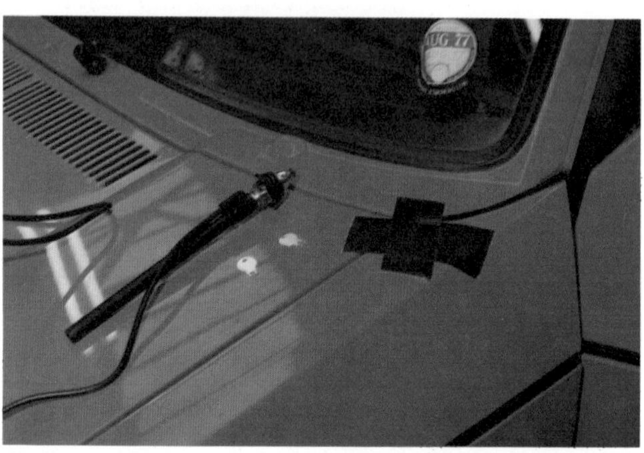

25 Alternatively, if you are worried that the drill bit might slip, make a cross with masking tape and do your marking out on that

26 Most aerials require a hole 22 mm (⅞in.) in diameter. Start by marking with a centrepunch and drilling a 3 mm (⅛in.) pilot hole

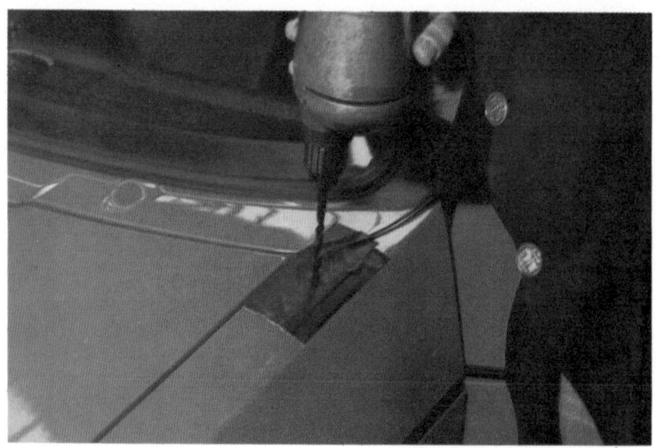

27 If you are using a hole cutter, next enlarge the hole to 15 mm (5/16in.) or larger, depending on the capacity of your drill chuck

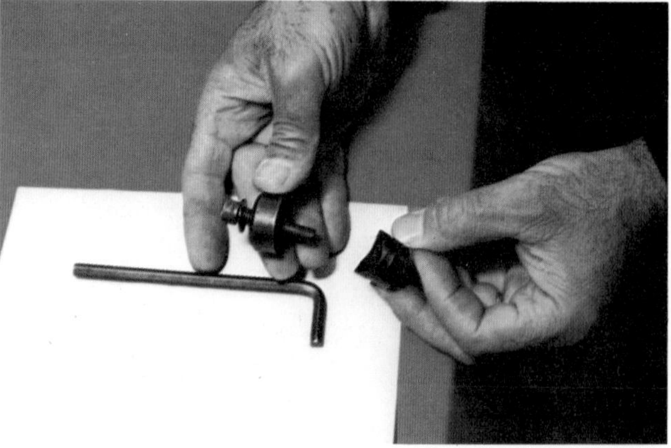

28 The hole cutter comes in two halves. One piece fits above the hole and one below, then the cutter is operated by an Allen key

29 It needs just a few turns to make a perfect hole. If no cutter is available, drill around the perimeter and knock out the disc

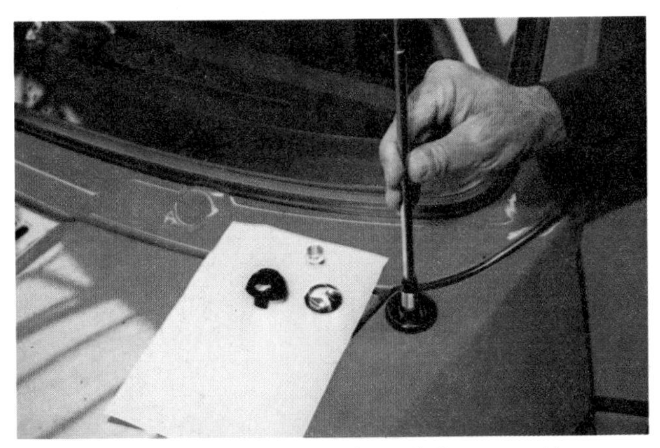

30 Push the aerial in place from underneath the car, making sure that its serrated teeth grip the underside, and fit a grommet

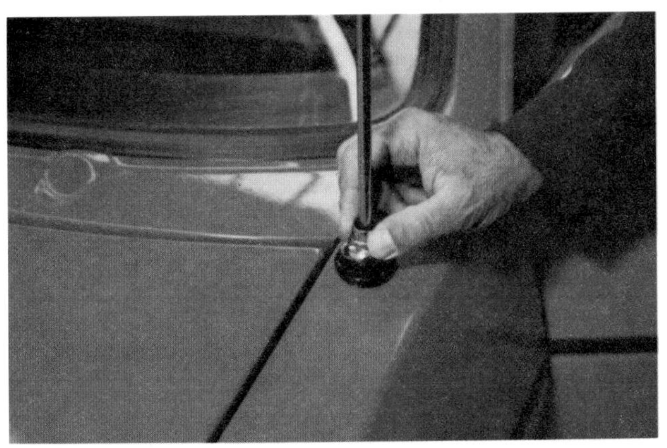

31 Next, fit the finishing cap. On this aerial, it must be rotated so it covers the drainage hole but excludes rainwater penetration

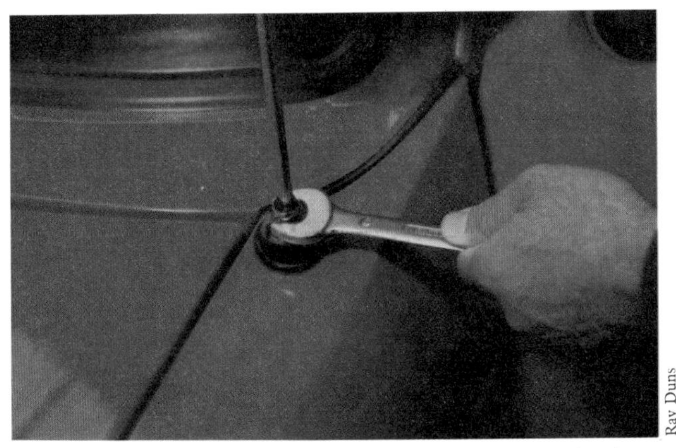

32 Having aligned the aerial by eye, ensuring that it is not leaning out from the car where it could be damaged, tighten the locking nut

Ray Duns

connect the aerial and speakers, and tune the set to a weak FM station where there is plenty of interference. Switch on the car's engine and touch the aerial to different places on the car until you find the place that produces the least interference. The aerial should be mounted as close to this spot as possible.

The fitting instructions with the best sets provide precise details about aerial fitting, in many cases including a template for drilling.

Before you start drilling, make sure there is no double-skinning or box section where you are planning to fit your aerial. If you are planning an installation near a wheel—in the front wing, for instance—measure the clearance above the wheel with the suspension both loaded and unloaded, to make sure the wheel cannot scrape the aerial base.

Fitting the aerial

The aerial hole is usually about 22 mm ($\frac{7}{8}$in.) in diameter, but always drill to the size specified in the fitting instructions. A good way to start is to cover the area immediately around the hole with masking tape. This will make marking out easier and also help to stop your centre-punch or drill from skidding and scratching the paint-work.

Start by centrepunching at the middle of the proposed hole, or by drilling a small pilot hole. To enlarge the hole, a cheap tool that can be used in an electric drill is a hole saw—a tubular cutter with a sawtooth edge. A simple-to-use alternative is a tank cutter, a device which is located on the pilot hole and tightened with an Allen key until the hole is cut. A third alternative, but the least accurate, is to mark out the hole required and then drill a series of small holes right round, and inside the perimeter line. The hole is cleaned up and smoothed with round and half-round files.

A good earth on the aerial mounting is essential to stop interference. The aerial mounting will incorporate some device for earthing—it might be a serrated ring, perhaps, or a similar sharp-toothed clamp. Before fitting the aerial, clean all dirt, rust and paint from the area that the clamp will touch (under the wing or wherever) until you have shiny metal. After the aerial has been fitted, the exposed metal around the earthing device can be protected against rust with an anti-corrosion primer or an underbody sealant. Be careful, however, not to get paint or primer on the good earth you have just created.

If possible, take the aerial cable straight into the passenger compartment without running it through the engine bay, which could cause interference. Where the lead passes through a drilled hole in a bulkhead, fit a rubber grommet to protect it from chafing.

Do not be tempted to alter the length of the aerial lead; you could get a severe signal drop—perhaps as much as 75 per cent. If the aerial needs lengthening use an extension lead, of the same make as the aerial and capacity compensated.

Now the aerial can be plugged in, the set finished off and the battery reconnected. Switch on the set and tune it to a weak station around 200 m on the medium wave band. Turn the aerial trimmer—a small screw usually fitted to the front of the set—until the best reception is obtained. This matches the radio to the signal characteristics of the aerial.

One task remains: to suppress the car against radio interference. This is covered in the next chapter.

Suppressing radio interference

Interference to a car radio comes in several forms. It may be a whine, a screech, a whistle or a persistent staccato crackle. It also affects different cars in different ways, sometimes being easy to cure and sometimes requiring considerable detective work.

The one thing you can be sure about is this: having installed your stereo/cassette player, you will find that some kind of interference suppression is necessary.

What causes interference

All the electrical current that flows around a car, operating the ignition, starter motor and other electrical devices is direct current (DC). That is, it is current which flows only one way around a circuit.

In older cars, a dynamo is used to generate this DC current.

In newer cars, an alternator generates an alternating current (AC)—that is, a current which continuously reverses its flow. But, because the car's battery can be charged only by DC current, the alternator has built-in components called diodes to convert its output to DC.

So the end result with both old and new cars is the same: DC current is produced.

Radio interference is caused by magnetic fields that build up around the ignition and charging circuits and various accessory circuits in the car. These fields can generate a small alternating current in any nearby electrical component.

This small alternating current can reach the set in two ways. It can be picked up by the radio aerial (radiated interference). Or it can travel via connections to the set, such as speaker leads or the power supply lead (conducted interference).

The objective of suppression, then, is to block off the alternating currents before they can reach the radio.

Built-in suppression

One technique for suppressing radiated (airborne) interference is to surround the offending components with an earthed metal screen. Most cars already have two of these.

One is the engine compartment, normally a metal box which effectively surrounds most of the car's electrical equipment.

The other is the metal box in which the radio itself is encased.

But these are not effective against conducted interference—the most common kind, and one with which you will have to deal.

Suppression devices

Several different types of component are available for interference suppression.

The first is the *capacitor*, a device which is automatically by-passed by DC current, but diverts to earth (in this case, the car's body) the AC pulses that would cause interference.

The most common type of capacitor is the parallel type, with a short lead at one end and an earthing clamp around its body. The earthing clamp is bolted to the car body, while the capacitor lead is taken to the live terminal of the electrical device you are suppressing (fig. 2).

1 A parallel capacitor is often used to suppress the coil. Undo the coil's mounting bracket in order to earth the capacitor

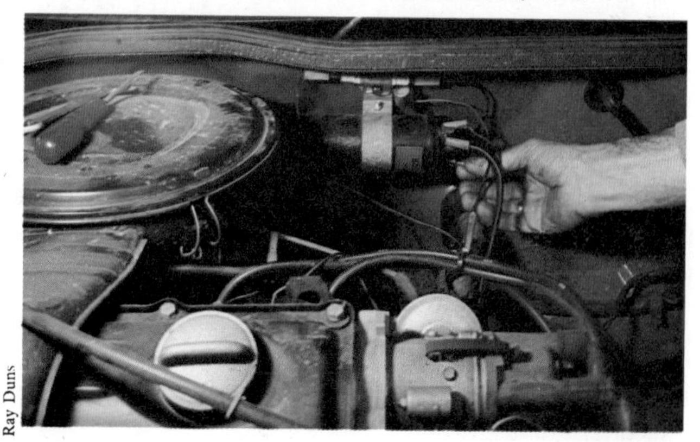

2 Connect the capacitor to the SW, BAT, or + terminal. For AM/FM suppression fit a 1mfd capacitor, and for FM, a 2.5mfd capacitor

Ray Duns

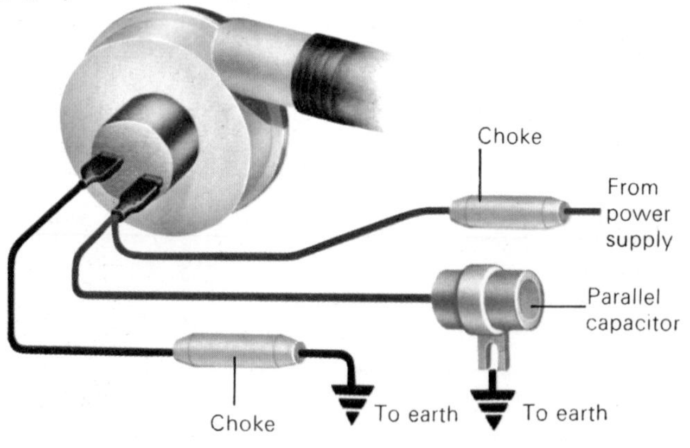

3 To suppress the heater, connect a choke in both the earth and live wires. Also fit a parallel capacitor to the live terminal

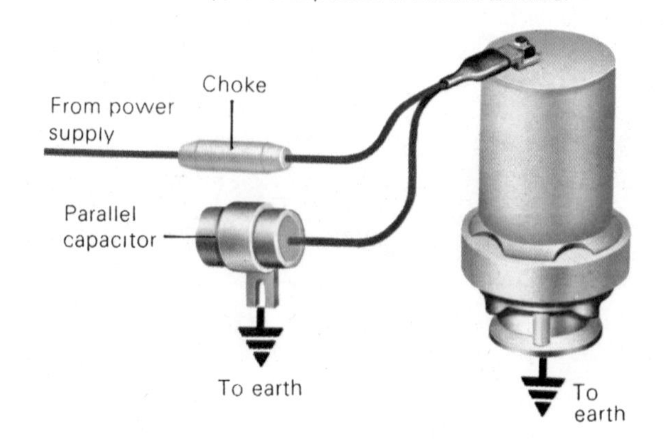

4 On an electric fuel pump, connect up a parallel capacitor to its live terminal. Then fit a choke in the pump's live wire

Lucas Electrical/Tri-Art

Another type of capacitor is the coaxial or feed-through type, which has a lead at each end. The capacitor is earthed as before, but this time you cut the supply wire to the electrical device you are suppressing and connect the capacitor's two leads.

Capacitors are used for suppression on the LT side of the ignition and for sundry other suppression jobs (see below).

The *resistor*, also used for suppression, slows down the flow of AC current so that it can no longer interfere with the DC current. It is used on the HT side of the ignition (see below).

Another type of suppressor is the *choke* which, like the other two, damps down the oscillations of alternating currents. It is wire-wound like a transformer. The DC supply current passes straight through the winding, but any stray oscillations of AC are blocked. The choke is fitted to the LT side of the ignition (see below).

The *earth bonding strap*, yet another suppression device, is a flat band of woven metal. It is used to suppress parts of the car which are not usually electrically alive, but have become so because they are near a magnetic field—the exhaust system can be one example. Earth bonding straps carry the interfering currents straight to earth on the car body.

Capacitors, resistors and earth-bonding straps can often be bought from a motor accessory retailer. If you find you need more sophisticated components, try a specialist car radio installer or a good auto electrician.

Order of work
Before starting work on any suppression, check three things:

First, that the aerial mounting is making a really good contact with the metal body of the car.

Second, that there is also a good earth contact between the radio casing and the car.

Third, that the whole of the car's electrical system is in good order. (Terminals should be clean and tight and properly insulated, spark-plugs should be correctly gapped and all the leads must be in good condition. Pay special attention to the HT leads, as described below, as these can play quite a large part in suppressing interference from the ignition).

For successful radio operation, three parts of the car must be suppressed: the coil, the generator, and the engine/exhaust system.

Once these have been done you can try your radio and, with luck, no further work will be necessary.

If it is, a series of tests will be needed to tell you which other car components are causing trouble.

Suppressing the coil
If your radio is an AM/FM set, suppress the coil with a parallel capacitor of 1mfd (microFarad) capacity as shown in fig. 2. It goes on the coil connection marked SW, BAT or + (on a positive-earthed car, —).

If this does not work (see interference tests, below), try using a 3mfd capacitor instead.

For an FM radio, start by fitting a 2.5mfd parallel capacitor to the coil. Then, if necessary, add an earth bonding strap between the coil mounting bracket and the engine.

Suppressing the generator
Your car owner's manual should tell you with what type

5 The HT lead between the coil and the distributor will often generate interference. First, use a sharp knife to cut the lead

6 Then you will need either a 5K or 10K resistor to join the two leads. Make sure that the resistor is held firmly in place

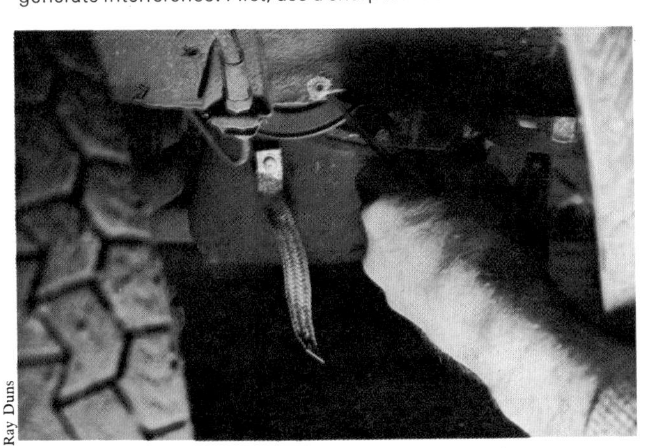

Ray Duns

7 An earth strap is a useful suppression device. Make sure that the two surfaces it joins are as free from dirt as possible

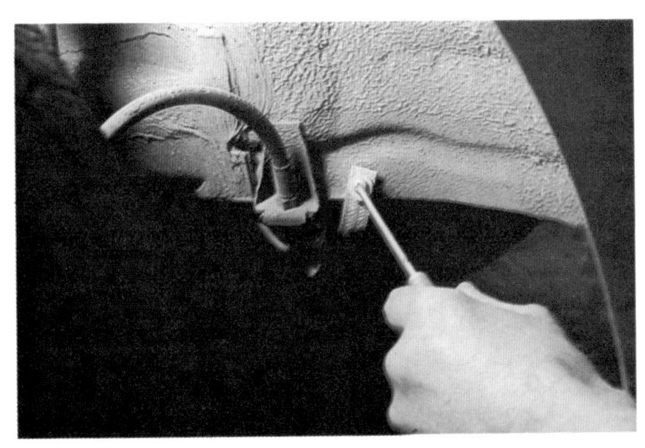

8 Tighten the earth strap securely. When in position, this strap will carry radio interference straight to earth on the car body

of generator your car is fitted: alternator or dynamo.

If it is an alternator, find the thicker wire (the output wire) coming from the back. For AM radio suppression, fit a parallel capacitor of 1mfd capacity to the terminal to which the wire is connected. For FM suppression, fit a 3mfd capacitor.

If a dynamo is fitted, you begin by fitting a capacitor exactly as you would to an alternator (figs. 10 to 13). But in this case the control box will also need to be suppressed, since it can produce a chattering, crackling interference.

Here you have two choices. You can replace the control box with a new one, with built-in suppression. Or you can suppress the old one, by fitting a 1mfd or 2mfd capacitor to the D terminal. (Do not suppress the F terminal.)

Suppressing the engine/exhaust

The engine and exhaust are suppressed as one unit by bolting one end of an earth bonding strap to either engine or exhaust, and the other to a nearby 'clean earth' on the car's body.

To find the best place to fix the earthing strap, take a long file—around 30 cm or 1ft—and lie under the car while a helper listens to the radio for you.

With the engine running, tune the radio off-station and turn up the volume so that all you get is loud interference. Now rest one end of the file against a suitable spot on the engine or exhaust and touch the other end to various parts of the car's underneath (for example, the front cross-member).

By trial and error, you will find the place where the radio interference is least. This is the ideal place for the earth strap.

If the strap cannot go at the ideal spot—for example, because it would mean drilling into the sump—fix it as close as possible.

Interference tests

Having suppressed the coil, the generator and the engine, you may still find that the level of interference is unacceptable. If so, a series of tests will help you pinpoint the trouble.

Some sources you may be able to identify by sound alone:

A *ticking* noise, the frequency of which alters with engine speed and which stops when the ignition is switched off, indicates that the ignition is the cause. In other words, the spark-plugs, distributor, or the heavy leads to the plugs and coil from the distributor (HT leads).

A rapid *ticking* noise at speeds over about 1,500-2,000 rpm can be caused by the points opening and closing in the control box.

A *whining* sound which increases in pitch as engine revs rise is likely to emanate from the dynamo or alternator.

Crackling or *buzzing* noises often come from accessories;

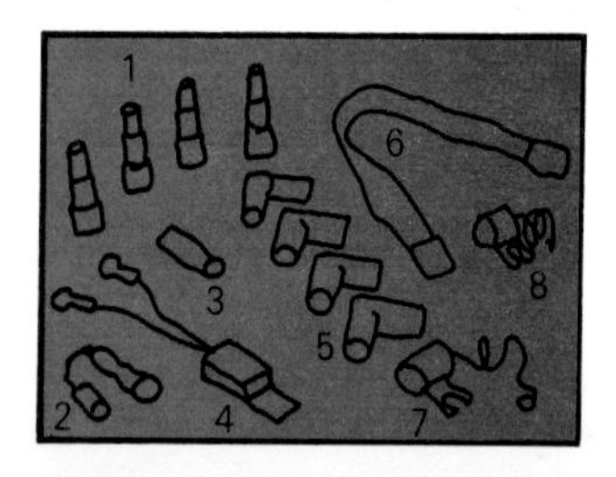

9 Suppression components that are often used. (1) straight screened plug caps (2) a choke (3) a resistor (4) a coaxial capacitor (5) right-angled screened plug caps (6) an earth bonding strap (7) and (8) parallel capacitors

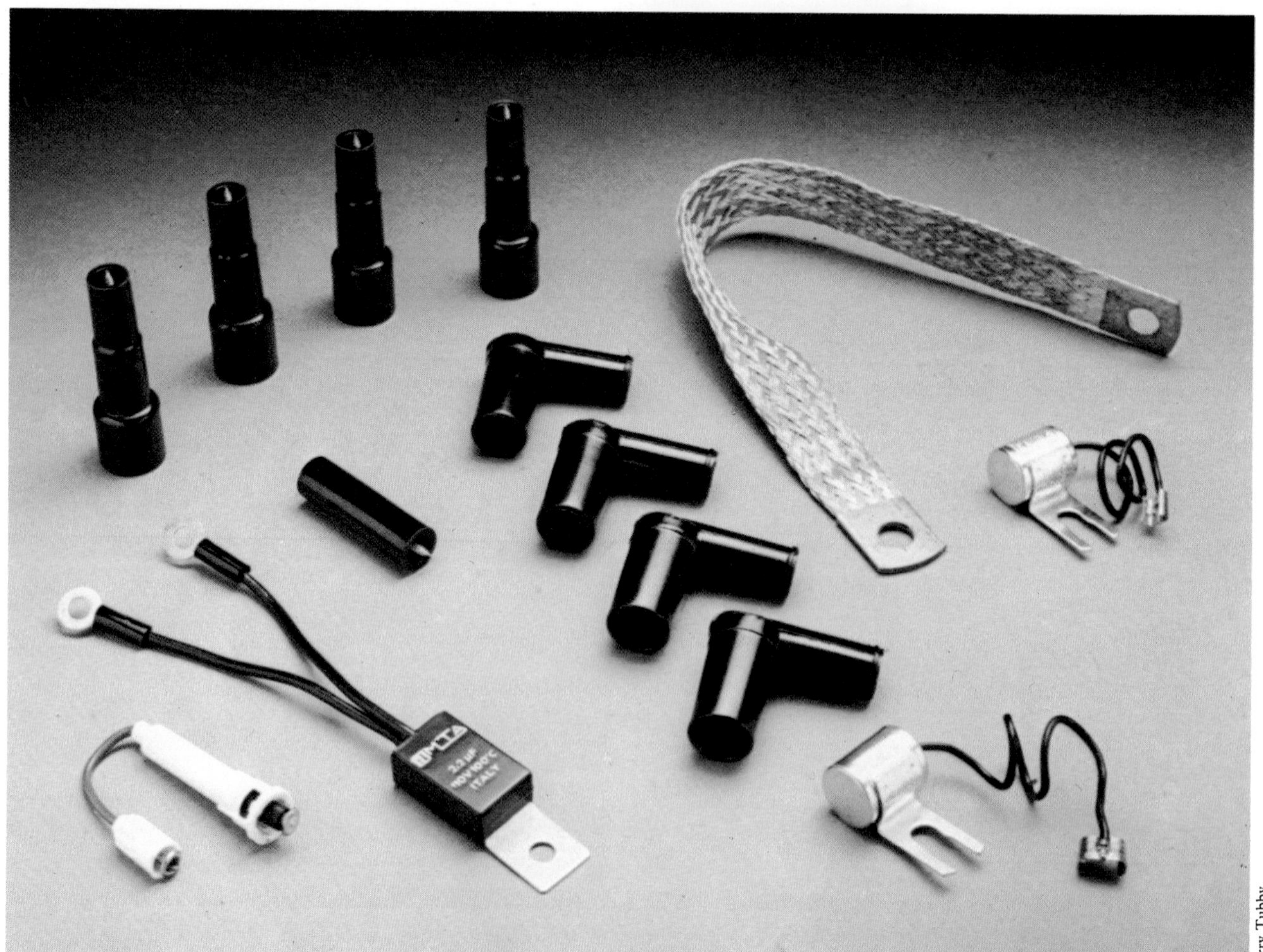

Jerry Tubby

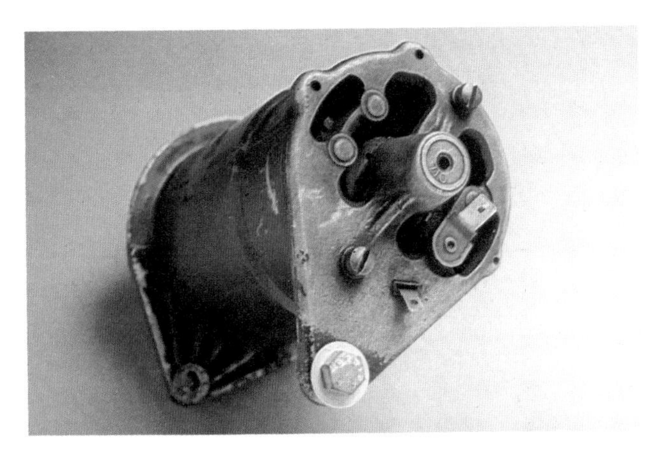

10 To cure any interference that may be coming from the dynamo first find the largest terminal on the back of the dynamo

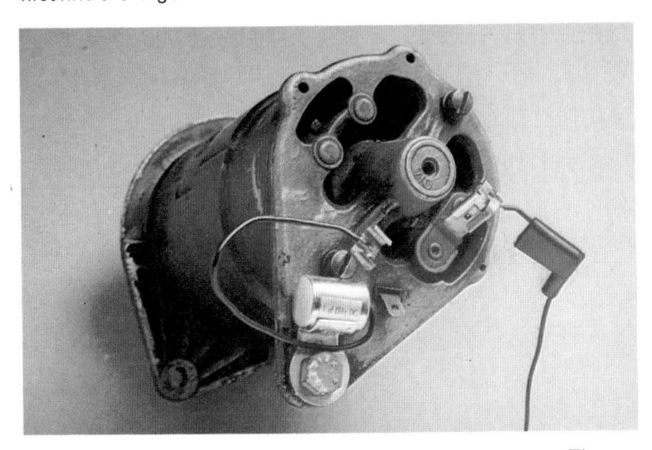

11 Pull back the insulation sleeve to expose the connector. Then use the mounting bracket of the dynamo to earth the capacitor

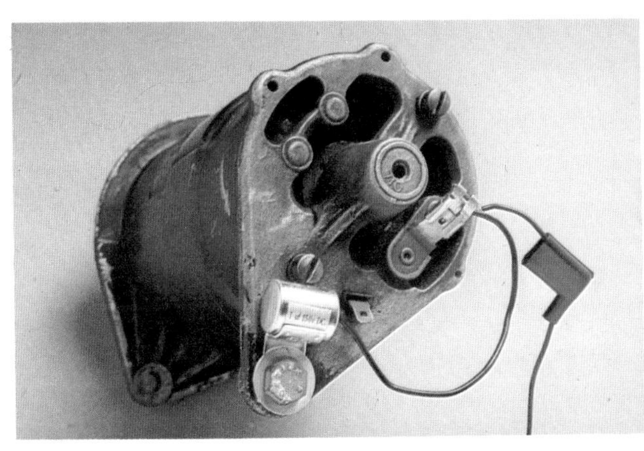

12 The wire from the capacitor is then joined to the connector on the dynamo. Make sure that they are held together securely

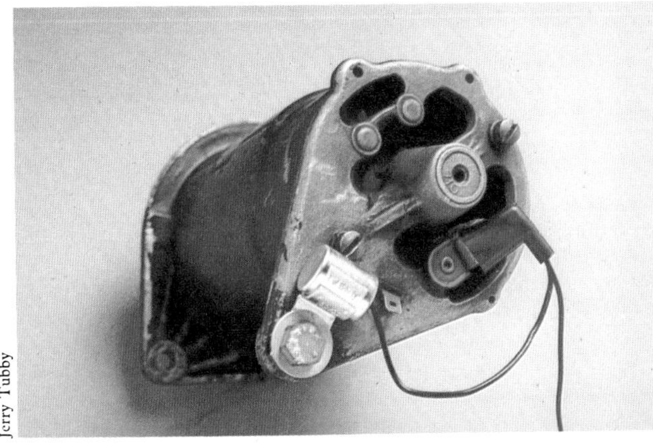

Jerry Tubby

13 Finally, push the insulation sleeve back over the connection. Adopt exactly the same procedure for suppressing an alternator

they appear as the component is switched on and disappear as it is turned off. Usually it is an electric motor, like the wiper motor, heater fan motor or screen washer motor. If it is causing interference, the indicator flasher motor will tick rhythmically through the speakers in time with the direction indicator dashboard warning light.

Intermittent *buzzing* noises, particularly at higher engine speeds, could be caused by the voltage stabilizer. This is a small electrical device linked in some cars' instrument circuit to smooth the current which operates the instruments and prevent it from fluctuating due to sudden voltage changes. (To find out if your car has a voltage stabilizer, look at the petrol gauge and switch on the ignition. If the needle moves right across and gives an instant reading, no voltage stabilizer is fitted. If the needle rises gradually, there is.)

If the interference noise is still difficult to identify, some tests you can carry out will help to isolate it.

First, with the engine ticking over, tune to a weak station on the radio. Pull the aerial out of its socket in the back of the set. If the interference disappears or lessens, it must be radiated interference picked up by the aerial or its lead.

Next, turn off the engine. Any interference that remains now must be conducted via the speaker leads or the power supply leads.

For the next tests, you need to check in advance that you can switch off the ignition without engaging the steering-column lock, if any, and to find a quiet road where you can 'coast' legally with the motor off.

First, with the radio tuned to a weak station, switch the engine off while the car is moving. With the clutch still engaged and the car in gear, the forward motion of the car will keep the engine turning over. Any interference noise that disappears will, therefore, have been coming from the ignition.

Try the same test again, but this time disengage the clutch. The engine will come to rest completely. If there is a difference between the two levels of interference (clutch in or clutch out) the cause will be the charging system.

Another test that works well with FM radios is to find a sheet of steel or copper about 25 cm or 10in. square, drill a hole and bolt a long lead to it. Attach the other end of the lead to a clean earth on the car's chassis. Again with the radio on a weak station, grip the metal plate with a pair of insulated pliers, then move the plate into various positions in and around the car, so that the plate acts as an interference screen.

When you find a position where the radio reception improves, then that is the source of the interference and you can take steps to deal with it. A poorly-earthed bumper bar, bonnet or body panel or perhaps a badly insulated silencer or suspension unit can be found by this method.

Suppressing the ignition

The basic ignition suppression that is required by law to prevent car engines from interfering with TV reception is built into new cars before you buy them.

Some suppression is carried out by the high tension brush in the distributor—the small spring-loaded brush in the centre of the distributor cap which, because it is carbon, is itself a resistor.

Sometimes extra suppression is provided by means of special resistive HT leads (fig. 15) between the coil, the distributor and the spark-plugs. These are made of cotton, nylon, rayon or silk, impregnated with carbon.

These carbon-trace leads are quite capable of damping out interference from the HT side where they are fitted, but can deteriorate with age or because of damage. For this reason, many car radio specialists prefer to use the traditional copper-cored HT leads (fig. 15), plus resistive-type spark-plug caps (the hooded type).

If your ignition system is causing interference, first check that all its components are tightly secured and in good repair. Then fit a resistor of either 5K (Kilo-ohms) or 10K into the HT lead from the coil to the centre of the distributor cap (figs. 5 and 6).

Should tests show that you still have interference, try a resistor on each plug lead. There are two types—the in-line type that fits into the plug lead itself (fig. 5), and the plug-in type, which pushes into the HT lead housings in the distributor cap and the leads then plug into the suppressors.

As a final step, the plug caps can be changed for the shielded type. These have small metal shrouds which cover the plug cap and which should be earthed. They incorporate a resistance of 1K each.

It is important, however, to make sure that the total resistance you build into the power line to any one spark-plug (including what you fit to the coil lead or distributor cap, plug-in or line suppressor, resistive-type plug lead and plug cap and shield) does not exceed 25K. A higher resistance than this could affect spark-plug performance.

Further suppression

If other components are causing interference, deal with them as follows:

Aerial and lead: Ensure the aerial is properly earthed. If this fails, enclose the lead in braided metal sheath and connect the sheath to earth.

Voltage stabilizer: Fit a 1mfd capacitor on the stabilizer's battery terminal (marked B) and a 1 amp choke on the other terminal. If the wiring behind the dashboard is a printed circuit, a special plug-in stabilizer will have to be obtained from the vehicle manufacturer.

Coil: If the coil is not already mounted on the engine, try an earth-bonding strap between the coil mounting bracket and the engine.

Non-electrical components (body panel etc): Bolt an earth bonding strap between the offending component and the chassis.

Ancillary motor (eg, windscreen wiper motor): If the radio is AM only, try a 1mfd or 2mfd capacitor on its supply lead as in fig. 3. If the radio is FM, fit a 7 amp choke in series with the supply lead, again as in fig. 3. Make sure the motor body is well earthed.

Direction indicators: Ensure that the flasher unit is well earthed. Fit a 1mfd capacitor on the 'battery' side of the unit.

Clock: Deal with this as with direction indicators.

In almost every case, these measures will suppress interference even on a troublesome car. If none of them works, however, you will need specialist help.

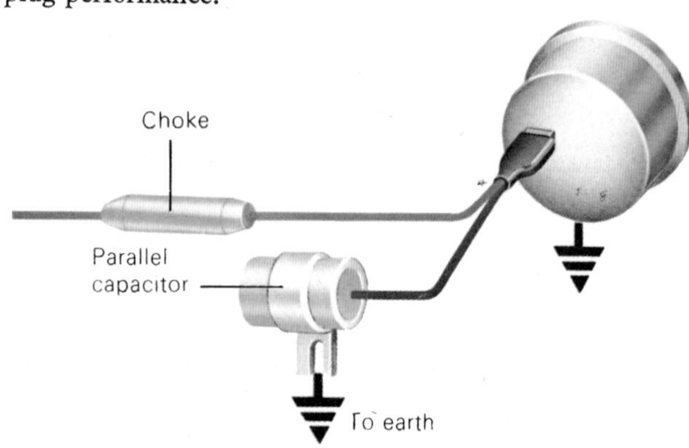

14 You can suppress a car clock by inserting a choke in its live wire and connecting a parallel capacitor to the live terminal

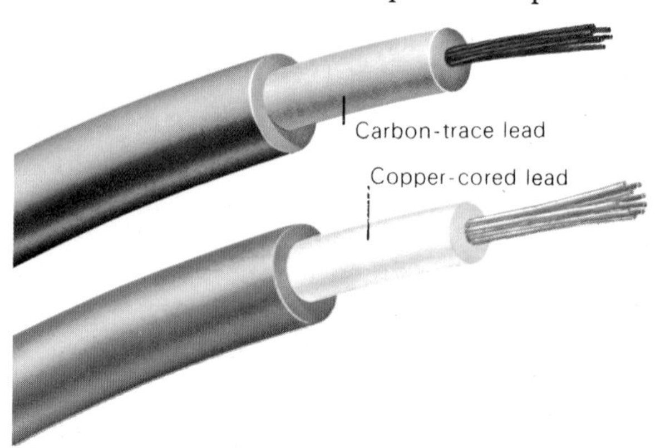

15 Carbon-trace HT leads can often cure radio interference. But some experts prefer copper-cored leads with resistive plug caps

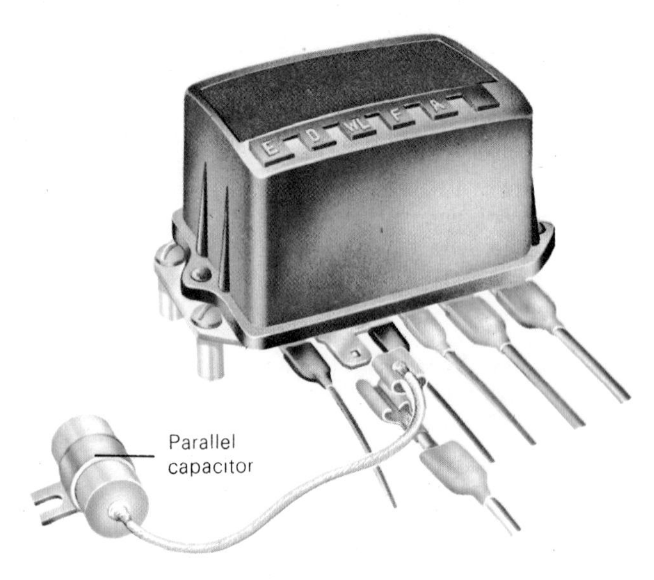

16 To suppress a control box, fit a parallel capacitor to the D terminal. Alternatively fit a new box with built-in suppression

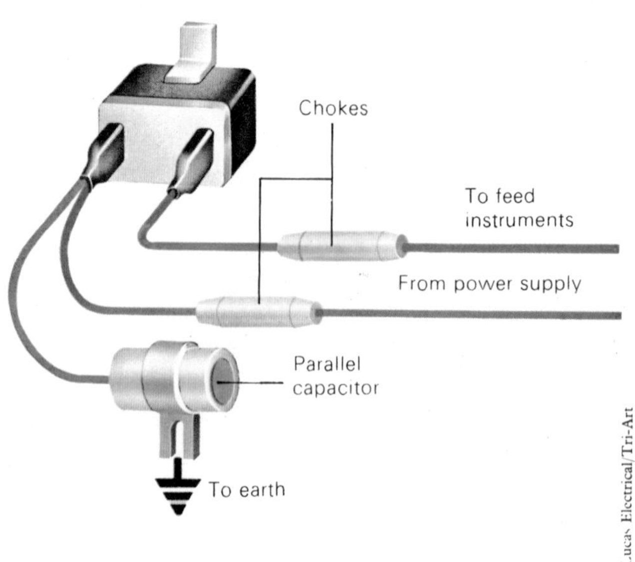

17 On a voltage stabilizer, first fit a choke in both of its leads. Then connect a parallel capacitor to its live terminal

Lucas Electrical/Tri-Art

Fitting a console

One of the most difficult problems the home mechanic is likely to encounter when fitting accessories to his car is lack of space. The dashboards of most modern cars are designed with all the necessary instruments clustered in front of the driver. Padded trays or recesses take up the rest of the fascia space and there is often nowhere to cut a hole or even to fit an extra panel. The answer is to fit a central console, running from below the fascia, along the car floor or transmission tunnel, and over the gear lever. In many more expensive cars they are standard equipment, and usually house radio or tape equipment, auxiliary instruments and switches, and extra storage trays and compartments.

Accessory consoles come in all shapes and sizes, to suit many popular makes of car. The typical 'short' console (fig. 2) is designed to extend only as far as the gear lever, as on the Ford Escort illustrated. It is primarily intended to house a radio receiver for which it has a special hole, but it also has a slotted panel behind which a speaker may be fitted. The console is covered in black leather-look vinyl.

By contrast the 'long' console (fig. 2) extends back between the front seats, the armrest unit covering the handbrake. Under the armrest is a small compartment for storing cassettes or odd items, and at the front of the console is a plain wooden panel which can be cut to house accessories. Both consoles are constructed from hardboard and plywood and feature a plastic gaiter which is drawn tight around the gear lever.

Choosing a console

There is no shortage of consoles on the accessory market but they vary a great deal in both design and quality. The first step when buying one is to find out exactly what is available for your car, by quoting the make, model and year to your stockist or manufacturer.

Examine the range, and decide exactly what sort of console you want. Some drivers find the full-length ones too cramping; others appreciate the centre armrest and storage compartment. If you are fitting or transferring instruments to the console, make sure there is enough room in the one of your choice. Think about colour as well—you should be able to find one that blends with your car's interior.

Finally make sure the console is of reasonable quality. Many accessory consoles look rather cheaply made. Yours should at least be rigid, with no loose trim strips or peeling vinyl. Do not expect any fitting instructions—in most cases they are not given. Self-tapping screws are provided to secure the console to the car floor, but the brackets supplied with them are rarely strong or numerous enough to keep it firmly in position. The best way to determine what brackets will be needed is to locate your console in position in the car. On a short console three or four will probably be enough, but on the full-length version three brackets on each side may be required. Use L-shaped ones, made of metal thin enough to bend to shape. The self-tapping screws provided with the console may not be long enough to screw through the bracket carpet and floor, in which case you should buy longer ones, or use thin bolts. If you use screws make sure that you have a drill bit of the correct size, usually 3-4 mm ($\frac{1}{8}$in.).

Fitting a short console

The short console illustrated is supplied with three brackets already attached—one on each side at the front and one at the back. The two front ones are designed to be bent outwards slightly so that they clasp the sides of the transmission tunnel, or in the case of front wheel drive cars the remote gearchange housing. The rear bracket sticks out behind the console and is screwed down straight into the floor.

If your console does not have brackets already fitted, fix them at this stage, either by drilling the sides of the console

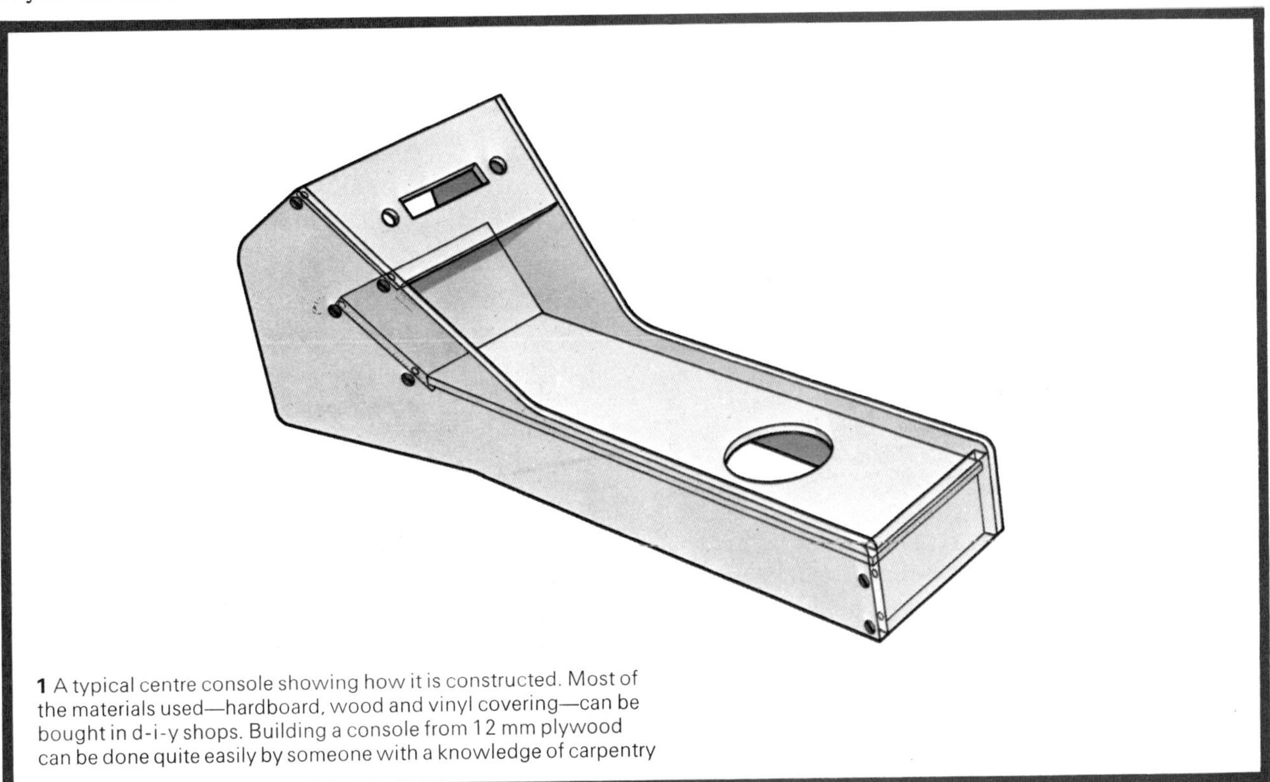

1 A typical centre console showing how it is constructed. Most of the materials used—hardboard, wood and vinyl covering—can be bought in d-i-y shops. Building a console from 12 mm plywood can be done quite easily by someone with a knowledge of carpentry

Bernard Fallon

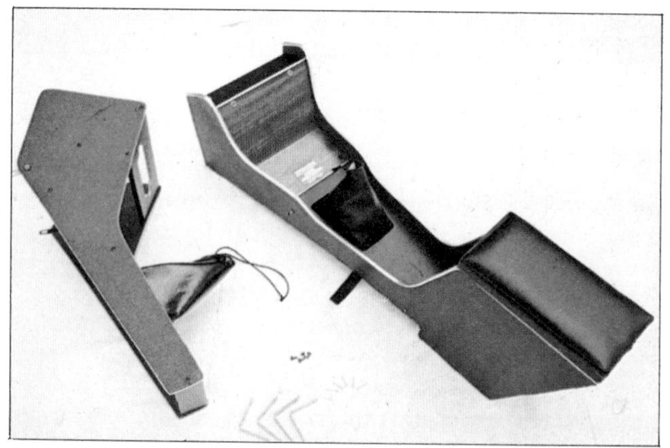

2 Two typical proprietary consoles. The one on the left is of the short variety while that on the right has a built-in armrest

3 This short console has brackets already fitted and these can be used as templates to drill screw or bolt holes in the car floor

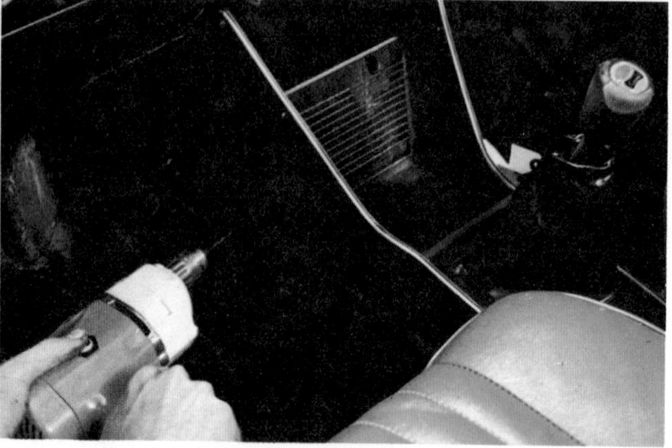

4 The front brackets are used in the same way. When you start drilling into the floor, be careful not to damage any brake pipes

5 On this console the slot for the radio is not big enough and must be cut to the correct size with a keyhole or coping saw

Jerry Tubby

6 Once the panel has been cut, it can be unscrewed and any rough edges filed down. Vinyl tape is used to stop the vinyl from peeling

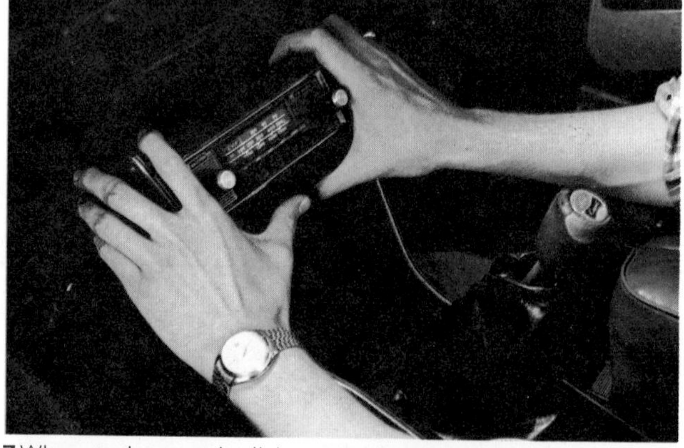

7 When you have made all the necessary connections to the back of the radio, slide it into the panel and locate it in position

and bolting them on, or by screwing them into the support brackets.

Locate the console in position, sliding the loose gaiter over the gear lever. Leave the brackets protruding, and bend them to shape. Mark the positions of the holes to be drilled in the floor, using a piece of chalk if necessary to avoid marking the carpet. If the console has been badly designed it will not match the contours of the car floor exactly, and you will have to trim it to fit. Mark the lines of the cut in chalk on the outside of the console, then cut the vinyl covering with a sharp knife and peel away the excess. Using a fretsaw, saw the wood or hardboard body of the console along the line, without chafing the covering. Rough edges can be filed down.

The next step is to drill the holes. If the console is being fitted to a rear wheel drive car it is likely that transmission components will prevent you from getting at the floor from underneath, so you will not be able to bolt it in place. You will have to use self-tapping screws. When drilling holes in the floor make sure they are the correct size and take care not to damage any components or brake pipes underneath. Check the path of the drill first by looking under the car.

When drilling the holes you may find there is not enough space to work in and you will have to move the brackets. Make sure the floor covering or carpet does not slip, or you will lose the position of the holes.

You can now turn your attention to the console itself, and decide exactly what you want to fit in it. The short console illustrated already has a hole cut to accommodate a radio but this may well have to be enlarged. Follow the same cutting procedure as on the sides of the console, using a keyhole saw to cut inside the hole. If you are transferring the radio from an under-dash panel, disconnect all the wires to it and

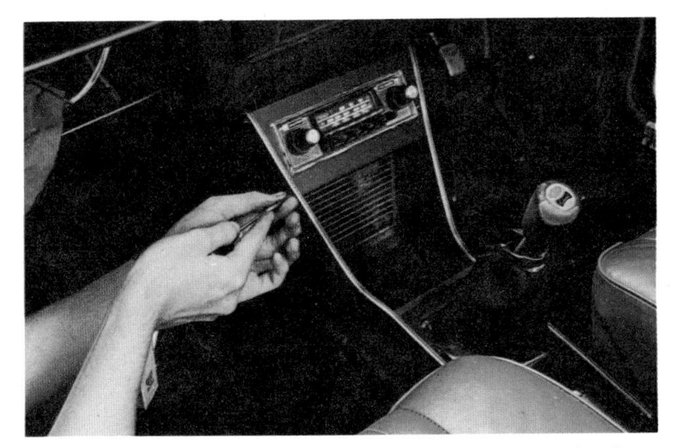

8 You can then refit the panel by screwing it in from the side of the console. Tape any obtrusive wires behind well out of sight

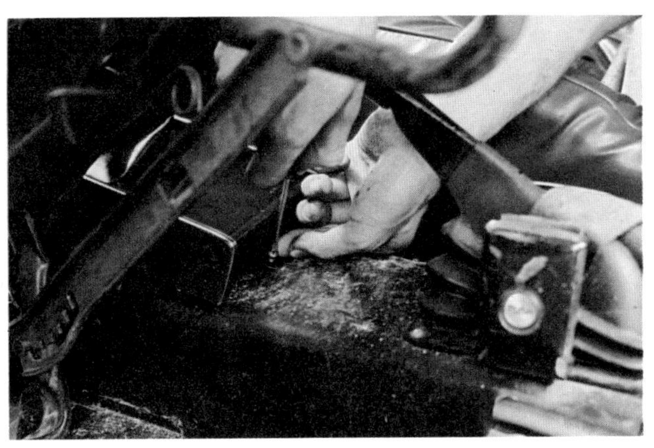

9 The console is now ready to be fixed in position. Here, self-tapping screws are being used to secure the brackets to the floor

re-route them down the front bulkhead and into the back of the pod. Any extension to the wires must be fixed with proper bullet or screw connectors, and remember that the aerial connection can only be lengthened using a special lead. The radio itself can be fixed to the console in a variety of ways, depending on the make. Some clamp on from the back, some screw in from the front, and others have L-shaped brackets at the side, to be fixed with screws to the back of the console panel.

In the console illustrated, you can fit a speaker below the radio. Screw it in at the back of the panel, using short self-tapping screws which will not protrude right through. This particular console does not have any provision for auxiliary instruments, but there are plenty of short ones available with plain front panels should you wish to fit extra gauges rather than a radio.

With all the desired accessories in place, locate the console in its position. If you have marked the holes correctly, it is now a simple matter of screwing or bolting the brackets to the car floor. Make sure that the unit is firmly fixed and does not vibrate with the engine running. If it does, you may need to fit more brackets or tighten the bracket screws and bolts. Check also that the accessories work properly. With all these steps completed, finish by pulling the drawstring tight round the top of the gear lever gaiter and tying.

Fitting a full-length console

Full-length consoles generally pose more fitting problems than short ones because there are more fixtures to obstruct them, such as front seats and handbrake. However they are ideal for small front-wheel drive cars like the Mini which has

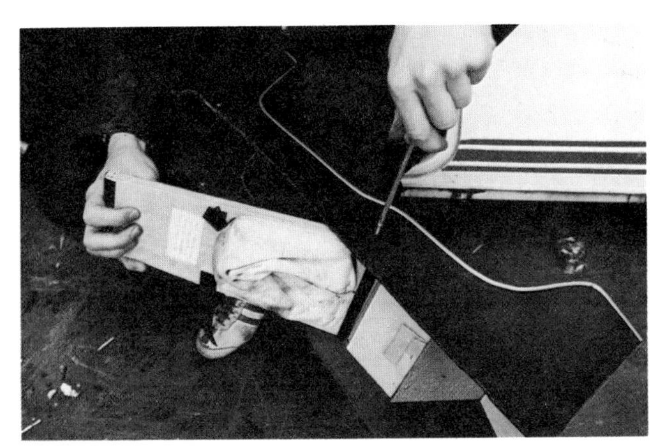

10 On this full-length console, the centre panel and gear-stick gaiter are unscrewed first to make locating it in position easy

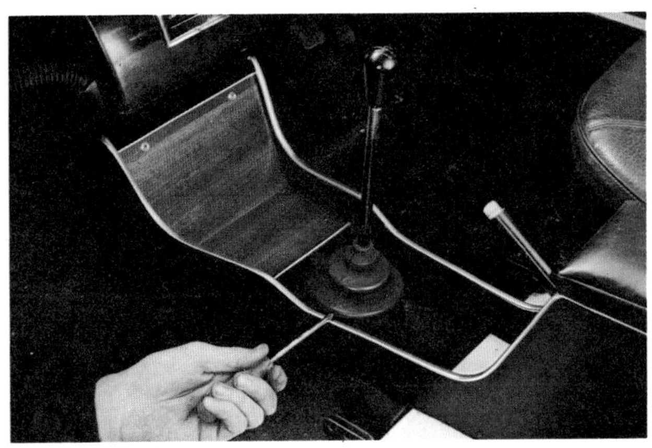

11 With the console in position, it can be seen that the centre panel will foul the gear linkage—it will have to be cut down

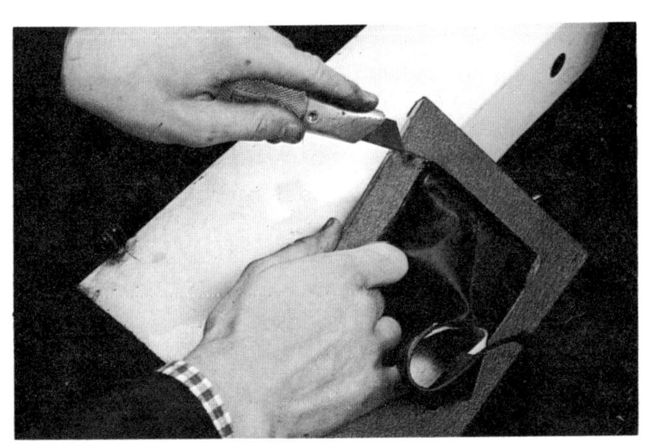

12 First the vinyl covering is cut with a sharp knife and peeled back, so that the edges will stay smooth when the wood is sawn

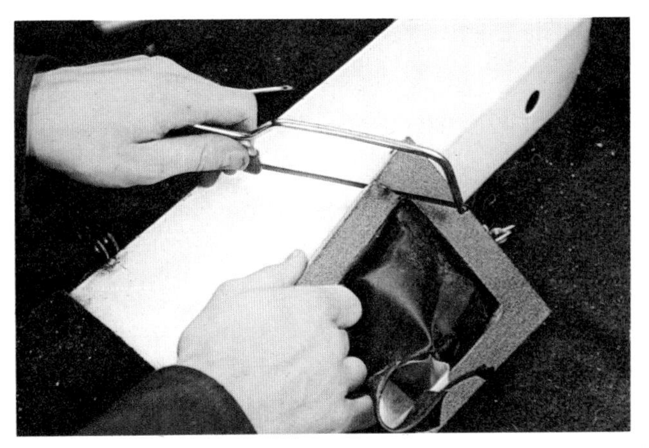

13 The panel can now be cut to shape using a hacksaw. Use a chalk mark as a guide if you are uncertain of the cutting line

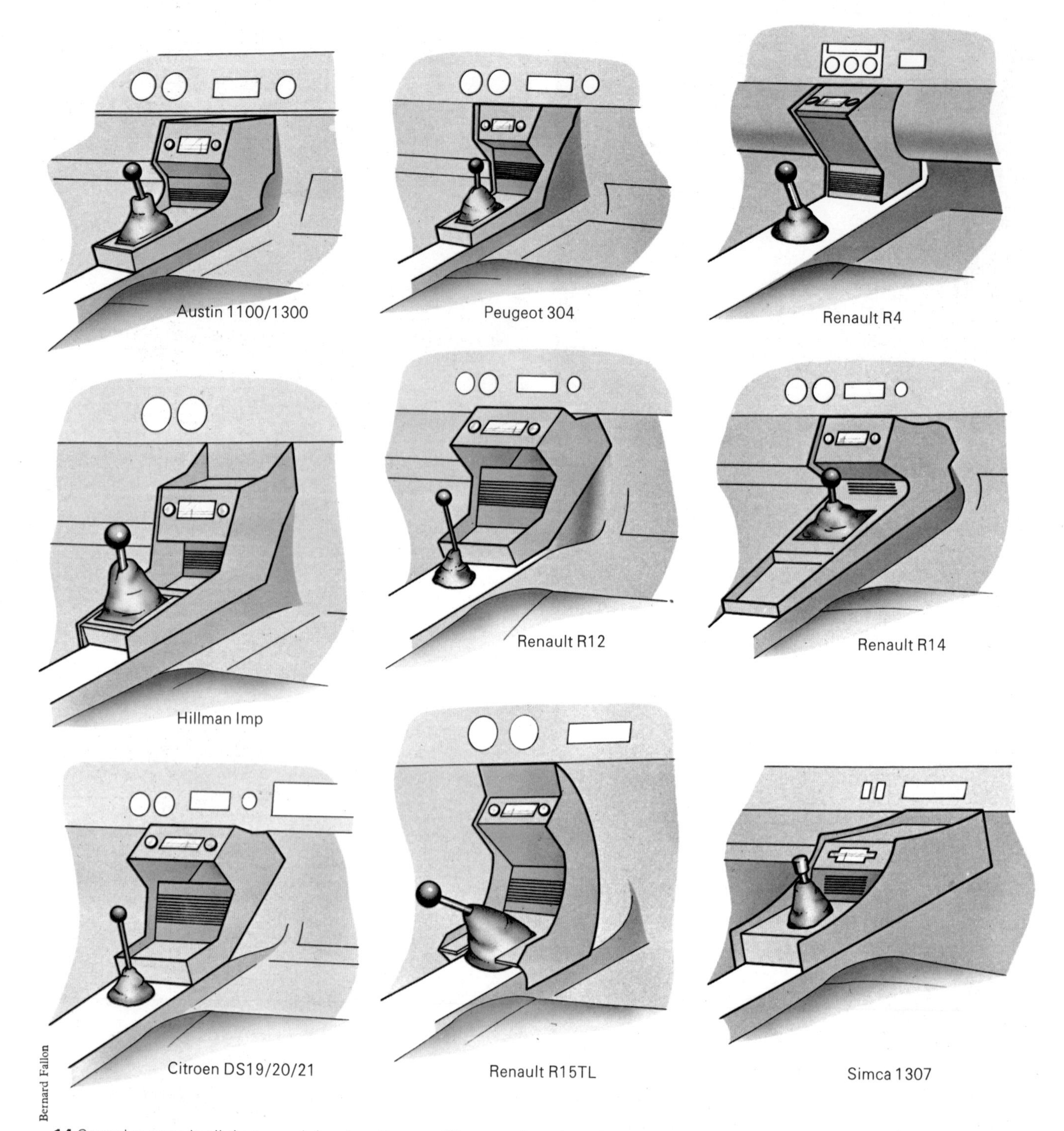

14 Consoles come in all shapes and sizes to suit many different makes of car. These are from Sprint

little dashboard space, plenty of room on the front floor, and an awkwardly protruding handbrake. A console like the one illustrated offers a wide panel for gauges, and covers up most of the handbrake while leaving it free to be operated safely.

Start by locating the console in position. You may find that there is not enough room between the front seats to fit it in, and one seat will have to be removed, by unbolting it either from the floor or from its two sliding brackets.

You should now decide what to fit in the console. If yours has a plain front panel, any holes to be cut in it are best done on the bench. The one illustrated is to receive two gauges, previously fitted in a panel under the fascia capping. To fit an instrument start by scribing a circle on the panel with a pair of dividers (fig. 15). The diameter of the circle should correspond to the inner width of the gauge. Drill a small hole or two just inside the edge of the circle, insert a keyhole saw blade and carefully cut round the circle (fig. 16). File down any rough edges. The instrument can now be inserted through the hole and secured by screwing its screw-clamp against the back of the panel. If instruments are being transferred to the console, all connections must be re-routed to run in from the back, as on the short console.

If you are transferring instruments from a metal dashboard or panel, separate earth connections will have to be made because the console panel itself is insulated. On each instrument, first attach a wire to the clamp at the back. Next run it to a convenient earthing point, such as a screw under the dashboard, and fix it firmly in place (fig. 18).

If you want to fit a radio measure it and scribe a rectangle the size of the casing in the front panel. Drill holes just inside the edges of all four sides to give a clean cut with the keyhole saw. The procedure for fixing is the same as on the short console.

With this particular full-length console there is no

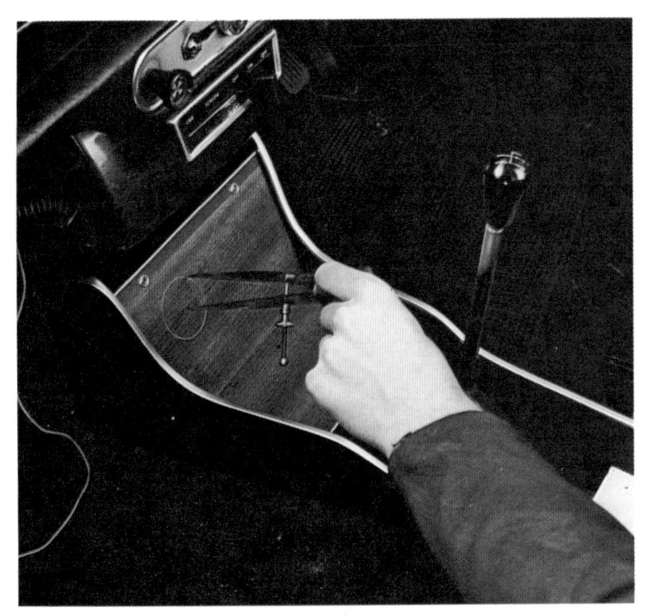

15 Holes for the auxiliary instruments are scribed on the veneer panel with a pair of dividers, set to the width of the gauges

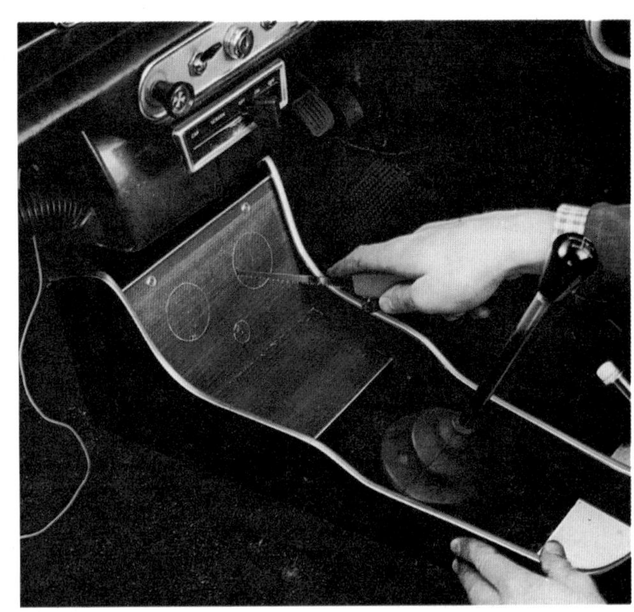

16 After you have drilled a small hole on the edge of each circle, you can insert the blade of a keyhole saw and cut out the holes

17 The accessories are then pushed through the holes and clamped from behind. Connect all necessary wires at this stage

Jerry Tubby

18 Because instruments are insulated in the panel, they require a common earthing wire. This one runs to a dashboard fixing bolt

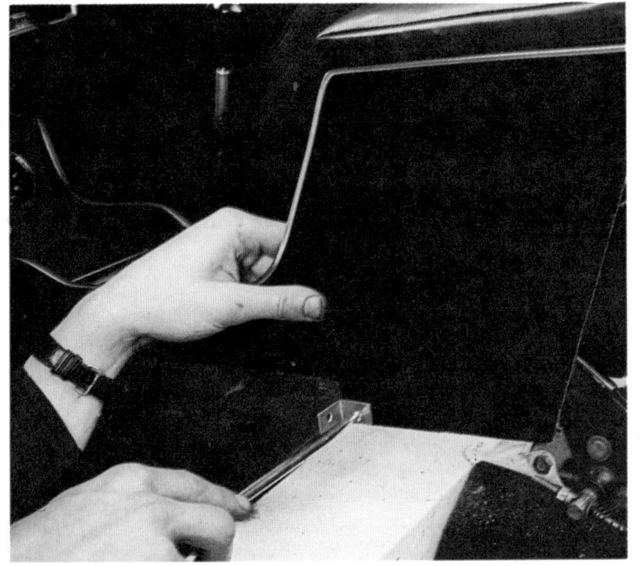

19 Having estimated the best position for the mounting brackets, they can be screwed or bolted in place on the console

provision for a radio speaker, but the tray panel round the gear lever gaiter allows room for such things as foot light switches, a hazard warning light switch or an extra ashtray if required. Be careful to allow sufficient clearance below the console, otherwise it will not fit flush against the floor.

In the case of the type illustrated, the console will completely overlap the gear linkage tunnel, and L-shaped brackets will be needed to screw it straight through the floor. These need only be of thin flexible metal, but start by choosing suitable places for them to go, with the console located in position. Drill the sides of the console and bolt or screw brackets onto the inside, making sure that you do not split what is often rather flimsy material. If the console has to be trimmed to fit, do it at this stage. Continue to follow the steps outlined above for marking the holes, checking, and drilling. When drilling through the floor pan in front-wheel drive cars take care not to pierce the exhaust pipe, which often runs close to the underside of the car. If you do have room to work from below, a couple of bolts will hold the console more firmly than screws.

Before you go any further check the handbrake. When full

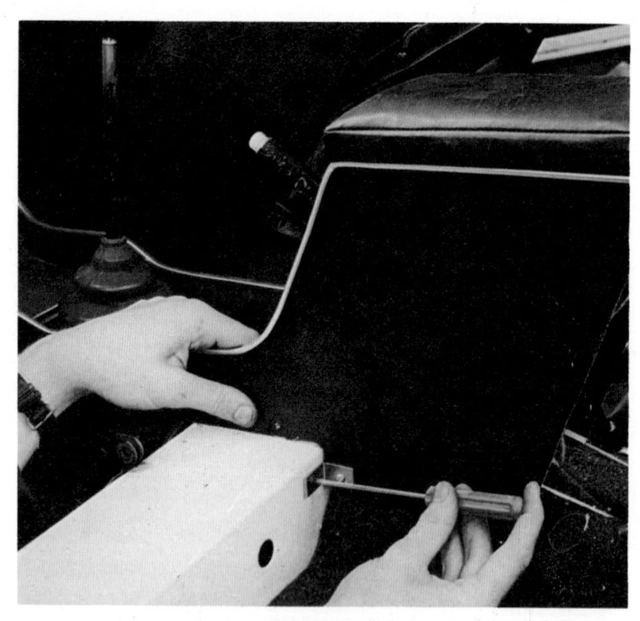

20 Once more, locate the console in position and mark the holes for the bracket screws in the car floor with a screwdriver

21 The holes can now be drilled. If they run through carpet, it may be easier to mark them with chalk or take the carpet up

22 Secure the console in place by screwing down all the brackets. Again where there is carpet, use longer screws or bolts

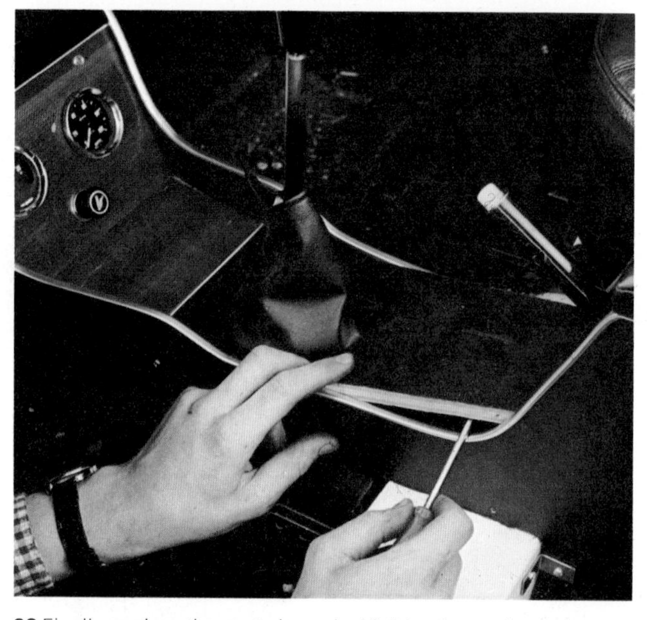

23 Finally, replace the central panel which has been trimmed to fit. The gaiter slides over the gear lever and is tied at the top

Jerry Tubby

24 The finished console in position in the car. The centre arm-rest, with a compartment underneath, is particularly useful

on it must not foul against the armrest casing. If it does, the handbrake will have to be adjusted to give less movement in the lever.

When all the accessories are in place locate the console once more, and screw or bolt the brackets to the floor. Check that it is firmly in position, and finally tie up the gaiter round the gear lever (figs. 19 to 24).

Soundproofing

If you are unlucky the hollow cavity inside your console may amplify any transmission noise in the tunnel beneath it. If this happens, remove the unit and pack it with suitable damping material such as cotton wool or foam rubber.

Fitting a cigarette lighter

One accessory which particularly lends itself to being fitted in a console is the electric cigarette lighter. Not only is a lighter easier to use than matches while driving—it is also safer. Unfortunately, its depth prevents it from going into the tray panel on most consoles, but it should fit easily in the front panel.

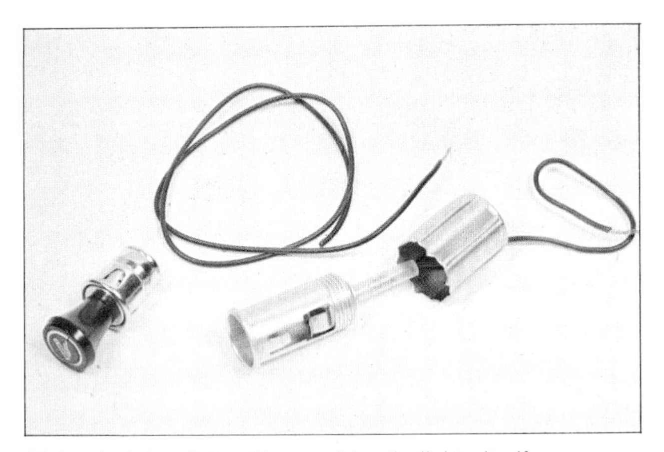

25 A typical cigar lighter kit comprising the lighter itself, an electric socket, a screw-on clamp and an optional earth wire

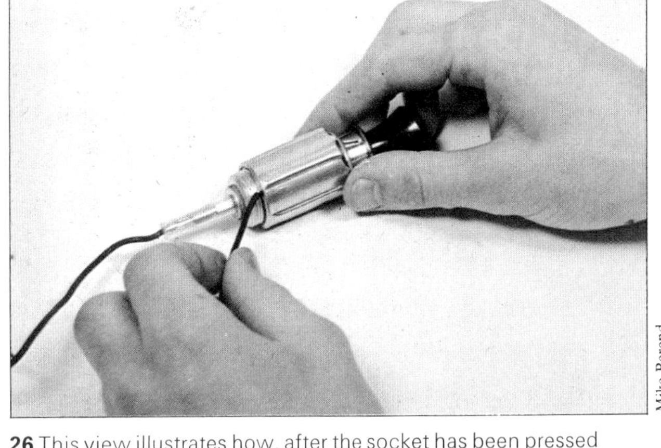

Mike Berend

26 This view illustrates how, after the socket has been pressed into a convenient hole, the clamp screws on behind to secure it

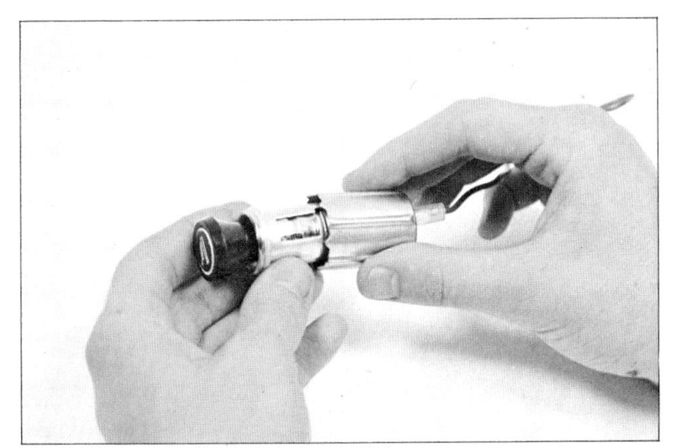

27 If the lighter is going into an insulated panel, the bared end of an earthing wire must be screwed on with the securing clamp

28 The lighter in place, seen from the back of the console. The earth wire is held by the tight clamp and can be connected up

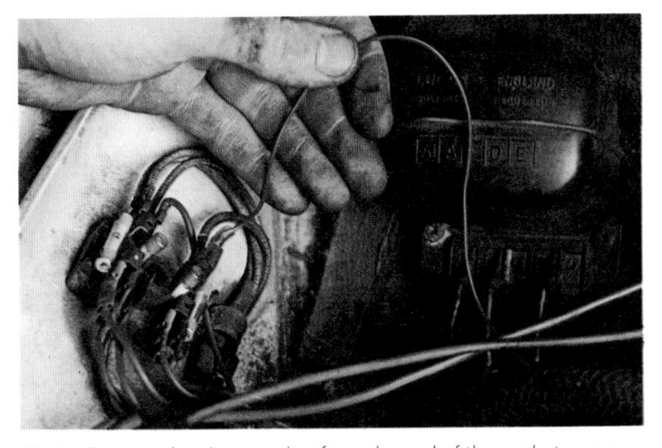

29 The live supply wire, running from the end of the socket, goes to a spare terminal on the ignition switch side of the fusebox

Start by unscrewing the metal sleeve clamp from the holder unit, then measure the width of the holder with a pair of dividers. Scribe a circle of this diameter on the console panel. To cut the aperture, either drill a hole just inside the scribe mark and saw round the circle with a keyhole saw, or simply drill a 'chain' of holes round the circle, push out the centre, and file down the jagged edge (see page 167).

The holder unit can now be pushed through the hole and secured by screwing the metal sleeve against the back of the panel (fig. 26). Before fitting the lighter, however, consider the problem of the earth. On most lighters the holder and fixing sleeve or clamp are 'earth'. This means that if they are in direct contact with an earthed part of the car, such as a metal dashboard, no separate earth wire is needed. The panel in a console will not be earthed so an earth connection must be made. To do this, take an adequate length of wire, bare the ends, and 'catch' one end between the sleeve and the holder unit as you screw the sleeve on (figs. 27 and 28). If you have a soldering iron solder the wire onto the sleeve for a more secure contact. Run the other end of the wire to a suitable earthing point such as a fascia fixing screw or bolt. Undo the screw, wrap the bare end of the wire round it and retighten.

The only other connection to make is to the live supply. A wire will probably be provided, but it is unlikely to be long enough so extend it using a bullet or a screw connector. Connect one end to the terminal on the back of the lighter unit, then run the wire up to and through the engine bulkhead to the fuse box. In order that you may use the lighter at any time, it is best fitted to a fused circuit not operated by the ignition switch. Identify the spare terminals using a 12v test lamp. With the lamp connected between each terminal in turn and earth, you will soon find which terminal lights it with the ignition on or off. Crimp or solder a spade connector onto the bare end of the lighter wire and connect it up. If there is another accessory already on the terminal, simply use a double spade connector. Because the holder unit gets hot during operation, it is as well to ensure that there are no wires or wads of soundproofing running too near to it, as this could start a fire.

After fixing the console in place, test the lighter by pressing it down into the holder and waiting for it to pop up when hot. The tray panel on a full-length console is a good place to fit an ashtray to complement the lighter. Cut a rectangular hole in the panel (it can often be removed for access) using the same methods as for fitting the gauges above. You can then push the ashtray into the empty recess.

Fitting a custom fascia

Barbara Bellingham

1 A custom fascia can give your car some of the character normally only associated with exotic models like this Aston Martin DBS V8

When a car manufacturer is trying to cut costs, elaborate and attractive instrument panels are one of the first things to be sacrificed. The basic versions of several popular cars have purely functional fascias which are cheap and easy to install. While these may be adequate they can also be ugly and inconvenient, especially if you want to fit extra switches and gauges. The answer is to fit a custom fascia. Your car will not only be better to look at but also more pleasant to drive.

Accessory fascias are now available for several cars in a variety of different styles. Although fitting them is sometimes an awkward job, no special knowledge or tools are required. The greatest difficulty you are likely to encounter is choosing what will be mounted in the panel before it is installed. A custom fascia provides an excellent site for accessory instruments but you must have these ready to fit, together with their connections, before the panel is actually fitted in place. Fitting accessories at a later date may mean removing the fascia and this is not always easy so it pays to do a fully comprehensive job.

Buying a custom fascia

There are two basic types of custom fascia available—the one-piece plastic moulding and the veneered wood panel kit. The plastic moulding types have been designed primarily for the enthusiast who wants to give his car's interior a more sporting image. Most of the products available have ample provision for extra switches and gauges and holes for these are easily cut in the plastic moulding. A fascia of this type will enable you to change the position of any existing instrument which you feel are badly sited. For example, using one of these fascia conversion kits the central speedometer on a Mini can be transferred to a more visible position in front of the driver.

In some cases, the moulded fascia does have the disadvantage of using up parcel shelf space, as on the Mini for instance, but this may not concern you. The Autoplas Mini dash illustrated (fig. 18) is one of two designs marketed by Screenoprints Ltd., the other one being suitable for either left or right-hand drive cars. The Madadash and Novadash Mini dash panels and the Escort and Anglia panels marketed by Brown and Geeson are similar. Like the Autoplas fascias, they are vacuum-formed, one-piece mouldings.

There are a number of wood panel kits available and although they are usually more expensive than the plastic panels they are also more solid. The idea behind these kits is to give your car a touch of quality for wood veneered dashboards are now only found as standard fittings on luxury and/or some high-performance cars.

The Rokee Mini dash panel illustrated (fig. 32) is typical of the products on the market. The kit is supplied in three pieces to allow you some flexibility during installation and these bolt together quite simply once they have been located in position. A feature of this particular dashboard is the proper glove compartment built into one of the panels which is always a useful fitting. One possible disadvantage is that cutting holes in the wood veneer may be tricky, but this will only arise if you are planning to fit a variety of extra gauges.

Rokee also market similar kits for the BL Mini Clubman, Allegro, Marina and Princess and for the Ford Escort and

Fiesta. Where the panels fit over existing instruments, holes will already have been cut; again, you should not have any problems if you retain your original layout.

Custom fascias are usually sold in the larger car accessory shops or by tuning specialists and it pays to have a good look round before you commit yourself. By doing this you will get a good idea of what is available for your car and which unit best suits your requirements. Having made a choice, inspect it before buying and decide what extras you want and where you can fit them. You can then buy these at the same time. Remember also to quote the make, model, chassis number and year of your car as there are often detailed differences between models which might not be immediately apparent.

What you will need for the job

Custom fascia kits are nearly always supplied with the self-tapping screws, bolts and brackets needed to fit them. But, just to make sure, have a look in your kit before you buy it. At the same time, consult the kit instructions and make a note of any recommended drill sizes. You must have the correct "bit" if self-tapping screws are being used.

With one-piece moulded fascias, you will probably have to cut holes for gauges. The simplest way of doing this is to use a hole-saw attachment on an electric drill. It should have a diameter of 52 mm (2ins). If you do not have one of these, the holes can be cut by drilling a series of holes and sawing out a circle with a keyhole saw or following the steps outlined on pages 167 to 169. Whichever method you use, a pair of dividers will be needed to mark the holes first. On some mouldings the holes for gauges are indented in the plastic. If this is the case with yours, you can deepen the marks by scoring them with the dividers and then cut round them with a sharp knife.

When you are installing this type of fascia you may find that instrument wires need extending. It is therefore a good idea to have a supply of electrical wire, a selection of crimp-on terminals and some screw or Scotchlok connectors. If you have a mechanical oil pressure gauge with a metal feed pipe, the pipe may not stretch to the new dashboard, in which case you will have to replace the pipe with the flexible nylon type. These can be bought in most accessory shops. Mechanical water temperature gauges may create similar problems. If they will not extend as they are, they will have to be replaced with more suitable units (see page 162).

Most custom fascias have provision for the speedometer to be left in its original position. If you want to move it remember that the cable may not be long enough. Make sure that you can get an extended one before attempting the job. You will probably find that a cable from another car in your manufacturer's range will be suitable.

If you are fitting extra gauges make sure you have them ready and that you have enough wire and terminals to connect them up to the engine. An ammeter, vacuum gauge and rev counter are all useful additions (pages 167, 192, 173). The same goes for additional switches.

Wood panel fascia kits, like the one-piece dashboards, should be provided with all the necessary screws and bolts. You may, however, need an impact adhesive (e.g. Bostik, Evo-stik or Superglue) to glue trim strips in place but check this with the kit instructions. Otherwise, the same things apply as for the plastic fascias. Remember though, that these kits usually provide for existing instruments and switches to be left in their original positions so there will be less extension work to be done.

Holes may be cut in the same way, but because of the problems of working with wood veneer a great deal more care will have to be taken (see below).

Fitting a one-piece moulded fascia—BL Mini

To fit a one-piece fascia, start by studying your original panel to see just what will have to be moved. Consider what form the new layout will take and where any extras are to be fitted. You will then be ready to begin fitting the moulding. First, disconnect the battery. This will eliminate the risk of short circuits later on when you are extending the wiring. On the Autoplas unit shown, the next step is to disconnect the choke cable at the carburettor end and the heater control cable from its valve on the engine block (fig. 2). Follow this by unscrewing the switch panel and loosening it from its location (fig. 3). On the Mini Mk II, the screws are accessible from underneath and behind.

2 Disconnect the inner and outer parts of the heater control cable by loosening the screws which secure the cable to the valve

3 The switch panel is recessed into the padded edge of the parcel shelf. Remove it by undoing the Phillips screws at either end

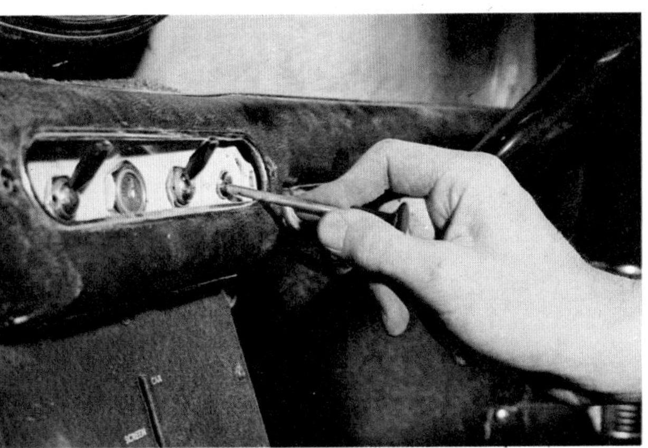

Nelson Hargreaves

4 Having loosened the choke and the heater cables at the engine, pull them out. Note where they pass through the bulkhead

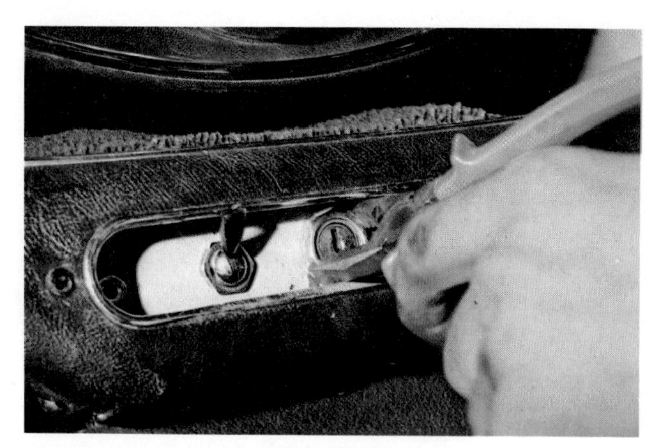
5 The ignition, light and wiper switches are all held in place by nut-shaped bezels. Unscrew them with pliers or a spanner

6 With the switches loosened and the switch panel removed, bolt on the two cable brackets. Make sure they are the right way round

You will now have to remove the choke and heater cables completely. They are secured to the switch panel by means of lock nuts. To reach the lock nuts you will probably have to lie on your back across the car. Loosen them from underneath the panel with an open-ended spanner and you can then unscrew them by hand. Before you pull the inner and outer cable assemblies together through the switch panel (fig. 4), have a look in the engine compartment to see where the cables pass through the bulkhead. They must be returned through the original grommets. Do not forget to retain the rubber grommets as the cables come out. They must be re-fitted too, or renewed if perished. Next, unscrew the switch bezels using an open-ended spanner or pliers to loosen them (fig. 5) and push the switches through the loose panel. Take care not to accidentally disconnect any of the wires behind. Pull out the switch panel, bending it slightly if necessary.

Before actually fitting the two cable support brackets to the new panel, check that the cables pass right through the bracket holes. The lock nut threads must also pass through. If they do not, carefully open the holes slightly with a round file. The two brackets can now be bolted in to place (fig. 6).

The above procedures apply generally to all one-piece Mini fascias featuring a moulded, projecting switch panel although there may be detailed variations according to individual manufacturers.

If your Mini has the three-gauge instrument cowl, this must now be dismantled to allow the two smaller gauges to be transferred to the new fascia. On Mk I Minis, the cowl is unscrewed and the panel light switch, if fitted, removed (fig. 7). The cowl itself may be discarded and the light switch can be re-positioned on the new fascia. The metal panel behind is then unscrewed to reveal the back of the gauges (fig. 8). They can be unclamped (do not disconnect them yet) and the panel discarded as well. From the Mk II onwards, there is no metal panel and the cowl itself supports the speedometer. Having unscrewed the cowl, unclamp the two gauges. Unless the speedometer is being re-positioned, replace the cowl to support it.

You should now be ready to position the gauges, together with any extra ones, on the new fascia. Having decided what to fit you will have to cut holes for them. If your car has ball air vents on either side holes may have to be cut for these too. Mark the holes by scribing circles of the appropriate diameter on the back of the fascia (fig. 9). Make use, if possible, of any indented marks provided by the manufacturer. The best way of actually cutting holes in the moulding is to use a hole saw as shown in fig. 10, taking care to centre the saw in the middle of each scribed circle. Another method is to drill a ring of small holes around each circle, press the hole out and then file it smooth. Alternatively, you can drill a series of holes to make a space big enough to push a keyhole saw through and then saw the hole out. Again, the hole will need to be filed smooth. If the plastic mould is quite thin, the holes can be cut with a knife. If you do this though, the scribed circles must be scored as deeply as possible to act as a guide.

On the Autoplas fascia, holes for the speedometer, switches and cables are already cut. If your fascia has no such holes, cut these in the same way as for the gauges above.

With the holes cut, press in the gauges being fitted as extras. The holes may need a bit of extra filing before the gauges will go in but a smear of lubricating oil on the casings also makes this job a lot easier (fig. 11). Next, disconnect the electric water temperature gauge, marking

7 The instrument cowl is held on by four Phillips screws. Having unscrewed them, you will be able to pull the cowl away

8 The two smaller gauges are held to the speedometer binnacle in a metal panel. Unscrew the whole assembly from its two brackets

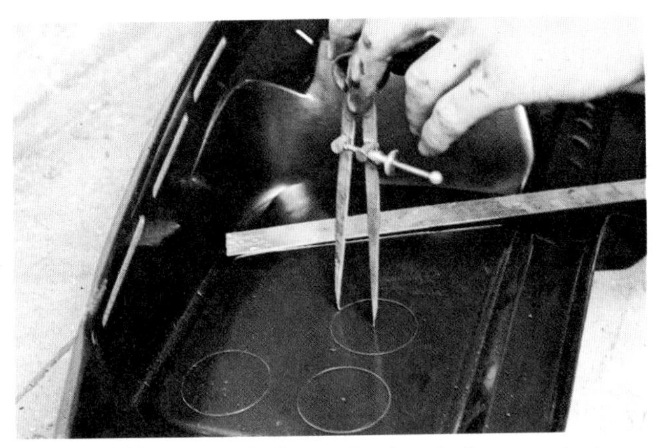

9 To fit auxiliary gauges in the new fascia, select a convenient site and then scribe the hole marks with a pair of dividers

10 By far the easiest way of cutting the gauge holes is to use a hole saw—it gives the job a smooth and well-rounded finish

11 With all the holes cut, you can push in the gauges. A drop of oil on the body of each gauge will help it to slide into place

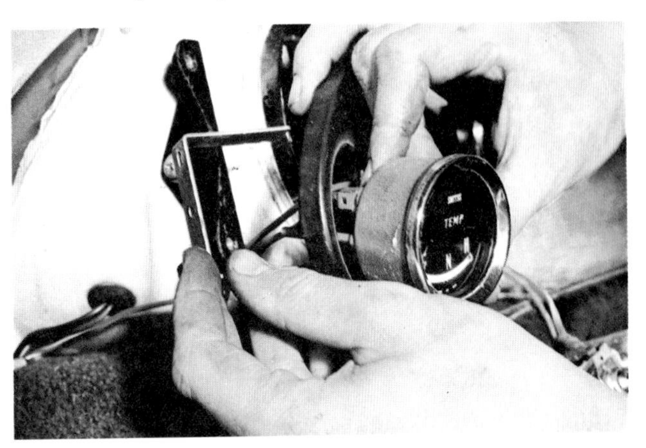

12 You can now remove the original auxiliary gauges from their mounting panel and fit them into the fascia in the same way

which wire goes where with pieces of tape, and press the gauge into the fascia as well. Finally, disconnect the oil pressure gauge by undoing the union nut at the back and add it to the other gauges on the fascia.

Offer the fascia assembly up so that it is fairly close to its final position but with the backs of the instruments readily accessible. You will then be able to see what wires need extending. These normally include all connections to the temperature gauge, to the panel light switch and the earth and illumination wires to the oil pressure gauge. Make sure that you use proper connectors for this job, otherwise you might be plagued later with short circuits. If the metal oil pressure pipe will not stretch to the gauge's new location, remove it and fit one of the flexible nylon type in its place.

Next, connect up any accessory instruments that are being fitted. Remember that in the plastic fascia, they will not be earthed unless connections are made to a metal part of the bodywork. To simplify the wiring, the panel light wires from all the gauges can be connected together and joined to a common supply wire. The same may be done for the earthing wires.

With the gauges connected, fit the switches in place in the projecting panel. The wires here should all be long enough. Push each switch through its respective hole and secure with the appropriate bezel. Add any extra switches at this stage as well, connecting them up before fixing them in the panel (fig. 15).

If the speedometer is being moved, all the wire connections from it must be extended to the central loom and a new cable fitted. A suitable hole for the cable must be drilled in the bulkhead and a rubber or plastic protective grommet should be fitted.

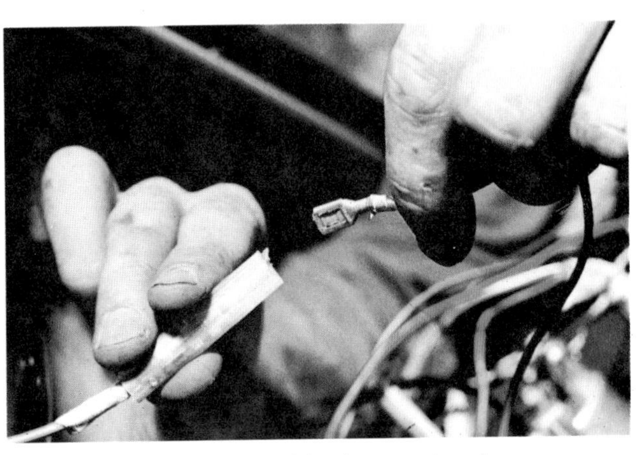

13 If you have to extend any wiring, be sure to use the correct connectors. Failure to do this could result in short circuits

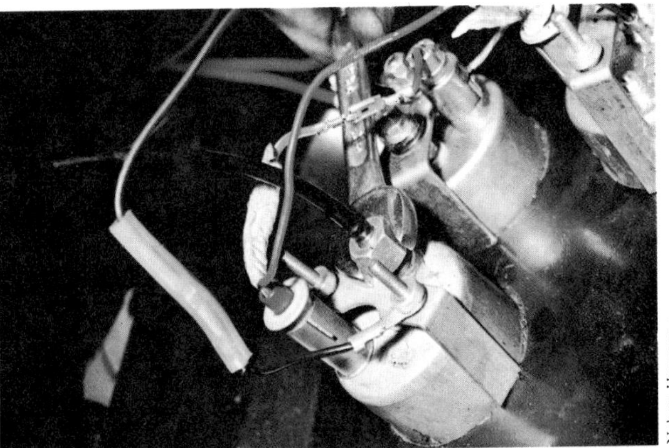

Nelson Hargreaves

14 If you are fitting a new nylon oil pressure pipe, feed it to the gauge and tighten the union nut to avoid leaks

When you have finished connecting the wiring, it is as well to check that everything works correctly. Temporarily re-connect the battery and run through every switch and gauge in turn. Pay special attention to warning lights and to the main light switch. Also, carefully check that every gauge illuminates properly.

Assuming that the gauges have been wired up correctly, any faults will probably be due to loose connections or to a loosened connector. Wires can often come astray from the barrel connectors near the main loom which is behind the speedometer. These wires can be checked from the engine compartment side of the bulkhead.

With everything apart from the choke and heater cables fitted and connected to the new fascia, pull away the rubber door trim locally around the front panel. Locate the fascia in position, mark all the screw holes and then punch and drill them using the drill bit size recommended by the manufacturer. Next, screw the fascia down with the self-tapping screws provided with the kit (fig. 16). Replace the door trim.

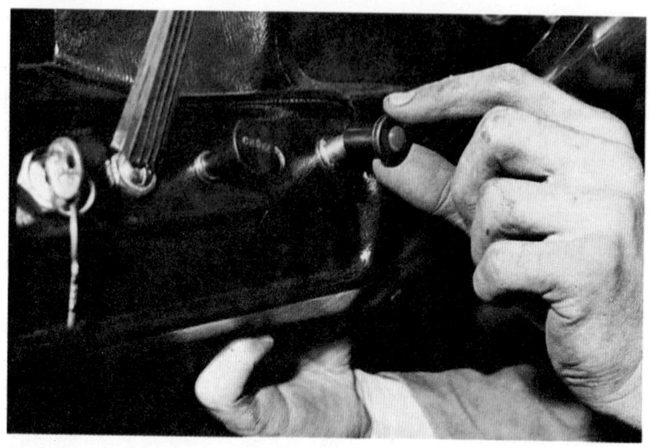

15 Extra switches are easily fitted into the new fascia's pre-cut switch panel. The original ones are also re-fitted at this stage

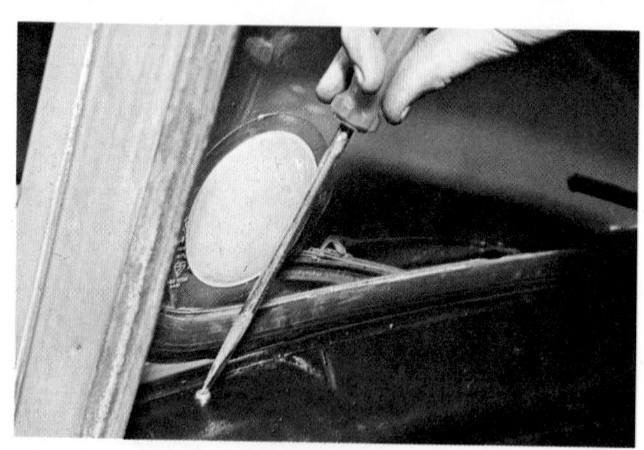

16 Having drilled two suitable holes, screw down the new fascia at either end of the metal panel running below the windscreen

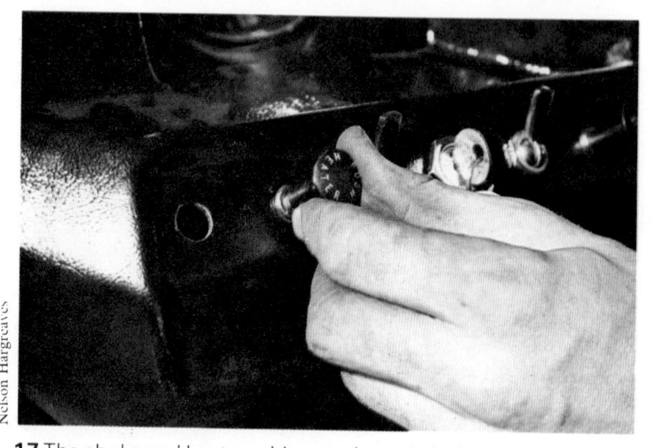

17 The choke and heater cables run through the brackets bolted to the parcel shelf. Secure them from behind with the nuts provided

Nelson Hargreaves

On fascias with a projecting switch panel, such as the Autoplas unit illustrated, all that remains is to fit the heater and choke cables. On the Autoplas dash these are pushed through their relevant holes, through the brackets behind and then fed back to the engine compartment. Before you feed the cables through the holes in the bulkhead, do not forget to thread on the lock nuts and washers. Press the cables right through until their handles are flush with the fascia and then secure them with the lock nuts from behind, screwing them up tight against the brackets.

Moving to the engine compartment, thread on the rubber grommets and seal the bulkhead holes. You can then re-connect the cables making sure that the inner parts are pulled through as far as possible. When you have tested the operation of the cables and are satisfied that they perform correctly, fitting is completed.

Fitting a one-piece fascia—Ford Escort Mk I/Anglia

Fitting a one-piece moulding to an Escort or Anglia is much easier than installing one in a Mini, but the general principles are the same. The central instrument binnacles are retained on both cars and additional instruments are fitted by the methods described above. The same applies when cutting holes for the ventilation outlets. The problems of re-locating switches and choke and heater cables do not arise, because of the design of the dashboards.

Fitting a Rokee wood panel fascia kit

The Rokee wooden fascia kits are designed to be easy to fit. As in the case of the Mini 850 illustrated (figs. 23 to 32), the fascias avoid existing switch panels and this, in turn, eliminates the need to re-locate any switches. Holes for existing instruments are pre-cut, so again there are no problems unless you intend to fit additional gauges.

The component parts of the fascia bolt together over the existing dashboard and are secured with self-tapping screws. Trim strips, supplied in the kits, are then stuck on with impact adhesive to complete the finish.

Cutting the wooden panels

On the backs of the panels in certain kits, indentations are provided to make cutting holes for extra gauges easier. Unfortunately, this does not get round the problem of cutting through the polished veneer which is very brittle and prone to crack and chip. Great care must be taken if you decide to attempt this particular job yourself, otherwise

18 A completed installation in a BL Mini 850 Mk.I. This fascia gives the car's interior a far more sporting image

19 The first step when cutting a hole in a veneered fascia is to drill a pilot hole. This will act as a guide for the hole saw

20 Before using the hole saw, smear it with cooking oil. The oil cuts down friction and lessens the risk of the veneer cracking

21 With the veneered side uppermost, locate the hole saw guide in the pilot hole and lower. Keep the saw as level as possible

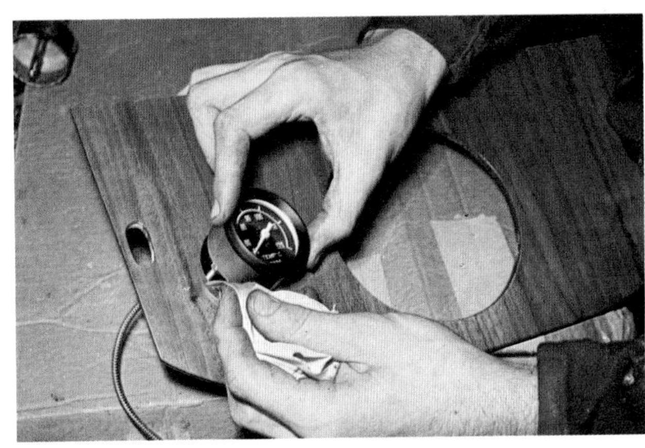

22 As in the case of the plastic fascia, a little oil smeared on the gauge will help it to push-fit into the newly cut hole

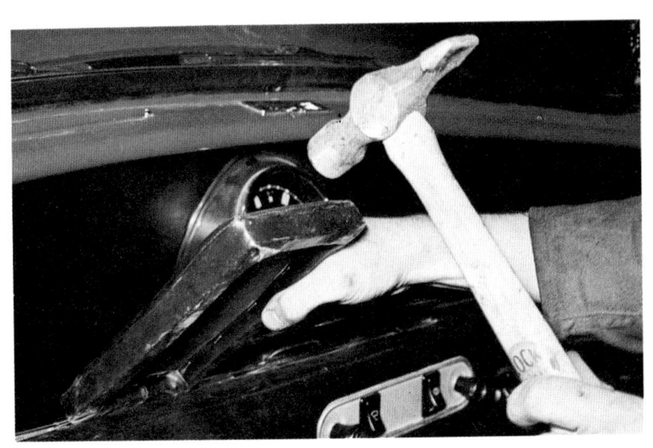

23 The first step when fitting the Rokee kit is to knock off trim strip which runs along this Mini's padded parcel shelf

24 You can now slot the centre panel into place. The chrome trim around the speedometer fits inside the large, pre-cut hole

25 Before fitting the side panels, you must screw on the brackets which are used to secure the panels to the car bodywork

Jake Wynter

26 Fitting the side panels. The fixing bolts on the inside locate in corresponding holes on either side of the centre panel

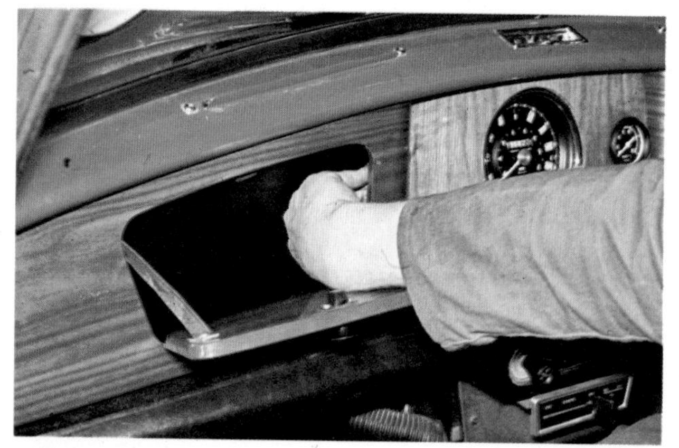

27 By reaching inside the glove compartments, you can screw the nuts provided on to the fixing bolts to form a single rigid panel

28 The next step is to glue down the extra black trim strip. This hides the small gap between the new fascia and the parcel shelf

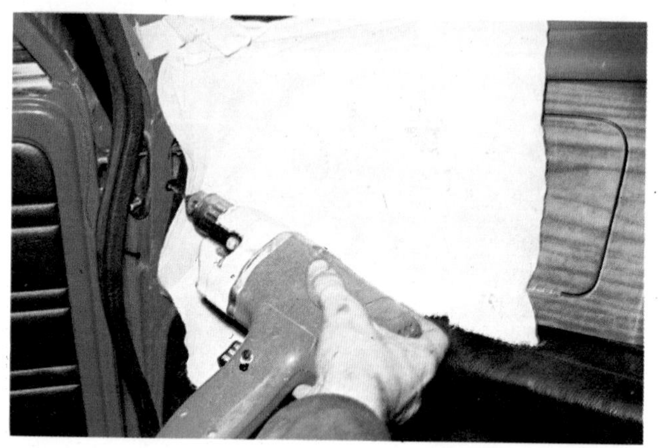

29 Use the panel brackets as templates for the side holes. Make sure that you cover the veneer first in case the drill slips

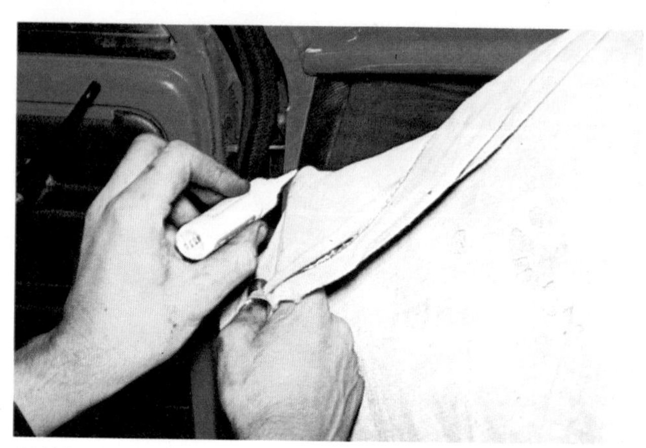

30 When you have screwed down the brackets, glue the vinyl flap on the end of each panel over the top to disguise them

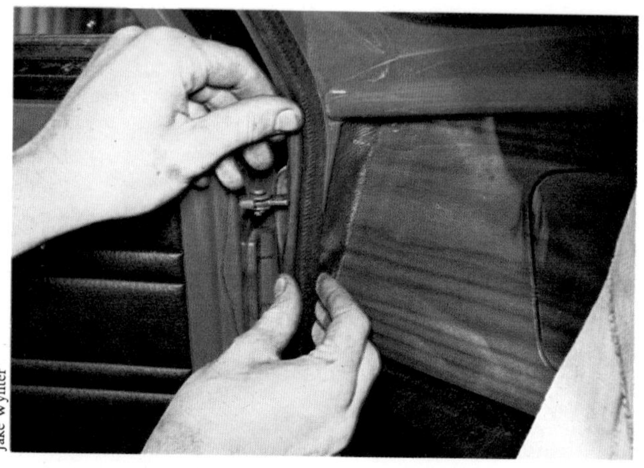

Jake Wynter

31 The job is completed by pressing back the clip-on door lining. Try if possible to overlap the edge of the vinyl flap as you go

32 The finished job. If the fascia vibrates when you start up the engine, re-check all the bolt and screw fixings for tightness

the appearance of the whole fascia may be ruined.

Start by laying the panel on a firm, flat, soft-covered surface, such as a bench, with the veneered side down. If there are no indented marks, scribe one (diameter 52 mm—2ins) with a pair of dividers. Estimate the centre of the circle and drill a pilot hole (fig. 19).

The next step is to cut the hole using a 52 mm (2ins) hole saw attached to a power drill. First, lubricate the outside of the saw with a drop of cooking oil (fig. 20). Turn the panel over and locate the pilot drill of the saw into the hole you have just drilled. Keeping the saw as level as possible, lower it gently but firmly on to the panel until it has cut through (fig. 21).

The gauge can now be pushed into the hole—the slight marks made around the apertures in the veneer will be hidden by its bezel—and then clamped in position.

If there are no indentations to guide you on the back of the panels, you should remember that too many holes could weaken the fascia's structure. Fitting large numbers of extra switches to a wooden fascia panel is also unadvisable; a better idea is to mount them on a separate switch panel, held by self-tapping screws, under the parcel shelf. If you intend to install really comprehensive instrumentation, the plastic moulding type of fascia would be a much better buy. Finally, when customizing the interior, always take great care to ensure that the fittings do not project in such a way as to create a hazard in the event of an accident.

In Australia, custom fascia kits are not generally available to the DIY mechanic. Larger motor accessory stores will, however, order a kit from the UK if requested.

Fitting a soundproofing kit

MIRA

1 Wind tunnel testing is one way of identifying the cause of wind noise which plagues both manufacturers and owners of cars alike

A noisy car is not only unpleasant to drive, or in which to be a passenger, it can also be dangerous as it creates driver fatigue and may prevent you from hearing warning sounds from other road users. However, by fitting one of the soundproofing kits that are available from the accessory market you can make a considerable reduction in the interior noise level of your car.

There are several kits to choose from at most accessory shops. Although your choice will probably be dictated by financial considerations, it is worthwhile selecting a more expensive kit if funds allow, as this will usually contain materials of better soundproofing quality. However, if the noise level in your car is not too high, one of the less expensive kits may suffice.

When you have purchased the kit that you feel will be most effective in reducing the noise level inside your car, it is a good idea to spend some time on preparations. Check the contents against the list given on the outside of the packet or in the instructions. If any pieces are missing, return the kit to wherever you bought it and exchange it for a complete one. Do this even if only a small piece is missing because noise, like water, will enter a car even through the smallest gap in the insulation. The effectiveness of the kit when fitted, therefore, could be drastically reduced even if you miss out just one piece of material and you will waste both your time and money. The basic principle to bear in mind when you are insulating a car is that it is the parts that you do not soundproof at this time that may continue to cause a noise problem later. Therefore, it makes sense both practically and economically to purchase the best and most comprehensive soundproofing kit that you can afford.

Preparing the car

Depending on the type of kit that you decide to fit, you will have to remove certain items from the car to apply the soundproofing materials to the bodywork. With even the most basic kits you will have to remove the carpeting and with some of the more extensive kits it is wise to try and gain as much access as possible to the areas which you will be covering with the materials in the kit. The Super soundproofing kit (fig. 2), from Sound Service Ltd, covers a great deal of the floor area of the passenger compartment, including the area under the rear seat, as well as areas under the bonnet and boot. Although it is not absolutely necessary to remove the front seats, it is desirable to do so in order to give yourself extra room in which to work. Removing as much of the interior floor covering as you can will also allow

George Wright

2 Using six types of soundproofing material, this extensive kit yields a substantial reduction in the car's interior noise level

3 Prior to fitting the soundproofing kit, you will need to prepare the car. First, remove the rear seat cushion from the vehicle

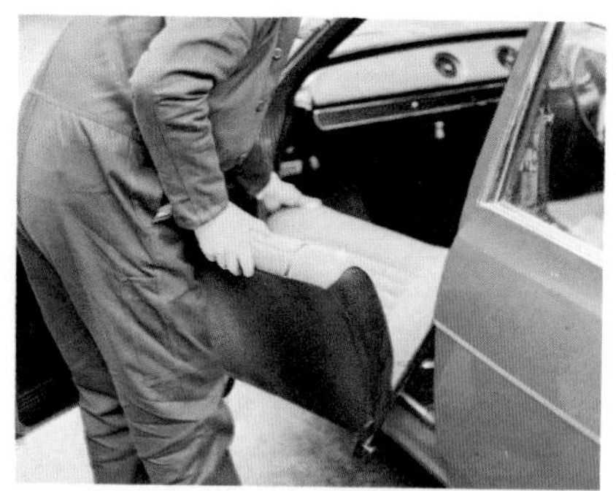

4 Undo their retaining bolts and take out the front seats. On some cars, the seats can be simply slid off their runners

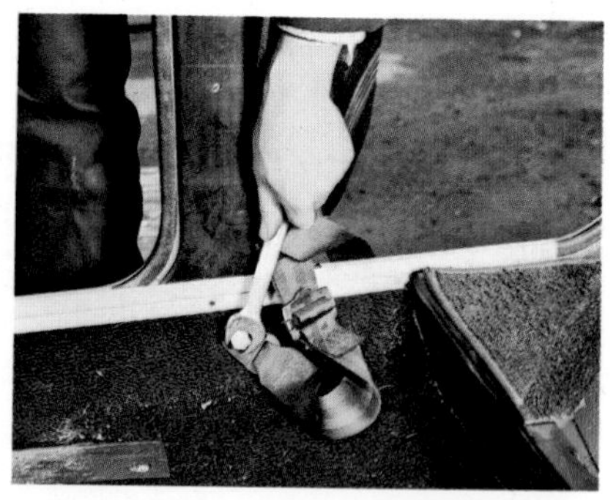

5 To remove the carpet, you will need to undo the lower mounting bracket for the seat belts. Note the position of any spacers

6 Next, undo the series of screws retaining the metal door trim and remove the trim from the car completely

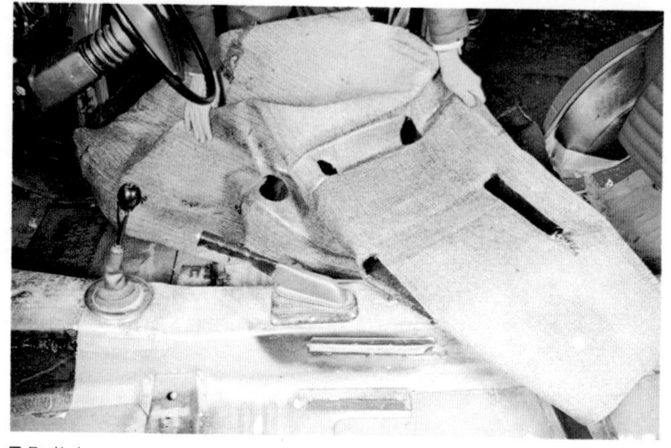

7 Pull the carpet out of the car. If this is difficult, check that you have unfastened all of the retaining studs around the carpet

you to make a closer inspection of the floorpan for any holes. These should be blocked to prevent air leakage from/to the passenger compartment causing wind noise and will also inhibit the ingress of water. Any rubber drainage plugs that are missing should be renewed.

To remove the interior trim, first take out the rear seat cushion (fig. 3). On the early Ford Escort to which the kit shown was fitted, this is fastened into position by clips. To remove the cushion, simply pull it up and away from the base of the seat. On other cars, the rear seat cushion may be retained by nuts and bolts or may simply rest in place, so make a thorough inspection before trying to lift it out. Once removed from the car completely, store the cushion where it will remain clean and dry.

It will also be wise to remove the front seats from the car. The subframe of most car seats is held to the floor by a number of bolts. The number varies according to whether the car has two or four doors. On two-door cars the seats usually tip forward to give passengers access to the rear so this can create a further complication. Some seats are mounted on runners. In this case, simply slide each seat forward as far as possible and then lift it out of the car. The seat runners can usually be left in position. Note carefully how your seats are retained and, if necessary, draw a diagram to help you remember the location of the nuts and bolts. Sliding the seat as far forward as possible is sometimes helpful as it can expose the rear bolts. Remove them (fig. 4) along with any brackets and keep them in a bag with each seat. Store the seat along with the rear seat cushion away from the work area.

Before you can take out any carpeting which may be fitted inside the car, you will probably have to undo and remove the lower mounting bracket of the seat belts. Undo the retaining bolt with a large spanner (fig. 5) and either let the belts hang outside the car while you are working or, remove the upper brackets as well and take the seat belts out altogether. Again, it is most important that you note the position of any spacers that are used to enable the belt bracket to swivel to ensure that you replace them correctly. While the belts are out of the car, you can take the opportunity to clean them and inspect the webbing for signs of wear. Only use warm, soapy water to clean the belts and then let them dry naturally. Do not place them in front of a fire or you may melt the nylon webbing.

Most carpets are located by plastic push-fit studs and a strip of metal along the inside of the door sills. Undo the series of self-tapping screws that hold the metal strip in position (fig. 6) and then pull it away from the sill. If the trim does not come away easily, check that you have not left any screws in position and then, using a screwdriver as a lever under one end, lift it away from the sill. Next, work your way around the carpet and pull all of the studs out of their fasteners. Make sure that you also release the studs that hold the carpet in position at the bulkhead as these are often obscured from view. If your car is fitted with a centre console (see pages 579 to 585), or anything else which fits over the carpet, remove this next and then lift the carpet over the gear lever and the handbrake (fig. 7), where floor-mounted, and out of the car. Beneath the carpet you will probably find that there are already some sound insulating panels. These will have been fitted to the car by the manufacturer and, unless they have deteriorated badly, can be left in place with the new insulation simply fitted over the top of them.

Once you have sufficient access to the floorpan and the bulkheads to fit the soundproofing materials, check where the under-bonnet and boot materials will need to be positioned to see whether there is anything that you will need to remove. With some kits you will be applying insulation to both sides of the front bulkhead and you may, therefore, need to remove items such as the windscreen washer bottle and its pipes (fig. 21), before you can position the foam or felt. It will rarely be necessary to disconnect any cables as the pre-cut kits make allowances for these. However, if you have fitted any accessories to the car that require wires or pipes to pass through the bulkhead, you will have to cut the material to accommodate them. When you do this, cut slits, not holes, so that the material will close up tightly around the cable to prevent any noise from getting through the gap. In the boot of the car, remove the spare wheel if it is located in one of the wings or on the floor and then empty the boot of all of its contents and any carpeting which may be fitted.

Now that you have gained access to the necessary panels, clean off all dirt and grease. The panels that fit under the bonnet must be glued into position and this will not be possible if the bulkhead is greasy. Use one of the proprietary cleaners, such as Gunk, for this. Inside the passenger compartment remove any of the nuts and bolts that you may find. Do not be too surprised by the presence of these. But, while it is unlikely that they will have worked loose from a component, you should check to see if any parts appear to be loosely mounted. A possible explanation for their presence is that the nuts and bolts were left in the car while it was on the production line, the carpeting being laid over them. With all of the loose debris removed, use a vacuum cleaner to remove remaining dust and fluff. You are now ready to fit the soundproofing kit to the car.

How the insulating materials work

The insulating materials used in soundproofing kits vary, though felt is the most common. The reason for the variation is that, although all of the materials are used for the same purpose, that is to eliminate noise, there is more than one way of tackling the problem due to the fact that noise enters the car via different routes, and each of these routes requires individual treatment.

The kit illustrated (fig. 2), for example, employs six types of sound insulating material. Other kits may use fewer materials but in all cases, an understanding of how they work will help you to appreciate the importance of fitting all of them correctly.

The first of the materials used is a sound barrier mat (fig. 8). This is in the form of a sound absorbent foam pad backed by a layer of a dense, black, rubber-like substance that reflects the sound back in the direction from which it has come. The sound barrier mat is applied to the metal panels with the black surface outermost. As the panel vibrates, the noise generated is transmitted into the foam and, while trying to push its way through the foam, the sound loses some of its energy. This is, in fact, transformed into heat, though this is so small that it could only be measured using laboratory equipment. The sound that does manage to get right through the foam is then bounced back off the reflective layer towards the metal panel from which it originated. The sound is therefore contained between the metal panel and the reflective layer until most of its energy has been absorbed. It has been estimated that only one per cent of the sound originating from the metal panel actually enters the passenger compartment when this type of sound barrier mat is used. When used in the engine bay, the black shiny surface prevents the foam from absorbing any oil and becoming a fire hazard.

Acousticell, an 18 mm ($\frac{3}{4}$ins) thick mixture of dense PVC foam and fabric, is the second of the materials used in the kit (fig. 24). The Acousticell acts as a sound absorber, dense enough not to need a reflective layer, and as a body panel damper. This means that it helps to prevent the energy in the vibrating panels from actually becoming noise. The density of the Acousticell is carefully controlled during the manufacturing process and it is tough enough to be used on the floor of both the passenger compartment and the boot and cannot become trodden down, one of the disadvantages of using felt in these areas. As the thickness of the felt is reduced, so is its ability to absorb sound. This is because sound absorbent material needs to be of the open cell construction, that is, containing many small pockets of air in which the sound can expend energy while trying to work its way through them all. If the size of the cells is reduced or if they are squashed altogether, the material will no longer be able to absorb sound as effectively.

Although felt is not used in the passenger compartment or the boot, the Super kit is supplied with a heavy felt pad for use under the bonnet (fig. 20). If the sound barrier mat is applied correctly to the bulkhead, this felt pad will not normally be necessary. However, although it is not such an efficient absorber of sound as Acousticell, the pad will help to reduce the amount of noise that bounces off the walls of the engine compartment and therefore the amount of noise that would normally try to penetrate the sound barrier mat on the bulkhead. This will have a slight effect in reducing the interior noise level and will also help to reduce the

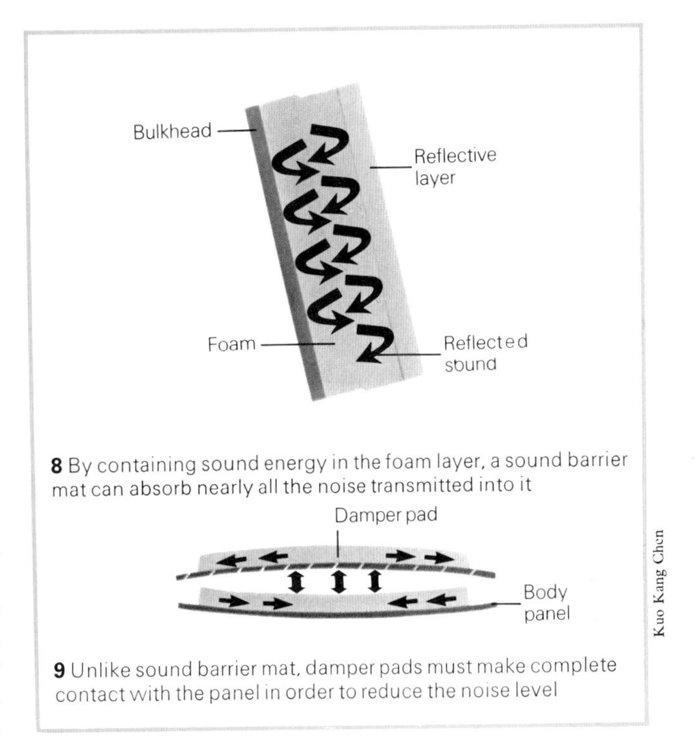

8 By containing sound energy in the foam layer, a sound barrier mat can absorb nearly all the noise transmitted into it

9 Unlike sound barrier mat, damper pads must make complete contact with the panel in order to reduce the noise level

Kuo Kang Chen

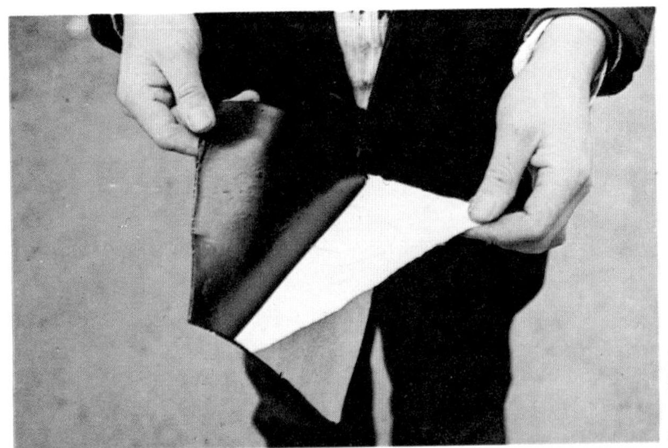

George Wright

10 Before positioning the damper pads, you will need to warm them until they become supple and then peel off the backing paper

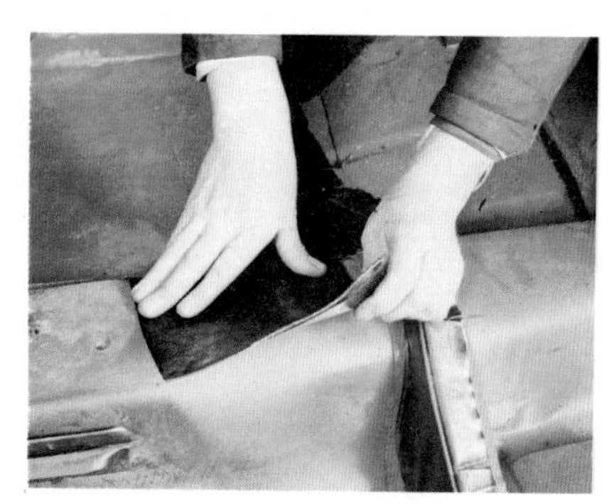

11 Apply the damper pads to areas prone to excessive vibration. The transmission tunnel is one such area

12 Also position a pad in the front or rear foot wells. Press them down firmly to ensure good contact with the metal

13 If you have warmed them enough, the pads should stick quite satisfactorily to the most awkward of panels

George Wright

14 When fitting sound barrier mat to the bulkhead, position it first and then apply some adhesive to the corners

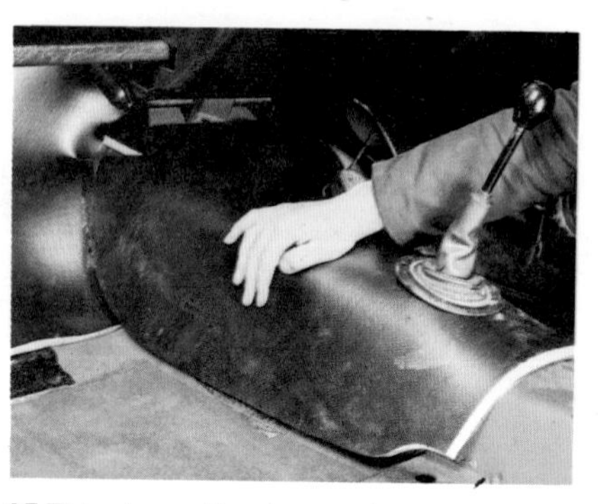

15 This piece of barrier mat does not need to be stuck in position. When re-fitted, the carpet will prevent it from moving

16 Before fitting the pieces of mat with cut-outs in them, check that they are the correct way up

exterior noise level by preventing the metal bonnet from transmitting sound into the atmosphere.

The remaining parts of the kit used as sound insulators are damper pads, sealing mastic and Airseal tape. The self-adhesive damper pads (fig. 9) should be positioned on any panels of the car's bodywork that are particularly prone to vibration. The floorpan is one such area as much of the engine and suspension vibration is fed directly into it. The pads work by actually flexing with the body panel as it vibrates, though obviously the amount of movement is very small. By flexing with the body, the pads absorb the energy that would otherwise manifest itself as sound. This transformation of vibrations into heat energy instead of sound energy is a common method of noise control.

The last two parts of the kit are both designed to help combat the problem of wind noise caused by air entering or leaving the passenger compartment, especially when the car is driven at high-speed. The putty-like sealing mastic (fig. 25) should be used to seal any holes in places such as the bulkhead where cables pass through. Even if a grommet surrounds the cable, mastic pressed around it will make it completely air-tight. The mastic is pliable enough to be used to fill the most awkward holes. The Airseal tape (fig. 27) is designed specifically to tackle the problem of air leaking out of the car through the door frames, by taking up any gap between the doors and the sealing rubbers.

Fitting the kit

Fitting one of the more comprehensive soundproofing kits can be tackled in three stages; the passenger compartment, the under-bonnet area and the boot. Some other kits are only fitted to the passenger compartment and the engine bay so check the instructions carefully. In all cases, hold the parts of the kit in position before you start to actually fit them. In this way you check they are properly trimmed.

Soundproofing the passenger compartment: The very first material to use in this area is the damper pads. Six of these are supplied with the Sound Service Super kit and although you can fit them wherever you want to, it is usual to use three in the passenger compartment and three in the boot. Before you can stick the self-adhesive pads in position, you must first warm them slightly so that they will adhere to the metal. Do not warm the pads for too long or they will crack. If you do not warm them for long enough, however, they will crack when you try to bend them to shape, so warm them slowly in front of a fire until they become supple but never leave them unattended. Then peel off the backing paper (fig. 10) and stick the pad firmly into position. Because the pads flex with the floor they must be in complete contact with it to work properly unlike some of the foam which only rests in position. Use one pad on the transmission tunnel (fig. 11) and one in each of the front or rear foot wells (fig. 12). You will find that they can be shaped (fig. 13) to fit any curves. If there are already some damper pads fitted by the manufacturer, you can either stick the new panels on top of the old ones, if they have cracked, or you can position the pads elsewhere on the floor area. Going over the pads with a wallpaper roller will press them down firmly if you have any trouble making them stick by hand.

Next, you can start to fit some of the barrier mat to the bulkhead. As the mat will be on a vertical panel you will have to use some of the adhesive that is supplied with the kit. This is a highly inflammable substance which gives off unpleasant and heavy petroleum vapours. Only use this adhesive with the car doors and windows open and in a well ventilated space and on no account smoke while you are working. The adhesive is best applied to the mat with an old paint brush and it is a wise precaution to wear an old pair of gloves to protect your hands. Do not cover the entire area of the mat with adhesive, just the edges of the corners will suffice. If you apply the adhesive to the mat only, you will be able to position the mat on the bulkhead and slide it around until it fits into its exact position. If you apply the adhesive to the bulkhead as well as to the mat and then

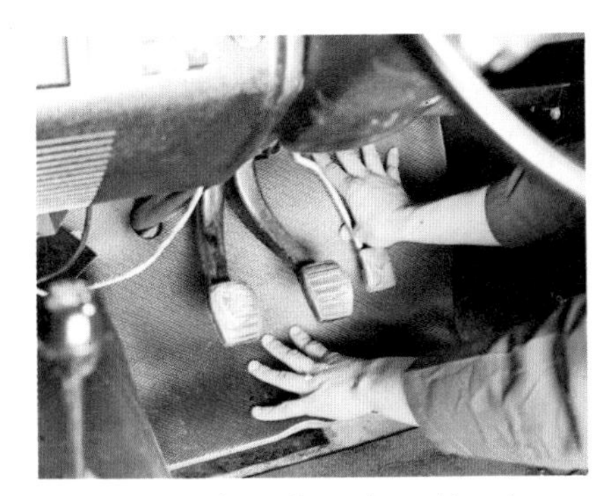

17 To prevent loss of travel, position the barrier mat around the pedals carefully. If necessary, cut some of the foam away

18 The Acousticell panel that fits under the rear seat should be rested in position only. Do not apply any adhesive to it

19 When fitting barrier mat under the bonnet, use adhesive to prevent the panels from falling on to the engine

20 Fitting the felt pad under the bonnet may require lots of adhesive. If it will not stay in place, discard it completely

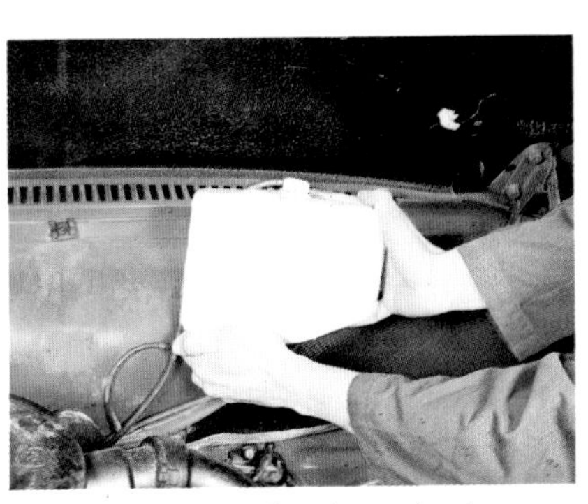

21 After soundproofing the engine bay, re-fit the windscreen washer bottle and any other items previously removed

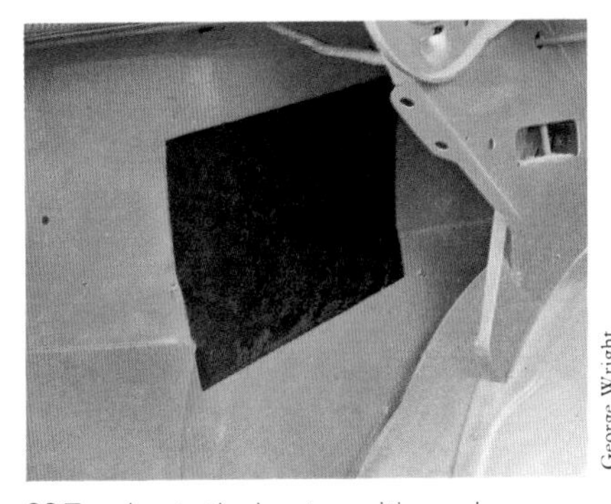

22 Turning to the boot, position a damper pad on the inside of the rear wing. Other pads can be fitted to the petrol tank

George Wright

allow both to become tacky, you will find that when you press the two together the mat will stick in position immediately and you will not have the chance to move it or change its position if it is in the wrong place.

First, identify the piece of sound barrier mat that should be stuck on to the passenger's side of the lower bulkhead. The pieces in the Sound Service kits are numbered according to model and the instructions tell you where each piece should go. Position the bulkhead mat and then peel back the corners and apply some adhesive to them (fig. 14). Press the mat back into position and allow the adhesive a few minutes in which to set. Then position the sound barrier mat that fits over the gear lever and sits on the prop-shaft tunnel (fig. 15). Do not use adhesive on this because when you re-fit the carpet, its weight will hold the mat in position. Using as little adhesive as possible gives you the advantage of being able to remove the insulation easily, if necessary, but using too much can actually prevent the insulating material from working properly because the sound cannot penetrate the adhesive and will be unable to enter the foam. On the Ford Escort kit illustrated there is also a piece of sound barrier mat, with a cut-out for part of the wiring harness (fig. 16), that should be positioned above the parcel shelf. There are similar pieces of barrier mat in the kit that should be carefully applied to the bulkhead.

The front foot wells can now be covered with some of the Acousticell pieces. Do not use adhesive on these because in order to perform their damping function, they need to be able to vibrate slightly with the floor. It is as they do this that the sound energy of the floorpan is transformed into heat. You can, of course, lay the carpet on top of the Acousticell with no detrimental effects to its sound insulating qualities as the amount of movement of the Acousticell that is required is very small.

Next, identify and position the Acousticell section for the rear foot well and the large area under the rear seat cushion (fig. 18). Press the Acousticell firmly into place where it fits under the rear seat cushion or you will not be able to re-position the cushion correctly. The insulation of the passenger compartment for the Ford Escort illustrated is now complete. The shape, size and number of pieces of material used will vary from kit to kit so always check your instructions carefully to ensure that you do not forget to fit any of them. You can now move on to apply the sound insulation materials to the engine bay.

Soundproofing the engine bay: With the early Escort there are only four pieces of insulating material to be fitted under the bonnet. Identify the relevant pieces for your car and make sure that you will be able to fit them without any problems. You may, for example, need to remove the windscreen washer bottle and pipes and you may have to cut some of the material that fits on the bulkhead if there are any extra wires passing through it (see below).

Apply some adhesive to the panels that should be fitted on top of the bulkhead near the bonnet hinges and stick them into position (fig. 19). When fitting the sound barrier mat on to the back of the pedal mounting, hold it in position first to make sure that you will be able to fit it around the cables when you are ready to glue it in position. The final part of the under-bonnet insulation is the heavy felt pad which you must stick to the bonnet (fig. 20). If there is already some thick, black, anti-drumming paint applied to the bonnet, you may experience difficulty in making the felt pad adhere properly. All you can do is to try to stick it in position and see if it stays there. If it stays in position for an hour or more then the adhesive will have had time to set and the pad will remain in place permanently. However, sometimes the adhesive attacks the anti-drumming paint causing the two to mix and the adhesive will be unable to form a satisfactory bond. If you cannot make the pad stay in place, do not use it. If you have applied the sound barrier mat to the bulkhead in the correct manner you will find that the felt pad is not essential anyway (see above).

If the pad were to become unstuck while the car was in

23 Next, empty the boot of all its contents and take out any carpeting. Block any holes in the floor with mastic

24 Lay the large Acousticell panel on the boot floor and then re-fit the carpet and replace your tool kit

25 To eliminate wind noise, you will need to block any holes with mastic. This is a pliable, putty-like substance

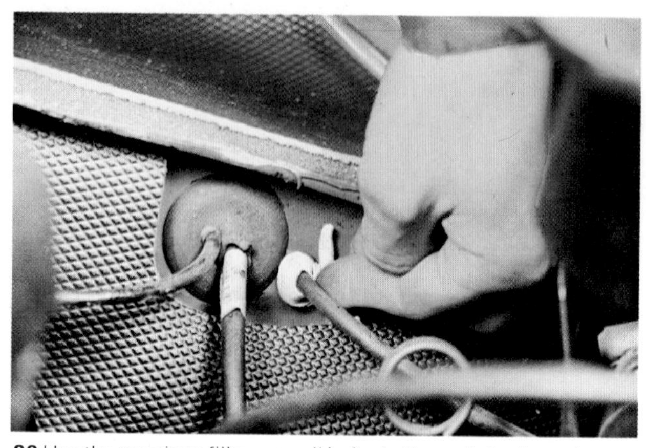

26 Use the mastic to fill any small holes in the car's bodywork, particularly where cables pass through the bulkhead

27 Finally, apply strips of Airseal tape to the door frames to form an air-tight seal between them and the doors when shut

motion it could become entangled with the fan blades or begin to smoulder and catch light if it rested on the exhaust manifold. When fitted normally, the felt pad is not a fire hazard as it is self-extinguishing. This means that when the source of flame is removed, the pad will no longer burn.

When you have completed the insulation of the engine bay, re-fit any components that were removed and remember to re-connect anything else that you may have disconnected (fig. 21). You can now insulate the boot.

Soundproofing the boot: If you have used three damper pads in the passenger compartment you will have three left to use in the boot. Typical positions for the damper pads here are on the petrol tank or tanks, on the inside of the rear wing (fig. 22) and on the underside of the boot lid itself. When you have fitted the pads, using the same method as that described for fitting them inside the passenger compartment, lay the final piece of Acousticell soundproofing material on the boot floor (figs. 23 and 24).

Before re-fitting the seats, carpets, pieces of trim and everything else that you have previously removed from the car, check that there are no pieces of the kit left over, bearing in mind that there may be some scraps which have no numbers because they have been used as packing material to protect the actual kit. Then check that you can obtain full travel of all of the pedals. If the sound barrier mat fitted around the pedal area prevents you from depressing them fully, remove the mat and then cut some of the foam away from the reflective layer. Never cut any holes in the reflective layer itself though. Due to the thickness of some of the insulating material, you may need to use slightly longer retaining screws for items such as centre consoles. It is preferable to use longer screws than to cut some of the foam away from the panels as this reduces their insulating properties. With everything re-fitted to the car, move on to the final stages of soundproofing.

Eliminating wind noise

As already explained, wind noise is caused by air entering or leaving the passenger compartment and is most pronounced at speed (fig. 1). Two items of the soundproofing kit are devoted to solving this problem, the sealing mastic and the Airseal tape. Check for any obvious holes in the bulkhead, fill any with mastic (figs. 25 and 26) and then test drive the car. At this stage, if you have carried out all the checks and maintenance mentioned in the first part of this article, you should notice a marked decline in the interior noise level, especially if you have correctly fitted one of the extensive kits. However, wind noise will probably still be a problem so you must identify where the noise is coming from and then eliminate it completely by using the wide variety of techniques available to you.

The best way to do this is to have a friend drive your car (having made sure that your respective insurance policies permit this) while you check the interior of the car. Most wind noise will be immediately apparent but when you have located a noisy area you must pin-point the exact position of the leak. This can be done by using a length of rubber tube as a stethoscope. Work your way round the doors and the bulkheads, making sure that you do not disturb the driver or obscure his vision. You will have to tackle the driver's door on a trial and error basis as you cannot test it while the car is in motion. Block any holes with mastic and apply the Airseal tape where required (fig. 24). Re-test the car. Repeat the process for as many times as necessary until you have satisfactorily eliminated all wind noise, bearing in mind that total elimination may not be possible.

Once you have completed the fitting of a soundproofing kit you should notice a significant reduction in the overall noise level of your car that will enable you to drive longer distances without feeling tired or strained and thus contribute to peace of mind and road safety.

Non-standard steering wheels

All cars are fitted with a serviceable steering wheel when they leave the manufacturer's factory and many drivers find them perfectly acceptable. One way to improve the appearance of a car's interior, however, is to fit a non-standard steering wheel which may also offer improved grip for the driver's hands and endow the steering with a more direct "feel".

There is a wide range of non-standard steering wheels (fig. 2) on the car accessory market and although they all perform the same function, there are differences in the various models that are available which could affect your choice. Many people buy the smallest wheel that they can fit to their car because they have seen small steering wheels fitted to racing cars and therefore assume that the smaller the wheel is then the better it must be. This, however, is not necessarily the case. Racing cars are fitted with small wheels for several specific reasons. The first of these is that racing car cockpits are often very cramped and there is no room for a larger wheel. Secondly, racing cars are fitted with high ratio steering racks which means that the steering wheel has only to be moved by a small amount to actually turn the front wheels of the car through a wide angle. You will find it very tiring to steer a car at low speeds if you fit a really small steering wheel in place of a large diameter one because you will have to make more effort to exert greater leverage. Before going to buy a non-standard wheel, therefore, you should familiarise yourself with all of the variations available and, if necessary, ask the advice of your local accessory dealer. He should be able to tell you the optimum size of wheel that can be safely fitted to your car. It is important to remember also that if you fit a wheel which is too small, your ability to control the car may be impaired.

John Harwood

1 Visually appealing and good to hold, the better non-standard steering wheels feature hand sewn leather rims with integral thumb spats and, if fitted properly, can only help to improve your driving

Steering wheel construction

Individual manufacturers have devised their own methods of steering wheel construction but, in most cases, the frames are made in steel, aluminium or an aluminium alloy and they are often designed so that the wheel will deform progressively in an accident and thereby absorb a proportion of any impact. An international standard against which steering wheels can be measured is gradually being introduced. Many manufacturers have already developed their own methods of testing and these comply with the national standards applicable in other countries in which the wheels are sold, such as the stringent TUV requirements in Germany. It is, therefore, reasonably safe to assume that the majority, if not all, of the non-standard steering wheels offered for sale through motor accessory shops and other outlets are made to a high standard in terms of safety.

Non-standard steering wheels will usually be judged on the basis of appearance, comfort and safety. They possess several advantages according to the purpose and the viewpoint of the purchaser and there are few disadvantages provided that a sensible choice is made and that the fitting is carried out correctly. Black leather or simulated leather are the most popular materials for trimming the wheel cover and, apart from constructional methods, there is one other detail that may assist in making a choice from similar wheels. Some wheels have extensions of the wheel trim that cover the joins between the spokes and the wheel rim (fig. 1). These are known as "spats" and while they improve the appearance of a wheel they also make it more comfortable for the driver to hold. More than most other accessories, the selection of a non-standard steering wheel is very much a matter of individual choice.

Buying a wheel to suit your car

Cheaper non-standard steering wheels are often sold with the boss attached to them and this means that they have a limited range of application. In virtually every case the packaging will tell you which cars the wheel will fit. Other steering wheels are sold in two parts. The first part comprises the wheel and its centre hub and the second comprises the special boss. This is an adaptor unit that will allow the wheel to be fitted to several different makes of car simply by using the relevant boss. The steering wheel is attached to the boss by nuts and bolts or small set-screws.

When deciding which wheel to buy, therefore, it is essential that you take along with you full details of the engine and chassis numbers of your car, as well as its year, make and model. You should bear in mind that if you do succeed in forcing an unsuitable boss to fit your steering column you may well be endangering your own life, the lives of pedestrians and other road users and that you may also invalidate your car insurance.

Choosing between a dished or a flat wheel

Apart from considering what size diameter of wheel you intend to buy you should also decide whether you want a dished or a flat wheel. The term "dish" relates to the distance between the hub of the wheel and a straight-edge placed across the rim of the wheel directly above the hub. If you fit a deeply dished wheel instead of a flat one (fig. 3), the wheel rim will be brought nearer to you. This is useful where a driver with short arms cannot obtain a satisfactory driving position using the normal seat and/or steering column adjustments.

Selecting a suitable wheel covering

Some drivers find that the grip provided by the rim of the steering wheel fitted to their car is not to their liking. This is usually because the rim is made of plastic and does not absorb perspiration from the driver's hands. There is, therefore, more of a chance of the wheel slipping from the driver's hands, especially during hot weather. The driver may also decide that the rim on his wheel is not thick enough. In general, non-standard wheels are fitted with thicker, padded rims which the majority of drivers find more comfortable to hold.

Most of the non-standard wheels on the accessory market are now covered in leather or a material with a similar feel to it. The wood-rimmed wheel, as fitted to many older sports cars, is now declining in popularity owing to the fact that many countries have legislated against such wheels because of the risk of them splintering in an accident. As different steering wheels provide different grips or feel, it is most important that you actually hold the wheel in the shop to make sure that you will find it comfortable once you have fitted it to your car.

The market

Most accessory shops sell non-standard steering wheels, though few offer the full range that is available. However, once you have visited several shops you will have seen most of the different makes and had the chance to compare prices. Below is a list of some of the more notable names that you are likely to encounter and the types of wheel that each manufacturer or importer is marketing. Addresses of major suppliers and manufacturers are listed in the "Where to buy it" section on page 246.

Alexander: Displayed in boxes that emphasise the racing connotations attached to non-standard steering wheels, Alexander market their products (fig. 2) under the Springalex brand name. All of their steering wheels are manufactured from materials which deform at a pre-determined rate to minimize injury to the driver in the event of an accident. They have steel inner rims for maximum strength and the spokes are made from 4 mm (5/32ins) thick NS6 alloy, mostly with rounded edges for comfort and safety. An exception to this is the Solo model which has steel spokes with squared edges.

Astrali: This company is one of the leading suppliers to the UK after-market and one of the largest in Europe. Their range starts with the Successor, a 330 mm (13ins) wheel with a simulated leather cover which has a thick-grip feel and is hand-stitched in a contrasting white thread. Its three spokes have a metallic silver finish and the wheel is sold assembled to a boss ready for fitting to many popular cars. Another model is the Sport available in 330 mm (13ins) and 356 mm (14ins) sizes. It is similar in many respects to the Successor except that a black anodized finish on the spokes is offered as an option and the boss is sold as an extra. Piccadilly models are made in 280 mm (11ins), 305 mm (12ins), 330 mm (13ins), 356 mm (14ins) and 381 mm (15ins) sizes. The covering is of vinyl combined with leather maxi-grip sections and it is perforated to reveal a red lining, giving an eye-catching effect. The spokes have either a polished or black anodized finish and bosses are supplied separately. Astrali's top of the range model is the Regent and it is available in a similar range of sizes to the Piccadilly. Its maxi-grip rim incorporates integral thumb spats formed on a resilient polyurethane material encased in hand-stitched leather.

Formula: Formula is a Company with steering wheel designs to cover more than 400 different car models. Wheels are available with either 343 mm (13½ins) or 381 mm (15ins) diameter, finished in mahogany or polyurethane foam covered in leather or vinyl. A choice of three dish depths is available for both diameter sizes; 25 mm (1ins), 92 mm (3½ins), and 127 mm (5ins) for the 343 mm (13½ins) models and 50 mm (2ins), 76 mm (3ins) and 115 mm (4½ins) for the 381 mm (15ins) models.

All Formula steering wheels have drilled and polished aluminium spokes. Leather and vinyl covered versions are available with black or silver enamelled spokes. For competition driving there is a 305 mm (12ins) solid-spoked wheel with 50 mm (2ins) dish finished in leather and 254 mm (10ins), 280 mm (11ins) and 305 mm (12ins) leather covered, thick-rimmed versions with black spokes and spats and undrilled centres.

Intersport: Made in France, Intersport steering wheels have aluminium frames riveted and welded on to a rolled-steel rim. The rim is given an initial coating of polystyrene to provide a firm but pliable grip and then this is covered with hand sewn leather to include thumb spats. A wood-rimmed model is also available. Sizes start at 305 mm (12ins) and all are slightly dished. Three spokes is the normal configuration but a four-spoke model has recently been introduced. All of the wheels can be attached to the steering column with a boss designed to collapse progressively in the event of an accident.

Momo: Momo offer a range of Italian wheels which are fitted as standard on all Ferrari cars including the Ferrari Formula One racing machines. They have hand-stitched leather covers and incorporate anti-corrosive alloys and special high-density foam rubber. There are 10 models, four of them named after well-known Formula One drivers. The Alpina is a four-spoke 381 mm (15ins) diameter wheel with a 25 mm (1ins) thick rim and a leather-covered padded centre. The Cavalino wheel, derived from the model fitted to the Ferrari Formula One cars, is semi-dished with three solid spokes and is sold in two diameter sizes. The Indy model is sold in three diameter sizes, starting at 317 mm (12½ins) and has three, drilled, silver-finished, semi-dished spokes. Finally, there are the Prototipo and PT.26 models.

Motec: Marketed by Brown and Geeson Ltd, there are three 330 mm (13ins) diameter Motec wheels, each with three steel spokes and a steel rim. The wheels are available with a 25 mm (1ins) or 63 mm (2½ins) dish and differ only in the level of finish. The least expensive model is the Competitor with a simulated leather covered rim and spokes finished in matt black. The European is similar except for chrome treatment on the spokes, while the Motec Leather, as its name implies, has real leather on the rim and chrome on the spokes. The centre boss cap provided can be used as a horn button or a headlamp flasher.

Moto-Lita: This brand is approved as accessory equipment by SAAB, Peugeot, Renault, BL, Opel and other car manufacturers and is supplied as original equipment on some American cars. There are five basic models starting

2 These wheels from Momo (A, C, D), Moto-Lita (B, trimmed with red leather by Wood and Pickett Ltd.), 100+ International (E), Intersport (F), Alexander (G and H) and Mountney Motor Products (I) illustrate the variety in colour, style and size of non-standard steering wheels that is available to the DIY enthusiast

A
B
C
D
E
F
G
H
I

3 You could fit either of these two wheels to your car though your choice would be governed by the depth of dish. The wheel on the left is effectively brought nearer to the driver due to its deep dish while that on the right is barely dished at all

John Harwood

with the Turbo which is a four-spoke design with leather over a natural rubber underlay. Sizes available are 330 mm (13ins), 356 mm (14ins), and 381 mm (15ins) in a flat or dished configuration. The Mark III model is available in three similar sizes, with flat or dished shapes and with a choice of three plain, drilled or slotted alloy spokes. Standard finish for the spokes is polished alloy but black, silver or anodized gold finishes are optional. The wooden rims are built from timbers which are cross-laminated, bonded and riveted to a one-piece alloy frame and finger notches are cut on the underside of it.

The basic version of the three-spoke Mk. IV model, offered in four sizes, is all black with a leather-over-rubber covering that incorporates integral padded thumb grips. The Mk. IV version has the same spoke options as the Mk. III, with the addition of tan as an alternative colour for the rim. The Mk. V model is available in three diameters with a leather-covered rim and has a traditional "Gunsmith" pattern engraved on the three spokes. These may be polished or finished in black or gold. This particular model is slightly dished.

The Mk. VI is a leather-covered wheel of four-spoke design, complete with thumb spats. The spokes are treated in similar manner to the Mk. V.

Mountney: Mountney Motor Products offer steering wheels with diameters ranging from 254 mm (10ins) up to 356 mm (14ins). The wheels are available in colours designed to match the interior of many cars, for example, black, red, tan and blue finishes are readily available.

Four depths of dish are offered and the alloy frames may be polished or black anodized. A thick grip wheel is one of the more recent additions to the range. Mountney also market a chain link steering wheel which is basically intended for customizing enthusiasts.

100+ *International:* This Company produces a very wide range of wheels with frames that are cut from one-piece alloy with a steel reinforcing rim to assist rigidity. The rim and spats are moulded in a thick layer of polyurethane foam and are covered with hand-stitched leather. The wheels are interchangeable with the boss kits which are each designed to fit specific cars and there is a special set of 254 mm (10ins) designed wheels for racing cars. The 305 mm (12ins) model has a plain frame while the 330 mm (13ins), 356 mm (14ins) and 381 mm (15ins) models have three drilled spokes. The standard finish on the frames is polished alloy but a black anodized non-reflective finish is optional. The four-spoke design is the only wheel with 25 mm (1ins) dished frame as standard, all the others can be supplied with a flat frame if required. A budget-priced wheel is available in a three-spoke design and has no thumb spats.

It is impossible to select any one non-standard steering wheel from the market and recommend it as being the best one to buy. Every driver will have his or her own tastes and requirements, some preferring one of the cheaper wheels to the more expensive ones. All that can be said is that if you choose carefully, not only will you buy a steering wheel that improves the appearance of your car but it may also help to improve your driving.

Choosing a car horn

Whether you use your car horn frequently or just on the odd occasion, the time may come when it could save you from having a serious accident. To be really effective a horn must be heard by other road users even under the most testing conditions. But it must also be subdued enough not to cause a nuisance when it is sounded in built-up areas.

For this reason many of the more expensive, high-performance cars on the market have two horns. One is for town use and the other for use where the conditions are more exacting. A large number of cars, however, are still equipped with single, subdued horns. While these may never be a source of annoyance in built-up areas, under motorway or country driving conditions they can often fail to fulfil their main purpose which is to give other road users adequate warning of your approach or presence. To overcome this problem, it is well worthwhile looking at the wide range of horns available on the car accessory market which can be fitted either to supplement or replace the existing unit. A look around a selection of accessory stockists will enable you to price them.

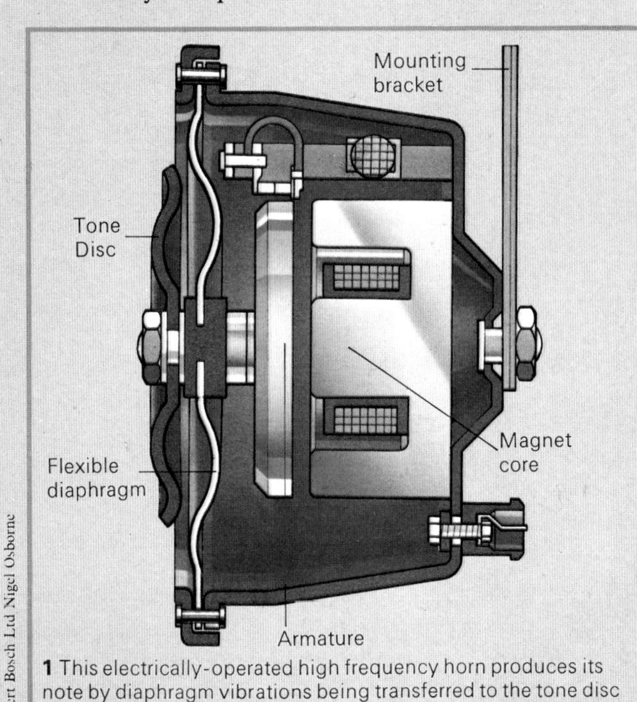

1 This electrically-operated high frequency horn produces its note by diaphragm vibrations being transferred to the tone disc

Robert Bosch Ltd Nigel Osborne

Horns and their uses

In most countries, there are laws which govern when you can use your car's horn. In the UK, for example, you cannot sound it between 11.30 pm and 7.00 am in built-up areas, nor may you use it when the car is stationary. During the day a blast on the horn is an effective way of warning other motorists that you are coming, though at night flashing headlights are usually a better alternative.

The two main characteristics of any horn are its range and its audibility; that is, the ease with which the horn can be heard. Under urban or city centre driving conditions, where traffic usually moves slowly and noise levels are generally low, neither are very important. The range need not be great because the low traffic speeds do not call for a great deal of advanced warning. Audibility is not a crucial factor either because wind and road noise in town are unlikely to drown the horn's sound.

On motorways, the situation is different. Here, the high speeds involved dictate that the warning note should carry as far forward as possible. It should also be loud and strident in order to compete with the wind and road noise surrounding other drivers. On country and mountain roads also a powerful long-range horn can prove to be a very useful accessory. To give an adequate warning as you approach a bend, for example, the sound from the horn will have to overcome such audibility barriers as high banks and hedgerows.

So, when you are buying a horn, consider carefully under what conditions the bulk of your driving will be done, in built-up areas, open country or on the motorway.

On the other hand, if you expect to do a lot of motorway or country driving, a powerful horn really is a worthwhile investment. Remember, though, that these horns are not suitable for use in towns. The ideal arrangement is to keep your standard horn, or an uprated version of it for use around town and to have the additional, powerful horn operated by a separate switch.

Apart from the penetrating, single-note horns, there are also several types of multi-note and musical horns available on the accessory market. These automatically sound off several different notes in quick succession, sometimes forming snatches of popular tunes. Many of them can be set for either single or multi-note functions. Horns like this are popular with customizers and owners seeking to add an extra distinctive touch to their car. From the safety point of view though, there is little to be said in their favour. In most countries, the use of such horns is quite heavily restricted by law.

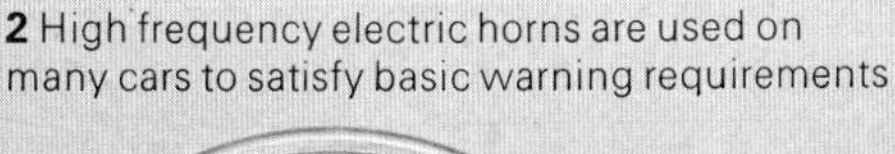

2 High frequency electric horns are used on many cars to satisfy basic warning requirements

Nigel Messett

Legal restrictions

In the UK, there are two restrictions on the use of multi-tone horns. The first bans all two-tone alternating horns, the reason being that these could be confused with the klaxons used by the police and emergency services. The second restriction states that no multi-tone horn of any description may be fitted to a car registered after August 1st, 1973. Any car breaking these regulations will also automatically fail the Department of Transport tests.

The laws in most other countries are similar, but if you are in any doubt at all you should consult your dealer. It would be extremely unwise of him to give you inaccurate information on this point.

There are also various laws in existence which govern the power and stridency of all accessory horns. In the UK, they take the form of an EEC directive. All the reputable manufacturers take care to keep their products inside the laws of the country in which they are being sold and they usually state this somewhere on the packaging. It is, in any case, unlikely that your dealer would risk selling an "illegal" horn, so you may reasonably assume that the one of your choice satisfies all the prevailing noise and stridency regulations of your country.

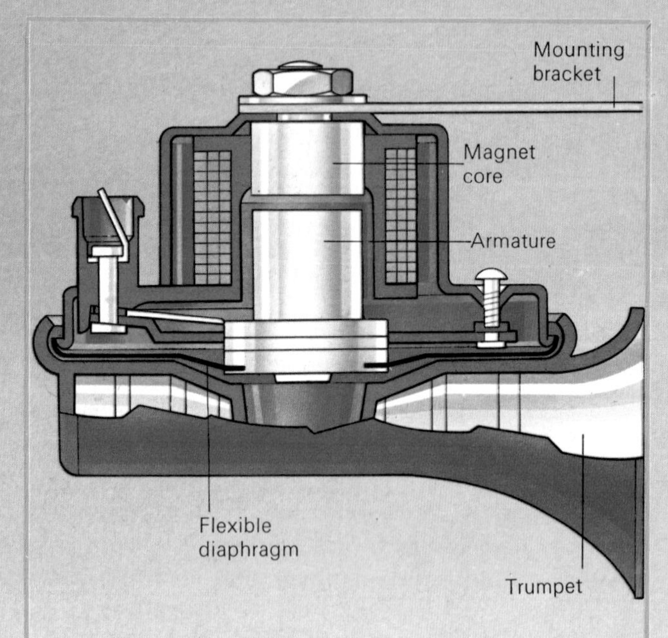

3 Unlike a high frequency horn which uses its tone disc to help produce a note, this windtone horn uses its trumpet. Air inside the trumpet is vibrated by the movement of the flexible diaphragm and the result is a softer and more musical note than is obtained from the high frequency units. As they are sometimes fitted in matched pairs, windtone horns can be used to give two similar notes for country purposes and a single, and less strident note in town conditions

Robert Bosch Ltd Nigel Osborne

Types of horn

There are now three basic types of horn available on the car accessory market. Categorized by the way in which they work they are: the high frequency horn, the windtone horn and the compressor horn. By understanding how they all work you will have a clearer idea of which one best suits your particular needs.

High frequency horns

High frequency horns are the type found on most inexpensive cars as standard equipment. They are relatively simple, both in operation and construction, but they do not have a particularly high sound output. Even so, they have to produce three separate components of sound for the horn to be usable and efficient.

A typical high frequency horn is the Lucas 6H model. When you operate the horn switch or lever, electric current flows to the armature. This moves slightly, taking the diaphragm to which it is attached (fig. 1) with it. At the same time, it momentarily stops the current, returns to its original position and then repeats the process. Because the armature moves the diaphragm back and forth at high speed it starts up a low frequency vibration. This is transferred to the tone disc (resonator) where it creates the high frequency vibrations which give the horn its characteristic note and is one component of the overall sound.

The diaphragm, which vibrates at between 300 and 500 cycles per second (cps), produces a note which is low in frequency but high in energy and it is this note which is penetrating and therefore carried away from the horn the desired distance and is the second component sound. The tone disc vibrates at about 2000 cps and emits the third component, this, being a high-frequency, low-energy note, adds a fresh character to the sound and enables anyone

4 A selection of windtone horns. These use more current than high frequency horns so they are sometimes sold complete with a voltage relay in the fitting kit

Nigel Messett

hearing it to pinpoint its origin. This aural phenomenon is well-known amongst hi-fi enthusiasts.

High frequency horns form the bottom end of the market and those which are available are usually designed as simple, standard, replacement parts (fig. 2).

Windtone horns

Windtone horns differ only slightly from the high frequency type but their output is greater and the tone is usually richer-sounding. It is because of this that windtone horns are often found as standard equipment on mid and upper range cars. Sometimes they take the form of matched pairs with each horn designed to sound a slightly different note simultaneously. On other cars two separate windtones of varying output give the driver a choice of town and country applications. Some cars equipped with high frequency horns also have this feature.

Like the high frequency horn, the windtone (fig. 3) has a vibrating diaphragm arrangement but instead of a tone disc there is a hollow trumpet. The vibrations from the diaphragm cause the air inside the trumpet to vibrate to produce a softer sounding, less strident and more musical note than the equivalent high frequency horn. The length of the trumpet determines the pitch of the horn while the shape regulates the overtones and therefore the quality of the note produced. The trumpets may be made from die-cast metal, spun metal or plastic and they are often rolled up like a French horn in order to save space. As a consequence, relatively long trumpets can be used.

As windtone horns often require up to double the current of their high-frequency equivalents, they are consequently more susceptible to changes in voltage and may need a voltage relay (fig. 7) to be wired into their circuit. This permits the high current carrying wires to the horn to be kept relatively short, so minimizing the possibility of voltage drops which would impair the horn's performance. If they are necessary relays are almost always included with the horn kit but it is worth checking with your dealer just to make sure.

Neither windtone horns or the high frequency models (see above) can be "tuned" but both types usually have some form of adjustment screw to take up any wear in the armature contacts.

Compressor horns

Compressor horns (fig. 6) form the expensive end of the market but they are very popular because of their comparatively high output.

The typical basic compressor horn equipment comprises an air compressor (fig. 8), air tube(s) and trumpet(s). The compressor itself consists of an electric motor coupled to a vane-type compressor. The motor is operated by a conventional horn switch or button and there is also a voltage relay incorporated in the circuit, as there is in the case of the windtone horn.

When the horn is activated, the compressor generates a powerful jet of air which passes through the air tubes to the trumpets of which there are usually two or more. Horns which have the facility for sounding each trumpet individually in quick succession, such as fanfare or musical horns, have a slightly more complicated compressor. In this case, the compressed air passes over a rotor which then distributes a jet to each trumpet in turn. Every trumpet has its own air tube and individual nozzle on the top of the high-speed air compressor.

At the base of each trumpet the jet of air passes over a tuned diaphragm (fig. 9) similar to the reed in a wind instrument, thereby creating a note. As with windtone horns and wind instruments this basic note is modified by the length and shape of the trumpet.

A simple, twin-trumpet, compressor horn has unequal length trumpets which produce simultaneous notes—one short and high-pitched, the other low-pitched and longer.

5 From top to bottom these horns are ; the Jubilee Diesel Tone, Bull Horn, Ol' Timer and Wolf Whistle. Basically novelty items favoured by customizing enthusiasts, they are often used more for creating amusement than as serious warning devices

6 Although costly and space consuming, compressor horns are popular due to their high output. Each trumpet's note is governed by length and shape. Musical horns (top) need a more complex compressor in order to play a tune

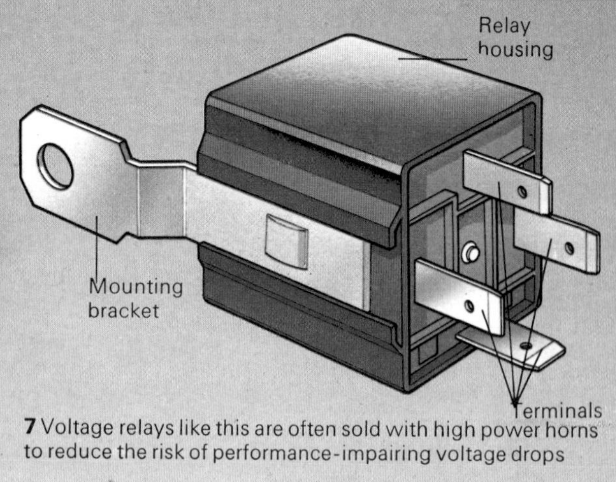

7 Voltage relays like this are often sold with high power horns to reduce the risk of performance-impairing voltage drops

The combination gives the horn great penetrative power and range but keeps the sound reasonably harmonious.

Vacuum-operated horns
Vacuum horns are rather different from the three basic types of accessory horn but their use is now confined only to novelty items like the "Wolf Whistle" (see below). The power for these horns is drawn from the inlet manifold.

Buying the horn of your choice
When you finally go to buy the horn of your choice, make sure that you have a good idea what type you want, bearing in mind that the ability to give a safer warning should be your main concern. At the dealer's, quote the make, model and year of your car. Also tell him whether there is a 6 volt or 12 volt electrical system and either positive or negative earth on your particular car.

When choosing, do not forget guarantees. These can be quite comprehensive with some horns and may help you to come to a decision. The other point to consider is how complete the horn kit is. A good one should include comprehensive fitting instructions, a relay, where necessary, adequate lengths of wire and fixing brackets, as well as the horn itself and, of course, the guarantee.

The market
Below is a selection of some of the most popular car horn ranges available on the market.
Alexander: This firm markets the Mixo range of horns. The twin and triple trumpet air horn kits are fully synchronized and feature bright red, plastic trumpets as well as being available for both 12 volt and 6 volt electrical systems. The company also offers the Stritone horn which is a development of the conventional windtone variety.
Autocar: Offer the Jubilee range of distinctive sounding horns. The 15/150 Veteran and 29/030 Ol' Timer models are compressor horns, the latter with a Klaxon sound. The 29/040 Diesel Tone and the 28/240 Twin Van are windtone horns—the 29/040 sounds like a diesel locomotive and the 28/240 has straight, chromed trumpets for external mounting by customizing enthusiasts. The Wolf Horn and the 29/050 Bull Horn are vacuum-powered, novelty horns with a strictly limited appeal (fig. 5).
Bosch: The range from this well-known German firm includes two, standard replacement, high frequency (HF) horns, the Fanfare horn set which is a windtone device and twin and triple trumpet compressor horn kits. The Europa Supertone HF horn features optional high and low notes.
Hella: Another comprehensive range of continental horns

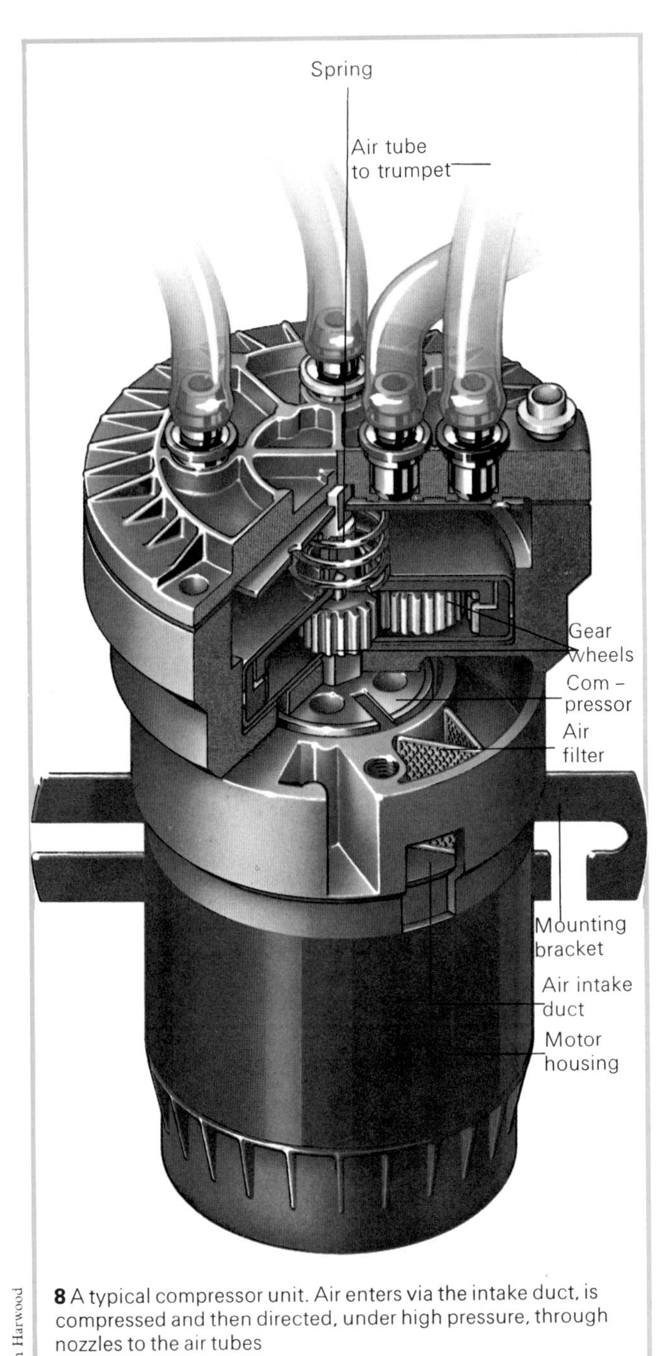

8 A typical compressor unit. Air enters via the intake duct, is compressed and then directed, under high pressure, through nozzles to the air tubes

John Harwood

including two, disc-type, HF horns: a twin windtone horn set and twin and triple trumpet compressor horn sets.

Klamix: A large range of continental horns which offers a very wide choice. The HF102 HF horn has a high and a low note while the KM4 and KW9 HF Beep horns can be used singly or in high/low note, matched pairs. The TR89 and TR129 Mixo windtone horns come in high and low note versions. Klamix are another firm marketing the Stritone-developed, windtone horn and also on offer is the similar Seatone set which features twin, matched, chrome trumpets. Both of these windtone models are available in high or low note versions as is the Riviera S, twin-trumpet, compressor horn. On the novelty side is the motor-driven Klaxonnet which is claimed to give a vintage klaxon sound.

Lucas: An internationally famous range of HF and windtone horns—including the 6H HF model—which are available in high or low note versions and in standard or uprated form. The 9H windtone model follows a similar specification and the 7H windtone is available as an alternative in high or low note versions and in standard or uprated form.

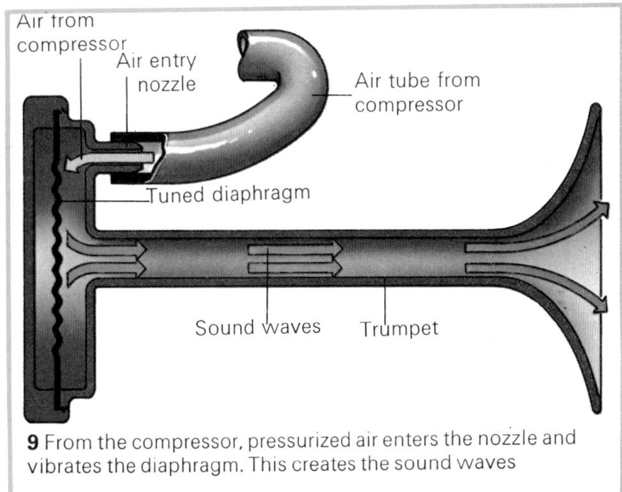

9 From the compressor, pressurized air enters the nozzle and vibrates the diaphragm. This creates the sound waves

Lyall Lusted: This firm markets the Svezia range of horns which is made in Italy. The Elektro-Vintage is a windtone horn; the Alpine and the Nice are twin and triple trumpet, compressor horns respectively.

Mill Accessory Group: Better known by the Group's Paddy Hopkirk brand name, this firm markets the well-established Fiamm range of horns. The Super set consists of matched, high and low note, windtone horns. The Mercury, Sport and Gran Turismo models are high and low note, twin-trumpet, compressor horns with different pitches and outputs. The Triple Three, triple-trumpet, compressor horn sounds three, simultaneous, blended notes. The Trio is similar to the Triple Three but has the facility for sounding the three notes in rapid succession. The most expensive models in the range are the Musical, multi-trumpet, compressor horns which can be bought to play snatches of a variety of different tunes including "Colonel Bogey" and "La Cucaracha". A range of chromed windtone and compressor horns is also available. These are designed for external mounting and are aimed mainly at customizing enthusiasts.

Harry Moss: Offering the well-known Maserati range of compressor air horns. The TS 6/12/24 Sprint model has twin, red plastic trumpets and a high-power compressor. It produces a penetrating, discordant sound with a high note. The T3 Minor, available in 6 volts or 12 volts form, has three trumpets which can be sounded in unison or individually, in quick succession. Musical compressor horns which play "Colonel Bogey" and "La Cucaracha" are also available.

Sprint: This firm markets the Stebel range of continental-made horns, some of which are quite unusual. The EMS2 is a windtone set with twin, red and black trumpets. The DEM2 is similar, but with chromed trumpets. The JEDP2 and JEDP3 models are compressor horns with two and three trumpets respectively. The BDP Brio is another triple trumpet, compressor horn set, but the notes can be sounded in fanfare or in unison. Similar to the Brio is the MDP3, but this horn has a more musical sound. Also available are more complex five and six trumpet, musical, compressor horns. Novelty items from this firm include the "Wolf Call" air horn; the klaxon-sounding, motor-driven, Ol' Timer horn and the Diesel Tone windtone horn, which is also marketed by Autocar; plus a musical, windtone horn that can be "played" on a three-button keyboard fiitted to the car's dashboard.

Wipac: This firm also markets some of the French Mixo/Klaxon range offered by Klamix but under the Clearhooters brand name.

Fitting a map light

Reading a map in your car during darkness can be a frustrating exercise. Many courtesy lights are simply not powerful enough for you to recognize the quickest route or locate road numbers on a normal map. There is an answer to the problem—fitting a purpose-built map reading light.

There are several types on the market: some feature a flexible tube which can be manipulated into several positions, some have mechanical linkages or some, which have to be hand-held, simply clip into a retaining bracket when not in use.

Simple map lights which plug into the cigar lighter socket are available but most need to be fixed permanently and wired into the car's electrical circuit.

When buying the particular map light you want, remember to check that all the screws and wires necessary for fitting are provided. If you wish to hide the wiring behind a panel in the car, rubber grommets will also have to be purchased.

Positioning the map light

Always carefully consider where to position the map light before you actually begin the job. It should be placed near the centre of the fascia so that the passenger can read maps while the car is moving and the driver can also use it when the car is stationary. Make sure that it will not be in the way when not in use. If a spring clip is provided to hold the lamp end of the flexible tube type of map light when not in use, make sure that this clip can be fixed rigidly and in a convenient position.

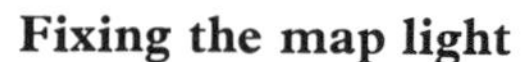

Fixing the map light

Most map light kits include self-tapping screws so that they can be fixed to a metal panel in the car. These can also be used if the light is being fixed to a wooden or plastic surface.

Before marking the drill holes, ensure that there are no obstructions or wires behind the panel. Mark the holes, using the base plate of the lamp as a template, and then, after re-marking with a centre punch, drill the holes.

If you wish to keep the wiring out of sight, you will need to drill an extra hole for this. Fit a rubber grommet in the wiring hole to stop the wires chafing on the edges.

Electrical connections

Two wires must be connected before the map light can be operated—the earth and the live supply. The earth can be connected by attaching a tag connector to the earth wire and screwing this to a metal part of the car.

The map light may be needed at any time, so it will be better to wire the light so that it operates even with the ignition switched off.

This is best done by attaching the live wire to a suitable terminal on the fuse box. To find which terminal to use, connect a 12-volt test lamp to earth and each terminal in turn with the ignition switched off. Attach the live wire to the terminal which lights the bulb.

Some fuse boxes do not have a permanently live terminal. In this case an alternative is to wire the lamp so that it works only with the side lights switched on. Carry out the test lamp method with the side lights switched on and attach the live wire to the terminal, or the lead, which lights the test bulb.

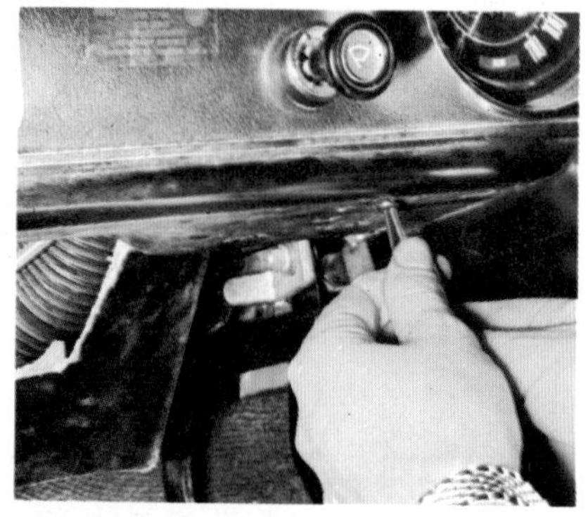

1 After drilling the required holes in the fascia and fitting a rubber grommet to the wire hole, feed the wires gently through

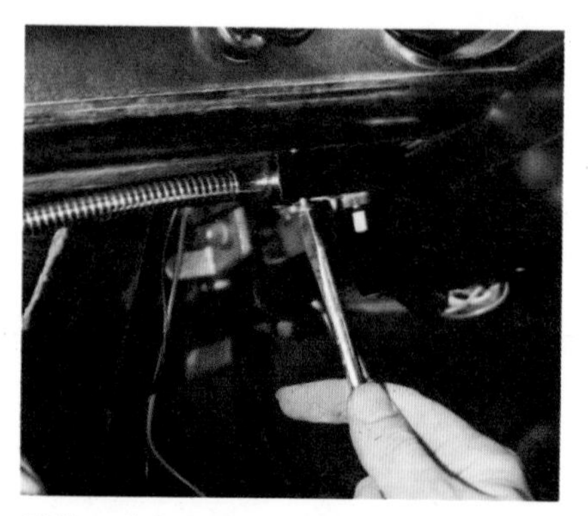

2 When fixing the map light base plate in place, tighten each screw lightly before finally turning the screws firmly home

3 The earth wire must be fixed to a part of the car's chassis. Here the earth wire has been secured by a fascia fixing screw

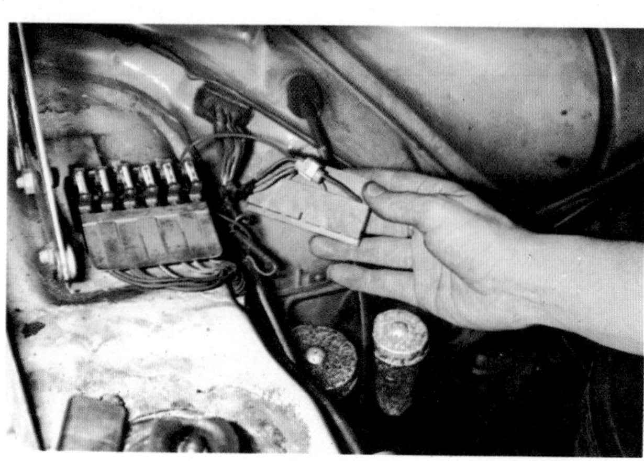

4 The live wire can be attached to a terminal of the fuse box, or to a wire leading to the fuse box, using a suitable connector

Jake Wynter

5 The map light fixed in place. It is within reach of both the driver and passenger yet remains out of the way when not in use

Buying replacement seats

Whenever you travel in a car, whether as a driver or a passenger, your body is in contact with the car seat. It is therefore not surprising that the design of the seat will have a more immediate effect on your comfort than any other part of the vehicle. Expensive cars have always used seats designed to a high specification with both the comfort and safety of the occupant in mind. By contrast, however, the seats in less sophisticated cars have often left a great deal to be desired in terms of comfort, especially on long journeys.

Only in recent years, with the growing recognition that safety and driver comfort are closely allied, have manufacturers begun to seriously consider the design of the seats that they fit to their cheaper models.

To cater for the owners of older cars fitted with seats that are a continual source of discomfort the accessory market has also developed an interest in this area and now offers a wide selection of replacement seats for the majority of mass-produced cars (fig. 1).

The makers of these non-standard seats are not bound by the same constraints as the major car manufacturers. For the latter, the biggest single consideration is the production cost of a seat and the effect that this cost will have on the overall price of the finished car. Non-standard seats are usually considerably more expensive than standard seats but they are designed from the outset to be far more comfortable, safer and usually more attractive.

1 These seats from (1) Wolfrace, (2) Mill Accessory Group, (3 and 5) Wood and Pickett Ltd., and (4) Stylex Motor Products illustrate the variety in colour and design available. The Recaro seat (5), with combined head restraint and speaker system, is adjustable by means of a push-button console

The importance of well-designed seats

A well-designed seat is not only important from the point of view of the occupant's comfort; it also makes a major contribution to the overall safety of the car, especially in an ergonomically-designed vehicle where the seat is part of a total design concept. It is an acknowledged fact that uncomfortable seats, by increasing fatigue, can actually have an adverse effect on the capability of a driver as the longer a driver sits on an uncomfortable seat the more pronounced the fatigue-induced effects become. A comfortable, well-designed seat is usually of most use to those who make frequent long journeys or who spend an appreciable time driving in heavy traffic. On shorter runs, there is unlikely to be enough time for the cumulative effects of a badly-designed seat to show themselves.

Seat design considerations

When a designer sets out to create a new seat he aims to produce one that will comfortably support the body of the occupant and cushion it effectively from vibrations, undulations in the road surface and the rolling movements created by the motion of the car as it is driven round corners. It is most important that the seat offers the correct amount of support to each part of the body with which it is in contact. If any one area of the seat offers dramatically better support than another, any initial feelings of comfort will soon give way to feelings of discomfort as the softer area will pull at the occupant's body and, in time, cause it to ache.

For this reason, many correctly designed seats will often feel quite uncomfortable when you first sit in them. After a short journey, however, the benefits of full, all-round support begin to show. Some drivers bolster their standard production seats with cushions in an attempt to counter the inherent deficiencies of the basic design. Far from solving the problems, this is likely to make the situation worse by adding to the uneven support that the body receives.

The designer must not only give the seat good supporting qualities which act when the car is moving in a straight-line; the seat must also offer resistance to the forces which induce involuntary body movements as the car is driven round corners, braked and accelerated.

Sideways movements, such as those incurred during cornering, can be counteracted by incorporating raised sections on each side of the seat squab, the horizontal part of the seat. These lateral supports do not have to be very pronounced in order to be effective, it is the way they are constructed that is important. On a specially-equipped rally car the lateral supports will be far more pronounced than those on a seat intended for an ordinary road car as they must cope with far greater sideways body movements caused by very rapid cornering. This causes the rally seat to take on the familiar "bucket" shape (fig. 2). Unless you are considering using your car for continually swift cornering, you will probably not require a very deep "bucket" seat and you will probably find that a shallower style of seat is quite satisfactory for everyday use.

The lower part of the backrest of a correctly designed seat should also support the lumbar region of the occupant when he or she is resting in the normal sitting position. Many accessory seats are made either with fixed or adjustable backrests but both types can incorporate a special, separately adjustable support pad for this sensitive area. It is also important that the backrest should not give during hard acceleration as this can also be very tiring on a long journey at high speeds.

A separate head restraint system, which is sometimes an extension of the backrest rather than a separate component of the seat, can extend support to the occupant's neck during hard acceleration and can also act as a brace in the event of a crash. The function of a head restraint is often misunderstood, mainly because it is sometimes wrongly referred to as a "head rest". Far from resting the head, which is neither practical nor desirable, the head restraint is designed to protect your neck and spinal cord from the possibility of a "whiplash" injury in the event of an impact. On accessory seats, the head restraint is either built into the one-piece structure or else it locates into sockets in the backrest. A well-designed seat will have a restraint just large enough to give the necessary support without unduly obstructing rearward vision. If it is of the locating type, it must also be secure when in position. A head restraint which comes loose is more dangerous than no restraint at all.

Like the squab, the backrest part of a replacement seat will probably have some extra lateral support at either side to help control body movement during cornering. In the case of rally-type seats, the backrest and squab supports are usually combined, tapering out at either end.

The other part of a replacement seat which usually offers extra support is the front of the squab. The extra resistance here helps to prevent the body moving forward under braking and supports the thighs when they are in the normal driving position. In a well-designed seat, this area of support should be firm but not uncomfortable.

2 Giving maximum lateral support, rally seats play a major role in enabling the crew to keep the car under control at high speed even over the roughest terrain

When all the support functions of a car seat are considered and combined together in a unified design the result is the basic seat shape commonly used. How refined and well-researched this shape becomes during the design and manufacture of a particular seat will, to some extent, determine how comfortable the seat is. But, comfort is also related to use and a seat that is comfortable for a rally driver will probably not satisfy a family motorist even if it is fully adjustable. This is why there are so many different shapes and sizes of seat available on the accessory market. All incorporate the considerations listed above but the majority are modified in some way to suit different uses. You should therefore have a clear idea which type of non-standard seat best suits your needs before making your choice.

Seat construction

In seat construction, as in seat design, the makers of non-standard seats have a lot more freedom than the cost-conscious car manufacturers. Although limited to an extent by price considerations, they are nevertheless in a position to use the best materials available in order to produce a superior product.

To ensure that they have sufficient strength and rigidity virtually all seats are fitted with steel frames. The framework may be either tubular or square-sectioned but, whatever form it takes, the non-standard seat is sometimes a good deal stronger than a basic, mass-production car seat.

The skeleton inside both the squab and the backrest of a typical standard seat is made from stretched rubber webbing, secured to the frame by steel hooks. Even though ordinary seats share this feature, the webbing in a non-standard seat will most probably be more highly resilient and stretch-resistant. Around the skeleton and giving the non-standard seat its characteristic shape, is the special padding. In order to reproduce intricately shaped designs as effectively as possible, seat manufacturers usually mould the padding in large sections. The materials used are either foam rubber or polyurethane foam, both materials being strong, light and easily workable. Where extra resistance is called for in certain parts of the padded structure, such as the front section of the squab, the foam is usually given a higher density to lessen its cushioning effect.

In the case of reclining seats, the relatively simple structure of the one-piece type is complicated by the incorporation of a mechanism designed to allow the occupant to alter the rake of the backrest. The mechanism may take the form either of a winder or a lever-operated ratchet on one side of the seat. It is safe to assume that the adjuster will have been fully tested for rigidity under crash conditions. The range of adjustment, however, is something which varies from seat to seat and this is a point you should bear in mind when you come to make your final choice of replacement seat.

The external covering of a seat is the aspect of seat construction which is usually of most concern to a prospective buyer. Specialist seat manufacturers have a wide choice of materials with which to cover their products and most offer several trim options on each model in their range. Plastic sheeting as a covering material is totally unsuitable for any seat because it does not "breathe". Lack of ventilation will cause a build-up of perspiration on the seat which, in turn, will make the occupant feel uncomfortable. Instead, vinyls are used on cheaper seats. Their ventilation characteristics are better than those of plastic but they, too, can cause a seat to feel clammy, especially on a hot day.

For this reason, most of the popular seats employ fibrous materials, to cover either the whole seat or just those areas most in contact with the driver. Collectively, these materials are usually referred to as cloth and they include cord, brushed nylon, polyester, Ambla and Dralon. Seats designed specifically for race or rally use often have more sophisticated developments of the standard types of covering material.

Ford Motor Co. Ltd Peter Dazeley

Buying non-standard seats

Perhaps the biggest worry for anyone contemplating buying seats is whether or not they will be able to find a model that fits their particular car. The answer is that most of the seats now available are complemented by various adaptors or subframes which enable a single model to be fitted to a variety of different vehicles. Standard seat fittings without runners to provide fore and aft movement can usually be modified to take non-standard seats mounted on their own special runners. Existing runner fittings can also either be modified or replaced completely so that the new seat offers a greater range of adjustment than before. A specialist seat dealer should be able to give you specific advice on which seats in his stock will fit your car providing you quote the make, model, year and chassis number. Remember, though, that the subframes are usually sold as extras and may not be included in the price of the seat.

The next consideration to be borne in mind is, inevitably, cost. If you want to transform your car's interior overnight, then you will obviously need to purchase a pair of front seats and this could prove expensive. A better idea, providing you are prepared to ignore the interior's appearance temporarily, is to buy one really good seat that suits you perfectly and then to install a matching one on the passenger side at a later date.

Whether any particular seat suits you perfectly can only be ascertained after it has been installed in the car and used on a long journey. When you sit in one at the dealers, though, it should at least feel comfortable. If you are trying the full rally-type seat, you will have to allow for a slight restrictive feeling created by the increased lateral support. Nevertheless, you should not feel cramped or be forced into an unnatural position. However, if all the seats that you try give the initial impression of being hard and uncomfortable, remember that your existing ones may well be past their best. Seats which have softened through age may seem comfortable at first but they are unlikely to remain so over a journey of any appreciable distance.

Whether you are drawn towards one-piece, rally-style seats or towards the fully adjustable, reclining variety really depends on what sort of driver you are. Seats based on rally designs have the distinct advantage of giving you full support under hard cornering or heavy braking; the involuntary body movements that take place under these conditions are one of the main causes of driver fatigue. A disadvantage of this type of seat is that your driving position is largely predetermined by its shape. This will not suit the driver who likes to adjust his seat according to his mood or the prevailing driving conditions.

Reclining seats are more expensive than the non-reclining type because of their extra complexity. While, perhaps, not offering the same degree of support, they do have the advantage of versatility; a seat which reclines completely may be used as an emergency bed or to increase loading space. Remember also that if your car has two doors the seats of your choice must have a tip-forward facility, in the form of either a hinged backrest or a hinged base.

Whether or not a seat will obstruct rearward vision is another point which should be considered. Although any seat fitted with a high backrest or an integral head restraint will, to some extent, obstruct rearward vision, it stands to reason that a really large seat will not be suitable for most small car applications.

When you have decided on the type and model of seat you require, you will still be left with a choice of coverings. Seat covering is really a matter of personal preference but your choice may be dictated by the availability of materials to match your car's interior. If you expect the seats to get dirty, choose a covering that will be easy to clean; your dealer should be able to advise you on this point.

Finally, if you cannot find a seat that fits you or your requirements, do not be tempted to compromise. There is a large enough selection available to cater for most people's needs and it is worth spending time making your choice.

Accessory seats pose a slight problem to Australian buyers, however. Because of Australian Design Rules the various State transport departments refuse to register cars fitted with other than approved seats. Only two brands have, at this time, such approval, Recaro and Scheel. Recaro seats are approved for most makes and models but Scheel seats, so far, only for Ford Falcon XA, XB and XC models. Most of the brand names listed in the accompanying tables are available through major accessory shops in Australia along with two local brands, Viking and Stratos, but intending purchasers should check their local regulations regarding fitment before buying a seat. If State approval has not been given to a seat it can only be fitted to rally or race cars and buyers who fit them to their road cars are warned that they could be forced to remove them at the time of annual registration inspection.

Selected seats

Here is a selection from the ranges of some of the best known seat manufacturers and importers.

ASS: This German firm offers the expensive but very high-quality 203S and 501S reclining seats which are optional extras on BMW and Porsche cars. The bases of both models are tailored to fit individual makes of car and are fully adjustable for fore and aft movement, height and rake.

Cobra: One of the best known names in the custom seat market, the Cobra range includes both one-piece and reclining seats with high or low backrests. A tilt-forward facility or electric operation is optional on some models and the choice of coverings includes brushed nylon, flame-resistant cropped polyester, and Dralon.

Corbeau: Another well-known range of seats, all of which have been designed using race and rally experience. Standard and high-backrest seats are available in both one-piece and reclining form. The standard models have provision for optional head restraints and most of the range feature a variety of trim options as well.

Huntmaster: Stylex Motor Products offer a wide selection of seats, the most popular of which is the Targa. Available in one-piece or recliner form and providing an exceptional degree of lateral support, it has found particular favour with rally drivers. All Huntmaster seats have welded steel frames, Pirelli suspension and cellular foam padding. Trim materials include vinyl, brushed nylon and simulated sheepskin.

Karobes: Included in this firm's range of seats are the one-piece High Back and Sportsman models. The High-Back incorporates an integral head restraint while the Sportsman is a low-backed seat. Both are trimmed in vinyl.

Mill Accessory Group: This firm markets a comprehensive range of custom seats under the Paddy Hopkirk and Billover brand names. All the seats have Pirelli suspension and a choice of trim colouring, apart from the top of the range Sports Master Race/Rally seat, which has a flame-resistant covering. As with some other seat firms, a medical consultant assists in the design of all models.

Recaro: A German-made range of seats, Recaro are imported into the UK by Wood and Pickett Ltd., the interior re-furbishing specialists. Like the ASS range, Recaro seats are expensive but of high-quality and sophisticated construction. The Ideal C seat is perhaps the ultimate in custom seating and is fully adjustable. Its high price also ensures exclusivity.

Restall: Another firm offering a comprehensive range of reasonably priced seats. Both one-piece and reclining models are available.

Ridgard: Apart from manufacturing a wide range of one-piece, reclining and bucket-style seats, Ridgard offer a particularly large selection of sub-frames. This enables the company's range of seats to be fitted in to virtually any car.

Wolfrace: This firm markets a one-piece and several reclining types of seat, one of which, the 400, is designed specially for vans. The recliners all have a tip-forward feature and the entire range is trimmed in beige, stain-resistant material.

Anti-theft devices

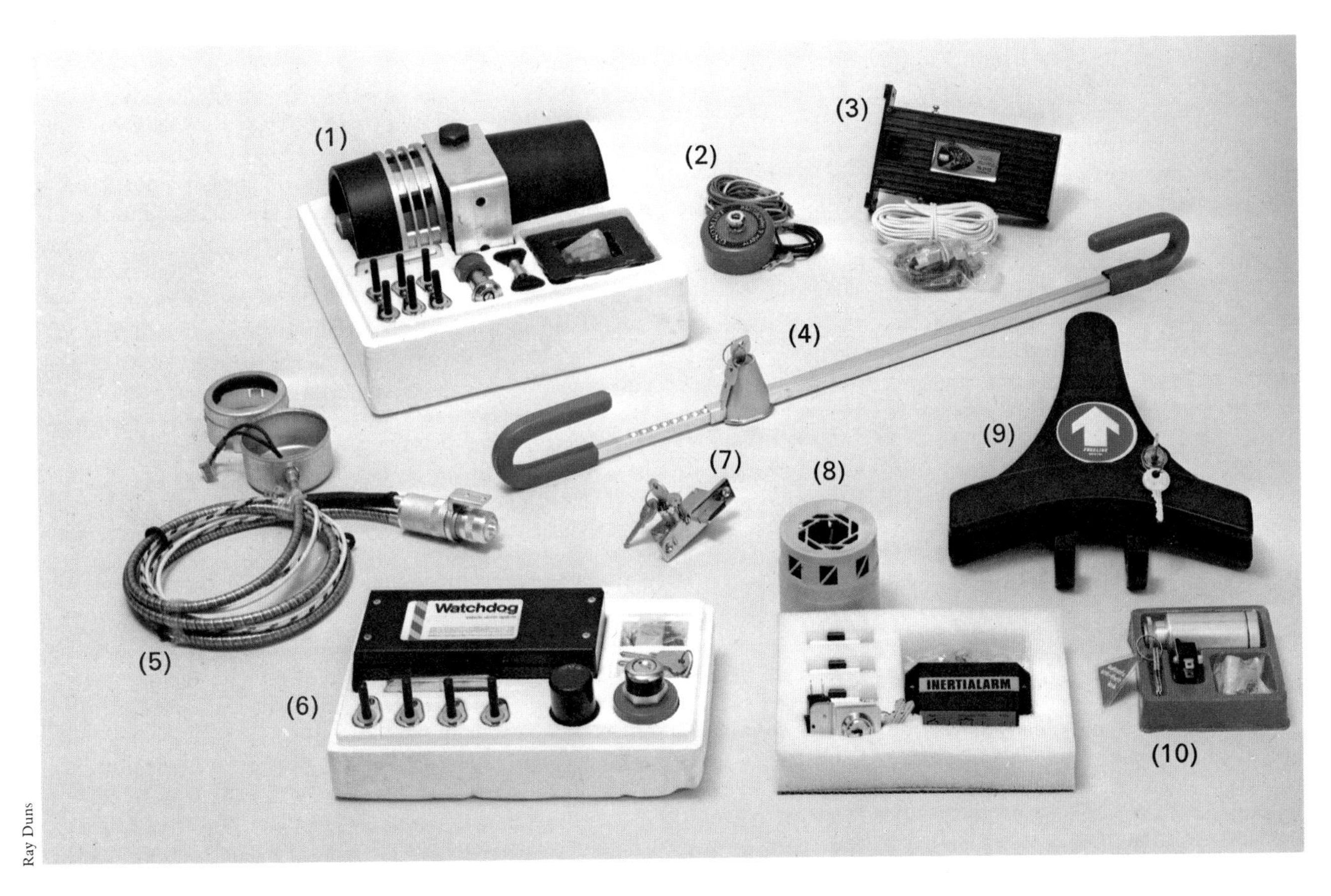

Ray Duns

1 Some of the many types of anti-theft device kits available (1) the Watchdog ESM/12 alarm (2) the Gnomist immobilizer-alarm (3) the Tragonic Tiger alarm (4) the Krooklok immobilizer (5) the BMS Immobiliser (6) the Watchdog VDL immobilizer-alarm (7) the Simba high-security deadlock (8) the Simba Inertialarm immobilizer alarm (9) the Freeline Autoguard immobilizer (10) the Autosafe brake immobilizer. These kits are supplied complete with full fitting instructions

The number of car thefts and break-ins increases almost every year. In England and Wales, for example, Home Office figures for 1976 showed that more than 264,500 cars were stolen, compared with about 184,000 in 1972.

If you regularly keep your car in an urban area, you could run a high risk of having it stolen or broken into. Insurance cover may protect you financially against any loss or damage, but you still suffer the inconvenience of waiting to get the damage or loss put right.

Many motorists try to beat the car thief by fitting their cars with steering-column locks. But thieves are increasingly tempted to break into cars not only to steal them, but also to take accessories and valuables left unprotected inside. The standard lock fittings on the boot, bonnet, doors and even the steering of many cars pose few problems for the really determined thief, who will be quite prepared to use brute force to gain entry. So there is a clear case for providing your car and its contents with extra protection.

Basically, anti-theft devices fall into four categories: immobilizers, alarms, immobilizer-alarms and high-security locks.

Mechanical immobilizers

Several types of immobilizer are available. All are designed to prevent the car from being moved or driven away, but do not necessarily prevent a thief from getting inside it. So if you do not keep valuables or have any removable accessories inside your car, and are mainly concerned with preventing the car itself from being taken, you may want to fit an immobilizer.

Immobilizers operate either mechanically or electrically, depending on the type. Some systems are very easy to install, while others need to be fitted by a skilled mechanic. Their prices differ widely.

Some of the immobilizing devices available are as follows.

The Freeline Autoguard (fig. 2), is one of the simplest anti-theft devices in every respect. It is manufactured in pvc and shaped to fit over the rim of the steering wheel. Two protruding hooks are pushed in to lock the device to the wheel. The Autoguard limits movement of the wheel, as any attempt to turn the steering brings the projecting stem into contact with the car door or windscreen. When located with the stem pointing downwards it can also prevent the driver's seat from being occupied. The device is released with a key and is removed and stored when not in use.

The Krooklok (fig. 3), not only limits the movement of the steering wheel, but also (on cars with manual transmission), immobilizes the gearbox. This is achieved by an extendible steel bar with a hook at either end. One hook goes over the rim of the steering wheel and the other fits under the clutch pedal (or brake pedal on automatics). When the bar is drawn together and locked with a key, the clutch pedal cannot be depressed and the wheel cannot be turned. Like the Autoguard, the Krooklok is removed when not in use.

Both these immobilizers are simple steering locks. They

have an advantage over column locks in that they are visible from outside the car. For a casual thief may damage a car getting into it, only to abandon the attempt to steal it when he finds that it is column-locked. But if a locking device can be seen beforehand, the thief may be deterred altogether, thereby preventing any damage to the car.

Electrical immobilizers

Electrical immobilizers work by cutting off the power to an electrical component or by interrupting the wiring circuit so that the engine cannot be started. The most common method involves immobilizing the ignition system by directing its electrical current through a lockable switch.

The BMS Immobiliser (figs. 1 and 4), is basically a switch which stops electricity from reaching the coil. It does this by directing the power supply to the coil through a multi-pin socket and plug switch. When the removable plug cap is in place, electricity flows to the coil normally, but when it is removed the circuit is broken and the coil cannot operate. A metal coil cover, incorporated in the system, fits over the coil and protects the connections from being rewired should a thief try to by-pass the switch. Some of the wires which lead from the switch to the coil are encased in flexible steel tubing as a further precaution against any attempt to rewire the system. The plug and socket can be fixed underneath the dashboard or hidden from view somewhere else inside the car. BMS devices are wired and coded individually so that thieves cannot possess a cap that will operate any other switch.

The Petromag (figs. 1 and 5) is a dual-purpose immobilizer arranged as a combination of a petrol tap, switch and lock. The key-operated lock unit cuts off the petrol supply to the carburettor and puts the coil out of action when the key is removed. The locking tap is connected to the fuel line with a length of flexible hose, ideally somewhere between the carburettor and the fuel pump. An electrical lead is also taken from the tap to intercept the ignition circuit between the coil and ignition switch. The lock unit is mounted on the dashboard.

The Autosafe (figs. 1 and 6) is a brake lock and ignition cut-out switch. A lockable valve mounted inside the car allows the brake hydraulic system to work in one direction only. When the valve is switched on with a key, and the brake pedal is depressed, hydraulic pressure is maintained at the wheel cylinders. The brakes are locked on and are released only when the valve is switched off. The Autosafe is an effective immobilizer, as the car cannot be moved or even towed away. The system cannot be by-passed because its valve is connected directly into the hydraulic system. This fact, however, means that installation—which involves modifications to the brake hydraulics—is not easy for the amateur.

Alarm systems

Anti-theft alarms do not physically prevent a thief from gaining access to the inside of the car. They are intended to defend the car and the interior against attempted break-ins by drawing attention to the fact that it is being tampered with. The warning alarm is usually a loud siren or car horn activated by switches or sensors mounted on the car at the most likely points of attack. To be effective, the alarm warning signal should be given before the thief gets into the car so that he is panicked into abandoning the attempt. Not all alarms do this, and so do not adequately protect either the car or its contents.

Some systems employ switches which activate the alarm. These can sometimes prove tricky to fit, but in some cases the existing courtesy light switches in the car can be used, saving the need to rig up a new circuit. These types of device work when, for example, a switch mounted in the door pillar is set off. But if the door has to be opened, however slightly, before the alarm is sounded the thief has time either to make a quick snatch for any valuables or even to get in and drive away regardless of the noise. This

2 The Freeline Autoguard locks on to the steering wheel rim

3 The Krooklok. It locks round the wheel and clutch pedal

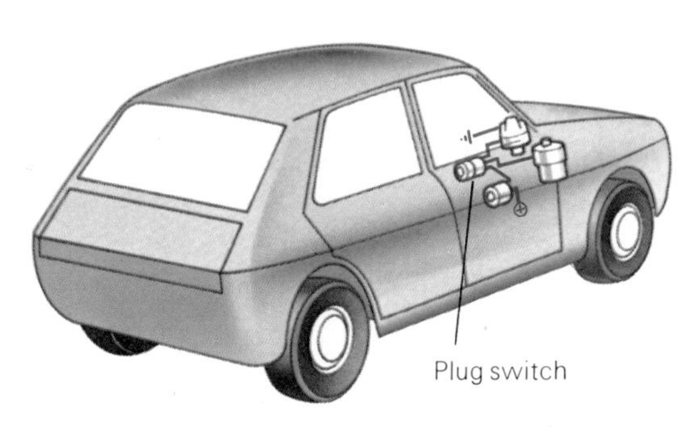

4 The BMS Immobiliser cuts off the power supply to the coil

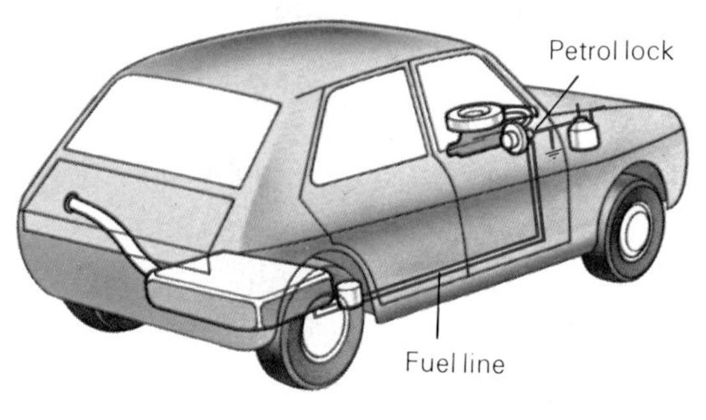

5 The Petromag intercepts the petrol supply and the ignition

Nigel Osborne

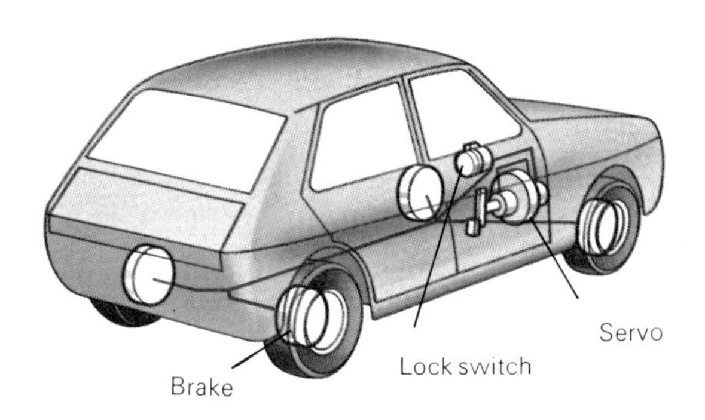

6 The Autosafe device locks the brakes on at all four wheels

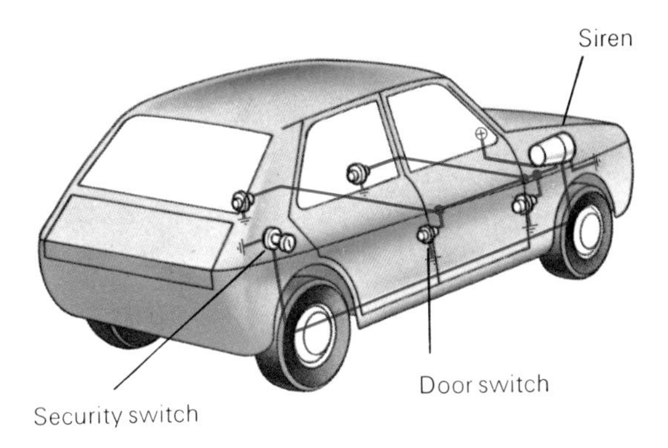

7 The Watchdog ESM/12. Door switches activate a siren alarm

8 The Tragonic Tiger. A sensor operates the headlights and horn

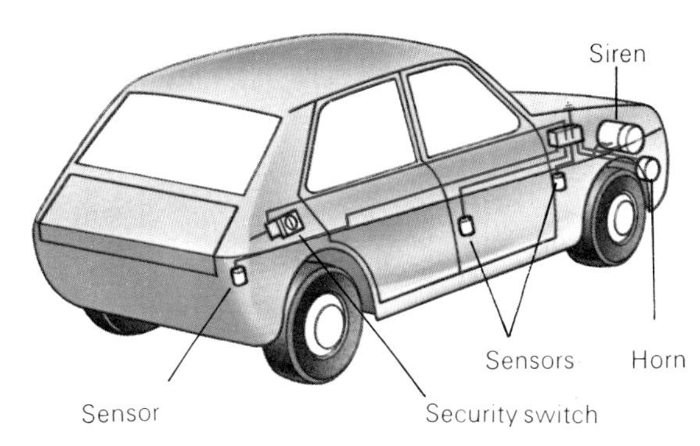

9 The Simba Inertialarm. Small sensors activate a siren or horn

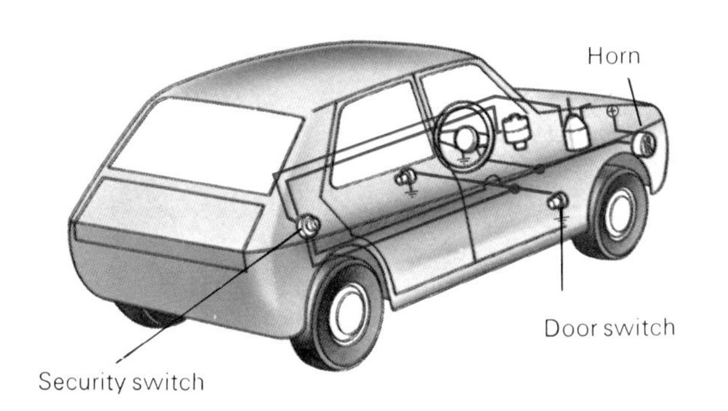

10 The Gnomist. Door switches cut off ignition and sound the horn

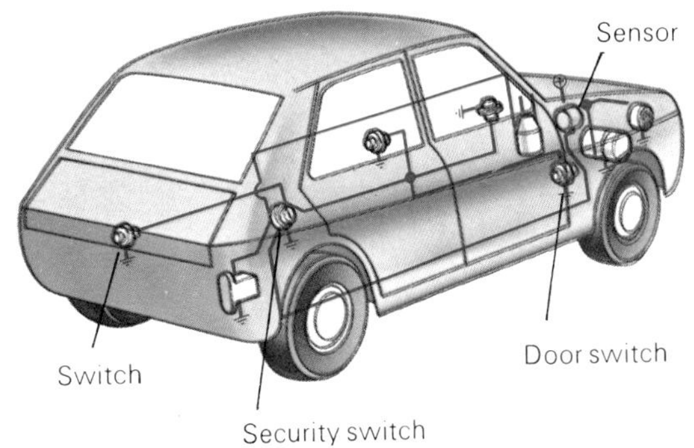

11 The Watchdog VDL. Sensors operate an immobilizer- alarm

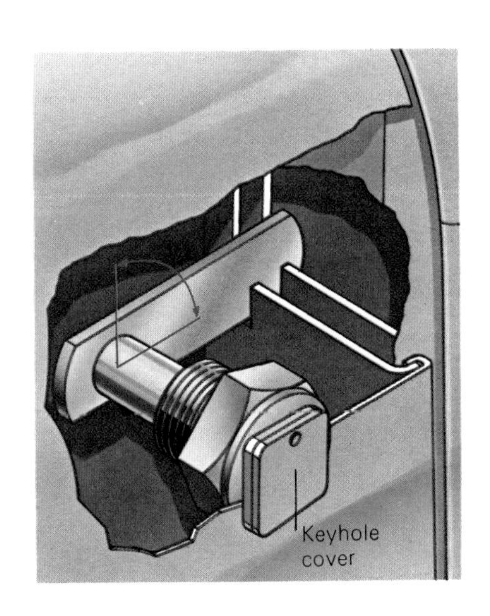

12 The Lander Universal Mini-Lock

13 A Simba high-security mortise deadlock

Nigel Osborne

illustrates the shortcomings of this type of system: the thief is not deterred before the car door has been opened.

Sensor systems can usually be fitted quite easily. They respond to movement or vibration and in some cases can be adjusted for sensitivity. Set at their most sensitive, sensors sound an alarm long before the thief can get into the car and this is usually an effective deterrent. But such sensitivity often makes these systems prone to false alarms from, for example, high winds rocking the car, people inadvertently brushing against it and other vehicles passing by.

At the other end of the scale, a sensor which is set to compensate for false alarms may be no more effective than a switch system. And unless the alarm is of the automatic type which sounds for a limited time and then re-sets itself, it will continue to sound until switched off. This could be particularly inconvenient if the car is left a long way from where you happen to be. In the meantime, the car battery (as well as people in the area) will be suffering.

On both switch systems and sensor systems, the security switches which set the systems ready for operation usually have to be mounted outside the car with just the keyhole showing, so that the wiring connections are inaccessible to the thief. The most popular place for these switches is in the front wing or rear wing of the car and fixing them in position involves drilling a hole through the bodywork.

The Watchdog ESM/12 (figs. 1 and 7) is an alarm system which uses switches to activate a siren. Six switches need to be installed in the car to protect all the door, boot and bonnet openings. Alternatively, the existing courtesy light switches can be employed to save putting in new ones. The key-operated security lock is mounted on the outside of the car and its location can vary according to which place is most convenient. The large and loud siren sounds for a limited time, adjustable from about five seconds to two minutes before it stops and re-sets itself automatically. The siren will continue to sound for its pre-set time even if the circuit to one of the switches is opened and then closed immediately. The system comes complete with all the necessary wires, brackets and switches.

The Tragonic Tiger alarm (figs. 1 and 8) consists of one main sensor unit which is connected to the car horn and headlights. The sensor can be adjusted for sensitivity and is mounted in the engine compartment (well away from the heat of the exhaust) or, where possible, in the boot. The sensor unit itself is an enclosed spring-steel strip which when shaken or vibrated makes a contact with the electrical circuits connected to it. The alarm responds by sounding the horn and flashing the headlights for as long as the sensor detects interference. This type of device is one of the easiest systems to install because of its simplicity.

Combined immobilizer-alarms

As their name suggests, immobilizer-alarms incorporate features of two types of anti-theft device. They sound an alarm when the car is interfered with and back this up (usually with an ignition immobilizer) for further protection.

Unless of the sensor-operated type, immobilizer-alarms function mainly to protect the car itself rather than its contents. The immobilizer part of most units is fairly straightforward, however, and installing them usually entails making simple wiring connections into the ignition circuit.

The Simba Inertialarm (figs. 1 and 9) is an ignition immobilizer coupled with a horn or siren alarm which is activated by sensors mounted in the car close to the door, bonnet and boot. These sensors are made to be particularly sensitive to vibration, but are not prone to false-alarm calls through accidental knocks. The alarm system stays on for a limited time and the ignition is immobilized until reset by means of the outside security switch. Extra sensors can be bought to protect other parts of the car.

The Gnomist (figs. 1 and 10) is one of the simplest and cheapest immobilizer-alarms available. It can be set up to work in one of two ways. First, it can be wired into the ignition circuit so that the alarm is sounded and the ignition is cut off when the ignition switch is operated or by-passed. Second, it can be connected to the door courtesy light switches and the ignition circuit so that the alarm sounds when the doors are opened. The alarm stays on only for as long as the switch remains in the open position, but the ignition remains dead until it is reset with the key. If the first system is used the security switch is mounted inside the car. With the second system it is mounted outside the bodywork. In both cases installing or concealing the switch depends entirely on individual ingenuity. Extra switches can be included in the system to protect the boot and bonnet openings.

The Watchdog VDL (figs. 1 and 11) has a double-system alarm and ignition immobilizer. Switches protect the door, bonnet and boot openings and in addition a single, large sensor unit is mounted in the boot to detect interference from an attempted entry. The alarm signal comes from the car horn and sounds for about 30 seconds before it stops and resets. If the thief tries to enter through an opening protected by a switch, an intermittent alarm will sound even after the door (or whatever) has been closed again. The ignition is immobilized automatically when the alarm is set off. The security switch is mounted in the boot.

Security locks

The standard door or boot locks on a car can be supplemented with high-security locks. These present a physical barrier to the thief, who, short of smashing his way in, cannot gain access to the interior and thus cannot drive the car away. Mortise deadlocks and rackbolts which cannot be effectively 'picked' offer maximum security for the contents of the car.

Many insurance companies insist that this type of anti-theft device be fitted to cover cars that regularly carry valuable goods. If you want this kind of security and are prepared to carry out some modifications to your car, you can fit one of the many types of high security lock systems.

The Lander Universal Mini-Lock (fig. 12) is based on a conventional car door lock. It has an extended barrel which fits through a hole drilled into the car door or pillar. A cam fixed to the barrel moves through 180° when the key is turned so that the door is effectively blocked and cannot be opened. Each lock is supplied as a universal fitting and therefore has to be modified slightly to fit different types of car. The existing door locks are left in place and can be used normally. When this unit is fitted each door has the advantage of two-lock protection.

The Simba mortise deadlock unit (fig. 13) is fitted into each door that needs protection and locates into a corresponding door pillar. The existing door locks are left in place and the system does not interfere with the normal locking procedure. Each deadlock has its own key and the sliding lock bar or bolt cannot be moved without it. In principle, fitting a deadlock should be straightforward. In practice, installing one could involve a lot of cutting and drilling of the door or door pillar—though this is balanced out by the high degree of protection it gives. This type of lock can also be fitted to protect a boot or hatch-back door.

Part 2

Outside the car

Fitting spring assisters

If you decide to load your car up heavily at the back, either with luggage or extra passengers, there will be a great deal of weight on the rear suspension. Attaching a trailer or caravan will increase this even further and may well impose a strain on the rear springs far in excess of what they were designed to take. This will result in low clearance at the back—your exhaust or differential may then run the risk of being scraped. Handling will also be affected by the uneven weight distribution, making the car dangerous to drive.

Fitting suspension aids, or spring assisters, will overcome these difficulties. They effectively uprate a car's suspension system under load and restore its balance. At the same time, by taking the strain, they minimize the danger of your original spring components failing. Providing the assisters fitted are of high quality, your car's ride and handling under normal loading conditions should not be unduly affected.

Choosing assisters

Spring assisters fall into four main categories: hollow rubber or rubber and coil springs; air cushion springs; coil spring damper units; and air-adjustable damper units. Because of wide variations in suspension design, the choice of what to fit is likely to be restricted to one or two types. Leyland front-wheel-drive cars, for example, have unconventional Hydrolastic and Hydragas suspension units mounted above independent trailing arms. They can be fitted only with the rubber, or rubber and coil type, of assister. Fortunately, suspension aids usually come in complete kits, designed around a specific car, so there should be no mistake providing that you quote the make, model and year of your vehicle to the dealer.

If you do have to choose between two different types of spring assister, you should bear in mind that the cheaper ones will not be as efficient as the more expensive, complex designs. A simple rubber spring may have good load-bearing characteristics, but it will not give such a smooth ride unladen as a progressively-sprung damper unit. In the spring-damper market, where several manufacturers offer a similar product, it is generally accepted that the more expensive ones give a better ride and last longer. If you intend to make use of your spring assisters only once or twice a year, it may well be worth spending a bit more to ensure a comfortable ride for the rest of the time.

Preliminaries

Fitting suspension aids is a relatively straightforward job, and you will not require any special tools. The kit of your choice should contain all the necessary parts and a set of instructions referring specifically to your particular car. Always start by checking the kit to see that it is complete, and identifying each part in turn. In every case when fitting assisters, the car must be jacked up and supported—either on body jacking points, chassis box sections, or subframe members—so that the back axle hangs freely from the suspension. For this, use either axle stands or wood blocks with a base area of at least 30 x 30 cm (12 x 12in.). Never leave the car supported on a jack, which may fall over or collapse; or bricks, which might crumble. In order to make the rear suspension more accessible, you should also remove the back wheels.

If you want to fit the air cushion, hollow rubber or rubber/coil type of assister, measure the distance between the centre of one of the rear wheels, and the top of its wheel arch, while the car is still on the ground. This will help you to check later that the assisters are correctly fitted.

Before beginning any further work, read the kit instructions and get some idea of where the spring assisters are going to be located. Remember that the principle of all spring assisters is to provide extra resistance between a car's unsprung weight (body, chassis, engine and so on) and its sprung weight (including axles, wheels, trailing arms and so on).

Fitting coil spring damper units

The coil spring damper is an expensive but efficient assister which replaces a car's original shock absorbers. There are units available for most cars with conventional dampers and some others as well and they have the advantage of doing two jobs at the same time. The coil spring part provides the extra assistance while the damper acts in the normal way, controlling the car's pitching motion (fig. 4).

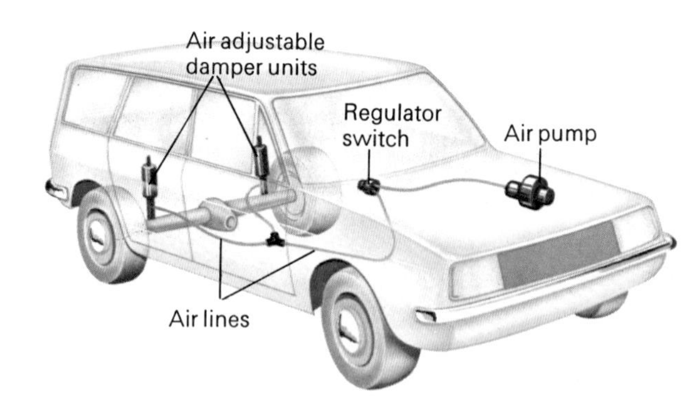

1 Air-adjustable dampers normally feature an air-pump mounted in the engine compartment and controlled by a dashboard switch

Identify your original shock absorber and note what type of fixings it has to the axle and car body—they will be of either the 'pin' or 'eye' variety (fig. 2). The pin fixing consists of a threaded bolt which goes through a locating hole, with rubber grommets and washers either side. It is secured by means of a locknut. The eye fixing has the threaded bolt running through a rubber bush at right-angles to the damper and is secured in the same way. The car illustrated has two pin-type fixings but others may have two eyes or a combination of both types. The procedure for dismantling them is the same in both cases.

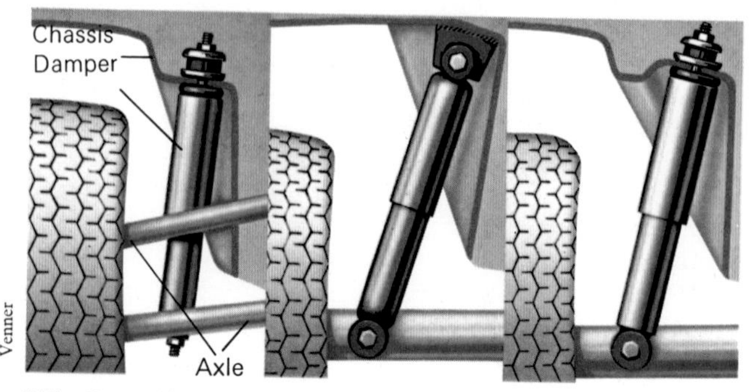

2 The three different types of damper fixing. From left to right: pin to pin, eye to eye, and pin to eye

Start by finding out where the damper is connected to the body inside the car. It will be in the boot or, in the case of a hatchback or estate car, in the passenger compartment, but you may have to undo a bit of trim in order to see it (fig. 5). Undo the locknut (fig. 6) and note the position of the grommets and washer, as the new ones supplied in the kit must go back in the same place. Move back under the car and undo the bolt securing the bottom of the damper in the same way. Grip either end of the damper firmly, in both hands, and press the two halves together. The damper can now be removed.

Some cars with trailing arm suspension, such as the Citroen 2CV, have their dampers mounted horizontally (fig. 3). The method of removal is, however, exactly the same.

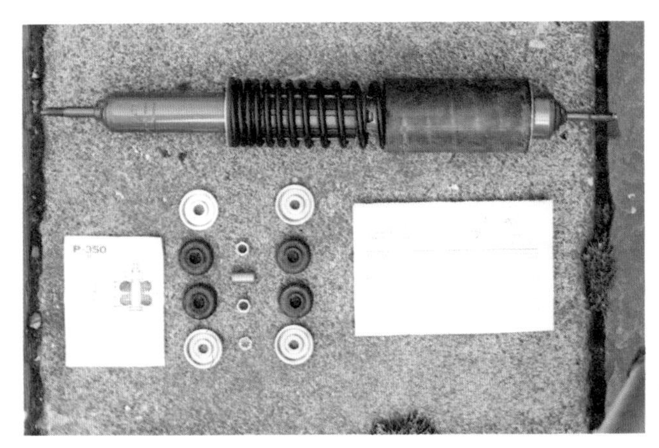

4 This Monroe Loadleveler is typical of the medium-priced dampers available. The kit comes complete with new washers and grommets

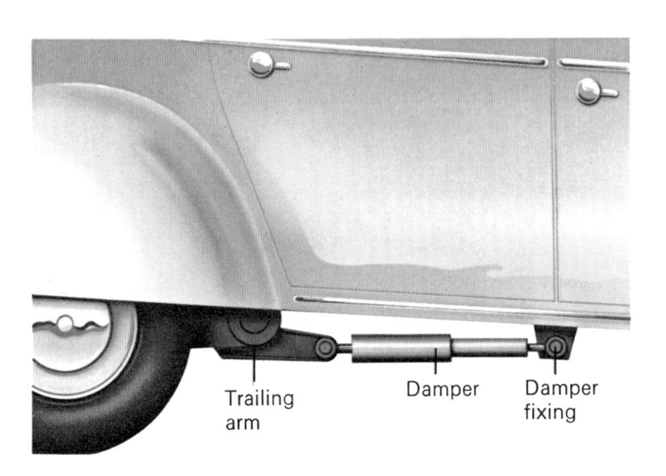

3 On some cars with trailing arm rear suspension, like this 2CV6 Citroen, the dampers are horizontally mounted

5 Unscrewing and prising away the boot trim is often the only way to find the top damper nut and its mounting pin

To fit the new unit, begin by putting new washers and grommets or bushes on the end pin or eye fixings. The kit instructions will show you the exact order of assembly. Next, compress the unit and insert the pins on either end into their locating holes on the bodywork and the suspension (fig. 7). If there is an eye fixing on one end, make sure its locating pin goes through the rubber bush properly.

Any further washers and grommets must now be placed on the pins, and the locknuts screwed on (figs. 8 and 9). They must not, at this stage, be tightened up.

Repeat the above operations for the other side of the car.

With both units in place, it is now necessary to check that the brake pipes and exhaust do not foul them. This is something which the kit manufacturers do their best to avoid and if they cannot, they usually give detailed instructions on how to overcome the problem. Sometimes, however, difficulties can arise, especially if your car has non-standard pipe fittings. If the brake pipes are too close, try to reroute them by bending or altering the position of their support brackets. You should not attempt to bend the pipes themselves. Do the same for the exhaust pipe whose mounting will probably be easier to modify.

When you are sure that the new springs can move freely, refit the roadwheels and lower the car to the ground. With the weight of the car on the wheels, tighten all the nuts and bolts on both units. Bounce the car several times and make sure that the springs are still free of obstruction.

6 Undo the mounting nut and remove the grommet and washers, then repeat the operation for the bottom mounting assembly

Anthony Kay

7 When fitting the new damper, or removing the old one, position the top fixing, compress it upwards, and slide it into place

8 Fit the new washers and grommet according to the manufacturer's instructions. A bit of Coparslip on the pin will prevent rusting

9 The bottom mountings are fixed in exactly the same way. Ensure that everything is replaced in its correct order

Fitting hollow rubber springs

The hollow rubber spring assister is a simple device which is both easy to fit and relatively cheap. In this case, the 'wasp-waisted' design of the spring provides a progressive resistance under load, by fitting between the rear axle and car bodywork. The exact method of fitting varies according to individual cars but the kit instructions will refer specifically to your vehicle. Check the kit instructions carefully before starting any work.

Cars with live rear axle suspension

On cars with live (or "beam") rear axle suspension, start by jacking up the car, supporting it safely, and removing the wheels. The first part of the kit to fit will be a metal plate (known as the reaction plate). This must be attached to the chassis or car bodywork, above the point on the axle where the spring will go. When the spring is compressed it will strike the plate, which in turn takes the strain. On some cars, there will be a small rubber bump stop already fitted above the axle to stop the suspension fouling the bodywork under bumpy conditions. This should be unscrewed or unbolted first.

The next step is to drill a hole through the box section above the axle (fig. 11). The reaction plate can now be fitted by bolting it on through the hole (fig. 12). The rubber spring itself must now be secured to its mounting bracket. This will involve inserting a bolt through the spring and out of the other end. Stick the bolt to a screwdriver with a bit of plasticine and it can then be easily guided through the holes (fig. 13). Check with the instructions that all the washers provided are in the correct order, and then tighten the locknut on the bracket (fig. 14) until the spring is firmly held, but not distorted.

Place the bracket and spring assembly on to the axle, underneath the reaction plate. Fit the two U bolts provided underneath the axle and through the locating holes in the bracket (fig. 15), screwing down the nuts loosely. If there are brake pipes running along the axle, try first to divert them slightly be undoing the nearest securing clip. If this cannot be done without damaging the pipes, then the aluminium bracket must be cut to accommodate them, according to the manufacturer's instructions.

With the spring now loosely fitted in position, you must carefully jack up the hub until it is at its normal height. You can tell this by measuring from the centre of the hub to the wheel arch and comparing it with the measurement taken when the car was on the ground. The car's suspension will be compressed to its normal unladen position, and at this point there should be a small gap (never greater than 5 cm or 2in.) between the rubber spring assister and the reaction plate. If there is no gap, and the rubber spring is compressed, lower the hub and remove the spring/bracket assembly. The bracket must be cut down with a hacksaw, along the V section marked. Reposition it and check the clearance again.

When the correct clearance has been obtained, make sure that the contact faces of the spring and the reaction plate are parallel, and tighten the locknuts on the U bolts.

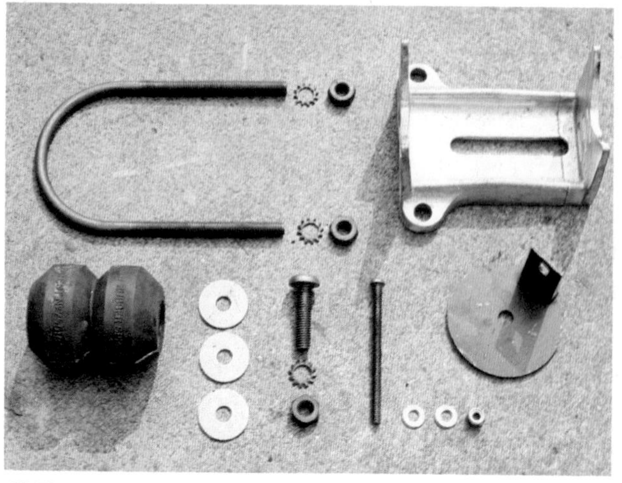

10 The Aeon rubber spring kit comes complete with spring, fixing bolts, bracket, reaction plate, and a selection of washers

11 To fix the reaction plate securely, start by drilling a hole in the chassis box-section where the spring will strike it

The ends of the U bolts may now be too long, so use a hacksaw to cut them back to just above the locknuts.

Repeat the above operations for the other side of the car and then run a final check to ensure that nothing will foul the springs when they are compressed under load. The wheels can now be fitted, and the car lowered to the ground.

For a few cars, the springs are attached to the bodywork, and the reaction plate to the axle. Different brackets will be provided in the kits, but fitting procedure is basically the same.

Cars with trailing arm rear suspension

Cars with trailing arm rear suspension, such as the Leyland front-wheel-drive range, usually have the spring assisters fitted to the bodywork in place of the original bump stop. A wedge-shaped bracket will be supplied, and after this has been bolted to the spring according to the instructions in the kit, the whole unit can be bolted on to the bodywork. The reaction plate is then strapped on to the trailing arm. Make sure that the plate and the spring are parallel, and that everything is tightly fixed. Repeat the operation for the other side of the car, then refit the wheels and lower the car to the ground. Check that the springs are not compressed with the car unladen. If they are, and the car has Hydrolastic or Hydragas suspension, then the displacers will probably need pumping up. This should be done immediately at your local dealer. Remember also to make sure that nothing interferes with the free movement of the springs.

Fitting rubber/coil springs

The rubber/coil spring is a development of the hollow rubber spring assister, which combines ease of fitting with more efficient springing (fig. 16).

Start by completing all the preliminaries of jacking and supporting the car and so on. In some cases, the kit instructions specify that the bump stop must be removed or cut down. Do this only when the manufacturers say so. The coil spring is then strapped to the car axle or trailing arm by means of two large Jubilee clips (fig. 17). If there are any brake pipes running along the axle, then the curved bracket on the end of the coil spring must be slid underneath them before the clips are tightened. Now jack up the hub until the suspension is compressed to its normal level (see 'Fitting hollow rubber springs' above). Check that the spring assister is not compressed. If it is, then clearance may be obtained by sawing off part of the rubber stop at the top of the spring (fig. 19). This can be made a lot easier by dabbing some washing-up liquid on the saw blade first.

Ideally, with the car standing on its springs unladen, the spring assister should just be touching the car body, chassis or bump stop, but a slight gap is acceptable. Cars with Hydrolastic and Hydragas suspension may, in addition, need a pump-up to restore their correct ride height.

Fit the other spring in the same way, then refit the wheels and lower the car to the ground. Check that both springs are level and firmly in place. As with all spring assisters, check also that nothing will interfere with their free movement.

12 Secure the reaction plate by inserting the long bolt provided through the plate bracket and the hole in the box section

13 A piece of Plasticine on the end of a screwdriver will enable you to feed the bolt through to the other end of the spring

14 Make sure that you have got all the washers in their correct order, and then secure the spring firmly to its bracket

15 The unit in position on the axle. When you have tightened up the U bolt nuts, saw off the excess bolt to prevent fouling

Anthony Kay

16 The Sanlin spring kit is very simple, consisting only of two Jubilee clips, the metal coil and rubber spring top

17 Having put the rubber top on the coil, place the unit on the axle. Wrap the Jubilee clips around the coil and tighten

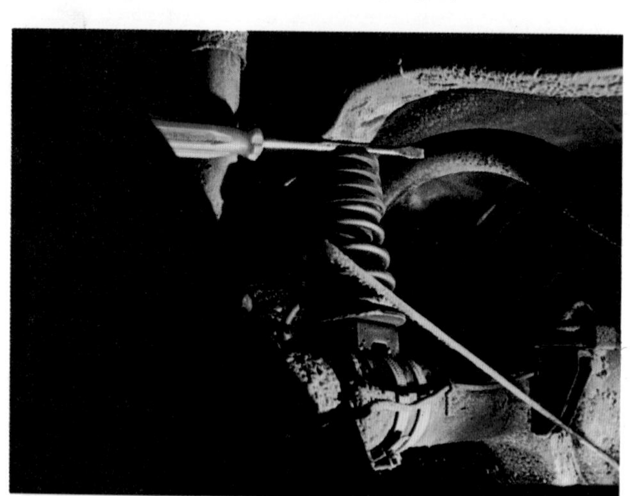

18 With the suspension jacked up to its normal height, check to make sure the spring is not compressed. A small gap is permitted

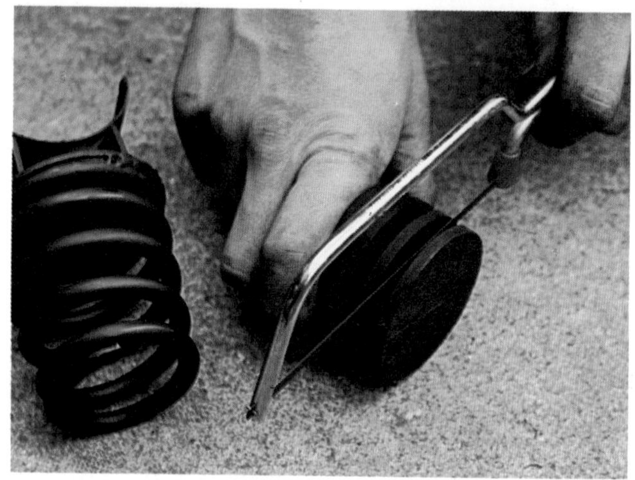

19 To obtain extra clearance, you can saw a section off the top of the rubber spring using an ordinary hacksaw

Fitting air-cushion springs

There is only one type of air-cushion spring on the British market: the Autoballans. It consists of a hollow ball, made of strong pvc, which is inserted between either side of the rear axle and the bodywork. Fitted with a Schrader needle air valve, it is filled with air under pressure to provide a simple and relatively cheap form of spring assistance.

Cars with leaf-spring suspension

On cars with leaf-spring suspension, having prepared the car as outlined above, take the Autoballans itself, and start by unhooking the metal outer spring clip from its lug. Now pull it through the inner rubber strap hook and unhook the rubber strap (fig. 21).

The next step is to insert the Autoballans between the leaf spring and the body or chassis, at a point about 15 cm (6in.) from the rear spring fixing (fig. 22). Make sure that the Autoballans, with the heat protector pad attached, is positioned with the pad nearest to the exhause pipe, as shown. If it is nearer than 2 cm, then the pipe will have to be moved farther away (see 'Fitting coil spring damper'). Next, wrap the rubber strap around the leaf spring and hook it together, holding the Autoballans in place. Follow this by hooking the outer spring around the strap and back on its lug. The extra plastic strap must now be secured around the leaf spring and up against the Autoballans, to hold it in position (fig. 24). Now carefully jack up the hub until the suspension reaches its normal height (see 'Fitting hollow rubber springs' above) and check that the Autoballans is not compressed. If it is, then it has been fitted too far back along the leaf spring. At the same time, make sure that there are no sharp protrusions likely to interfere with the ball when it is compressed under load, and that it remains the specified 2 cm from the exhaust pipe. Repeat the above steps for the other side of the car.

The air-hoses must now be fitted. This is done by fixing the valves in holes which you will have to drill in boot cross-members, then connecting these to the rubber hoses from the balls by means of plastic tubing. Start by drilling a 6 mm hole through either side of the boot floor, as close as possible to the springs. Take care not to damage the springs, the petrol tank or any other nearby components (fig. 25). Smooth off the rough edges of the holes with a file to avoid damaging the hoses. Now feed the rubber hoses from the two Autoballans through the holes until they protrude about 5 mm ($\frac{1}{4}$in.) and then cut them (fig. 26). Make sure that the hoses will not be pinched or cut in this position when the suspension is compressed.

Next, find two convenient bodywork support brackets at either side of the boot (fig. 27) and drill an 8 mm hole in each. Feed the clear plastic tubes, with valves attached, through the holes and then screw the valves tight (fig. 28). Pull the rubber hoses through the bodywork a further 25 mm (1in.) and push the plastic tubes into them, to a depth of about 10 mm ($\frac{3}{8}$in.) (fig. 29). Finally, push the rubber hoses, which will now have increased in diameter with the plastic tube inside, back through the holes in the boot until they are a tight fit. The roadwheels can now be

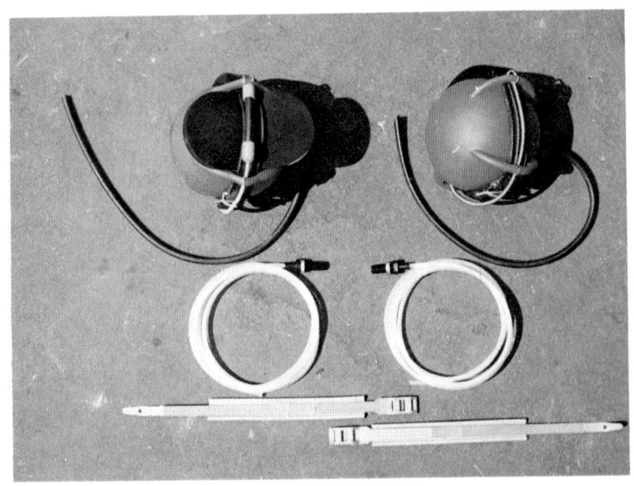

20 The Autoballans kit comes complete with plastic balls, straps, air lines and valves. The straps will be fixed around the balls

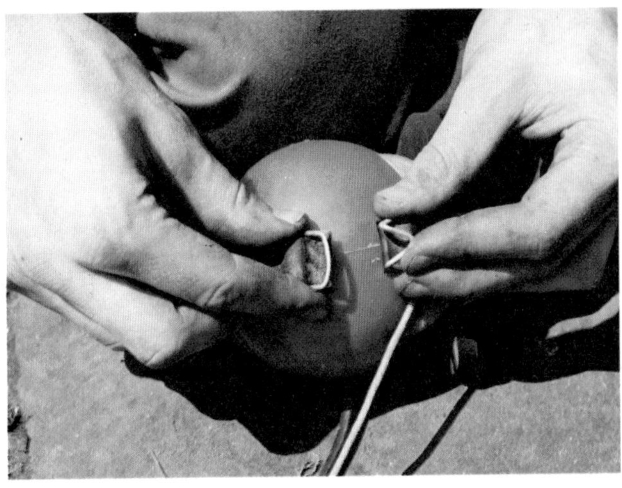

21 The inner and outer mounting straps are easily unhooked. This must be done before you locate the ball in place

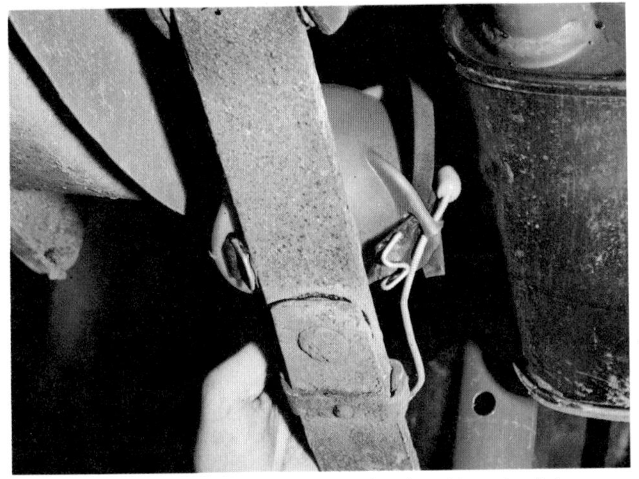

22 One Autoballans in place on the leaf spring. Note that it has a protective pad fitted to shield it from the heat of the exhaust

23 Hook the inner and outer straps around the leaf spring to hold the ball firmly in place. Make sure they are not twisted

24 The extra plastic strap in position around the leaf spring to stop the Autoballans gradually sliding out of place

Anthony Kay

25 When drilling holes for the rubber air hoses in the boot floor be careful not to damage the springs underneath

fitted and the car lowered to the ground. Check that the springs are still in position and not fouled in any way. They can now be inflated to the correct pressure by means of the valves in the boot. This is normally 0.4-0.8 bar (6-12psi) depending on the load to be carried.

Cars with coil spring suspension

The Autoballans can also be fitted to cars with coil spring suspension providing the coils are of a large enough diameter to accept the balls, and there are no obstructions, such as struts, running down the middle of them.

Having supported the back of the car and removed the road wheels, warm one Autoballans in hot water to soften it. Next compress it with your foot until it is flat and pinch the rubber hose to prevent air re-entering (fig. 30). Insert it between two coils, halfway up the spring, and use a piece of cardboard to wedge it in place (fig. 31). Repeat this for the other side of the car, and then remove the wedges.

The rubber hoses and air valves can now be connected in the same way as those on leaf spring suspension cars, as

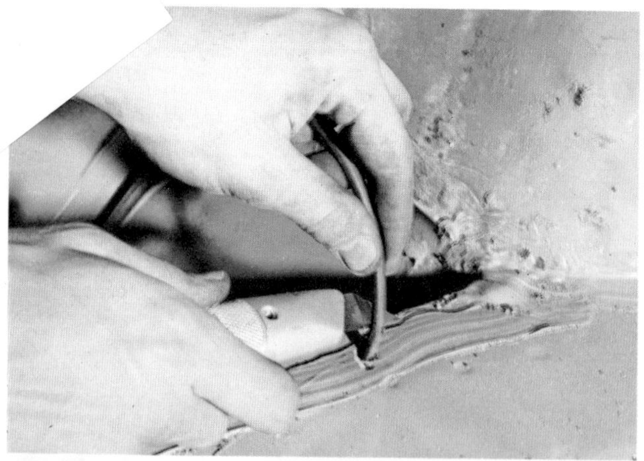

26 Having filed down the rough edges of the holes, and pushed the hoses through, cut off the excess leaving a little spare

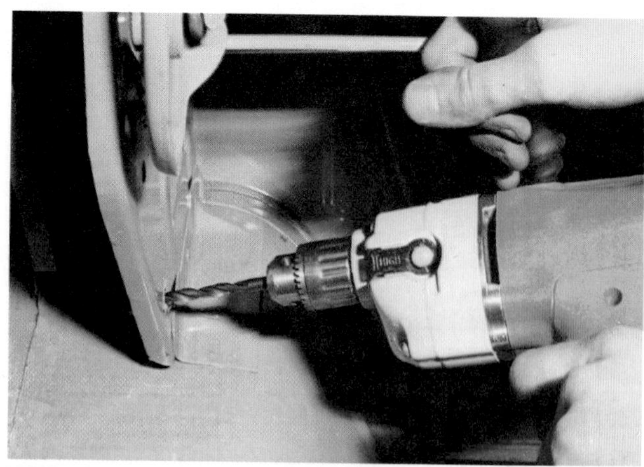

27 Any support bracket fairly close to the hoses can be drilled to accommodate the air valves

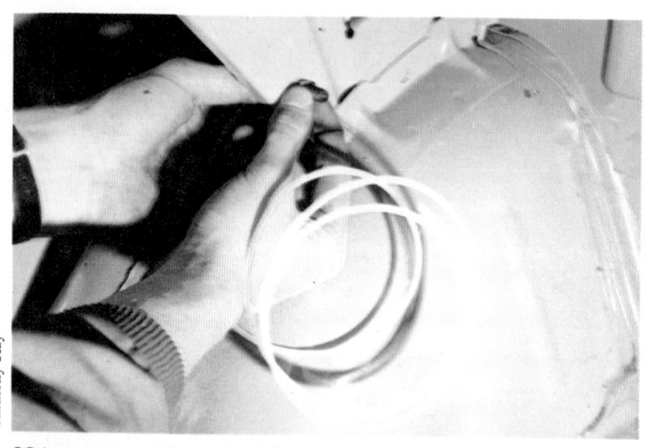

Anthony Kay

28 Insert the valve, with air line attached, through the hole in the bracket and then fix it tightly with the screw washer

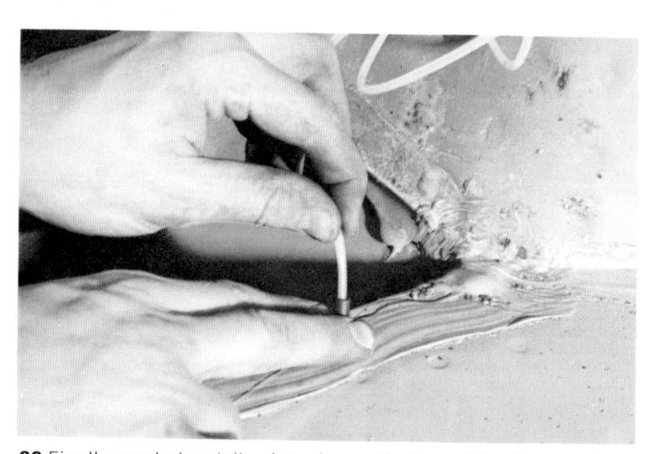

29 Finally, push the air line into the protruding rubber hose and force it back into the hole until the hose is a tight fit

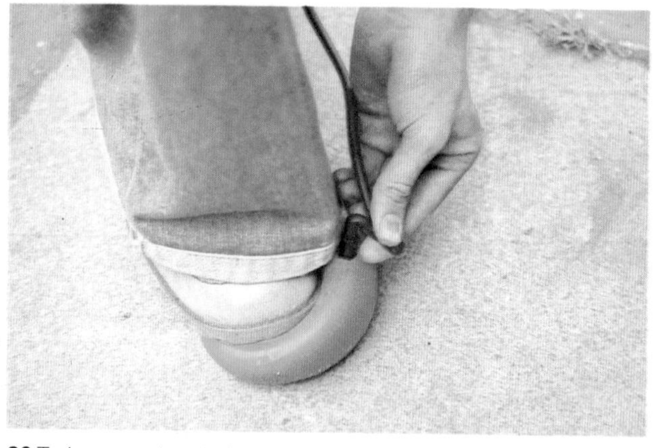

Nelson Hargreaves

30 To insert an Autoballans into a coil spring, start by treading on the ball to deflate it. Pinch the hose to stop air getting in

31 Next, push the flattened ball into the coil. When the pinched hose is released, the ball will revert to its normal shape

described above. Carry out the same checks for fouling, refit the wheels and lower the car. In this case, however, it is important to inflate the Autoballans to a pressure of 2 bar (30psi) for the first couple of days of use. This enables the springs to seat properly and to 'run in'. Having completed this period, deflate the Autoballans to the manufacturer's recommended pressure—normally 0.85-1.6 bar (12-23psi) with the car unloaded.

Air-adjustable dampers

Air-adjustable damper units are similar to the coil-spring dampers already described. In this case, however, the spring assistance is obtained by means of a pressurized air chamber rather than a simple coil spring. By filling the chamber to various pressures, ride height can be adjusted to suit different loads. The dampers are fitted in the same way as coil spring units, but the two air pipes running from them must then be connected to a common valve box. With an air-line connected to the valve, the dampers can be inflated to the correct pressure.

An advanced development of this idea, which comes in kit form, enables the air pressure, and therefore the ride height, to be adjusted from inside the car. This is done by means of an electric air pump, controlled by a switch mounted under the dashboard. This pumps air to the dampers at the desired pressure. A similar device has also been designed to complement the Autoballans (see above). It connects conveniently to the two valves exposed in the car boot. Unfortunately, although these systems are efficient, they are also complicated and expensive.

Fitting flared wheel arches

1 A wide range of flares is available, and a high standard of finish is relatively easy to achieve

2 A pop rivetter along with an electric sander are some of the tools you will need for fitting flares. The resin filler as well as the flares can be purchased from most motor accessory shops

Fitting wide wheels to a car usually means they protrude outside the car body to some extent and wider wheel arches have to be fitted to prevent stones being thrown up by the wheels to the detriment of other vehicles. (The law also demands this). Wheel arches, of course, can be fitted for fun, as on this Mini, for instance.

The easiest way of dealing with this problem is to purchase a set of ready-made glass fibre 'spats' or flares. You will also need quick setting resin filler paste (available at most motor accessory shops) and some paint. The few simple tools, pop rivetter and perhaps an electric sander can be hired, and you can then try your hand at fitting these embellishments yourself.

Although there are many spat designs on the market already shaped for individual cars, there are still many car models for which 'custom made' pieces are not available.

If you are unable to find a set to match your requirements exactly, buy some that are as near as possible to the right shape and modify them.

This is much easier than attempting to design and manufacture your own.

Here we have taken a typical Leyland Mini where there is no difficulty in obtaining the necessary parts and there is no need to cut away any of the existing wheel arches.

Be prepared to spend some time on the job as it will require care and patience to obtain a good marriage of the flare to the body—particularly in the final sanding off and finishing.

Wheel arch preparation

The first job to be done is to remove the bright trim around the arch. This will just pull off (fig. 3).

3 Remove the bright trim by levering it off. Place out of the way. If badly tarnished, replacement trim is available

4 Offer up the fibre glass flare to the car body noting what material must be removed to obtain a good fit

5 Mark with a wax pencil both sides of the car body to where seams have to be cut

Next examine the fibre glass flares and if needed, trim off any rough edges from these pre-formed shapes with a file or surform. Offer up each flare to obtain a good fit, noting any awkward spots on the body that will need attention (fig. 4). These parts need to be marked at the cutting points (fig. 5).

Now, using a hacksaw, cut through the body piece(s) to be removed (fig. 6). Take care that a fine toothed hacksaw blade is fitted in the frame. It is very easy when commencing a cut for the hacksaw to skate off the material and scratch the body. If you have a small file, make a small nick in the seam at the point on the body where you intend starting the cut, it will help you to avoid any unnecessary damage. Finally cut through the offending panel joints with a cold chisel (fig. 7). It is essential that the cold (metal type not wood) chisel is not blunted. A good plan would be to freshly sharpen it. A sharp chisel will require only light hammer blows to cut cleanly.

6 Cut through both sides of the seam with a hacksaw taking care that the saw does not slip

7 Finally remove the cut seam with a cold chisel and hammer. It is essential that the chisel is sharp

8 Clean up the whole area thoroughly with a wire brush to remove rust and loose paintwork

9 With the flare held in position mark round the edge of the flange with the wax pencil

10 Be sure to obtain a good scuffed up finish. Wear safety goggles if a power tool is used

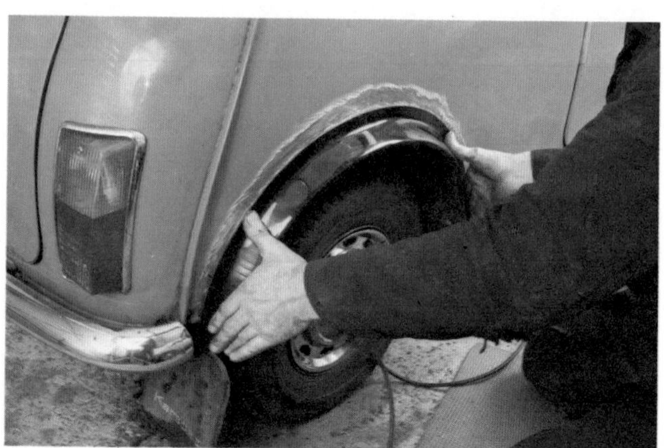

11 Check the position of the flare again to ensure that paint has been removed from the required area

Use a wire brush to clean up all around the wheel arches, removing rust and encrusted dirt (fig. 8) working well at them to prepare for a rubbing down.

Dealing with one wheel arch at a time, put the flare back into position and, using a wax pencil, run a line completely round the edge of the flange. This indicates the area which will have to be roughed up and from which the paint has to be removed (fig. 9). The help of two assistants would be useful at this stage one holding each flare carefully on the marked line whilst you view the car from a position where both flares can be seen simultaneously, any minor adjustments in height or angular positioning can be made so a balance is maintained.

Cutting back

From about 25-38 mm (1-$1\frac{1}{2}$in.) above the line cut back the paint down to the line, using a coarse 40 grit paper to achieve a rough finish. If a power sander is used for this make sure that safety goggles are worn to protect the eyes (fig. 10).

Finally recheck the flare position against the scuffed up area to ensure that sufficient paint has been removed (fig. 11).

Support the flare on a block of wood and mark drill holes around, spaced at about 75 mm (3in.) centres. Drill the holes using an $\frac{1}{8}$in. twist drill (fig. 12).

Replace the flare in position and bore a hole about half-way around into the body-work using the same size drill (fig. 13). Use a pop rivet in this first hole to hold the position (fig. 14) firmly and then continue to bore each hole—and pop rivet it—in sequence around the flare (fig. 15). This is necessary to avoid any distortion of the flare against the body-work. Completion of this part of the job is shown in fig. 16.

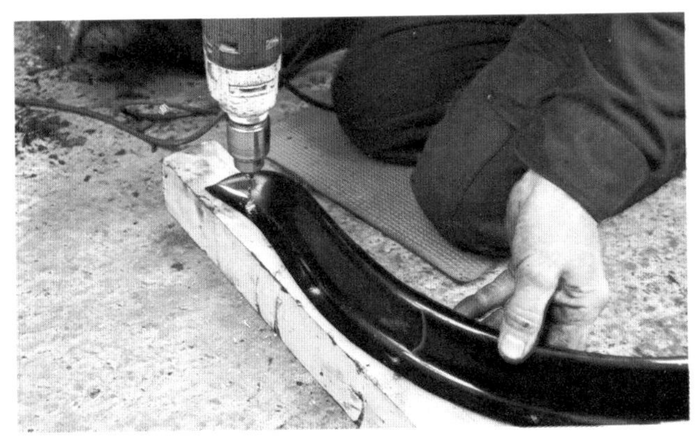

12 Pre-drill the flare with holes about 75 mm apart. Mark holes first with the pencil supporting the flange on a wood block

13 Drill the first hole through the body using the same drill as before, use the middle flare hole for this purpose

14 Pop rivet the first hole to hold the flare firmly in position on the side of the car body

15 With one pop rivet fixed, continue drilling and rivetting the rest of the holes in sequence around the flange

16 Rivetting complete and the flare fixed ready to be blended in with the body-work

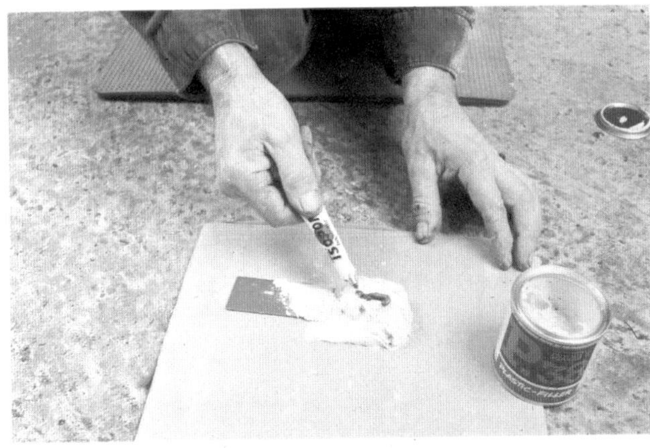

17 Mix the filler and hardener in the right proportions and thoroughly mix together

18 Apply the filler with long strokes, making the finish as smooth as possible. Do not leave mix standing

19 Take the high spots off the hardened filler with a rough, dry paper. An orbital sander could also be used

20 The first rough fill having been cleaned up, it is now ready for refilling with more filler

21 Obtain the correct contour with a second application of filler. Apply in same way as first application

22 Finally shape and cut back with rough, dry paper and then smooth off with wet and dry paper

23 The wet and dry paper is best cut in half and folded twice to make thirds to give alternate working surfaces

24 Remove dust with a cloth and then thoroughly wash off the work area

25 The final finish is achieved using fine wet and dry paper with plenty of water

26 Clean off whole area with sponge and water, leather and allow to thoroughly dry

27 To prepare for painting the whole area surrounding the work area should be well masked off

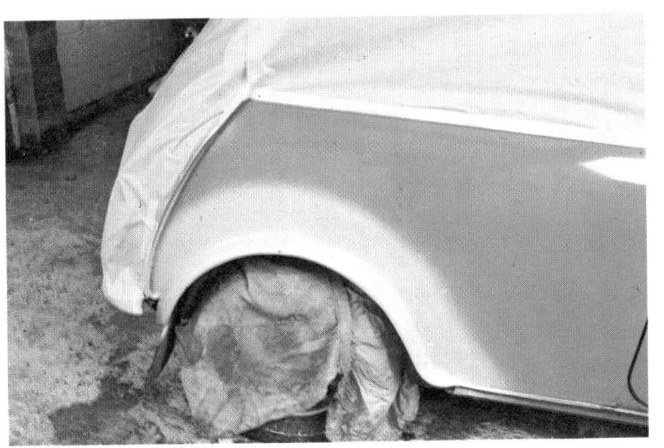

28 The primer coats having been applied, rubbed down and filled if necessary, the flare is ready for the finishing coat

29 An underseal should be brushed on underneath the wheel arches to protect any exposed metal

Marrying-in

The resin filler is used to smooth the flange of the flare into the body-work. This is readily available as a pack and is usually supplied with the filler mix contained in a large tube or tin and the necessary accelerator (or catalyst hardener) in a small tube.

Take a piece of cardboard or ply and put on a sufficient amount of filler. Squeeze out the recommended amount of hardener. You will need about 13 mm ($\frac{1}{2}$in.) of hardener to each tablespoonful of filler. Mix these together thoroughly, using the plastic spatula supplied with the kit (fig. 17).

Do not exceed this amount of hardener—there is sufficient in a small tube to deal adequately with the supply of filler. Also do not leave the complete mix standing as it will harden quickly. It must be used straight away.

Apply the filler with the spatula using long firm strokes, making the finish as smooth as possible, finishing off the ends carefully (fig. 18). Feather off the filler against the body, working fairly quickly and as soon as the filler starts to 'gel', leave it alone to harden. (The hardening time depends largely on the temperature, but in any case it normally takes only a few minutes).

When hard, take off the high spots with a rough 40 grit paper, used dry. An orbital sander can be used for speed, but it can be managed by hand (fig. 19) quite easily. This process will show clearly where some re-filling is necessary (fig. 20).

Mix up more filler and go over the whole area. It will be easier this time as the base filler underneath cannot move. Cover the low spots and any holes and work towards the correct contour. Allow it to harden off (fig. 21).

After this second hardening period, rub back again with the 40 grit paper—again used dry. This should be the final shaping before finishing, so take care to achieve the effect you want (fig. 22).

Now take a sheet of 180 grit wet and dry paper, cut it in half and fold each half into thirds to give alternative working surfaces (fig. 23). You will also need a bucket of water and a sponge. Put a little detergent into the water.

Thoroughly wash off the work area with the sponge (fig. 24), and commence rubbing down with the wet and dry paper using plenty of water to achieve the final finish (fig. 25). You will find that the fingers are better at spotting bumps and depressions than your eyes.

Clean off the whole area and leather it down. Dry it off ready for painting and don't touch it to avoid any slight grease mark (fig. 26). Now at last the surrounding body-work can be masked off, using paper and masking tape, to make sure no paint drift can get to any other paint work (fig. 27).

Finishing off

When you are satisfied with the shaping, a priming coat of paint can be applied. This should be a 50/50 mix of paint and thinners to obtain the right consistency for effective spraying (fig. 28). Examine the painted surface carefully and fill any pin holes or slight faults with a cellulose filler. Allow to harden thoroughly and afterwards rub down with the wet and dry paper and plenty of water. Spray again with the primer.

The last job here before applying the finishing coats is to paint under the flares with a good under-seal applied with a brush (fig. 29).

Later the trim can be cut to size and pushed back into position. If the trim is damaged or tarnished, now would be a good time to replace it.

Fitting a vinyl roof kit

A vinyl roof kit can improve dramatically the appearance of your car. Yet the kits, available custom-designed for most popular models, are quite reasonably priced, and only half a day's work is involved.

D-i-y vinyl roofing kits are most easily obtainable by mail order direct from the manufacturers, and are available for most cars.

Kits come in two kinds—the one-piece sort for cars with gutters that follow the line of the windows, and the three-piece sort for cars with gutters that run along the tops of the windows and across the rear pillars, such as Leyland Minis, Austin 1100s and early Ford Escorts.

Most kits contain the roof vinyl itself, already cut to size and with sewn seams, a pot of adhesive and a brief set of instructions. On receiving the kit it is advisable to lay the vinyl on the roof of the car to see that it has been cut correctly. The vinyl should overlap all the edges by at least 2.5 cm (1in.), as you will need to trim it later on.

Much of the work involved in fitting a vinyl roof will be easier if you have a friend to help you.

Preparing the roof

The first job, if you have ventilator grilles in the rear pillars of your car, is to loosen or remove them. If they are of the type that have a clear margin of bodywork all round them, they must be removed. If, like the car illustrated, they have at least one edge which adjoins a piece of trim or an edge of the bodywork they need only be loosened. The grilles will be held in position either by screws, in which case the screwheads will be clearly visible, or by bolts. These can be reached only from inside the car.

If they are held by screws, loosen them and ease the grilles about 6 mm ($\frac{1}{4}$in.) away from the bodywork.

If they are held by bolts you will have to remove the plastic covered boards which conceal the rear pillars on the inside of the car. First, if it is a four-door car, peel away the strip of door seal, from the top of the door-frame to the lock. There will be at least one screw at the bottom of the panel concealing the pillar. Remove it and carefully lift away the panel. This will allow you to reach the nuts holding the grille (fig. 1).

Many manufacturers recommend that before fitting a vinyl roof the chrome trim often fixed to gutters should be removed. This may be more trouble than it is worth as, with care, the vinyl can be made to run into the gutters while the trim is attached. Moreover, trim can be very difficult to refit.

The adhesive will need a clean, slightly roughened surface on which to grip, so the next step is to thoroughly

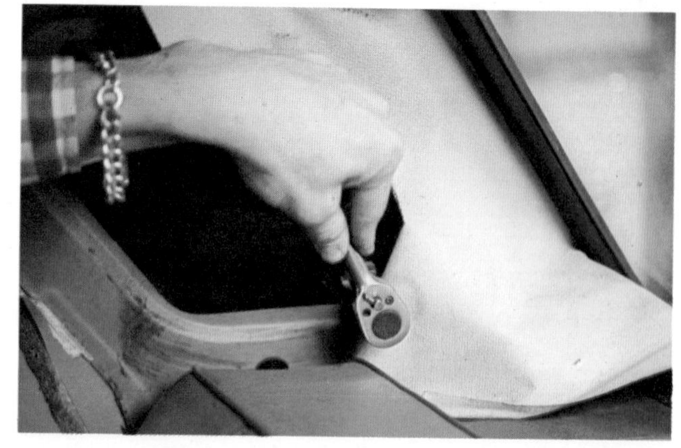

1 To remove the grilles, use a socket spanner or pliers to loosen the bolts behind the rear panel—there are usually four

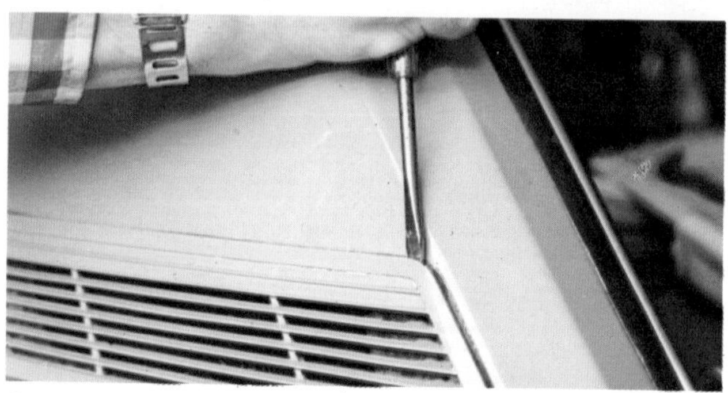

2 Ease the grilles away from the body by levering them out with a screwdriver. Leave a gap of 6 mm for the vinyl to fit into

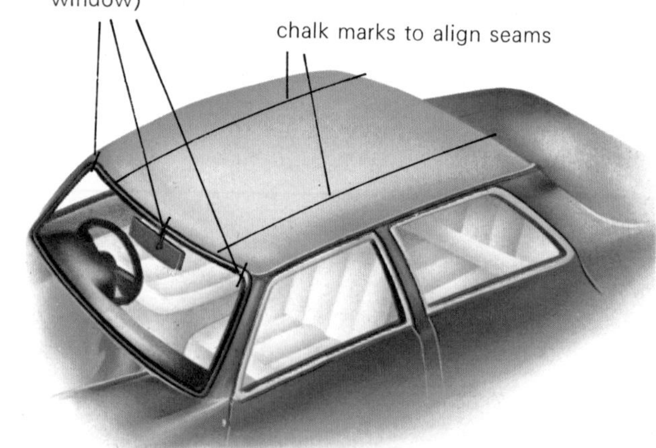

3 Make chalk marks on the window rubbers to match the position of the seams on the vinyl. Do this at each end of the car

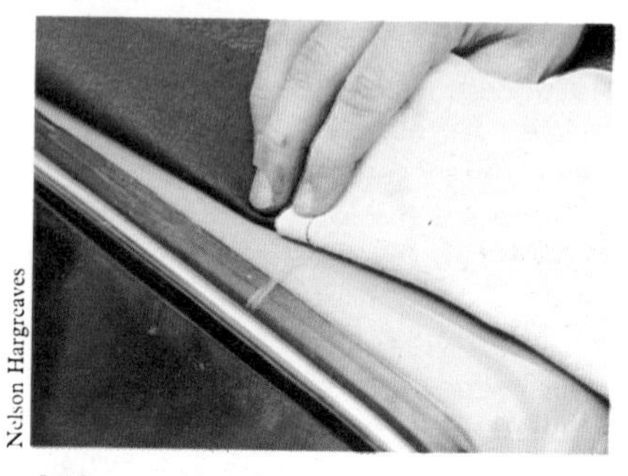

4 After marking, lay out the vinyl on the roof and check the accuracy of your chalk marks. If any are out, re-measure them

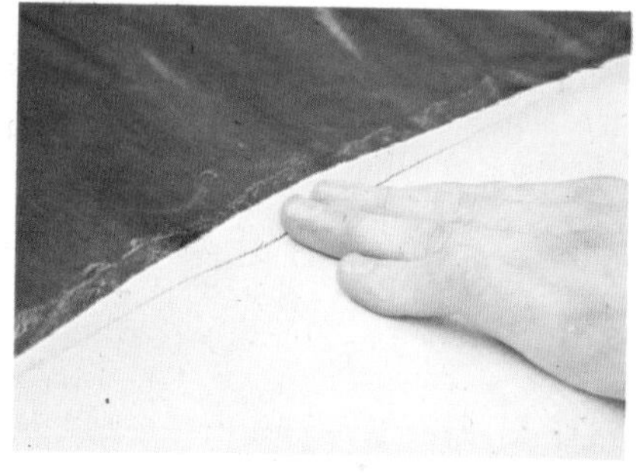

5 To fix down the seams, spread glue under them. Wait until the glue feels almost dry before pressing them down very firmly

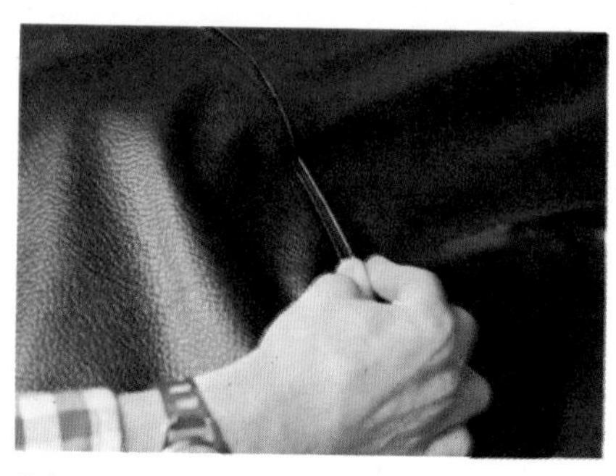

6 A good way to hold the seams in position is to pin through the vinyl and into the window surround at the rear of the car

7 Fold the vinyl in half before glueing, to leave the front half of the roof exposed. The top seams must lie on the lower ones

8 Glue must be spread evenly, but not too heavily. Use a piece of plastic or stiff card, as the glue will ruin a paintbrush

9 Lift the vinyl back over the roof, being careful to stop it touching. Bring the vinyl right forward before lowering it

10 Lower one seam at a time. Lay the first on the chalk mark and pull it taut. Do the same with the other and brush both smooth

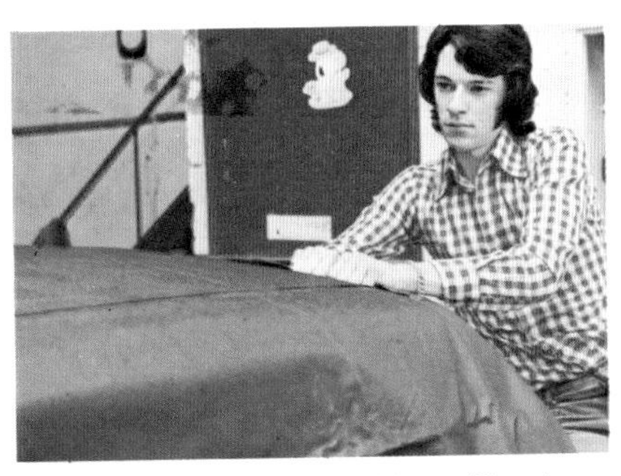

11 Creases can be removed by pulling the vinyl before the glue sets. If this fails, try rubbing them with a cloth pad

12 To fix the outside edges of the vinyl, first fold them back on to the roof. Then spread on the adhesive as before

13 Next run a line of glue down into the gutter. Make sure that it is clean and dry as dirt and water will weaken the adhesive

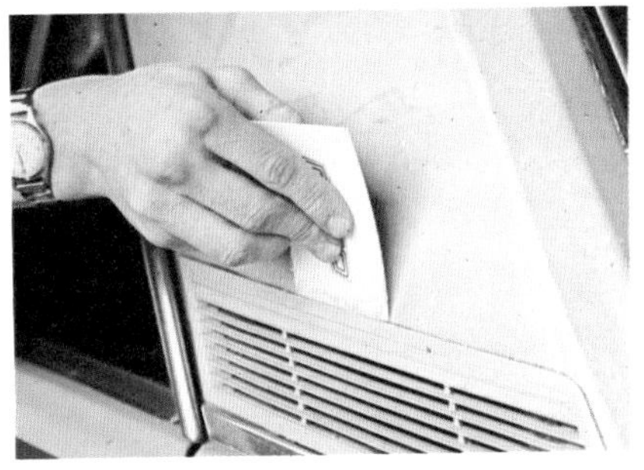

14 Repeat this on the ventilator grilles. Also apply adhesive to the pillars, from the roof to the top edge of the grille

15 Brush the vinyl down on the roof before pulling it on to the front pillar. See that it sticks at the top but leave the end free

clean the roof, rear pillars and (sometimes) a small strip below the rear window. First wash it down with a car shampoo or household detergent and rinse thoroughly. Then rub it down with a sheet of wet-and-dry abrasive paper to provide a key in the paint surface for the adhesive to cling to. Rinse the roof again and dry it off well.

Since roof vinyl 'flows' to fill bumps and hollows in much the same way that wallpaper does, any dents will show up on the finished job. So remove any loose or flaking paint, treat the underlying metal with rust killer, and make sure any holes are filled in.

Marking out

The seams which divide the vinyl into three will need to be laid accurately, or your finished roof will be lop-sided and the seams themselves crooked. So the next stage is to mark out the roof with chalk to show where the seams will fall. You will need a flexible steel tape for this job.

Fig. 3 shows how the roof should be marked.

Measure across the top of the windscreen and mark the centre on the black rubber surround with a piece of chalk. Do this above the rear window too.

Next lay the vinyl out on the roof. Measure the distance between the seams. Halve this and measure it out on either side of the central chalk mark. Make chalk marks here too—these will be the points where the seams will fall. Repeat this at the rear window. This gives you four marks to sight along when the vinyl is in position.

Check that your marking is accurate by unfolding the vinyl on to the roof—gently, so you do not erase the chalk—and making sure that the seams line up with the ends of their respective chalk lines (fig. 4).

Laying the vinyl

The easiest way to lay the vinyl is to fold it in half across the width of the car (fig. 7) and stick down one end at a time. You must place it accurately; once the adhesive grips there is little scope for adjustment. For this job you will need a small plastic card to spread the glue, a clean cloth pad, a large pair of scissors, a wallpaper scraper, a screwdriver, two 50 mm (2in.) nails and a bottle of white spirit for cleaning any spilled adhesive.

First turn the vinyl upside down on the roof of the car and glue down the underside of the seams (fig. 5). This will give a smooth finish to the roof. Then turn the vinyl over again and line it up with the chalk marks. Go round to the back of the car and push each of the nails through the seams and into the rubber surround of the window (fig. 6). These will hold the seams in position while the front of the vinyl is glued. Next fold the vinyl in half.

16 To cover the rear pillars, first pull the vinyl away from the roof with one hand and smooth out the section above the window

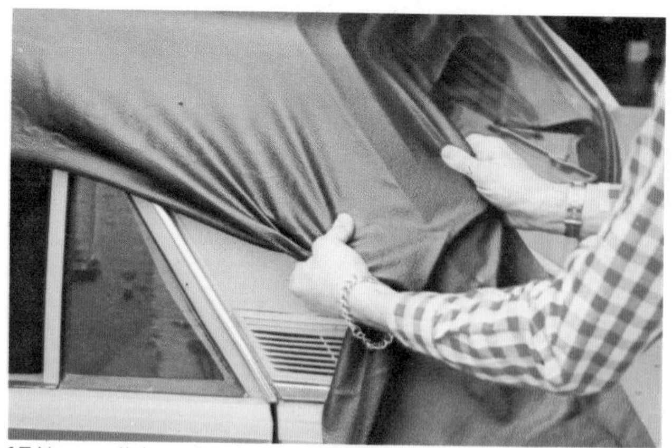

17 Next, pull down hard with both hands. Your assistant should brush it into place when it is taut, brushing from the top down

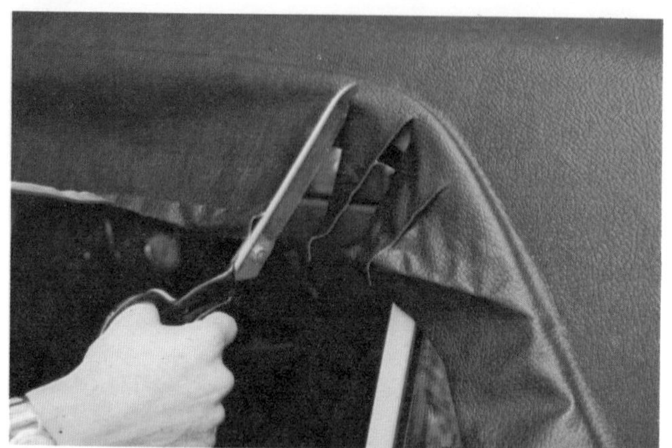

18 To trim the gutters, first slit the vinyl overhanging the curve in the gutter. Then push the vinyl down into the gutter

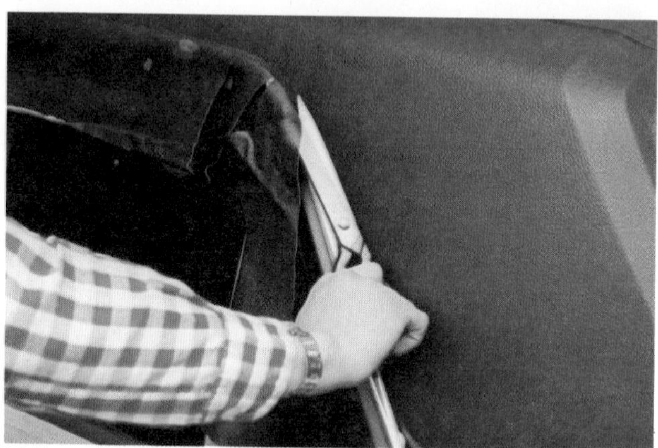

19 Next trim off the vinyl as close to the gutter as possible. Large scissors are best, though a very sharp knife can be used

20 Ease the slack vinyl into the gutter. This may produce a tongue of vinyl above the edge nearest you. This must be cut off

21 Trim the ventilators next. Tuck in the vinyl with the scraper while you hold the grille away from the body with a screwdriver

Nelson Hargreaves

Using a plastic card, apply the adhesive to the car roof and wait a few minutes while it becomes tacky. The adhesive must be even—or bubbles will appear on the surface of the vinyl—and not too thick. At this stage, spread the adhesive only from the centre line to just beyond the seam line (the area from the seam to the gutter will be treated later). Also, leave unglued a centimetre or two where the vinyl meets the windscreen and rear window.

Now, with your helper holding his side of the vinyl sheet well clear of the roof, very carefully lower your half of the vinyl over and into position on the roof. Lower it on to the paintwork very gradually to avoid creasing, and use the cloth pad to brush it into position as you go.

Should you get a crease, grip the vinyl in both hands at a point in line with the crease and pull hard (fig. 11).

Once this section of the roof is in place, check again that the glued seams are in position with the chalk marks. If one is out by more than about 3 mm ($\frac{1}{8}$in.), or if the seam itself looks crooked, try to ease it into place by pressing down and pushing with the palms of your hands—but do not push hard, or you will stretch the vinyl.

Now glue down the other half of the roof the same way.

Having fixed the vinyl sheet firmly in place you will be ready to tackle the edges of the roof. Apply an even coating of adhesive to both roof and vinyl on the strip between the seam and gutter. See that there is a line of adhesive down in the gutter itself—this is important as it will help to prevent the roof from slowly peeling off after fitting.

Covering the rear pillars

The procedure for covering the rear pillars varies according to whether you have a one-piece or three-piece roof kit,

22 To tuck the vinyl in under the window rubbers, trim off the excess material. Aim to leave a margin of at least 12 mm (½in.)

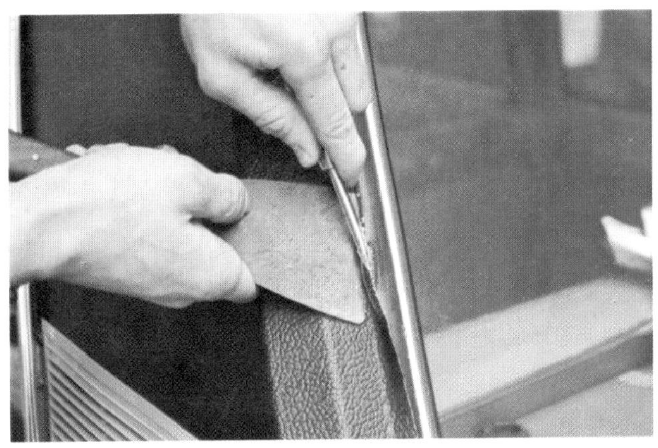

23 Apply adhesive to the vinyl, lever up the rubber with the screwdriver and use the scraper to work the vinyl in underneath

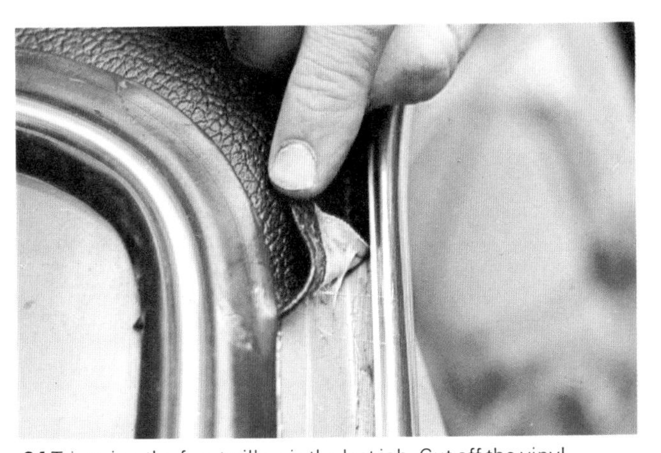

24 Trimming the front pillars is the last job. Cut off the vinyl about 8 cm down the pillar, tuck the edge under and glue it down

25 The finished job. Rub the roof down with a cloth pad and see that all the edges are well fixed. Re-glue any that are not

and on what type of ventilator (see below) you have.

If it is one-piece, follow the same procedure as for the roof edge. Brush adhesive on to the pillars and the reverse side of the vinyl, leaving a narrow strip around the edges unglued. The next step is to ensure that the vinyl runs smoothly over the 'shoulder' of the rear pillar. Pull the vinyl out from the car with one hand and with the other smooth out the area above the rear window—or get your assistant to do this (fig. 16). Next pull the vinyl down onto the pillar (fig. 17). Make sure that it is taut and free from creases before your helper brushes it into place with the cloth pad. Cover the pillars as far as the ventilator grilles. If there are no grilles carry on down to the foot of the pillars and leave to dry.

If the roof kit is a three-piece one, you first trim off the roof section to the line of the gutters, then start off again below the gutters. Make sure the top edge of each pillar section is pushed well upwards to cover properly the area just under the gutter.

Trimming round ventilators

With the grille eased away from the body, trim round the vinyl so that it overlaps the grille by 6 mm. Tuck the vinyl underneath with the scraper (fig. 21). If the grille has had to be removed, run the pillar vinyl over the ventilator.

When the vinyl is dry, you start from the middle of the hole and cut away all the vinyl you do not need, leaving a couple of centimetres' margin for the grille to cover.

Ventilator grilles which are an integral part of the bodywork are a little trickier, but it is still possible to obtain a neat finish. Fix the vinyl sheet firmly at the top of the pillar, but do not apply adhesive to any other part of the body or vinyl. Stretch the vinyl down on to the pillar. The outline of the grille can now be felt through the surface of the vinyl. Mark its outside edges very carefully with a soft pencil. Cut round well inside this line to avoid making the hole too large. Hold the vinyl down over the grille again to check the accuracy of the cut. Trim if necessary. Glue the vinyl down only when you are satisfied that you have a clean fit round the edge of the grille.

Trimming the gutters and windows

The next job is to run the vinyl into the gutters. First cut the vinyl in the curve of the gutter (fig. 18). Next push the vinyl down into the gutter with the scraper and trim off the excess vinyl as close as possible to the gutter (figs. 19-21).

Forcing the vinyl under the window rubbers is next on the list. First trim off the overlapping vinyl from front and rear leaving about 12 mm (½in.) spare to go under. Also trim the vinyl on the front pillars, allowing it to run no more than 7.5 cm down from the roof. Next loosen the rubber by pushing the blade of a screwdriver under the edge and pushing it all the way round the windows. Then apply glue to the edge of the roof and the back of the vinyl. Push the screwdriver under the rubber, lever it up and force the vinyl underneath with the scraper (fig. 23).

Finishing off

Wipe from the car's paintwork, using white spirit, any smears of adhesive which have 'strayed' from under the vinyl.

Replace the ventilator grilles.

Finally, with a soft cloth and working from the centre of the roof, press down the vinyl roof with firm, smooth strokes. Any air bubbles should disappear in a few days.

Pin-striping

Pin-striping—the art of applying fine lines to your car's paintwork—is a form of decoration long favoured by custom enthusiasts. Nearly every exotic custom car on the road uses some form of striping to highlight contrasting colours or accentuate styling. Owners of more conventional cars can also use pin-striping to good effect. One or two subtle lines will almost certainly improve the car's appearance.

Pin-striping designs range from the simple single line running along the side of a car to intricate swirling patterns covering a whole panel which often totally transform the car's looks. The design you employ will depend a great deal on your imagination and ambition, but you should bear in mind that complicated pin-striping, with curves and corners, is a lot more difficult than the single line and it can be done well only with a lot of practice. It is worth remembering also that there are wide variations in the methods used to apply pin-striping lines. Some are easy, some a great deal more difficult. When you are considering designs for your car, plan how you are going to apply them and avoid taking on anything too ambitious.

Methods of pin-striping

Pin-stripes can either be stuck on to a car like transfers, or painted on. The stick-on method, using a proprietary product, is quite simple but, unlikely to give a really professional finish. Painting the stripes, which can itself be done in a variety of ways, will give a far more pleasing and permanent result and a better appearance.

The masking tape method involves painting, with either a brush or a spray can, between two parallel lines of masking tape with a narrow gap between them (fig. 11). Pin-striping in this way can be difficult because it is often impossible to keep the two rows of tape straight and the same distance apart. An alternative is to carve a narrow section out of one strip of the tape using a sharp knife and a metal ruler, but again this is awkward. The tape must be laid out on a flat surface to be cut and it is hard to cut out a strip of uniform width (fig. 12). There are however, special "centre lift" tapes available on the accessory market. Using one of these products, you simply lay down a strip of the tape and peel off the centre section to reveal the line of bodywork to be painted.

An alternative to conventional masking tape is "spaghetti" tape (fig. 14). Because this is narrow and flexible, it allows you to create corners and curves as well as straight lines. It can either be used like masking tape, in rows with a small gap between, or in single strips if an overall respray is being considered. In the latter case you apply the tape as straight as possible then spray the car. When the car is dry the tape is removed very carefully to reveal a pin-stripe picked out in the original colour.

One method of pin-striping which is gaining increasing

3 (right) Fairly simple pin-striping on this Escort is made more effective by using a contrast of colours on both the stripes and bodywork

1 (above) The freehand designs on this Honda Civic help to break up its rather solid lines
2 (below) The styling of the TR7 is perfect for subtle pin-striping

4 (right) Gentle, curving lines show up the rounded appearance of this VW "Beetle". A thin stick-on stripe, like the Calcustom, is ideal for the job

Terry Allen Designs

popularity with customizing enthusiasts employs a special painting roller. This tool, which is imported from the United States, consists of a paint reservoir below which is a narrow knurled roller. You simply run the tool along your car's bodywork to produce a thin, even pin-stripe. In Britain the best known of these tools is the Beugler (fig. 8), which is well made but rather expensive. Less impressive but still efficient are the tools made by Murray Black. Their "A" model has a single roller. The more expensive "M" model comes with a selection of rollers and can be adapted to take two at the same time, for creating double stripes which can be of unequal thicknesses.

By far the most versatile method of pin-striping, once you have mastered the techniques involved, is to paint the stripes by hand. This is, in fact, the way most professional coachbuilders do it. Ordinary artist's brushes can be used for the job but you would be well advised to buy a dagger or a swordtail brush (fig. 9). These have a head of thick bristle running down to a fine point. This means that an adequate supply of paint can be held in the brush and a line can be painted without stopping. It also means that a line can be thickened or tapered according to how much pressure is applied. The type of paint you use is also important. Enamel paint is best—cellulose car paint has a fast drying time which can cause problems.

A complete alternative to paint is Indian Ink. This can be used to good effect to pick out thin lines round elaborate paintwork designs, providing it is protected afterwards with a coat of acrylic lacquer. The best method of applying it is to use a technical drawing instrument such as a crow quill pen, for which you can get a variety of nibs to vary the width of the lines.

Pin-striping designs

The simplest and most common pin-striping design is the single straight line, which is often employed by car manufacturers to enhance the appearance of their more expensive models. Because it involves no corner work, the design lends itself to the masking tape method of painting. The effect of the single line pin-stripes is subtle but it can often serve to accentuate a car's clean lines and divert attention from its less flattering points.

More awkward to produce are single lines running right round panels or areas of bodywork. They usually follow the swage lines of a panel—the lines created when it was pressed or moulded. An example of this sort of pin-striping could be seen on the old John Player Lotus Grand Prix cars. Because sharp curves are involved, this type of design should be done either with a roller tool or freehand. "spaghetti" tape is really only suitable for more gently curving stripes.

Both single and swage line patterns can be elaborated on by the addition of more lines, but this is a lot more difficult and requires some practice. It is most important to keep the lines parallel or the results will be poor (figs. 1 to 6).

Going beyond these relatively simple designs, which follow existing lines on the car bodywork, there opens up the much wider field of free designs to be found on many custom cars. If there are no indentations to follow, you should draw the proposed route of the pin-stripes with a

5 (right) Gold pin-striping, as used on this MGB, can be applied with good effect to any car with dark or silver coloured paintwork

6 (below) The angular lines of a Holden benefit a great deal from this particular pin-striping design

felt-tip pen. Cardboard templates can also help to produce straight lines across panels. Highlighting the outline of special paintwork is also popular and is best done with a pen and ink or a brush. With a little practice, a pair of compasses can be used in conjunction with an ink pen to produce either curving lines or intricate swirling patterns.

Surface preparation

Whether you are painting stripes or sticking them on, preparing the surface to ensure good adhesion is most important. It is usually a combination of dirt, grease and old polish which spoils a finished job and you must start by removing it from the area to be worked on. The best way of doing this is to rub in some rubbing compound until all traces of silicone polish have been removed. If the surface still seems too shiny, you can rub the area to be painted with extra fine wet-and-dry paper, but make sure that you have masked it up fully beforehand or the surrounding paintwork will be scratched.

Pin-striping with masking tape

Pin-striping with masking tape is perfectly straightforward. The most important precaution is to mask the surrounding paintwork with newspaper. First lay the tape in place to give the correct edge of the stripe, then fit on a second masking strip, with newspaper sandwiched between them, to cover the "blind" side of the pin-stripe.

Before you start to paint, press down the edges of the tapes with a fingernail, to prevent paint seeping under the edges and spoiling the line.

Once you have applied the paint, by whatever method, give the paint time to dry thoroughly before you lift the tape, otherwise you will damage the edges and end up with a ruined line. How long this takes depends on the type of paint. The manufacturer's instructions should tell you, but as a rough guide you should certainly wait until the paint is dry to touch.

The variety of effects you can achieve by creative use of masking tape is almost infinite. The most versatile version

7 On this Chrysler Imp, the square lines of the body panels have been picked out to produce a simple but effective striping design

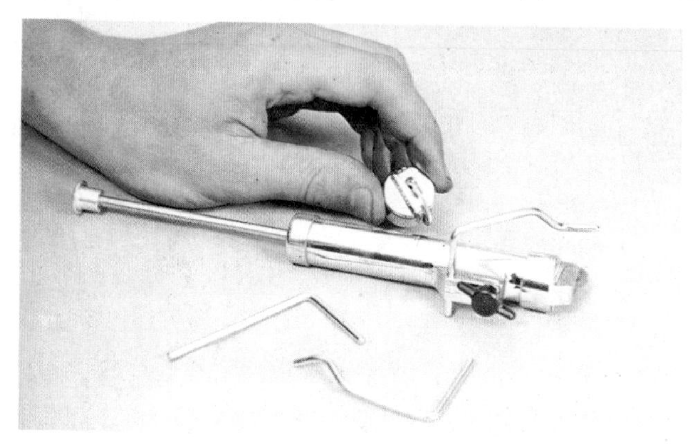

8 The Beugler roller striping tool comes complete with outriggers to help balance it during use, and two different widths of roller

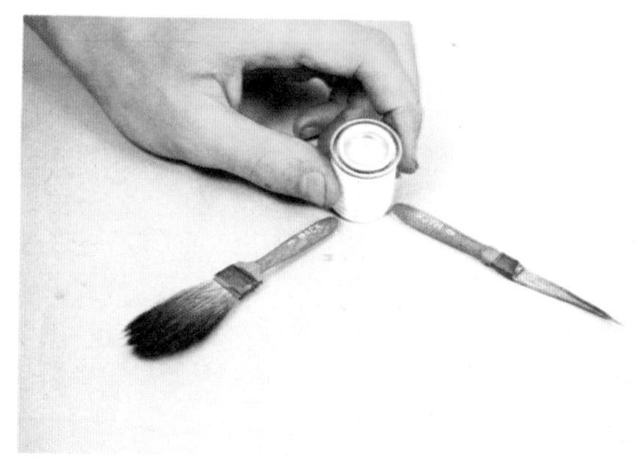

9 Two dagger brushes, for pin-striping by hand. The thick bristle heads are designed to produce a constant, narrow flow of paint

is probably the extra thin "spaghetti" tape. This will follow tight curves satisfactorily but requires even more careful masking around it than ordinary tape. One variation in using this tape is to apply it in a single width in the desired pattern on a single panel, and then carefully mask off the edge of this panel. Then spray in the whole of the panel using a contrasting colour to the original finish. Lift the "spaghetti" tape when the paint is dry, and you will be left with a thin line design picked out in the original paint colour amid the contrasting area. An effective refinement of this technique, if you have an airbrush or fine "touch-up" spray-gun, is to "fog in" a different shade of the original colour around the outer lines of the design rather than colour a whole area solidly.

When you contemplate producing a complicated pattern with "spaghetti" tape, it is wise to work out the exact design on paper rather than try it out on the car. If your design incorporates precise curves, you can cut templates from cardboard, using a pair of compasses to draw an arc, or a variety of household objects—plates, lids, coins—can give an exact circle.

Once you have settled your design, draw it out again on the car with a soft lead pencil. If you are using compasses place a square of masking tape under the pivot point to prevent damage to the paintwork. Alternatively use a loop of string, held firmly at the pivot point, to guide your pencil round an exact arc.

Freehand pin-striping

If you are confident enough to dispense with tape and enjoy the creative pleasure of painting on your design freehand, you must choose between using a brush and using the roller tool.

It is important to remember when planning a design that the line produced by a roller is slightly wider than the nominal wheel size because of the spreading of the paint. How much spread you get in practice depends on such factors as the type of paint used and the porosity of the

10 A selection of pin-striping products including stick-on stripes conventional and "spaghetti" masking tape and enamel paint

11 Parallel strips of masking tape with a gap in between can be used for pin-striping but they restrict you to single lines only

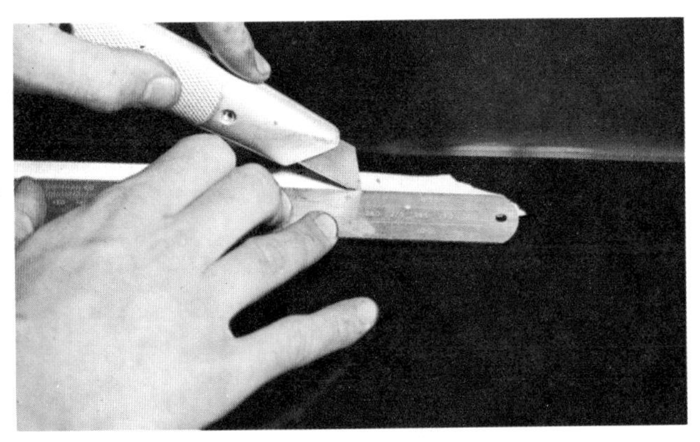

12 If you want to carve a strip out of one piece of tape, start by sticking it down and then score two lines with a sharp knife

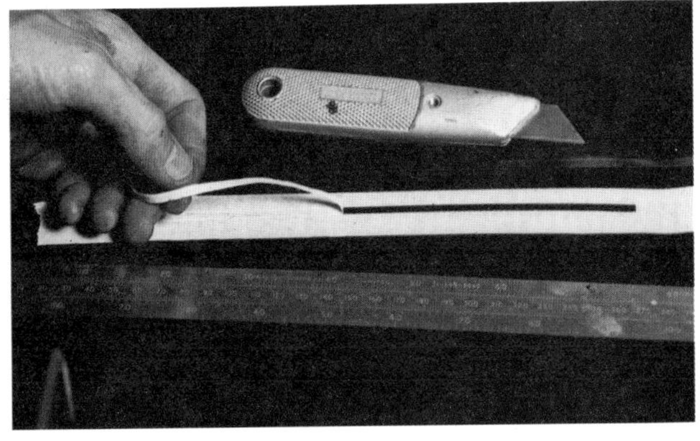

13 Next, flick the end of the strip up and peel it back. Finish by rubbing over the tape again to ensure that the edges are flat

14 "Spaghetti" masking tape is far more versatile because it can be formed into gentle curves with the fingers without crinkling

Mike Berend

15 When you have laid the tape in the desired position, make sure that it is completely flat and then carefully paint over it surface you are applying it to. Practice before using the tool on the car will show exactly what effect you will achieve (figs. 17 to 20).

The most satisfying form of painting is still the earliest method—by hand and eye using a brush. Professional-style pin-striping can be mastered by most people but it inevitably takes time, care and patience. And practice is essential before you start work on the car.

To ensure that you lay down a clean, even straight line, you must first master the correct hand stance. The aim is to use your fingers to maintain the correct and consistent brush-to-surface distance, preventing unwanted up-and-down movement which would vary the stripe width. You can grip either one-handed or two-handed.

In the single-handed grip the brush is held between thumb and forefinger with the handle resting against the fleshy part of the hand between the finger and thumb and the third and little fingers serving as the steadying outrigger (fig. 22). For the two-handed hold the idea is to clamp the brush between both thumbs and forefingers, with the two little fingers acting as outriggers (fig. 23). Keep a firm hold on the brush and use your little fingers to steady your hands as they move. To negotiate curves, you should keep a constant pressure whilst pivoting on the appropriate little finger. You can deliberately raise the brush at the end of a stripe to produce a tapered effect.

The paint used is more important in hand-brushing than in other methods of striping. Enamels are best, not least because if you make a mistake you have time to clean off the paint and start again. Acrylics and lacquers can be used, but because of their fast-drying properties you may need to employ a retarder to delay drying in order to ensure a good, clean stripe.

Using a retarder involves a knack which takes a little practice but pays considerable rewards. The idea is to dip the brush in thinners or retarder before dipping it in the pigment. Paint a few stripes on a piece of scrap paper to set the mixture flowing effectively, then gently wipe the bristles between the thumb and forefinger to relieve the brush of excess paint and work the tip to a fine point.

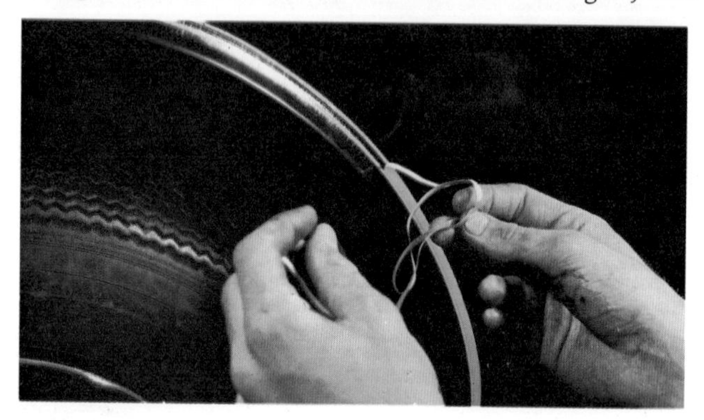

16 If you are using slow-drying enamel paint, you must leave at least two hours for it to dry before finally peeling off the tape

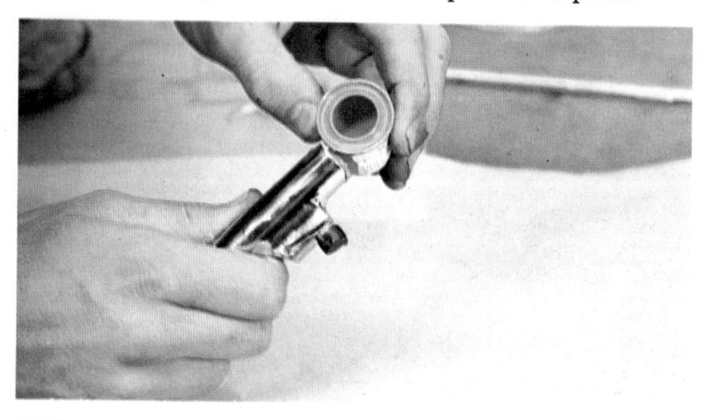

17 To use the Beugler tool, start by removing the roller head and then pour an adequate supply of enamel paint into the reservoir

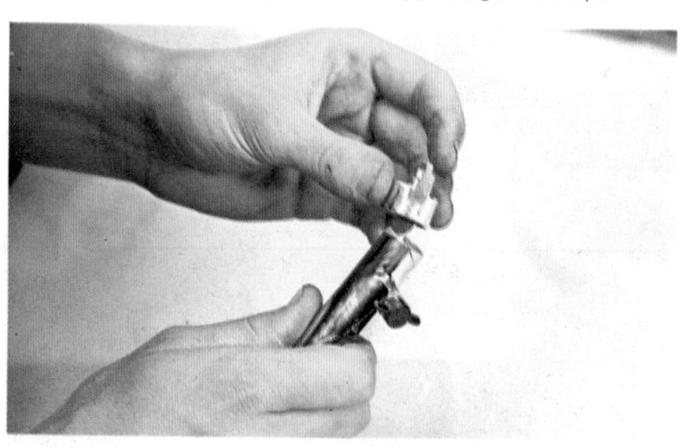

18 Replace the roller head and spin the roller itself to cover it in paint. You can now try a few practice runs on a flat surface

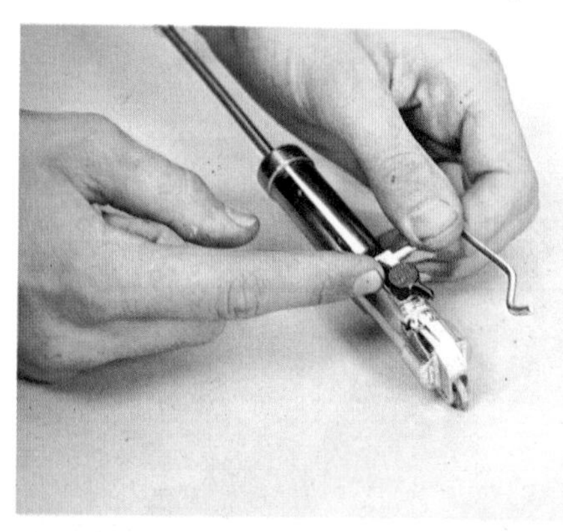

19 Before starting on the car, select a suitable outrigger. Screw it on to its mounting and adjust it until the Beugler is level

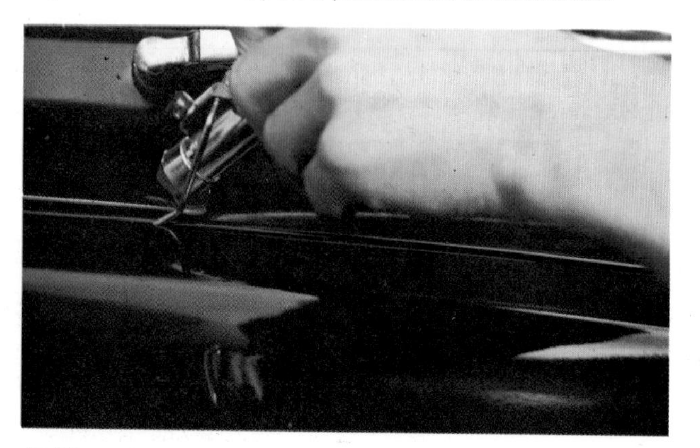

20 When striping on the car, always pull the Beugler towards you and ensure that the outrigger is constantly resting on the panel

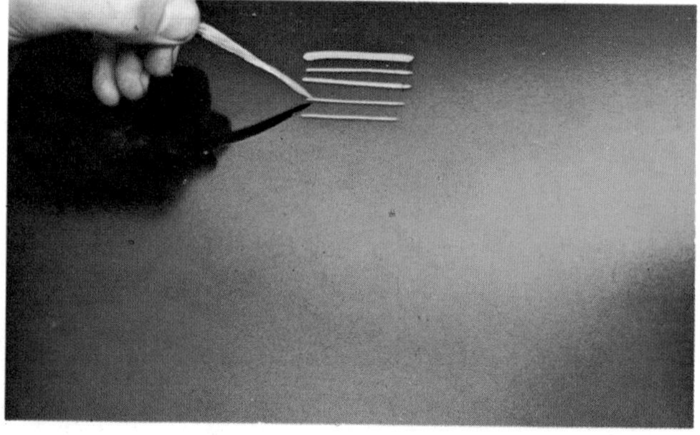

21 Painting stripes by hand requires a lot of practice. By varying the pressure on the brush you can produce different thicknesses

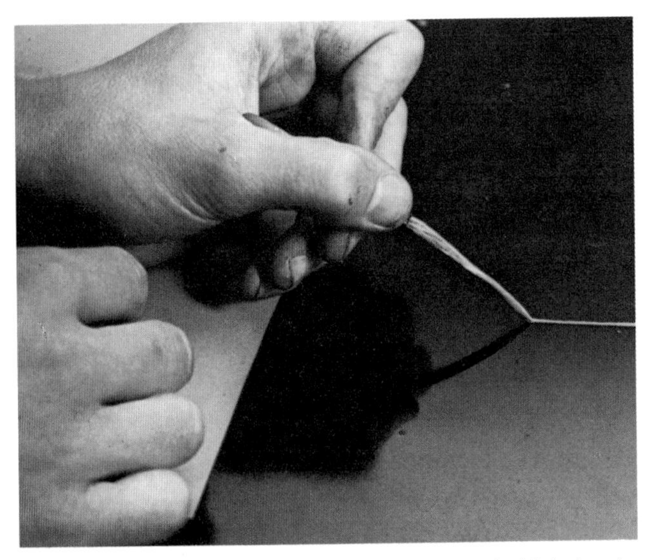

22 With the single-handed method of painting, you hold the brush between thumb and forefinger, using the other fingers to balance

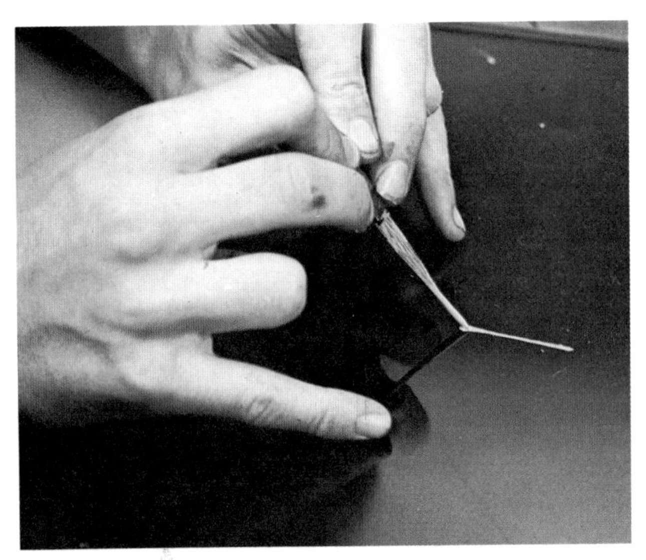

23 With the two-handed method, hold the brush as shown and make your little fingers into outriggers to keep it on a steady course

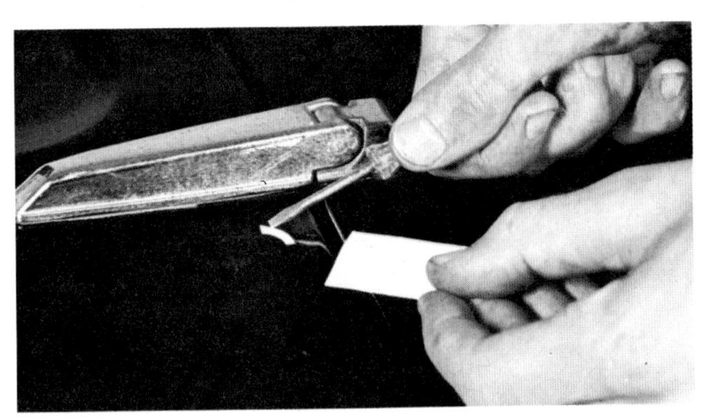

24 The Calcustom stick-on stripe kit comes with corner pieces. These should be stuck down first in the appropriate positions

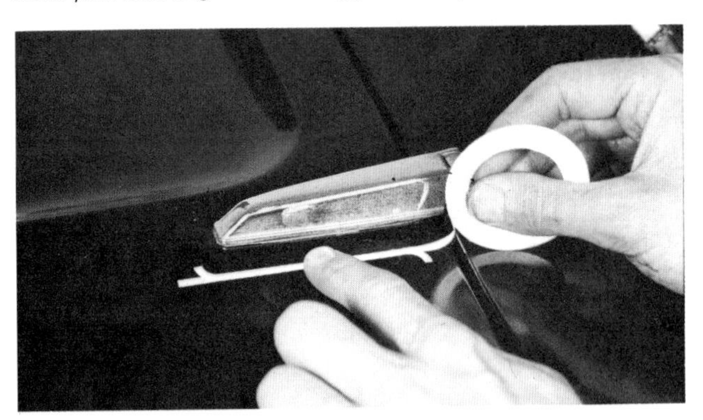

25 You can then join them up with straight striping from the roll. Lay it across the corners and trim it to fit with a sharp knife

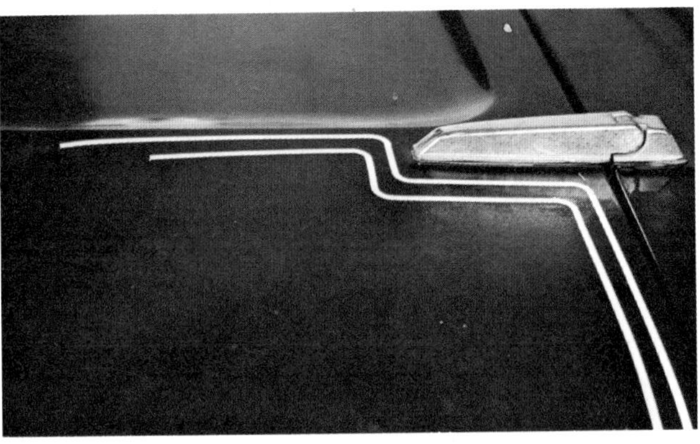

26 The finished design can certainly look effective providing you keep the stripes parallel. If necessary, use a stencil as a guide

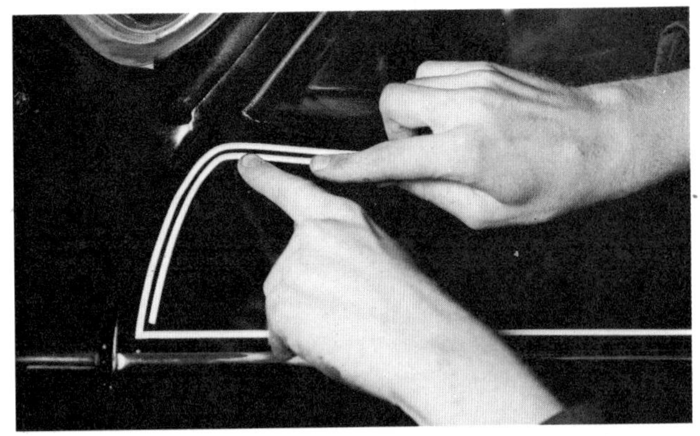

27 You can curve this type of striping tape quite sharply using your finger as a template and holding the roll in the other hand

28 With the tape in position, run over it again with the fingers to make sure that it is firmly stuck down to the bodywork

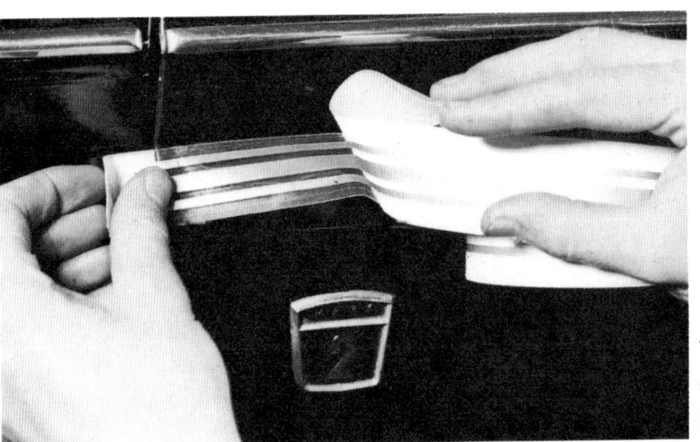

Mike Berend

29 This 3M striping tape is effective, but only for straight lines. Lay the tape by peeling it off the thick backing on to the car

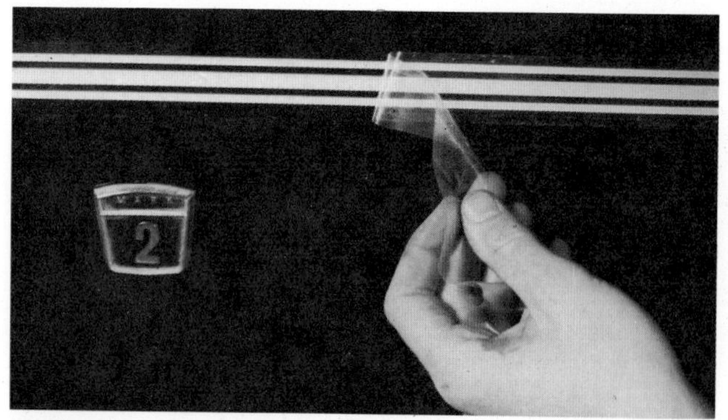

30 When it is in the desired position, give the tape a final wipe to stick it down and then peel off the transparent backing strip

31 The final result can look quite impressive. The stripes are so thin that it is hard to tell that they have not been painted on

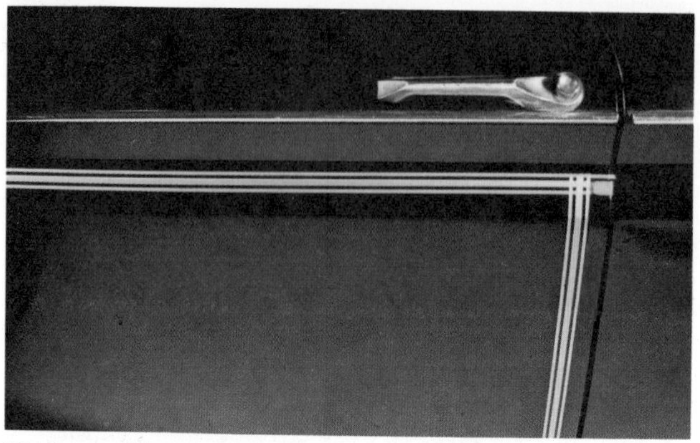

32 It is possible to use the 3M tape to pick out body panels by overlapping the strips and forming right-angled corners

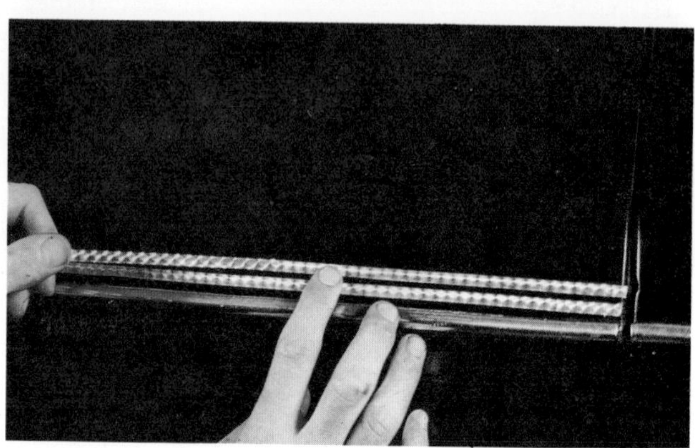

33 This Simoniz Prismatic tape is reflective. Popular with custom enthusiasts, it is especially effective laid in double strips

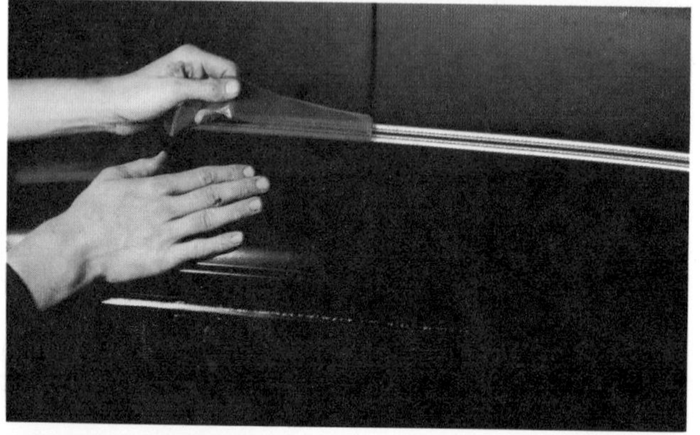

Mike Berend

34 A different type of stick-on striping tape, this time in white but with the same double backing. When laying it, keep it taut

35 It is used here to outline a sill. It is equally effective if applied in a single stripe over the bonnet, roof and boot-lid

Quills, pens and drawing instruments

For fine line rendering, the most useful drawing instruments include the crow quill pen (still used by some artists), the very fine-nibbed type of technical pen and the ruling pen. Fine round sable brushes may also be utilized.

The crow quill pen has a range of nibs from broad to fine and can be used to draw very clean thick and thin lines. The technical pen comes in a wide variety of nib sizes and produces a continuous flow and a line of constant thickness. The ruling pen, a common drafting instrument, is particularly effective for drawing straight lines and line width is adjustable by means of a side screw.

For the first two instruments, Indian ink rather than paint should be used. This takes quite well on acrylic paint provided that the surface is first rubbed down to a dull finish. It must, of course, be protected with a top coat of clear acrylic when dry. The variety of designs which can be created using these methods is virtually limitless. It is, however, a good idea to practice before attempting anything too ambitious.

Stick-on stripes

The final component of this group is the stick-on method of striping (see figs. 24 to 35). Stripes are created quite easily by simply sticking a special plastic tape to the car bodywork. This tape is inexpensive and usually narrow, so curves can be achieved with a little care. If they are clumsily applied, the effect is poor, since the edges tend to snag and begin to peel away when the car is cleaned.

There is little to be said regarding the application of these stripes. Once you have decided where you want to put them, you can either mark a line as previously described, or apply them freehand. In each case you must get it right first time, otherwise the backing paper will peel away when you try to re-position them.

A wide range of stick-on stripes is available from most accessory shops and motor factors, and it is possible to buy single, double or treble stripes. The double and treble stripes are too thick to form corners. Several colours are available, and there are even special diffractive stripes which refract and reflect different colours at different angles.

Fitting a spoiler

Barbara Bellingham

1 The finished job shows the improvement in appearance that a bolt-on spoiler can make to your car

Low protrusions under the front bumpers of most rally and racing saloons are a familiar but puzzling sight to the ordinary motorist. Yet more and more manufacturers are using their rally experience and incorporating an aerodynamic 'spoiler' in their road cars. There are two reasons. First, this type of fairing can appreciably reduce the car's wind resistance and increase its stability. Second, spoilers can give a characteristically 'sporty' touch to even the most modest family saloon.

Unfortunately for the home mechanic, it is unlikely that a bolt-on spoiler will cut wind resistance appreciably. To do so it would need to have been designed as an integral part of the original bodywork. But it will certainly transform the looks of the car, and many enthusiasts feel that for such a modest outlay the transformation makes fitting a spoiler well worth while. And it may aid the stability of the car at speed, by pushing air round the side of the car rather than underneath.

The range of bolt-on spoilers available on the accessory market has expanded dramatically since the revolution in glass-fibre began, and designs are now produced which suit most popular makes of car. When you buy a spoiler, give your dealer the details of your car and he should be able to find one to fit. Check it at this stage for any cracks in the glass-fibre. The spoiler will appear to be an extremely flimsy glass-fibre moulding, with its exposed face finished to a gloss (usually black). If you are planning to keep the colour and finish unchanged, make sure that the gloss surface is not scratched. Despite the apparent weakness of unfitted spoilers, they are so designed as to be surprisingly robust when fixed in place.

Preliminaries

The chances are that when you buy a spoiler, you will get only the moulding itself and a few basic fitting instructions. What other materials you will need depends largely on how complete a job you intend to do. Whilst it is relatively simple to bolt on a spoiler and leave it in its natural finish, far better results can be achieved if you invest in some extra materials and spend a little more time blending it in with the car bodywork. The spoiler can be fixed to the car with self-tapping screws, or for a more permanent finish with pop rivets. To pop rivet, you will need a riveting gun, which can be bought quite cheaply from most hardware shops, and a drill bit. The rivet manufacturer may specify the drill diameter; if not you should use a drill the same size as the rivet, usually 4.5 mm (5/32in.). Self-tapping screws are effective, but the finish looks less professional. The spoiler illustrated requires No 6 size screws, which should be bought together with a 2.35 mm (No 42) drill, although again the manufacturers may recommend a particular size. Buy at least twenty screws, to ensure that you have enough.

Although most glass-fibre spoilers are moulded as accurately as possible, and are in any case quite flexible, it is likely that yours will not fit absolutely flush along the front of the car. If you are aiming for a really good finish, it is therefore advisable to mould the edges of the spoiler into the bodywork with glass-fibre paste. Using glass-fibre matting and resin as well, you can also blend the sides of the spoiler in with the front wheel arches. This can all be done quite easily if you buy a good d-i-y glass-fibre kit, such as those made by Isopon or Holts.

In many cases, as on the car illustrated, the part of the bodywork to which you attach the spoiler will have become

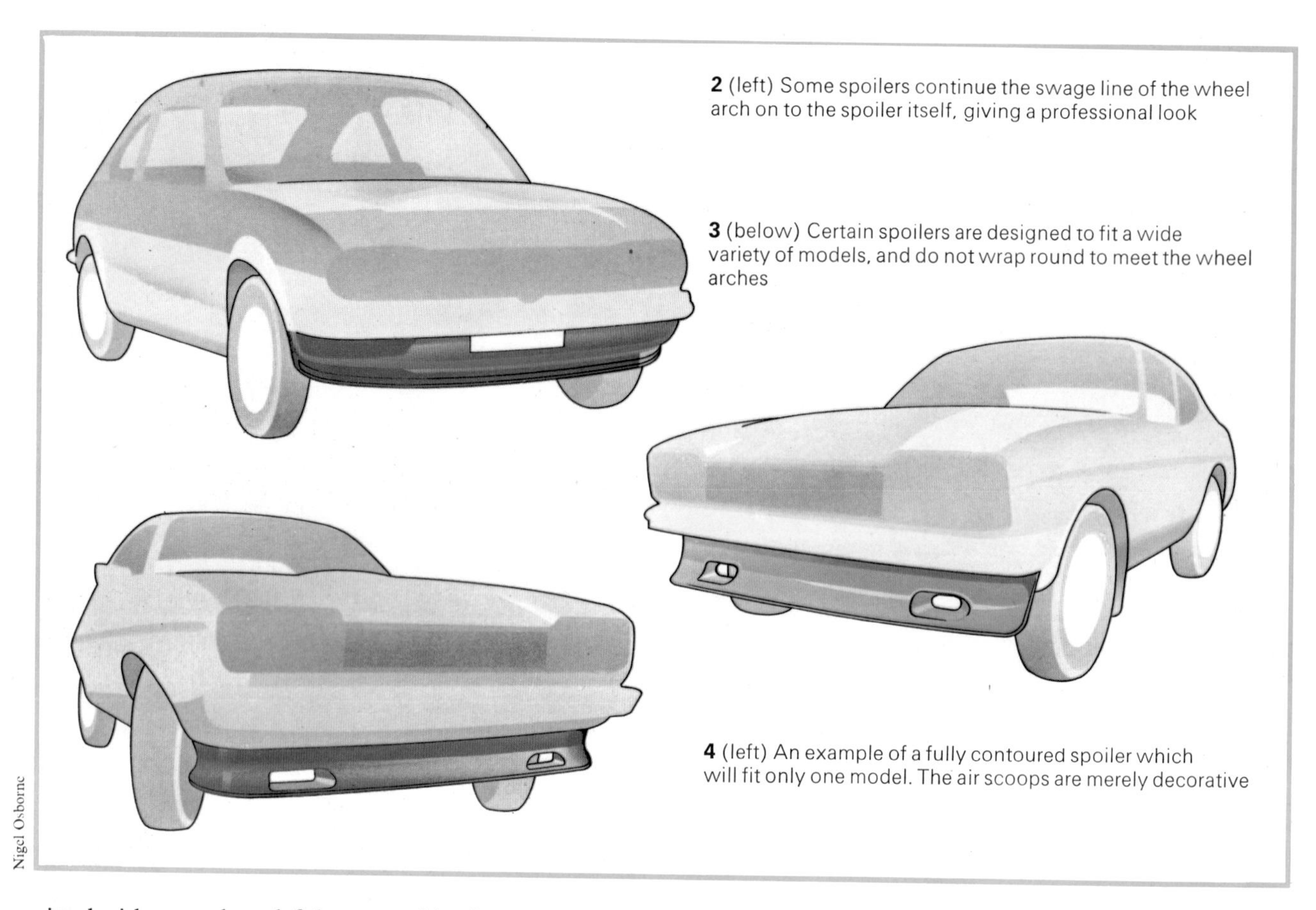

2 (left) Some spoilers continue the swage line of the wheel arch on to the spoiler itself, giving a professional look

3 (below) Certain spoilers are designed to fit a wide variety of models, and do not wrap round to meet the wheel arches

4 (left) An example of a fully contoured spoiler which will fit only one model. The air scoops are merely decorative

Nigel Osborne

pitted with rusty dents left by stone chips from the road, or covered in oily dirt. It is therefore a good idea to repaint it while fitting the spoiler, rather than fit a new spoiler on to deteriorating metal. Most enthusiasts agree that spoilers look better when they are matched to the car's original paintwork, and certainly this has the advantage of requiring only one colour. Two cans of proprietary touch-up spray should be enough to cover painting the spoiler and the damaged front of the car, but only if the areas are thoroughly primed first. For this you will need two cans of spray primer. If the front of your bodywork is badly corroded, you should paint it with rust inhibitor before spraying, so check this before starting the job.

Finally, you will need a selection of coarse, medium, and fine wet-and-dry paper, for rubbing down the paintwork and any glass-fibre. A sanding disc attached to a power drill will make this rather laborious task a lot easier, but the final rubbing down must still be done by hand.

Preparing the car

First jack up the front of the car and support it on axle stands, or drive it on to ramps. This will make working on the front end below the bumper less uncomfortable. Now, any obstructions must be removed for access. If your number plate is in the way, unscrew it from its bracket, then unscrew the brackets from the car bodywork (fig. 5). Accessories such as fog lights should be removed in the same way, leaving you with a clear front panel. If this panel is less than perfect you should renovate it at this stage. Begin by sanding it down either with a sanding disc (fig. 6) or by hand with wet-and-dry paper, until the rust and outer layer of paint have been removed. Next, tape newspaper over the bumper and any other chrome parts likely to be touched by the paint spray.

The next step is to clean the whole area thoroughly with a damp cloth to remove any unwanted dust. Inspect the surface, and if it still appears a bit chipped give it a coat of rust inhibitor. Leave the compound on for about ten minutes then wash it off with water. When the panel is finally clean and dry, you can begin to prime it.

Shake the primer can for about a minute. Then, holding it 20-25 cm (8-12in.) from the panel, begin spraying. Use deliberate sideways movements to keep the spray even, and do not try to put too much on with one coat. The paint dries rapidly and you can soon build up an even, layered finish which will make the final painting much easier, and give you a far more professional finish.

Fitting the spoiler

When the panel is dry, you can start to fit the spoiler. Begin by offering it up for a trial fitting, pressing it against the front of the car. Adjust the height until the sides of the spoiler fit flush against the sides of the car. Now, holding the spoiler against the car with one hand, run a pencil along the top edge of the spoiler to mark where it will come to on the panel (fig. 9). Put the spoiler down, locate its centre by measurement, and drill a hole at the centre about 6 mm ($\frac{1}{4}$in.) down from the top edge.

Again offer the spoiler up to the front panel until its top edge coincides with the mark you have just made. You can now use the spoiler as a guide to drill the central hole in the panel. You must be careful however not to let the drill slip and carve a slot in the glass-fibre, while making no impression on the metal behind. This first central fixing must be in the right position, and even if you intend riveting the spoiler, it is worth using a self-tapping screw to hold it temporarily in place in case you have made a mistake. With the hole drilled, screw in the self-tapper until it is tight and the spoiler holds firmly in position (fig. 12).

Stand back and look at the spoiler. It does not have to be level at this stage, but it must be centrally located. If it is not, unscrew it and drill a fresh hole. When you are satisfied that the spoiler is central, turn to the sides. They must be made level with each other, and the best way of lining up

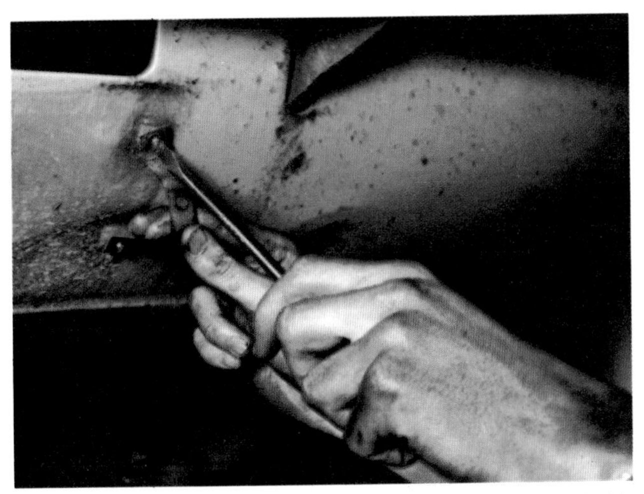

5 When you have removed the front number plate, you will probably find separate supporting brackets. These should be removed

6 With any projections removed, sand down the front valance with an electric drill and sanding disc, or use wet-and-dry paper

7 With the basic surface preparation completed, you should mask any areas likely to be affected by paint overspray

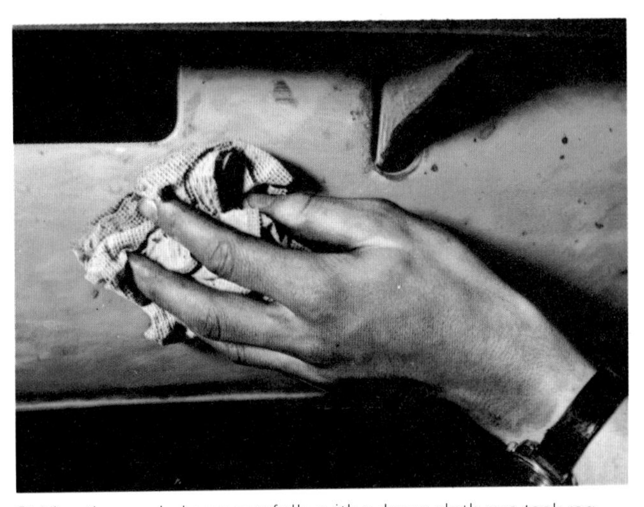

8 Wipe the sanded area carefully with a damp cloth or a tack rag. Ensure that all dust traces are removed to get a good finish

9 When you have rust-treated the panel and sprayed on some coats of primer, hold up the spoiler and mark its position by pencil

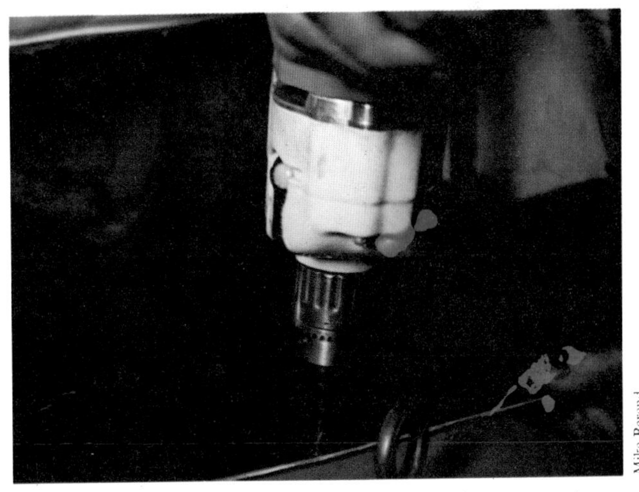

Mike Berend

10 With the spoiler on a block of wood, measure the centre point and drill a hole approximately 6 mm ($\frac{1}{4}$in.) below the top edge

the sides correctly is to tape one side to the wing to hold it in position (fig. 13) then move round and tape the other side. You can then make slight adjustments to get the spoiler absolutely level.

With the spoiler in its correct position, the next step is to drill the remaining fixing holes. Start with the two sides (fig. 14), then drill at regular intervals towards the centre. You must finish up with at least eleven fixing points, all 6 mm ($\frac{1}{4}$in.) below the top edge of the spoiler. With the holes drilled, screw in the screws (fig. 15) or fasten the rivets.

Having completed all the fixings, take a good look at the spoiler, especially where it joins the wheel arches. You may find that you want to trim it to blend in with the curve of the arch, although this is more a matter of personal preference than an absolute necessity. If the spoiler has to be cut, use a hacksaw or keyhole saw, and start by marking the line of the cut first in chalk. When you are actually sawing, do not allow the spoiler to bend or warp; keeping it rigid will reduce the risk of accidentally cracking it. Smooth the edges with a file or wet-and-dry paper.

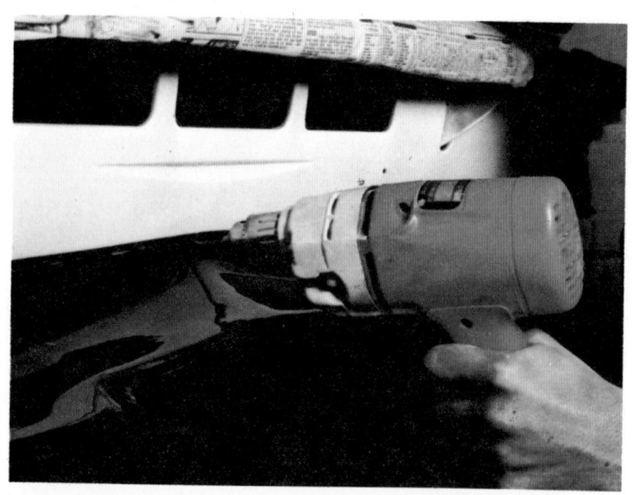
11 Hold the spoiler to the car as a guide and either drill a hole directly or make a pencil mark and begin the hole with a punch

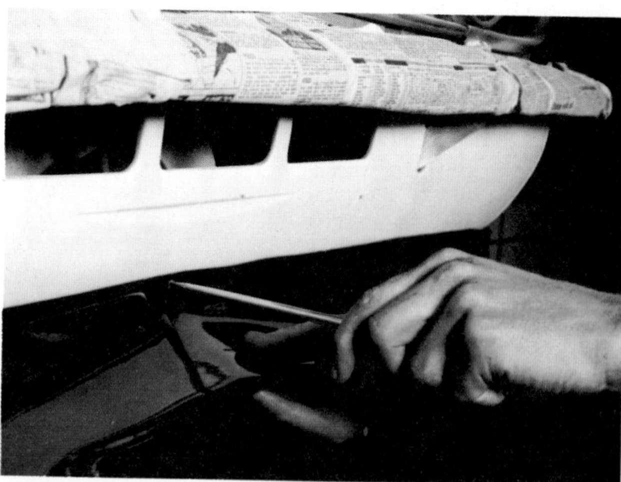
12 Use a self-tapping screw to hold the spoiler in position. At this stage it is important to check that it lines up correctly

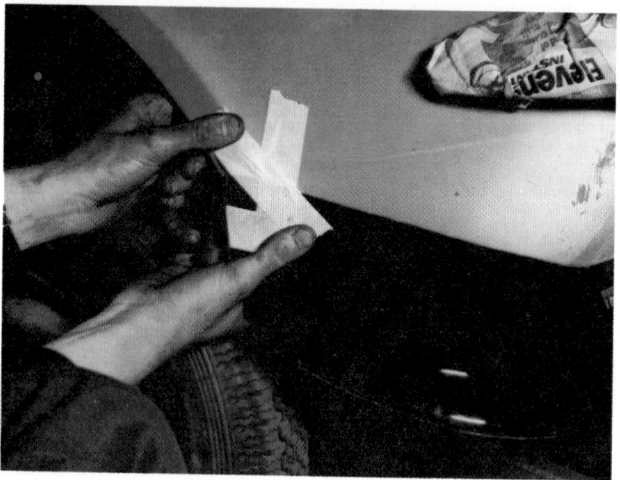
13 When you are satisfied that the spoiler is evenly mounted, use masking tape to hold the ends to each wing prior to drilling

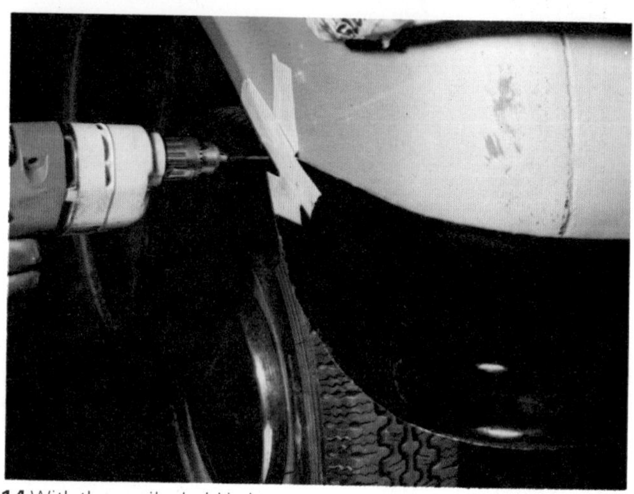
14 With the spoiler held in its correct position, the next step is to drill the remaining holes, working inwards from each end

15 Secure the spoiler with either screws or pop rivets, taking care not to buckle the top edge. Use at least 11 fixings

Mike Berend

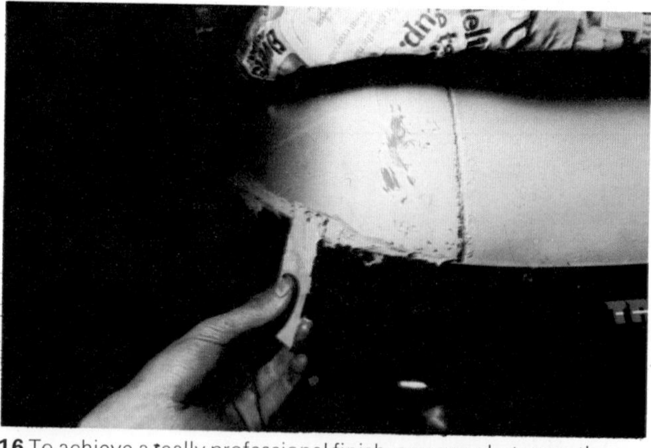
16 To achieve a really professional finish, any gaps between the spoiler and the bodywork can be eliminated with filler paste

Painting glass-fibre

When the spoiler is secured right round the front panel, it should be rigid and fairly strong. If you are lucky it will also be flush against the panel, but this is quite rare. There will probably be several small gaps, and to give a satisfactory finish these must be filled with glass-fibre. At the same time you can use the glass-fibre filler to blend the spoiler with the front panel. Most d-i-y glass-fibre kits contain a filler paste, together with a tube of hardener. Start by mixing the two together, referring to the instructions supplied with the kit. You will have to work fast, because the filler is designed to set rapidly.

Using a spatula or a piece of cardboard, press the filler into the gaps and try to smooth it on to the front panel (figs. 16 and 17). Leave the glass-fibre to dry through, then begin rubbing down with wet-and-dry paper (fig. 18). If you do not get a smooth finish first time, and lots of small indentations remain in the filler, apply another layer. Leave it to dry then rub it down again.

If you want to blend the sides of the spoiler in with the wheel arches, it should also be done at this stage. For this job you will need some fibre matting and resin to build a base on which to lay the filler. Prepare enough matting to make two or three layers. With the matting thoroughly

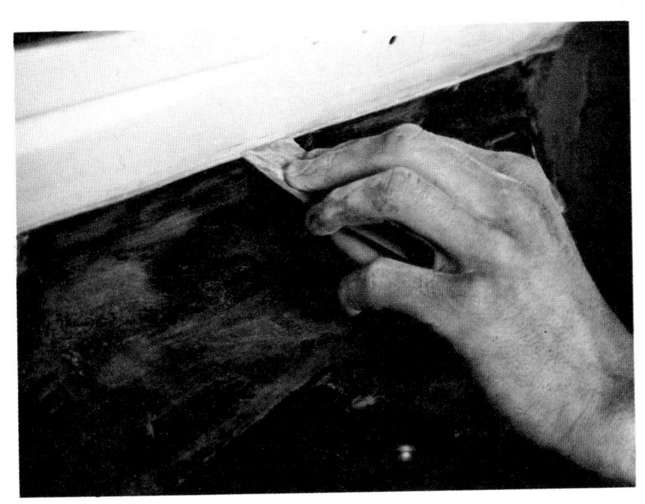

17 If there are any indentations in the first coat of filler, a second coat should be applied once the first has hardened off

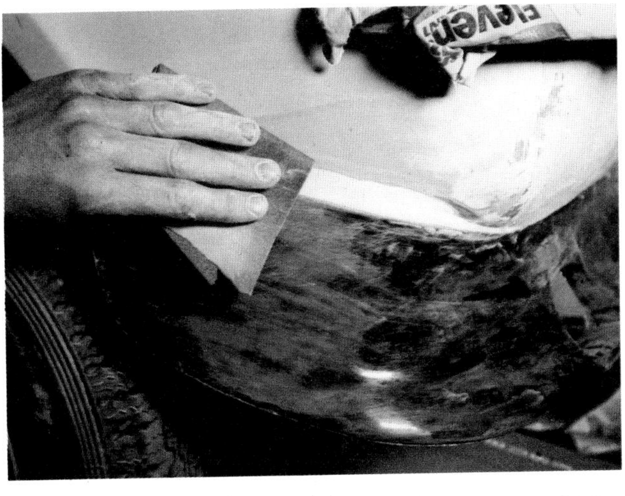

18 Use a coarse grade of wet-and-dry paper to remove any sharp points of filler, then use a finer grade for a smooth finish

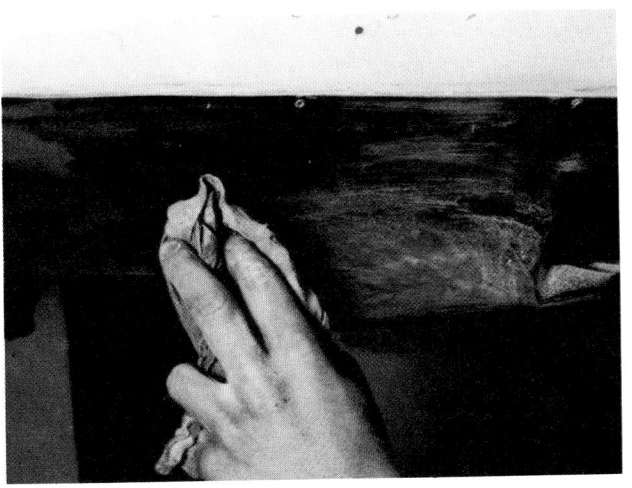

19 Make sure you have also thoroughly sanded down the spoiler, as this will give the paint a good key. Wipe off all the dust

20 Give the spoiler and front panel two or three coats of primer, holding the aerosol about 20 to 30 cm away, then apply the colour

21 The finished paint application should look like this, with a good shine. Use rubbing compound to blend the new and old paint

soaked in resin, lay it across the gap between the spoiler side and the arch and leave it to set. You may need more than one layer. Next, spread the filler paste over the top and mould it as far as possible into a smooth fairing. It can then be rubbed down in the normal way.

When the glass-fibre work is smoothed down and completely set, give the entire area, spoiler and panel as well, a final rubbing with fine grade wet-and-dry paper. It is especially important to roughen the glossy surface of the spoiler before applying any paint. Having completed this operation, it is even more vital to clean everything thoroughly. There will be a quantity of fine glass-fibre dust around, and this tends to gather in hidden corners, only to reappear when you begin painting. If possible use a vacuum cleaner to get rid of the debris, followed by a final wipe with a damp cloth (fig. 19) to give a totally dust-free surface.

With everything clean, apply a coat of spray primer, making sure it goes on evenly. Wait until it is tacky then spray again, to build up a reasonably thick layer of paint. Follow this with the final coat of paint, spraying the panel, spoiler and all hidden recesses behind them.

Refitting the number plate

With your spoiler fitted and painted, the only remaining problem will be refitting the front number plate. Many spoilers fit over the original bracket holes in the front panel and it is unwise to reposition the brackets on the spoiler itself. There are two ways of getting round this difficulty. The first is to fix the number plate above the bumper on the radiator grille, using the original bolts. Tighten them up through the grille slots. The main disadvantage of this method is that the number plate tends to spoil the frontal looks of your car. A better way is to modify your original number plate brackets so that you can reposition them on the front panel below the bumper, but above the spoiler. The most important thing to remember is that the plate must be easily seen from in front of the car. Having part of it obscured by the bottom lip of the bumper could lead to legal complications. If you cannot bend the brackets into the right shape, you will need new ones. Drill two holes and secure the brackets with self-tapping screws.

Choosing personalized wheels

Fitting a set of non-standard wheels to your car is one of the most effective ways of giving it its own individual character. The accessory market offers a wide range of wheels, manufactured to high standards of quality and safety. With a little patience, you are bound to find several designs any of which can be fitted to your car without much trouble.

Mike Key

1 Gleaming alloy wheels have long been a favourite with custom car enthusiasts, but they can also considerably improve the looks of an ordinary family saloon. The wheels here are Cragar GTs

Buying wheels can be expensive and the wrong ones may well spoil your car's handling. But the checks and tips below will help you to make the right decisions before you actually commit yourself to such a large outlay.

Standard or wide wheels?

The first thing to consider when buying non-standard wheels is whether or not you want to increase the width of the rims. Most wheel manufacturers make their products a 'size up' from a car's original equipment. This usually means a width increase of 10 mm to 25 mm (about ½in.-1in.).

Fitting wider wheels will certainly increase a car's visual impact but will not automatically result in better handling. Although wide-section tyres give a car better cornering, handling and braking, the balance of its suspension can be upset and undue strain imposed upon axles and half-shafts. Some cars fitted with excessively wide wheels have been found to handle appallingly, especially in the wet; their increased rolling resistance has also resulted in higher fuel consumption. Generally speaking a small increase in track width will not cause any problems, but do not expect any great benefits either.

The greatest advantage of wider wheels is that a much larger selection is available on the market. But before you buy them you must consider the problems which you will encounter in fitting them to your car. Not only will they have to clear bodywork and suspension, but they will also have to satisfy any legal regulations on wheels.

Legal requirements

In Britain, the law specifies that the entire circumference of the tyre tread enclosed by the car's body must be covered (fig. 2); other countries have similar regulations. It would, in any case, be anti-social to drive a car which constantly flicked mud into the eyes of following motorists.

Wheel manufacturers and dealers can usually tell you if your car will require bodywork modification to accept a wider wheel and supply a selection of glass fibre or aluminium 'spats' designed for this purpose (fig. 2). These are 'extras', however, that will not be supplied with the wheels themselves.

Wheel sizes

Wheel dealers' advertisements often quote wheel dimensions as a code—for example, '4½J x 10'. The first figure refers to the width of the rim in inches—most manufacturers start at 5in. (125 mm) and progress in ½in. (12 mm) sizes up to anything between 10in. and 15in. (250 mm and 415 mm). The letter following, normally J, is a code describing the distance in inches between the top lip of the rim and the part upon which the tyre rests. J means 0.68in. (17.5 mm). The final figure denotes the diameter of the wheel, rim to rim. This varies from 10in. on a standard Mini to 15in. or 16in. on a large saloon (fig. 5).

Inset, outset and offset

Inset and outset are terms used in the trade to describe the convexity or concavity of wheels. The measurements are taken from the centre of the rim to the part which bolts on to the car's hub (fig. 5). If the bolt-on part is nearer the hub, the wheel is concave and is described as having a degree of outset. If the bolt-on part is nearer the outside of the wheel, then the wheel has a certain amount of inset.

As well as having either inset or outset the majority of wheels are known as 'offset', meaning that the bolt-on face is offset to one side of the centre of the rim.

Making wheels with inset and offset enables manufacturers to cater for a wide range of vehicles. A car with a relatively protruding hub and axle will obviously require a wheel with a large amount of inset, if it is not to stick too far outside the bodywork (fig. 4). Some cars have shock absorbers or other suspension parts in prominent positions inside the wheel arches. They will need wheels with outset, to bring them away from the arches and thus avoid fouling (fig. 3).

Measuring the bolt pattern

It is important when buying wheels to make sure that they fit the existing pattern of hub studs on your car. This

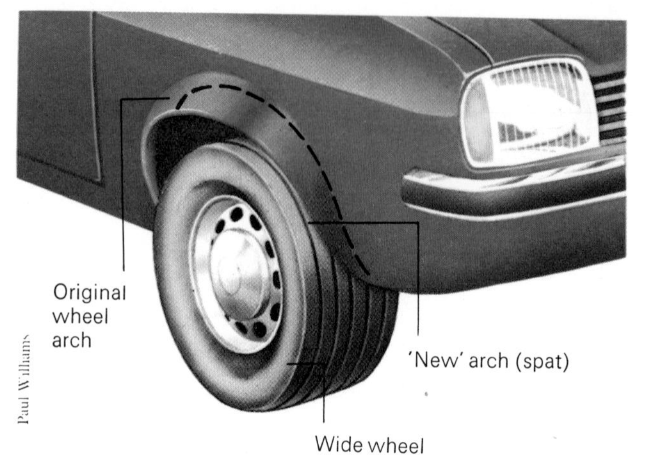

Paul Williams

2 When your tyre treads protrude illegally outside the bodywork, because wider wheels have been fitted, the only answer is to fit spats round the wheel arches

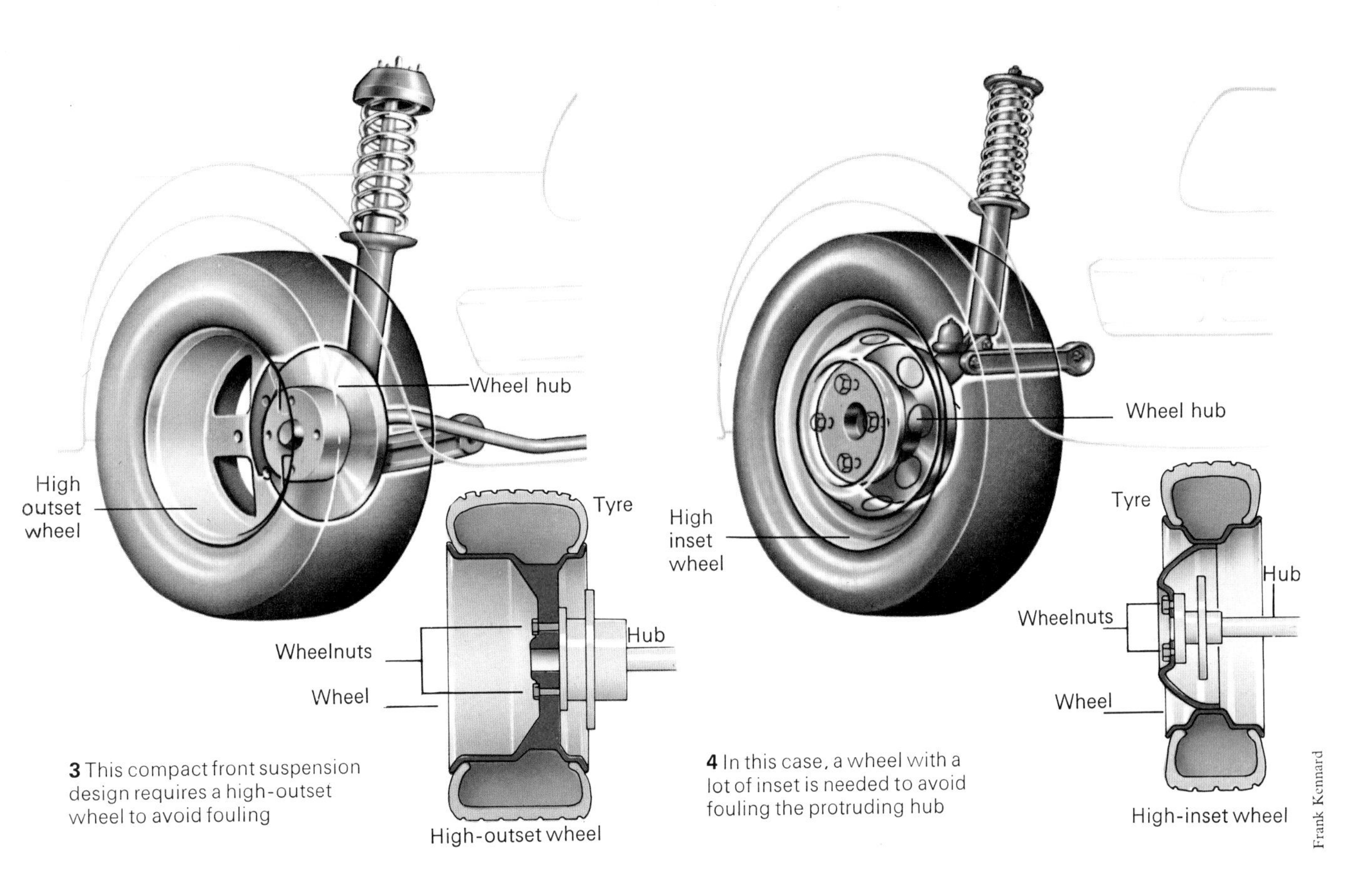

3 This compact front suspension design requires a high-outset wheel to avoid fouling

4 In this case, a wheel with a lot of inset is needed to avoid fouling the protruding hub

pattern is normally referred to as the PCD and is described in terms of the distance between two opposing studs (fig. 5). A good wheel dealer will almost certainly know the PCD for your car already, but it is still worth taking the measurement to make absolutely sure.

Many wheel manufacturers provide a comprehensive catalogue in which you will find a list of cars with the appropriate wheels next to them. But should you want to buy wheels second-hand, or if the dealer's information is inadequate, you will need to do your own measuring. You can do this by first raising your car on a pair of axle stands. With the wheels straight, make a note of the maximum clearance possible between them and the wheel arches. Now turn the steering wheel to full lock and again measure by

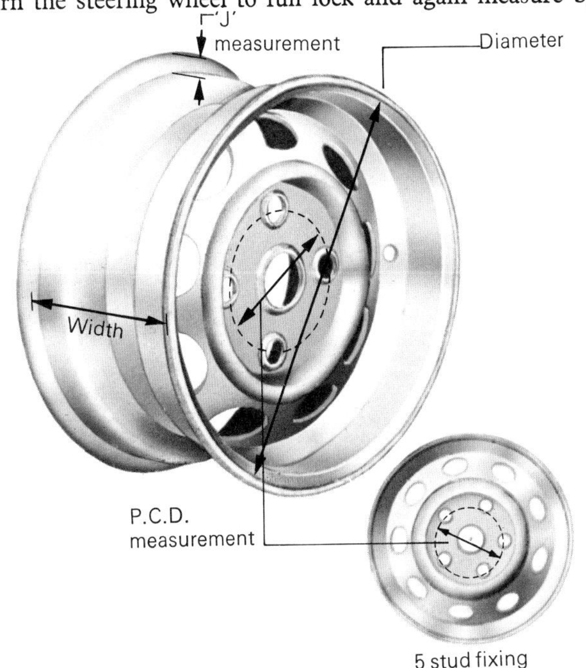

5 A typical alloy wheel showing all the measurements that you are likely to be given, or need, when you go to a dealer

how much the wheels can be widened, paying special attention to shock absorbers, springs, and wishbones. Repeat for the opposite lock.

The next step is to place a jack under one of the tyres and to carefully raise it until the suspension is compressed. You can now discover how much room there is between the tyre and the top of the arch, and whether or not wheels of a greater diameter may be fitted. Having dealt with these clearance checks at the front of the car, move to the back where trailing arms and shock absorbers could be more of a problem. You must not forget to make an allowance also for the bulge of a tyre's sidewall under load. Finally, with the car on the ground again, estimate how far the wheels can be widened without forcing the tyre tread illegally outside the bodywork.

Finally, before you buy, check that the amount of inset or offset on the wheels you want will be suitable for your car.

Slight modifications

You can make small modifications to your car if the wheels of your choice do not quite fit. Manufacturers themselves make spacers to enable certain cars to take their wheels, but do not buy these if they exceed 12 mm ($\frac{1}{2}$in.) in width. Although longer studs can be drifted into the hub to allow spacers to be attached, a large increase in track width is bound to impose more strain on the axle than it was designed to take.

One device which you might encounter is the bolt-on hub extension, often misleadingly referred to as a 'spacer'. This is a piece of metal which bolts on to the hub, the wheel being fixed to the other side of it, and is generally considered to be dangerous. It is possible, however, to buy adaptors which convert a five-stud hub (as found on VWs, Ford Transit vans and so on) to the more conventional four-stud fitting found on most alloy wheels, and similar adaptors for fitting five-stud wheels to four-stud hubs.

If a wheel looks as if it is going to foul the inside of the wheel arch, it is possible to dent the arch with a rubber hammer until sufficient clearance is obtained. Before attempting this, however, make sure that the area around and behind the proposed dent is free of components, pipes or attachment points.

Tyres

Buying a set of non-standard wheels slightly wider than the originals does not necessarily mean buying new tyres to go with them. Fig. 5 gives a guide to the maximum and minimum rim widths for particular tyre sizes, but again, this is a subject on which your dealer should be able to advise. Remember to allow for any sidewall bulge—slightly greater on radial tyres—when estimating clearances.

Alloy or steel wheels?

Most wheels on the accessory market are made of either aluminium or magnesium alloy. Magnesium wheels can offer a weight saving of up to 35% over their pressed steel counterparts and, at the same time, they are much stronger. Unfortunately, they have two great drawbacks—they are expensive, because of the cost of the metal, and they are prone to corrosion. Lead, as used in balancing weights, will quickly eat through the outer layers of the alloy, so it is important to use weights of the stick-on adhesive type and not the clip-on variety.

Even more of a problem is road salt, still widely used by many British local authorities in winter. Salt attacks both types of alloy, but is far harder on magnesium. The only solution is to make sure that your wheels have an adequate coat of protecting compound and that this is regularly maintained. Manufacturers have improved their anti-corrosion treatments enormously over the last few years, but you should still use wheel cleaning materials to help keep your wheels in tip-top condition.

Aluminium alloy wheels are by far the most popular. They offer a good compromise between price, strength and looks, and do not corrode so easily. A small chip or scratch will quickly develop an oxidized layer which prevents

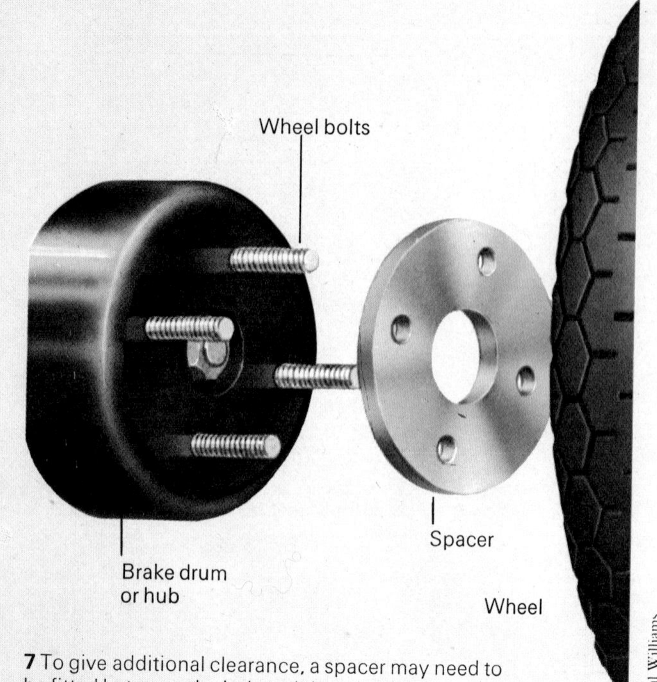

7 To give additional clearance, a spacer may need to be fitted between the hub and the wheel

6 Some typical alloy wheels. Left to right, Appliance Turbo-Vec; Shelby Cobra Supaslot; Appliance smooth centre; Appliance wire spoke; Wolfrace slot mag; Appliance wire mag

further deterioration. The material used is usually LM 25, an alloy which is much stronger and lighter than steel. It has another advantage in that it is more flexible than the stronger magnesium. Small knocks often produce only a slight warp, which can be repaired—but losing a large chunk of metal will mean a new wheel.

Pressed steel wheels are now a rarity on the accessory market, although the majority of production cars have them fitted as standard. Car manufacturers favour them because they are cheap and easy to produce, but they do take care to ensure that their wheels are safe—unlike some that have appeared in the shops. Steel wheels are about half the price of alloy ones, but you certainly will not get as much for your money. They are heavy, not as strong in relation to their weight, and they are not as attractive as an alloy wheel. Nevertheless, they do offer a cheaper means of personalizing your car, and are perfectly safe providing you select a reputable make, such as Dunlop or Weller.

Designs

Non-standard wheels come in an ever-increasing variety of designs, some of which have strange-sounding names. The slot-mag is the solid type of wheel with wide slots arranged in a circle around the hub. The dish-mag is a more concave version. The steel spoke wheel, as its name implies, has four or more spokes connecting the hub to the rim; it should not be confused with the fake 'spoke' wheel which has a larger number of small, solid, spokes.

Some manufacturers market a 'split rim' wheel with two halves which bolt together. By this means, a standard design of wheel can be given varying degrees of inset or offset, thus making it more adaptable in cases of difficult clearances. The most interesting steel wheel design is still the traditional, spoke, wire wheel. Unfortunately only a very few manufacturers make them and the choice of cars to which they can be fitted is restricted.

Wheelnuts

Some wheel manufacturers supply their products complete with nuts while others provide their wheels with steel inserts to allow you to use your original ones. Dealers also carry wide ranges of chromed nuts as extras, and these are often designed for a particular wheel. Another extra which could prove a good investment is a set of lockable nuts. Alloy wheels provide a tempting and surprisingly easy target for the car thief; locking your nuts will make it that much more difficult for him.

Besides the conventional mechanical locks on the market, it is now possible to buy a more expensive but more efficient electro-magnetic device to ensure that your wheels stay where they belong.

Balancing

Most high-quality alloy wheels are precision balanced at the factory, and will be unbalanced only by the tyres put on them. Self-adhesive weights are now available and these can usually be placed on the inside rim to avoid marring the wheel's appearance. Your dealer will advise you which wheels are hard to balance, and on whether the weights should go inside or out. Steel wheels tend to pose more of a problem and may have to be balanced in the normal way.

Buying from a dealer

When buying wheels, it is important to go to a reputable dealer or manufacturer, who will be qualified to advise you on your particular car. The wheel makers spend a lot of time and money designing and testing their products, and should know what wheel fits what car. In many cases, all that you need to do is give your dealer the exact make, model and year of your vehicle and he will show you an appropriate selection of wheels. If you want to be absolutely sure, or if your car is already to a non-standard specification, carry out the prescribed checks first. If a particular wheel catches your eye, then contact the manufacturers for advice, but remember that it is not worthwhile making extensive modifications just to accommodate a particular design.

Finally, spend a little more by going to a reputable dealer, rather than buy wheels from a large discount or cash and carry warehouse. By doing the latter, you cannot be certain of the quality of your purchase. You will also forego the detailed advice which ensures that you do not waste your money on wheels that won't fit.

Fitting exterior mirrors

Some motorists rely solely on their interior mirror to keep a check on following vehicles. As the density of traffic increases, however, all-round vision is becoming more important if accidents are to be avoided. There is a wide variety of wing and door mirrors on the market to help the driver interested in good all-round vision and safety for drivers, passengers and other road users.

Wing or door mirrors are relatively inexpensive and can be fitted without much difficulty, either by drilling the wing or door or, with some designs, simply by clipping the mirror in position. They can improve safety by eliminating the blind spots on the nearside and offside rear quarters of the car, giving the driver a much wider field of vision.

When overtaking other cars, the driver can double check that it is safe to pull into the outer lane, or on to the other side of the road, by using his interior mirror to detect vehicles travelling at a longer distance, and his wing or door mirror to make sure that he is not about to be overtaken himself by a closely following vehicle.

In dense traffic jams, nearside and offside mirrors allow the driver to keep a look out for, and check the progress of, any cyclists or motorcyclists who may be moving between lines of slow-moving vehicles.

Wing mirrors

Wing mirrors are available in two basic designs—the ordinary mirror on a supporting arm (fig. 9), and the bullet-shaped 'racing' type (fig. 4). They incorporate one of two patterns of glass—flat and convex. Convex glass tends to diminish the apparent size of following vehicles and makes them appear further away than they are. The advantage over flat glass is that they give a far wider field of vision, and the driver can see not only following cars, but enough of the road to give him a better perspective.

Generally the conventional wing mirror incorporates a mechanism which enables it to spring back into position if it is disturbed by vandals or by someone brushing against it. The arm can be reversed for fitting to either side of the car, and most new designs feature replaceable glass.

Adjustment is made by slackening a locknut, pivoting the mirror about a ball socket to give the required position, and tightening the locknut. 'Racing' mirrors do not incorporate spring-back and are mounted closer to the body of the car, usually by means of two nuts. They are streamlined in shape, and are adjusted as conventional mirrors. The finish may be chrome, unpolished stainless steel or matt black. Some racing mirrors can be sprayed to match the colour of the vehicle's bodywork.

1 Wing and door mirrors can not only improve safety by giving a better rear view, they can also brighten the appearance of your car

Door mirrors

Door mirrors are similar to wing mirrors. The conventional type tend to have shorter supporting arms, but some racing mirrors can be fitted to either wings or doors. Most people fit a mirror to the driver's door only. If you wish to fit one to the passenger door you will need to buy a left hand mirror as the majority of door mirrors are not interchangeable.

Many manufacturers now fit door mirrors as standard on some models. On less expensive models where the mirrors are not fitted, holes to accept a certain make of mirror may be pre-drilled. If this is the case with your car, check with a main dealer which mirrors will fit the holes.

Several manufacturers make door mirrors which clip on to the car. They do not require any holes to be drilled into the bodywork, but simply clamp on to the quarter-light frame or the edge of the door.

2 The Alexander right-hand bolt-on door mirror (left) and a left-hand McLaren door mirror of the type marketed by Harry Moss

3 The Paddy Hopkirk European door mirror is easily fitted, and is available in polished stainless steel or matt black finish

4 Two different 'racing' style wing or door mirrors, an Alexander Raceview Mk II (left), and the Italian Sebring Mach I design

5 The Hella 4004 GT wing mirror is manufactured by a German firm, and has a very streamlined shape. It is attached by two screws

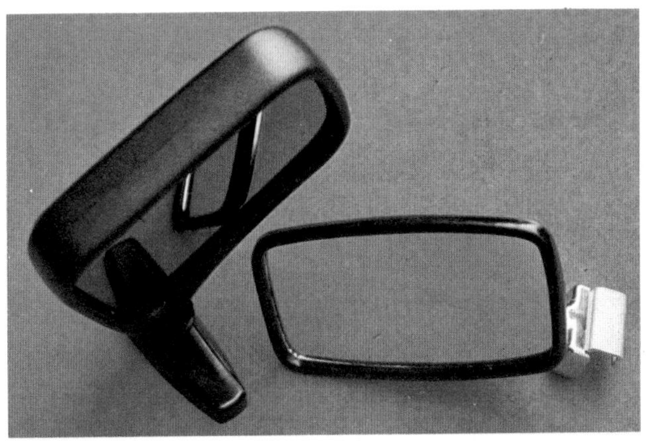

6 The Tornado door mirror marketed by Harry Moss, giving a large field of vision (left), and a clip-on-fitting door mirror

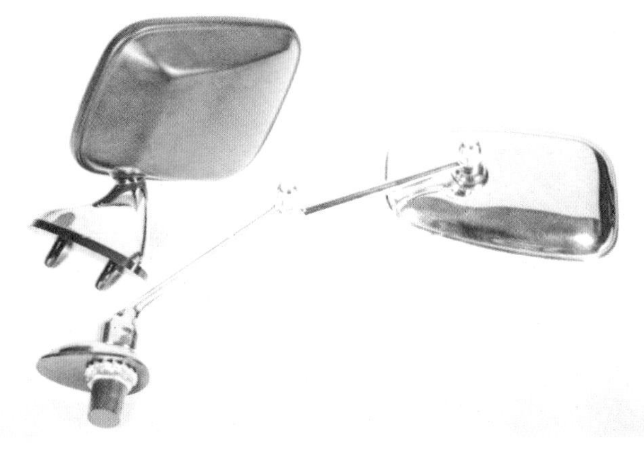

Mike Berend

7 Two products from the wide Desmo range, the Black Lance door mirror (left) and the extended 168 series mirror for towing

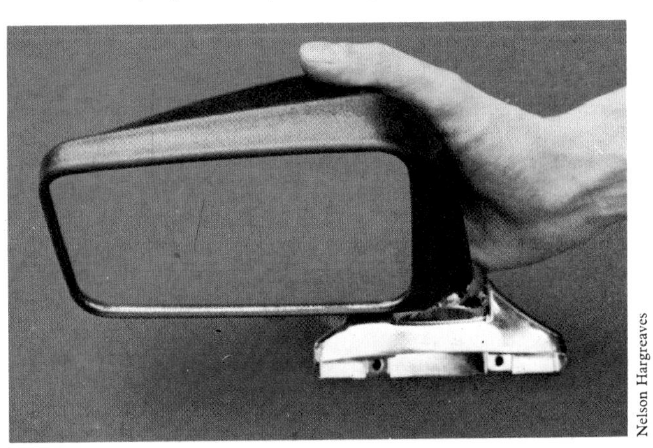

Nelson Hargreaves

8 The Britax Outrider door mirror, shown here in right-hand form, is easily fitted and adjusted. It has a black grained finish

9 Always start with the mirror on the driver's side. Have a helper hold it on the wing while you view from inside the car

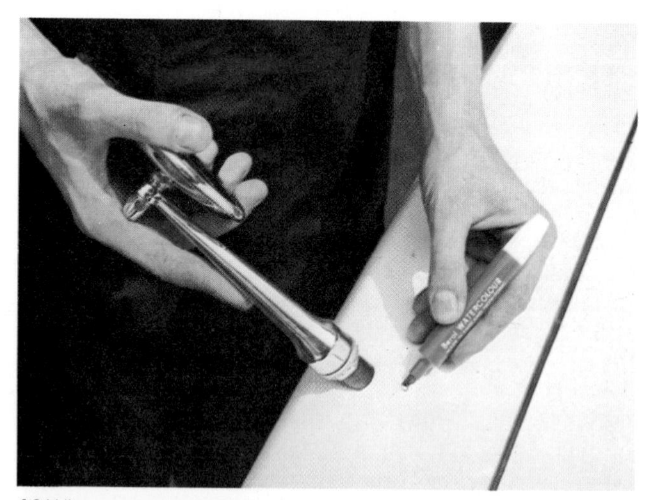

10 When you are satisfied with the position of the mirror, your assistant should mark the car wing with a felt-tipped pen

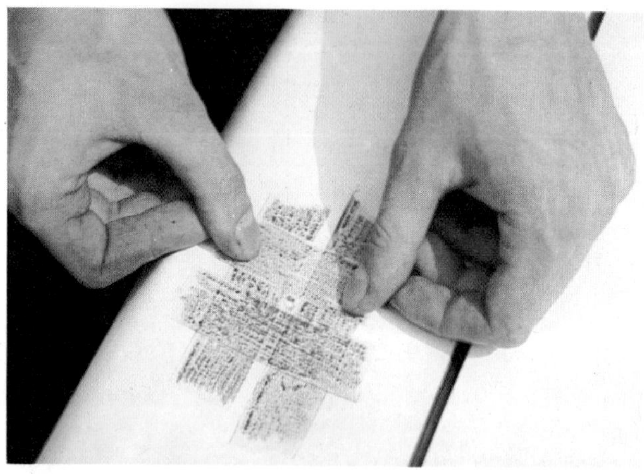

11 Place strips of masking tape around the felt tip mark. This will protect the paintwork in the event of the drill slipping

12 An alternate method is to place a strip of masking tape over the original mark and redraw the mark over this

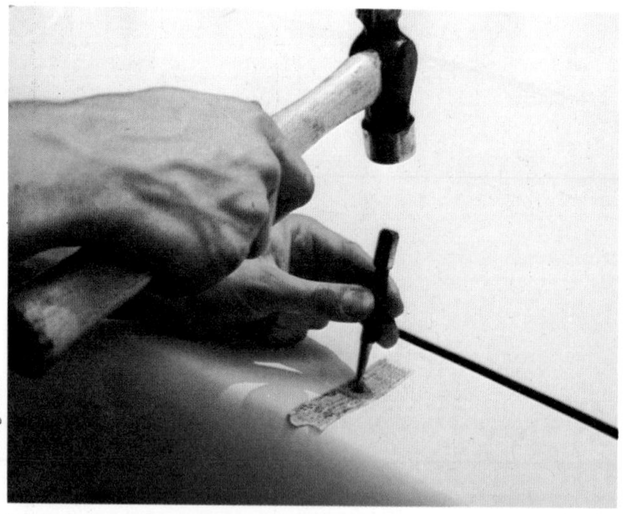

Nelson Hargreaves

13 Always begin a hole by marking it with a centre punch. This reduces the chances of the drill slipping and causing damage

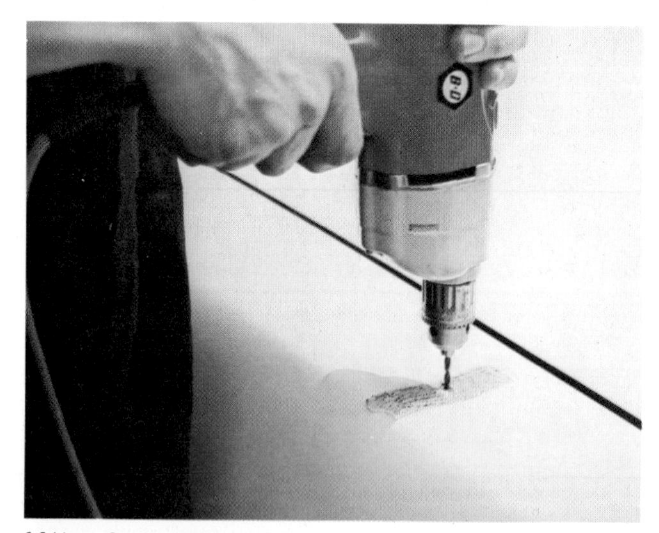

14 Use a 3 mm drill bit initially, as this will penetrate the car wing more easily. Then use a cutter to enlarge the hole

Towing mirrors

Towing imposes specific requirements when wing or door mirrors are being selected. The arms must be longer than on ordinary wing mirrors to allow the driver to see round, for example, a caravan, which may be considerably wider than the towing car. If mirrors are fitted on the front wings of a towing car, they must be of the spring-back type.

Perhaps the most refined towing mirror is the periscope type. This is attached to the car just above the windscreen, in front of the driver. As the name suggests, the mirror uses the periscope principle to enable the driver to see what is happening behind him.

The market

Many British and European firms produce wing and door mirrors, but the following provides a cross-section of the designs on the British market.

Desmo. A British manufacturer producing a wide range of mirrors. Types 166 and 168 in the Boomerang series have straight arms, the 168 being longer. Types 270 and 271 have

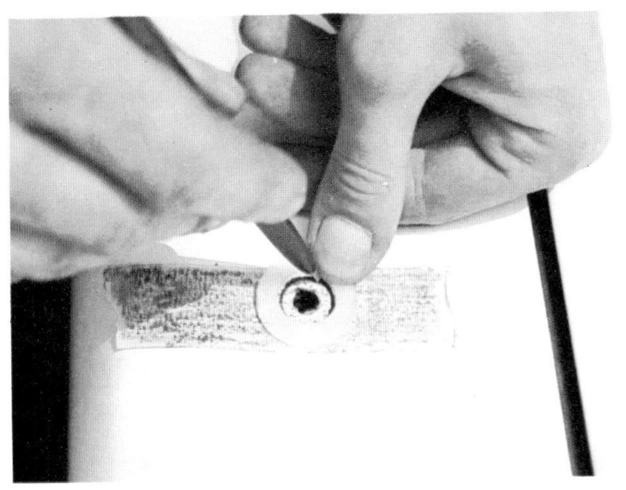

15 If you cannot obtain a cutter, draw around the inside of one of the washers from the mirror to determine the hole size needed

16 Open up the small hole to the required size with a round file, taking care that it does not jump out on the upward strokes

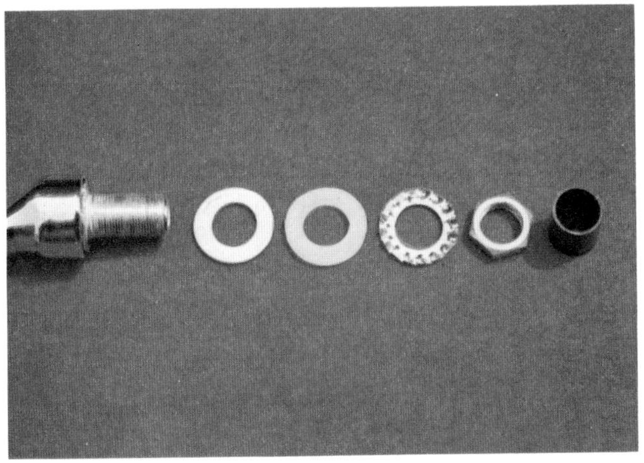

17 The wing mirror washers should be carefully assembled in the correct order, otherwise any spring-back mechanism will not work

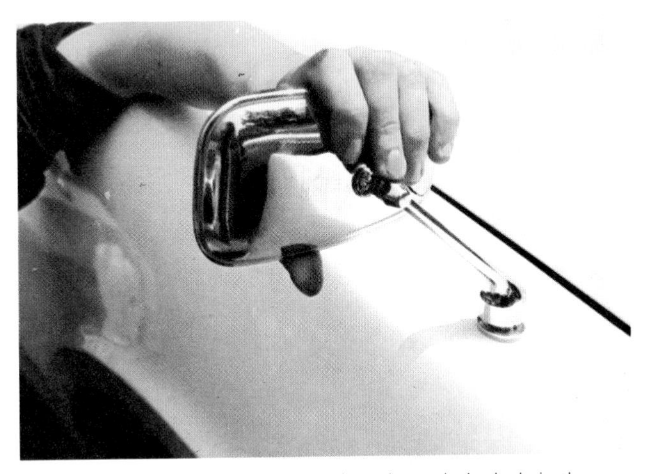

18 Slide the threaded stem of the mirror through the hole in the wing and attach the securing nut and washer from below

19 Tighten the mirror until the arm tries to turn, then spring the mirror back and fully tighten using a spanner on the flats

curved arms. All are chromed and have single nut fixings. The 1000 range of 'Eurovision' door mirrors is available in left and right hand form, and the mirrors feature a 'knock-away' facility to cope with casual knocks. They are produced in a variety of sizes. The company also make a clip-on door mirror. The newly introduced Black Lance model has shatterproof anti-dazzle glass. A derivative of the Boomerang mirror, the Boomerang Caravan mirror, is made for towing. It can either be bought complete, or an extension arm can be added to the ordinary Boomerang series. Various plinths to stabilize the extended mirror are supplied; they are useful for cars with sharp apex wings such as Rover 2000s.

Autosafe. This company markets a range of door mirrors. The standard model is available with flat or convex glass, finished in polished stainless steel or stove enamelled matt black, in right or left hand versions. The company also markets a version of this mirror electrically controlled from inside the car. A push-button regulates the adjustment, and can be operated in one of four directions.

London Bankside Products. One of the largest range of mirrors is offered by this company. The Solar door mirror is finished in black leather grain and chrome and fits right or left hand doors. The Eclipse Passing mirror comes in two sizes and clips to the quarter light. The International door mirror is available in chrome or matt black and can also be fitted to front wings. The Orbiter sports mirror has two alternative finishes, and is of hooded shape, as is the Floria sports mirror. The Apollo range of bullet-shaped racing mirrors features a circular, vibration-free lens in an aluminium casing. London Bankside Products also produce the Solar Tristar towing mirror. The unit has a long reach and a wide range of adjustment. It requires no drilling, but clamps firmly to the front wing at three points. When nothing is being towed it can be removed and stored.

Polco. Polco import French mirrors to Britain. Their range features a clip-on overtaking mirror, two sizes of wing or door mirror, and a rectangular wing mirror. The overtaking mirror is available only in flat glass, while the others are anti-vibration tested to 145kph (90mph). The wing or door mirrors have a spring-back action, while the head of

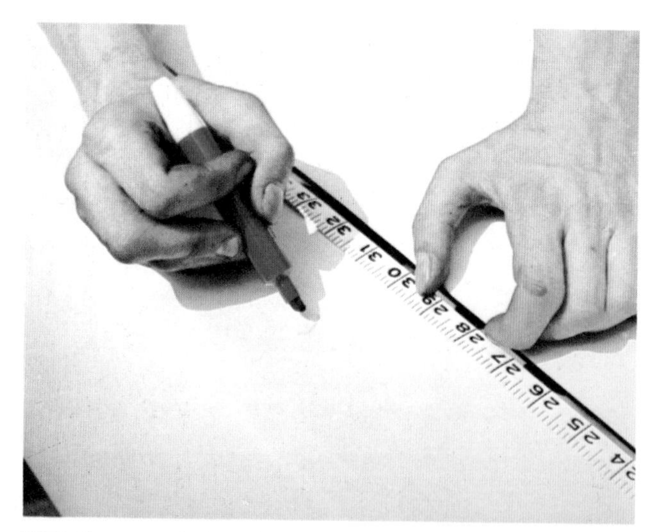

20 To fit a second wing mirror, measure the position of the first mirror, transfer it to the other wing and repeat the process

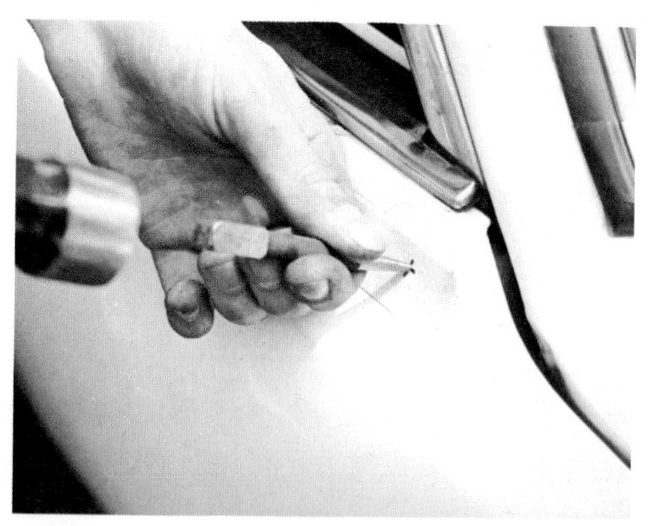

21 When fitting a door mirror, mark the positions of the screw holes on masking tape, and start them with a centre punch

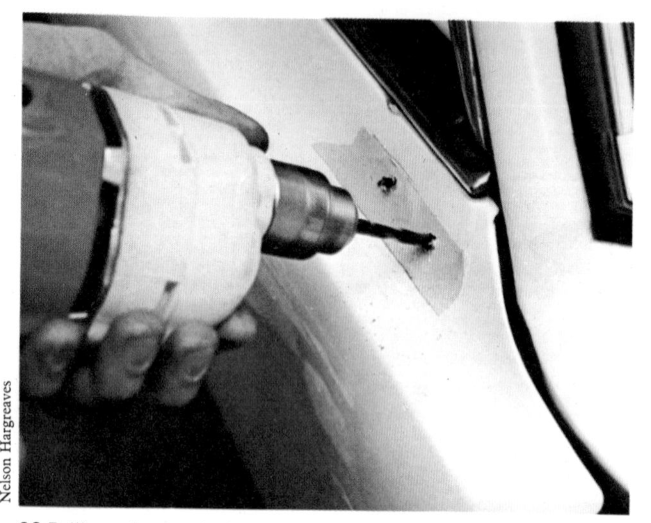

Nelson Hargreaves

22 Drill out the two holes, using the correct size of drill bit. If you use too large a drill the mistake is hard to rectify

23 With the majority of door mirrors, a plastic plinth has to be pushed into the holes, and is held in place by two screws

the rectangular mirror will rotate through 360° and will break off on severe impact (20 kg). They also market a telescopic caravan mirror. This has a stainless steel mirror head and measures 24 cm (9½in.) when retracted, and 33 cm (1ft. 1in.) when extended. It mounts on a plastic plinth supplied with the mirror, and is fixed to the wing by self-tapping screws.

Magnatex. This company is one of the largest manufacturers of mirrors in Britain. They market a large selection of mirror heads and stems, as well as complete units. The most recent model is the B9 wing mirror which incorporates spring-back action and stainless steel construction. They also produce a door mirror that has a stainless steel casing and anti-dazzle glass. It is available in flat or convex glass and right and left hand versions. The glass is covered with a special anti-shatter tape on the reverse side. A plastic plinth hides the securing screws. Magnatex have a new type of caravan mirror on the market. In normal use it serves as an ordinary wing mirror, with a swept-back arm. When the vehicle is used for towing the arm is snapped outwards from the car at an angle of 90°, and the mirror head is repositioned.

Claudet. This company markets a wide range of shaped mirrors. Most are wing mirrors with round or elliptical heads, but they have a clip-on door mirror which clamps on to the window surround, and a mirror suitable for wing or door mounting.

Hella. A German company producing a range of racing mirrors in streamlined bullet shape.

Raydyot. The Raydyot range includes a compact caravan mirror, which can be used as an ordinary wing mirror, or extended for towing a caravan. In either position it can be further extended by swivelling the head through 180°, giving a total of four positions.

Harry Moss. Harry Moss market several designs of mirror ranging from the Sprint, which has a swivelling base plate to keep the mirror-head horizontal, to their door mounting mirror. They also import Italian Sebring Mach 1 racing mirrors which can be supplied in lightweight plastic or heavy duty metal.

Alexander. This well-known firm make a bolt-on door mirror, in chrome or matt black; also the Raceview range of racing mirrors in a choice of finishes.

Barnet Plastics. They make the periscope type of caravan towing mirror, available from accessory shops.

Fitting wing mirrors

The most difficult part of fitting wing mirrors is deciding where to position them. Remember, once you have drilled the holes for the mirrors, you cannot change your mind unless you are prepared to undertake bodywork repairs. Patience and a little forethought are essential.

Select a level parking place that allows a good view rearwards. An ordinary suburban street is ideal, especially if

24 Clip the mirror in position over the plinth, having unscrewed a small retaining grub screw. Push the mirror firmly home

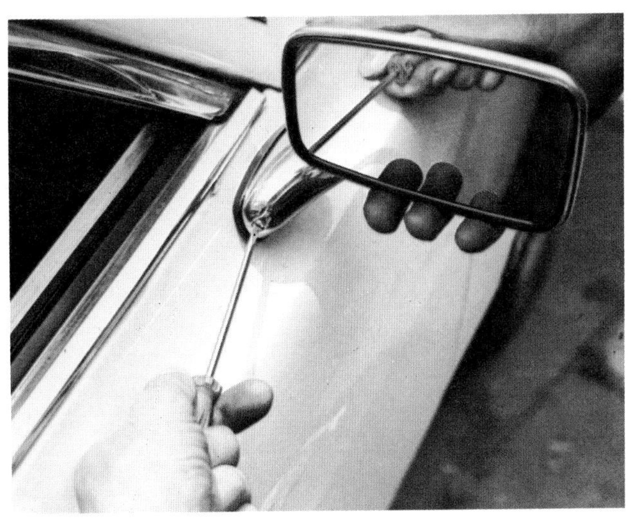

25 With the mirror properly fitted on the plinth, tighten the grub screw which holds it in place, and adjust the mirror by twisting

there are parked cars behind to give you a perspective as you align the mirrors.

Sit in the driving seat and make sure your interior mirror is correctly aligned. You should aim to reduce the blind spots on either rear quarter as much as possible when fitting your mirrors, at the same time making sure that the wing mirror allows you to see enough of the road behind to make fitting worthwhile.

Have an assistant hold the mirror upright on the wing. You should experiment with the exact position until you obtain the maximum field of vision. Bear in mind that when finally fitted the mirror will be about an inch lower, if it is a single bolt fixing. If you position the mirror too close to the windscreen pillar you may find you have to peer round the pillar. This defeats the object of the mirror, which is to afford easy rearward vision.

When you have the mirror in a satisfactory position, your assistant should mark with a felt tip pen the spot where the base of the mirror stem rests on the wing. Feel under the wing to make sure the position you have chosen is not double-skinned. If it is, find a point as near to the original as possible. Remember, the mirror stem can be mounted on the side of the wing if there is enough room to accommodate the securing nut and washer.

With the final position determined, mark it clearly with the felt tip pen, making two marks where two set screws will secure the mirror. Next place strips of masking tape around the pen marks to protect the paintwork from accidental damage when you begin to drill. Use a centre-punch to begin the hole, then drill a 3 mm ($\frac{1}{8}$in.) pilot hole. You can either use a suitably sized hole cutter—most wing mirrors with one bolt fixing are around 16 mm ($\frac{5}{8}$in.)—or enlarge the hole by using a bigger drill followed by a thin round file. If you use the second method, it is a good idea to remove the rubber or nylon washer from the mirror, place it over your mark, and scribe round the inside diameter to give the exact dimension of the hole. Screw-secured mirrors can be fitted by simply drilling two small holes of the size specified in the manufacturer's instructions included with the mirror. Make sure the insulating rubber is fitted between the mirror base and the car body, then secure the mirror with the self-tapping screws, or nuts and bolts, whichever are supplied.

Single bolt mirrors require a slightly different technique. Remove any protective dust cap from the threads on the stem. Take off the hexagon nut and the shakeproof washer. Insert the base of the stem through the hole in the wing, keeping the mild steel washer and the plastic washer on the stem. These protect the bodywork, and are important to the correct working of the spring-back action. From beneath the wing, fit the shakeproof washer and the hexagon nut, and tighten the nut, making sure the mirror arm is at the required angle from the side of the wing. To prevent the spring-back mechanism from working when tightening, two flats are provided under the skirt at the base of the arm. These are exposed by turning the arm through 90° (fig. 19). Tighten the mirror fully, making sure the arm does not go out of alignment.

With the mirror locked into the desired position, check that the spring-back action works properly. Replace the dust cap on the threaded section of the stem below the wing.

Fine adjustment can now be made by slightly slackening the locknut at the back of the mirror, which has the effect of releasing pressure on the ball socket. Your assistant can rotate the mirror while you check from the driving seat that the right position has been achieved. When it has, your assistant can carefully tighten the locknut.

If the single-nut mirrors are fitted with plinths, the stem passes through the steel and plastic washers, the plinth itself (which rests on the wing), the wing, and the shakeproof washer and nut.

Fitting door mirrors

Door mirrors are fitted in a similar way to wing mirrors, and usually have a two-hole fixing. Take care in siting clip-on mirrors on the window frame. You may find that your sideways vision can be blocked by the mirror particularly when entering roundabouts.

Most door mirrors use self-tapping screws. Some new cars are now fitted with pre-drilled holes and captive nuts. Where nuts and bolts are used, you will have to remove the interior trim on the door panel if no holes are already drilled. The procedure for removing the trim is outlined on pages 26 and 27.

Adjustment of the mirrors is by means of a concealed screw in some models, or a screw at the base of the mirror in others. Take care making adjustments. Some mirrors, such as those made by Autosafe, use adjuster screws operated by an Allen key. Right hand mirrors have left hand threads on the adjuster screws, left hand mirrors have a right hand thread.

It is quite possible to fit both wing and door mirror to your car, but be careful to line them up so that the door mirror does not obscure your view through the wing mirror.

Choosing auxiliary lamps

Fitting auxiliary lamps to your car can make all the difference to your ability to drive safely in treacherous conditions—or faster if the road is good. They come in three kinds—driving lamps, fog lamps and spot lamps—each with a specific purpose, and none costing more than a few pounds to install.

Driving lamps

Driving lamps are generally used to supplement headlamps for high-speed night driving. Their beam patterns are similar to those of normal headlights on main beam, with an intense core of light surrounded by illumination of reducing intensity (fig. 4). Although the filament may have the same power as that of the main beam in a twin filament headlamp bulb, the light projected is much more powerful than that of a normal main beam. This is because the driving lamp is designed as a single-function unit, whereas a headlamp, providing both main and dipped beams, is something of a compromise. Beam pattern is usually oval in shape, but the intensity of its core varies from lamp to lamp, even among models from the same manufacturer, and depends on two principal factors: the diameter and design of the reflector.

Spot lamps

Spot lamps can usually be recognized by their almost totally clear lens and are designed to project a pencil beam of very high intensity and little peripheral illumination. In this case, the core of the beam is circular, and its range is greater than that of the equivalent driving lamp. Since the beam is so narrow, spot lamps are suitable for use only where range is more important to a driver than lateral spread. Their purpose, therefore, is to illuminate the road well beyond the range of the car's headlights and to assist fast driving on straight roads by giving earlier indication of approaching hazards (fig. 1).

Fog lamps

Fog lamps are the most specialized type of auxiliary lamp, and are designed to help you see in conditions of very poor visibility. Recognizable by their deeply fluted lenses, they have a beam pattern which is fan-shaped, spreads out through at least 160°, and can be seen to end horizontally in line with the driver's eyes (fig. 5). The problem with car lights in fog is that light is reflected back into the driver's eyes by the minute particles of water. By eliminating light

2 Rally cars, like this Ford Escort, are usually equipped with a dazzling array of auxiliary lights to make night driving easier

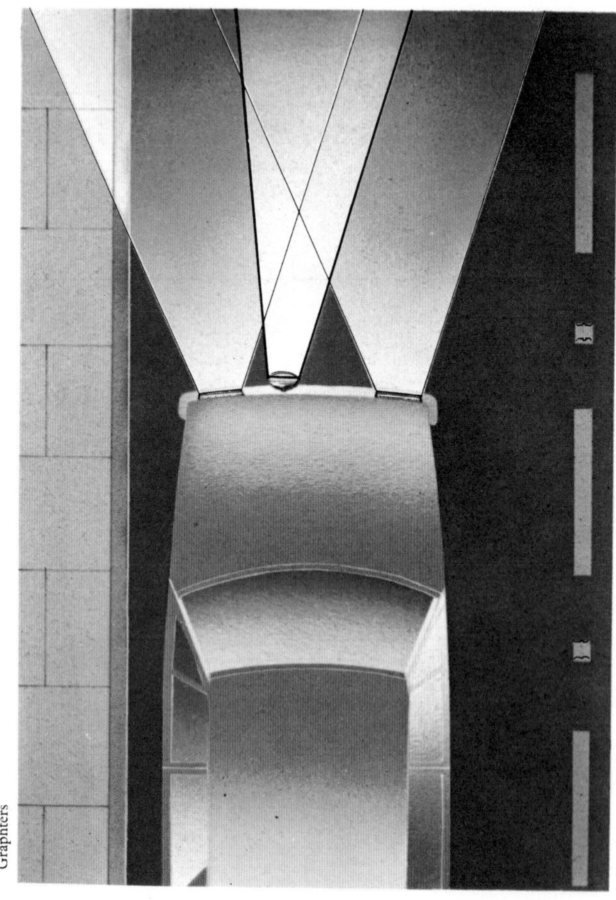

1 The narrow, pencil-like beam of a typical spot lamp. The wider angle of the car's headlamp beams enables the driver to see both the kerb and the centre of the road, while the spot lamp shines straight ahead to warn of any oncoming obstructions or hazards

3 A typical fog lamp beam in profile. By shining below the level of the driver's eyes, the beam cuts through the fog bank without reflecting any light back into them. It is this reflection which makes driving in fog with ordinary headlamps so difficult.

above the actual level of the fog lamp, such reflections are kept to a minimum and the beam can be seen to penetrate the fog, picking out obstacles to the front and sides (fig. 3).

The beam of a good fog lamp is at its most intense immediately below the 'cut-off point' (where it ends), and decreases closer to the ground to produce a carpet of light on the road surface. The wide-angled beam also serves to illuminate 'cat's eyes' in the centre of the road and the kerb; in fact, in areas where really thick fog is common, it is better to fit a pair of fog lamps rather than one spot and one fog lamp as is sometimes recommended.

Tungsten filament or quartz halogen?

The majority of auxiliary lamps on the market today use bulbs of the halogen type and, generally speaking, it is only the low priced models which still employ the conventional tungsten filament bulb. An ordinary tungsten filament must glow at very high temperatures in order to produce light. This causes it literally to evaporate and in time the tungsten molecules deposit themselves on the inside of the glass bulb. Thus, the filament gets thinner and thinner and eventually breaks, while the coating on the bulb progressively reduces light output—an effect commonly known as 'blackening'.

Halogen bulbs are described by various terms—quartz, quartz iodine, iodine vapour, IVB, quartz halogen, tungsten halogen, or just simply halogen—all of which mean the same. The bulbs, developed principally by Philips in collaboration with Cibié during the early 1960s, have far greater efficiency watt for watt than conventional bulbs. They give something like double the light for any given wattage. As in a conventional bulb, the filament is tungsten, but it is enclosed in a smaller quartz bulb filled with a gas derived from one of the halogen elements—iodine, bromine or fluorine. The smaller enclosure enables the filament to reach much higher temperatures, and consequently it emits a more intense, whiter light.

Another useful characteristic of the halogen bulb is that some of the evaporating molecules combine with the gas and tend to re-deposit themselves on the filament, thus prolonging its life and reducing 'blackening'. One thing you must remember, however, is not to touch a halogen bulb; perspiration will almost certainly shorten its life. Should you have to touch one, the bulb should be cleaned carefully using pure alcohol.

Quartz halogen bulbs have, by their greater efficiency, made a substantial contribution to safer night-time driving, and their many advantages far outweigh the extra cost. Furthermore, recent advances in bulb technology have been accompanied by improvements to reflectors which now provide clearer, crisper beams. Reflector quality is very important—they should be highly polished, precisely shaped and free from any irregularities which could produce stray beams. The glass used must be clear and pure, since any imperfections here will also reduce the effectiveness of the beam.

Lamp accessories and fitting

When buying auxiliary lamps, you will also have to purchase the correct mounting brackets, electric cable and switches. Using cable and switches of inadequate current-carrying ability could result in damage to the lamps and to your car's electrical system. Cables for fog or driving lamps should be in the order of 28/030 gauge. Switches should have a minimum rating of 10 amps, since each will be operating a pair of lamps (probably each rated at the usual 55 watts).

For higher wattages, even more substantial switches may be required, although the current through them can be reduced by placing a voltage relay—rather like a starter solenoid—near the lamps. Finer wires can then be safely employed between this and the switch. A further precaution is to place a fuse in the supply line to each pair of lamps, so that if one fails and causes a short circuit, only that par-

4 The beams of two auxiliary driving lamps, designed to act as a complement to normal main beam headlights. Fitting driving lamps puts a great deal more light at your disposal, making night-time driving safer. They also help to cover any 'blind spots'

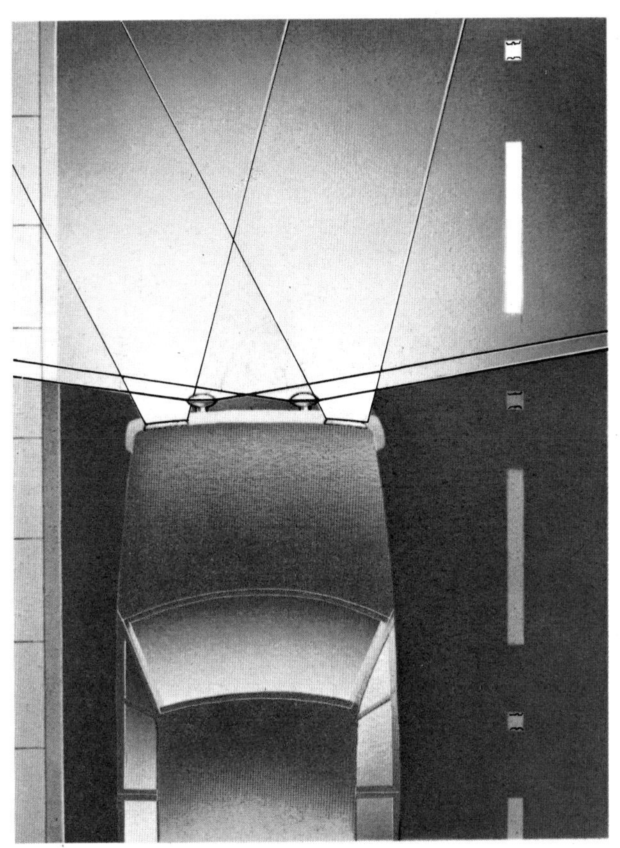

5 Fog lamp beams, as seen from above, have a much greater degree of spread than conventional headlights. This is because they are designed to cut through a fog bank, rather than pierce it, which would cause light to be reflected back into the driver's eyes

ticular circuit will go dead, nothing else will be affected, and there will be little risk of fire or burned electrical contacts. If you are buying a relay or fuse, get it at the same time as your lamp or lamps and consult your dealer as to the correct rating.

All good auxiliary lamps are supplied with some form of mounting spigot or plinth, but because of the frequent changes in frontal shape of modern cars, lamp manufacturers no longer provide mounting brackets with their units. In many cases, the spigot can be bent or adjusted so that it can be attached direct to the car bodywork; other lamps are designed specifically for back-mounting (that is, to the radiator grille). If a bracket is essential, however, it can usually be obtained from the manufacturer or your local dealer. When buying your lamps, make sure that you have a good idea of where they will go and that in this position, they comply with any legal requirements that may be in force—this will forestall any later problems when you come to fit them.

Legal requirements

British regulations governing forward facing auxiliary lamps state that if a pair is fitted, they must be positioned symmetrically and be of the same colour, either white or amber. If desired, a pair may consist of one fog lamp and a matching spot or driving lamp. Maximum height from the centre of any lamp to the ground must not exceed 107 cm (42in.) and if the lamp is placed between 107 cm and 61 cm (24in.), it must either be wired to extinguish when the headlights are dipped, or else be permanently fixed so as to avoid dazzling other drivers (fig. 6).

Lamps placed below 61 cm from the ground may be used only in conditions of poor visibility, such as in fog or when snow is actually falling. Both lamps in a pair must be mounted at identical heights and positioned so that they are the same distance from the centre of the front of the car. On cars first registered in the UK before December 31 1970, the distance between the inner edge of each lens must not be less than 35 cm (13.8in.), but on cars registered after this date, lamps must be placed so that they are not more than 40 cm (15.8in.) away from the outside edge of the car's body (measured to the outer edge of the lens) (fig. 6). Again, if a pair is fitted, they must always be lit at the same time and should not be used singly. Single auxiliary lamps, whether spot, fog or driving, may be used only in conjunction with headlights and never by themselves.

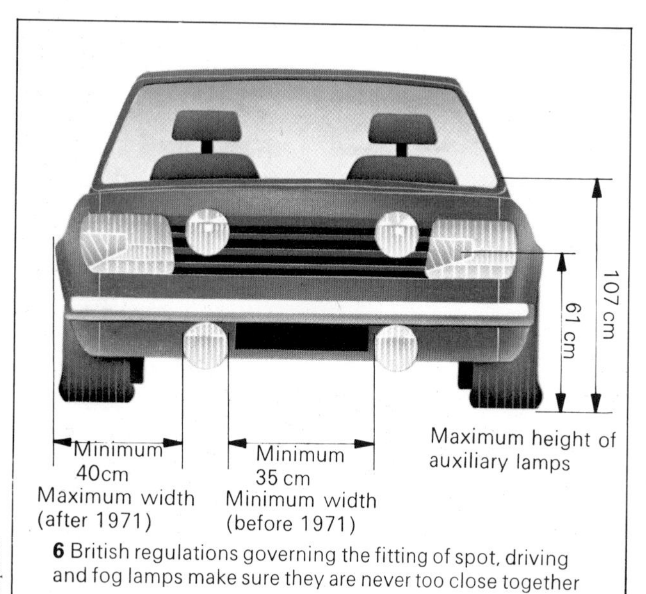

6 British regulations governing the fitting of spot, driving and fog lamps make sure they are never too close together

Graphters

Choosing your lamps

Before actually going ahead and buying lamps, be absolutely clear which kind you want. If you expect to be driving regularly in conditions of bad visibility, then choose either a pair of fog lamps or matching fog and spot lamps. High-speed driving outside towns may well become easier if you have a pair of long-range spot lamps, but remember that they are really useful only where prolonged use of main-beam headlights is possible. Driving lamps are the obvious choice if you feel that your car's headlights are inadequate, and at night they will give added lateral spread as well as filling any 'blind spots'.

The colour of auxiliary lamps—white or amber—is very much a personal preference. All lamps emit some light from the blue part of the spectrum, which scatters more easily than other colours and therefore tends to dazzle. By cutting it out with a yellow filter, dazzle is reduced but so is the beam's intensity. This leaves you with a choice between a brighter white lamp and a less dazzling but dimmer amber one.

The market

There are many British and Continental firms making auxiliary lamps, but the following gives a good cross-section of the different designs available.

7 This group of lamps includes (1) a Hella spot lamp (2) and (3) two Bosch Nighteyes fog lamps (4) a Stadium Satellite fog model (5) a Lucas Square 8 fog lamp (6) a Wipac Master Guide fog lamp and (7) a fog lamp from Raydyot

8 Here are two strikingly designed spot lamps—the SEV Marchal Starlux (1) and the Carello Luxor (2)

Bosch: This German manufacturer produces an extensive range of matching fog and driving lamps. The Nighthawk GT models are circular, with black Resicoat bodies, and are intended for upright mounting, while the Nighteyes range have similar bodies, but are rectangular and can be mounted either upright or suspended. Bosch also make the large, 100 watt, Jumbo Rally Floodlamp with a powerful spread beam.

Carello: This Italian firm produces another range of matching fog and spot lamps in varying sizes and of a distinctive design.

Ceag: This firm markets under the Lumax brand name. Both fog and spot lamps are available, with round or rectangular lenses. They have stainless steel bodies and are fitted by means of an ingenious ball joint bracket.

Cibié: One of the largest manufacturers: their products are generally expensive but of high quality. All can be mounted either upright or in the pendant position—pointing downwards—by means of a single 10 mm bolt and a swivel fixing to allow for angular adjustment. There are ten models in the range, both round and rectangular. Fog, spot and driving lamps are all covered, including the Bi-oscar combined fog/driving lamp, and all are supplied with a plastic protective cover.

Hella: This German firm produces eight models, for all of which there are fog and driving lamp versions. Bodies are either matt black with chrome rims or chromium-plated. Round models are mounted upright, while the rectangular ones can also be fixed downwards.

Marchal: This French manufacturer offers a comprehensive range of fog, spot and driving lamps. The Magnum range have chrome rims and silver-grey bodies, the Starlux are in stainless steel, and the Magnalux lamps have a chromium-plated finish. 100 watt bulbs are optional, on some models.

Lucas: This well-known accessory firm markets the Square 8 model, which is rectangular with a black body and chromed rim. Available in fog and spot forms, it can be mounted either in the upright or pendant position.

Raydyot: Three models are available from this maker, and all can be bought either as driving lamps with a clear lens, or as fog lamps with a choice of clear or amber. There are two round and one rectangular styles and bodies are in black or stainless steel.

Sedan: This firm, which makes all types of lighting equipment, offers pairs of matching fog/spot lamps in three sizes. Of all-metal construction, the smallest is available in either chrome or matt black, and the larger two in matt black only.

Stadium: This firm offers a pair of compact rectangular fog and spot lamps under the trade name Satellite. One excellent feature is their clamp-type brackets, which enable them to be fitted over the edge of the bumper and locked with a special key. They can also be bought with a Vario unit, which adjusts light intensity to suit prevailing conditions.

Wipac: This firm's principal model is the Hair Raiser rally lamp. With a silver-grey steel body and chromed rim, it is offered in three forms—standard lens, long range lens and short-range fog lens. It can be mounted upright or inverted. The Rally Major and slightly smaller Master Scout are made in stainless steel as are the rectangular Master Pilot and Master Guide units. The Big Imp models come in three forms—as dipping headlamp, driving lamp and spot lamp; the Big Imp Junior is a similar, but smaller, version.

9 Another sample of the lamps available including (1) a Cibié Apollo driving lamp (2) a Cibié Super Oscar spot lamp (3) a driving lamp from Ceag (4) a Wipac Master Scout driving lamp (5) a Cibié Iode 35 driving lamp and (6) a Hella driving lamp

Choosing and fitting reversing lights

A reversing lamp is undoubtedly one of the most important safety features on a car. Even in daylight it provides a clear warning to other drivers that you are about to reverse, and helps avoid the small but costly shunts that plague every motorist. Most new cars have reversing lights built into their rear light cluster. If your car does not, fitting one is a relatively easy job.

As there are many kinds of reversing lamp on the accessory market, supplied with a variety of fittings, you should easily find one that looks stylish on your car.

The market

Most major auxiliary lamp manufacturers offer a range of reversing lamps. As with fog and spot lamps (see pages 112 to 115), those made by the big European names—Cibié Bosch, Lucas, Hella—are expensive but of high quality. Some lamps are designed to fit in a particular way while others are supplied with universal fixings, so before buying take a good look at the back of your car to see where a reversing lamp will go. There are a number of lamps intended to fit flush against the car bodywork (fig. 2). Although they are compact and unobtrusive, they do require two holes to be drilled in the panel to which they are attached. Most larger reversing lamps are supplied with a single bolt bracket and securing nut (fig. 3). The bracket can be adjusted to hold the lamp in either an upright or pendant position, and the bolt itself is fixed through a hole drilled in the top or bottom of the bumper. Many firms now manufacture clamp brackets which eliminate the need to drill holes. Some lamps are supplied complete with these brackets. With others you have to buy them as an extra. The Hella Universal bracket, for example, can be clamped in a variety of ways to the lip of your bumper and is especially useful on cars with unusual bumper designs.

Having decided what type of fitting to use you can go ahead and buy a lamp. Among European manufacturers Bosch, Lucas, Cibie, Marchal and Hella all offer distinctive rectangular lamps with a variety of finishes and fixings. The Hella range also includes a round one. In the UK Wipac offer perhaps the widest range of reversing lamps, both round and rectangular. Lamps are also available from Lucas, Raydyot, Lumax, Sedan, Stadium and many smaller manufacturers. Stadium make two unusual lamps. Their Brilliant reversing lamp uses a quartz halogen bulb for extra brightness (see page 113), and comes equipped with a clamp fitting. The Stadium 'two-in-one' lamp has a red plastic lens cover which can be clipped on to convert it to a fog warning lamp. This, however, will only be usable if the lamp is operated by a dashboard switch and not actuated automatically.

Operating switches

When buying a reversing lamp you are unlikely to get anything more than the lamp itself. You will have to buy as extras an adequate supply of electrical wire and a switch.

There are two basic types of switch: a dashboard switch which the driver operates before selecting reverse gear; and a switch which goes into the gearbox. The gearbox switch is found on nearly every car which has reversing lights fitted as standard. As the selector fork in the gearbox moves into the reverse position it presses against a plunger in the switch, causing it to activate the light for as long as the car remains in reverse gear. A third type of switch fits

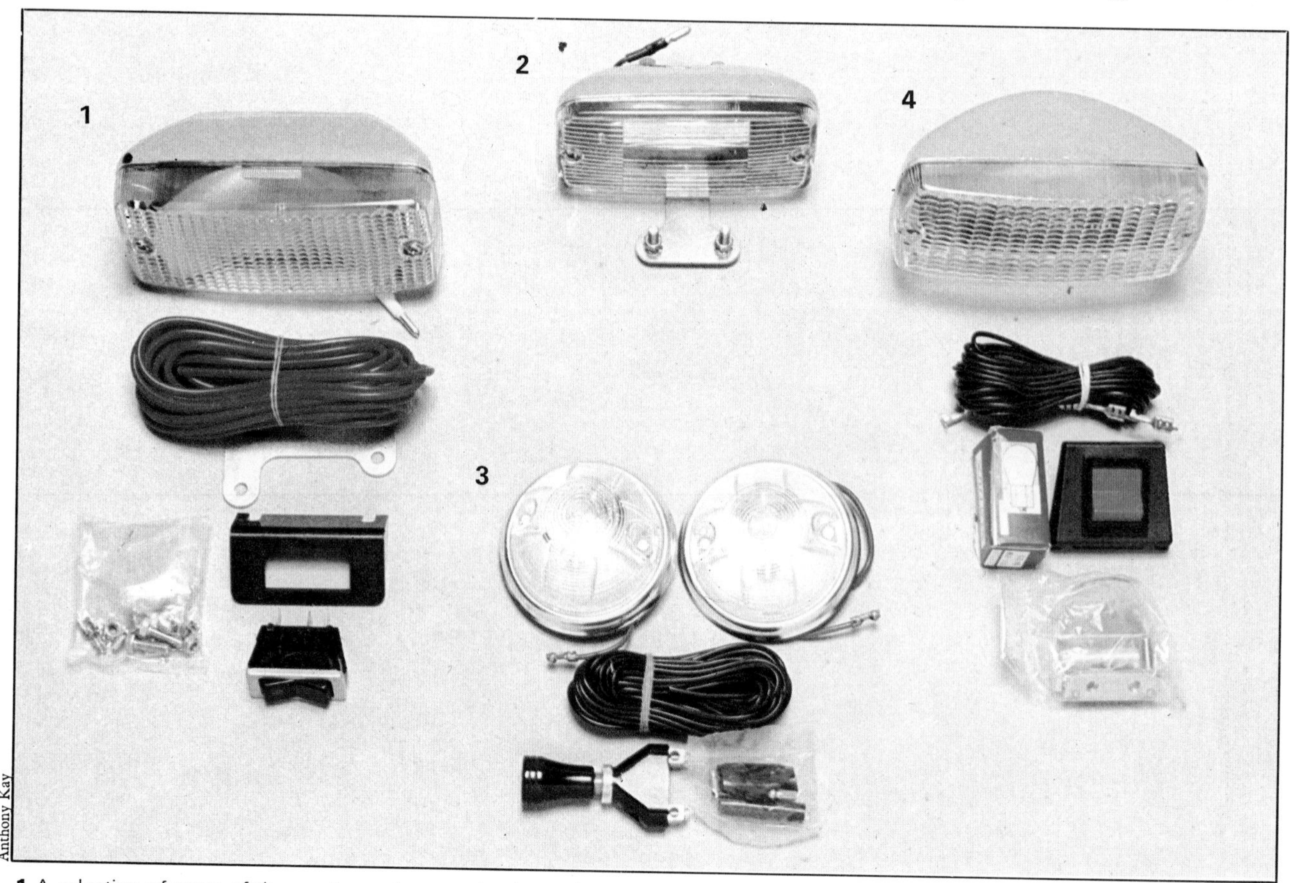

1 A selection of some of the most popular reversing lamps in the UK: (1) Cibié Super Marignan reversing lamp kit (2) Cibié Marignan reversing lamp (3) Britax twin reversing lamp kit with flush-fitting lamps (4) Britax RL 1 reversing lamp

the speedometer cable, but this kind of unit is now obsolete and is rarely encountered.

The obvious advantage in having reversing lights which work automatically is that you do not have to remember to switch them on and off. Fortunately, installing an automatic switch is not as difficult as it sounds because many gearboxes have provision for fitting one. Many manufacturers include switches in their parts range. To confirm that a switch can be fitted to your car contact your dealer. Ask specifically for a 'gearbox reversing light switch' and quote the model, year, and if possible chassis number of your car. If a switch is available, you can ask the dealer where on the gearbox the socket for it is located. You will probably be told that there is either a 'blanking plug' or a 'cover plate' which must be undone. The blanking plug consists of a plug with a nut on the end, screwed into the gearbox in place of the switch. The cover plate will simply cover the socket and be held by screws.

One problem with reversing light switches is that they may be difficult to buy off the shelf and must be ordered, so do not wait to buy one until you are ready to start the job.

If your car does not have provision for an automatic switch, or you do not want to work on the gearbox, the simple alternative is a dashboard switch. Remember though that in most countries (including the UK) the law requires the switch to have a warning light to remind you to turn it off. The best type of switch to use is one with a light built in and push-pull operation to prevent it being turned on accidentally. The switch can be fitted straight into a hole in the dashboard, but it is often easier to mount it in an individual panel which is secured with self-tapping screws underneath the dashboard.

Fitting a flush-fit reversing lamp

If you are fitting a flush-fit reversing lamp, you will have to drill three holes in the rear panel or boot lid of your car—two for the fixing bolts or screws and one for the supply wire. Start by inspecting the proposed site for the lamp, and decide whether it will be possible to bolt through the panel. If the panel has two layers, or a cross-member runs across where you want to drill, bolting the lamp on could be difficult and you will have to use self-tapping screws.

Having decided on the fixing method, buy the relevant bolts or screws, together with a suitable drill bit. Most manufacturers recommend specific sizes for their particular lamps, but if there are no instructions use a bit of about 3 mm or $\frac{1}{8}$in. diameter for screws, and 6 mm or $\frac{1}{4}$in. for bolts. You will also need a centre punch to make sure that the drill bit does not slip and mark the paintwork when you start to drill the panel.

Start by unscrewing the lens cover. Press the lamp against the fixing surfaces, and using the back of it as a template mark the position of the two bolt holes and the supply lead hole (fig. 4). Remove the lamp, and indent the marks using a hammer and centre punch (fig. 5). Now carefully drill the three holes. Feed the supply wire through the extra hole, screw or bolt the lamp in place (fig. 7) and refit the lens cover.

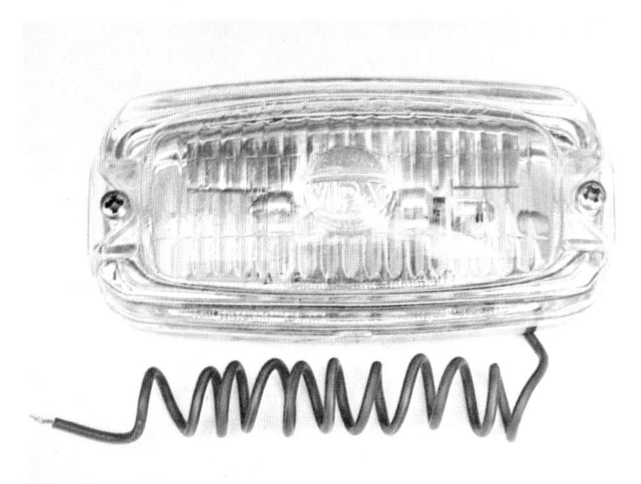

2 This Wipac Flushbeam reversing lamp is typical of the flush-fit type which mount straight on to a body panel without brackets

3 A more conventional Bosch reversing lamp. The body of the lamp is bolted to the mounting bracket, which is fully adjustable

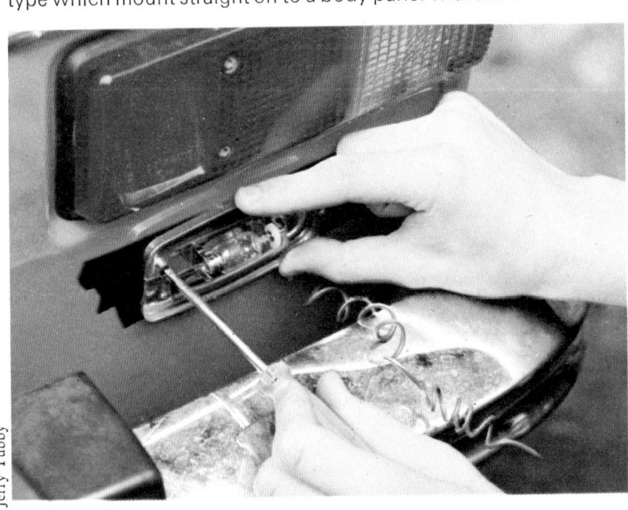

Jerry Tubby

4 With the flush-fit lamp, start by marking the drill holes. To stop the drill slipping, it is best to cover the area with tape

5 Having removed the lamp, which is used as a template, you can turn the marks into indentations with the aid of a centre-punch

Jerry Tubby

6 Having drilled holes of a suitable size, the live supply wire can be fed through the panel and into the luggage compartment

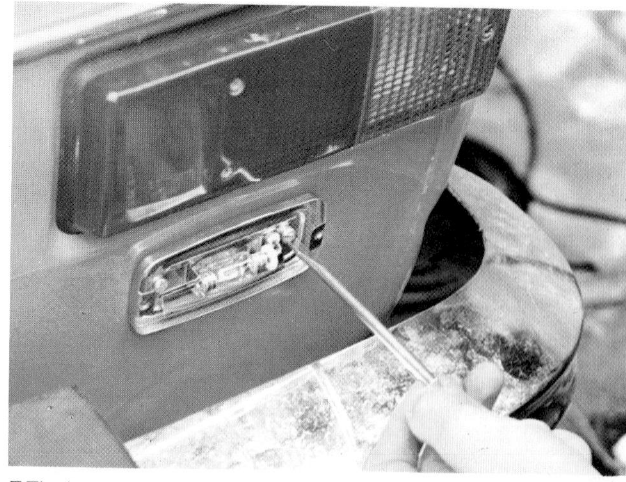

7 The lamp can now be secured in place by means of the screws or bolts provided. Do not forget to remove the tape first

Fitting a bracket-mounted lamp

To fit a bracket-mounted lamp, start by choosing a suitable site for it, making sure that it does not obstruct the number plate. If the lamp is to be mounted using only the bracket bolt, two holes will have to be drilled in the relevant surface—one for the bolt, and a smaller one for the supply lead. A 10 mm ($\frac{3}{8}$in.) drill bit should be large enough for the bracket bolt, but measure the diameter of the bolt to make sure. A 6 mm ($\frac{1}{4}$in.) bit will be adequate for the smaller hole. As with any holes being drilled in chrome or body work, take care to start them with a centre punch to give the drill an adequate grip.

If the lamp is to be fixed using a clamp, make sure it will fit both the mounting bracket you are using and the point where it will be attached.

The bracket-mounted lamp illustrated (fig. 3) is not supplied with any wires at all, and it will therefore be necessary to connect up a live supply lead. Start by unscrewing the lens cover. You will find a tab connection on the bulb holder. Solder or crimp a spade connector to the end of a piece of suitable insulated wire, attach it to the tab, and feed it out through the grommet in the lamp body. Screw in the bulb, if it is supplied as a separate item, and refit the lens cover.

Next, indent the panel or bumper where the fixing bolt hole is to be drilled (fig. 12), and drill it. Change to the smaller bit and drill the wire hole. Next, unbolt the mounting bracket from the lamp (fig. 14), insert it through the appropriate hole and tighten the locknut provided (fig. 15). With the bracket secured, the final step is to bolt the lamp itself back on to it. Adjust the lamp to the correct angle before final tightening.

Fixing the reversing lamp with a clamp is much simpler but less secure. Simply bolt the clamp to the lamp bracket, clamp it round the bumper lip, and tighten the clamp bolt.

Wiring-up to a dashboard switch

If you are fitting a flush-fit lamp, it will almost certainly be earthed through the back plate directly to the car body. On the other hand a plastic-bodied bracket lamp will have an earth wire, and it should be connected at this stage. Having fed it through the rear panel, find a convenient earthing point in the boot or luggage compartment. Any screw or bolt attached to the car body will do. Connect the bared end of the wire to it, using a tag connector if possible. In the unlikely event of there being no screws or bolts, use a self-tapping screw to make the connection.

The other wire (the only one if there is no earth) is the

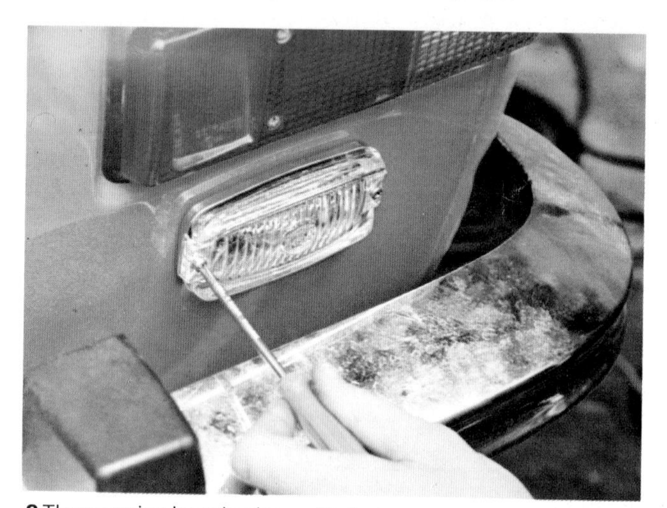

8 The reversing lamp in place with the lens cover screwed on. It will be earthed by its direct contact with the car bodywork

live supply. Some modern cars have wires built into the loom, as a provision for fitting reversing lights as optional extras. A wiring diagram is necessary to identify them, or you can consult your dealer to find out if your car has this facility. It is really much simpler to use your own wire. Connect a good length to the wire from the lamp, using a screw connector, and start to feed it, out of sight, towards the front of the car. You can make use of any interior panels by loosening them and running the wire behind. There will certainly be a hole in the rear bulkhead, if your

9 With a bracket-mounted lamp, start by unscrewing the lens cover to reveal the bulb holder and live supply connection point

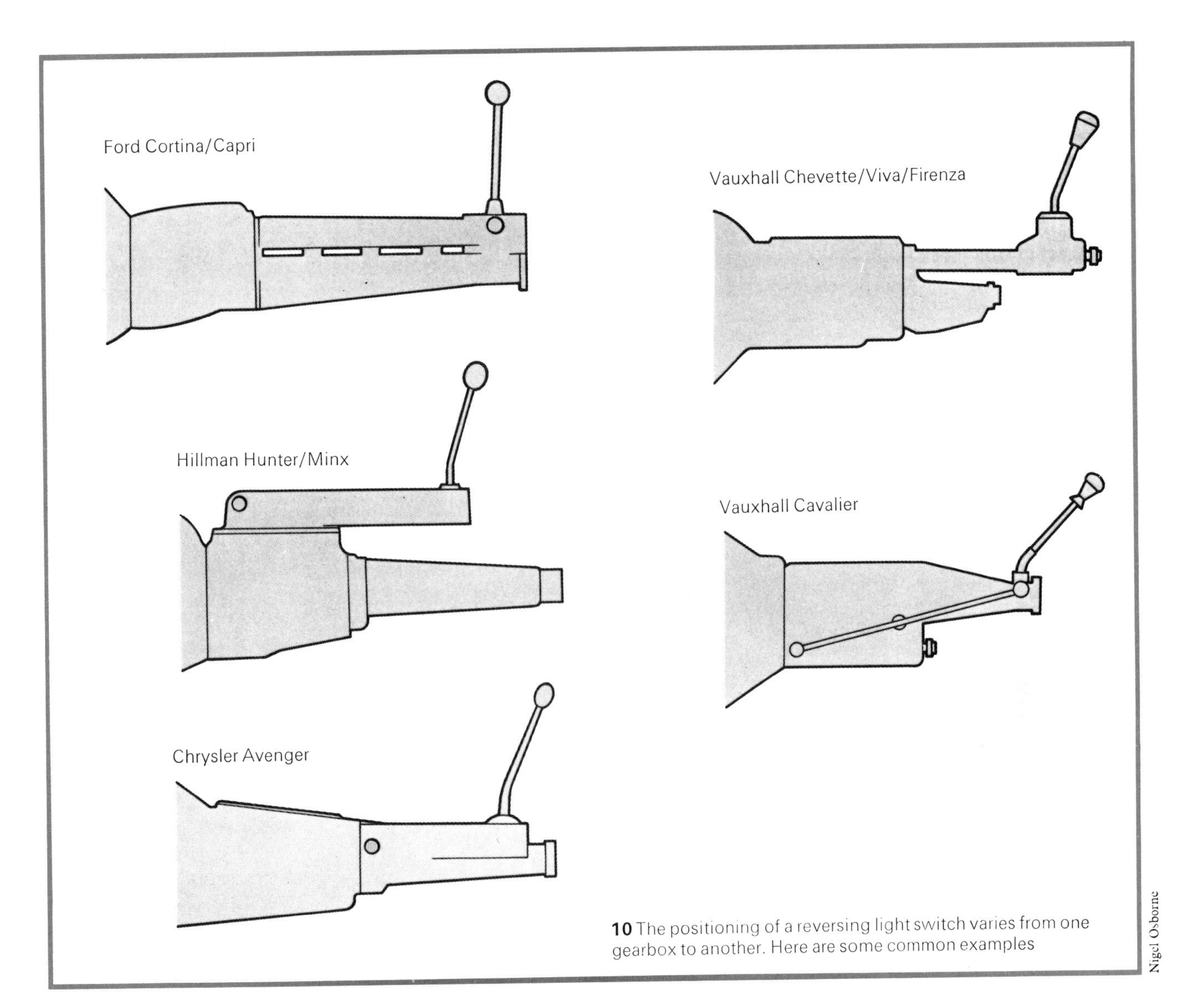

10 The positioning of a reversing light switch varies from one gearbox to another. Here are some common examples

car has a boot, and from there the wire can go under the back seat and carpet and up to the dashboard.

Using a spade connector, attach the loose end of the wire to one terminal on the reversing light switch (fig. 17). Take another length of wire, connect one end to the other switch terminal, and run it to the fusebox (fig. 18). The wire must be attached to a terminal on the fusebox which is activated only when the ignition is on. Identify this, either by consulting a wiring diagram or by using a test lamp. Once identified, secure the wire to it with an appropriate spade or bullet connector.

The final stage is to fix the switch in position. If it is to go in the dashboard, drill a small hole and enlarge it with a keyhole saw. File down the rough edges, unscrew the knob and securing ring on the switch, and feed it through the hole from behind. Screw the ring back on until the switch is tightly held, then refit the knob.

If you are mounting the switch in an individual panel, use the panel as a template and drill two holes underneath the dashboard. Fix the panel in place with two self-tapping

11 The live wire is then fed through the lamp body and connected to the appropriate (unearthed) tag on the bulb holder

12 Having chosen a suitable site for the bracket, like the bumper, stick on some protective tape and indent a mark with the punch

screws or a pair of bolts and attach the switch to it.

The lamp should now be ready for use. All that remains is for you to get into the habit of operating the switch every time you engage reverse gear.

Wiring-up to an automatic switch

To wire the reversing lamp to a gearbox-operated switch, follow the procedure for wiring up to a dashboard switch, until you reach the point where the supply wire has been fed under the carpet to the front of the car. You will now have to run the wire down to the gear change extension housing of your gearbox. There should be a convenient gap round the gear lever, once you have removed the carpet for easy access. If there are no holes you will have to drill one in the floor. In this case you must fit a rubber grommet round the wire to prevent leaks or short-circuits.

With the supply wire to hand, you can tackle the problem of fitting the switch itself. The typical switch (fig. 20), as fitted to the vast majority of cars, has a screw thread which goes into the gearbox. On the other end are two terminals; one for the wire from the lamp, the other for the wire from the fusebox.

Unfortunately, when you buy your reversing switch there will not be any instructions with it, so you must ask your dealer where the switch fits. If your car has provision for one, the threaded hole will have been blanked off in some way, generally with a plug which has a nut on the end. It is easily unscrewed with a spanner. On some cars there is a cover plate instead, but again it is simple to unscrew. The greatest difficulty you are likely to encounter is in actually finding the correct blanking plug. It can easily be confused with the gearbox bolts, drain plugs, and reverse stop

13 Do the same for the live wire hole on the rear panel and then drill on the punched marks which will stop the bit from slipping

14 To get more room to fit the mounting bracket, unbolt it from the lamp body, noting the position of all nuts and washers

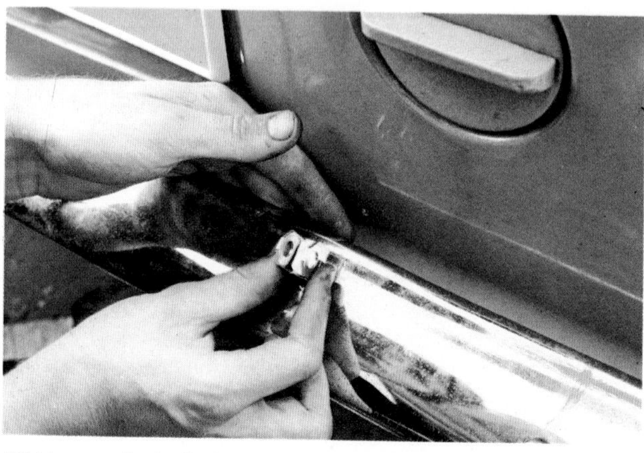

15 Next, undo the locknut on the bracket mounting pin. Insert the pin in the drill hole, replace the nut and tighten it up

16 Locate the lamp back on the bracket and replace the bolt which holds it. Adjust the angle of the lamp before final tightening

Jerry Tubby

17 The live wire is connected to one of the terminals on the dash mounted switch. This is fixed in place with two self-tapping screws

18 The wire connected to the other terminal on the switch is then run to an ignition-activated terminal on the fusebox

spring plungers. However a few general rules will help you to understand your dealer's more specific instructions. On front-engined rear wheel drive cars, the plug will almost certainly be on the gear change remote-control housing, either on one side or at the end. The same goes for most front wheel drive transverse-engined cars. On the other hand, on some front wheel drive cars such as the Renault 12 illustrated, the plug is located on the side of the gearbox casing (fig. 21).

Exactly how you approach fitting the switch depends a great deal upon its location. On some cars, where the blanking plug is near the base of the gear lever, it is possible to work from inside the car. Lift up the carpet and remove any cover plates for access. With other cars, like the one illustrated, you will have to work from underneath the car. Either way, it is best to jack up your car safely and have an exploratory look. Make sure that it is both well supported and secure on axle stands before you crawl underneath.

Having found the plug, unscrew it from the gearbox (fig. 21). Next screw in the switch and tighten it firmly with a spanner. Take the wire that you have run from the reversing lamp and solder or crimp a spade connector on to the end. Connect this to either of the two terminals on the switch (fig. 22). Do the same to the bared end of another length of wire. Connect this to the other switch terminal (fig. 23) and feed it up to the engine compartment. Tape it safely out of the way. The other end of this wire can now be connected to the fusebox in the same way as for the dashboard switch. Lower the car to the ground. Refit the gearbox cover in the passenger compartment if you have removed it, and replace all carpeting. You now have a reversing light system which works automatically.

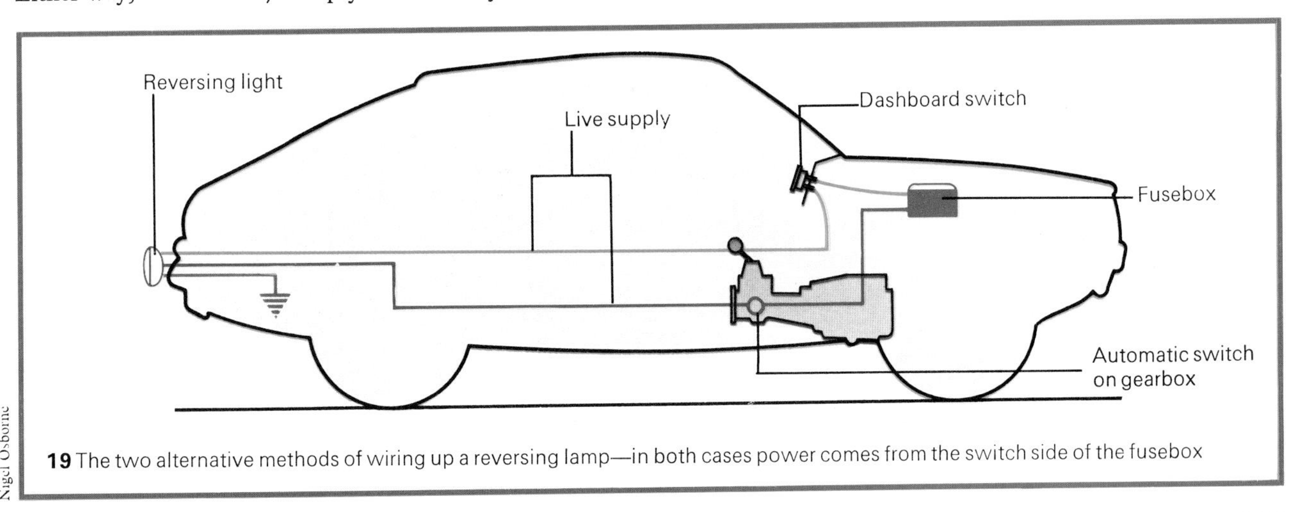

19 The two alternative methods of wiring up a reversing lamp—in both cases power comes from the switch side of the fusebox

Nigel Osborne

20 This typical gearbox reversing light switch fits a Renault 12. It operates by detecting movements in the reverse selector fork

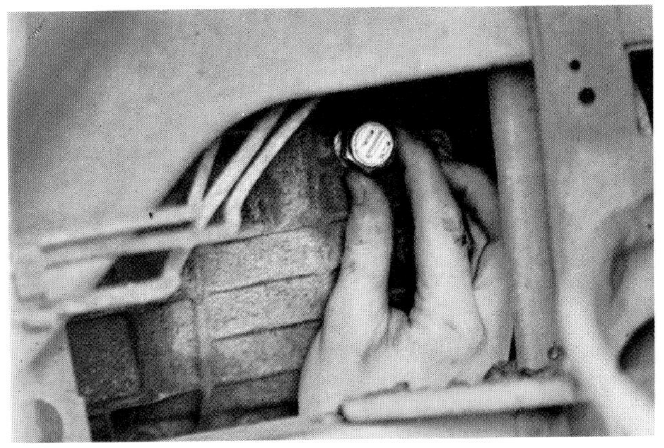

21 On this particular car, the blanking plug for the switch can be easily seen quite clearly on the side of the gearbox

22 The switch in position on the gearbox. As with the dash switch, there are two connections—the first will run to the lamp

23 The second connection is the one to the fusebox. The terminals on the switch should be tagged, so use spade connectors

Fitting an intermittent wiper control

When a car is being driven, it is imperative that the driver has clear vision through the windscreen. Normally the windscreen wipers and, if necessary, the washers can be employed to achieve this during both wet and dry road conditions. However, motorists will frequently encounter an "in-between" condition when there is only a slight drizzle that is just enough to wet the windscreen but which does not keep the windscreen wipers sufficiently "lubricated" for more than two sweeps of their operating arc. As the wipers clear the screen of water they begin to scrape over the temporarily dry surface and the driver is obliged to turn them off and then turn them on again very shortly afterwards as the drizzle wets the screen once more. This can be very irritating but the problem can be solved by fitting an intermittent wiper control unit.

Fitted as standard equipment on some cars, an intermittent wiper control unit delays the period between each complete sweep of the wiper blades. Most cars equipped with this feature have a fixed delay but the DIY car enthusiast can buy and fit a unit, such as that marketed by Hella (fig. 1), which has a variable delay of between four and

Jake Wynter

1 An intermittent wiper control kit. This Hella unit is simple to fit and available for a wide range of cars

20 wipes per minute. This means that very fine drizzle can be cleared from the windscreen just as easily as light rain. As the unit helps to prevent the wipers from operating on a dry screen, the wiper blades and the motor should last a great deal longer.

Buying an intermittent wiper control unit

Before you buy an intermittent wiper control unit, check that you can, in fact, fit one to your car. Some of the units will not operate when used on cars, such as some BL Jaguar and Rover models, where the windscreen wipers automatically park completely off the glass when they are turned off. If you are in doubt on this point consult your local dealer. The Hella unit can be used on cars with either positive or negative-earth but it cannot be used on cars with 6 volt electrical systems or without a self-park circuit. Once you have bought a unit make sure that the instructions and all the necessary fittings have been supplied with it. Hella in Australia supply fitting instructions for Australian-manufactured vehicles for which they supply kits.

Reading the instructions

Many car accessories are manufactured in one country and are intended for sale in many others. This is true of the Hella intermittent wiper unit which is made in Germany and exported for fitting to a wide number of models of car. Consequently, the instructions supplied with the unit are multi-lingual and cover the fitting procedure for several cars in a variety of popular manufacturers' ranges.

Before actually fitting the wipe control unit it is most important that you read and understand the set of instructions that are included in the kit. If you do not do this you are more likely to make a mistake at a later stage of the fitting procedure.

The instructions supplied with the Hella kit can be divided into three sections. The first of these can be found on the back of the kit's packaging. There are three pairs of wiring diagrams and the cars included on the instruction chart fall into one of the three wiring categories. Each pair of diagrams is numbered and shows the existing wiring for a windscreen wiper system and how the wiring should look once the intermittent wipe unit has been fitted. There is a key, beneath the diagrams, to explain what each of the symbols used in the diagrams mean. As everything on the back of the packet is explained in seven languages, put a ring around the wording that you will be using so that you can identify your instructions at a glance. Follow this practice as you work your way through all of the instructions.

To find out which of the three pairs of wiring diagrams is relevant to your car, consult the vehicle chart enclosed in the packet. This is the second section of the instructions. Locate your car on the chart and then look across to the first column. You will see there a number which corresponds to the relevant wiring diagram printed on the back of the packet in which the kit comes. The number in the first column for all of the Opel cars on the chart, for example, is "1". Thus if you own one of the Opel cars listed on the chart you will use the pair of diagrams on the back of the packet numbered "1". The remaining columns of the chart each contain an abbreviation of an instruction. These tell you how and where to connect the wire indicated at the top of the particular column relevant to your car. Using the Opel Manta as an example, the second column indicates that the "rt" wire must be connected to "WS 53a". The explanation of the abbreviations is contained in the instructions on the back of the chart. Once deciphered, the above instruction means that the red wire must be connected to terminal 53a which will be marked on your windscreen wiper switch. It is a simple matter, and advisable, to write down on the chart the meaning of all of the abbreviations. This will save you from having to continually turn the chart over to consult the other side, while you are working. If your car is not included in the chart, see below.

Next, examine the intermittent wipe unit itself. You will see that there are seven coloured wires emerging from the back of it (fig. 2). As the wires are uncoiled, you will find that two of these are, in fact, a single red wire which comes out from the unit and then goes back into it without a break. If your car's wiper motor draws its power supply via the main wiper switch, as with the first and third systems shown on the back of the packet, then you can leave the loop as it is. If, however, the wiper motor is earthed via the switch, as with the second system shown on the back of the packet, then you must cut the loop in two. Once the loop is cut, you will be left with two, short, red wires. Tape over the one that leads to the number 49 terminal, so that it cannot cause an electrical short-circuit and connect the other

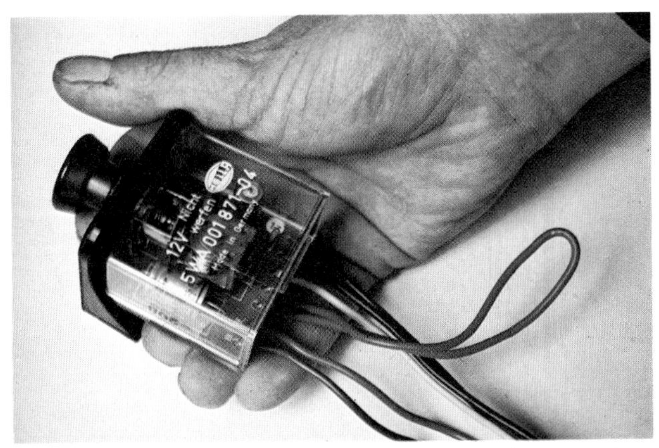

2 When uncoiled, you will see that there are seven wires emerging from the back of the unit. On some cars, the red loop must be cut

piece, leading to the 30/31 terminal, to a suitable earthing point on the car (fig. 17) or to the brown earth lead.

The remaining five wires to be considered are coloured one brown, one red, one yellow and two black. The points from which these wires emerge from the printed-circuit board at the back of the unit are numbered 31 (brown), 49 (red), 53 (yellow) and 31b1 and 31b2 (the two black wires). You will also find these numbers marked at the top of each column on the vehicle chart, next to the appropriate wire, as a further aid to identifying the wires.

Fitting the unit to the fascia

There are two methods of fitting the unit to the fascia. The first is to use the fixing bracket that is supplied with the kit to attach the unit beneath the fascia (fig. 6). The second is to discard the bracket and to mount the unit from behind the fascia after drilling a 6 mm ($\frac{1}{4}$ins) hole. This method can only be used where there is enough room behind the fascia to cater for the unit (fig. 4).

To fit the unit beneath the fascia panel first select a site (fig. 5). When doing this bear in mind that the control knob must be accessible to you while you are sitting in your normal driving position and that you should be able to operate it without taking your eyes from the road. It is best if you can position the unit so that you do not have to move your hand too far away from the steering wheel when you wish to operate it, though this may not always be possible. If the control knob is situated close enough to the main windscreen wiper switch, you will be able to turn one system on and the other off quite easily in the same movement. This will be useful if, for example, the rain becomes too heavy for the intermittent wipe unit to cope and you need to use the ordinary switch.

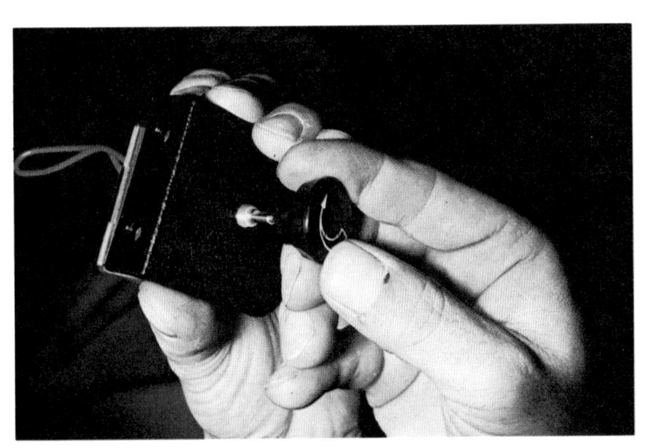

3 To remove the fixing bracket from the rest of the unit, first pull off the control knob. It is a simple push fit

With a site selected, disconnect the battery and check that there are no cables running behind the fascia at the point where you wish to drill. Then, using the fixing bracket as a template, with a centrepunch mark the position of the first hole. The fixing bracket can be removed from the unit by first pulling off the control knob (fig. 3). Drill the hole, secure the bracket loosely in position with a self-tapping screw and then, using the bracket as a template once more, carefully mark the position of the second hole, again using a punch. Now swivel the bracket out of the way and drill again (fig. 6). With the drilling completed, tighten both screws fully to secure the bracket (fig. 7) and then attach the rest of the unit to it (fig. 8). The unit should be held in place by means of the lock nut on the spindle. Finally, re-fit the control knob (fig. 9).

If you are going to fit the unit behind the fascia, you must

4 If you decide to fit the unit behind the fascia, check that there will be enough room for both it and the control knob

5 To fit the unit beneath the fascia, you may first need to remove items such as fuse box covers in order to gain working space

6 With the first hole drilled, and the position of the second hole marked, swivel the bracket out of the way and drill the second hole

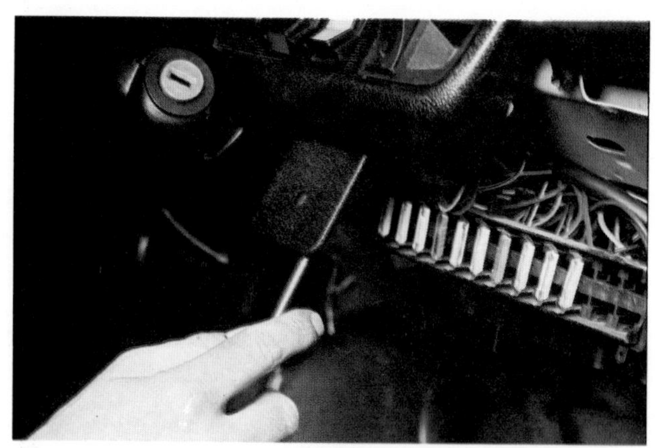

7 Secure the bracket firmly in position using the self-tapping screws supplied with the kit and a screwdriver

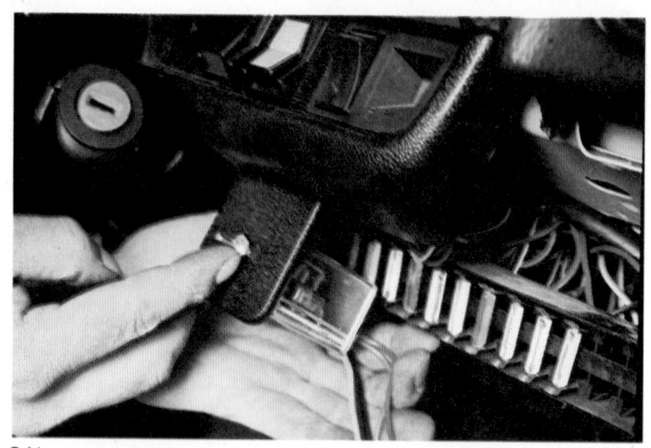

8 Next, attach the rest of the unit to the fixing bracket. The lock nut on the spindle should be finger tight

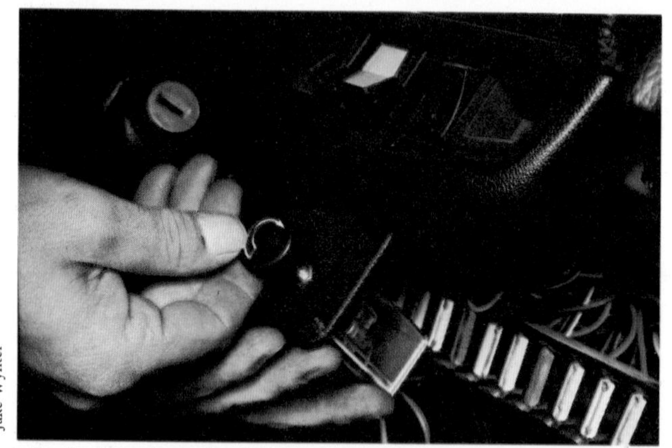

Jake Wynter

9 Re-fit the control knob to the spindle. The unit is now mounted and you can begin to connect the wiring

again select a suitable site but this time your choice may be restricted by other switches and wires already running behind the panel. When you have chosen a site, hold the unit in position to make sure that there will actually be enough room for it and estimate the point on the fascia where you will need to drill. Before you drill the hole in the fascia mark its position with a centrepunch. Drill the hole using short bursts of power so that the drill will be easier to control when it finally breaks through the fascia. Then, from the rear, push the control knob spindle through the hole in the fascia and use the lock nut to secure the unit in position. Lastly, re-fit the control knob.

With the unit mounted on the fascia, check the chart to see where you will need to make the electrical connections. On most cars, the connections have to be made at the existing windscreen wiper switch on the car but other vehicles require connections to be made at the cable leading from the wiper switch to the main wiring harness or at the ignition switch. You will need to gain access to the relevant control. If the wiper switch or the ignition switch is mounted on the fascia it can usually be removed from its hole by carefully unscrewing the outer locking ring and then withdrawing the switch from behind.

If the wiper switch is on the steering column, you will have to remove the column surround. This is usually located by several concealed screws which hold the two parts of the surround together and also secure the surround to the column. Look carefully underneath and check that you have not missed any screws before attempting to prise the two parts of the surround apart. If you are quite satisfied that there are no concealed screws, the surround may just be located by spring clips. Note carefully how the surround is made. Usually there is a seam in the moulding which conceals the joint between the two parts. Once you have identified the two parts, gently pull them away from each other. Do not be tempted to lever them apart with a screwdriver as this can damage the edges and spoil the final appearance.

When you have gained access to the necessary areas you can begin to connect the wiring.

Connecting the wiring

If you have studied the vehicle chart carefully, making the electrical connections should not present any real problems. However, be prepared to extend any of the wires from the unit if they are too short or to cut them if too long (fig. 10).

If you do need to extend any of them, use a piece of wire that is the same size and colour and make the join with a proper screw connector. Connect the wires in turn, starting

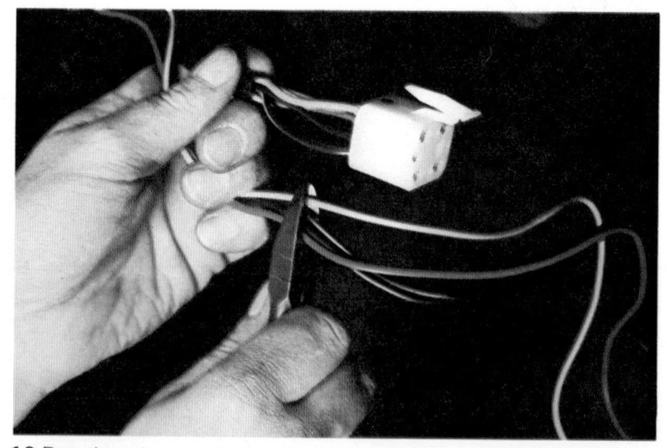

10 Run the wiper control unit wires to their connection points, and cut them to length if necessary

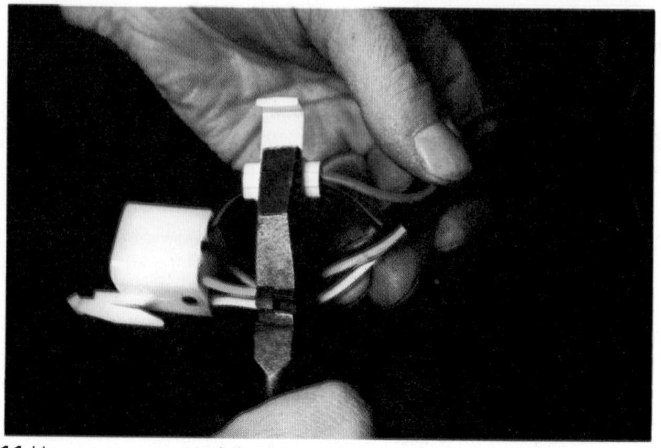

11 Use a connector to join the number 49 (red) wire, which provides the power supply to the Hella unit, with another wire

with number 49 (red) wire.

Number 49 (red): Consult the second column of the vehicle chart to establish where the number 49 wire should be connected. On most cars, this wire must be connected to a terminal on the main wiper switch. However, other cars require the wire to be connected to the fuse box and yet others require the connection to be made to the ignition switch. Once you have located the wire or terminal to which number 49 must be connected, you must decide how to make the join. If the connection is to be made to a terminal, then you may need to solder a spade connector to the wire so that you can push it on to the terminal. If the number 49 wire has to be connected to another wire, then use one of the Scotchlok connectors supplied with the intermittent wipe unit (fig. 11). Lay the two wires to be connected in the plastic connector, press the "knife" down, fold the tongue over the top of the connector "knife" and then press the tongue firmly home until it clips over the lug. The "knife" cuts through the insulation of each wire to make contact from one to the other.

Number 53 (yellow): The procedure for connecting the number 53 wire is the same as for the number 49 wire. Again, you must check the vehicle chart carefully to ensure that you connect the wire to the right place (fig. 12).

Number 31 (brown): This wire is fitted with an open-ended connector. On the majority of cars it must be connected to an earth (fig. 13); some bare metal under the

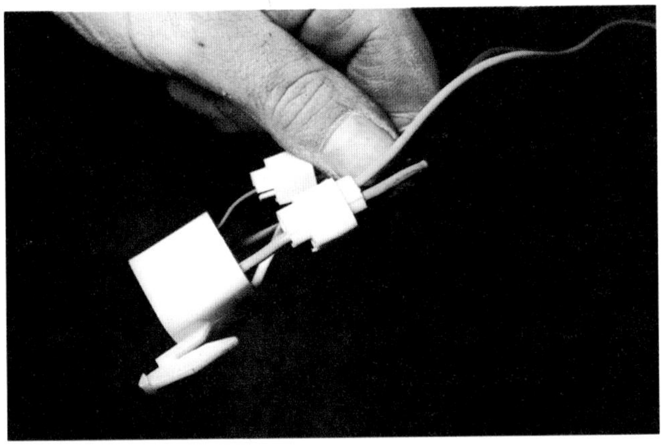

12 Next, connect the number 53 (yellow) wire from the unit. Here it is connected to the power supply to the wiper motor

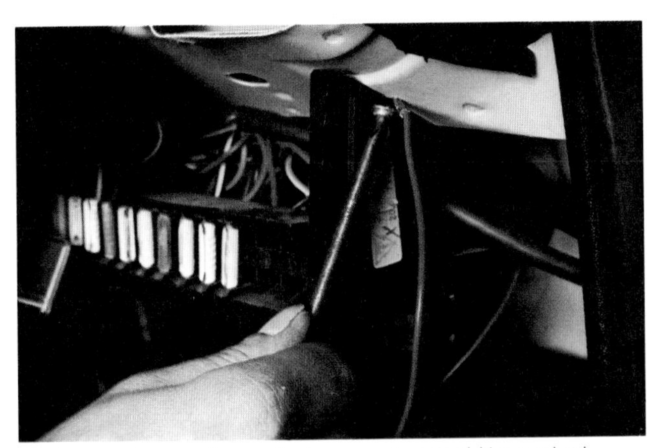

13 On negative-earth cars, the brown wire should be earthed. On positive-earth cars it must be connected to a special relay

fascia will be ideal for this and you will probably be able to make use of an existing screw or nut. If you cannot find a suitable place to earth the lead, scrape some paint away from a metal panel that is out of view and drill a small hole. You will then be able to fix the wire in position with a self-tapping screw. You may find that there is no need to drill a hole because you can make use of an existing one. If this is the case use a suitably-sized, self-tapping screw and make sure that it is a secure fit.

Some Renault cars require the number 31 wire to be connected to a special Hella relay instead, which must be bought separately from the unit, while the older Triumph Herald 1200 requires the connection to be made at the ignition switch, so once again check with the chart.

Numbers 31b1 and 31b2 (two black wires): On a few cars, such as the early BL Minis, Triumph Herald and some Vauxhalls, the installation of the wiper control unit is completed without actually fitting the two black wires. They can be neatly coiled or you can cut them off and seal the stubs with insulating tape. On the majority of cars, however, the black wires need to be connected as an interruption of

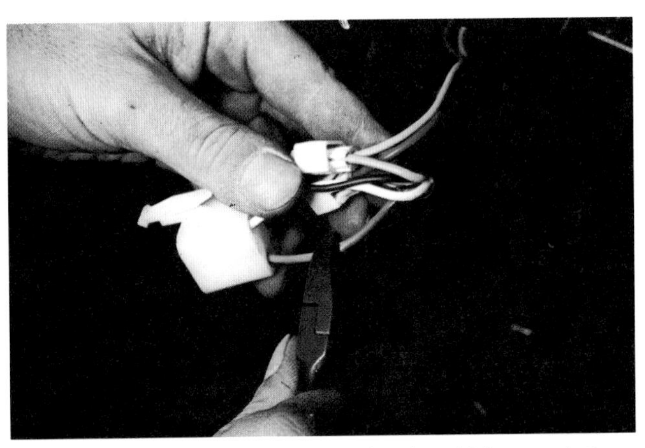

14 On some cars you will need to cut the wire which controls the windscreen wiper self-parking circuit. Here, it is the green one

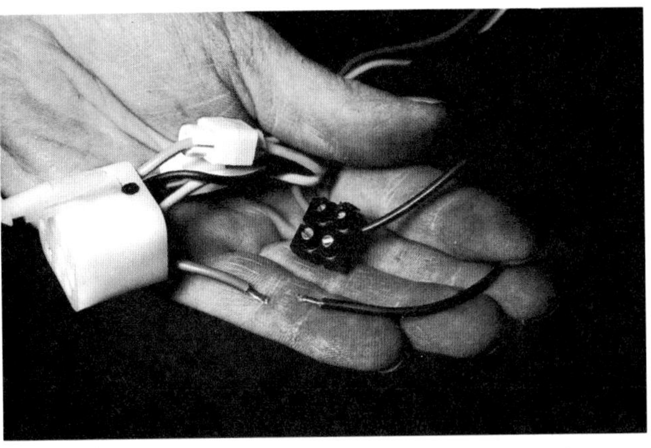

15 Each section of the self-parking wire must be connected to either of the two black wires from the wiper control unit

the wire for the windscreen wiper self-parking circuit. In the 31b column on the chart, against your particular car, you will find the abbreviation for the wire which needs to be cut and connected to the black wires. This connection generally needs to be made at the wiper switch or the wiper motor but on the MGB, for example, it can be made to the eight pole connector situated below the fascia. Cut the wire at any convenient point and bare the two ends (fig. 14). Then connect each end to one of the black wires using the screw connector provided (fig. 15). If you have dealt with the red loop of wire as explained earlier, the installation is now complete and the unit is ready for a test.

Operating the unit

After making sure that you have connected all of the wires properly, re-connect the battery and check the operation of

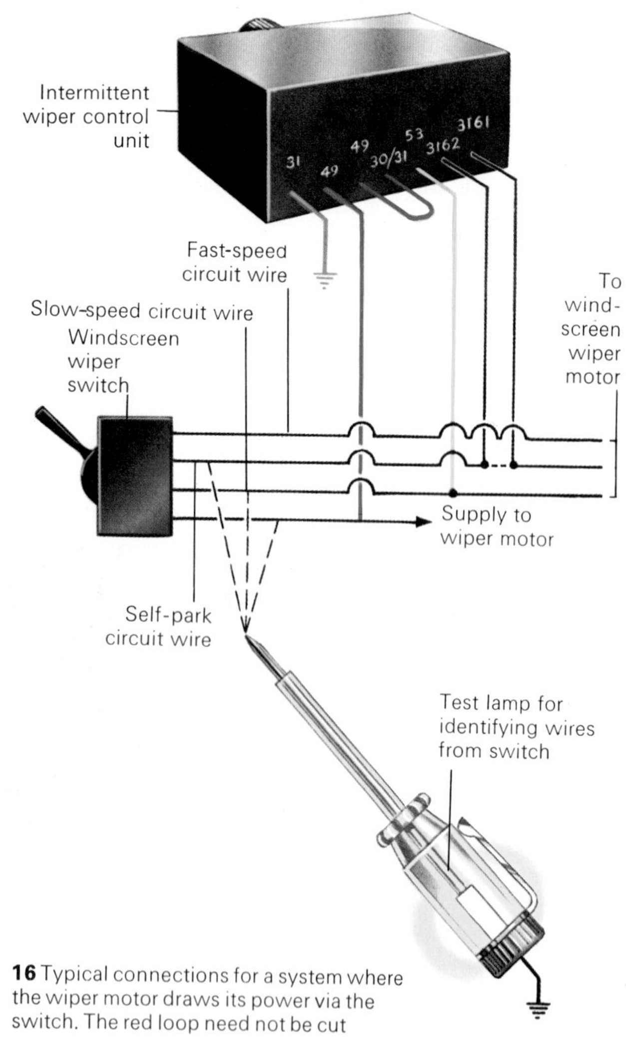

16 Typical connections for a system where the wiper motor draws its power via the switch. The red loop need not be cut

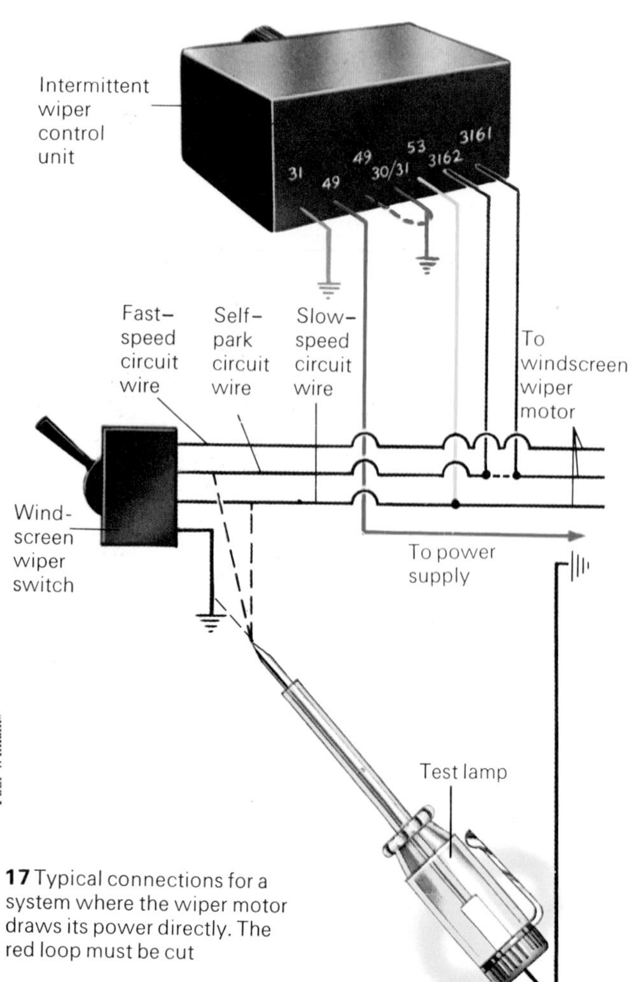

17 Typical connections for a system where the wiper motor draws its power directly. The red loop must be cut

the unit. Before you switch it on, pull the windscreen wipers away from the screen (fig. 18) so that they do not scrape on the dry glass. The wipers should operate normally from the main wiper switch. Intermittent wiping will be obtained if you turn the main wipers off and turn the Hella control knob clockwise. The more you turn the knob the longer the interval will be between each complete sweep of the wipers. You should be able to achieve a maximum delay of about 15 seconds depending on the type of wiper motor.

Fitting the unit to cars not covered by the chart

In most cases you will find that once you have mastered the rather unfamiliar instructions there should be few difficulties in fitting the Hella intermittent wipe control unit. Problems are only likely to arise in cases of old or unusual makes of car not covered by the instruction fitting chart. If this is the case, it will be necessary to carry out some simple tests to identify the wires at the wiper switch.

You will then need a 12 volt test lamp, the lead of which should be attached to a suitable earth on the car's chassis or bodywork. Now switch on the ignition, make sure that the wipers are switched off and probe all of the wiper switch terminals separately. If the lamp lights up at one terminal, make a note that this is the current supply and that the unit is of the type using an earthed motor, instead of earthing through the switch. To this wire or terminal connect the red lead from the Hella unit, number 49 (fig. 16).

If, with the ignition on and wipers switched off, all the terminals are "dead", this indicates that the wipers on your car are of the type having direct supply and that they are earthed through the switch. In this case, the red wire can be connected to any point on the back of the ignition switch, or to the main fuse box, which is live only when the ignition is switched on (fig. 17). Refer to page 24 for instructions on locating a live fuse.

Now switch the wipers on, with the arms pulled forward.

18 Before testing the wiper control unit, pull the wiper blades away from the screen to prevent them operating on dry glass

Identify the terminal or wire which is live in addition to the supply lead. This one is the slow-speed circuit to which the yellow lead, number 53, should be connected.

You may notice that another terminal, when checked with the circuit tester, gives a flash of light in rhythm with the wipers. This is the self-parking circuit and its wire is the one which must be cut and connected to the two ends of the black wires, numbers 31b1 and 31b2.

It is quite possible that these tests will not give a flashing light with the wipers running. In this case, the black leads from the unit are not required and can be left disconnected.

When neatly installed and working properly, the intermittent wipe control will serve as a useful refinement for safe driving as well as adding to your pride of ownership and a little to the value of the car.

Fitting a rear wash/wipe system

One problem for hatchback or estate car (station wagon) owners is that the large rear window, designed for good visibility, becomes clouded with mud and road dirt. Air turbulence, created at the back of the car as it drives forwards through the atmosphere, has the effect of throwing dirt up from the road and on to the rear screen and obscuring vision.

Losing rearward vision in this way is not only inconvenient but dangerous as well. The answer to the problem is to fit a rear screen wiper/washer system. The wiper used on its own will keep the rear window free of rain droplets, which can also cut down visibility: used in conjunction with the washer spray, it will also get rid of wet mud and dust, thus aiding safe driving.

Rear screen wiper kits are now available on the accessory market to suit nearly every car likely to need one. At a first glance they may look complicated and difficult to fit. In fact, the job is usually straight-forward and well within the scope of the DIY mechanic. You will be working at both ends of the car, however, so the process can become rather drawn out. To tackle it methodically, you should fit the wiper motor and jet nozzle first, followed by the wiper itself and the washer pump. Finally, connect the tubing and wiring as described on page 135.

The kit illustrated (fig. 1) is the Trico Rearview/Rearwash which comes in several different guises to suit a wide range of cars. The wiper part of the kit includes a wiper arm, motor, grommets and terminals. The Rearwash part comes in two forms. The first, which is designed for use in conjunction with an existing windscreen washer, has a special pump and tubing. The second type is a complete unit and has a combined pump and washer bottle.

Other rear wiper/washer kits are available, but these are similar to the Trico units and rely on a similar fitting procedure for successful installation.

Buying a rear screen wiper/washer kit

When you are buying your rear screen wiper be sure to quote the exact year, make and model of your car. The dealer may also need to know whether your car is positive or negative earthed (see page 23) and whether or not it

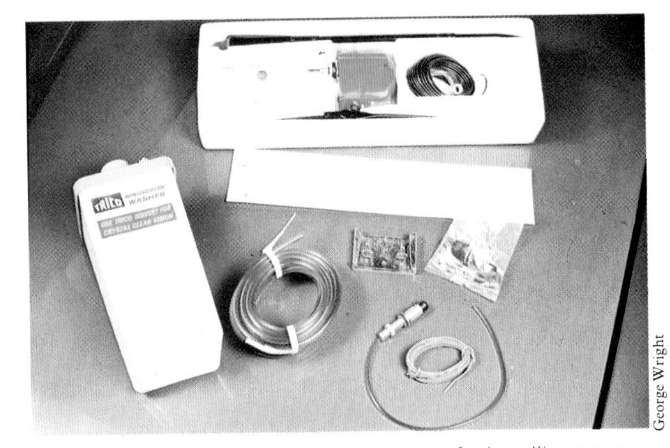

George Wright

1 The Trico kits contain all the necessary parts for installing a rear washer/wiper including wire, screws and spade terminals

2 The layout of the Rearview/Rearwash kit employing a combined washer pump and bottle as a supplement to existing units

3 The alternative type of kit which uses an existing washer bottle and a separate, bracket-mounted washer pump

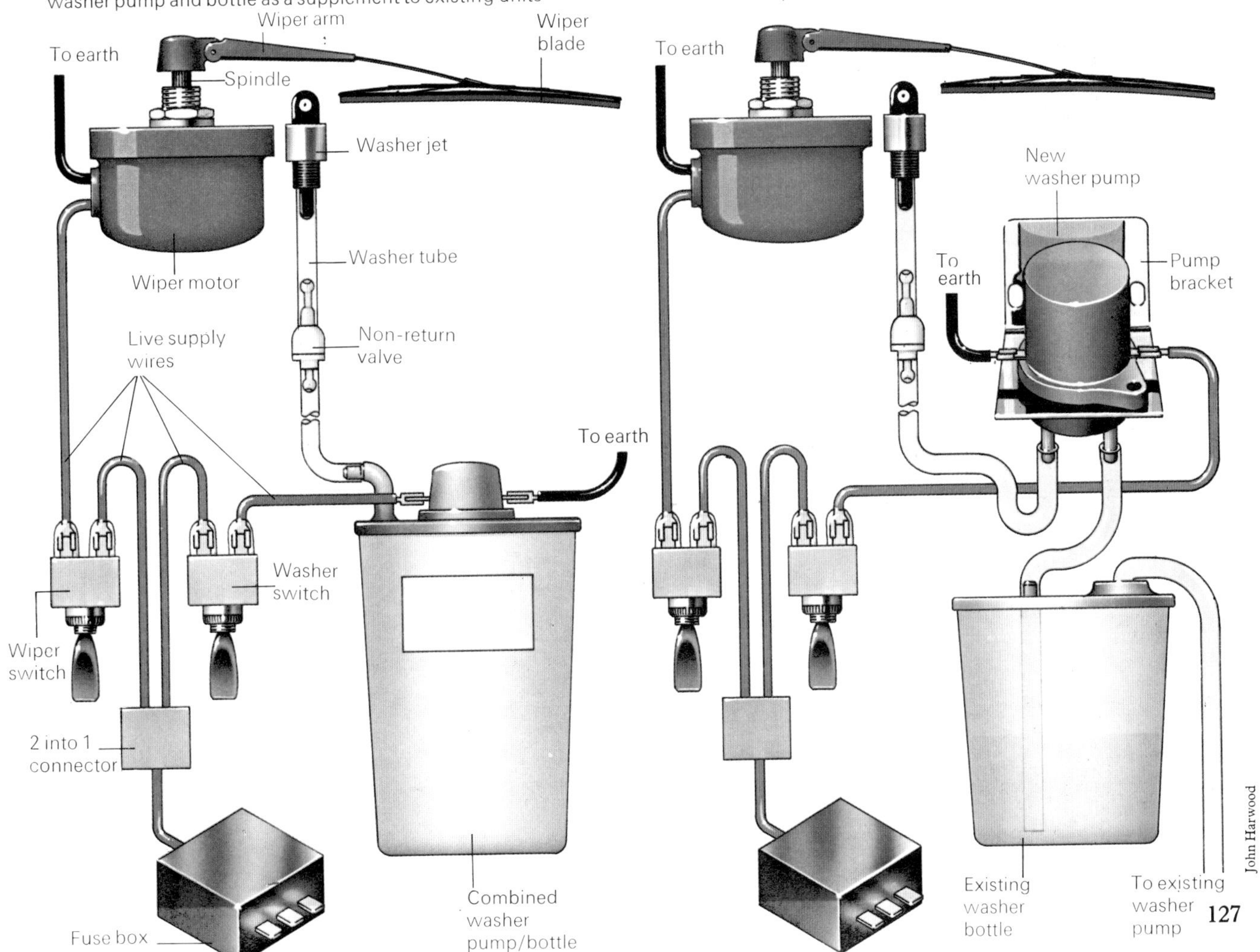

John Harwood

already has an electric washer for the front screen.

Some cars already have provision for fitting a rear screen wiper/washer as part of their standard specification. Check with your local franchised dealer to see if this is the case with yours. If so, you should be able to buy a compatible wiper/washer kit. This will enable you to make use of any blanked holes, wiring and tubing already built into the car on the production line.

What you will need for the job

Before starting the job, open up the kit and carefully read the manufacturer's instructions. Make a note of anything needed for the job that is not included in the kit such as switches, wire or terminals and purchase the necessary items. The Trico kit includes all these things but it is a good idea to have a few extra grommets and terminals and a length of standard electrical wire close by in case of unforeseen problems.

The switches operating the washer and the wiper will have to be mounted inside the car, either in or underneath the fascia. If you decide to mount them underneath, a separate panel will be needed with two self-tapping screws to fit it in place. If the fascia on your car has provision for extra switches, you may want to replace those in the kit with switches which match the existing ones. These can usually be bought from your local franchised dealer. A simple on/off switch will do for the wiper but the washer will require a spring-loaded switch biased towards the "off" position.

Fitting a rear screen wiper does not require any special tools but you will need a power drill and drill bits of sizes specified by the manufacturer of the kit. In the Trico kits 3 mm ($\frac{1}{8}$ins), 8 mm (5/16ins), 9 mm ($\frac{3}{8}$ins) and 11.5 mm (7/16ins) bits will be required. One or two additional sizes are needed for certain cars but these are specified in the kit's instructions.

Again on some cars, the inner skin of the rear panel or tailgate must be cut away to provide clearance for the wiper motor. You can be prepared for this by having either a short bladed padsaw or a sharp cold chisel. A metal working file will also be needed to smooth down any rough or jagged edges.

If you decide to feed the washer supply tube and the live supply to the wiper motor along box sections and door pillars or behind the interior trim, a length of stiff wire (3 metres or 10 feet approx.) will save a lot of trouble. A supply of Scotchlok or barrel connectors may also prove useful when you come to install the wiring.

Drilling the holes

Rear windscreen wipers like the one illustrated are operated by an electric motor. This is mounted on the inside of the tailgate or rear panel and the spindle attached to it protrudes through the body skin so that the wiper arm itself may be fitted on to it.

The jet for the screen washer also protrudes through the same panel; inside the car, a tube runs from it to the washer bottle.

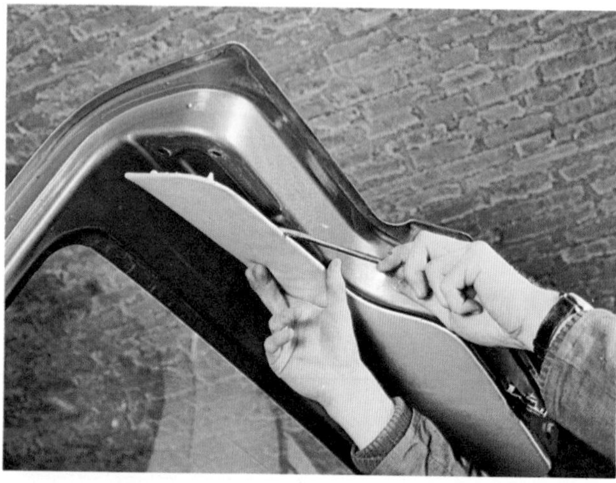

4 In most cases, the lining on the inside of the tailgate is held by press-on studs. Prise it away carefully using a screwdriver

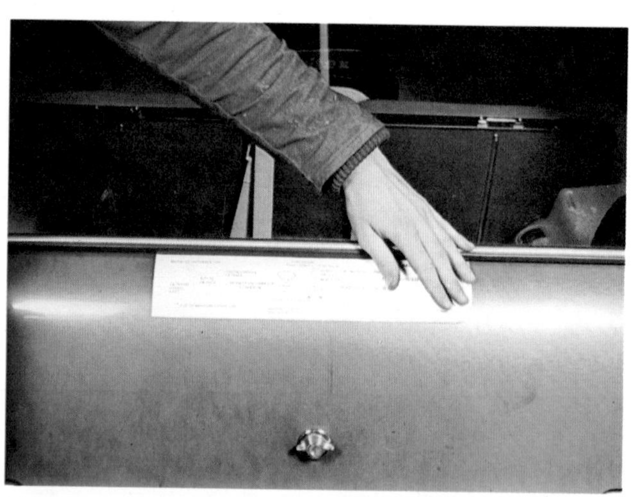

5 When you have positioned the adhesive template correctly, press it down on the outside of the tailgate and smooth out the bumps

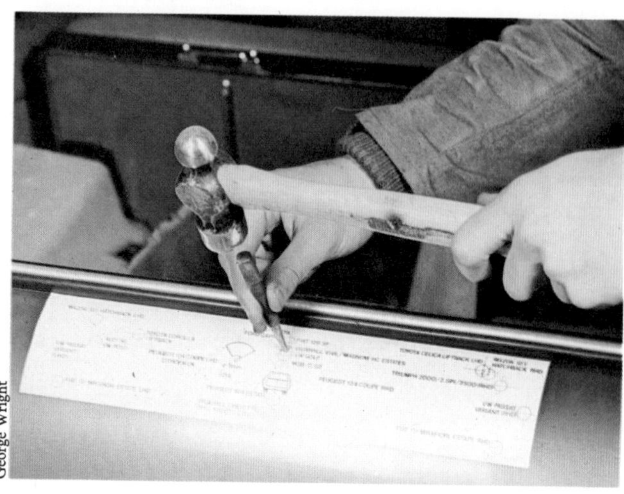

George Wright

6 Use the template to identify the correct location for the wiper spindle hole. Indent the circular mark with a centrepunch

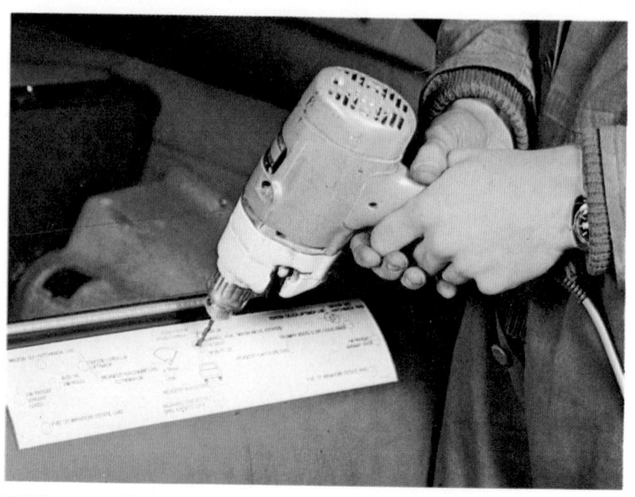

7 With a small diameter bit, drill a pilot hole through the mark. This will prevent the larger drill bit from slipping afterwards

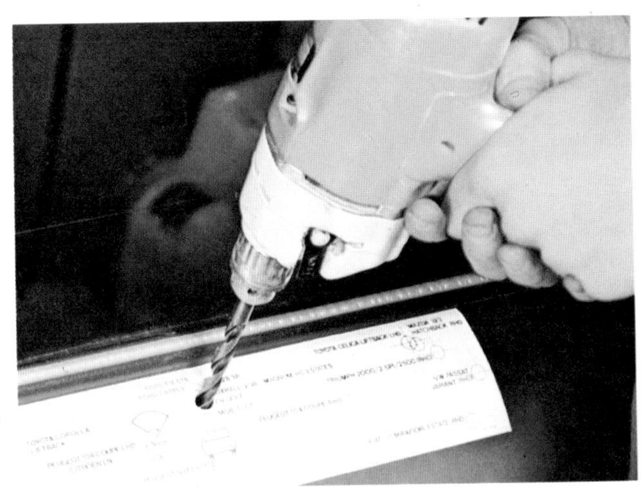

8 The large diameter bit may now be used to finish off the hole. File down any jagged edges and then check that the spindle fits

9 The washer jet is mounted to one side of the spindle. Indent a mark on the template and then repeat the drilling procedure

Before you start to drill holes for the spindle and the jet nozzle, the inside of the panel or tailgate must be exposed (fig. 4). On some cars it may already be accessible but on others there will be a trim panel to remove, normally secured by screws, press-on studs or fold-over metal clips. Make sure that you know how the panel on your car is secured and then carefully remove it, remembering that the materials used will probably be fragile and easily damaged if handled roughly.

On the BL 1100/1300 and the Ford Capri Mk I (1969-74), the rear parcel shelf must be removed; on the 1100/1300 this can only be done once the rear seat squab and backrest have been taken out.

With the trim removed the next stage is to mark the site of the drill holes. Many kits, including most of the Trico range, provide self-adhesive templates to make siting the wiper hole easier. Where one of these is provided, peel off the backing and stick it down on the outside of the tailgate or rear panel (fig. 5); the kit instructions will give its exact location.

Where no outer template is provided, dimensions will be given to enable you to measure horizontally from the edge of the panel and vertically in line with the boot catch or tailgate release. In order to mark the spot, stick the point of a felt-tip pen through a small strip of masking tape. Use the pen as a marker at the point where the measurements cross, stick the tape down and remove the pen.

If you are using a kit template, the hole for the washer jet nozzle may not be indicated. The jet should go on the opposite side of the tailgate/boot release centre line to the wiper spindle and it should be the same distance from the line. If the spindle is centrally located, mark the jet hole to either side (fig. 9) but do not forget to check if a hole here will foul the tailgate/boot release mechanism.

If there is no template, follow the above procedure for siting the jet hole and mark the site with another strip of masking tape.

With the sites correctly marked, make a final check to ensure that as they stand there is no chance of the holes fouling any release mechanisms, wires or trim brackets. Now take a centrepunch and indent the two holes through the template or masking tape (fig. 6), to provide a firm basis for drilling. Using a 3 mm ($\frac{1}{8}$ins) bit and holding the drill at right angles to the rear window, drill two pilot holes straight through the panel or tailgate (fig. 7).

These holes can now be opened up with larger drill bits to the sizes recommended in the kit instructions. With any of the Trico kits (apart from that for the Rover SDI series), use a 9 mm ($\frac{3}{8}$ins) bit for the motor spindle hole and a 8 mm (5/16ins) bit for the washer jet hole. The drill sizes and the fitting procedure are slightly different in the Trico kit for the Rover and a detailed instruction sheet is provided for this model.

Installing the wiper motor

The wiper motor is fitted from inside the tailgate or panel. Most rear panels and tailgates are constructed in two halves to keep them rigid. The outer half or "skin" is the

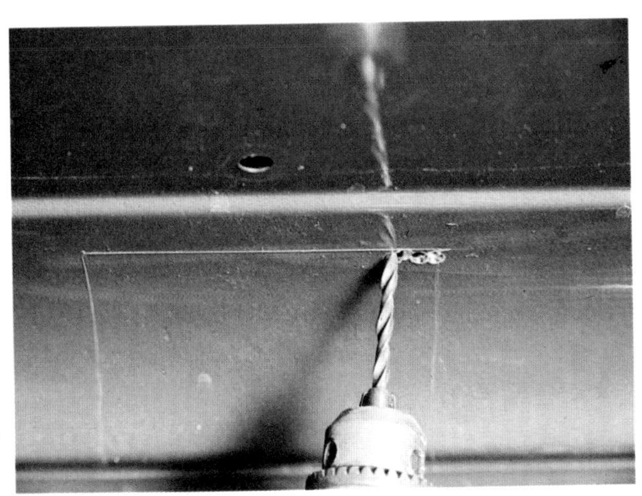

10 One method of cutting out the inner skin of the tailgate is to drill a series of holes at each corner of the marked out area

11 The holes should run into each other to form a slot. You can then insert a padsaw blade and saw around the remaining metal

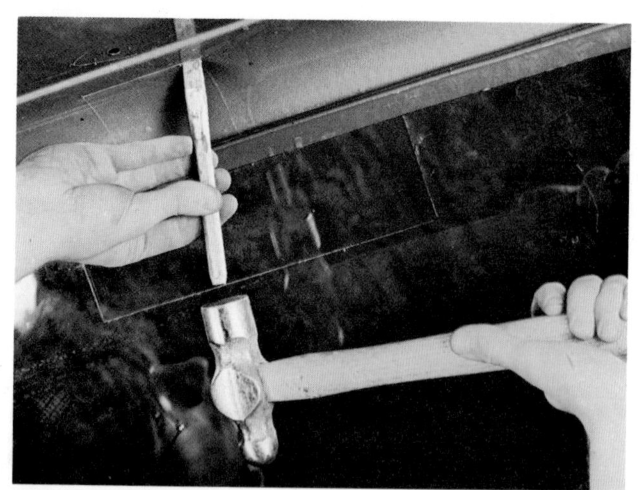

12 A less satisfactory method of cutting the skin is to drill-out the whole marked area and then knock it out with a cold chisel

13 If you use the chisel method, the jagged edges that are left must be filed down. The best tool for this is a heavy-duty rasp

14 The aperture left in the inner skin can be finished off by applying strips of tape to the edges to give a neater look

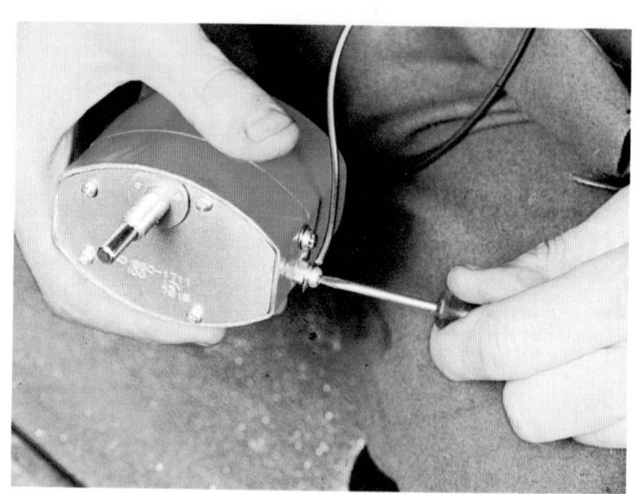

15 Use the kit instructions to identify the live supply terminal on the motor body, then connect a suitable length of wire to it.

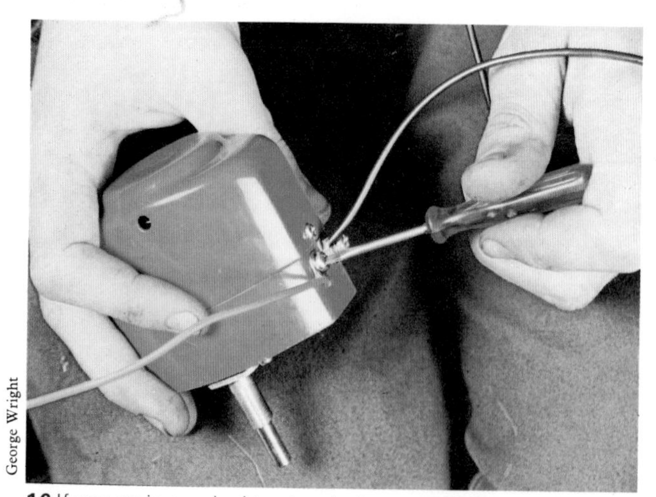

George Wright

16 If you are in any doubt as to whether or not the motor will be earthed when in position, connect an earthing wire to the body

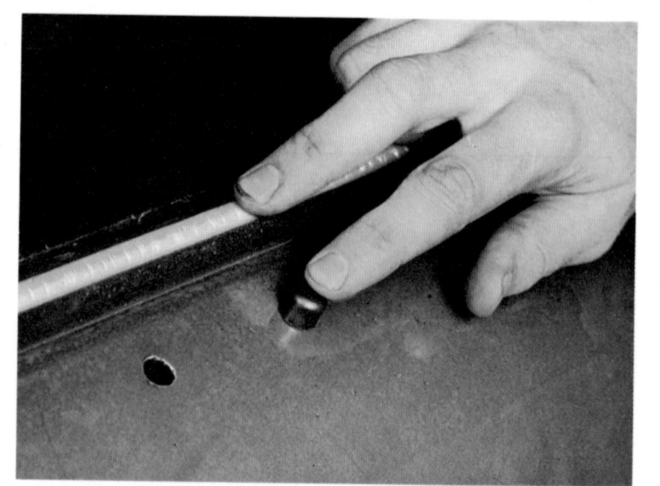

17 On this car, the spray from the unextended jet would clearly be obstructed by the rubber surround and trim of the rear window

surface you have just drilled through. The inner skin, revealed by removing the trim, may take one of two forms. On some cars, such as the Morris Marina Estate, it is not solid but split up into boxed sections. This saves the tailgate from becoming too heavy. Other cars however, such as the Citroen GS Estate, have solid inner skins.

Different wiper motors fit in different ways but it is often necessary to cut away part of the inner skin before the motor can be properly located. This must be done strictly in accordance with the kit instructions. Where the inner skin is in sections, cutting it is not difficult with a short-bladed padsaw. With solid inner skins like that on the GS Estate tailgate, a self-adhesive template is usually supplied to help you mark the cutting section. Stick this in place or, if there isn't one in your kit, mark the section with a felt tip pen according to the instructions.

Using a 3 mm ($\frac{1}{8}$ins) drill bit, drill a series of holes next to one another on the edge of the marked section (fig. 10). This will enable you to insert a padsaw blade into the space and saw around the template or boundary mark (fig. 11). An

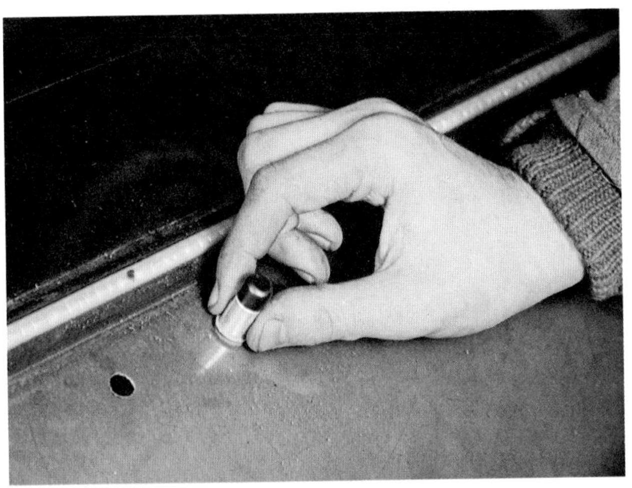

18 Once extended, the jet can be secured in position with the nut provided. Use the cut-out section in the inner skin for access

alternative method if a padsaw is not available is to drill holes round the edge of the section and knock it out with a sharp cold chisel (fig. 12). This, however, will leave a jagged edge which must be filed down before you go any further (fig. 13).

On some cars, such as the VW Golf, a small section of the parcel shelf may also have to be cut to fit the Trico kit. This will be shown in the kit instructions.

With the cutting completed, take the motor supply wire from the kit and connect one end of it to the insulated terminal on the motor body (fig. 15). To avoid any earthing problems later on, it is a good idea to connect another length of wire to the optional earthing terminal (fig. 16).

Fitting the washer jet and the wiper motor

In the Trico kit illustrated, the washer jet nozzle has an optional extension. This enables the same nozzle to be used for a variety of applications. To find out if the extension is required on your car, start by inserting the nozzle only through the relevant hole in the tailgate/rear panel. You can then estimate whether or not it protrudes enough to spray the window at the desired angle. On the car illustrated it does not; if the nozzle were left like this, the spray would fail to clear the window surround (fig. 17).

If you decide that the extension is needed, screw it to the nozzle when you have removed it from the hole. With the Trico kit, you will have to increase the mounting hole diameter to 9 mm ($\frac{3}{8}$ins). Having done this, replace the extended nozzle and secure it from behind using the lock nut supplied. If there is not enough room to screw on the nut because of the inner skin, you will have to continue the nozzle hole right through the skin. You can then secure the jet from behind as shown in fig. 18.

Next, take the plastic non-return valve supplied with the kit. Following the kit instructions, press the appropriate end of the valve into the length of tubing connected to the jet assembly (fig. 19).

To install the motor, fit the rubber mounting pad over it then feed the wire connections behind the inner skin of the tailgate/rear panel. Push the motor spindle through the appropriate hole until the motor is flush against the inside of the outer skin (fig. 20). Assemble the nut, washers and spacers according to the kit instructions and tighten until the motor is held firmly in place (fig. 21). The wiper motor in the Trico kit for the Ford Capri Mk I has an additional bracket. This must be secured with the two self-tapping screws provided.

As you fit the motor, however, bear in mind that you may need to remove it temporarily later on if access to the space between the inner and outer skins is limited. A much more professional look can be obtained by feeding the washer tubing and motor wires out of sight between the two skins and up to the headlining or tailgate hinge.

With the washer jet and wiper motor installed, the next step is to fit the washer pump, tubing, wiring and switches. Various layouts for these components of the Trico kit are described in fig. 22.

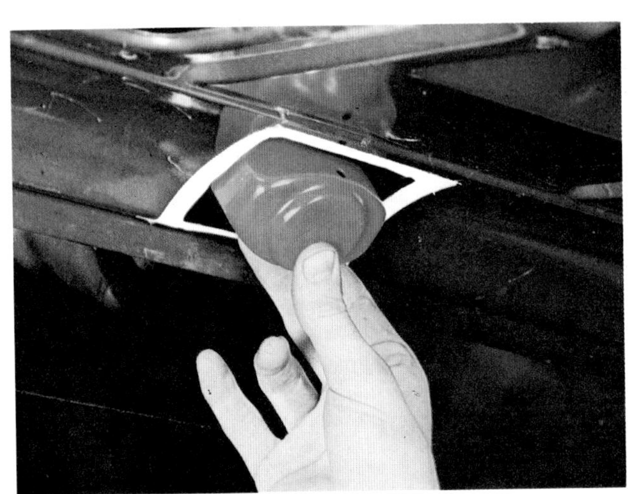

19 Working inside the tailgate, press the non-return valve on to the tube running from the jet. Make sure it is the right way up

20 The motor is fitted into the cut-out section, flush against the tailgate outer skin with the spindle fully exposed

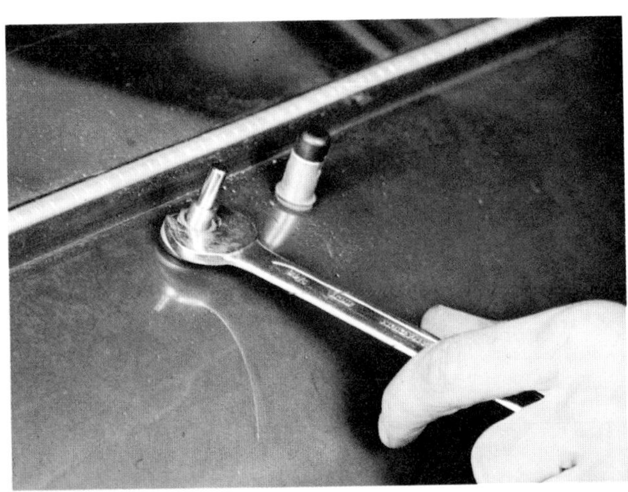

21 Secure the motor by tightening the lock nut on the spindle. Take care to assemble the nut and its washers in the right order

Tubing and electrical layouts

You are now approximately half way through the installation process of your rear wash/wipe system. From now on you will be working all over the car and it is as well to set aside at least half a day to complete the job. Because so many parts of the car, including the fusebox and fascia, will need attention, it is inadvisable to continue driving with the installation only partially in place.

Plan in advance the layout of your kit, noting where you will have to run the water tubing and electrical leads. You may be using the standard washer bottle and fitting a new pump (fig. 22A), or fitting a new washer pump and bottle combined beneath the bonnet (fig. 22B). A third possibility is to install the combined washer pump and bottle at the rear of the car. Each of these methods requires a completely different route for the tubing and wiring (see page 133).

Installing the switches

Start by installing the wiper and washer operating switches. If they are to be mounted on a panel under the fascia, mark and drill the holes for the securing screws using the mounting panel as a template to guide you. Tighten the panel securing screws and install the switches. Leave the switches slightly loose until you have connected up the electrical leads (figs. 34 and 37).

If you are fitting switches that match those already on the fascia, cut out the appropriate blanking plates with a sharp knife but do not mount them at this stage. Wait until you have run the electrical leads behind the fascia and through

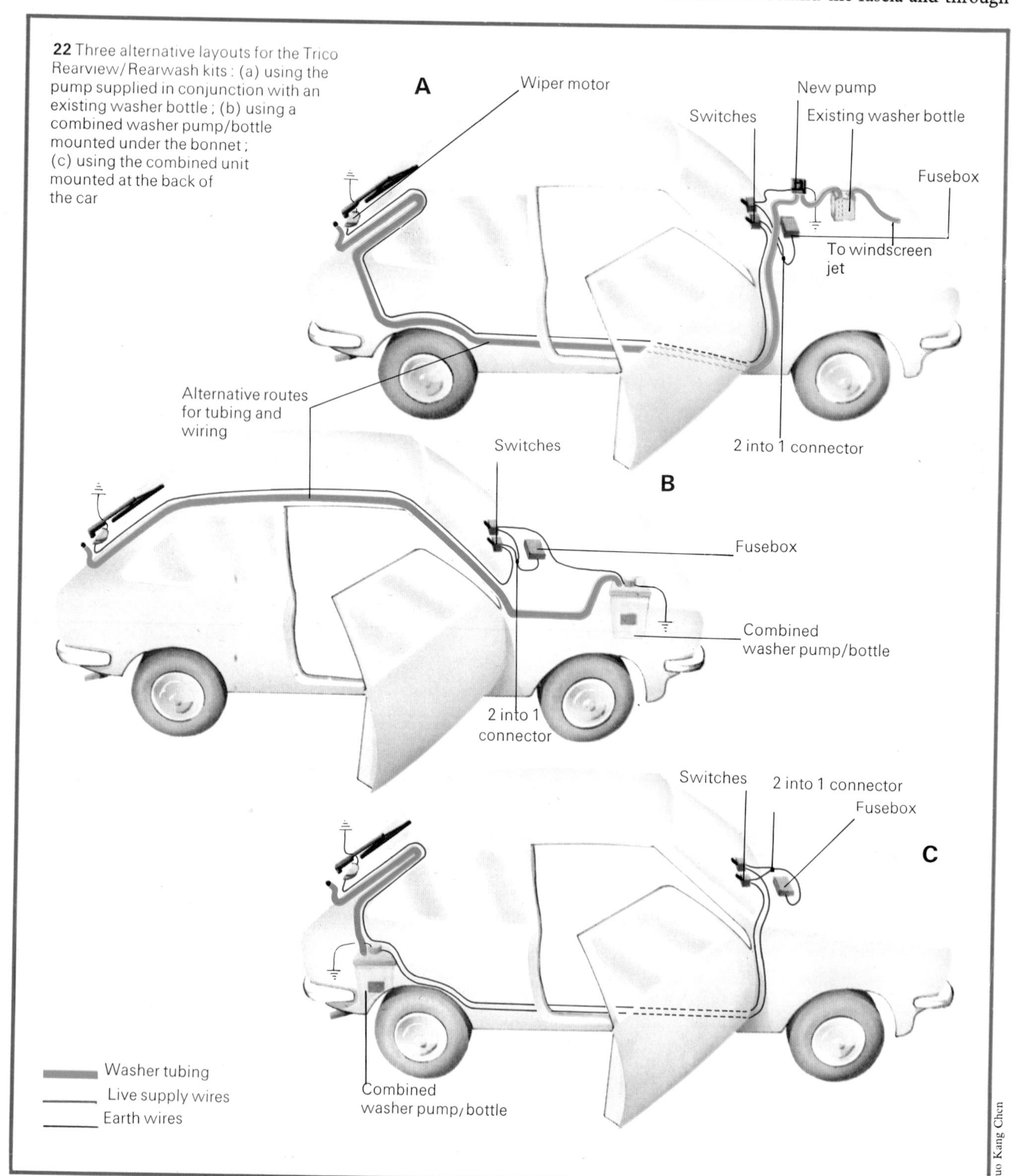

22 Three alternative layouts for the Trico Rearview/Rearwash kits: (a) using the pump supplied in conjunction with an existing washer bottle; (b) using a combined washer pump/bottle mounted under the bonnet; (c) using the combined unit mounted at the back of the car

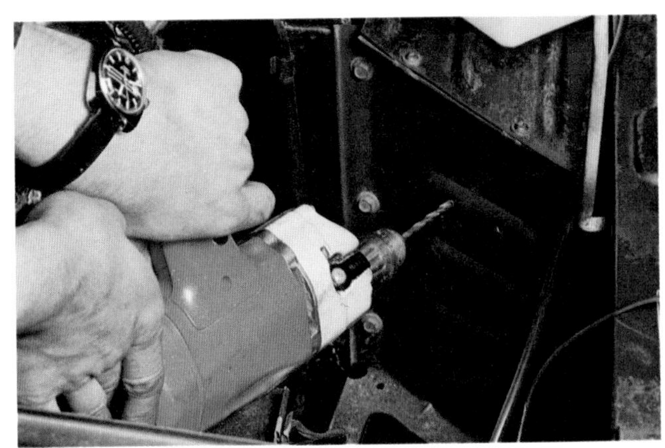

23 First select a site for the washer pump or pump/bottle unit. In this case, an underbonnet location is chosen and the holes drilled

24 When mounting the pump or, as shown here, the pump/bottle bracket, attach the earthing wire to one of the screws

the switch holes (see below). You will now find it much easier to connect the leads to the terminals on the switches. Once connected, these switches can then be pressed into place. If you fit the switches before positioning and attaching the wires you may experience difficulty gaining sufficient access behind the fascia to connect them.

Installing a pump using the existing washer bottle.

If the washer in your kit is designed to be used with an existing washer bottle only an extra washer pump will be provided (fig. 1).

Start by mounting the new pump under the bonnet close to and slightly above the existing washer bottle. Use the pump bracket as a template and drill two holes to take the self-tapping screws that come with the kit. Take care not to make the holes too large. Place the the pump in position and then tighten the screws.

Next, drill a hole—to the size recommended by the kit instructions—in the top of the washer bottle. Push the rubber sealing grommet provided into the hole and then insert the special length of tubing that comes with this type of kit. The tubing should be pushed down until it almost touches the bottom of the bottle. This helps to make sure that the system will pick up water even when the bottle is nearly empty. Connect the other end of the tubing to the appropriate nozzle on the new pump. This is usually marked "inlet" but if it is not the instructions in the kit will tell you which nozzle to use. When pushing the tubing over the nozzle you may find it easier to first gently heat the end of the tube. This can be done using hot water or a carefully applied flame. If you apply flame, do it away from the car and do not allow it to linger at any point on the tube. A few seconds is sufficient to soften any tubing.

Installing a combined pump and washer bottle

Some kits incorporate a combined washer pump and water bottle (figs. 22 and 32). As these kits can be mounted at the rear of the vehicle they allow you more freedom in deciding exactly where to fit the equipment. This type of unit could also cut down on the amount of tubing you will require and save the need to route the tube behind the headlining or under the carpet (see below).

The biggest problem with the combined unit is finding a suitable position for it in the luggage compartment so that it will not be affected by the movement of any luggage when the car is in motion. If you succeed in finding a good position, secure the holding bracket supplied with the unit in the manner described earlier. If you have mounted the pump close to the washer jet nozzle, and in such a way that any tubing need not be routed behind the headlining, you can now fit a length of tubing to the pump and then connect it to the non-return valve described on pages 127 to 131. If the washer pump and bottle unit is mounted some way from the washer jet nozzle you may have to disturb the headlining to conceal the tubing (see below).

If you are unable to find a good mounting position at the rear of the car, fit the unit in the front of the car in the same manner described above for fitting an extra pump to the existing washer bottle (figs. 23 and 24).

Routing the tubing and electrical leads

Routing the water tubing and the electrical leads from the rear of the car to a front-mounted pump bottle unit may be the biggest problem that you will encounter when fitting a wash wipe unit. Considerable lengths of tubing and electrical wiring will have to be routed from the rear of the car to the front on most cars, those with rear-mounted engines or a combined washer bottle and pump mounted in the boot being exceptions. This tubing and wiring should be concealed and protected as much as possible so that passengers do not trip over them or cause them to become disconnected. As this part of the job is usually time-consuming and awkward, you should install both the tubing and the wiring at the same time.

Some kits give detailed instructions on the best route for the tubing and wiring on specific cars. If no advice is given, you are faced with a choice. You can either run these connections underneath the carpets or behind the headlining. Whichever method you use, run the connections along that side of the car on which the pump bottle unit for the front windscreen washer is fitted.

Running the connections underneath the carpets is the easier method as most carpets are removable and are usually held down by press-studs. Once these have been pulled away the carpet can be lifted and then clipped back after the tubing and wires have been laid in position. You may find, however, that pressure from a passenger's feet pressing on the carpet may stop the flow of water to the washer jet if the tubing is not run as close to the bottom angle of the door sill as is possible.

Hiding the tubing and wiring behind the headlining is a neater, more permanent method but it can be a difficult operation, especially where the headlining is cloth. The headlining may be secured by one of several different fixing methods so you should study it carefully. Look for any securing clips or push-fit trim behind which the headlining may be trapped to hold it in place. If you are in any doubt ask your dealer about the method of fixing used.

Once you have decided on which of the two alternatives you want to take you can begin work. The tubing and wiring will not be pre-cut to the correct length (apart from

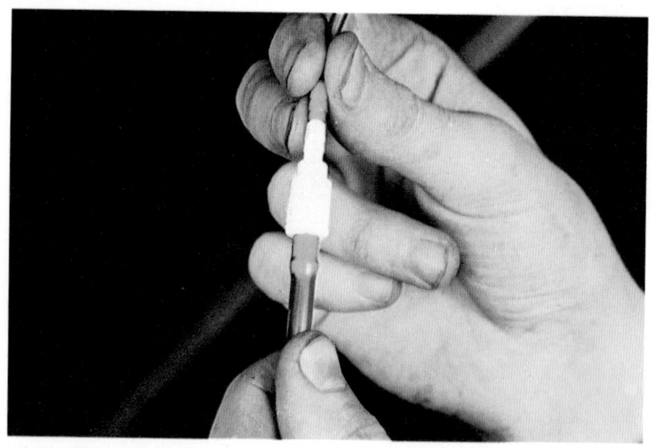

25 Connecting the washer tubing to the non-return valve. The tubing at the top of the valve should already be connected to the jet

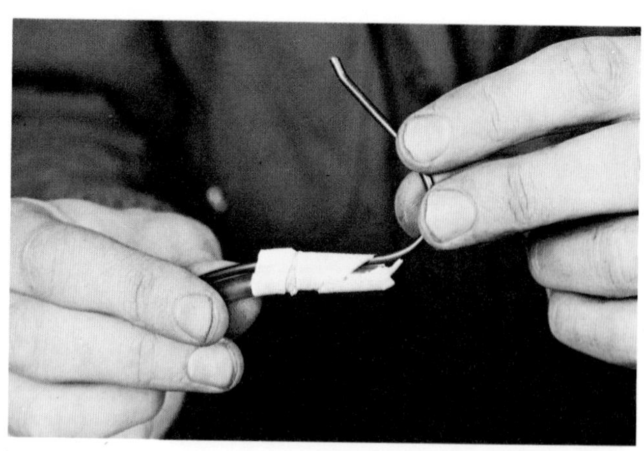

26 Before you start feeding the washer tubing and the live supply wire through the car, tape them together in a tapered joint

27 If you are using stiff wire as a trace, feed it behind the panel concerned, tape the tube to the end and pull the assembly through

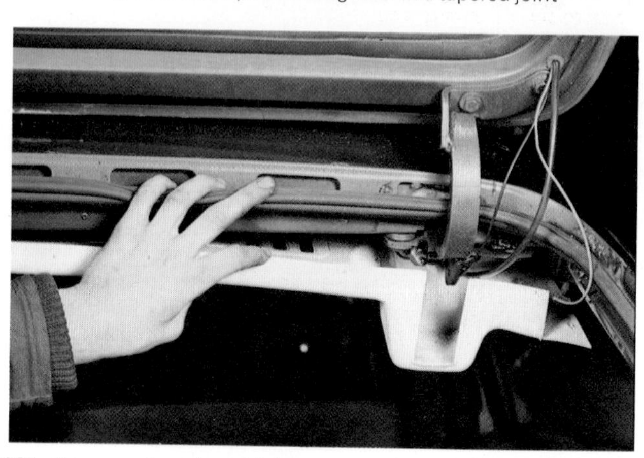

28 In this case, the tube and the supply wire can be fed from the tailgate hinge to the headlining via an unscrewed rear trim panel

the special length already mentioned above) but you will need to fit oversize lengths anyway and then trim them when you make the connections.

Using an existing water bottle

If you have a saloon car—and you want to run the tube/wire under the carpets—first connect the tubing to the non-return valve (fig. 25) and the wiring to the wiper arm unit. The same applies to an estate car or hatchback but in these cases, you may find it necessary to temporarily remove the wiper motor for access (see pages 127 to 131). Re-fit the motor when you have routed the wires and tubing.

You will now be able to run the tube/wire connections under the rear parcel shelf, if one is fitted, and then down the side of the rear seat until they can be routed under the carpets. When you reach the front foot-well, detach the relevant side trim-panel and run the tube/wire behind it. At all times you should avoid pinching the tubing as this will affect the flow of water to the washer. Where the tubing alone passes through the front bulkhead, protect it with a rubber grommet. You may find that you can make use of an existing grommet instead of having to drill a fresh hole. The wiring can be routed behind the trim panel and under the fascia to the switch mounted on the fascia. The tubing and wiring are now ready for connection (see below).

If you have an estate car or a hatchback and you want to route the tube/wire in the manner described above, connect them to the arm/nozzle and then route them across the inner body panel and out of the relevant top corner of the tailgate (fig. 28). Feed them under the trim on the rear pillar tailgate. Feed them back under the trim on the rear pillar, if there is any, until they reach the carpets. You may find

29 The headlining is easily peeled back on this car, once the trim strip has been unclipped. Hide the tube and wire behind it

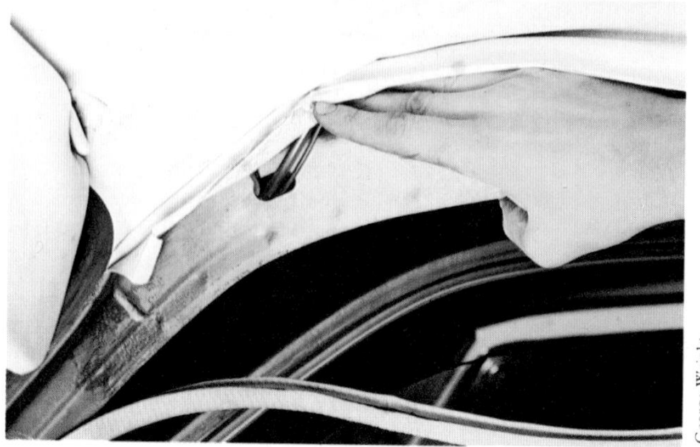

George Wright

30 There will almost certainly be some sort of hole at the top of the windscreen pillar down which to feed the tubing and the wire

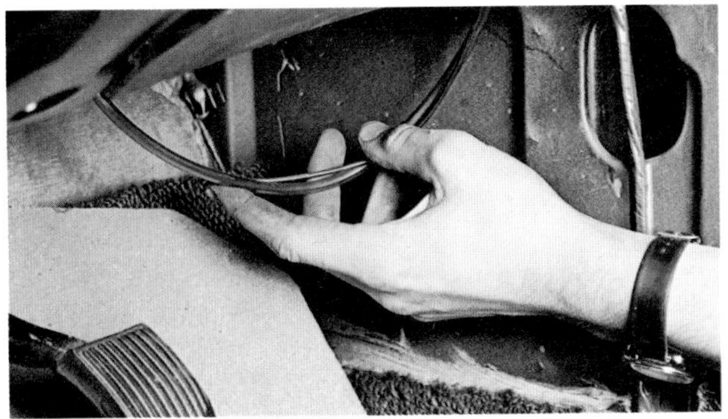

31 At the bottom of the pillar, the stiff wire trace will emerge from behind the footwell trim panel. Pull the wire right through

32 An alternative site for the pump/bottle unit at the back of the car. The unit is secured to the spare wheel with an elastic clip

that you have to drill a hole right through the rear pillar in order to feed through the connections. If so, use grommets to protect them. You may also decide to loosen the side trim panel and hide the connections behind it. Always make sure that you leave sufficient tubing and wiring for the tailgate to open to its fullest extent without stretching them. Also make sure that the tubing is not kinked when the tailgate is raised or lowered.

If you have a saloon car and decide to route the connections behind the headlining, fit them to the relevant units at the rear and feed them under the rear parcel shelf. It will probably be necessary to peel away the headlining in places. as this will expose the metal of the bodyshell. On some cars the supporting pillars or framework of the bodyshell are hollow whilst on others they have a gutter behind the headlining in which the connections can be run. If you are uncertain which type of framework you car has, your dealer should be able to tell you.

Where the framework is hollow, less of the headlining has to be disturbed. Peel it back at the base of each pillar. Bind the free ends of the tube/wire together with tape, making sure that the join is smooth enough to pass over any obstructions (fig. 26). Poke a length of stiff wire along the cavity above the doors until it works its way along to the front door pillar. You may have to remove the relevant side trim panel in the footwell to see where the wire reappears. When it has passed right along the cavity, tape the tube/wire to the end protruding from the rear pillar and then pull it through until it is visible by the front pillar. The tube/wire can now be routed behind the trim panel in the footwell. Temporarily hook the wiring to one side under the fascia ready for connecting to the panel switch (see below). The tubing should be fed through the bulkhead into the engine bay as described earlier.

If you have to remove the headlining along the top of the apertures, peel it back carefully until you expose the gulley along which the tubing and wiring are to be run. Try to disturb as little of the headlining as possible .The curvature of the framework will usually serve to hold the tubing and wiring in place but in some cases you may have to tape them in place. Do not replace the headlining or trim panels until you are sure the systems work properly (see below).

Using a rear-mounted pump and washer bottle

If you are fitting a kit with a combined pump and washer bottle and you are able to find room to locate it at the back of the car then the process of routing the tubing and wiring is both different and easier. The tubing will be much shorter and you will simply have to run it from the washer bottle to the washer jet, hiding it as described. You will still have to route the wiring through the car however and, again, you have the choice of tucking it under the carpets or behind the headlining. As you are routing only electrical wiring you can run the wiring under the carpet and avoid the necessity of disturbing the headlining (fig. 22).

Where your car has a top-hinged tailgate you may want to hide the tubing and wiring behind the trim of the door pillar so that it emerges from behind one of the top corners of the car's tailgate.

Connecting the washer tubing

When you have routed the tubing from the back of the car and through the bulkhead you can connect it to the washer pump (fig. 33).

Arrange the tubing under the bonnet so that it cannot touch any moving parts and in such a position that it will not be melted by heat from the engine. After cutting off any excess material, connect the tubing to the jet nozzle on the combined pump and bottle unit, or to the nozzle specified in the instructions (usually marked "outlet") if you have a separate washer pump.

If you have mounted the pump bottle unit in the back of the car near the jet, simply cut the tube to a suitable length and then connect the free end of the tubing to the pump as described previously.

Connecting the wiring

To connect the wiring of the wash/wipe units (fig. 22) begin with the supply wire which you have fed from the back of the car to the switch. Connect this to the terminal on the wiper operating switch as specified in the instructions provided with the kit.

Next connect a suitable length of wire to the non-earth terminal on the washer pump or the combined pump/bottle unit. This should be identified in the instructions. Connect the other end of this wire to the appropriate terminal on the washer switch. If you find later that the washer sucks instead of blowing, simply reverse the connection at the washer pump.

Now connect separate lengths of wire to each remaining terminal on the two switches. One of these wires should be long enough to reach the fuse box, the other can be joined to the longer wire using a "two into one" junction (fig. 35). The longer wire connected to the fusebox will supply the power to both the wiper motor and the washer pump. You should take care to connect it to the live side of the ignition so that the circuit only works when the ignition is switched on.

Finally make sure that both the wiper motor and the pump are earthed. If they have been mounted against metal parts of the car bodywork and are making metal to metal contact, they will be earthed already. If they are insulated or mounted on rubber you have to run separate earth wires from the appropriate terminals on the units (detailed in the

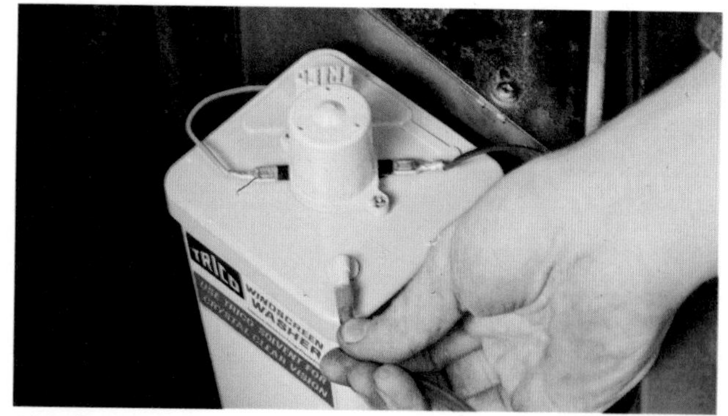

33 With the live and earth wires already connected to the pump/bottle unit in the engine compartment, the washer tube is fitted

34 The wiper and washer operating switches are held in brackets under the fascia. Use the screws provided to secure them

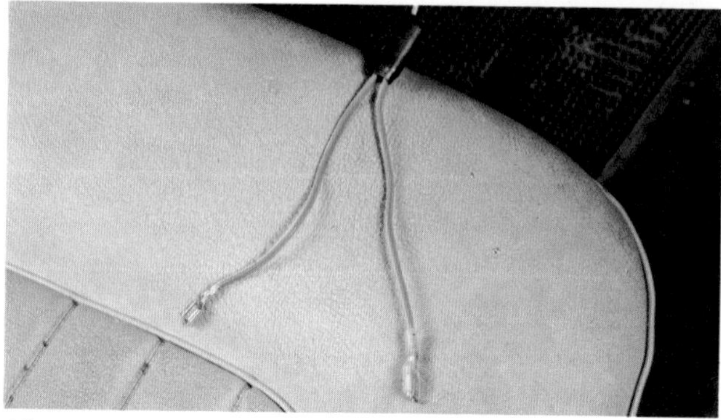

35 The wiring from the fusebox to the switches can be simplified by joining the two supplies together with a suitable connector

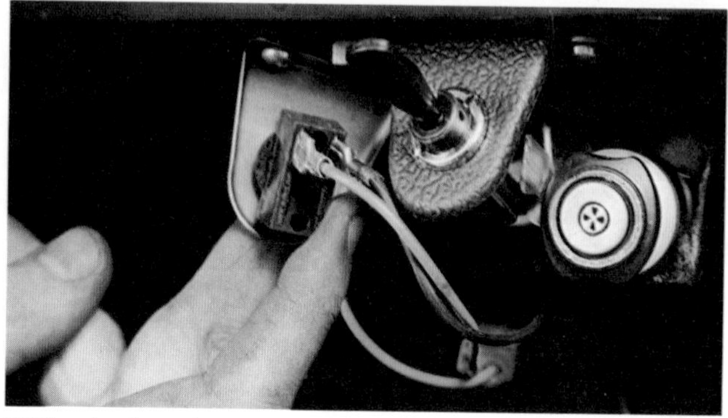

36 To wire the switches, temporarily remove one screw from each bracket. You can then turn the switches round to obtain acces

instructions) to an earthing point on the bodywork. This can be a suitable screw or nearby nut and bolt.

Provided that your kit is designed for both positive and negative earth applications (see page 23) you can now test the washer unit to make sure it is wired correctly. Ask an assistant to press the washer switch while you watch the bottle. Remember that it will take some time to prime the system if you have fitted the water bottle to the front of the car. If the pump sucks rather than blowing water to the jet, reverse the two electrical connections to it.

Fitting the wiper arm

To fit the wiper arm and blade, start by placing the arm only on to the motor spindle. Tighten the lock screw temporarily and pull the arm slightly towards you so that it cannot scratch the window. Have an assistant switch on the wiper motor and then stop it as the arm reaches the limit of its travel. Keep adjusting the position of the arm on the spindle until the optimum area of the screen is being swept. Lock in position. The wiper blade can now be clipped to the arm and pulled out as necessary until you get maximum window coverage without the wiper straying off the edge.

Adjusting the washer jet

To make sure that the washer jet sprays the window as effectively as possible it may be necessary to adjust it. You should already have decided whether or not the extension is needed and fitted it accordingly (pages 127 to 131); even so, the jet may require some adjustment.

To do this, have an assistant operate the wash switch. Note where the spray strikes the window (it may miss it altogether) and consult the kit instructions. In the Trico kits, the spray should strike 25 mm (1ins) below the top of the wiping arc.

If the spray needs adjusting, slightly alter the position of the ball nozzle in the jet with a small pin. Check it again and continue adjusting until you reach the right spot.

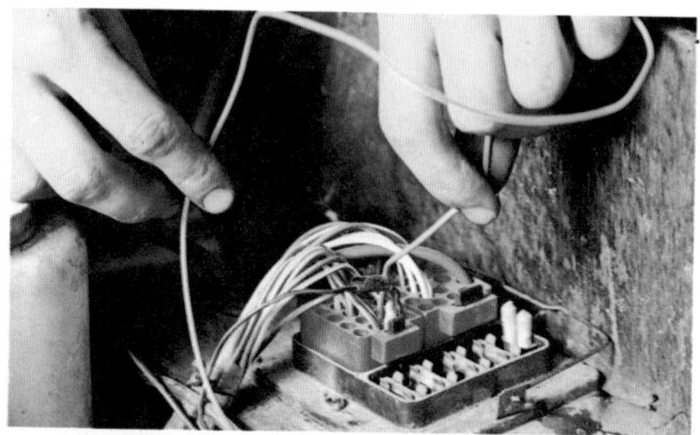

37 Complete the wiring by connecting the single supply wire from the switches to the appropriate terminal on the fusebox

George Wright

38 The completed job. The wiper arm and blade has been fitted to the motor spindle and the washer jet correctly aligned with a pin

When you are sure the unit functions properly refit any trim or headlining that was disturbed during the installation process. If you have a hatchback or an estate (station wagon), check that the tubing is not fouled by the tailgate hinge.

Fitting a rear screen heater

A real must for winter weather is the rear screen heater, which combats ice and misting up, and ensures good rearwards visibility.

An integral screen heater is fitted by many car manufacturers now as standard equipment or optional extra on most cars in their ranges. The heating element is bonded into the glass and in this form is relatively expensive to buy and fit, as the job will have to be done by a professional screen fitter.

There is, however, a large range of kits available which come complete with element, switch, warning light, flex and connections, designed for the DIY enthusiast. They are cheap to buy, easy to fit and very efficient.

Heaters come in sizes suitable for almost every make of car. Smaller, square grids are also available for vans, and so preference really comes down to selecting the best size for your car.

One of the trickier parts of the job is aligning the heater element on the window. Start by laying the whole thing on the outside of the glass in the intended position, and when you are satisfied that it is correctly placed, mark up the glass around the edge with crayon or masking tape, so that the shape will be seen from the inside (fig. 2).

Inside the car, the window must be very clean, and wipe it over thoroughly with methylated spirits (fig. 3). For fitting, the glass must also be perfectly dry. Use a hair dryer for this purpose.

Next, lay the heater down on a clean surface with the backing paper uppermost. Peel this off, and cut vertically into two halves (fig. 4). Replace the backing paper, only with a gap of about 50 mm (2in.) down the centre of the heater element (fig. 5).

Hold the element up to your pre-marked position and check once again for centering. It is best to have someone outside the car assisting you in this.

(fig. 6). Smooth down the exposed two inch strip onto the window. Remove each half of the backing paper in turn, smoothing the element outwards as you go with a soft rag, ensuring that there are no kinks. When in position, use the rag to smooth out any lines, ensuring good adhesion all over. This can be checked from the outside.

It is essential that on estate cars the electrical connections are uppermost to facilitate opening the rear door. It is a good idea to observe this practice on saloon cars as well, as objects on the parcel shelf could damage the wiring.

The switch must now be positioned on the dashboard or console, and the warning lamp must also be used.

A lot of kits feature switch and lamp together in a small panel that can be simply fitted where you please with two small screws. Care must be taken when drilling the screw holes to ensure that there are no wires behind the panel you are drilling. If you choose to mount a switch actually in the dashboard, it is likely you will have to drill one hole for the switch, and one for the lamp (fig. 7). An alternative is to buy a switch which incorporates a lamp, necessitating only one fitting.

A single wire will have to be run from the switch under the carpet to the rear of the car. To prevent the wire being damaged by being trodden on, keep it to the edge of the carpet, and should only be necessary to keep it in place with two or three strips of adhesive tape placed at regular

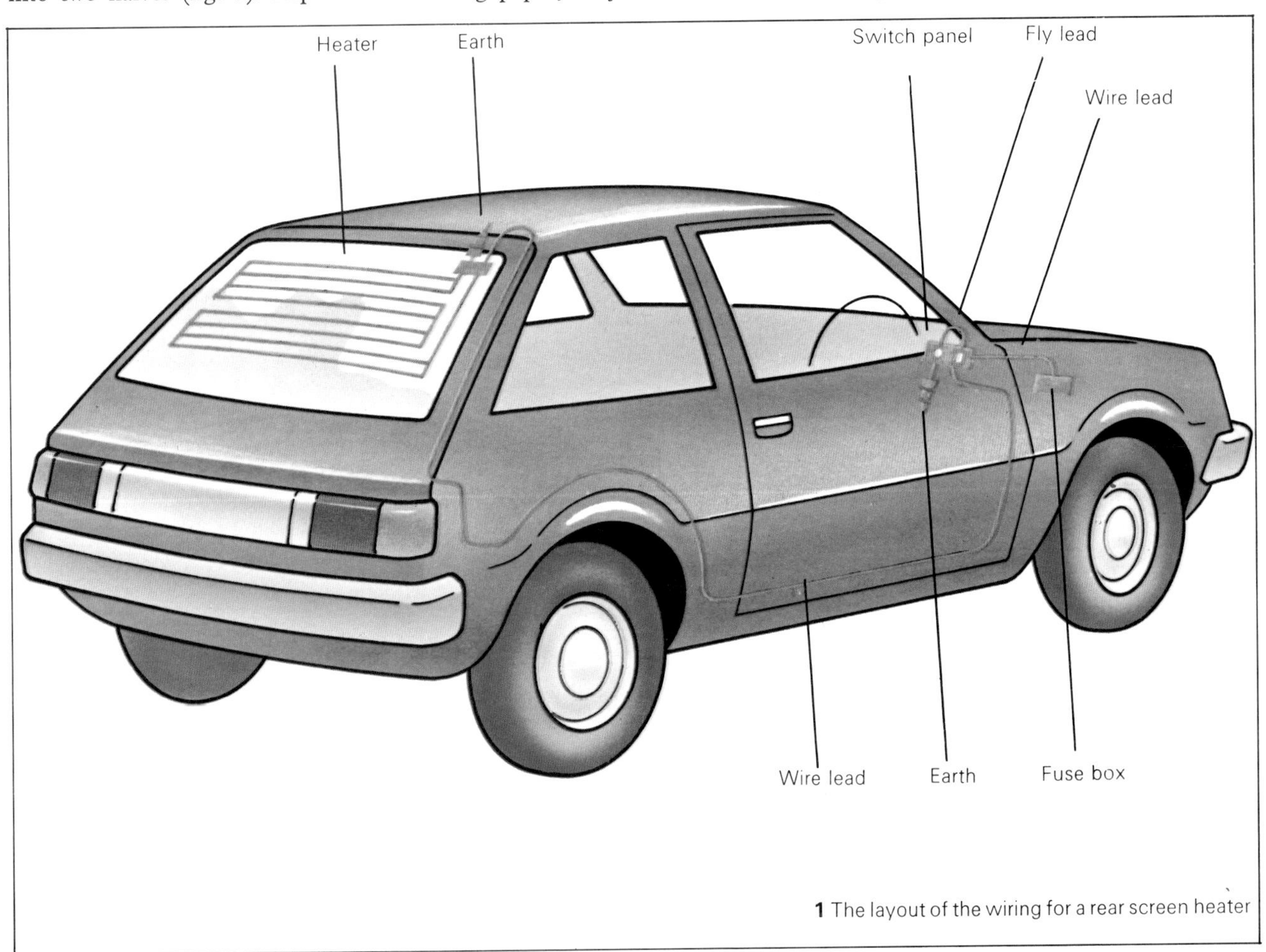

1 The layout of the wiring for a rear screen heater

intervals along its length. The carpet will do the rest.

Run the wire under the rear seat and into the boot compartment, making sure that it is free and not in a position where it might be chafed when the seat is in use. A small hole should be drilled up through the parcel shelf and then fitted with a rubber grommet of suitable size. A second wire must be run from the boot through the same grommet. Prise back the window surround rubber and lay the wires inconspicuously behind it to give a neat appearance. Bare the two wire ends and fit spade connectors, which can then be fitted to the screen terminals (fig. 8). The other end of the wire in the boot should be fitted with an eyelet type connector and fixed to the body to make a good earth with a screw or bolt. An existing screw to earth may be used, but the surrounding area should be rubbed to bare metal and greased to ensure good contact.

For the final stage of wiring, the battery must be disconnected. The long wire from the heater should be connected to one side of the switch. A live feed must be taken to the other switch terminal either from the fuse box or ignition switch. If the wire is taken from the fuse box, ensure it is an outlet which is only live when the ignition is on (fig. 9). A wire taken direct from the ignition must be fitted with an in-line 35 amp fuse. Thread wire through bulkhead (fig. 10) and connect to switch. Connect one terminal of the lamp to the heater side of the switch (not the feed side) (fig. 11). Connect the other terminal of the lamp to a good adjacent earth and wire up lamp (fig. 12).

Finally fit switch and lamp (fig. 13) to dashboard and re-connect battery.

Switch on heater for 5-10 minutes running thumb over heater outline to make good contact with glass. Switch off and then slowly peel off transfer paper (fig. 14).

Run thumb again along edges to ensure good adhesion. Also press terminals firmly onto glass. Secure and conceal wiring (fig. 8).

The consumption of electricity by a screen heater is about the same as for your headlamps, so it should not be left on unnecessarily. It will require only a very short time to do its job but should never be left on when the car's engine is off. This can be ensured by choosing the correct terminal on the ignition switch or fuse box. It will then be switched off automatically when the engine is off. Great care must be taken of this type of heater as they are inclined to be a little vulnerable to the heavy-handed cleaner! When cleaning is necessary, use a little spirit to start with, and finish off gently with a clean duster.

Ensure that the final leads to the panel are firmly fixed and out of the way of any prying fingers.

2 Position template on outside of rear window and mark with masking tape. Check position in mirror

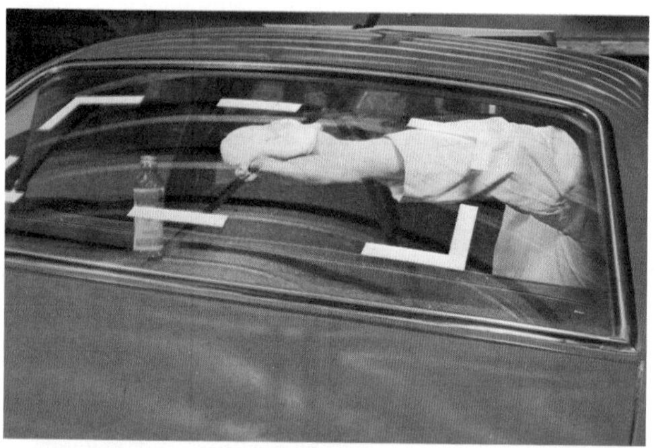

3 Thoroughly clean inside of rear window with spirit. Dry off with a hair dryer or vacuum cleaner blowing tool

4 Lay heater panel down with backing paper upwards. Peel off backing and cut vertically into two halves

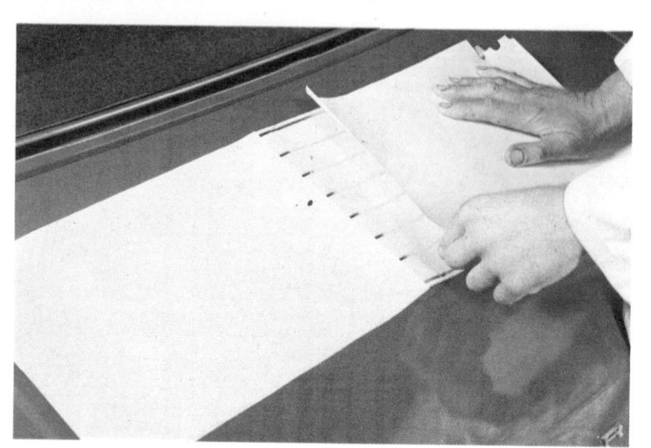

5 Replace backing paper leaving a 50mm (2″) gap down the centre of the element

6 Centre element on inside of window. Stick down 50mm strip and remove backing strips in turn. Smooth outwards

7 Mark positions on dash for switch and warning lights. Check that the space behind the door is clear before drilling

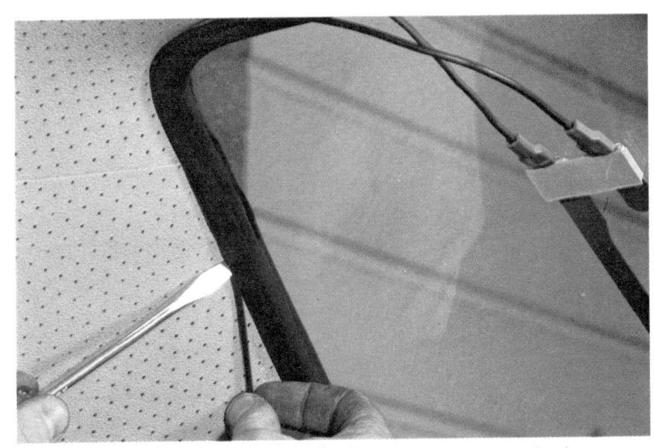

8 After connecting the wires to the heater element terminals feed them under the rubber window beading for neatness

9 Connect live feeds for switch from a fuse box outlet controlled by ignition switch

10 Feed the wire through the bulkhead, following the loom to the heater switch. Connect to one terminal of the switch

11 Connect the long wire from the heater to the other terminal of the switch

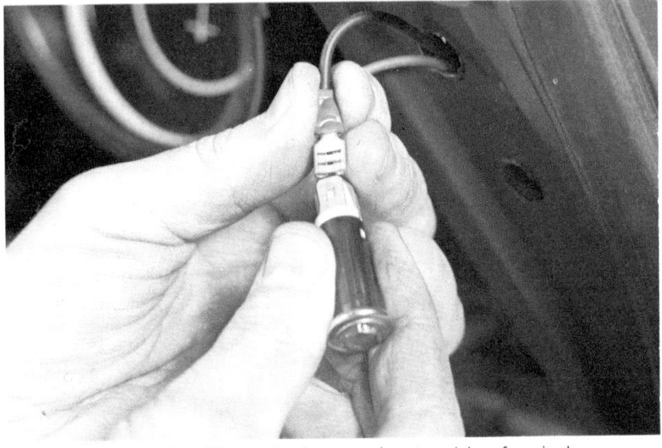

12 Connect one lead from the lamp to heater side of switch. Connect the other lamp lead to an earth

13 Position and secure the switch and lamp to the dash, then re-connect the battery

14 Switch on for 5-10 mins. Run your thumb over the heater outline, then slowly peel off the transfer paper

Custom spraying

Spray-painting stripes, designs or emblems on your car can make a dramatic difference—for better or for worse—to its looks. What matters is not whether you choose a bold, brash design rather than a more subdued one, but how well your design is integrated with the car's basic lines.

Personalizing of this sort is fun to do. It is not difficult. And the materials are cheap: all you need is masking tape, some scrap newspaper and cardboard, and a can or two of aerosol spray paint.

Designing your colour scheme

The design of your colour scheme can be sketched directly on to the car, but it is easier to work it out first on a sheet of paper. A photograph of the car is a great help: you can fix it to a board with drawing pins, lay a sheet of tracing paper over it and get a close idea of how your design will actually look.

Unless you are an experienced designer, the actual design should follow closely the styling lines of the car body itself. Custom painters sometimes produce really striking designs that violate every body line, but this needs real skill—and, even then, failures are quite frequent.

So, for beginners, it is safer to stick to designs that relate to the shapes of the car and of its individual body panels, as in figs. 4 to 7. Straight lines, for example, are best for cars (or vans) of angular appearance, while curving or flowing lines are best on cars with more rounded contours.

Colour choice is obviously important too. Different tones of the same colour—for example, dark brown lines on a light brown car—will produce colour schemes that are discreet and sophisticated. Stark contrasts—for example, red areas on a white background—will give you schemes that range from vivid to eye-popping.

Remember, when drawing up your scheme, that large areas (such as a whole car panel) will look much brighter than small areas (such as the colour sample on a card or can) of the identical colour.

Masking off

Once you have decided on your design, the next step is to transfer it to the car. Then you have to lay masking tape right round the borders of each new colour you intend to apply.

Ordinary-width masking tape (25 mm or 1in.) is best for marking out straight lines. But if you propose to paint curves or intricate designs you will also need 6 mm ($\frac{1}{4}$in.) masking tape from a specialist supplier. This extra-narrow tape bends easily to outline curves.

The basic technique for masking off is on pages 8 to 10. But because designs of this sort are more complicated than plain painting—it is impossible, for example, to mask off simultaneously two adjoining panels—you will need to improvise a little, depending on the design you are using. A suggested order of work is:

First, mark out your design on the car body with chalk or a felt-tipped pen. This will let you see that the whole design looks right before you commit yourself to painting part of it.

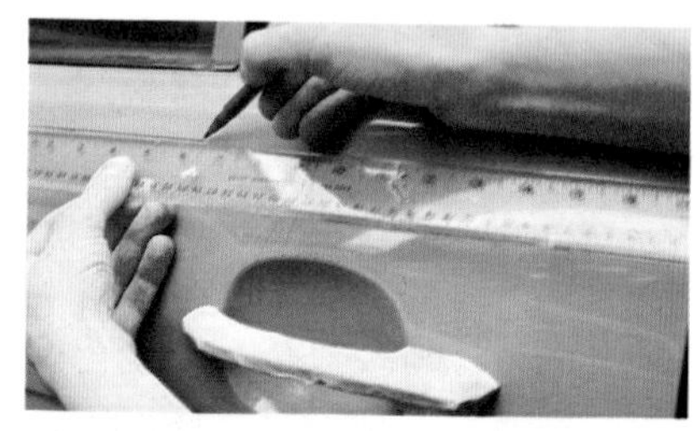

1 Mark out the design, using a felt-tip pen or chalk and a ruler as a straight edge

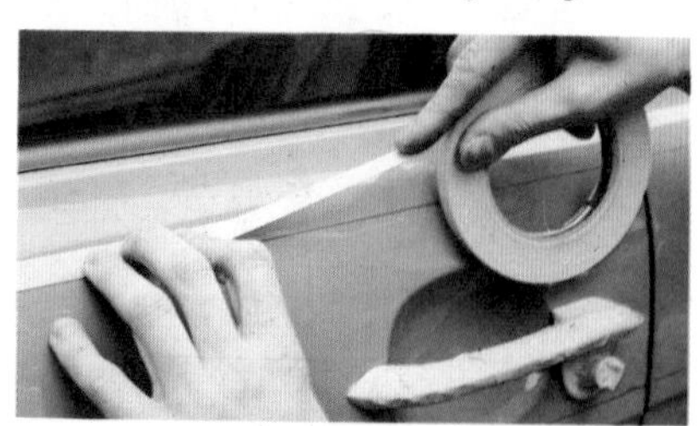

2 Mask around the outer perimeter of the design, first using narrow masking tape

3 Thoroughly mask any brightwork to avoid having to remove overspray later on

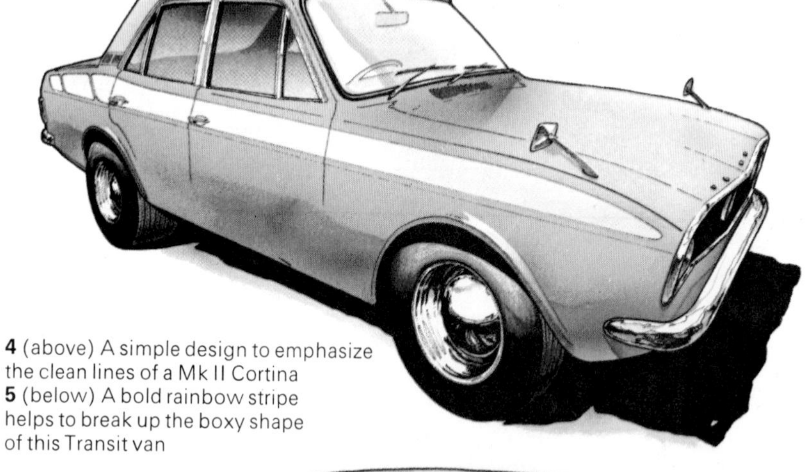

4 (above) A simple design to emphasize the clean lines of a Mk II Cortina
5 (below) A bold rainbow stripe helps to break up the boxy shape of this Transit van

Second, use narrow masking tape to outline the whole area to which you intend to apply your new colour or colours, so that the felt tip marks are just visible.

Third, rub down with wet-and-dry abrasive paper the area to be sprayed, using first 400 grade and then 600. This will get rid of any wax or grease on the panel.

Fourth, dry the area to be sprayed with a chamois leather, making sure to remove all trace of moisture and the felt tip or chalk marks.

Fifth, mask with newspapers the main area which is not going to be covered by the first of your proposed new colours.

Some further tips for the masking stage:

Balance is important. When you have drawn your design with chalk or pen, check that both the area you are going to paint and the area that you are *not* going to paint are not 'lopsided'. Good eyesight and good judgement are better than a ruler for this task; precise measurements are no guarantee that the finished product will look right to the eye—but you will be able to see and 'feel' whether your lines, or whatever, are straight and balanced-looking.

Angles are best dealt with by running two pieces of masking tape to meet and overlap each other, and then cutting away the tape that is not wanted (fig. 8).

Sharp curves are easiest to do if you use a length of extra-wide masking tape to cover the whole area. Mark out the curve on the masking tape, using an ordinary compass, and cut away with a handyman's knife the area you want to paint. Be careful not to cut so deeply that you reach bare metal. Alternatively, use 6 mm masking tape, bending it round the corner.

Chips in the existing paint need special attention at the rubbing down stage. These small holes in the bodywork collect grease and wax which can repel the new paint, leaving 'fisheyes'—blotchy areas—to spoil the finished job. Chips should be cleared of all wax, grease, rust and flaking paint and, if necessary, apply some new primer to protect the surface.

Spray painting

Ordinary car aerosol paints, from a chainstore or motor accessory shop, are quite suitable for spray painting personalized designs. But before you buy, make sure that the paint you propose to use will be compatible with that already on the car.

Before painting, wipe any dust off the design area with a duster—but not with your hands as, however clean, they will transmit grease. Spray according to the instructions, keeping a flexible wrist to achieve an even coat.

After applying each colour, do not wait for the paint to harden before you remove the masking tape—you might damage the paint edge as the tape comes off. Instead, wait only until the paint is tacky. You can test it by putting your finger on the masking tape, without touching the actual painted panel.

First get rid of the newspaper. Then use a sharp knife to lift the end of each piece of tape, and peel off the tape very slowly. If the paint has not stuck properly to its base coat and tends to lift off with the tape, gently run a sharp-bladed knife along the edge of the masking tape so that you cut the paint free. The tape should then peel away without difficulty.

Wait until each colour has dried hard (it could take anything from 24 to 48 hours) before re-masking for the next colour.

6 (above) Colourful flames emphasize the curves of this Morris 1000

7 (below) 'Panels within panels' give this Hunter a distinctive look

Chris Mynheer

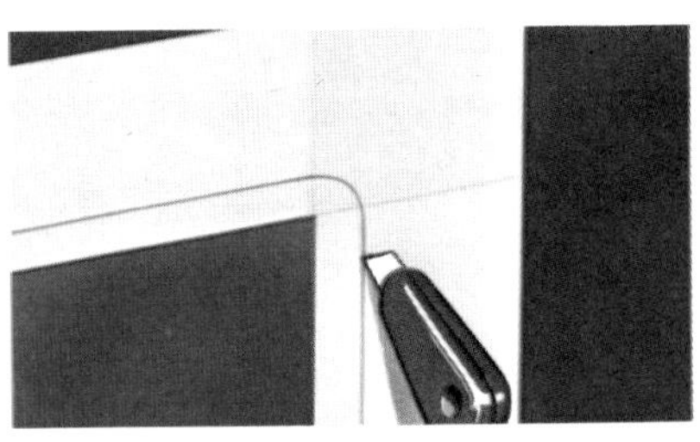

8 To form angles, overlap the tape, then cut away the area that is not required

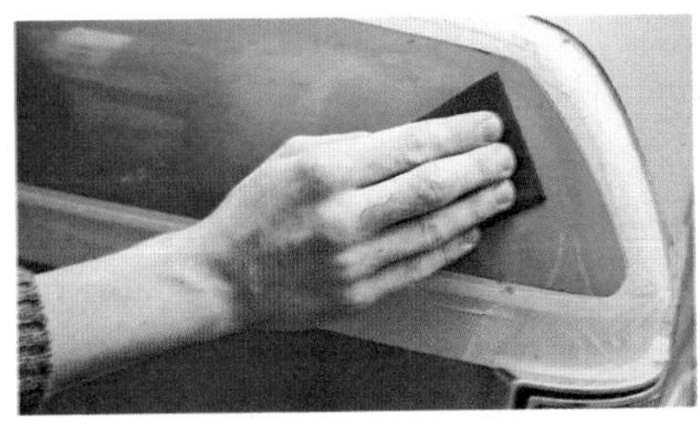

9 Rub down the area to be sprayed, using wet-and-dry paper, until it is smooth

Jerry Tubby

10 Thoroughly mask off with newspaper any paintwork that is not to be sprayed

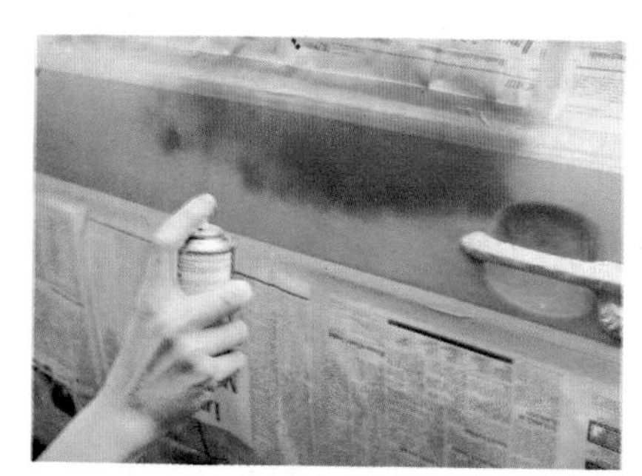

11 Practise with a light coat, making sure you hold the aerosol vertically, about 9in. to 12in. away from the masked panel

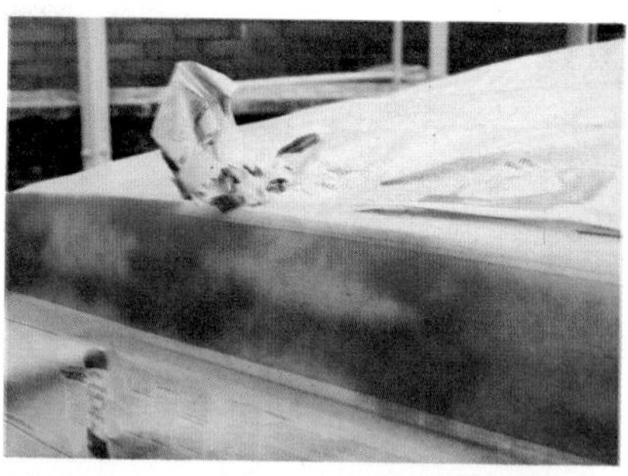

12 When you feel confident, tackle a panel at a time, applying thin coats and taking care not to overpaint, as this causes runs

13 Do not expect to achieve an immediate result with one coat, but gradually build up the paint depth required

14 Run a sharp knife or scalpel round the edge of any brightwork, where the paint may build up, before lifting the tape

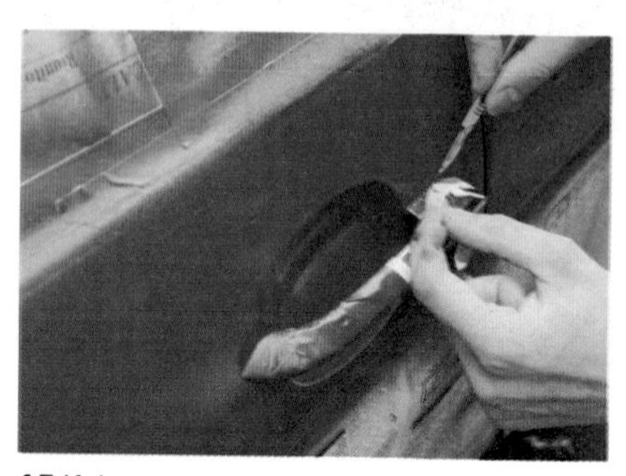

15 If there is heavy paint build-up around the edge, cut along the edge to avoid the risk of tearing the paint

Jerry Tubby

16 The remaining masking tape should peel off easily, but it is a wise precaution to follow along with the scalpel just in case

Special effects

Several unusual effects can be achieved with aerosol sprays. Stars, circles, boxes, emblems and similar small designs can be painted by cutting a sheet of cardboard and using it as a template, or stencil. Make sure you leave enough card around the required shape to prevent any overspray from hitting the rest of the car.

The best way to spray such shapes is to hold the template firmly against the panel with your left hand, so that you get a sharp edge to the paint, while you use the aerosol can in your right, spraying very lightly. This method is highly versatile: the card and aerosol are easily moved, so you can spray patterns at random over the car's panels.

Because the density of the shapes themselves depends on the number of coats you spray—the more coats, the bolder the image—you can if you wish mix solid shapes with soft, 'ghosted' ones.

By using the aerosol in a different way you can achieve the effect known in custom circles as 'fogging'. What you do is to spray so that only half the spray cone (fig. 17) falls on the car panel, the rest ending up on the newspaper mask. When the newspaper is removed, the result is a colour which starts with a hard edge and gradually fades away.

'Fogging' requires a little practice, so it is wise to try it on a sheet of scrap material before venturing near the car.

Once fogging has been mastered, you can combine it with 'random' masking to produce effects such as those in fig. 6. Or combine fogging with stencil work to produce a whole series of other, unusual patterns.

Lacquering and compounding

The ideal protective coating over your finished panel or panels is a layer of clear lacquer, since it gives a highly 'polished', unmarred surface.

Lacquers, like paints, can be bought in aerosol form. But again you need to make sure that the one you choose will be compatible with the existing paints; cellulose will probably be the safest bet.

When thoroughly dry, the surface should be compounded. This is a hand-finishing method which removes a very fine coat of paint or lacquer to produce a flatter, smoother surface—and gets rid of any dust which has settled on the finish while it was drying.

Compounding is done with a cutting paste, such as T-Cut car polish, and a soft rag. The paste is applied with a circular movement, following the maker's instructions, and then rubbed off.

Trevor Lawrence

17 To achieve the effect called 'fogging', allow only half of the spray cone to actually fall on the unmasked panel area

George Wright

18 The paint needs 48 hours to harden before it is compounded and then finished off with a good coat of wax polish

Part 3

Improving the engine

Engines and engine power

All cars and motor-cycles in current production are powered by internal combustion engines, in which the force needed to propel the vehicle is generated inside the engine itself. Since many of the chapters in this section of the book deal with tuning and improving the car's performance, it is useful to understand the layout of a typical engine.

Internal combustion engines used in motor vehicles are of two main types. The first is the spark-ignition engine, in which fuel vapour mixed with air is ignited by an electric spark, and the expansion of the air caused by the heat of the combustion is used to drive a piston or rotor. Spark-ignition engines are usually fuelled by petrol, although propane gas is sometimes used.

The second type is the compression-ignition engine, which also uses the heat from a combustion process to drive a piston, but in which no spark is needed. Instead, the fuel is vaporized and injected into air which has been heated to a temperature at which the fuel becomes self-igniting. Compression-ignition engines are driven by fuel oil, or 'dieseline'.

The force which drives either type of engine is not, strictly speaking, an 'explosion'. The fuels used ignite readily, but burn relatively slowly as compared with, say, dynamite. This characteristic allows the piston to be pushed down its cylinder without damage, whereas an explosion would wreck it.

The vast majority of internal combustion engines used in motor vehicles are of the reciprocating type, in which the up-and-down movement of a piston or pistons is converted by means of a crankshaft into a rotary motion—in much the same way that the more-or-less vertical movement of a cyclist's legs is used to rotate a

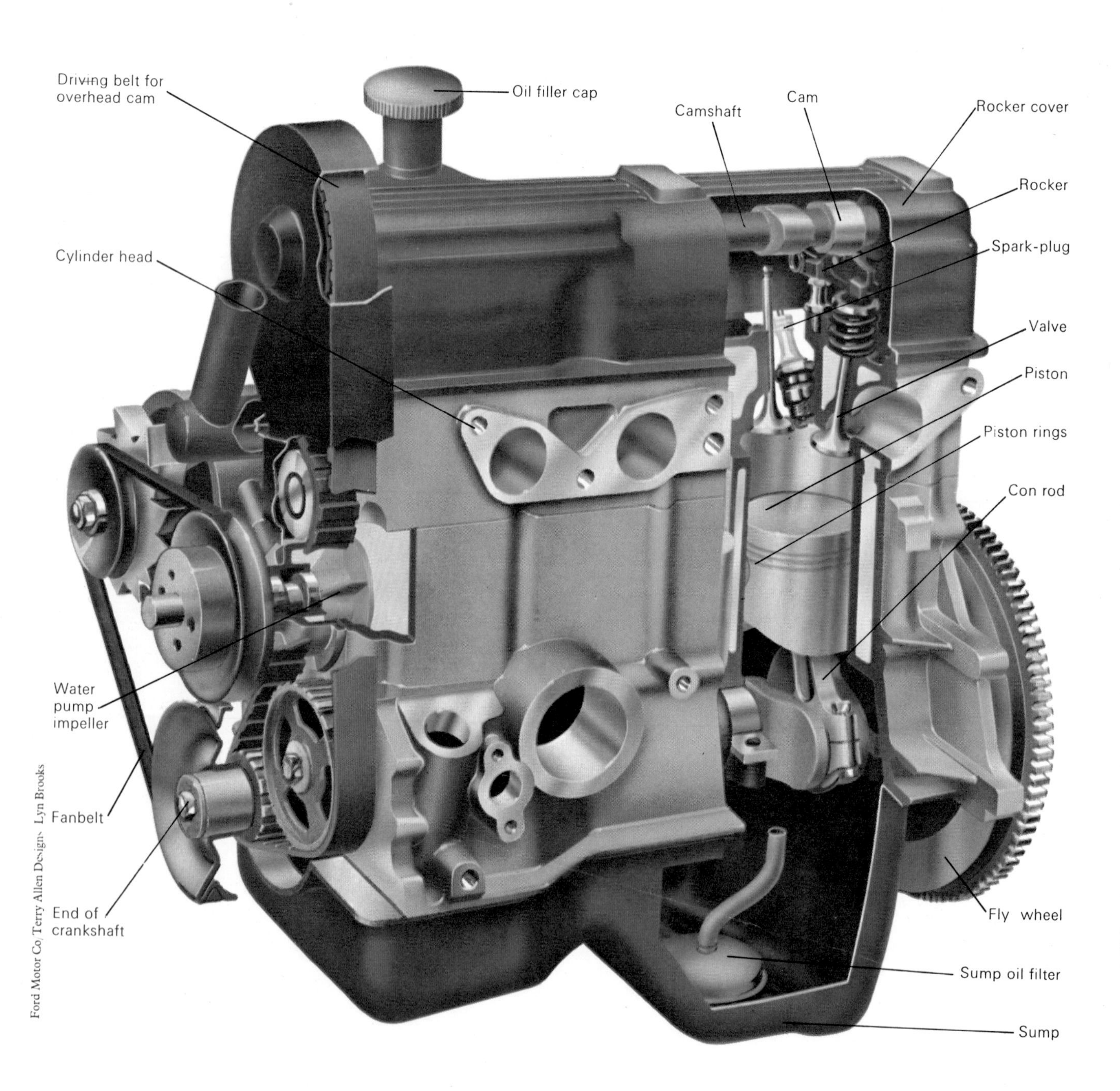

Ford Motor Co/Terry Allen Designs Lyn Brooks

cycle's chain wheel.

Reciprocating engines, in turn, are of two types. In the two-stroke engine, driving force is imparted to the piston once for every revolution of the crankshaft (or two strokes of the piston). In the four-stroke engine, force is imparted once for every two revolutions of the crankshaft (or four strokes of the piston).

How an engine works

To obtain work from combustion, the source of the combustion must be confined and its energy directed. Putting a match to a saucer of petrol would produce a 'whoosh' as it caught fire—but little else, because the energy generated by the burning would be dissipated in all directions.

So the basic part of an automobile engine is a cylinder, machined from the engine block so that it is closed at the top (fig. 1). Inside the cylinder is a closely-fitting piston which acts as a seal for the lower part of the cylinder so that the force of the combustion is fully contained. At the same time, the piston is free to move up and down.

Each time combustion takes place, the piston is driven downwards and its motion is transmitted by a connecting rod to a rotating crankshaft. From there the motion is directed, via the vehicle's gearing and transmission system, to the driving wheel or wheels.

The top of the cylinder is not totally sealed at all times, however. Two (sometimes four) openings permit the ingress of fuel and the expulsion of exhaust gases resulting from combustion. These orifices are opened and shut at appropriate intervals by valves, whose movement is controlled by a camshaft driven (indirectly) by the crankshaft. This ensures that the frequency at which fuel is ingested by the cylinder matches the speed of the engine. Another device, the distributor, is also driven by the engine to ensure that the charges of fuel are ignited at the correct intervals.

All reciprocal engines must be started by an outside agency, such as a self-starter motor, kick starter or (on older cars) a starting handle supplied as a defence against self-starter failure. From that point the operation of four-stroke and two-stroke machines is somewhat different.

Four-stroke engine

The four-stroke spark-ignition engine used in the majority of modern motor vehicles was invented—twice—in the nineteenth century.

The first inventor, in about 1862, was the Frenchman Alphonse Beau de Rochas. The second, about 1875, was the German Dr N. A. Otto. Since neither knew of the other's patent until engines were being manufactured in both countries, a lawsuit followed. De Rochas won a sum of money, but Otto emerged with the fame: the principle of the four-stroke engine is still known as the 'Otto cycle'.

In any reciprocal engine, the two extreme positions between which a piston can move are called top dead centre (TDC) and bottom dead centre (BDC). In a four-stroke engine (fig. 2), each piston starts its pattern of work from TDC. As it begins its first downwards movement, an inlet valve in the top of the cylinder opens to admit petrol vapour mixed with air. By the time the piston has reached BDC it has induced, or sucked in, a full measure of this fuel. This first movement is therefore called the induction (or inlet) stroke.

During the next—upwards—stroke, the inlet valve is closed while the piston compresses the fuel mixture so that it will readily ignite. This stroke is therefore known as the compression stroke.

As the piston approaches TDC, an electric charge jumps between the electrodes of the spark-plug and ignites the fuel vapour concentrated in the top of the cylinder. The resulting combustion, in which the temperature of the burning fuel can reach 2,000°C and the force as much as 2 tonnes, drives the piston downwards—the power stroke.

By the time the piston has again reached the bottom of the cylinder, the force of the combustion has been expended. All that remains is to allow the waste products of combustion to escape into the exhaust system and hence into the atmosphere. So at this stage a second valve in the cylinder, the exhaust valve, opens. This

1 (opposite and below) Cutaway and three-quarter views of a typical four-stroke car engine, showing its principle components

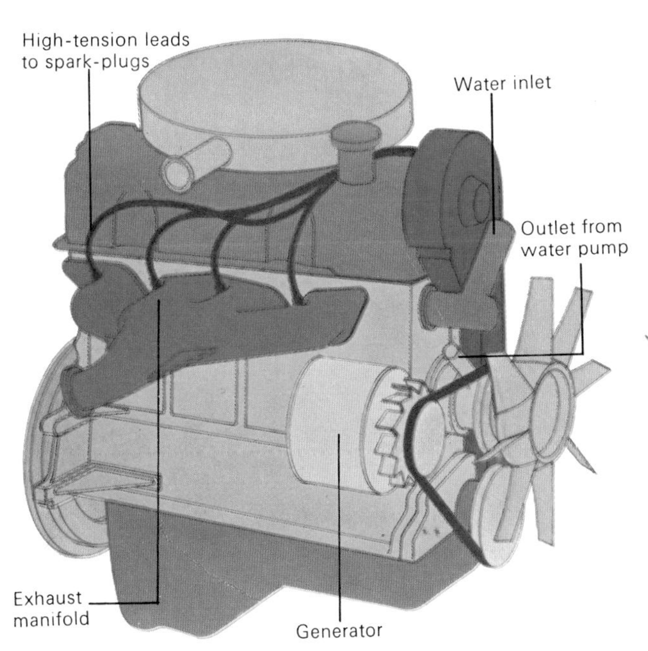

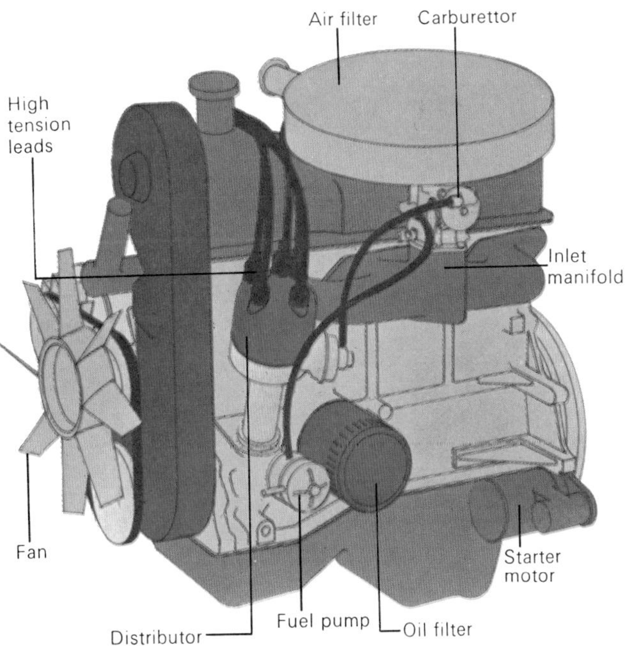

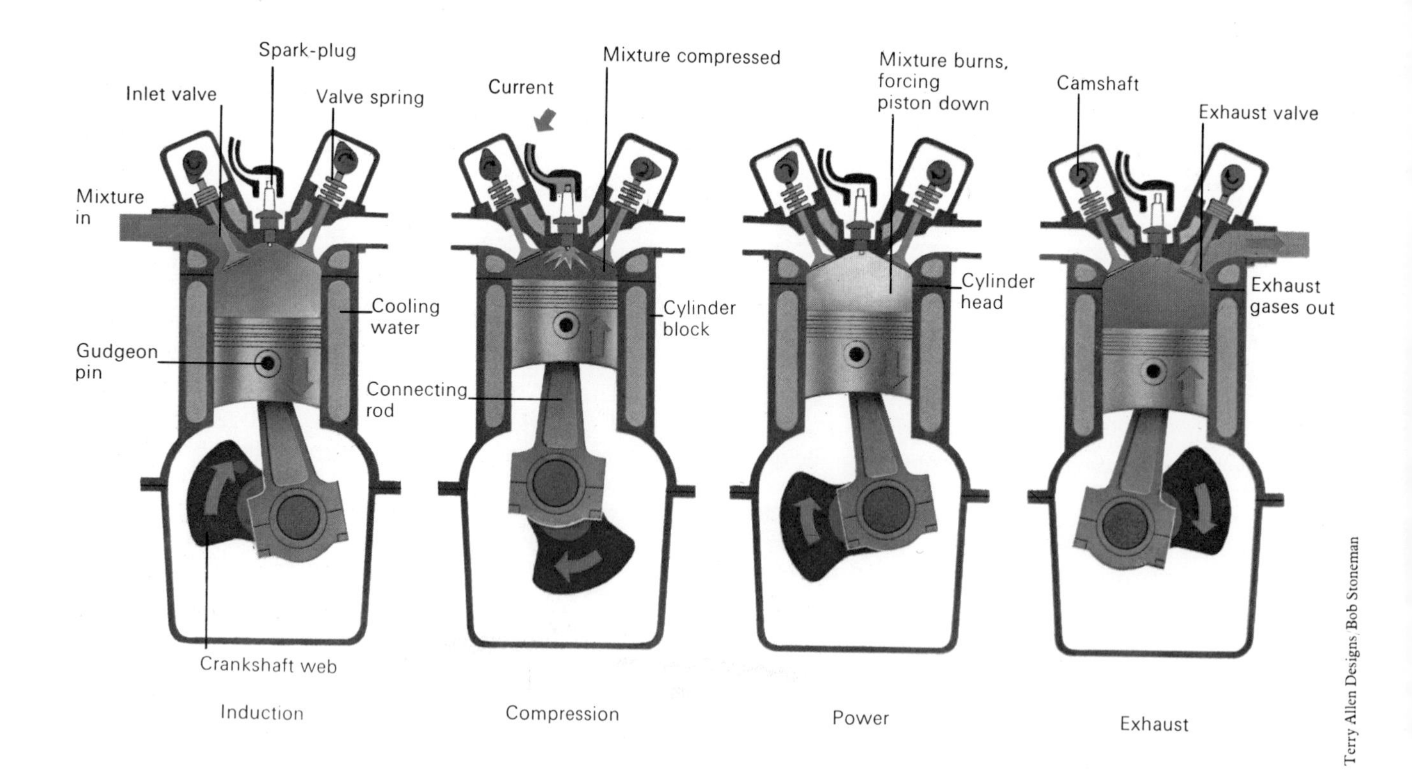

2 (above) The four-stroke cycle

3 (below) The two-stroke cycle

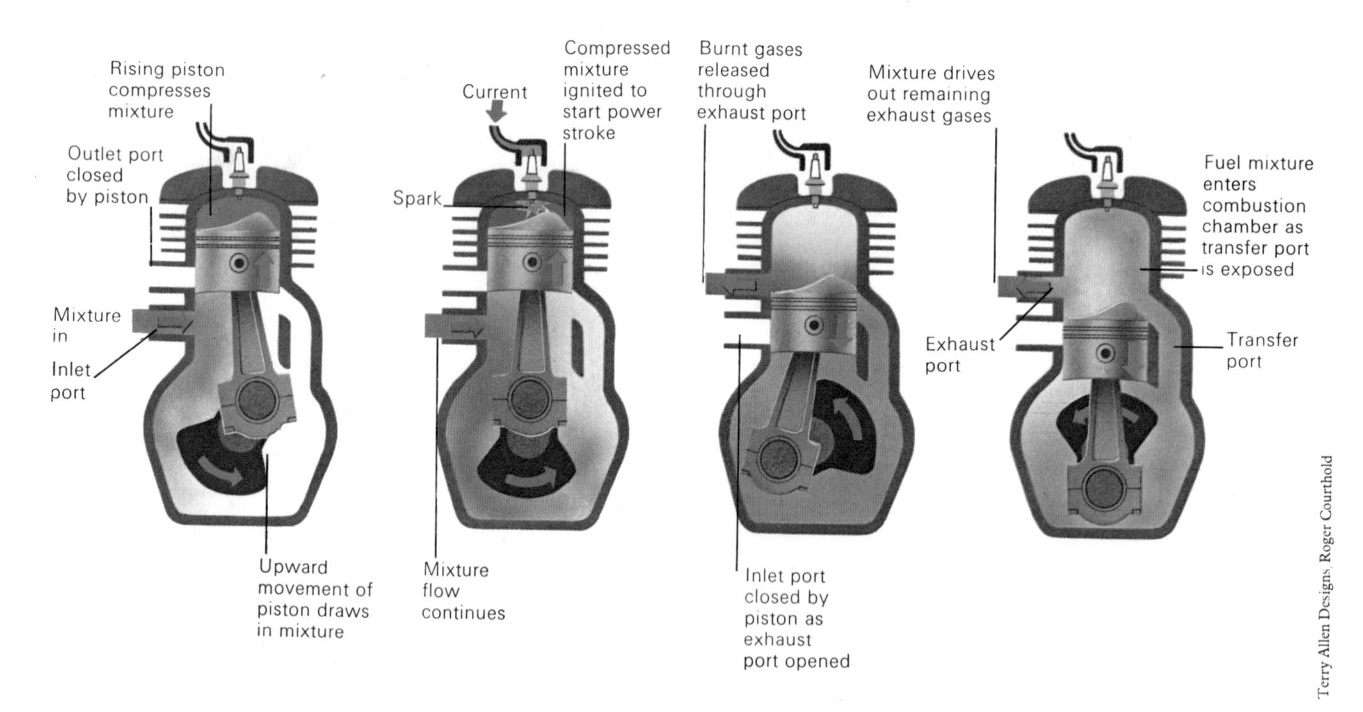

allows the piston on its fourth, or exhaust, stroke to push the gases out through the top of the cylinder.

That is the theory of the four-stroke operation, but in practice the different stages are not as neatly separated as the theory suggests. For example, the engine will generate maximum power if combustion is at its peak when the piston is at the top of its stroke. But burning is not instantaneous; instead, it begins in the fuel mixture that is nearest the spark-plug and fans outwards until all the fuel is burned. To allow for this delay, ignition has to take place a fraction of a second—or a few degrees of crankshaft rotation—before the piston reaches TDC.

Similarly, there is a delay between the instant that a valve begins to open and that at which fuel vapour, or exhaust gas, can flow through it at full pressure. So both inlet and exhaust valves are often made to open a few degrees early (a process called valve lead) or close a few degrees late (called valve lag) to increase the engine's efficiency. Such intervals are, of course, only fractions of a second, since even at idling speed a piston in a typical family car moves upwards or downwards about 1,600 times a minute.

Manufacturers plot the valve lag and valve lead—together called valve overlap—for each individual engine on a valve timing diagram (fig. 5). Generally, the faster an engine is designed to operate, the greater the amount of valve overlap.

Although the piston has to make four movements to

complete one cycle of work, the shape of the crankshaft means that each piston can make only two strokes—one upwards, one downwards—for each revolution of the crankshaft itself. So any one piston can apply driving force to the crankshaft only once every four strokes, or two revolutions.

It is perfectly feasible to maintain the turning momentum of the crankshaft between power strokes by means of a flywheel or similar device, and hence to build a four-stroke engine with only one cylinder. But the vibration set up by the spasmodic firing of such an engine would impose an excessive load on both the engine itself and on the vehicle as a whole. Rather than having one huge cylinder, therefore, four-stroke car engines usually have four or more smaller ones which fire in rotation.

Two-stroke engine

Since the four-stroke engine was seen to be relatively inefficient, delivering only one power stroke in four, inventors sought a way of improving it. By 1878 a Scot, Dugald Clerk, developed an engine whose work cycle was completed in two strokes, using a secondary cylinder and piston to feed the fuel mixture into the main cylinder. In 1891 Joseph Day modified Clerk's engine to dispense with the second cylinder, substituting instead an airtight crankcase through which the fuel could be fed on its way to the firing chamber. But the basic principle of the two-stroke engine is still called, after its original inventor, the Clerk cycle.

The two-stroke engine (fig. 3) has a cylinder, piston, crankshaft and spark-plug as does its four-stroke counterpart. But there are no valves. Instead, three holes—the inlet, exhaust and transfer ports—are cut into the cylinder itself and are blocked or left open by the piston as it moves up and down.

The two-stroke engine must accomplish induction, combustion and exhaust in one up-and-down movement of the piston. The work cycle starts with the piston rising from BDC to uncover the inlet port, thereby inducing a charge of fuel into the airtight crankcase. As the piston continues to rise, it seals off the exhaust and transfer ports and completes the compression of the fuel mixture in the combustion chamber.

Just before TDC, the mixture is ignited and the piston is pushed downwards. As it descends it uncovers the exhaust port to allow the burned gases to escape. At the same time, the bottom part of the piston acts as a pump to force the mixture in the crankcase up the transfer port and into the combustion chamber ready for ignition.

The head of the piston is shaped to reduce the amount of unburned fuel vapour that can mix with the exhaust gases while the piston is around BDC. And, in modern two-stroke engines, the transfer port is shaped to direct the fuel vapour towards the top of the cylinder, away from the exhaust port. But some mixing of unburned and burned gases is inevitable.

Because each piston produces a power stroke for every revolution of the crankshaft, a two-stroke engine should theoretically be twice as powerful as a four-stroke engine of the same cylinder dimensions. In practice it is rarely more than $1\frac{1}{2}$ times as powerful.

There are a number of reasons. One is that the induction and transfer ports are unalterable openings whose band of operating efficiency is relatively narrow. If the ports are designed so that a large amount of fuel is used, the engine will tend to work well only at high speeds. If on the other hand the ports are designed for small amounts of fuel, the engine will perform well at low speeds but badly at high. Further, because the piston moves twice as quickly as it would need to in a four-stroke engine of similar revolutions-per-minute, it is subjected to greater heat—but its extra role as a port sealer requires that it be manufactured and maintained to closer tolerances. So higher wear than in a four-stroke is inevitable—and more damaging to performance.

Finally, in spite of advances in design, it is impossible to prevent some of the unburned fuel vapour from mixing with the exhaust gases as it drives them through the exhaust port. As well as wasting petrol and increasing pollution, this can cause deposits of lubricating oil to foul the exhaust port and spark-plug.

So although many motor-cycles and mopeds still had two-stroke engines, there was a strong trend in the 1970s towards four-strokes, particularly for motor-cycles of larger engine capacities. And the use of two-strokes in cars was confined to one or two models.

Compression ratios

Both spark-ignition and compression-ignition engines compress each charge of fuel before it is ignited. This increases the temperature of the fuel, making it easier

4 (below) Ford experimental stratified-charge engine. This varies from the standard four-stroke in two ways. It uses direct-cylinder fuel injection instead of a carburettor, and the piston head itself is a combustion chamber of high compression ratio. The engine's 'programmed combustion', first in the piston head and then in the cylinder, saves fuel and reduces air pollution

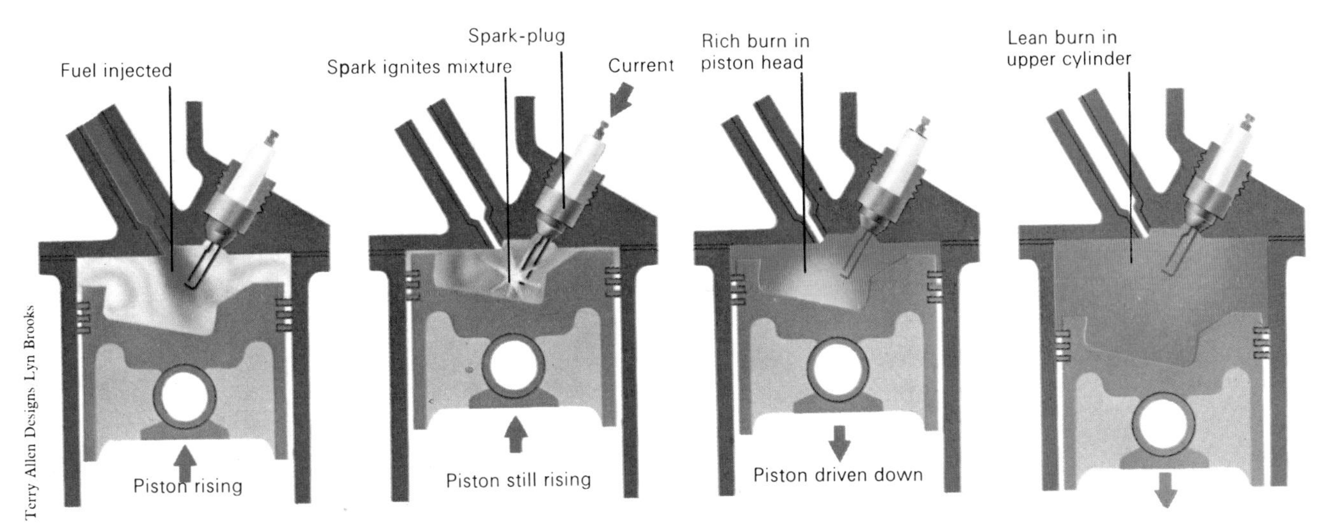

to ignite; helps ensure that it burns completely; and increases the pressure—and hence the power delivered—after burning.

The amount by which the fuel mixture is compressed is called the compression ratio. It is calculated by dividing the 'swept' volume of the piston (ie, the volume traversed by the piston from BDC to TDC) by the volume of the compression chamber (ie, the volume above TDC). For example, a cylinder with a swept volume of 100 cc and a combustion chamber volume of 10 cc would have a compression ratio of 10:1. In the petrol engines of production cars, compression ratios vary from about 7.5:1 to about 11:1. In diesels, the usual compression ratio is around 20:1.

Everything else being equal, the higher the compression ratio of a cylinder the greater the power it can deliver. One of the first steps in converting a conventional engine to high-performance, for example, is to machine a small amount (perhaps 0.75 mm or thirty thousandths of an inch) off the top of the cylinder head. This increases the compression ratio by reducing the volume of the compression chamber.

However, a high-compression engine is also a less flexible engine, because its usable band of engine speeds is narrower than a low-compression engine's. On low-octane petrol, for example, an engine with a compression ratio of 10:1 would perform poorly in a high gear at low speeds, whereas a similar engine with an 8.5:1 compression ratio would manage easily. The reason is that extremes of pressure and temperature cause the mixture to explode instead of merely burning rapidly.

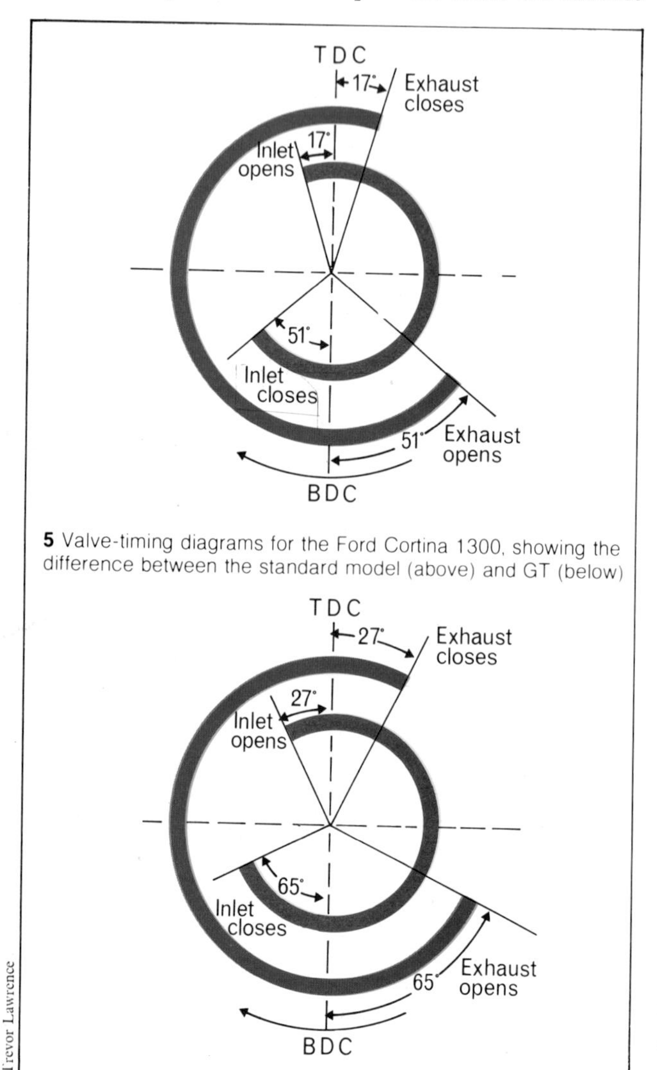

5 Valve-timing diagrams for the Ford Cortina 1300, showing the difference between the standard model (above) and GT (below)

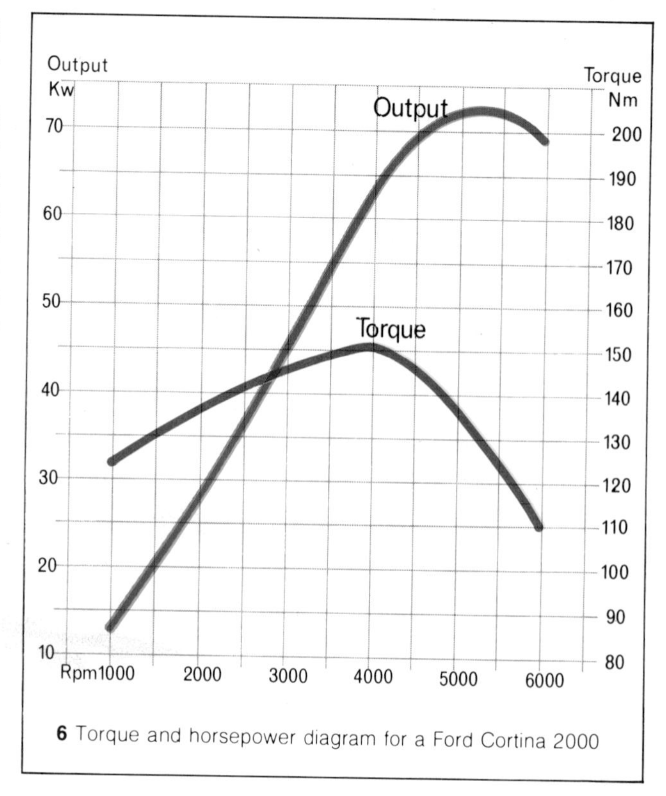

6 Torque and horsepower diagram for a Ford Cortina 2000

To counteract engine knock, lead is added to petrol; the higher the octane rating (or 'star' rating) of the petrol, the greater the amount of lead that has been added. The use of petrol with a high octane rating makes it possible for cars whose engines have a high compression ratio to be driven without constant gear changing. A car whose engine has a compression ratio of 11:1, for example, will normally use the best available fuel.

Until recent years there was a tendency for the compression ratios of production car engines to be progressively increased. In both the US and Europe, however, legislation has been introduced to limit the amount of atmospheric pollution produced by cars' exhausts. So by the late 1970s the trend was the other way, with some new Continental cars having compression ratios of as low as 7.5:1.

Engine power

The power developed by an engine can be measured in several ways, the most common being indicated horsepower and brake horsepower. Indicated horsepower is a measurement of the power generated inside the cylinders. Brake horsepower is a measurement of the power remaining after losses from friction and pumping inside the engine itself (but not losses in the gearbox or transmission) have been deducted. It is usually about 85 per cent of indicated horsepower. One horsepower is 33,000 ft/lb/min—the power needed to move 33,000 lb one foot in one minute—and equals 0.746 kilowatts.

Another way of expressing the performance of an engine is to quote its maximum torque. This is the turning force exerted by the engine, and is normally expressed as a load at a radius—for example, kilogramme metres, Newton metres or foot pounds.

The engine speed which produces the maximum horsepower is not the same as that at which maximum torque is generated, however. Maximum torque usually occurs at around two-thirds of the engine speed that produces maximum horsepower.

Trevor Lawrence

Tuning the engine

Nelson Hargreaves

1 This selection of tuning parts for a Vauxhall includes Dellorto carburettors with special manifold and airbox, two gas-flowed exhausts, a modified cylinder head and electronic ignition

Tuning your engine—for economy or performance—need not necessarily be confined to the odd check on the points or the carburettor. Nor is it essential to give an engine a major rebuild in order to extract more power or achieve a lower fuel consumption. In recent years, a variety of bolt-on tuning accessories have become available to the DIY mechanic. Choose the parts carefully and you will be ready to transform not only your engine but the character of the entire car.

The engines which offer the greatest scope to the home tuner are those in the cheap and medium-priced mass production cars. There are two basic reasons for this.

To begin with, a manufacturer must strike a balance between the efficiency of his design and how much it will actually cost to make. Twin carburettors, for example, may be an efficient way of providing the engine with fuel but on an ordinary family saloon, one will do a good enough job for less than half the cost.

The manufacturer must also make his engine to comparatively wide tolerances. This allows for mass production and for the matching of parts from a variety of different sources. Unfortunately it also leaves the finished engine with quite a large number of 'rough edges'. This often impairs efficiency and, as a result, restricts performance.

Engines manufactured to high tolerances and with expensive materials are certainly more efficient, but they are not an economic proposition on a mass-production car. With different parts often coming from different sources, a car manufacturer has little choice but to allow margins for error in his design, consequently, some efficiency is sacrificed because of this.

All in all though, the compromise usually works well. Prices are kept down and so are servicing costs because parts are standardized and are kept relatively simple. An engine in a low state of tune will not be working to its full potential and will therefore often cover high mileages without the need for an overhaul. A good example of this is the VW "Beetle". The engines on these cars have a solid reputation for long life and this has been gained to a large extent by restricting their performance. The rev limit is set at a relatively low figure and other aspects of the design give a deliberately low power output in relation to the engine's cubic capacity and tuning potential.

DIY tuning

As a DIY tuner, you will not be bound by the constraints put on the car manufacturers. Starting with their basic engine, and a reasonable sum of money, you will be in a position to build up a more efficient unit to suit your own personal requirements.

There are engine parts available which, if used properly, can transform an engine from its basic state up to racing standards. In many cases they will be better made and of better quality than the manufacturer's originals because more time has been spent making them. They will, of course, be more expensive.

For many car owners, though, the investment is a worthwhile one. You do not have to stretch your resources to match the budgets of racing specialists in order to achieve results. Quite worthwhile improvements can be made, especially in power output, for about half the cost of a new engine. The brake horse power of a basic BL Mini, for example, can be almost doubled just by changing the carburettor, cylinder head, camshaft and exhaust. This may sound like a lot of work, but all the parts can usually be bought on an exchange basis from a tuning specialist and removal of the standard part and fitting the modified ones is well within the capabilities of the DIY mechanic.

In short, the basic idea behind engine tuning is that you make the proper use of the parts and the expertise available. There is no reason at all why you should not be able to create a really individual, practical and reliable car.

When to tune the engine

If you decide to tune your engine, the parts which you have modified or replaced should certainly be able to cope with the extra strain, but those which have been left as standard may not. After a certain amount of wear has taken place some parts may become liable to break up under stress. Increasing your compression ratio, perhaps by fitting a modified cylinder head, inevitably places a greater load on the piston rings. If they are worn, you will not get much benefit from your expensive tuning equipment.

Engine wear is difficult to assess because it varies so much from car to car but tuning experts usually agree that with an engine that has covered more than 48,000 km (30,000 miles), tuning and major modifications should be considered only as part of a major overhaul.

This is not a hard and fast rule, though. It depends to a large extent on how complete a tuning operation you plan to undertake. For instance, fitting a new carburettor and a new exhaust manifold to an old engine would be all right providing the unit was in good overall condition.

If you are in any doubt about your own engine you should carry out a few simple checks for wear before investing in tuning equipment. The most effective check is the compression test (page 161). When you run it, you should find that all your engine's cylinders give a similar reading, close to the manufacturer's original specification. If one or more vary a great deal from the others, suspect worn bores and pistons, broken rings or badly seating valves. You may have to consider an engine re-build.

If possible, and unless one is already fitted, it may be worthwhile to connect up an oil pressure gauge to the engine. A low reading here could warn you of imminent bearing failure. You can learn a lot by just listening to the engine. If it sounds particularly noisy, the valve gear and the timing chain may be in need of adjustment or replacement and may not stand any additional stress. The most important thing to remember when you start engine tuning is that you must have a sound basis on which to work.

Weak engines

Another point to bear in mind before you invest in tuning parts is whether or not your engine is inherently strong enough to take more power. There are several older engines which have a bad reputation with tuning experts and you should seek their advice. If you own such an engine, you should think about changing the entire unit rather than risk any modifications. Among the most common are the old Leyland "A" series 803 cc engines, which some experts consider not to be strong enough for tuning. The 1098 cc unit as fitted to the 1100 range does not have a very good reputation either, although the engines fitted to the 1100 Sprite and Midget have larger big-end bearings and, therefore, are considered to be a much better foundation on which to work.

The V-4 unit found in some British Ford Corsairs and Zephyrs is another which is not suited to tuning—a complete engine swap is a better proposition. The Chrysler Imp Mk I engine has a weaker block and head which cannot be stressed too heavily and the old Minx/Rapier 1600 cc unit is yet another engine with a poor reputation for strength.

If you are in any doubt at all about the suitability of your engine for tuning, either because of its condition or the age of the design, consult a tuning specialist. Be prepared to be disappointed if he tells you that the engine cannot be tuned—it is far safer to check at this stage and avoid wasting a lot of money.

Economy or performance

Contrary to the popular myth, fitting a pair of twin carburettors to your car does not make it use twice as much fuel. The difference between tuning for performance or for economy is not as clear cut as that. The basic idea of increasing power output is to make the engine more efficient. If this is done, fuel consumption as well as power output will benefit from the improvement and the engine will be, potentially, more economical. In practice though, the increased power can tempt you to make more use of the performance in which case the fuel consumption will most probably increase.

Certain modifications do make a lot of difference to the amount of petrol the engine uses but these are at the more advanced end of the tuning accessory market. They are designed mainly for the racing enthusiast, primarily interested in maximum performance.

Generally speaking, rectifying the imperfections in a standard engine, improving the way in which fuel gets into it and smoothing the way in which the exhaust gases get out, all help to improve economy as well as power. Which kind of benefit you reap really depends on how heavily you use the accelerator pedal and the power available.

Engine tuning and safety

Tuning up an engine means increasing your car's potential performance beyond the limits of the original design. This in turn places a question mark over the ability of your brakes and suspension to cope with the extra power. It is very important, both from a safety and from a legal point of view, that your car is fit to drive in its modified form.

There are large selections of brake and suspension tuning components available on the accessory market, specially designed for engine tuning enthusiasts. If you are only considering a mild tune you may not need to make use of them, but you should still check with a tuning specialist to make sure. More substantial increases in engine power will certainly call for the brakes to be uprated, so bear in mind the cost of doing this before you commit yourself. A reputable tuning-part stockist should certainly be able to tell you what the implications of tuning your engine to a certain stage are, and whether you will need to modify the brakes and suspension.

Warranties and insurance

New-car warranties can be jeopardized if you start fitting unauthorized parts to your engine within the guarantee period. Some manufacturers do offer approved tuning kits which can be incorporated into the warranty—Leyland ST Pluspacs come into this category—but it is as well to check with the dealer from whom you bought the car.

Like a warranty, your insurance cover may be invalidated if you tune your car's engine beyond its original specification, as this may move it into a higher insurance rating group. The answer here is to always make sure that your insurance company is kept informed of any modifications. Depending on what they are, you may or may not have to pay a slightly higher premium. It is probably best to plan all your modifications and then ask your insurance company before proceeding.

Nelson Hargreaves

2 Hand polishing the cylinder head ports. Gas flow is improved after the ports and the combustion chambers have been machined

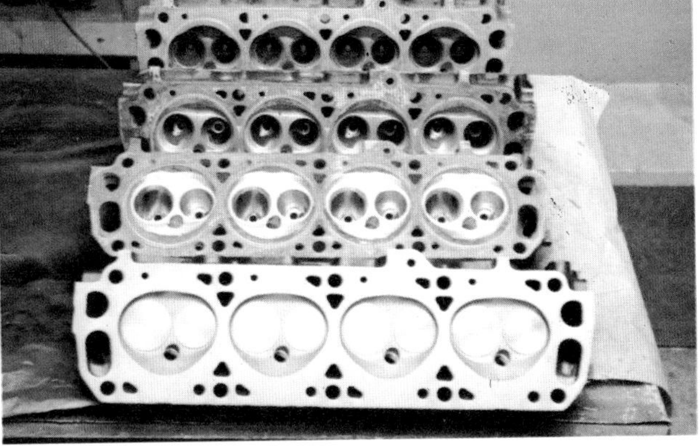

3 Four stages in cylinder head modification. From top to bottom: a standard head, machined, polished and finally sandblasted

The basics of engine tuning

Because engine tuning is mainly about improving your engine's efficiency and turning it into a more refined unit, there is a lot that you can do without buying any parts at all. Great improvements can be made to your original cylinder head, for instance, by polishing the inlet and outlet ports and by 'trimming' the combustion chambers so that they are all the same size and match their opposite halves on the engine block.

The accessory market offers a wide range of components (cylinder heads included) where this work has already been done, and all you have to do is to find out what is available and choose the right parts for your particular engine (see pages 155 to 160).

The car manufacturers who offer tuning parts for their cars, like Ford and Leyland, often refer to 'stages of tune'. There are usually three and each stage encompasses a list of modifications to improve the performance of your engine. Stage one is normally designed to give a modest increase in performance. Stage two involves more modification but gives a correspondingly greater increase. Stage three is basic competition standard and will commit you to considerable expense if you decide to modify to this standard.

The reason for grouping tuning modifications together in this way is that no single component can be modified or changed without its relationship with the rest of the engine being affected. For example, if you change your carburettor to enable the engine to burn more fuel, there should be a more powerful explosion in the combustion chambers and therefore more power. But this will only be possible if the engine can suck the extra fuel in and for it to do this properly, you will have to fit a new camshaft and perhaps you will also need to fit bigger valves.

Even then the story may not be over—if the gases in the combustion chamber cannot escape smoothly and efficiently then the engine's power output will still be restricted. In this case you will have to consider the purchase of a new exhaust manifold as well.

Carburettor, camshaft and exhaust manifold changes are among the easiest modifications that can be made to a basic engine and, more often than not, they should be done together. As you progress to more advanced stages of tune, so more components will require attention, including the distributor and the cylinder head. Even this does not take into account modifications to the lower half of the engine—the pistons and crankshaft—and to the lubrication and cooling systems. These particular modifications are covered in the next chapter.

Because of the inter-relationship between tuning components, you should be prepared to buy several items at the same time. Leyland 'Pluspacs' are kits of components designed to bring an engine up to a certain stage of tune and when you buy one you can expect to be told exactly how much performance increase it will give.

Although kits like this make buying tuning parts simpler, there is a wide range of individual products to choose from. You may well find it cheaper to shop around, seeking the advice of various dealers and specialists. Tell them the sort of improvements you are looking for and how much you want to spend. They should then be able to advise you on what is available for your particular car and perhaps they will make up a kit for your car. In Australia manufacturers do not, as a rule, offer performance kits. The parts needed to uprate performance are usually available through specialist outlets. Some Australian tuning shops will obtain Leyland SP Pluspacs to order and Australian six-cylinder and V-8 engines are suitable for tuning.

Tuning in detail—cylinder head

The cylinder head is at the heart of the engine and the starting point for any really comprehensive tuning operation. A change of carburettor, exhaust manifold and camshaft will all contribute to a power increase, but if you have a good cylinder head as well, the benefits will be all the more apparent.

The cylinder head on a mass production car engine usually has many rough surfaces within the inlet and exhaust ports. These inhibit gas flow and so restrict power output. The surfaces of the combustion chambers may not be completely smooth and the chambers themselves may vary slightly in size. The inlet and exhaust ports can be machined and smoothed as can the combustion chambers. You can do these jobs yourself but it is far easier to buy a cylinder head on which the work has already been done (figs. 2 and 3). Although cylinder heads are expensive items a tuning specialist should be able to provide one in part exchange for your original unit.

Tuned cylinder heads vary in price according to the work that has been carried out. The basic, 'stage one' head usually has the rough surfaces discussed above smoothed so that the engine becomes more efficient. The inlet and exhaust ports and the combustion chambers will have been polished to a condition well beyond the manufacturer's original specification. The chambers will also have been 'matched' so that they are exactly the same size and correspond to their opposite halves on the block. A 'Stage one' cylinder head is normally part of a fairly mild tune—the carburettor and exhaust manifold may be changed but you would leave in your original camshaft.

The more advanced (and expensive) Stage two and three

cylinder heads have some additional modifications. These usually take the form of bigger inlet and exhaust valves and stronger valve springs. This enables the heads, in conjunction with a 'higher lift' camshaft, to take more petrol vapour in and let more exhaust gases out. The power of your engine can therefore be substantially increased as can its performance at higher engine speeds. Stiffer valve springs help to eliminate valve 'bounce' which sometimes occurs when an unsophisticated engine is pressed hard.

Buying a modified cylinder head can be expensive, even on a part-exchange basis, so think carefully before making your choice. Decide how much tuning you want to do—a simple, 'Stage one' head will be cheaper but it will not leave much room for future modification. Ask your dealer's advice about what other modifications you may need to make as well. A highly modified cylinder head may not give you any improvement in power at all if it is not properly served by the rest of the engine.

As with other tuning components, modified cylinder heads are available for a large number of cars through specialist firms and the quality is generally very high. Some manufacturers, such as Ford and Leyland, offer their own modified products. Do not forget to consult them first if your car is still under warranty.

Tuning in detail—carburation

Your engine's fuel system is one of the first things to consider when you are buying tuning parts. You will almost certainly have to change your original carburettor and possibly the inlet manifold—there is little to be gained by swapping the jets or needles around—and this could involve major expense.

The amount of power developed by an engine depends a great deal on the amount of fuel it is able to burn. The ideal arrangement—from a performance point of view—is to have one carburettor serving each cylinder so that as engine revs increase there is sufficient fuel available to be sucked into the individual combustion chambers. On most cars though, this arrangement would be too expensive and too complex for a manufacturer to consider. The

4 Perhaps the ultimate in performance carburation, this selection of Weber carburettors includes (1) a 28/36 twin-choke conversion kit for a Cortina Mk I (2) a 40 DCOE sidedraft conversion for a Mini with its special manifold (3) a downdraft IDA unit as fitted to the Porsche 904 (4) a triple set-up of 40 DCOE's on their one-piece manifold. This sophisticated conversion is for a Datsun 240Z

James Johnson

5 One of the simplest tuning modifications on a BL Mini or 1100 is to replace the SU HS2 carburettor with this larger HS 4 unit

average four cylinder car has only one carburettor serving all four cylinders. This set-up works well enough under most conditions but whenever you accelerate sharply and the engine requires a lot of petrol very quickly, the chances are that it will not get it, or it will be inefficiently supplied. The result is less power and acceleration than the optimum.

On performance engines the relative inefficiency of the single carburettor is overcome by the use of twin installations or a single twin-choke unit. The twin-choke carburettor has a 'second stage' which comes into operation under heavy acceleration and provides an extra flow of petrol when it is most needed. A twin-carburettor installation also provides more fuel when it is needed—in this case because it is a step nearer the ideal of one unit per cylinder.

Changing your carburation is one of the first steps towards tuning the engine and making it more efficient. For this reason there is a large selection of conversions available to the DIY mechanic. Both SU and Stromberg

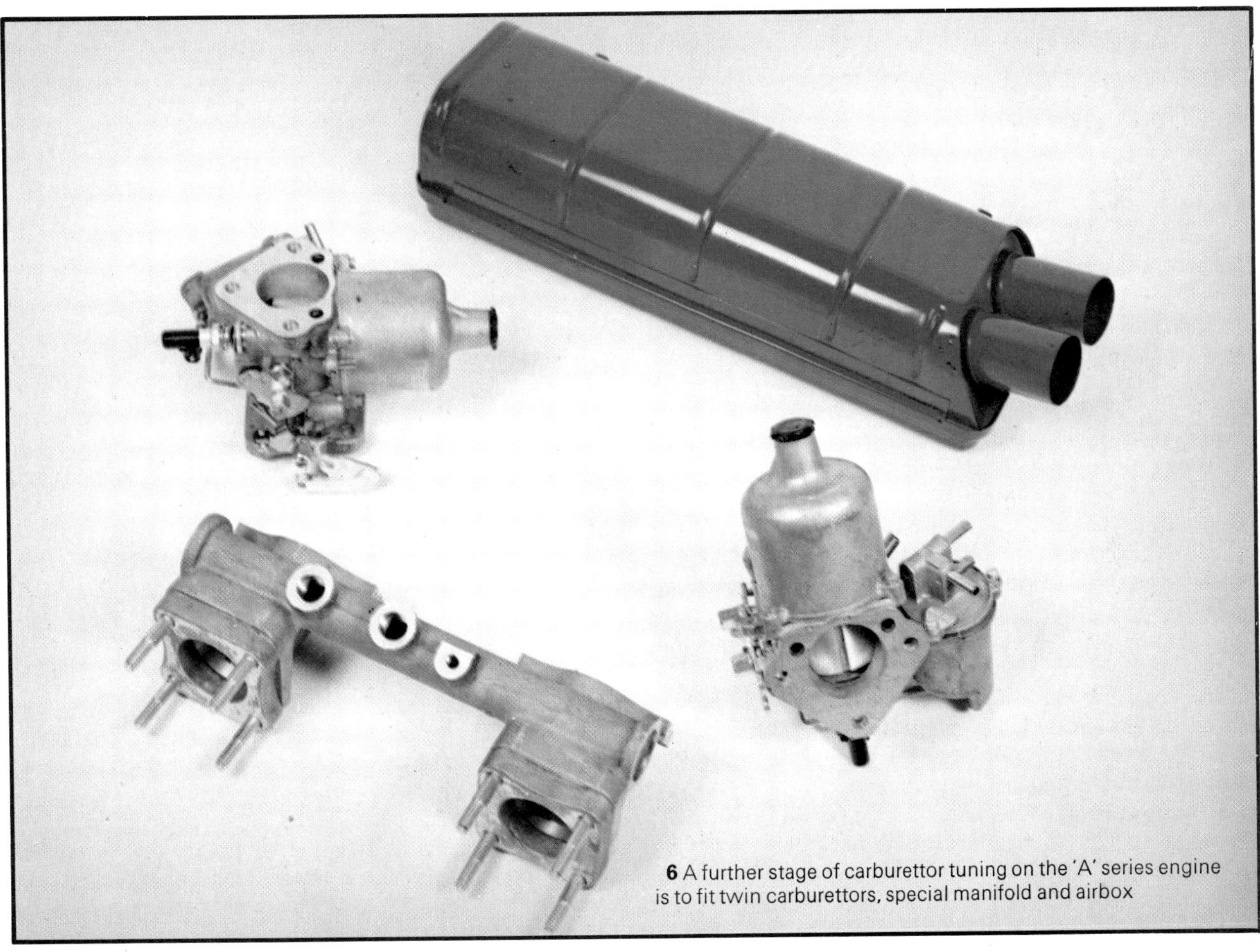

6 A further stage of carburettor tuning on the 'A' series engine is to fit twin carburettors, special manifold and airbox

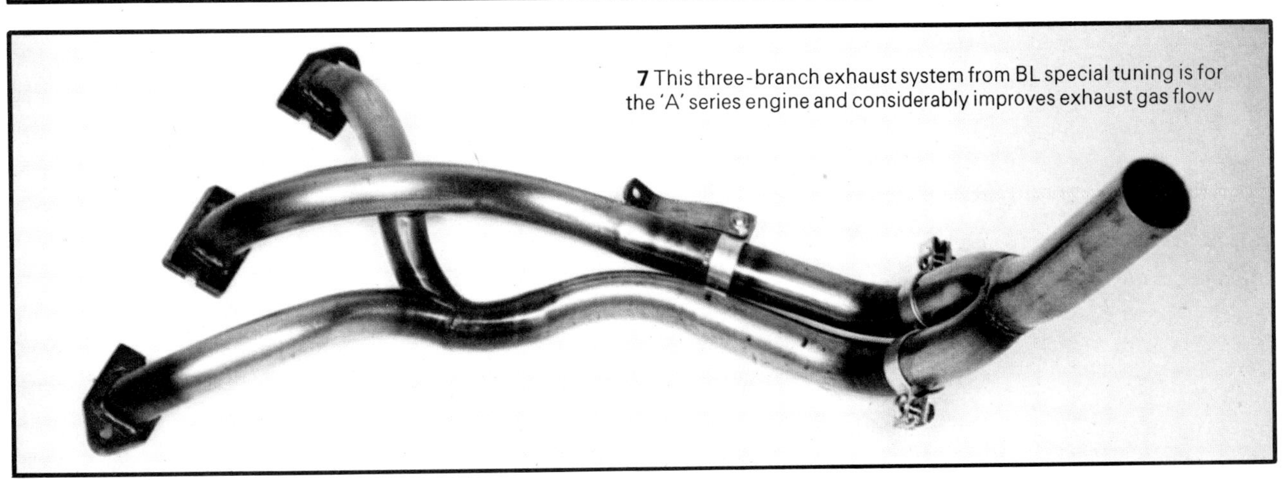

7 This three-branch exhaust system from BL special tuning is for the 'A' series engine and considerably improves exhaust gas flow

8 Standard (above) and modified (below) camshafts. The modified camshaft lobes differ slightly in profile from the standard version and alter the valve operation

market twin carburettor kits for a wide range of cars. These are provided complete with a new manifold and accelerator linkage to suit a particular car and they can usually be bought on a part-exchange basis. The most famous names in twin-choke conversions are Weber and Dellorto. These carburettors have a good reputation for reliability and economy, relative to performance. Webers may be fitted to some cars as standard but are available for a great many more as a tuning conversion (fig. 4). Two basic types are offered. The 28/36 series are downdraft units intended mainly for 'mild' tuning. They combine a useful performance increase with good economy and are more than adequate for most road car applications. The Weber DCOE sidedraft carburettors are a good deal more expensive but they are considered to be approaching the ultimate in performance carburation. Although they, too, are available for a wide range of cars they will not really prove their worth unless fitted as part of a comprehensive tuning operation. Similar in performance and operation are the Dellorto range of carburettors.

The Japanese Nikki twin-choke range is also becoming increasingly popular and is similar in specification to the 28/36 Weber. Like the Webers, they are marketed in kits complete with all the necessary ancillaries.

Because uprated carburation is one of the most basic forms of engine tuning, many enthusiasts are happy to simply change their carburettor. While it is true that a twin-carb or twin-choke installation will, on its own, give you a power increase, you cannot expect to reap the full benefits without some further modifications.

Tuning in detail—exhaust

The exhaust manifolds on many mass-production car engines are relatively inefficient. Designed for cheap and easy manufacture, they tend to restrict the flow of exhaust gases out of the cylinder head so restricting the engine's ability to produce power. In fact, it is possible to design a manifold which actually speeds up the exhaust flow and therefore helps to develop engine power. The 'extractor' type of manifolds, which you can examine at a tuning specialist shop, go a long way towards this ideal. Even so, they will still be slightly restricted when properly silenced to satisfy local noise regulations.

Fitting an extractor manifold is another of the most basic tuning modifications and will certainly help you to get more benefit from a change of carburettor. In many cases though, exhaust tuning accompanies a change of cylinder head and camshaft and you should consult your specialist dealer before deciding to commit yourself to a manifold which matches your standard head. It may well be more beneficial to save up and buy all the components together.

There is a wide selection of extractor manifolds on the tuning accessory market to suit many different cars. Some car manufacturers, such as Leyland and Ford, market their own products as part of their special tuning ranges. On some cars, it may be possible to fit some form of tuned exhaust from the high performance and/or GT model variants in the same manufacturers range. Tuning specialists and dealers often market their own makes of extractor.

Tuning in detail—camshaft

The camshaft on your engine controls the opening and closing of the inlet and exhaust valves. It therefore plays a major role in the flow of gases into and out of the cylinder head and, consequently, with the power developed.

The camshaft on a standard engine is designed as a compromise between high-speed power and low-speed torque so that the engine is reasonably flexible. A fully modified camshaft, designed solely for performance, has a higher "lift" than its road-going counterpart (fig. 8). This means that it opens and closes the valves over longer periods, letting more petrol vapour in and gases out. The result is that the engine develops greater power at high engine speeds but loses a lot of its basic tractability.

There are, however, camshafts available which fall in between the two extremes. A 'mildly tuned' camshaft will give a slightly higher lift than a standard one to exploit the benefits of uprated carburation without sacrificing too much torque at low revs. In this case, if you make full use of the gearbox, the difference will hardly be noticed.

Tuning specialists and dealers normally carry a range of camshafts for each car and can advise you on their different characteristics. Remember, though, that to change yours, you may have to remove the radiator, or even the engine unless it has an overhead camshaft. For a mild tune, a camshaft change is desirable but not essential.

Buying tuning components

Nelson Hargreaves

1 Specially modified components like these balanced pistons help to give a tuned engine its high performance characteristics

Changing the cylinder head, carburettor and exhaust, as described in the previous chapter, can produce quite startling results—in many cases doubling the engine output. It is easy though, to forget the numerous other components in the engine which have all been designed to work together in the most efficient way possible. The balance between them may be upset if you intend to make really extensive modifications to your car's engine.

Most car engines, apart from those which are already highly tuned, operate some way below their full capacity. More often than not, they are specifically designed to do so in the interests of prolonging their life. A "mild" tune, such as a carburettor and exhaust change, should not impose too great a strain on the rest of the engine.

When the cylinder head and the camshaft are changed as well, however, the situation becomes more complicated. Engine output will be substantially increased and you will obviously make use of the extra power. If a highly-tuned camshaft is fitted, the benefits will only really become apparent at higher revs and you may find yourself driving at consistently greater speeds. Under these conditions, many of the ancillary components on the engine may need uprating to cope with the additional stress.

If you want to go further still and run your engine at speeds above the manufacturer's recommended limit, then internal components like the crankshaft, pistons and fly-wheel may well have to be toughened or lightened.

Australians considering this kind of major tuning should make inquiries with the motor registration office in their State. Varying rules apply which effectively limit what can and cannot be done to a vehicle. For example in NSW, as a general rule, you are not allowed to change the horsepower of your car's engine to greater than the horsepower available from an optional engine for that car. In other words the owner of a 3.3-litre Holden is not permitted to raise that engine's horsepower above that of the 5-litre V-8 unit.

Buying components

As with the components described in the previous chapter (page 149), the best place to buy tuned ancillaries and engine parts is the tuning specialist. To cater for the increasing interest in tuning, the accessory market offers an ever-widening range of parts to suit most cars. In many cases, components which have been discontinued by the car manufacturers themselves are copied by specialist firms to ensure a continuing supply. The specialist dealer is in a good position to advise you on what will be needed in your particular case. He will have the data and information available to tell you what modifications are required to achieve a certain level of tune.

Some manufacturers, like Leyland and Ford, offer special services themselves as an alternative source of tuning parts. If you have a new car, you may be obliged to take advantage of this sort of facility in order to protect your warranty. The main disadvantages of dealing with a manufacturer direct are that you may not get such personal service and that you will not be able to "shop around" for the best value. On the other hand, their advice should be both informed and accurate and their products will be of a guaranteed high quality.

Be sure to give your dealer the correct information about your engine when you discuss buying tuning components. You must quote the engine number to avoid any costly mistakes and you should be clear in your own mind as to how much tuning you intend to do. Before making a decision about this, bear in mind that you will probably still want reasonable fuel economy and a degree of low-speed tractability from your engine.

Ignition tuning

If you decide to explore the more advanced areas of engine tuning, the ignition system is one of the most important things to consider. An engine which has been given a change of carburettor, exhaust, cylinder head and camshaft will probably only begin to show a substantial power increase

Courtesy of Fiat Motor Co. (U.K.) Ltd

2 The 2-litre engine in this Fiat 131 Abarth rally car develops more than twice the power of equivalent mass-produced engines. Fuel injection and a 16-valve cylinder head are just two of the advanced tuning modifications employed in the unit

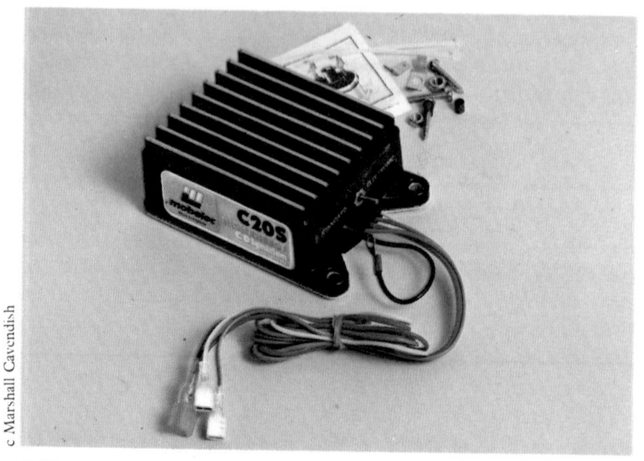

c Marshall Cavendish

3 Electronic ignition systems, like the one shown here, represent one of the most effective ways of uprating your original ignition

4 A thermostatically-controlled fan like this keeps an engine at its most efficient working temperature. It will also save power

Nelson Hargreaves

5 On this highly-tuned, Burton, hot-rod engine, the special water pump is driven by a toothed belt from the crankshaft pulley. This will keep the pump operating effectively at speeds in excess of 9000 rpm and ensure adequate cooling under racing conditions

above 3000 to 4000 rpm. To get the most from the change, it is desirable to have a distributor which has been specially designed to function efficiently above these higher engine speeds and a tuning shop should be consulted.

A tuned distributor, therefore, has different advance/retard characteristics from one built for a standard, mass-production engine where the chief consideration is low-speed torque (see page 176). Your dealer should be able to advise on the correct part for your particular engine. In many cases it will be the distributor fitted to the high-performance model of a range. When you buy a distributor do not forget to ask about timing the engine. Depending on what other changes have been made, the timing may have to be altered and the dealer should have the information you require to enable you to set the timing correctly.

Changing the specification of the spark plugs is not normally necessary except in the case of highly-tuned racing engines where virtually the entire design of the unit is altered. However, your timing specialist may advise

George Wright

6 This Leyland ST oil cooler is designed for a racing Mini. At high engine speeds it keeps the oil at its optimum temperature

7 A special, dual-purpose pump used in converting Leyland "A" series engines to high-efficiency, dry-sump lubrication for racing

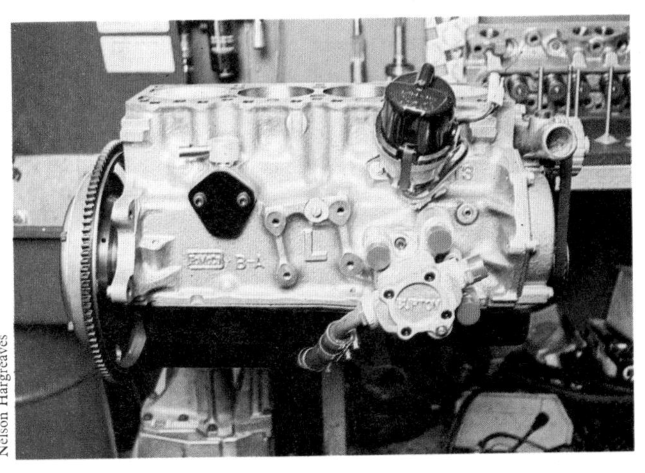

Nelson Hargreaves

8 This Burton-modified engine has a dry-sump arrangement. Oil is collected by the pump, pumped to a tank in the back of the car and then re-circulated. The chief advantages of the system are better weight distribution and more effective cooling of the oil

using a slightly "cooler" plug if the engine is to be run at consistently high revs.

A change of coil, on the other hand, is a good idea and usually accompanies a distributor change. The coils used in tuned engines are described as "heavy duty" which means that, like tuned distributors, they are designed to provide a strong spark at higher engine speeds.

The final things to check when tuning the ignition system are the high-tension leads. If they are in bad condition, any extra loads may cause them to start breaking up. It is really best to include a new set as part of your list of tuning components.

Electronic ignition

The most important characteristics of electronic ignition systems are the reduction of the loads on other parts of the ignition system and, in some cases, elimination of the contact breaker points altogether. This can be especially beneficial where tuned engines are concerned, because electronic components are less likely to be affected by high revving then their mechanical counterparts. For this reason it is worth considering investing in an electronic system, such as that in fig. 3, as part of a comprehensive tuning programme.

Replacing the timing chain

Although not strictly part of the ignition system, the timing chain can, if "stretched" or worn, produce symptoms similar to those normally associated with ignition faults. For this reason, your original chain is worth replacing with a heavy duty one as part of a tuning programme. As with distributors, the chain from a high performance model in the same range as your car is usually suitable.

Tuning the cooling system

On most cars with a conventional, engine-driven fan, the cooling system should be able to absorb the modest increases in temperature which accompany tuning modifications. In some cases though, especially where the engine is consistently being run at high speeds, the system may become over loaded. To avoid over heating, it must be modified to disperse more heat at a faster rate.

The simplest way of doing this is to fit the fan and radiator from a high performance model in the same range, or similar components from a larger car. A tuned BL Mini 1000, for example can make use of the radiator fitted as standard to the Mini Cooper S. Although radiators can be bought in part-exchange, a breaker's yard can be the best source of such parts (see pages 233 to 242).

It is important to remember, however, that your engine must not be over cooled. Often, the slight increases in temperature which result from engine tuning turn out to be beneficial and actually improve combustion. Over cooling can produce excess condensation and at the same time increase petrol consumption.

There are no set rules for when and when not to tune the cooling system and it is, therefore, best to try out your standard system first to see how it copes. Do not forget though, that your radiator cap should be in good condition. If it is worn or defective, it will not keep the coolant under pressure and it will boil at a lower temperature.

One modification, which tuning enthusiasts often find worthwhile, is to fit a thermostatically-controlled, electric fan (see pages 209 to 222) if one is not already fitted as standard. An electric fan will enable you to keep your engine at a constant, slightly higher, temperature, thus increasing its efficiency. From the point of view of extra power, an electric fan also has the advantage of replacing the engine-driven unit which normally absorbs up to 5 bhp of an engine's total output.

Tuning the lubrication system

Efficient lubrication is important in any car engine but it becomes especially so when the engine is stressed beyond its original specification. At high engine speeds, your engine's oil pump has to keep the oil flowing very quickly indeed. The oil itself has to absorb more heat and take a greater buffeting from moving parts.

Nelson Hargreaves

9 The pistons in the Burton-tuned engine are all-steel for extra strength at high revs. The crowns and skirts are special designs

George Wright

10 Standard (left) and modified pistons. The dished crown of the modified one is shallower in order to raise the compression ratio

In the past, this resulted in the oil over heating in highly-tuned engines which made it less effective and caused rapid wear. Modern engine oils, however, are a great deal more robust and can operate effectively over a wide temperature range. In fact, the oil in a standard engine rarely reaches its optimum temperature, about 100°C, during normal road use. This leaves plenty of capacity to absorb the extra heat caused by mild tuning, providing it is pumped around the engine properly.

From a tuning point of view, the oil pump is, therefore, the vital component in the lubricating system. For a modest tune-up, all you will need is a pump in good condition and, providing your basic engine has not covered too high a mileage, the existing pump should be usable.

More advanced tuning and running an engine at high revs may require you to fit a larger oil pump to keep the oil circulating efficiently, although this varies according to the engine. Your specialist dealer should be able to advise you on this particular point.

Oil coolers

Because of the efficiency of modern motor oils, oil coolers are rarely necessary on anything but highly-tuned, competition engines. It can actually harm an engine if the oil is over cooled and not allowed to reach its most favourable operating temperature. You should seek advice as to whether or not a cooler need be fitted before committing yourself. Sometimes an oil cooler is desirable on an engine tuned for towing purposes, especially if the car in question has automatic transmission. Similarly, air-cooled engines, which have different cooling characteristics, usually require an oil cooler with anything but a very mild tune. If you do need an oil cooler, you will find quite a large range of kits on the market. These all consist of a small radiator which is mounted in the engine compartment and pipes enabling it to be plumbed into the oil system. Most oil cooler kits have a thermostat, available at extra cost, which diverts the oil through the radiator only when it reaches a certain (pre-set) temperature. In the interests of making sure that the oil is not over cooled, this is a worthwhile investment.

If you are advised against fitting an oil cooler, but are still worried about the oil over heating, an oil temperature gauge is the best solution. It will set your mind at rest for a fraction of the cost. Fitting one is covered on page 196.

Advanced engine tuning

Advanced engine tuning is usually taken to mean modifications to the lower half of the engine and really only concerns the enthusiast who wishes to take his engine a great deal further than the manufacturer's specifications. At very high revs, the stresses and strains on components like crankshafts and pistons become enormous. Those fitted to standard production engines are not usually designed to take this sort of stress, so you may have to replace them with special, precision-made items or have the units modified. This kind of tuning is, therefore, only possible if it is included in a complete engine re-build.

Despite the rather limited number of enthusiasts who tune their engines to such advanced levels, special crankshafts, pistons and other components, to suit a wide range of different makes, are stocked by most tuning specialists.

Pistons

Performance pistons are usually produced by specialist manufacturers and you will often find a choice of products available, varying both in cost and sophistication. They are all made from complex aluminium alloys which are light but very strong and well able to cope with the higher operating temperatures and pressures that are created by high-revving engines. In some cases, the pistons may be designed in such a way that they raise the compression ratio of the engine, as well, to produce even more power. Piston rings of a different pattern and thickness usually accompany special pistons and are designed to complement these high-performance characteristics.

Crankshaft, bearings and connecting rods

Like the pistons, the crankshaft, bearings and connecting rods on a highly-tuned engine have to operate under enormous loads and there are many specialist products specifically designed for the job.

A modified crankshaft has, first of all, to be strong. Special cranks, therefore, undergo a series of hardening processes

George Wright

11 This con-rod from a Leyland "A" series engine will take a great deal of stress in standard form. Only the bolts are "tuftrided"

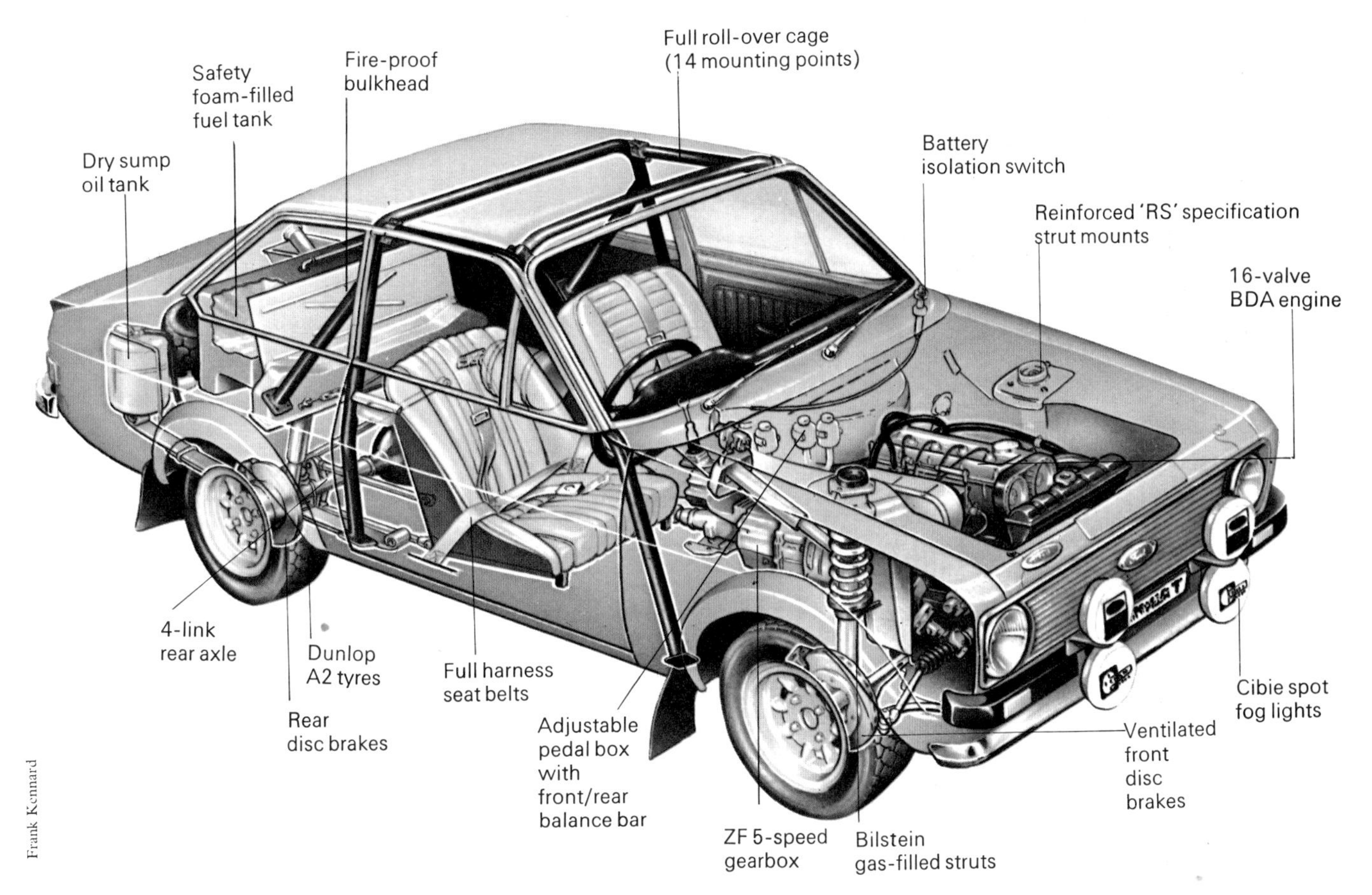

Frank Kennard

12 The Ford Escort Rally car illustrates what can be done to an ordinary family saloon. Virtually the whole car has been modified in some way so that it can safely cope with the power of the highly tuned 16-valve BDA engine and the stresses of rallying

George Wright

13 Crankshaft grinding and modification must be left to a specialist. Here, a crankshaft is being modified

Nelson Hargreaves

14 The special clutch and lightened fly-wheel on a modified engine help to reduce power losses

George Wright

15 A Burton-modified clutch and fly-wheel assembly from a BL "A" series engine.

16 The first stage in balancing con-rods and pistons is to weigh each component of a set individually to find the lightest

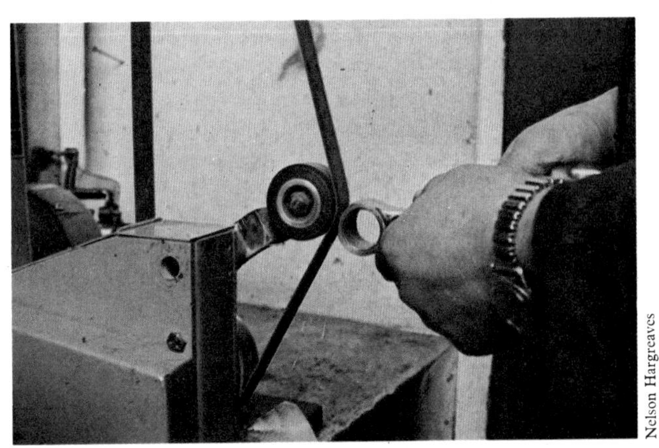

Nelson Hargreaves

17 The heavier components in the set are then matched to the lightest by skimming off small amounts of metal

18 Crankshaft balancing requires more sophisticated machinery. The shaft is mounted on rollers and bolted to a motor which spins it

19 Readings can be taken to determine where and by how much the crankshaft is out of balance. It is then skimmed accordingly

20 Extensive engine tuning often requires block modification. The block shown here is being re-tapped to take a dry sump pump

21 Larger valves, stronger valve springs and specially-designed, steel, spring caps—vital in any really high-revving engine

Nelson Hargreaves

22 The cylinder head of the Burton-tuned engine. At full power, the stresses on the OHV rocker gear are enormous

23 A tuned engine. With twin DCOE Weber carburettors and a special exhaust manifold, this 1700 cc unit can produce 184 bhp

which vary according to individual manufacturers. This is what is meant by terms such as "tuftriding" and "nitriding". It is possible to have your existing crankshaft treated in this way at a reasonable cost. To cut down internal stress within the crankshaft as it turns at very high speeds, it is also specially balanced.

Special connecting rods can usually be bought to match performance pistons and will be made of similar light but strong alloys. These should also be matched as a set by a specialist supplier of tuning equipment to further improve the overall balance and performance of the finished engine.

The fly-wheel

One of the jobs of the fly-wheel is to absorb the minor imbalance of components which becomes all the more apparent at higher engine speeds. On a tuned engine, which is much better balanced than its standard counterpart, this job will not be so difficult. Thus the fly-wheel can be made lighter, in which case it will absorb much less of the engine's output. As with bearings, lightened fly-wheels are usually designed as a complement to a tuned crankshaft. You should bear in mind that a lightened fly-wheel is likely to cause the engine to run considerably less smoothly in the lower rev range.

Balancing

To extract the most from your tuned engine, it is wise to have the crankshaft, connecting rods, fly-wheel and clutch balanced as a unit. This work should be carried out by a reputable machinist who specialises in your particular unit. The work is not unduly expensive and will give your work the final touch.

Compression testing

Carrying out a compression test is a useful way to check the internal condition of your engine. All you need is the tester itself (fig. 1), a plug spanner, soft brush and a small amount of engine oil.

Start by removing all the spark-plugs, remembering to clean around the sockets with the brush before the plugs are completely unscrewed, then screw the tester into the plug socket of No.1 cylinder. (Some testers are a push-fit.) If your starter solenoid has a push-button, turn the engine over so that each piston reaches top dead centre at least once. If your starter solenoid has no button, have an assistant turn the ignition switch.

The dial on the tester will register and retain the maximum compression figure for the cylinder. Note this, reset then repeat the test on the other cylinders.

You can now compare your readings with the manufacturer's recommended figures, which are obtainable from your handbook or local dealer. The readings should be within 1.05kg/cm^2 (15 psi) of one another and above the minimum acceptable figure quoted by the dealer.

If a reading is low, pour a teaspoonful of engine oil through the spark plug-hole of the relevant cylinder. Reconnect the tester and repeat the procedure. If there is an improved reading, the loss of compression is due to worn bores or piston rings. The oil you have just poured into the cylinder will have formed a seal round the rings and temporarily improved the compression. If the reading is the same, compression is low due to worn, badly seating or burnt valves, or a leaking head gasket and must be dealt with.

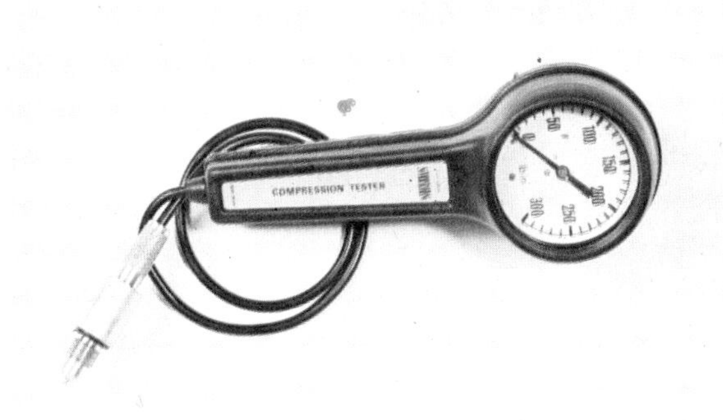

1 There are various types of compression testers. This tester is a dial gauge type, manufactured by Smiths

2 After detaching the high tension leads and moving them out of the way, remove all of the spark plugs with a plug spanner

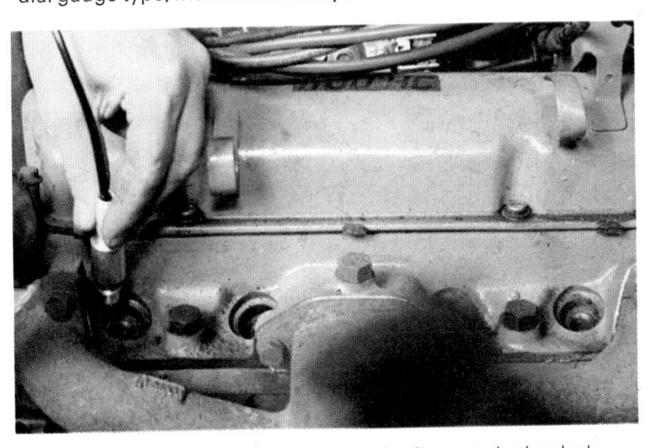

3 Screw the compression tester into the first spark plug hole. Some types of tester have to be hand-held in position

4 After removing one of the low tension leads from the ignition coil, turn the engine over with accelerator pressed hard down

5 After noting down the reading from the first cylinder, check the compression on the remaining cylinders in the same way

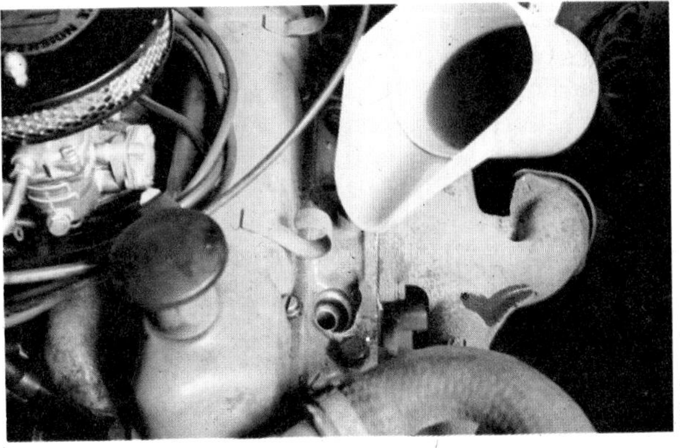

Mike Berend

6 To check for wear, pour a few drops of oil into the cylinder and take another reading. A higher reading indicates bore or ringwear

Fitting a water temperature gauge

Overheating is one of the most common, yet most unpredictable, problems for every driver. Your car's cooling system relies on perishable components like rubber hoses and paper gaskets; when any of these fail, and they usually do when you least expect it, water is lost and the temperature of the engine soars.

If you have no means of spotting the trouble quickly, the chances are that the engine will seize up and you will be faced with a costly overhaul. A water temperature gauge is a worthwhile investment if you want to avoid such disasters.

Although most modern cars are equipped with some form of temperature indicator, many drivers fail to take advantage of it. Because the indicators are usually built into an instrument cluster, or inside a speedometer dial, it is easy to get so used to looking at them that you miss the point when the needle flicks into the danger zone. For many motorists, the first sign that their car is overheating is when steam begins to emerge from the engine compartment. By then it is often far too late.

By fitting a temperature gauge, either in a single mounting or with a group of supplementary instruments, you can get into the habit of watching it and taking notice of the warning signs. An accessory temperature gauge will also give you the benefit of a graduated scale showing the actual temperature of the water—something which few ordinary indicators do. This is especially useful if you want to keep your engine running at its most efficient operating temperature (see below) or if you are considering fitting a thermostatically-controlled fan (see pages 209 to 222).

Types of water temperature gauge

Two basic types of water temperature gauge—electrical and capillary—are available and each has advantages and disadvantages over the other. Most experts agree that of the two, the capillary type is the more accurate and also more responsive to temperature changes. A sensing bulb is screwed into the engine, somewhere on the water cooling jacket, and this is attached to the gauge by means of a solid (usually copper) capillary tube.

But herein lie the chief drawbacks of this type of gauge. The bulb, capillary and gauge are all permanently joined together. This means that you have to cut quite a large hole in your engine bulkhead to feed the bulb through. Also, because the capillary must not be bent sharply or twisted, it cannot be squeezed into tight spaces, at either the dashboard or the engine end. The tube has to be carefully treated and the manufacturer's instructions usually specify that it must be coiled and tied back at various intervals, to prevent damage through fouling or vibration.

The electrical gauge is not so accurate, but is considerably easier to fit and for some cars, where space is limited, it may be your only choice. Once again, a sensing bulb has to be screwed into the engine, but this is likely to be more bulky than its capillary counterpart and you should consider this before buying one. The sender connects to the gauge with an ordinary wire and further connections are made from the gauge to a live supply and to earth. There are therefore no large holes to be cut in the engine bulkhead and the all-wire connections will allow you greater flexibility when mounting the instrument on the dashboard.

Both types of gauges will be provided with illumination wires which connect into the existing panel light circuit. For the capillary gauge, a separate earth connection will have to be made if the instrument is mounted in an insulated panel. Both types cost about the same.

Finding a site for the sender or sensor bulb

All water temperature gauges work by means of a sender or sensor bulb which transfers the relevant information to the gauge itself. The sender should preferably be located in the heart of the cooling system—the engine water jacket. There, the water is doing its job of picking up excess heat from the cylinders for dissipation through the radiator and the most accurate temperature readings can be obtained.

If your car already has a temperature indicator, there will be some kind of sender tapped into the engine with a wire running from it. It will probably be located somewhere on the cylinder head, usually near the thermostat housing. On a few cars, the sender is tapped into the water jacket further down on the block. Be careful, though, not to confuse the temperature sender with the one for the oil warning light. This is always found lower down on the engine, in most cases near the oil filter.

When fitting a new temperature gauge, the basic technique is for the old sender to be unscrewed and the new one

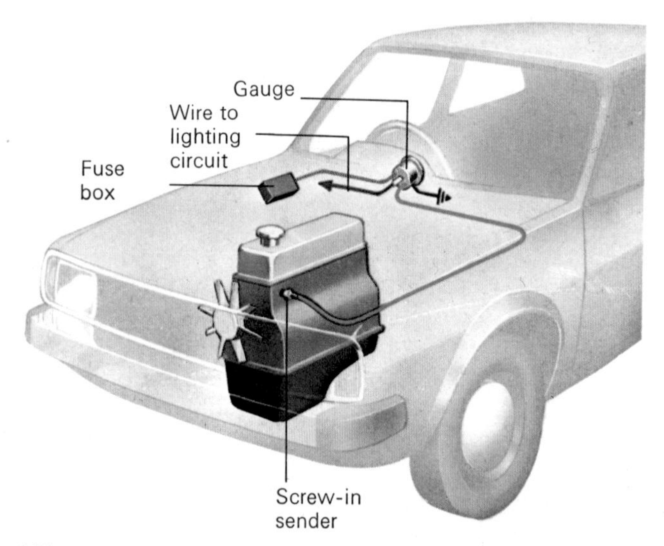

1 The electrical gauge has two additional connections. One goes to the sensor in the engine block and one to the fusebox

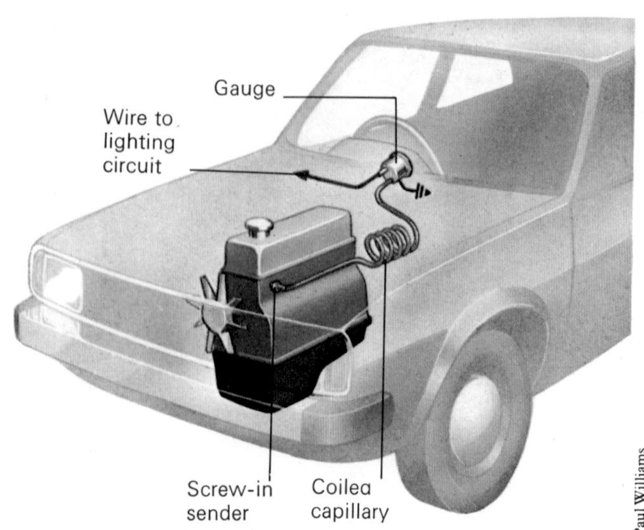

2 With the capillary type of water temperature gauge there are only two electrical connections—the earth and the light wire

Paul Williams

screwed into the tapping in its place.

If your car does not have a temperature indicator, it will almost certainly still have a tapping in the engine for one to be fitted. This will have been closed off with a nut-shaped blanking plug and you should look for it in the same way as for the indicator sender above. Fitting the new sender will again be a simple matter of unscrewing the plug and screwing the sender into the tapping.

If you are in any doubt about where the old sender or blanking plug is on your car, your local franchised dealer will be able to tell you.

In the unlikely event that your car has neither an indicator sender nor a blanking plug, it is possible to drill and tap the radiator header tank. This, however, will not give you an accurate reading. Combine this fact with the risks of damaging the radiator and you will probably decide that the job is not worthwhile.

Buying a water temperature gauge

The first thing to decide before buying a temperature gauge is what type will best suit your particular car and requirements. If you are considering the capillary type, bear in mind that the capillary will have to run more or less straight from the back of the instrument and through the engine bulkhead, in which you will need room to cut a hole. Next, look at the proposed location of the sensor bulb on the engine. Lack of space here could mean that the capillary will have to be bent too sharply (it must never be less than 25 mm (1in.) radius).

With the electrical gauge, space under the dashboard and at the bulkhead is not such a problem. You should still make a careful check, though, that there is enough room to fit a sender on the engine.

Cars with restricted space in this area include all UK Fords manufactured after June 1965 and the Austin Maxi range. Smiths are among the instrument manufacturers who cater for this particular problem by producing a special 'small-bulb' capillary gauge.

Another point to remember when buying an electrical gauge is polarity—you must be able to tell the dealer whether your car is positive or negative earth (see page 23) so that he can supply the correctly wired instrument. Check with your car dealer if in doubt.

Once you have decided which type of gauge to buy, you can consider the problem of whether or not the sensor bulb or sender will screw into your engine. Unfortunately, the tappings on car engines vary in size, even among the same make and model. If you are able to find out the size of your tapping by consulting your local franchised dealer, you can check when you buy the gauge. If you cannot get this information, you will have to rely on the instrument dealer. Quote the make, model and year of your car together with the engine number if possible and he should be able to supply a gauge that fits. The chassis number will also be helpful. If he cannot, go to someone who can.

Several manufacturers provide adaptors with their gauges to suit two or more fittings. This does not justify taking a chance on the tapping size when buying your gauge, but the adaptor may be useful if you decide to transfer the instrument to another car.

What you will need

Apart from the gauge of your choice, you can save a lot of time by buying the other bits and pieces needed for the job before you start. Consider where you are going to place the gauge. Singly, it can be mounted in a pod beneath the dashboard. If it is to be part of a group of accessory instruments, then it can go in a multiple panel (see page 168). You can of course cut a hole in a dashboard panel (see pages 167 to 168) if there is room, but modern fascia designs rarely allow enough. If you opt for a pod or panel, make sure that you have a sufficient supply of self-tapping screws to fix them in place.

With a capillary gauge, you will need to drill a hole in the bulkhead large enough to pass the bulb through. The manufacturer of the gauge will probably specify a certain size of hole; a typical size is 22 mm ($\frac{7}{8}$in.). (This is too large a hole for most household drills to handle, but an alternative method is described below.) A grommet to seal the hole may be provided. If not, buy one which will both fit the hole and allow the bulb and capillary to pass through it.

Both types of gauge may need a supply of ordinary electrical wire, spade and screw connectors. The capillary gauge will require wire connections to the panel light circuit and possibly to earth as well. The electrical gauge will also need these, plus further connections to the fusebox and to the engine.

Finally, you will need a roll of vinyl tape or something similar to tie back the loose capillary or wires.

Mounting the gauge

Choose a site for the gauge where it can be seen without difficulty from the driving seat. If a capillary gauge is being fitted, it should be mounted in such a way that the capillary can pass straight out and through the bulkhead.

If the gauge is going in a separate pod or panel, use the pod brackets or the panel as a template and mark holes for the fixing screws above or below the dashboard. You can then drill the holes and also fix the gauge itself in its mounting. Whether the gauge is going in a panel, a pod or the dashboard, you should leave the final fixing until all the connections at the back have been made.

Wiring for illumination—all gauges

All accessory water temperature gauges have an illumination wire which has to be connected into the panel light circuit. If your car has the older type of instrument circuitry, there will be wires running from the illumination bulbs on your existing instruments. Find out which they are, either by tracing them back under the dashboard or consulting a wiring diagram.

If your car has printed-circuit instrumentation, or there is not enough room to trace the wires, loosen the light switch away from the dashboard, taking care not to disconnect any wires behind. Turn the switch to the 'side lights on' position and check that the panel lights are also on. Disconnect one terminal at a time from the back of the switch until the panel lights go out. Make a note of which terminal, by being disconnected, causes this to happen.

Next, identify the illumination wire on the back of the gauge using the manufacturer's instructions. Lengthen it if necessary with new wire and a screw connector until it stretches to the connection point. If you have isolated a panel light wire, then the connection point may be anywhere on it. You can splice on the new wire using a Scotchlok connector (pages 169 and 171). Otherwise you will be connecting to the terminal which you have just isolated on the light switch. In this case, crimp a double spade connector to the new wire, slide it on to the terminal and fit the old wire on to the spare tag.

Whether you are fitting an electrical or a capillary gauge, it will not light up if it is not properly earthed. This will happen if, for example, it is enclosed in a wooden dashboard or plastic panel. To earth the gauge, take a piece

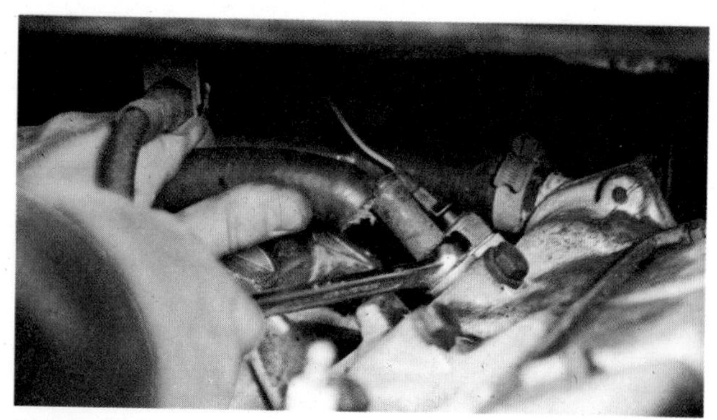

3 To fit an electrical gauge, start by finding the blanking plug or original sender. Here, a water pipe is removed for access

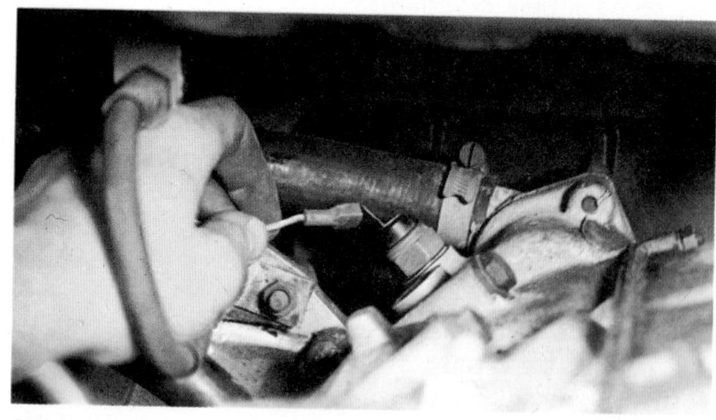

4 This Chrysler Imp has a sender already, but it only operates a warning light. Start by removing the wire connected to it

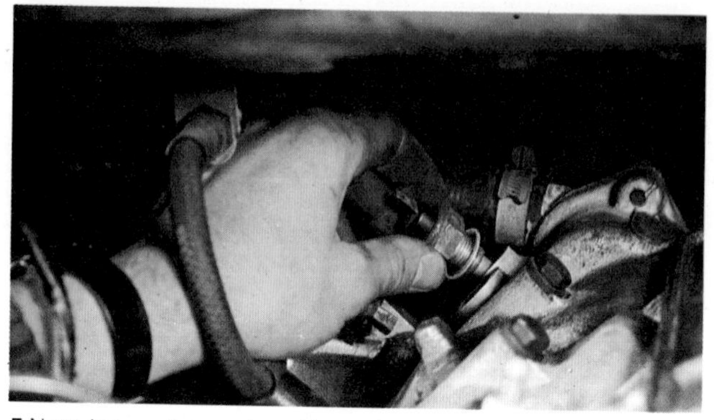

5 Next, loosen the sender with a spanner and unscrew it from its location on the cylinder head near the thermostat unit

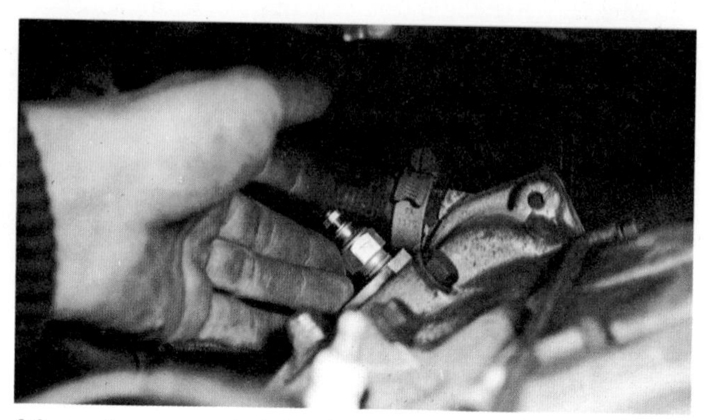

6 Screw the new sender in its place. Use a spanner to tighten it up but be careful not to overtighten and destroy the thread

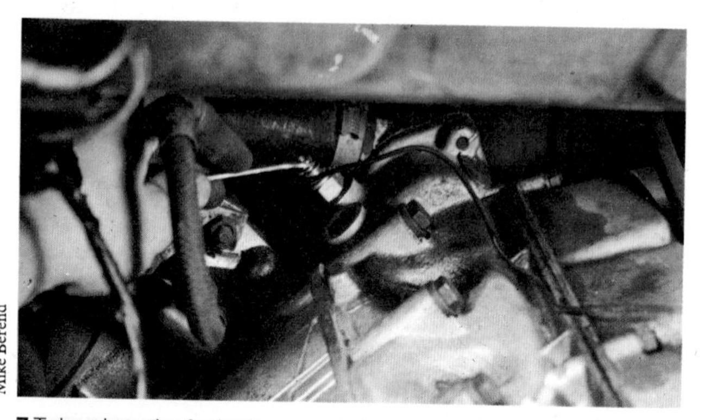

Mike Berend

7 Take a length of wire long enough to stretch from the sender to the gauge. Connect one end to the screw terminal on the sender

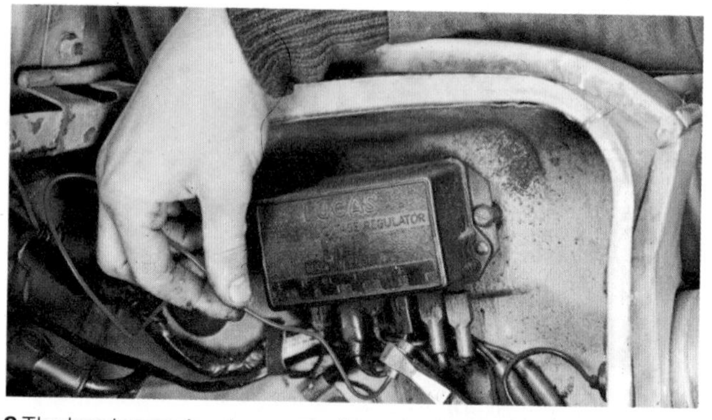

8 The Imp has no fusebox so the live wire, which must also run to the gauge, has to be connected to the voltage regulator

of wire and secure it to the appropriate place on the body of the instrument, again following the manufacturer's instructions. Run the wire to an earthed point on the car, such as a dashboard fixing screw. Make sure both connections are both clean and tight.

Fitting an electrical water temperature gauge

To fit an electrical gauge, start with the sender. Part-drain the water out of the engine by undoing the radiator drain tap or, if there is no tap, by disconnecting the radiator bottom hose. Having identified the original sender or blanking plug, unscrew it from the engine. If there is a wire running from the old sender, it should be disconnected and taped back to the wiring loom in case it is required at some time in the future.

Next, screw in the new sender carefully, checking again that the tapping on the engine matches its thread. Tighten it firmly, but be careful to avoid using undue pressure which might damage it.

With the new sender in place, all that remains is the wiring up. If you have followed the instructions above for connecting the illumination wire and earthing the gauge, you will have only two connections left to make. One will be from the gauge to a live supply, such as the fusebox, and the other will be to the sender on the engine. Start with the live one. Connect a length of wire to the back of the gauge, using the manufacturer's instructions to identify the correct terminal. Run it to the fusebox, if necessary passing it through a convenient gap in the front bulkhead.

At the fusebox, the wire must be connected to a spare terminal on the switched circuit as opposed to the non-switched circuit which carries a live supply at all times. To find which is which, turn the lights on and disconnect one wire in turn from the ignition switch side of the fusebox. Note which disconnected terminal causes the lights to go out. It will be on the non-switched circuit. Now you can connect the gauge to the spare terminal on the other one.

If the spare terminal already has something connected to it, you can splice the wire from the gauge on to the wire running from the terminal using a Scotchlok connector.

To connect the sender wire, start by fixing it to the correct terminal on the back of the gauge and then run it through a convenient gap in the bulkhead to the engine compartment. Keep the wire away from the hot engine, tying it back with

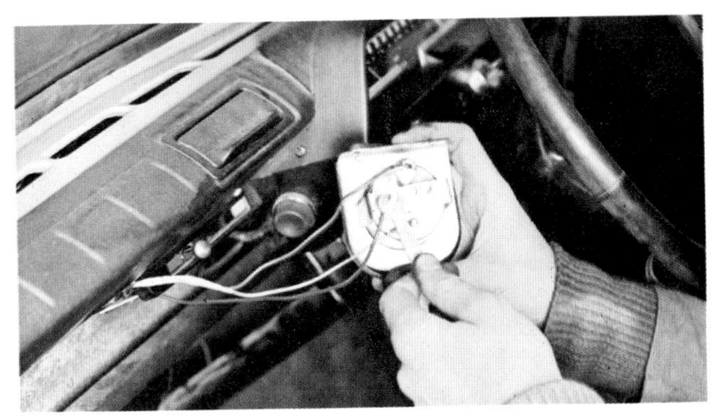

9 With the panel light and earth wires already connected to the gauge, the live wire can be attached to the appropriate terminal

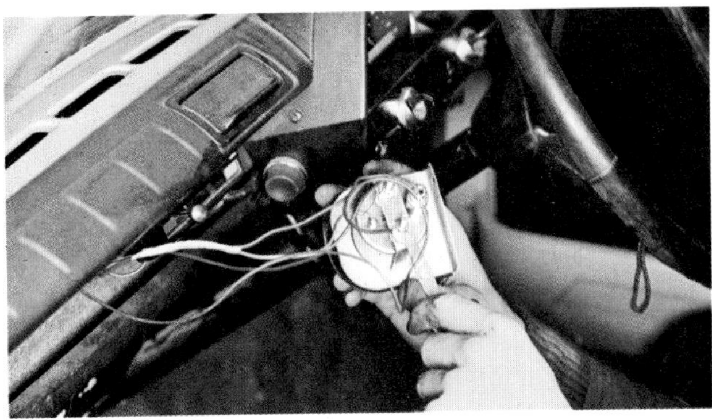

10 Follow this with the sender wire. On this gauge, the two screw terminals also serve to hold the panel clamp tightly in place

tape where necessary, as you run it down to the sender. Attach it to the sender terminal with an appropriate tag or with a spade connector.

Fitting a capillary water temperature gauge (large bulb type)

To fit a capillary gauge, start by bearing in mind the following important points:

1. At no time must the capillary or sensing bulb be disconnected from the gauge

2. The capillary must not be sharply bent or twisted

3. All bends in the capillary must be made with the fingers and should never be less than 25 mm (1in.) radius.

The first step is to feed a rubber grommet on to the capillary tube. This should be of a suitable size to fit the hole which will be drilled in the bulkhead to feed the capillary through. Not only will the grommet prevent draughts, but it will also stop the capillary from chafing on jagged metal.

Next, cut a hole in the bulkhead immediately behind the gauge's intended mounting position. It should be large enough for the bulb on the end of the capillary to pass through, but an exact size will probably be specified by the manufacturer of the gauge. If your drill will not accept a bit of the correct size, use a 3 mm or $\frac{1}{8}$in. bit to drill a series of holes around the circumference of the proposed larger hole, knock out the metal disc and clean up the rough edges with a half-round file. Carefully feed the bulb through into the engine compartment and straight down to the tapping in the engine (see above). As under 'fitting an electrical gauge', part-drain the cooling system and remove the old temperature indicator sender or the blanking plug which will be fitted in its place.

With the large-bulb capillary, there are two different methods employed to fit the bulb into the tapping. On some gauges, the bulb is inserted into the tapping and the locknut above it is screwed in tight to hold it firmly in place. On other gauges, such as the Smiths TB and GTB types, you screw a brass union into the tapping first. The bulb then goes through it and is tightened with the union nut above. Where an adaptor is required, this will screw into the tapping in the same way as the union.

When the bulb has been connected, all that remains is to route the capillary tidily. Different manufacturers recom-

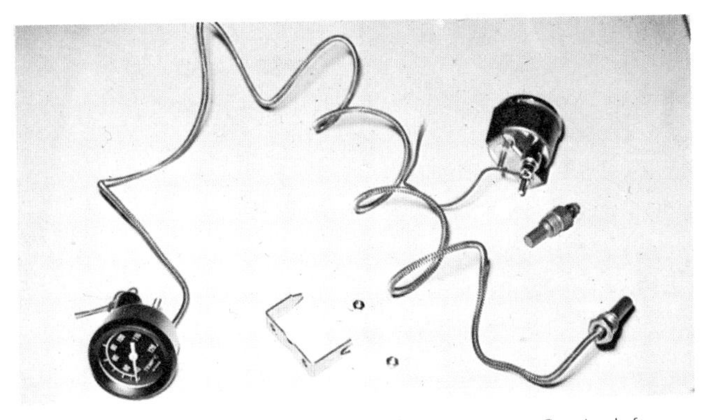

11 Two different types of water temperature gauge. On the left a capillary gauge and, on the right, an electrical one with sender

12 When fitting a capillary gauge, you should start by deciding where the capillary is to pass through the engine bulkhead

13 On this BL Mini, there is a convenient hole in the binnacle holding the speedometer. The plastic plug is simply pressed out

Jake Wynter

14 In this case, the gauge is mounted in a custom fascia panel. Clamp the gauge in place and then feed the capillary through

15 This car does not have a sender already fitted. Instead there is a blanking plug which must be unscrewed with a spanner

16 You can then feed the capillary sensor into the hole and screw down the union nut which holds it tight and prevents leaks

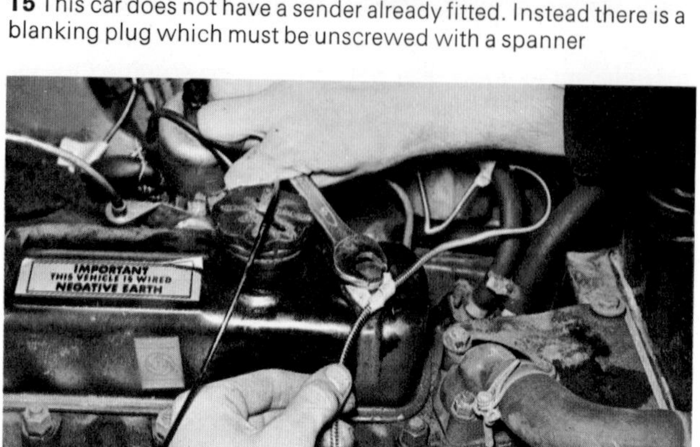

17 The first cleat on the capillary must be made to a cool part of the engine, not too far from the union nut. Avoid sharp bends

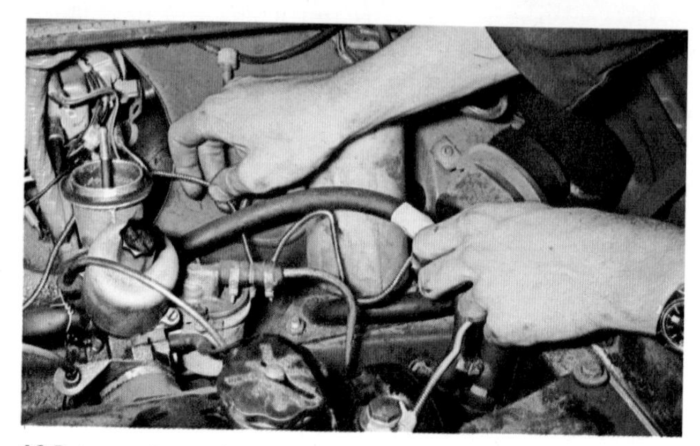

18 Between the engine and the car bodywork, coil the capillary to absorb engine vibration. Make the coils as large as possible

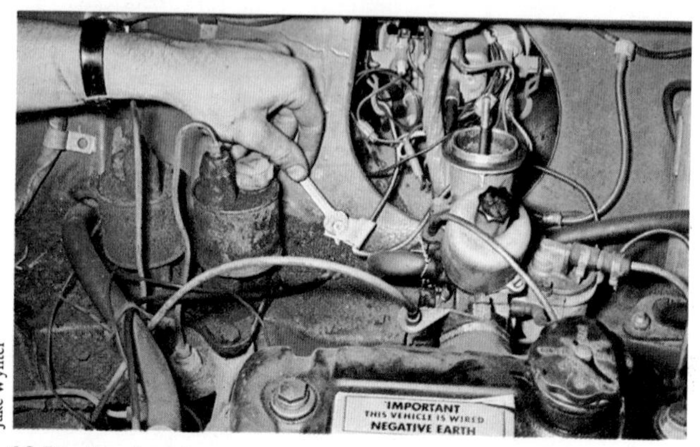

Jake Wynter

19 Finally, cleat the capillary to the bodywork. You can make the cleats from cardboard, scrap plastic or pieces of thick wire

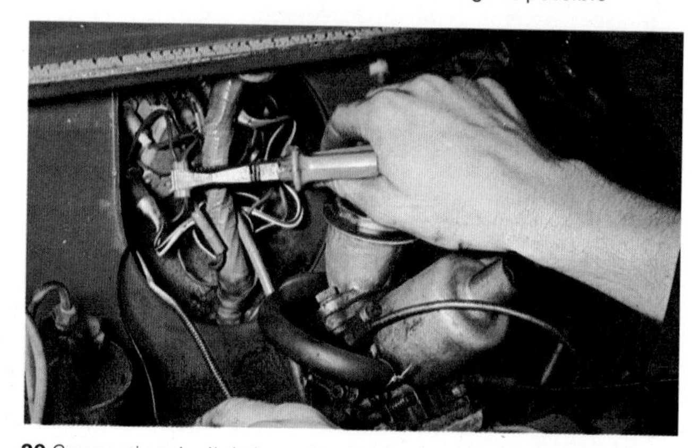

20 Connecting the lighting wire. On this car the instrument wires are exposed and it is easy to splice into the panel light circuit

mend different ways of doing this but the following instructions form a safe guide:

1. Run the capillary as straight as possible to the edge of the engine and tie or cleat it with a scrap of wire to a convenient point. Make sure that the tube avoids all the areas which are likely to get very hot.

2. Between the engine and the bodywork, make three coils in the capillary of not less than 51 mm (2in.) radius, using your fingers as guides. These will help to absorb engine vibration and reduce the risk of fracture.

3. Run the rest of the capillary along the bodywork inside the engine compartment and up to the point where it emerges through the bulkhead. Cleat it to the body with wire or tape at intervals of about 200 mm (8in.) and make more coils if there is any excess length to take up. These, too, should be carefully cleated to the bodywork.

When you have connected the earth and illumination wires as described above, and fixed the gauge in its mounting, it should be ready for use.

Smiths TB-SC small-bulb temperature gauge

The sensor bulb on the Smiths TB-SC gauge is specially designed for engines where access to the tapping into the water jacket is limited (see above). The gauge is fitted in the same way as the large-bulb type above, apart from the bulb fitting, which is slightly different.

In this case, insert the bulb into the tapping, holding both the bulb and the capillary. The bulb should be screwed in using a spanner. At the same time, make sure that the capillary winds round the protruding mandrel in neat and tidy coils.

To be absolutely sure however, that everything is working correctly, start up the engine. Under the bonnet, watch out for leaks. The most likely place is at the union where the capillary runs into the block. If there is any sign of water at all, stop the engine. Tighten the union nut slightly and then re-check it. It is also a good idea to check the capillary coils and cleats. Make sure that they are not disturbed by engine vibration.

Fitting an ammeter

Failure of the car to start because of a flat battery can be very irritating. But for a reasonable outlay, and a few hours' work, you can fit an ammeter which will allow you to monitor the perfomance not just of the battery, but of the whole electrical system.

The ammeter measures the value of an electrical current, the unit of measure being amperes (amps), and so enables you to monitor the rate of charge or discharge of the battery.

The ammeter dial has a central needle operating on a graduated scale. One side denotes discharge (—) the other charge (+). The scale usually reads up to 30 amps, depending on the make, and the type of charging system it is designed to monitor.

There are quite a number of ammeter kits available on the market, in varying sizes and dial shapes. Some of the most common makes are Smiths, Jaeger, Time, Speedwell, Yazaki and Veglia Borletti.

Siting the instrument

Some cars have provision for an ammeter. This takes the form of a blanking plate, often situated in an existing dial which houses two or three other gauges. You may need to fit a specific ammeter as intended by the manufacturers.

In the majority of cases, no such provision exists. You will have to fix the instrument either by cutting a hole in the fascia panel, or by adding an extra panel to accommodate it. Before any steps are taken to fit the instrument, however, the exact location must be decided.

Ideally, the ammeter must be placed in such a way as to be easily visible to the driver at all times. It must also permit easy routing of the wiring and not interfere with the functioning of any other controls. If the instrument is to be fixed in the fascia panel, there should be enough space behind this to accommodate the bulk of the ammeter and its securing clamp. If it is fixed to an additional panel, make sure this is not positioned in such a way as to cause injury in an accident.

1 Most ammeters are circular, with black or white faces on which a graduated scale is marked up to plus or minus 30 amps

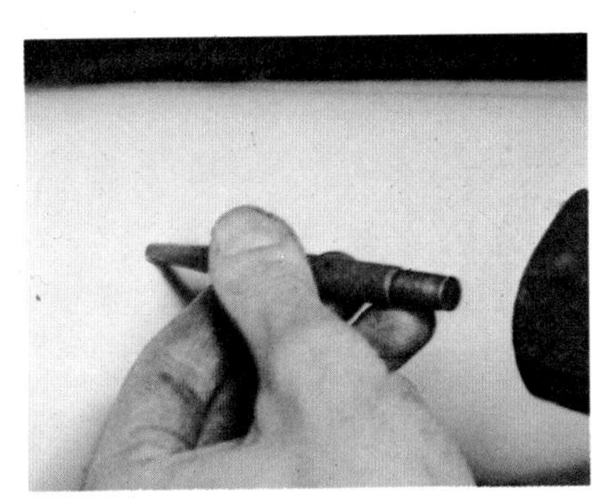

2 When the instrument is to be mounted in the fascia the easiest way is to use a hole saw. Begin by marking with a centre punch

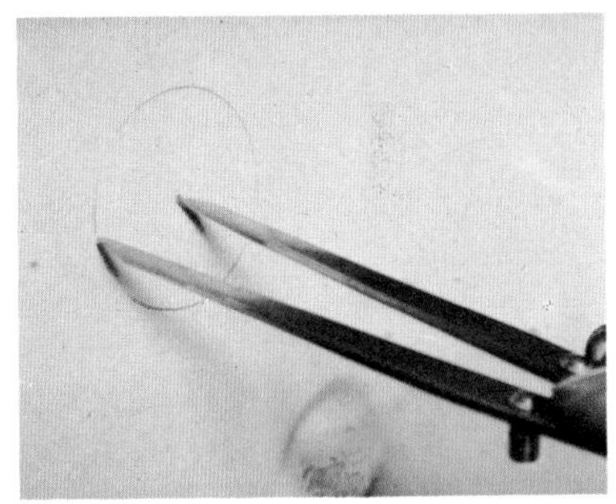

3 With a pair of sharp dividers, scribe a circle of the right diameter, usually 52 mm, using the punch mark as the centre point

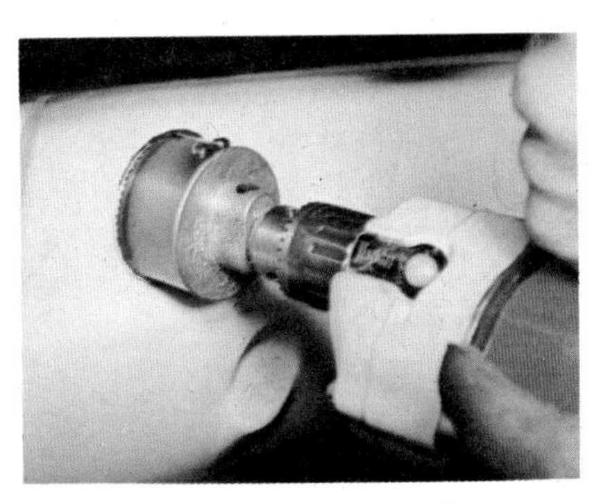

4 With a hole saw of the correct diameter (just under 52 mm to allow for the width of the cut) drill through the centre point

5 With the metal disc removed from the hole test the fit of the ammeter dial. The edges may need to be filed before it will fit in

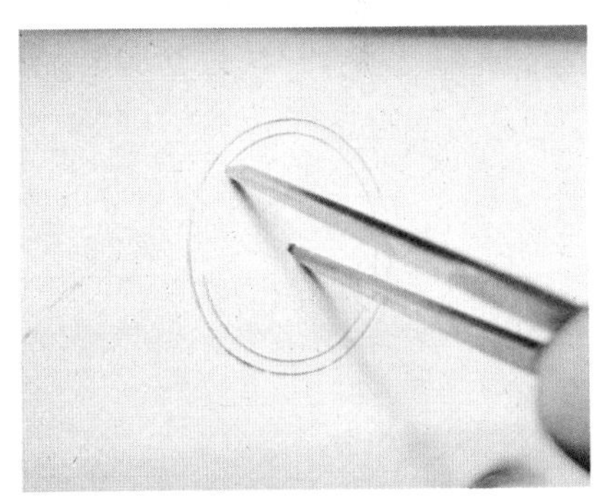

6 If no hole saw is available, scribe two circles, the second 3 mm (0.125in.) inside the first. This is half the drill diameter

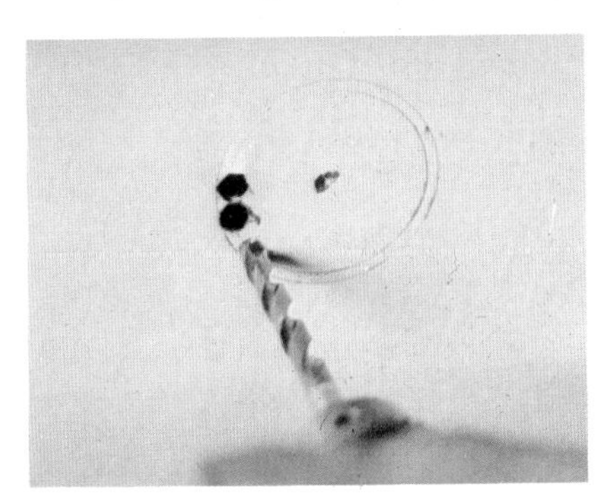

7 Using a 6 mm drill bit, carefully drill a series of closely grouped holes around the circumference of the second, inner, circle

8 With the series of holes drilled, check that they are as close together as possible then tap out the panel with a screwdriver

9 The edge of the circle will be very rough and this will prevent the instrument from being inserted. So use a file to smooth it

Nelson Hargreaves

If you are considering fitting several extra instruments, there is a wide variety of floor consoles on the market which can be used to house dials and switches. These are available from most accessory shops. Also available are roof consoles which are fitted above the windscreen.

Fixing the instrument

If you are fitting an instrument into a larger dial that holds two or three others, remove the main dial. Undo the clamp at the back of the instrument and ease it forward. Take care not to break any connections. It will probably be necessary to disconnect the leads, in which case you should mark them carefully so they can be replaced in the correct position. With the instrument removed, it should be possible to remove the blanking plug and screw in the new ammeter. Reverse the procedure to refit the main dial.

Where no special fixing exists, the easiest way to make a hole in the fascia panel, be it metal or wood, is to use a circular saw, or hole saw. After deciding on the location, mark the centre of the area where the dial is to be fitted with a centre punch. Most dials are 52 mm (2in.) in diameter, but some may differ. Check the size of your instrument and then, using dividers and the punch mark as the centre, scribe a circle. Using a hole saw of the correct diameter, drill out the panel. This will produce a neat hole which should require no filing.

If a hole saw is not available, an effective but more time-consuming method may be employed using an ordinary power drill. Scribe a circle the size of the instrument, as before. Select a drill bit of around 6 mm (0.25in.). Then scribe a second circle, just inside the first and about half the diameter of the drill bit, in this case 3 mm (0.125in.)

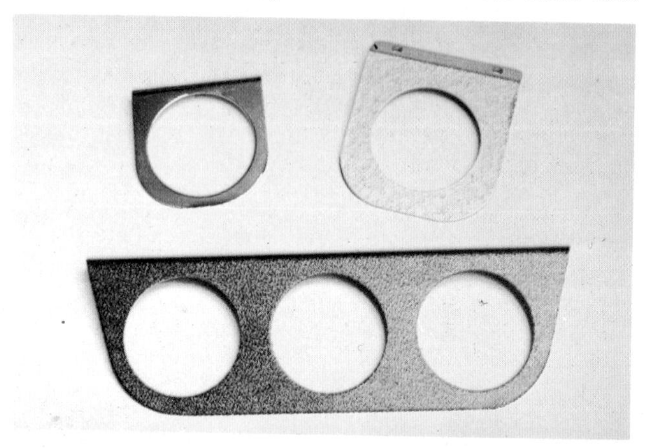

10 Fixing panels for auxiliary instruments are obtainable, in a variety of designs and colours, for up to three instruments

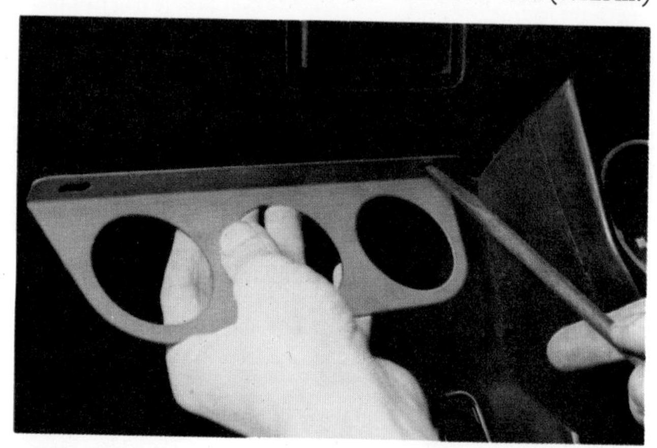

11 As it is intended to fit more dials to this Leyland Mini at a later date, a large panel is being used. Mark out its position

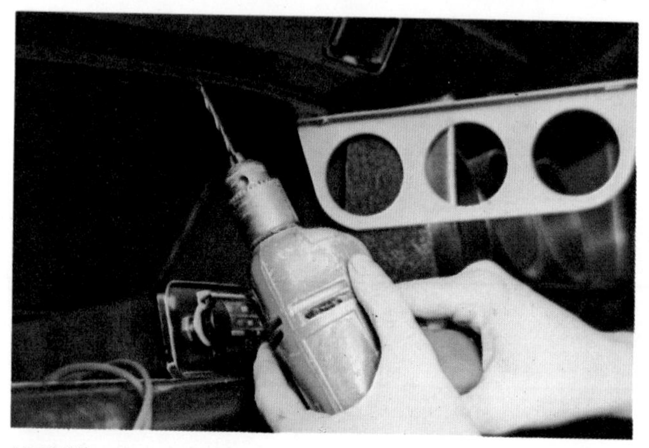

12 Drill one hole to begin with, and secure the panel by self-tapping screw. Then swivel the panel and drill the second hole

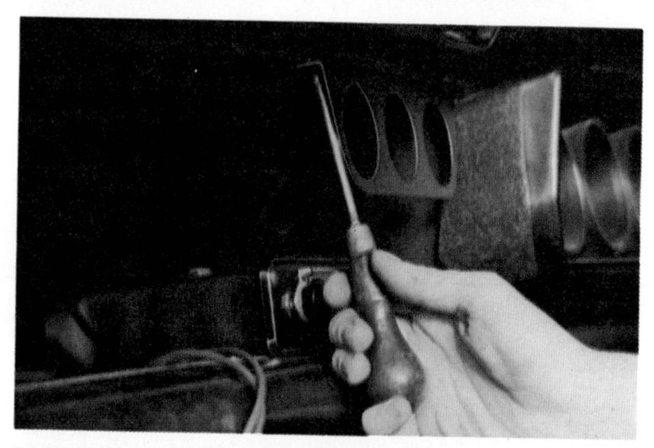

13 Fit the second self-tapping screw to hold the panel securely and fully tighten the first screw. The panel must not be loose

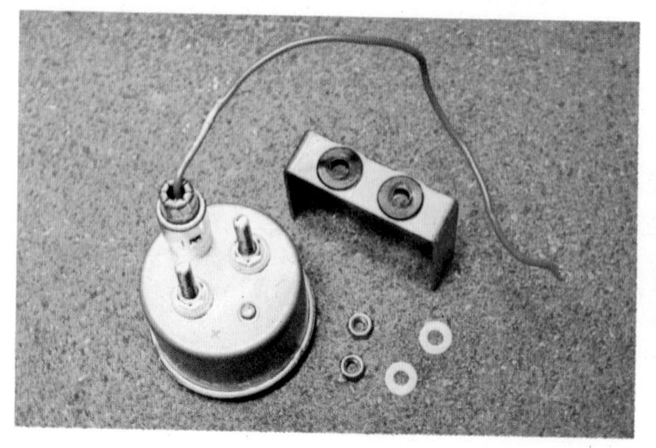

14 The ammeter is secured by a bracket on the back which itself is held by two knurled nuts. The illumination bulb is visible too

15 Insert the instrument into the panel until it lies flush with the panel face. Make sure it is upright, then tighten the clamp

16 A selection of connectors. Top, left to right: Scotchlok; tag; rubber grommet. Bottom, left to right: spade; bullet; piggy-back

away from it. Now drill round on the inner circle, grouping the holes as close together as possible (fig. 7). It should then be easy to punch out the metal within the hole with a hammer and screwdriver. Finish off by filing the edge of the hole until it is smooth.

Unfortunately, many modern fascia panels are so designed that there is little room for the addition of extra instruments. The answer is to fit a separate instrument panel. Some ammeters come complete with a matching single mounting plate but multi-instrument panels in various shapes and sizes can also be obtained.

Panels are usually fixed with self-tapping screws but in some instances self-adhesive pads are supplied with the panel. If neither of these methods is satisfactory, small nuts and bolts can be used.

With the mounting for the instrument prepared, remove the securing clamp from the back of the ammeter. This is held by one or two knurled nuts. Insert the gauge into the mounting hole until it lies flush against the dial surround, then attach the clamp from behind. Tighten the clamp nuts, ensuring the gauge is straight and upright.

Tools for wiring the instrument

Several tools are required to wire the instrument.

A small electrical screwdriver will be needed for any terminal screws.

A pair of bull-nose insulated pliers will suffice for crimping connectors and will be even more useful if they incorporate a wire-cutter. If they do not, it is advisable to obtain wire-cutting pliers and a wire-stripping tool. A penknife may substitute for the latter as a last resort, but it is not really suitable for cutting wires 'in circuit', as there is always a tendency to stretch the wire while doing this, thus loosening connections.

If you have ideas of undertaking further electrical work, a professional crimping tool might be a worthwhile investment. This will cut, strip and crimp any number of different sized wires and connectors and is relatively inexpensive.

Failing this, the number of smaller items required will include heavy-duty bullet connectors, heavy and light insulated spade connectors and a roll of plastic insulating tape.

Correct fitting of wire connectors

If bullet connectors are used anywhere in the main circuit a soldering iron, solder and flux will also be needed. This is because the only really secure connection with bullet connectors is one where the wires are soldered to the male bullet and its female barrel.

An ammeter is wired in series in the battery charge and

17 The voltage regulator box is usually mounted on a bulkhead in the engine bay. This Leyland Mini has the 'two-bobbin' type

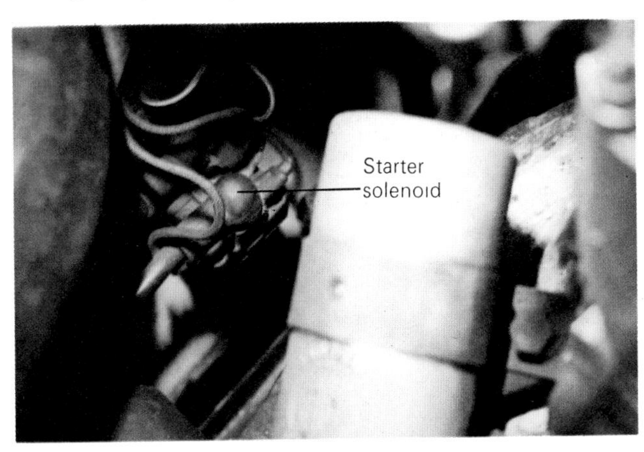

18 The starter solenoid is also located in the engine bay, but may be harder to find. On the Leyland Mini it is by the clutch

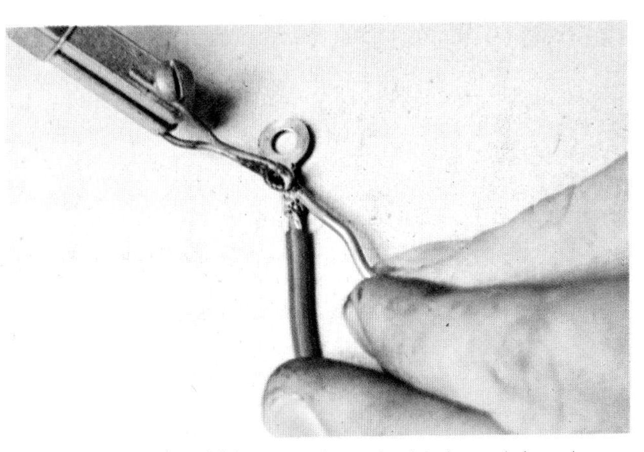

19 Cut two lengths of 44 gauge wire and, with the ends bared, a tag connector should be soldered to one end of each wire

Nelson Hargreaves

20 Poke the two tag connector ends of the wire through a grommet in the bulkhead and connect a wire to each terminal of the dial discharge circuit. This means that all current from the generator to the battery and from the battery to the car's electrical system (excluding the starter motor) passes through the ammeter.

Due to the strong current being passed through the ammeter it is particularly important that heavy-duty leads are used to wire it up. If the leads are not already supplied with the ammeter, or if additional lengths are required, suitable gauge wire is 44/0.012 if the car has a dynamo, or 65/0.012 if it has an alternator.

It is extremely important that circuit connections should be made using heavy-duty bullet connectors or by soldering the joint, or both. The connection is made by stripping a length of insulation from the wire end, fractionally longer than the male plug, and then 'tinning' the bare wire. This entails applying a thin coat of solder to the wire. It should then be inserted into the male plug and soldered.

The terminal connections on the back of the ammeter should always be made with heavy-duty spades, although these will already be fitted where the wiring is supplied with the ammeter.

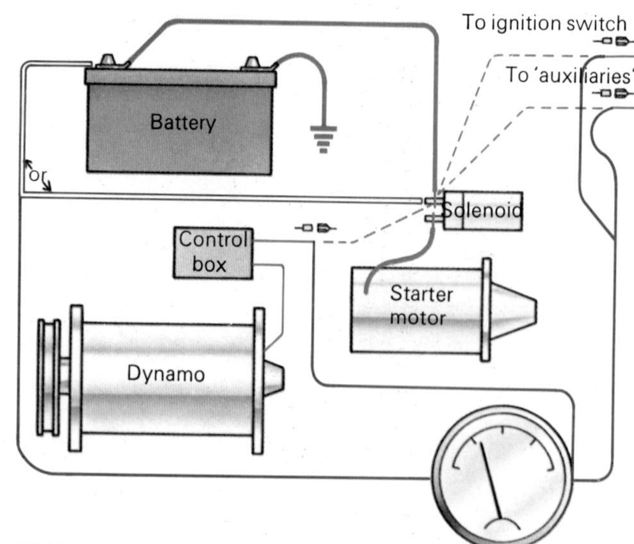

21 How you wire an ammeter depends on your car's original wiring scheme. In this one, charging is by dynamo and control box. One terminal on the solenoid is the starting point for both the wire to the ignition switch and the wire or wires to the 'auxiliaries' —lighting system, wiper motor, radio and so on. The red lines show the new wiring you will need for the ammeter

Locating the starter solenoid and regulator box

You will need to locate the starter solenoid (fig. 18) and the regulator box (fig. 17) before wiring begins.

The position of the solenoid varies, depending on the make of car. It may be mounted on a bulkhead inside the engine bay or, in some cases, it may be on the starter motor itself. Regulator units are almost always found in one corner of the engine bay, on a bulkhead, or under the fascia.

Protecting the wiring

Wiring from the ammeter to the engine bay will have to be routed from the car interior through the front bulkhead. The easiest way to do this is to find a grommet. This is a rubber bung with a hole in the centre which is used to protect wires passing through metal holes where the sharp edges may damage them. Push the two wires leading from the ammeter through an adjacent grommet. If there is no grommet within reach of the ammeter location, drill a hole under the fascia or the carpet where it will be least noticeable, and fit a grommet of suitable size. Never be tempted to omit grommets. If the wires do chafe through on a plain metal hole, the most likely outcome is a short circuit.

Wiring the instrument

Before beginning to wire up the ammeter, check the earthing of your car. This can be done by checking which lead on the battery is connected to the bodywork of the car (it should, of course, be disconnected while you are working). This is the earth terminal; the other one is the live terminal, which the car's electrical circuits are connected to. You will find that there is a thick heavy-duty cable running from this terminal to the solenoid. A similar cable runs from another solenoid terminal to the starter motor. These cables should be left alone.

Next you will need to find the point(s) to which the wire from the ignition switch, and wire or wires to the car's other electrical systems—lights, wiper motor, radio and so on—are connected. Sometimes they are connected to the solenoid (figs. 21 and 22), sometimes split between one terminal on the solenoid and one on the battery (fig. 23). There is no mistaking these wires; they are much thinner individually than the heavy cables mentioned in the last paragraph.

The ammeter has to be wired between the battery and all the electrical circuits, so that it shows all charges and discharges. The only exception to this is the starter motor: this takes such a high current that the ammeter would be destroyed. So whatever you do, never connect the heavy-duty starter cable to the ammeter so that the starting current flows through it.

Whichever way your car is wired, the principles you have to follow in wiring up the ammeter are the same:

1: From one terminal of the ammeter, run a wire either to the non-earthed terminal of the battery, or to the solenoid terminal to which the battery is directly connected. (It doesn't matter to which end of the battery-to-solenoid cable you connect, since this cable and its terminals are, in the electrical sense, all one unit.)

2: Next, you must intercept the wire that runs from the alternator (or control box) to the solenoid, and divert it instead to the ammeter.

3: Then you must intercept the wire from the ignition switch to the solenoid and divert it to the ammeter.

4: Finally, you must intercept the wire from the 'auxiliaries'—lights and so on—to the solenoid and divert it too to the ammeter.

Note that the wires mentioned in paragraphs 2, 3 and 4 all go to the same terminal on the ammeter.

Figs. 21 to 23 show how this is done in theory. In practice, how you go about it will vary from car to car, depending on convenience—on where it is easiest to connect to an existing wire. There are no 'rules' for this, because cars' wiring systems vary so much. All you can do is to study the diagrams until you understand the objectives, and then hunt out the right wires on your own car.

If, when the job is done, the ammeter reads 'back to front' there is no great problem. You just swap over the terminals on the back of the ammeter itself.

A cautionary note: cars with ammeters already fitted, or with wiring installed, may require a different type of instrument called a *shunt* ammeter. This does not carry the full charge/discharge current, so you cannot replace one by the ordinary series type dealt with here.

Fixing the illumination light

Apart from the main wiring, the ammeter will also have an illumination light for night use. This must be wired into the car's panel light circuit. The bulb will be found in

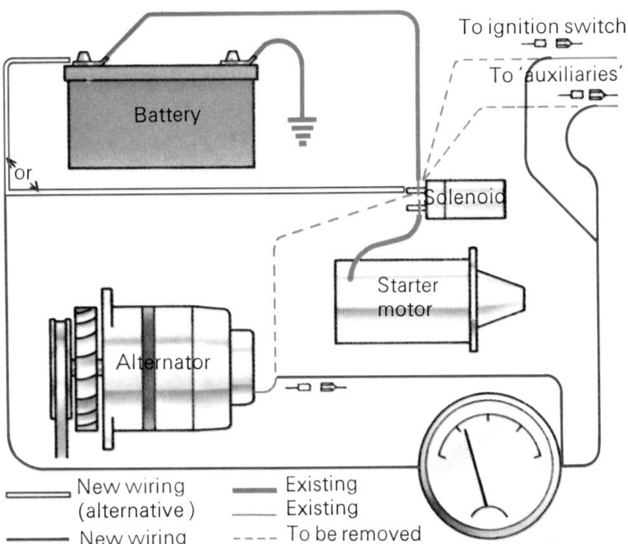

22 A similar system, but this time using an alternator instead of a dynamo. The connections to the ignition switch wire and 'auxiliaries' wire can be made at any convenient point, except of course at the solenoid itself. You can recognise these wires because they are single thin wires, or a bundle of thin wires, whereas the cable from the battery to the solenoid is thick

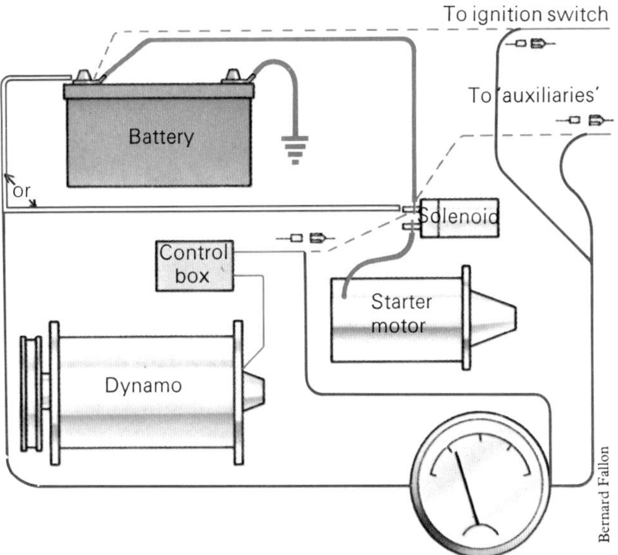

Bernard Fallon

23 Split systems like this are found on a few cars. Instead of being wired to the same terminal, the ignition switch wire and the 'auxiliaries' wire(s) start out from opposite ends of the battery-to-solenoid cable—electrically it makes no odds, since the cable and its terminals are virtually one unit. And the basic principle of wiring the ammeter is exactly as before

a socket on the back of the instrument. It may have a single light-gauge wire already attached or there may be provision for a wire in the form of a small spade terminal. The easiest way to connect the light is to wire it directly into the panel light circuit under the fascia.

Look behind the fascia from below and locate the speedometer. A similar bulb should be visible on the back of this instrument. A single light-gauge wire is attached to this and the ammeter light wire should be connected to it. The best way of doing this is with a Scotchlok clip. This is a special type of clip and is used to connect a supply lead such as the ammeter light wire directly to an insulated wire. The supply lead is laid in the clip alongside the insulated wire and held in position by grooves. The clip is hinged in two halves and these are then pressed together. The metal plate is squeezed home with pliers and the clip locks with a snap-round insulator. Scotchloks should not be used on wires that carry a high current.

Sometimes it is not possible to connect the ammeter light in this way. Instead, a connection will have to be made to the sidelight wiring. If trouble is experienced in tracing the wiring, or in cases where a printed circuit is fitted, connect the ammeter light to the sidelight terminal on the fuse box (fig. 28).

The fuse box will be situated either under the dashboard (usually on the passenger side) or under the bonnet on a bulkhead. Check the circuit diagram in the car's handbook to ascertain which fuse box terminal carries the sidelight power. The relevant spade connector can then be detached and a 'piggy-back' (double) connector clipped on to the terminal. Spade connectors are attached to wire ends by stripping the insulation, inserting the wire into the insulated spade end, and crimping the two together.

Once again, if they are to be used anywhere in the heavy-current circuit, as on the main ammeter terminals, heavy-duty spades must be used and soldered as well. In fact, it is far better to solder all joints to be really sure of good, permanent connections.

Reconnect the sidelight-wire spade, solder a spade to the ammeter bulb wire and clip this to the second tongue of the same terminal.

The only remaining job is to see that the instrument itself is earthed. If in fitting it into the car the metal instrument case is in good contact with a metal surface, nothing more need be done. Otherwise you will need to run a wire from the case to a known clean earth.

Using the instrument

When the engine is first started and the car is running over 20-25mph, the ammeter should indicate a charge (+) rate of up to 30 amps. This figure may vary depending upon the individual car's generator output to rpm ratio. As a general

24 With the 'two-bobbin' type of regulator box, remove the wire from the A terminal and tuck it away from the other wires

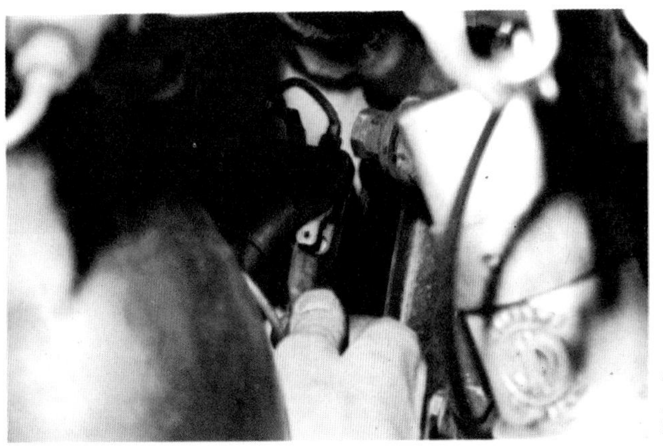

Nelson Hargreaves

25 Remove the other end of the wire from the starter solenoid. The wire could be discarded but it is easier to tuck it away

rule a dynamo should put out 15-20 amps and an alternator a slightly higher current.

After a few minutes constant running, the charge should drop to 0-5 amps as the regulator system cuts in to prevent overload to the battery.

At no time should a discharge be apparent with the car running above 2,000rpm or about 30mph. A slight discharge is acceptable at idle speed, except in cars fitted with alternators. These are designed to prevent discharge at low rpm.

The generator can be tested by switching on the headlights and heater fan blower and running the engine at about 2,000rpm. If your car has no tachometer, this is a little faster than twice the normal idling speed. If the ammeter needle drops below the 0-5 amp charge (+) mark, it could be that the fanbelt is slipping, the generator is in need of service or the battery is in poor condition.

A dynamo-powered system does have limitations and may not be able to cope with the consumption demanded by, for example, the use of headlights, heater blower, windscreen wipers and a heated rear window simultaneously. In this instance the operator must decide which equipment demands priority, and which must be turned off. Prolonged running with a discharge rate in excess of 1 amp will drain the battery.

If the system will not charge without turning off the headlights, either the dynamo is faulty or there is an overload and too much current is being used in the system. Again, the remedy is either to fit a new battery or to have the generator serviced.

An alternator, as mentioned, is better designed to cope with low rpm. It can also cope better with ancillary equipment. It has a higher current output than a dynamo throughout its range. As a result, any recurrent ammeter discharge reading should be investigated.

If the electrical system usually copes with a full load, but discharges under certain engine speeds, the fanbelt is probably loose. Tighten it and recheck with a full load and the engine revving. If the discharge is still evident, the fault will lie in the generator or the regulator. Sticking or worn brushes may produce a spasmodic discharge or a flickering reading.

When the direction indicators are operated, one side at a time, there should be an even discharge reading that is the same for both sides. If the two readings are uneven, it points to a faulty earth, a poor connection in the circuit or a blown bulb.

The ammeter reading should always be steady. If it flickers abruptly, turn on different electrical systems, one by one, until that which is causing the fluctuation is isolated. It will then be necessary to investigate that circuit for a poor connection.

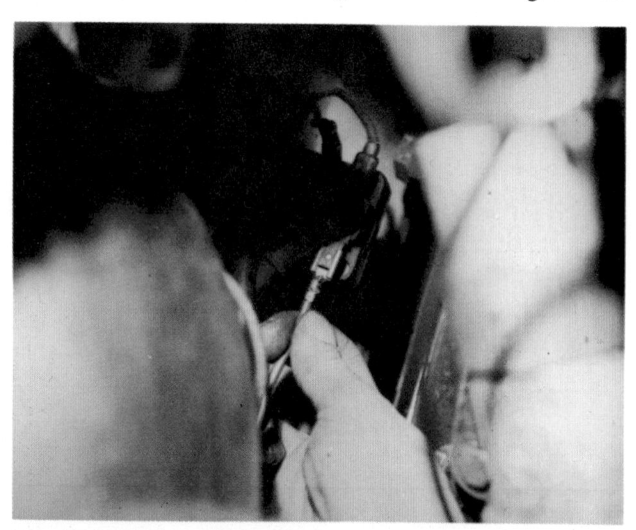

26 With a heavy-duty spade connector soldered to the end of the relevant wire, attach the wire to the starter solenoid terminal

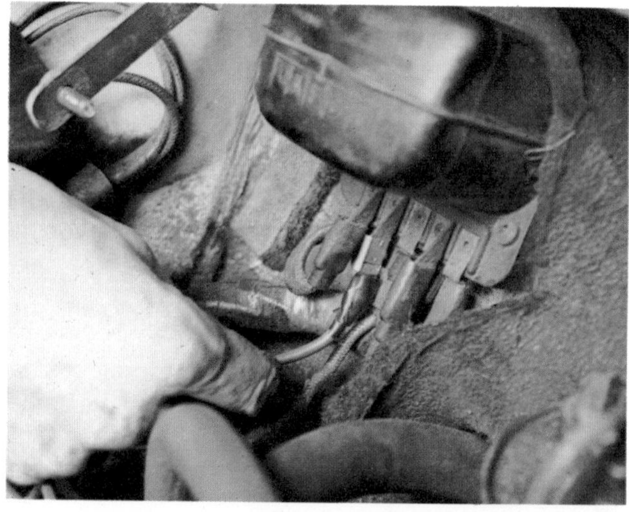

27 Another heavy-duty spade connector should be soldered to the remaining wire. Connect the wire to the regulator box A terminal

Nelson Hargreaves

28 To wire up the instrument illumination on some cars, it will be necessary to locate the fuse box, situated in the engine bay

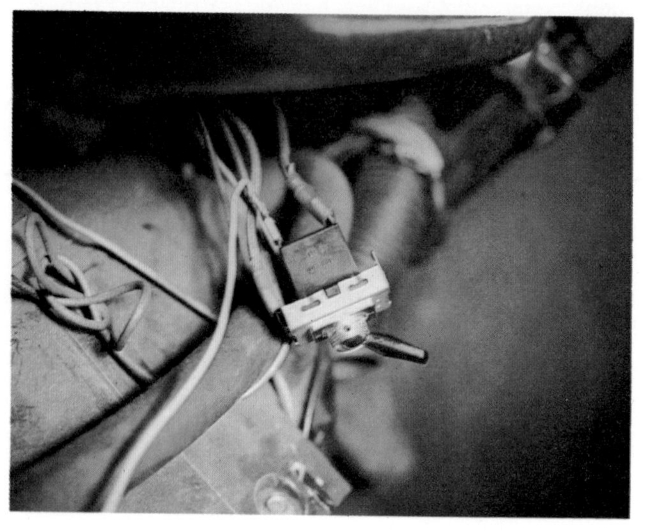

29 Where there is a printed circuit, but it is not possible to wire to the fuse box, connect the wire to the panel light switch

Fitting a rev counter

The tachometer, or rev counter, is an extremely useful addition to any car which does not already have one fitted as standard. By skilful reading of the instrument, it is possible to tell at what point your engine is developing maximum power, and also when it is at its most efficient in relation to the amount of fuel consumed. For a relatively modest outlay, it enables you to get the most from your power plant without risking the serious damage caused by over-revving.

Two basic kinds of tachometer are generally available on the accessory market—the 'pod' type, which is mounted in its own casing on top of the fascia; and the more conventional dial type, designed to be mounted in the fascia panel itself. Both are electronic in operation and work by detecting the impulses in the car's ignition system which occur when there is a spark at one of the plugs. The number of sparks per second is then converted into the number of engine revolutions per minute or rpm.

Siting the instrument

To get the most use from a tachometer, you should be able to keep an eye on it in the same way you would a speedometer—that is, you should be able to see it out of the corner of your eye while you are driving. Siting it is therefore of prime importance. You may be tempted to mount it on a little panel under the fascia, but here you will not be able to see it and keep your eyes safely on the road. The pod type of tachometer is the easiest to fit because it does not require any hole cutting in the fascia panel, and can be transferred to another car without difficulty. The instrument should be positioned just to the left or right of the centre line of the steering, so that it is in the field of vision while driving, but not a source of distraction.

1 This tachometer will suit either four- or six-cylinder cars. It is important to set the switch at the back before you start

If you are going to fit the larger dial type, find a site where it can be seen clearly with your hands on the steering wheel in their normal, straight ahead position. If it is located in the fascia panel, there must be sufficient space behind it for wiring, and in practice this is often hard to find on modern production saloons. The first task when buying a tachometer is, therefore, to investigate possible locations and any obvious fitting problems before choosing a particular type of instrument.

Other preliminaries

Before buying a tachometer, make sure that the one of your choice is suitable for use with your engine and electrical system. Some instruments are designed to operate only with four-cylinder engines; others are specifically for sixes and eights. Make sure yours is compatible, or that it has an adaptor switch on the back like the Sanpet S-500A illustrated (fig. 1). The tachometer must also match the polarity of the car to which it is fitted. Check whether your car is positive or negative earth by noting which battery lead runs straight to the car body—this is the earth—and buy a tachometer to match.

If your car has a 6-volt electrical system rather than the usual 12-volt, you must buy a 6-volt tachometer. The wires provided with accessory instruments are often not long enough, so be prepared for any extension work with extra wire and a supply of screw connectors.

If you have electronic ignition, you must buy a tachometer which is compatible with it (see below).

Installation—pod type

Your instrument will have either a screw-on bracket like the one illustrated, or a self adhesive pad. With the screw-on type, place the bracket where it is to be fixed and mark the two holes. If it is to be fixed to metal, drill the holes and then fasten. Otherwise, simply screw into the plastic fascia capping with two self-tapping screws (fig. 2). With an adhesive fixing, make sure that the location is clean and dry; peel off the protective backing and then press the bracket firmly in position. In cold weather, extra adhesion may be obtained by heating the base beforehand.

If necessary, the instrument pod can now be attached to the bracket (fig. 3). Next, feed the wires from the back of the pod through a convenient demister slot, or around the fascia capping and down a door pillar (fig. 4).

Installation—dial type

With a conventional dial type instrument, choose a convenient space on the fascia panel, which will accommodate

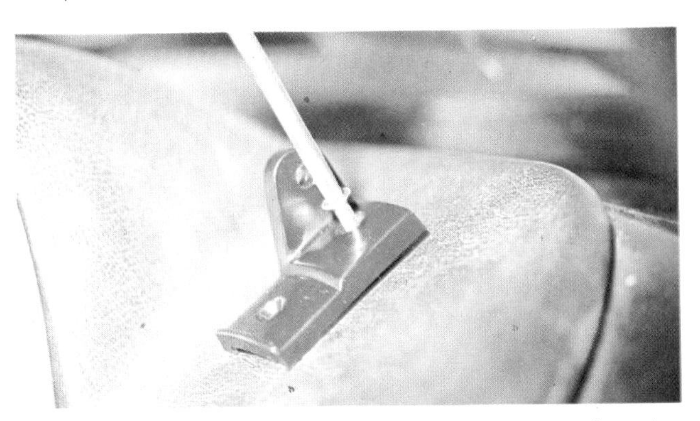

2 Screw the mounting bracket down on to the fascia capping using self-tapping screws. You may have to drill the holes first

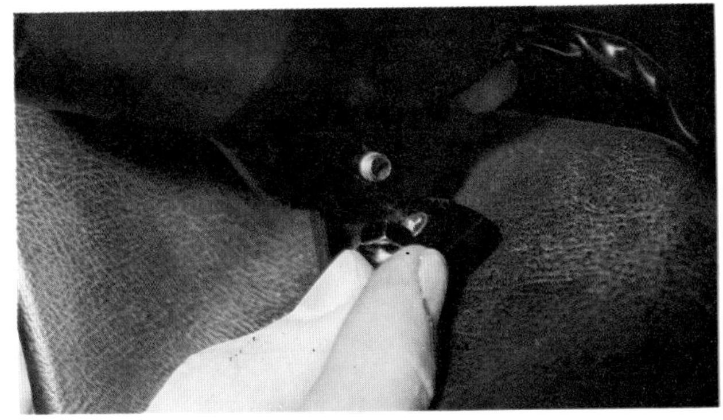

3 With the bracket firmly in place, secure the instrument pod to it using the small nut and bolt provided in the kit

the bulk of the tachometer comfortably. Now carefully cut a hole as described on pages 167 to 168. Feed the wires at the back of the instrument through the hole, making sure that they are still accessible, and then fix it in position by means of the screw clamp provided.

Wiring—illumination

Whichever type of tachometer you have chosen, it is important at this stage to familiarize yourself with the wires at the back of the instrument by matching their colours with the manufacturer's individual instructions. One of these will have to be wired into the panel light circuit to provide night-time illumination; find out from the instruction leaflet which one this is.

Many modern cars have printed circuits to which it is difficult, or impossible, to add an extra wire. So connect the illumination wire instead to the sidelamp/headlamp switch, which has a separate panel light wire. Loosen the switch so that the terminals at the back are accessible and the wires visible (fig. 5 and 6). Disconnect each wire in turn and try the switch until the side and headlamps go on but the panel lights do not—that is the one you want. Connect the illumination wire to the same terminal as this wire (fig. 7), using a spade connector if necessary.

Alternatively, the circuit may be broken into in the same way at the fusebox if this should prove more readily accessible (fig. 8). If a wiring diagram is available, you may be able to find the correct colour wire under the fascia and splice the new wire with a Scotchlok connector. This procedure is the same for both pod and dial tachometers.

You will now be left with three connections to make into the ignition circuit—one to earth, one (the 'triggering' lead) to the distributor side of the coil, and one to a live voltage supply.

Wiring into the ignition

Begin by rechecking which wire is which in the manufacturer's instructions, as any mistake could damage the instrument. Take the earth lead first. This must be fixed to any metal part of the car in contact with its main body—usually a fascia panel fixing bolt is ideal (fig. 9). Make sure the connection is clean and tight.

The next step is to connect the triggering lead, which is the one that actually provides information on the number of engine revolutions per minute. To do this, trace the low tension wire running from the side of the distributor back to the coil—even if it disappears into the wiring loom, it should still be easy to match the colour up when it reappears; this will be at the 'distributor side' of the coil (fig. 10). Feed the two remaining wires from the tachometer through the engine bulkhead, remembering to fit a rubber grommet to prevent fraying if a fresh hole has to be drilled (fig. 11). If the wires have to be extended, use proper screw connectors and make sure that you can still identify the wires correctly at the other end (fig. 12). Solder or crimp a spade connector to the triggering lead, and attach it to the distributor side of the coil using a double spade connector (fig. 13).

On some cars, the coil terminals will be marked CB and SW, in which case connect the triggering lead to the CB one. On later negative earth vehicles they may be marked + and – ; here, connect it to the – side.

Wiring the live connection

The final wire is the live one which provides power to the circuit when the ignition is switched on. Different manufacturers recommend different points at which to make the connection, but there are basically only three—the switch (SW) side of the coil; a spare terminal on the fusebox connected to any circuit which becomes live when the ignition is switched on; and a spare terminal behind the ignition switch itself. With the Sanpet S-500A, for example, it is a simple matter of connecting the live lead to the opposite side of the coil to the distributor (fig. 14). In other cases follow instructions carefully and ensure the terminals needed are accessible by unscrewing the ignition switch or removing any trim around it. There will almost certainly be a spare terminal provided, specifically for such accessories, and the lead can be attached by means of a standard spade connector. If the ignition switch is impossible to get at, then the fusebox is a good alternative. The correct terminal should be identified using a wiring diagram.

Electronic ignition

Some earlier types of tachometer, such as the Smiths RVI, work by sensing complete breaks in the current through the coil instead of the minute voltage variations sensed by later units. These are not compatible with

5 Loosen the light switch from the dashboard. Some switches just pull out, while others have a securing clamp behind the panel

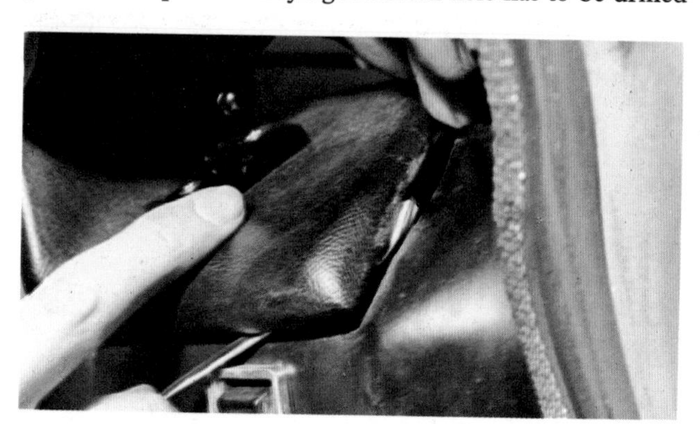

4 Here the fascia capping is prised open to allow the wires from the pod to be hidden. Alternatively, feed them down an air vent

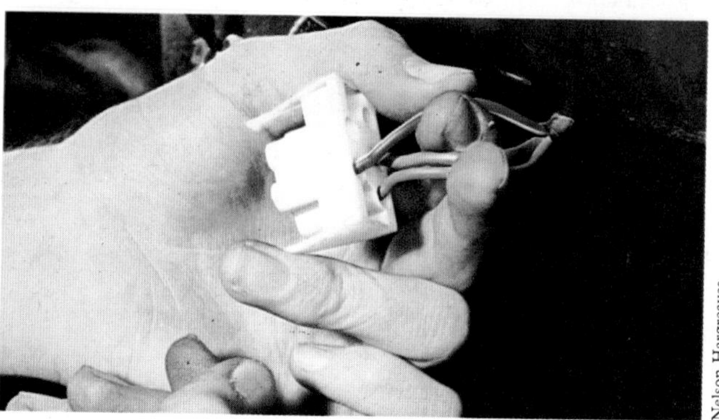

Nelson Hargreaves

6 The wires to the switch are now exposed. In this case they are fixed to a terminal block which clips on to the switch itself

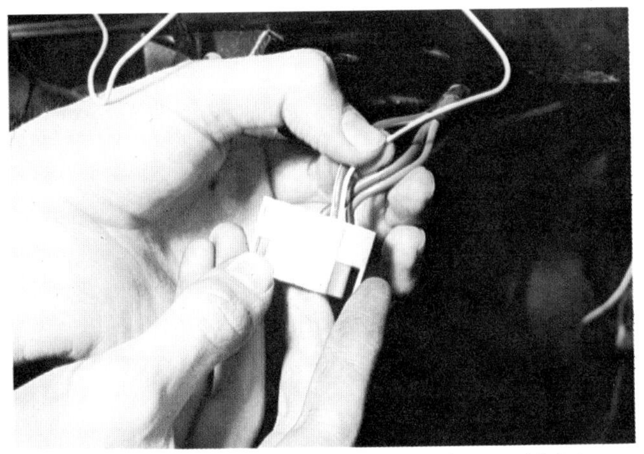

7 After you have found out which wire runs to the panel lighting circuit, connect the illumination wire from the pod to it

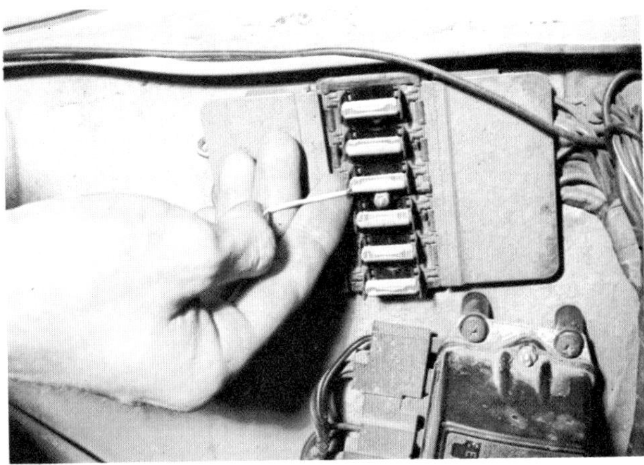

8 If the light switch proves to be inaccessible, you must attach the illumination wire to the appropriate fusebox terminal

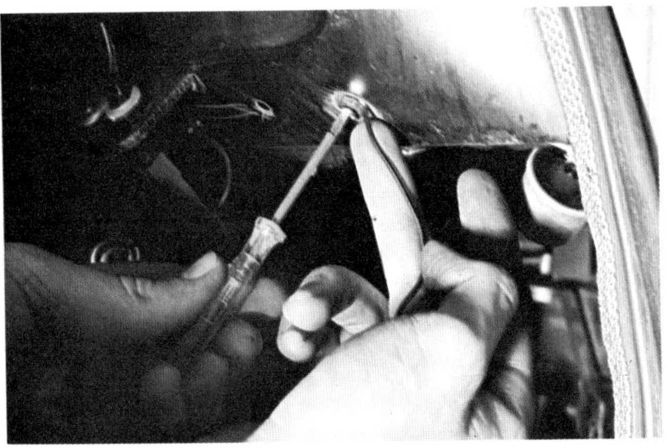

9 Fix the earth lead to any metal part of the bodywork. If there are no convenient bolts to use, drill a hole for a new screw

10 Identify the low tension lead running from the distributor to the coil. Do not confuse it with the thick, black HT lead

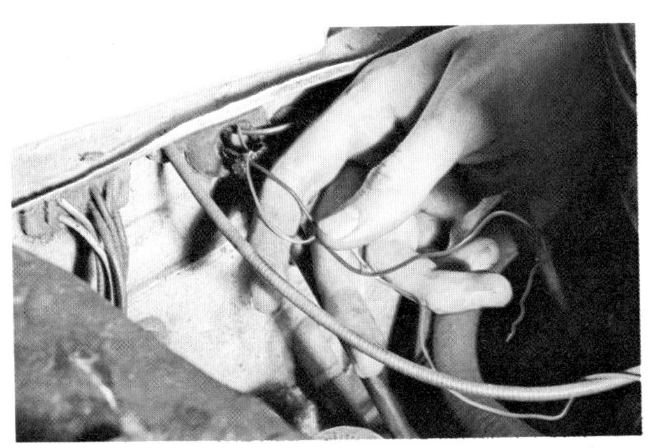

11 Feed the wires from the pod inside the car through the engine bulkhead. Make use of any existing holes where possible

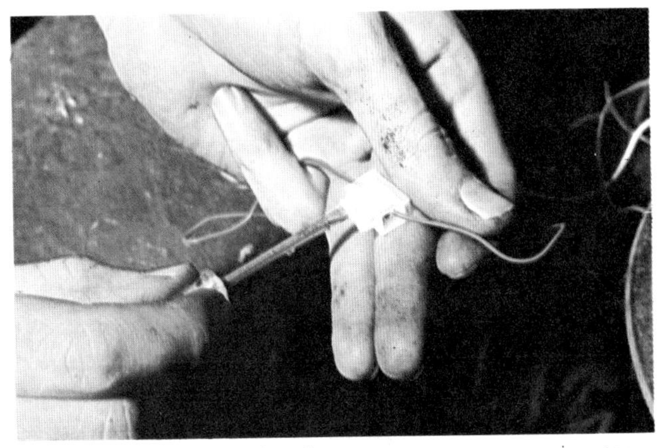

12 If you have to extend the wires, use a proper screw connector to do it. Do not simply twist the bared ends together.

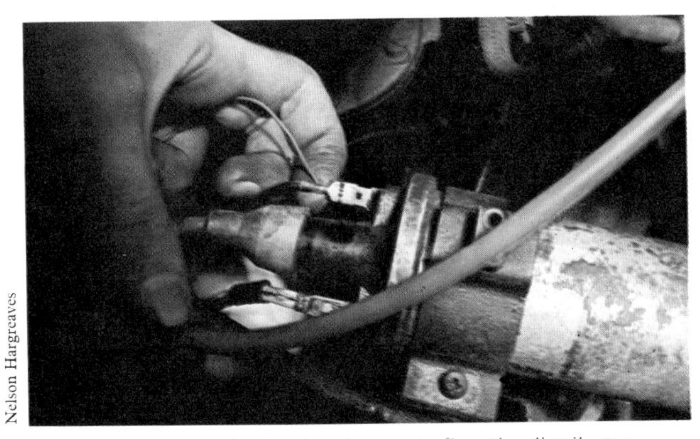

Nelson Hargreaves

13 Attach the triggering lead to the terminal on the distributor side of the coil. Do not forget to replace the low tension lead

14 The finished job, showing the live supply lead attached to the other terminal on the coil, in the same way as the trigger lead

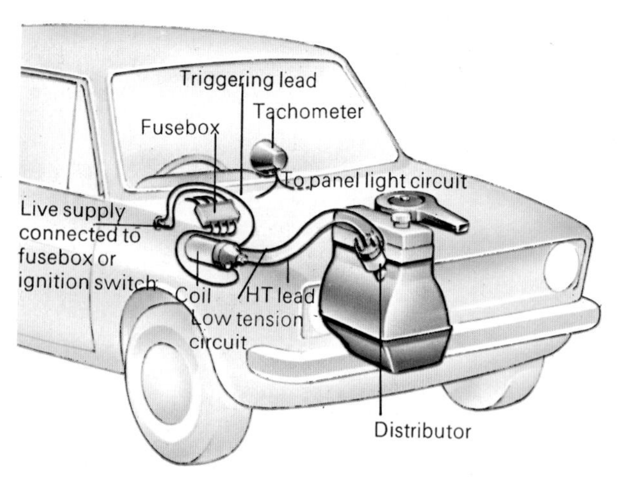

15 One way to connect up a tachometer, with the live supply as well as the triggering lead conected to the coil. The makers' instructions will tell you which method to use

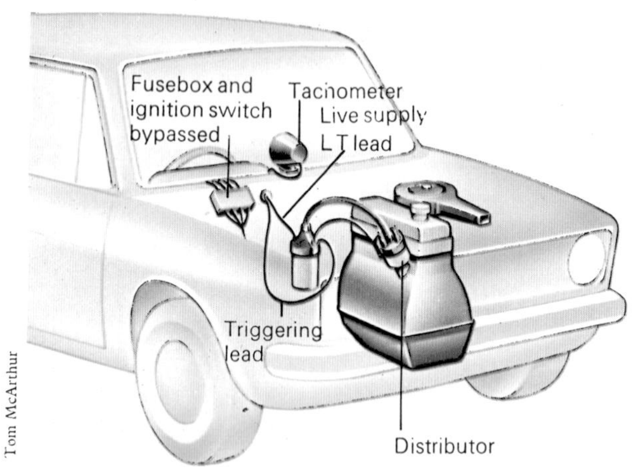

Tom McArthur

16 The alternative method. The live supply is connected further down the ignition circuit, either to the ignition switch side of the fusebox or to the ignition switch itself

certain types of electronic ignition, and require an additional adaptor to be fitted. If you already have an electronic system, check with its manufacturer that your tachometer will be compatible. If considering buying one, do not forget to get the appropriate adaptor as well if you already have a tachometer.

Counting the revs

All tachometers are calibrated per thousand rpm. Sometimes they run 1, 2, 3, etc., with a small motif on the dial face saying 'X 1,000'. Others go 20, 30, 40, etc., with 'X 100' underneath. Most of the instruments on the accessory market are provided with an extra, movable

17 The tachometer dial, showing the rev limit indicator adjusted to 5500 rpm. At this speed, the red warning light below comes on

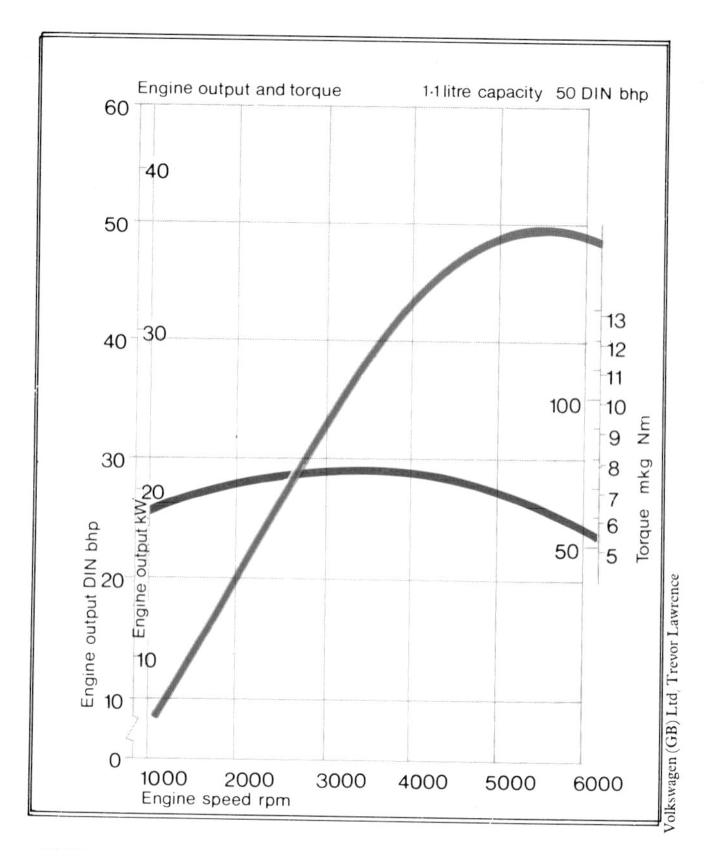

Volkswagen (GB) Ltd Trevor Lawrence

18 The engine output and torque curves of a VW Derby. The engine output curve climbs steeply to its peak at 5500 rpm, leaving the torque curve much flatter with a slight peak at 3500 rpm

needle which enables you to set on the dial the upper limit at which your engine should be revved (fig. 17). On tachometers fitted as standard equipment, there is usually a red sector on the dial which ends at the maximum rev limit. This indicates that the driver can keep his engine turning at such high speeds only for short bursts of time; the needle must not pass this point.

In practice, the upper rev limit may be taken as that at which the engine develops maximum power, and this information can always be found in the data section of the car's handbook. It must be strictly adhered to.

Far more useful, in the course of normal motoring, is the rpm figure at which the engine develops maximum torque—that is, when its 'twisting' power is at its peak in relation to the force imposed against it by the weight of the car. At lower or higher revs, the relationship becomes less favourable, but at this figure—again obtainable from the car's handbook—you can be sure that you are getting the most from your engine in terms of speed for fuel consumed (fig. 18). It is also the optimum engine speed at which to climb hills—especially important if you are towing a caravan. Some tachometers have warning lights which come on when the engine reaches a certain speed. The Sanpet S-500A, for example, is provided with an automatic warning light which comes on when the indicator needle reaches the red hand. Set the hand at the maximum rev limit and the light will warn of over-revving. Alternatively, set it at the maximum torque figure and the red light will indicate optimum engine speed.

If you know the tickover speed of your engine (usually around 800rpm), a tachometer is an invaluable aid when adjusting the carburettor, and can warn of over-fast running. Finally, remember that it is often possible to rev your car excessively, with detrimental effects, so you should pay special attention to the tachometer when accelerating hard or overtaking.

Fitting oil temperature gauges

The oil in your car's engine is designed to operate at an optimum temperature. This is determined after comprehensive, combined research by the car manufacturer and the oil company. If the oil falls too short of this temperature, or if it exceeds it by a large amount, the oil loses efficiency and engine damage may result.

If you have tuned your engine, or use your car regularly for long-distance motoring or towing, an oil temperature gauge (fig. 1) will warn you as soon as the oil begins to deteriorate. On some cars it is not possible to fit an oil temperature gauge (see below) but it is a relatively simple job on others and is well within the scope of the well-informed DIY mechanic.

Engine oil is not only used to lubricate an engine, it also helps to cool it. When the oil flows near the hottest parts of the engine, the cylinder bores and the pistons, it absorbs a great deal of the surplus heat produced during combustion. It carries this heat back to the sump which, because it is sited under the engine and exposed to the airflow, is relatively cool. The oil, therefore, transfers its heat to the sump casing, cools itself in the process and is then pumped back through the engine to repeat the cycle (fig. 2).

Under normal conditions, in an engine in good working order, the oil is never allowed to overheat; the sump always absorbs the excess temperature before the oil is re-circulated. In fact, manufacturers often design their engines with sumps which slightly overcool the oil. This allows a safe margin of error for moderate temperature increases, such as those caused by hard driving or unusually hot weather. However, if the engine is not in good condition, this safety margin will quickly be taken up.

Overcooled oil allows water, which is produced as a by-product of combustion, to condense in it. The water is then carried round with the oil and eventually mixes with it to form an emulsion. The emulsified oil is just as incapable of lubricating moving parts as overheated oil, rapid engine wear is the inevitable result. The emulsion can sometimes be seen as a creamy substance (commonly referred to as "mayonnaise") inside the rocker cover.

Initial checks

Before you buy a gauge, make sure that it is possible to fit one to your car (fig. 18). Some accessory gauges connect to the sump in place of the drain plug and the manufacturers produce adaptors for this purpose to fit a variety of different cars. There are two disadvantages in this arrangement. First, every time you drain the oil, the gauge connection will be disturbed and may possibly be damaged. Second, if your car has a magnetic drain plug to catch any metal particles in the oil, the plug will have to be sacrificed. You should also check with your dealer that a capillary can be fitted in this position. In some cars the sump filter prevents this.

Most oil temperature gauges, however, are fitted to the sump by a separate connection. Before starting to fit this type of gauge consider the problems involved in removing the sump. On some cars, the bolts or screws holding the sump pan to the crankcase are inaccessible because they are obscured by sub-frame cross-members or steering components. In cases like this, the engine must be unbolted from its mountings, fully disconnected from the rest of the car and raised with a hoist to give sufficient clearance. You may not consider it worth going to all this trouble to fit an oil temperature gauge.

On other cars, like the BL, tranverse-engined, front-wheel drive range, the sump also serves as the transmission casing. To remove a sump of this type you will have to dismantle the engine and transmission unit. For this reason the fitting of an oil temperature gauge is not a practical proposition unless the engine has been highly-tuned and warning of a rise in oil temperature is vital. Unfortunately, it is not possible to fit a gauge which connects to the drain plug socket either. Nearly all the cars with gearboxes in the sump have a magnetic drain plug which should not be discarded (see above).

If your car has a more conventional sump which is free from obstructions, fitting an oil temperature gauge with an independent sump connection should be practical. In this case, a further check has to be made in order to avoid problems later on. Using a flexible rule, measure from the

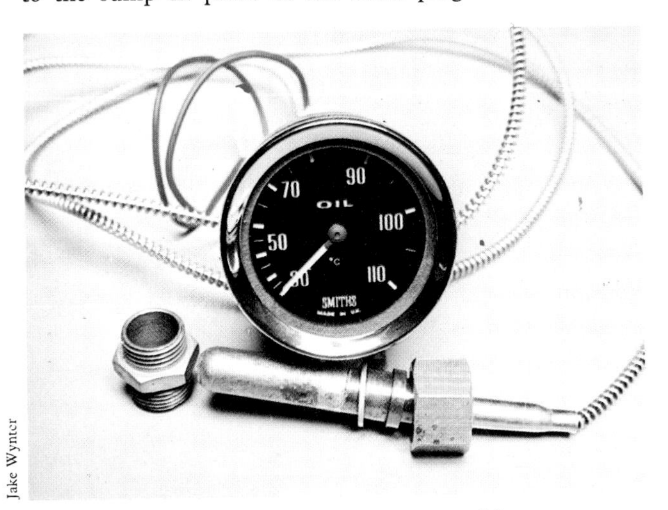

1 A typical oil temperature gauge kit consisting of the gauge, adaptor, sensor bulb and lock nut, capillary and wire for the light

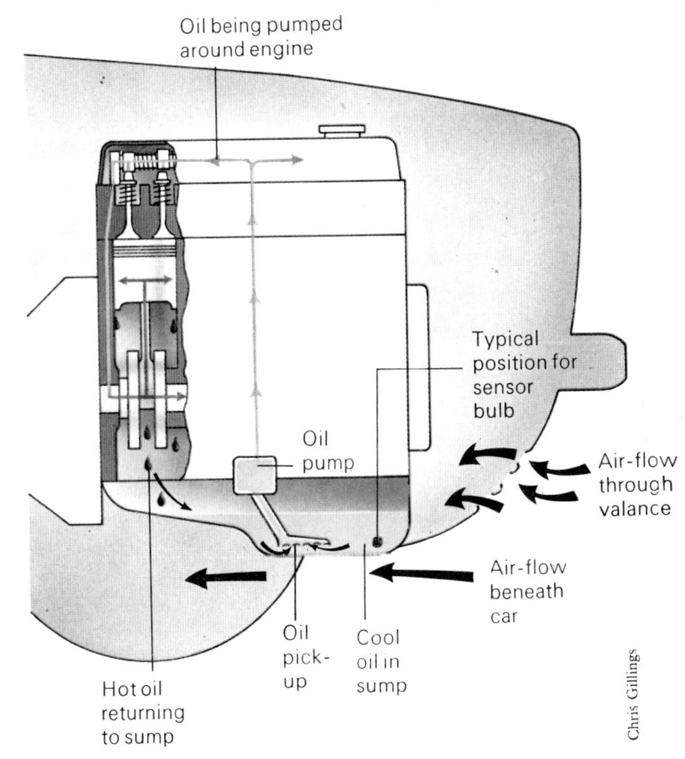

2 If the oil returning to the sump is not being sufficiently cooled by airflow, a temperature gauge will indicate this

engine bulkhead down to the sump and estimate how much further the capillary which connects the gauge to the sump will have to stretch. Allow for the fact that the gauge itself will be mounted somewhere on the fascia panel. By having some idea of how long the capillary must be, you can check the gauge of your choice at the dealers' and avoid buying an unsuitable one.

Buying a gauge

When you go to buy an oil temperature gauge, make sure that you know what type of fitting you want. If you want the type of gauge that connects to the drain plug socket, quote the make, model and year of your car so that the dealer can supply you with the appropriate adaptor. On all gauges, check the length of the capillary and check the width of the sensor bulb on the end of it. You may have to drill a hole in the engine bulkhead in order to pass the bulk of the tubing through from the fascia.

If the sump on your car is a thick aluminium casting you will need to drill and tap it to screw in the capillary bulb. The gauge fitting instructions should specify what sizes of drill tap will be needed; in the case of the Smith's OTB unit illustrated, the tap required is 5/8ins UNF and the drill is 15 mm (19/32ins). It may not be possible to tell much about the construction of your sump just by looking at it, in which case you should consult the manufacturer or your local franchise dealer.

Fitting the gauge

Because the capillary which connects the gauge to the sump is permanently attached to the gauge body and cannot be removed, you must start by fitting the gauge inside the car.

First, disconnect the battery (fig. 3). Position the gauge in the fascia or fit the mounting panel (figs. 4 to 7) or pod underneath. To cut a hole in the fascia, you will need a

3 Before starting work on your car, disconnect the battery. You may wish to remove it from the car altogether

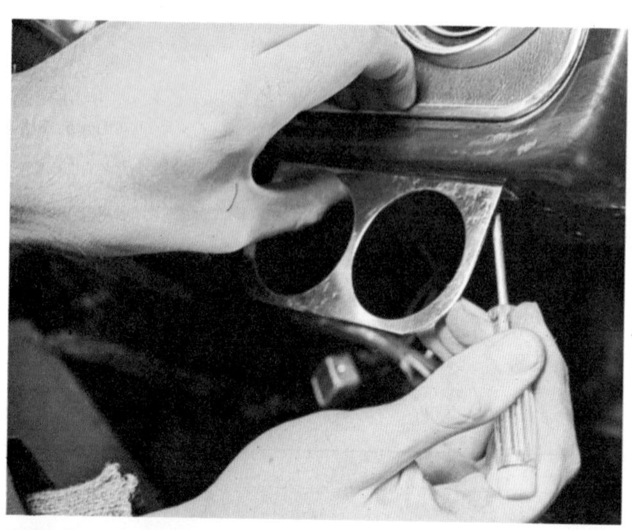

4 Having selected a position for the gauge, scratch a mark where you are going to drill. Use the mounting bracket as a guide for this

5 After checking that there are no cables behind the panel, mark the hole's position with a centrepunch and then drill it

6 Now offer up the mounting bracket to the hole and secure the bracket in position with a self-tapping screw

7 Swivel the bracket around until it is in the desired position and, using it as a template once more, drill the second hole

Jake Wynter

52 mm (2ins) hole saw (see page 28).

Before actually securing the gauge by means of the screw-clamp behind it, sort out all the connections. Start with the capillary. Once it has been fed through the hole for the gauge and under the fascia to the bulkhead, estimate the point at which it must pass through into the engine compartment. From the engine side, drill a pilot hole at this point, taking care not to disturb any existing wires or tubes. Next, carefully open up the hole with a larger drill bit or a file so that the bulb on the end of the capillary can just be passed through it.

Returning to the inside of the car, push the capillary through the hole (fig. 8). Fit a grommet into the hole to prevent the possibility of the metal round it chafing through the pipe. Attached to the rear of the gauge you will find a short length of red wire. This should be connected into the panel light circuit. To give yourself some extra flexibility, extend the wire using a spare length and a screw connector (fig. 9). Next, temporarily re-connect the battery. Following the procedure described on pages 174 to 175, identify the wire carrying the live supply to the panel light circuit. Connect the wire from the gauge into this supply wire, using a Scotchlok connector (figs. 10 and 11).

If the fascia, panel or pod to which the gauge is being secured is made of insulated material, you will also have to make an earth connection. To do this, take a suitable length of wire and connect it to any convenient screw or bolt which is in contact with the earthed part of the car. A fascia fixing screw will usually be suitable. Connect the other end of the wire to the body of the gauge. There is often a screw provided for this purpose but if you cannot find one, solder a tag connector to the wire and fit it to one of the screw-clamp bolts.

Before finally securing the gauge in its mounting, turn on the lights and make sure that it is illuminating correctly. If it is not, check both the wire connections and then the bulb. This is either screwed or clipped into its holder.

When you are satisfied that the gauge is lighting up properly, switch off the lights, and secure the unit in position by means of the clamp unit provided (fig. 12).

Now drain the oil from the engine into a suitable receptacle by undoing the drain plug on the sump, and once again disconnect the battery. Jack up the front of the car and support it on ramps or axle stands (fig. 13).

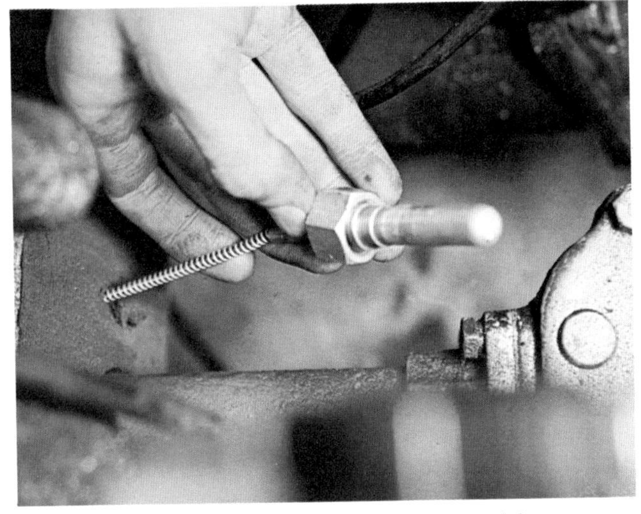

8 This sensor was pulled through the soft pad around the steering column. Therefore the bulkhead did not need drilling

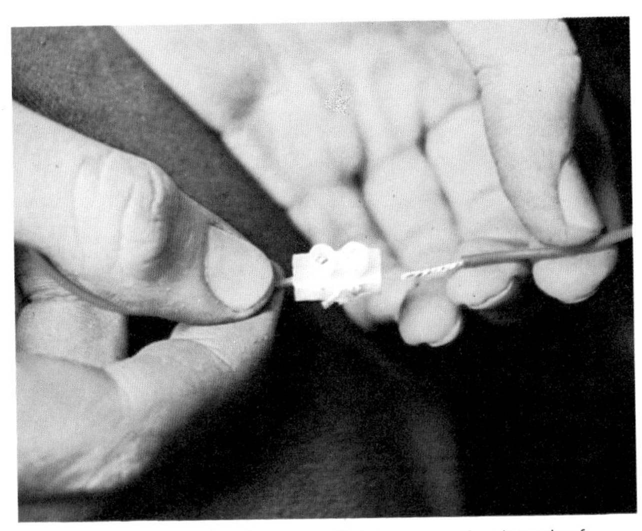

9 To extend the wire for the gauge light, use another length of similar size and colour and join the two with a screw connector

Fitting the capillary in the drain plug sockets

Once you have checked with your dealer that you can fit a capillary in the drain plug socket, simply insert the sensor bulb and screw in the adaptor provided with the gauge. Screw down the locking union to form an oil-tight seal. Re-fill the engine with oil and follow the procedure outlined under Final checks. The fault you are most likely to find is an oil leak. Always make sure that you cure this or your car's engine could suffer irreparable damage.

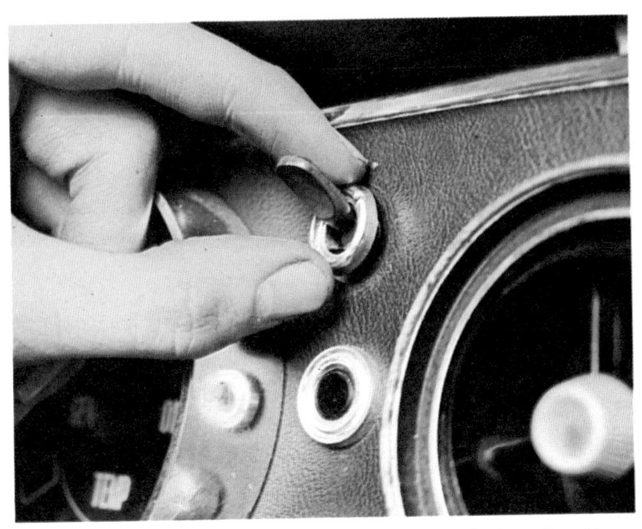

10 You will need to connect the gauge lighting wire into the side light circuit. To do this, first remove the light switch

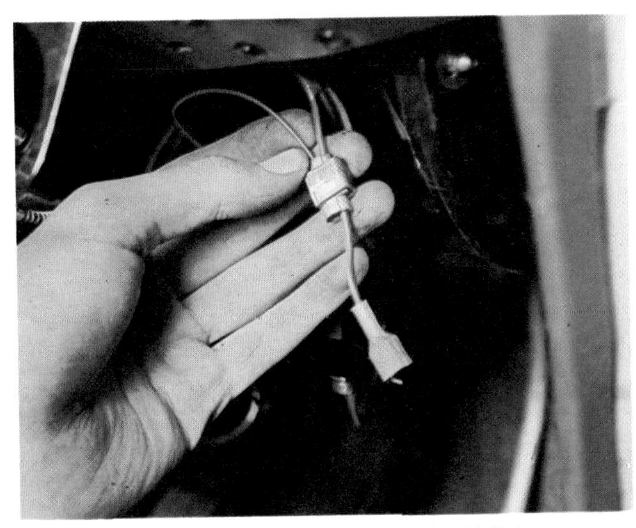

11 Having identified the live supply wire for the sidelights, connect the gauge light wire to it with a Scotchlok connector

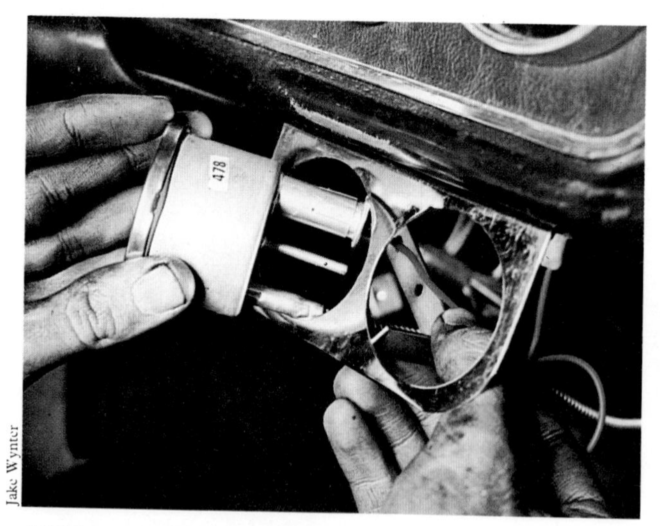

Jake Wynter

12 When you are satisfied that the gauge light is working, secure the gauge in the bracket by means of the clamp provided

13 Before removing the sump, jack up the car and support it on stout axle stands positioned under the body frame side-members

Fitting the capillary to the sump casing

If you are fitting the type of gauge which has its own independent connection to the sump, then you will have to remove the sump. This is because you will have to drill a hole in it. If you leave the sump in place when you drill the hole, swarf (metal shavings) will fall into the oil and may damage the engine by blocking the oil-feed pipes.

Removing the sump: Providing there is sufficient accessibility (see below), sump removal is a matter of undoing the bolts or numerous screws which hold it to the crankcase. This, however, can be a rather messy job because oil may drip down as you remove the sump and expose the engine. Make sure that you are suitably dressed.

If some of the sump bolts are inaccessible, you may be able to get extra clearance by loosening the engine mountings and raising the unit slightly. You should only do this where absolutely necessary. Take care not to strain any other mountings, the radiator hoses or any linkages.

When you have taken off the sump, clean it thoroughly in petrol or paraffin (kerosene) until all the dirt, oil and accumulated sludge inside it have been removed. Thoroughly clean the filter if one is fitted. Chip off and discard any old pieces of gasket around the top edges of the sump. You will now be ready to fit the adaptor into which the capillary sensor bulb and locking union nut are screwed.

Fitting the adaptor: To fit the adaptor, you must first of all select a site for it on the sump, bearing in mind that the sensor bulb which will be connected to it must not foul any moving engine parts, the oil pump or the sump filter.

You can safely judge this by holding the clean sump adjacent to the bottom of the engine and noting where the protrusions are. Mark the chosen site with chalk or paint. Next, consult the gauge fitting instructions and note whether the manufacturer recommends a specific site. Modify the chalk mark where necessary and then re-check the site against the bottom of the engine.

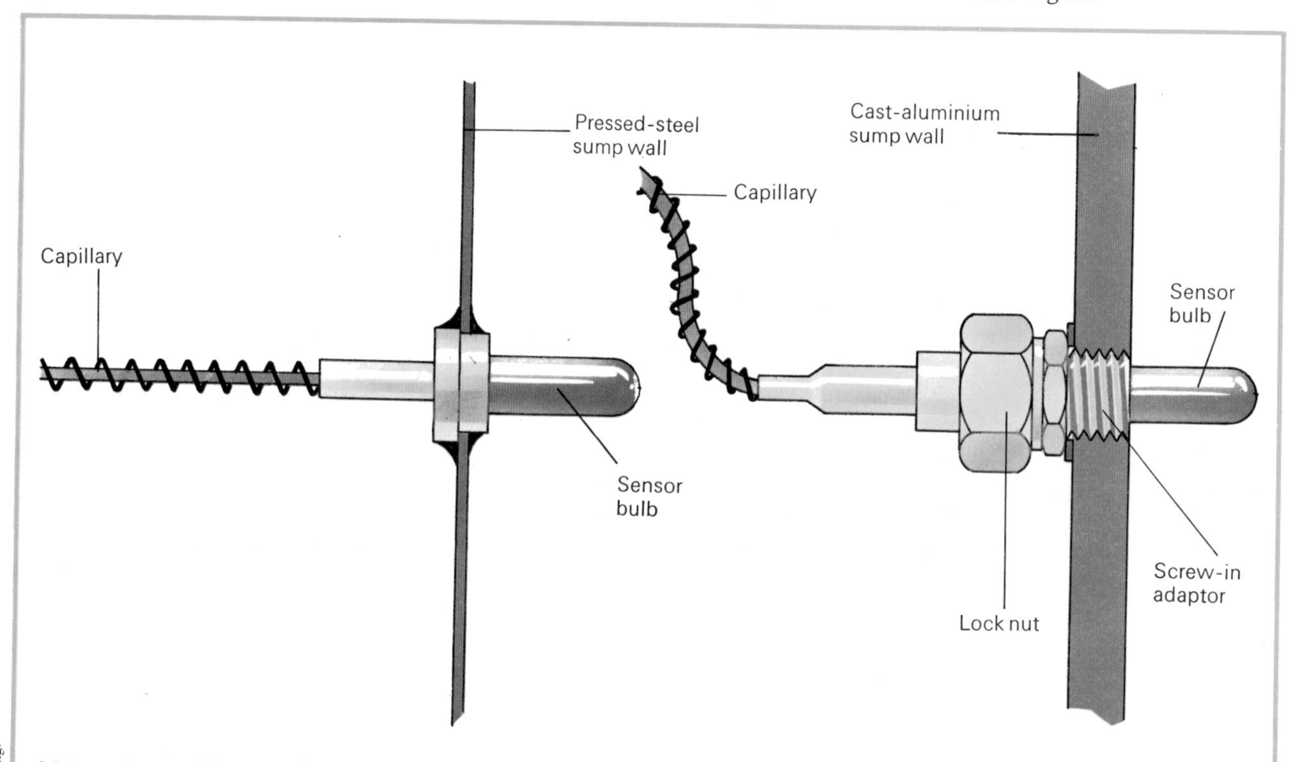

Chris Gillings

14 It may be possible to braze the sensor into position without the adaptor. However, this is not a recommended procedure

15 If the sump wall is thick enough, it can be drilled and tapped. The adaptor can then be screwed, instead of brazed, into position

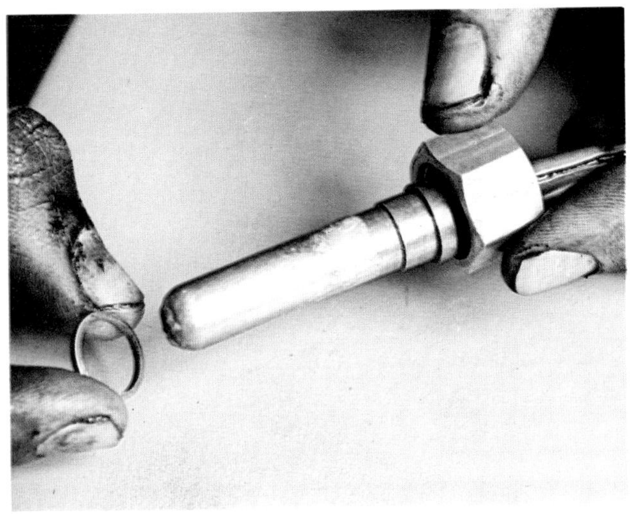

16 Prior to screwing the sensor unit into the adaptor, make sure that the copper sealing washer is in position

Using the drill size recommended by the gauge manufacturer, drill a hole in the sump and then carefully clean away any swarf. At this stage you should inspect the sump casing to see whether it is thick enough to be tapped for the screw-in adaptor. If it is cast-aluminium, then it almost certainly will be. If, however, it is pressed-steel (or, more rarely, pressed-aluminium) the metal will be too thin to be tapped effectively (figs. 14 and 15).

If you can tap the sump, use the tap size recommended by the gauge manufacturer. Again, clean away any swarf on the casing and then apply a light coat of gasket sealant to the adaptor. Screw it into the tapping, taking care not to over-tighten it. If your sump casing is unsuitable for tapping the adaptor will have to be brazed or silver-soldered (sweated) in place instead. This is not a DIY job, but it can be done quite simply and quickly by someone with the right tools and experience, such as a welder or metal worker. It ought to be possible for the job to be done efficiently while you wait.

Re-fitting the sump: With the adaptor in place, the sump will be ready for re-fitting to the engine. Before attempting to do so, thoroughly clean away any oil and dirt from the mating surfaces on the crankcase. Dry them completely using a soft, fluff-free rag.

Now coat all the surfaces in gasket sealant, paying special attention to the two seals at either end of the crankshaft. Before the sealant can dry thoroughly, stick the new sump gaskets to it, making sure they are in their correct positions. Apply a further coat of the gasket sealant to the corresponding surfaces on the sump and then offer it up and into position.

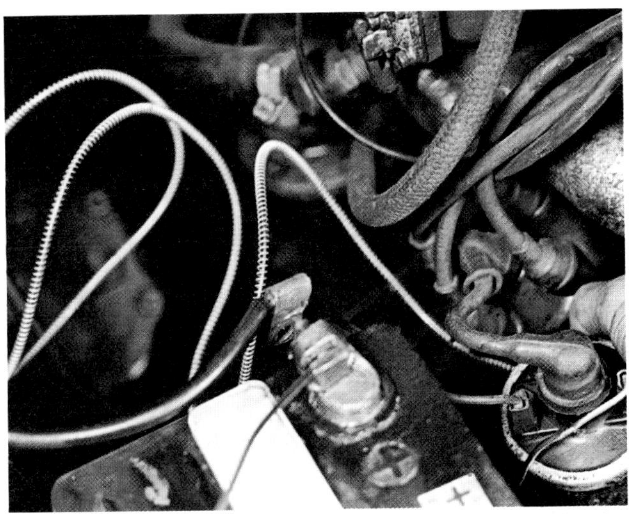

17 Wind the capillary into 125 mm (5ins) coils from the bulkhead to the sensor bulb. This helps to absorb any vibration

While holding it in place, insert the securing bolts and screw at least four in before you let go of the sump. Re-fit the remaining bolts (or screws) and tighten them up firmly.

With the sump back in place, the capillary sensor bulb can be fitted (fig. 16). Insert it through the hole in the adaptor and then lightly screw down the union locking nut attached. Before you fully tighten the locking nut, however, make sure you hold the adaptor nut with an open-ended spanner. This precaution will stop the tapping or brazing around the adaptor from becoming damaged during the tightening process. When the capillary is tight and you have replaced the drain plug, re-fill the engine with oil. If you have loosened any engine mountings to obtain extra clearance, re-tighten them. Check that no connections or linkages to the engine have become displaced.

Final checks

Whichever type of temperature gauge you have fitted, the next step is to coil the capillary into 125 mm (5ins) coils where it runs between the sump and the engine bulkhead (fig. 17). This will help to absorb any engine vibrations which might otherwise loosen the connections or damage the capillary tube. Make sure too that the capillary cannot get in the way of any moving parts. If there is a chance that it might, tie it back at convenient points using the appropriate number of pieces of stiff wire.

Re-connect the battery and start the engine. Check for oil leaks, not only at the drain plug or adaptor, but also all around the sump and crankcase joint. If there are any they will almost certainly be from the latter, probably due to a mis-fitting gasket. If tightening has no effect, the only solution is to stop the engine, drain the oil and remove the sump once more, making sure this time that the oil seal is tighter and that the gasket is properly located when it is re-fitted between the sump and crankcase.

Using the oil temperature gauge

Having fitted the gauge (figs. 19 and 20), it is important to know how to make best use of it. The first thing to do is find out, from your car's manufacturer, the recommended working temperature range of the oil. Once you have the minimum and the maximum figures, you will be ready to compare them with the readings on your gauge.

Providing your engine is in good condition and fully warmed up, there should be no problem with the readings, an occasional glance at the gauge should confirm this. The only times when the oil might get excessively hot are after a spell of hard driving, with the engine revving near its limit, or when you are towing a caravan or trailer. Under these conditions, the usual methods of cooling the oil may prove inadequate and the only answer will be to fit an oil cooler. Fitting an oil cooler is covered on pages 196 to 201.

If your oil starts to exceed the manufacturer's maximum recommended temperature and you have not been stressing the engine or towing, the first thing to suspect is a low level of oil in the sump. Too little oil in the engine can, of course, upset the normal oil cooling process so check the reading on the dipstick straight away.

The next thing to check, if the oil level is correct, is the crankcase breather system. If this is at fault, then the gases building up in the crankcase may be causing the oil to exceed its normal operating temperature.

Other possible causes of overheating oil are usually

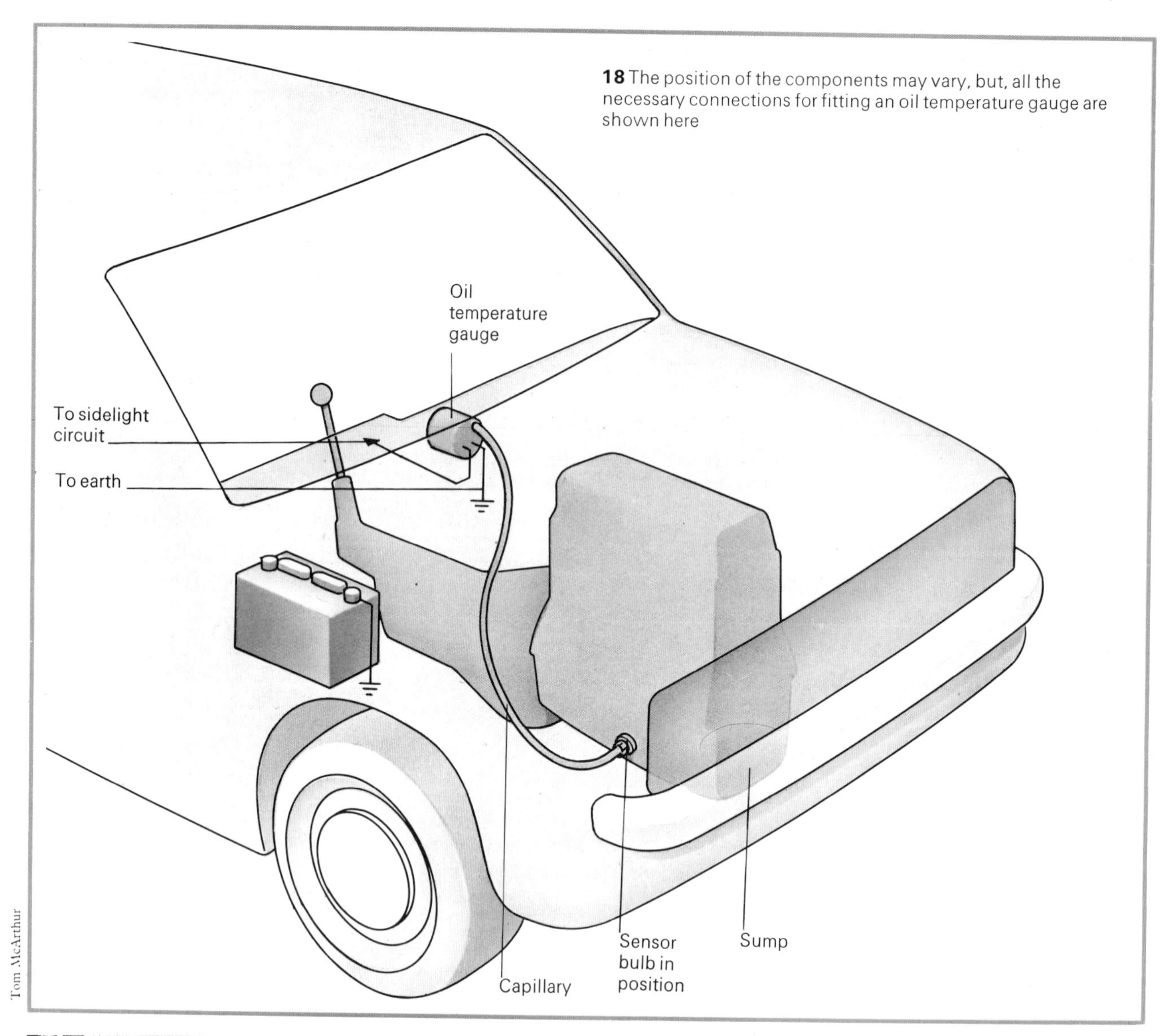

18 The position of the components may vary, but, all the necessary connections for fitting an oil temperature gauge are shown here

19 If you mount your oil temperature gauge in a double bracket, you will have a ready-made mounting position for another gauge

20 With another gauge fitted, you will have a neat and useful assembly that will be a valuable source of information to you

connected with an engine which is badly worn. Gases blowing past worn bores and piston rings, for example, can often have the same effect on the engine oil as a blocked breather system would have.

Your oil temperature gauge can also be used to diagnose faults connected with overcooled oil. If you consistently find that the oil stays below the recommended minimum temperature, start by checking the radiator pressure cap. If this is faulty, the water cooling system may not be reaching its designed temperature, in which case it will have a detrimental effect on the oil.

If the problem appears to be general overcooling, as sometimes happens in very cold weather, the solution may be to blank off part of the radiator or to fit a thermostatically-controlled cooling fan (pages 209 to 222). The latter will allow your engine to run at more efficient temperatures.

Buying exhaust systems

A smell of exhaust fumes as you are driving, headaches after a long journey, increased noise and strange knockings from underneath the car are all tell-tale signs that your car's exhaust system is no longer in a useable condition. Even if you only own a car for a year or two, you will most probably have to face the problem of replacing a defective exhaust and of entering one of the most competitive and confusing sectors of the spare parts market. However, with a full knowledge of the products available and a good idea of what you are really looking for, there is nothing to prevent you from buying a good exhaust system at a reasonable price.

When to replace your exhaust

Unless it actually falls apart, it is often hard to decide whether or not an exhaust needs replacing. There are, however, several symptoms which give a warning of imminent failure. The first is excessive noise. Whenever an exhaust system corrodes so that tiny holes appear, or part of it becomes disconnected, there will be an increase in the noise level. This will be more noticeable outside the car than inside it. Sometimes the noise can increase imperceptibly and if you drive your car every day you may not notice the increase until it becomes excessive. It is, therefore, a good idea to make the occasional comparison, where possible, with another car of the same make, year and model as yours. If your car appears appreciably noisier, suspect a defective exhaust system as the cause.

Exhaust fumes leaking into the passenger compartment is another sign commonly associated with a corroded or damaged system. The fumes, which contain Carbon Monoxide (CO), can be lethal if allowed to accumulate in a confined space such as a garage. In a moving car, the fumes can cause nausea and drowsiness which are both unpleasant and possibly dangerous. If you suspect that a faulty exhaust system is the cause, check it as soon as possible.

Metallic knocking noises under the floorpan complete the trio of warning signs. Exhausts come adrift from their mountings far more often than other parts of the car and the knocks will probably be due to a fractured mounting. This does not mean that you can ignore the noises. If the mounting has broken, it will not be long before the exhaust piping itself starts to crack due to the lack of proper support. Having been warned by the symptoms above, the next step is to make a visual inspection of the exhaust and find out exactly where the trouble lies. Use ramps or jack the car up and place it on axle stands. If you use ramps, pull the handbrake on as far as possible, select neutral (or "P" if you own a car fitted with automatic transmission) then chock the rear wheels of the car.

Start the engine and, operating the throttle linkage, rev it a few times from under the bonnet. As you do so, listen carefully for a blowing sound around the area of the exhaust manifold. Assuming that the manifold itself is not loose or cracked, concentrate your attention on the joint with the first part of the exhaust pipework, the downpipe. This is a common area for leaks and a worn gasket or loose clamp can make your car's entire exhaust system easily sound as though it needs renewing.

Finally, make a note of any corroded patches, cracks, loose joints and broken mountings and assess the condition of each section. Due to the amount of heat involved, and their location, all exhausts look rusty but a few sharp taps with a screwdriver should clearly reveal whether or not they are structually sound.

You should now be able to decide on a course of action. If

1 Either chromed and highly polished or simply left with the matt finish of the Thrush Outsider (top), exhaust components such as these attract the eye and can improve the appearance of most cars. Manufactured to high standards of durability in order to preserve their appearance, custom exhausts can be purchased from many accessory stockists along with a full range of adaptors (bottom)

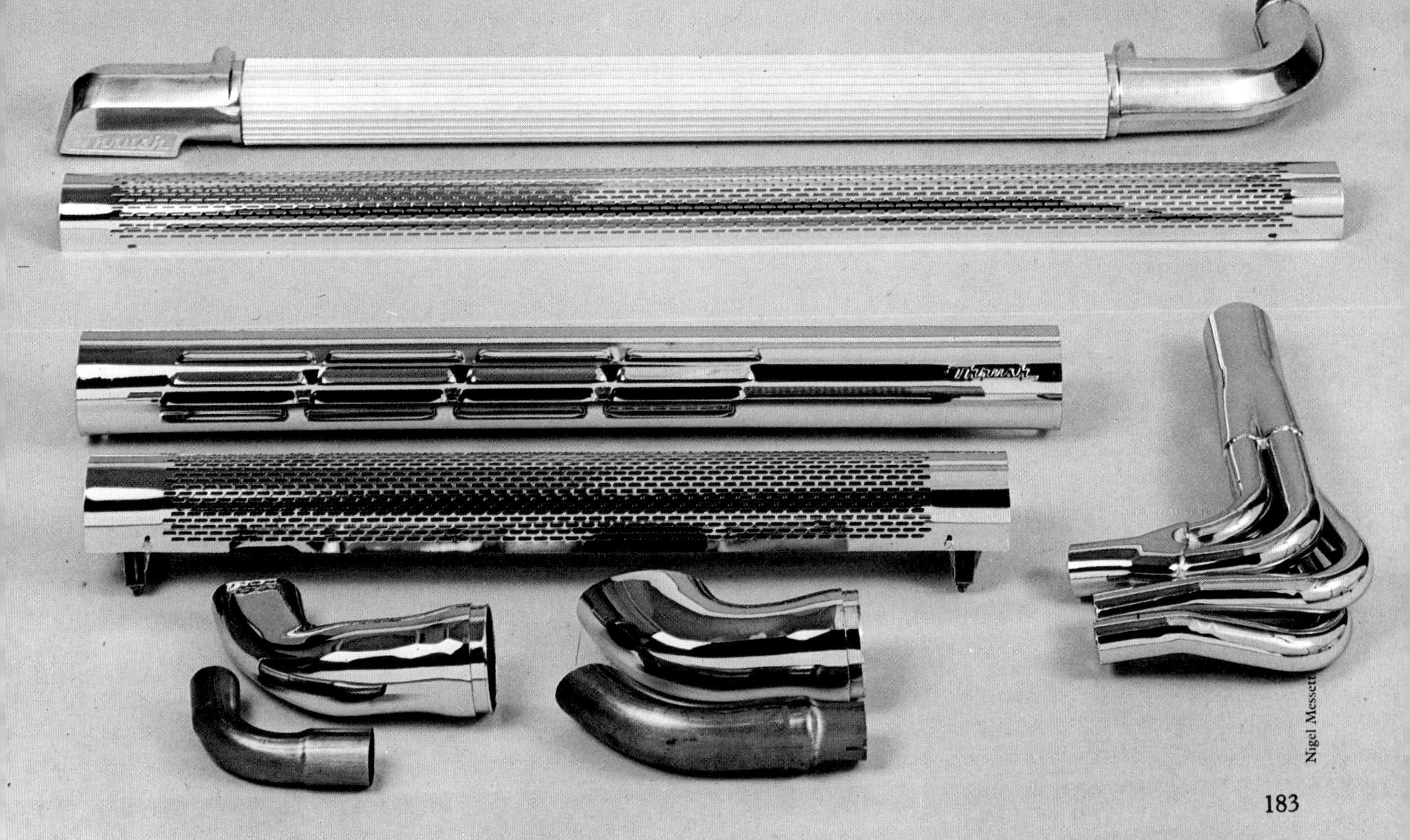

Nigel Messett

it is just the mountings which are broken, you can buy new ones from an exhaust specialist or your local dealer (see below). The same goes for any sheared clamp bolts and any badly worn clamp gaskets.

If the damage is within the structure of either the pipes or the baffles, try to determine its extent and whether it is confined to one section of the system or to the whole exhaust. You will then be able to consider replacing the damaged parts alone, although when one section of an exhaust has corroded, you can generally be sure that the rest of the system will soon follow.

In the case of small holes, that is those under 12 mm (½ins), you can also consider the possibilities of making a temporary repair, using a proprietary exhaust repair kit. This may or may not be advisable, according to your future plans for the car.

Types of replacement exhausts

Once you have decided to replace your exhaust, or a section of it, you will have to choose between the considerable variety of different types of system that are available on the market. Replacement exhausts fall into three main categories: standard mild-steel systems; customized or tuned mild-steel systems and stainless-steel systems.

Mild-steel exhaust systems are the units that are fitted as standard to most mass-produced cars. Although manufacturers are well aware that mild-steel exhausts only have a limited life, they argue that the extra cost of using longer lasting materials would not be particularly acceptable to the majority of new car buyers.

When new, a mild-steel exhaust looks remarkably tough. On average though, it will be subjected to rigorous use. Not only must it bear the enormous heat and pressures of the gas flowing through it, it must also undergo quite rapid temperature changes and will be subject to corrosion, both internally and externally. Water is a by-product of combustion and often condenses in the pipes and baffles. It stays there, combining with the air and acidic vapours in the system, to eat away at the metal whenever the car is not in use. This is largely unavoidable.

Despite the disadvantages though, mild-steel exhausts are cheap and this is their greatest advantage. There is little point in investing in an expensive exhaust system if you are not going to keep your car long enough to realize the benefits. Because mild-steel exhausts continue to be the most widely used type, it follows that they have the widest range of applications. If you have an old or rare car the chances are that you will have to choose mild-steel as a replacement because no other types exist unless, of course, you have one specially made.

Custom and tuned exhausts

To cater for the motorist who wants his car to sound "sporty" or who needs an exhaust system to compliment a tuned engine, the exhaust market offers an extremely wide range of specialized products (fig. 1).

Custom exhausts (figs. 2 to 4) look impressive and make the engine sound powerful but they are unlikely to improve your car's performance in any way. In the UK, Peco Silencers Ltd., offer perhaps the largest range of custom exhausts. This includes the Sportwinder side-mounted exhaust with chromed heat shield, either plain or perforated. Special exhaust conversion kits, sold separately, enable you to convert your existing exhaust to take the Sportwinder system. The Peco Big Bore and Sport silencer exhaust range offers a selection of large-diameter exhausts which are claimed not only to look and sound sporting but also to improve performance by giving better gas flow. In fact, unless you also modify the exhaust manifold in some way (see below), the improvement will be so small as to be almost totally unnoticeable.

Tuned exhausts (see page 154) vary in detail from the custom type in that they are designed solely with performance in mind. Improvements are usually obtained by enlarging the diameter of the pipes (as against the standard equivalent), re-designing the baffles so that they are less obstructive to the flow of gas and by paying careful attention to the layout of the system. These modifications allow the exhaust gasses to be emitted efficiently and this improves engine performance. However, because the speed of gas flow is at its most critical at the start of the system, it is the tuned exhaust manifold which offers the greatest benefits.

Tuned manifolds are engineered to high standards and tend to be expensive. There is, however, little point in buying the rest of your exhaust in tuned form without also purchasing this vital component. In fact, a tuned manifold coupled with a standard exhaust will offer far greater improvements in performance than a system which is put together the other way round.

Stainless-steel exhausts

Stainless-steel exhausts are initially an expensive alternative to mild-steel standard replacements. The extra expense goes into the costs of materials which are usually guaranteed to last as long as your car does. This is one reason why

Custom Car

2 Using a V12 engine demands that two lots of exhaust pipework be fabricated. The exhausts emphasise the car's design symmetry

manufacturers such as Rolls-Royce fit stainless-steel systems to their cars as standard equipment. The available range of stainless-steel exhausts and exhaust sections has expanded rapidly in recent years to cope with the increased demand. There are now systems to suit most current mass-produced cars and the number of manufacturers involved in the market grows yearly.

Where to buy an exhaust

Deciding where to by an exhaust system can be the most confusing part of the replacement process. The three main sources are the parts' department of a franchised dealer; car accessory shops and specialized exhaust fitting centres.

Parts' departments

The parts' department of your franchised dealer will supply you with a manufacturer approved, replacement, mild-steel exhaust for your particular car. If the dealer also offers a special tuning service, he will, in addition, stock tuned exhaust components approved by the car manufacturer.

The greatest advantage of going to this source for your exhaust is that you are unlikely to be supplied with the wrong parts. You will also have the manufacturer's seal of approval on those you do buy. However, against this must be weighed several disadvantages.

To begin with, the other two sources of exhaust listed may well offer less expensive products. This does not necessarily mean that they are inferior either. Most of the major car manufacturers turn, at some time or another, to outside firms for their exhaust systems.

Exhausts made by specialist firms such as T. I. Bainbridge, Peco and Bosal are just as likely to be sold over the parts' counter as they are in an accessory shop or a specialist fitting station. Another point worth remembering is that your parts' department may be unwilling or unable to split up a complete system just to supply you with one section.

If you do decide on a parts' department purchase, however, you must carry out a complete check on your old exhaust first. Bear in mind that a new exhaust will require a completely new set of mountings and jointing clamps. If the joint with the manifold is made using a gasket, you must buy one of those too and remember that a proprietary sealing compound (see pages 187 to 191) will help in keeping the joints gas-tight.

One situation in which it is always advisable to go to your franchised dealer is when the car is still under warranty; parts which are not approved by the manufacturer could invalidate your guarantee.

Car accessory shops

Some car accessory shops carry a range of mild-steel exhausts designed to be compatible with the existing system on your car. Some also serve as outlets for one of the manufacturers of stainless-steel systems, Grundy and Peco being the best-known names in the UK. So if you go to an accessory shop, you may well be faced with the question: stainless or mild-steel? To decide, think first about whether you will be keeping your car long enough to reap the benefits of a stainless-steel system. If you are still faced with a choice, compare prices. You may be surprised to find that a stainless-steel system is only slightly higher than a comparable mild-steel one though a 50 per cent increase is normal. If you are seriously considering a stainless-steel exhaust, compare the prices of them with those at exhaust fitting stations (see below). The fitting stations may well be more competitive. When buying a stainless-steel system, make absolutely sure that you are

Custom Car

3 Each serving a single cylinder, these pipes fully complement the high standard of finish achieved on the other engine fixtures

supplied with all the necessary parts, including any conversion kits which you may need.

Accessory shops can often be the cheapest places to buy mild-steel exhausts though you should consider all of the implications first. The shop owner, who may have neither the expertise of the franchised dealer nor the specialist knowledge of the fitting station mechanic, could supply you with the wrong parts, or you could forget to ask for all the extras such as mountings and clamps.

There is one other criticism that has, in the past, been levelled at cheaper exhausts. It is that they may have been manufactured to an inferior specification. This does not mean that they are dangerous or unlikely to pass a road-worthiness test. It does mean though, that they may be made of thinner metal, might sound less refined and may not last as long as a more expensive mild-steel system. So when you are considering an exhaust that seems well under the market price, go carefully into the question of how long a guarantee it has.

Custom exhaust parts are usually only obtainable from specialist accessory shops and dealers. They will inevitably be more expensive than standard items but you should at least be able to check that a part does have the visual impact for which you are looking. Tuned exhausts and exhaust components can be obtained from specialist tuning shops or manufacturers. Like custom parts, they will be more expensive than standard replacements but you will be assured of a high standard of workmanship. Moreover, the advice of the dealer on what to fit and what not to fit to your car can, in this case, prove invaluable. In the UK, Howe and Janspeed are the best-known manufacturers of tuned exhausts outside the major car manufacturers themselves. In addition to the systems, the two companies also offer compatible manifolds, mountings and clamps.

Exhaust fitting stations

The number of exhaust fitting stations specializing in the replacement of exhausts and sometimes of tyres as well, has increased spectacularly over the past few years. Their appeal lies in the fact that they are convenient. You can drive into a station, wait while the exhaust is fitted and then

4 As distinctive as the car itself, this multi-pipe exhaust system is a strong feature of the car's identity. Although not fitted with visible silencers, the bore of each pipe has been carefully blocked to partially obstruct, and therefore silence, the gasses

Custom Car

drive out again with a new exhaust. As an extra attraction, no labour charge is made for the work, you pay the cost of the parts alone. The station owners claim that they can afford to do this because they specialize in only one job and buy their materials in bulk, at large discounts.

So when you visit a "free-fit" station, you have two options: to simply buy the parts and fit them yourself or have them fitted free at the station while you wait.

Taking the former case, if you go to a fitting station just to buy your exhaust, you should not expect to pay the price quoted to customers having one fitted. Obviously, some account of the cost of labour will have been taken when the price of parts was fixed and you should be able to arrange some sort of discount on that basis with the station manager. You can then compare the quoted price with other sources but do not forget to include "extras" such as mountings and clamps in your estimate. The question of a guarantee should also be investigated. Although most stations offer a guarantee, it may not cover parts which are bought and then which are fitted elsewhere.

The quality of the exhaust that you buy may well vary. The same criticism of "cheap exhaust, poor quality" has been applied to fitting stations as well as to car accessory shops. Your only safeguard here will be the reputation of the station concerned and the terms of the guarantee supplied with the exhaust. You should be able to take it back if you are not satisfied with its quality or if it has not been fitted correctly and has leaks.

If you decide to go to a fitting station with the object of having a new exhaust both supplied and fitted, it will probably be because you have reasoned that some extra money will save you a great deal of time and trouble. However, do not rush into the final decision.

When you arrive at the station, read the terms of any guarantees pinned on the wall. They should cover both parts and labour for a reasonable period of time (1 year or 20,000 km (12,000 miles) is the norm). Also read any other notices that are posted up concerning extra charges outside the cost of the parts. They may include a time surcharge, for jobs which are abnormally lengthy or what is known as a "foreign car surcharge". This latter charge is quite common in most fitting stations and it usually applies to all cars manufactured in foreign countries.

Before you proceed, ask yourself whether you are really happy to have the fitting done by someone else. If you are, the next stage is an inspection of your car's old exhaust system by the fitter. You should be allowed to be present while this takes place but in some establishments insurance considerations do not permit this. During the inspection, you will have to judge for yourself whether the fitter is using his experience in telling you what new parts are needed or just simply employing sales talk.

Try to make sure that you have at least some idea of what is wrong and do not be persuaded into accepting a whole new exhaust system if it is just a loose clamp that needs tightening or a single section that needs replacement. Be ready to decide too, whether you want a standard or a stainless-steel system (see above) and do not accept one just because the station has not got an alternative in stock. Always make sure that the station has the correct unit in stock before you allow them to proceed.

On the other hand, be prepared for a small labour charge if repairs to your old exhaust do not call for any new parts. This is only fair to the station from whose equipment and expertise you have benefitted.

Ultimately, the choice is entirely up to you, so make sure that you have all of the relevant facts at your disposal before you make the purchase. Give yourself time and do not be rushed into a purchase unless you are satisfied that it fulfills your particular requirements.

Improving the exhaust system

Because of the intense competition in the trade, prices of exhaust systems in Britain are fairly low. As stated in the previous chapter, most factors and exhaust centres offer to fit a new system quickly and free of charge. However, checks and temporary repairs you can make will ensure the exhaust lasts as long as possible. If you do decide to fit a new system yourself there are a few firms which sell d-i-y kits at a discount. Fitting a new system is best done as a whole, which means a new pipe, silencer, clips and any other pieces necessary.

The main function of the exhaust system is to take the exhaust gas from the engine and push it into the atmosphere. This is done by a pipe which runs from the exhaust manifold on the engine to the rear of the car. Since the action of the internal combustion engine generates a great deal of noise, the exhaust system incorporates a silencing device.

Some manufacturers simplify production and reduce costs by making exhaust systems as one complete unit — that is, the pipe and silencer are combined in one piece with no provision for dismantling them. Other systems are made in several pieces, often when the exhaust pipe has to follow a complicated route under the car. This facilitates dismantling, but the extra support clamps and brackets become added corrosion risks. And since a number of separate components costs more than a combined system —and each individual component is likely to wear out at the same time as the others anyway—a built-up system may well cost more to replace than a combined one would.

Ordinary mild steel exhausts are sometimes guaranteed, but in Britain their lifespan is sometimes as short as one year and a severe winter. Salt used to de-ice roads, flying stones and wet conditions all attack the metal from the outside. Internally the exhaust is subjected to an even greater battering. Exhaust gas carries with it water in the form of steam, acid produced by combustion and unburned petrol. All have a powerful effect on the metal (fig. 1).

The rate of corrosion will be greater in a cool-running engine than one which is thoroughly warmed up. A car whose working life consists mainly of being driven to the shops or railway station, for example, will suffer from exhaust corrosion much more than a car which is regularly used for long, fast runs.

On top of all this is stress from constant vibration, which can easily fracture or eventually destroy the system. The exhaust is mounted on, or suspended from, brackets cushioned by fibre. These can conceal the fact that the exhaust is in imminent danger of falling to pieces.

A good deal can be done, however, to ease the working conditions of the exhaust system if regular checks are carried out.

Checking the exhaust system

Perhaps the most important check is that the various nuts and bolts along the exhaust system line are tight. This should be carried out as part of a normal annual servicing routine.

Begin with the joint between the exhaust manifold and pipe. This joint may be one of two basic types. The less common of these employs a flange on the manifold which mates with a similar flange on the pipe. The two are joined with nuts and bolts and often there is a heat resistant gasket or 'O' ring between the flanges to make a gas-tight seal (fig. 3). More popular is an arrangement in which both the manifold and the exhaust pipe are belled out to offer a perimeter flange (fig. 4) and the two sections are locked together with a V-section clamp. The clamp draws both ends tightly together and prevents gas blow-by around the perimeter of the joint when the nuts and bolts are secured.

If the nuts work loose and the tiniest gap appears between manifold and pipe, flames from the exhaust will

1 These worn exhaust systems show clearly how corrosion can eat away from the inside until the walls are paper-thin

George Wright

2 Rolls-Royce exhaust, above, is stainless steel and has silencers for different sound frequencies. It costs 15 times as much as the Leyland Mini system, below

char the edges of the bell mouths and start a leak that will rapidly worsen if left. The intense heat around the joint can make the nut and bolt connection stick together so the clamp appears to be tightly secured when, in fact, its hold on the two parts may be just slack enough to allow a leak to start. So make sure the nuts really are tight when cold.

An engine on which the mountings are worn or loose will rock about, and this excessive movement is the worst possible treatment for an exhaust pipe. Cars with transverse engines are particularly prone to this trouble. Some motorists, too, slow down the idling speed of the engine in the interest of fuel economy, and this encourages the engine to rock quite violently and can cause exhaust pipe fractures. Check the engine mountings and ensure that any stabilizing bars are tightened up.

Mounting brackets under the car have to be tight, otherwise the exhaust pipe will have too much movement and be prone to breakages. Examine the fibre cushions or suspension straps on the mountings, too. If any are broken or weak replace them, or the weight of the pipe may stress some other part or member and again damage will result. There may be four or more such mountings at intervals along the length of the entire exhaust system.

This mounting arrangement varies according to the pipe layout. There may be two small silencers instead of one, or a twin-pipe system. The pipe may hump over the back axle and have a support at the top of the curve. Some systems are even more elaborate. But the principles of servicing them are much the same.

The first mounting is often just behind the bulkhead, underneath the car or even, in some instances, on the gearbox. This support is usually the first to hold the free length of the exhaust pipe after it has left the manifold, so it takes the brunt of the vibration from the engine and may be particularly prone to shaking loose. In addition the pipe changes from vertical to horizontal just before this point and the bend is a corrosion trap where moisture collects.

The silencer is often the heaviest component in the system, so there may be a support mounting at either or both ends of the unit. If one or both fail, then extra weight stress will fall on some other part. So check these regularly and replace the straps or cushions when they show signs of wear. On most modern cars, this is simply a matter of attaching the new straps over the hooks on the mounting (fig. 7). The older cushion type (fig. 8), is a block of rubber through which a nut and bolt or just a bolt passes,

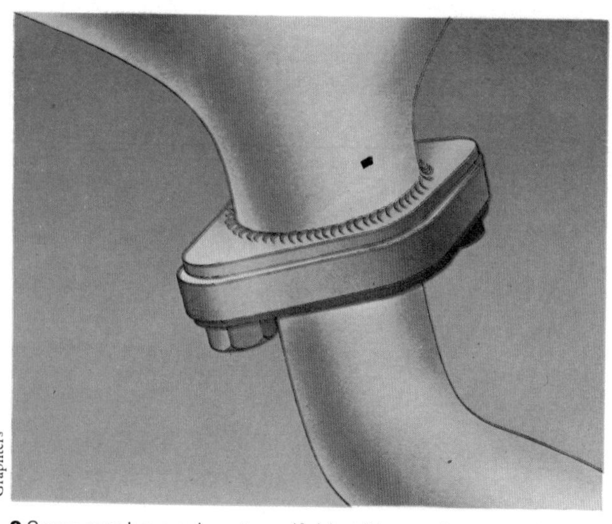

Graphters

3 Some cars have exhaust manifolds with a ready-tapped flange, to which the exhaust pipe is bolted directly

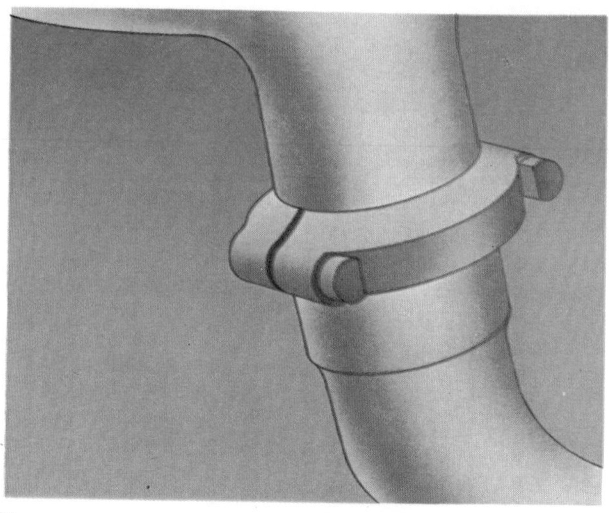

4 The more common system uses a pair of clamps, held with nuts and bolts, which fit over the ends of both pipe and manifold

5 Flexible straps must be replaced before they fail, to avoid placing great strain on the remaining exhaust supports

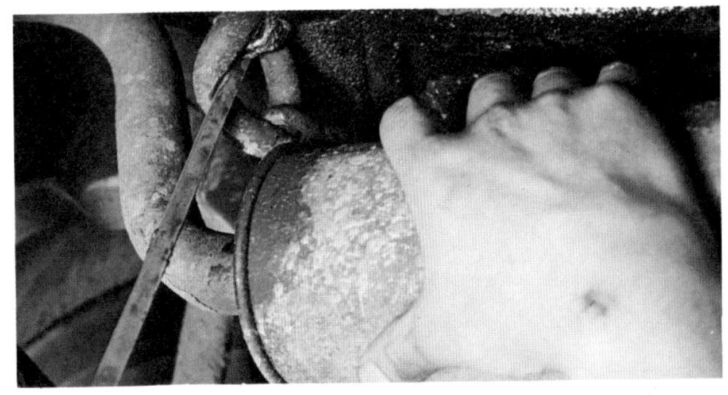

6 To remove a strap, lift the exhaust and prise off the strap using a suitable bar—a large screwdriver will do

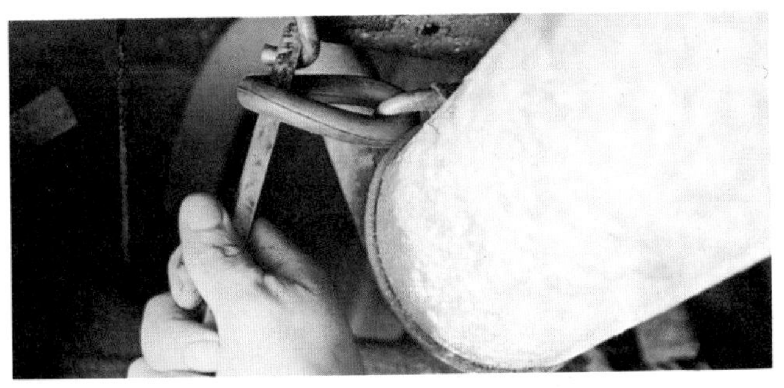

7 Fit the new strap to the exhaust first, then lever it over the hook with the bar, as shown here

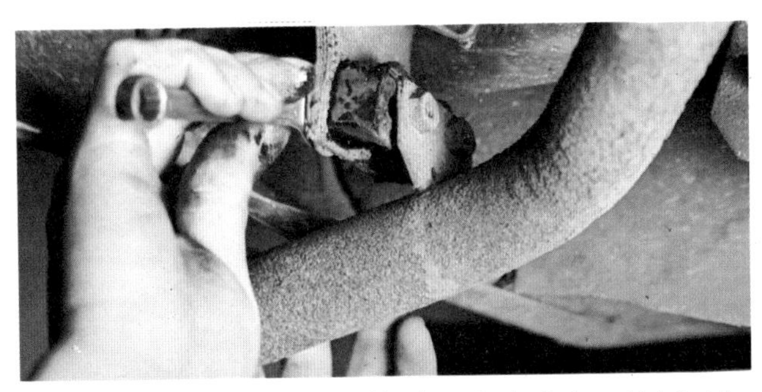

8 To replace a perished cushion block, undo the bolts which hold it to the fibre strap—penetrating oil will make this easier

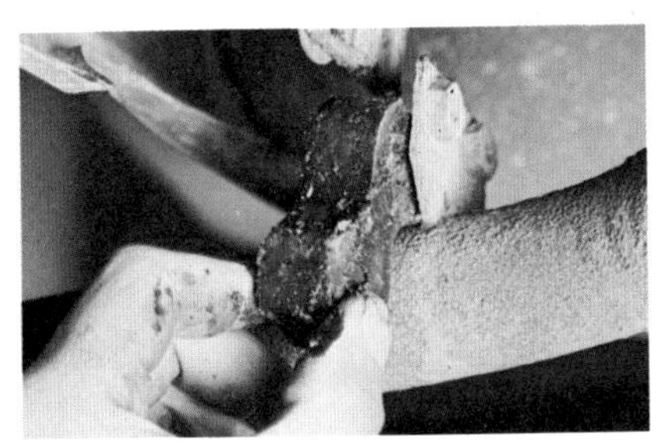

9 The nuts are fixed, and cannot be undone. The fibre strap itself may need replacing

10 Car-sickness may be due to a leaky tail-pipe which needs replacement

11 The push-fit extension can improve the car's appearance, as well as being safer

George Wright

joining a bracket on the pipe or silencer to another bracket on the bodywork. The rubber block may eventually harden and lose its insulating properties, causing vibration to set in. So replace any hardened or perished blocks.

Finally, there is a support clamp for the tail-pipe, which may also need tightening or replacement.

Repairing the exhaust

The tail-pipe can suffer heavy wear, as the exhaust gas passing through it has cooled and condensation is deposited. A ragged, rusty tail-pipe detracts from the appearance of a car. So, until a new silencer or complete system is fitted, try attaching a tail-pipe extension (fig. 10). This ensures that poisonous carbon monoxide exhaust gas is carried away from the car, whereas a short or leaking tail-pipe may allow the gas to collect in the draught underneath the car and find its way to the interior.

Extensions are usually a force fit over the existing pipe, so take care when pushing them on a corroded tail.

If you find a gap between two sections of pipe that fit into each other, it should be filled rather than trying to over-tighten the clamp to crush the metal together. A good material for this purpose is ordinary cooking foil. This is heat-resistant and even when folded tightly has a high degree of compressibility. Undo the clamp and separate the two sections of pipe a little. Tear off a strip of foil, fold it to the required thickness and insert it into the gap, then re-tighten the clamp (fig. 14).

Repairs to a damaged silencer are possible if done properly, but if corrosion is the source of the trouble, the silencer will have to be replaced eventually.

Damage to the exhaust pipe before the silencer will result in an increase in noise noticeable to both the driver and the police. A loss of performance, sometimes quite drastic, may be noticed too. Such damage is unlikely to be local; the rest of the pipe may be paper thin and subject to repeated trouble after one repair has been made. But as an emergency expedient, special impregnated bandage can be wound round the damaged area and held in place with wire clips (fig. 17). The heat developed in the exhaust bakes the bandage into place to form a solid seal. An alternative is a stiff paste which can be bought, mostly in tube form. This is used to seal leaky joints, including any round the manifold clamp. A similar paste can be spread over any small holes in an exhaust pipe or silencer (fig. 20). Such repairs must be regarded as temporary, however. If a crack should develop between the paste or bandage and the surrounding metal, highly-toxic carbon monoxide gas could leak into the car, to the danger of its occupants.

Another method of repair involves cutting out the damaged length of pipe completely and replacing it with a length of flexible metal exhaust hose, which again is available from factors and accessory shops. The hose comes in different bores and lengths, and its flexibility makes it suitable for replacing curved sections. Buy a hose with a slightly larger diameter than the existing exhaust pipe so

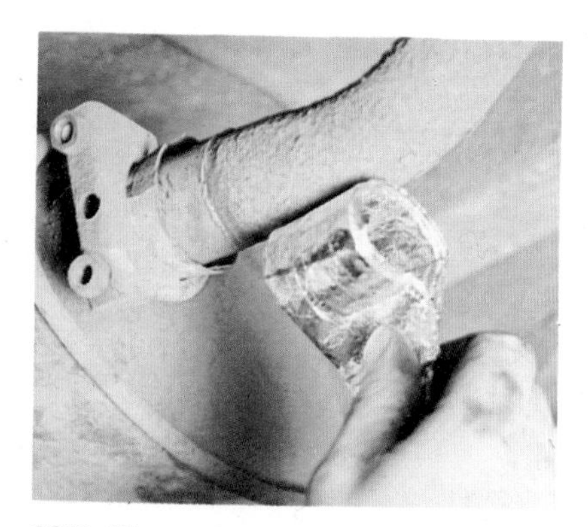

12 To fill a gap between loose-fitting pipes, fold a piece of baking foil several times and cut it to the required length

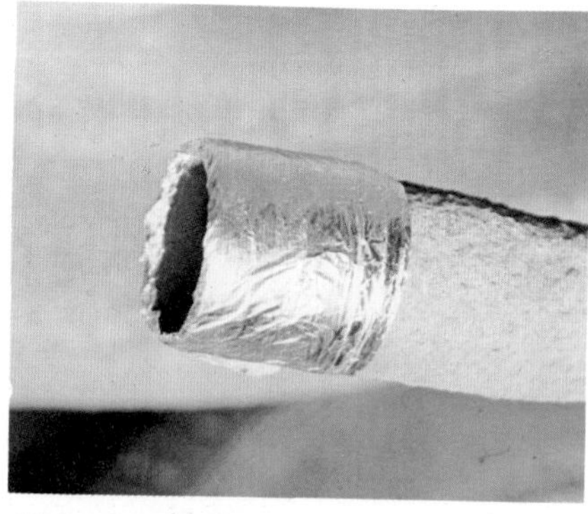

13 Once you have cut it to the right circumference, wrap the foil tightly round the end of the smaller pipe

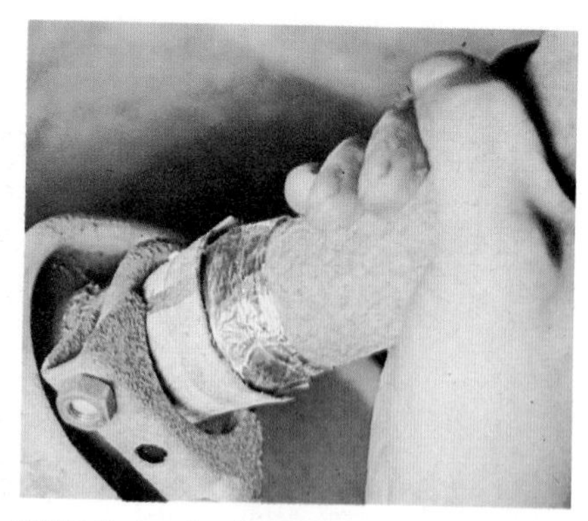

14 Push the pipe back into the joint, and tighten up. If there is still a gap, use a greater thickness of foil

15 Emergency repair packs make roadside repairs possible. The first stage is to lay the aluminium foil over the hole

16 The bandage material is damp so it is easy to wind round the repair, completely covering and overlapping the aluminium

17 Wrap the wire supplied round the repair to hold it while it sets. The repair is only suitable for fairly small holes

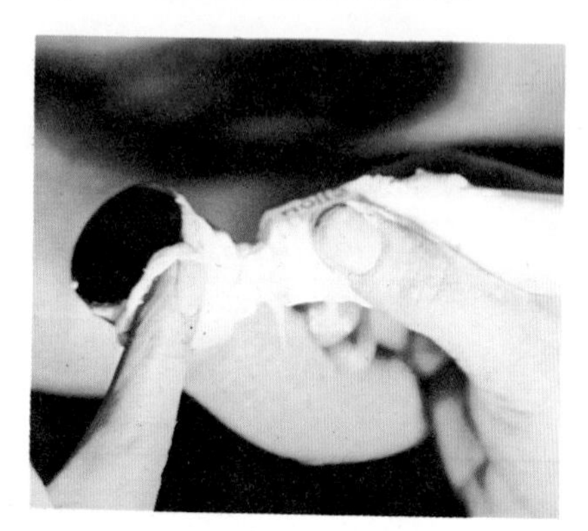

18 Leaky joints can be a problem. Paste such as Fire Gum hardens rapidly—so replace the cap when not using it

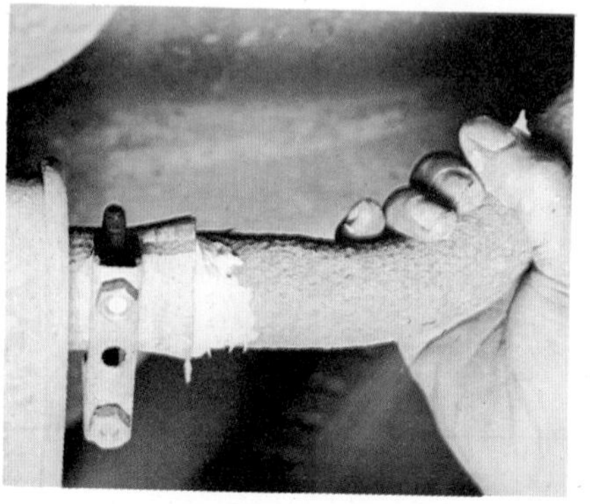

19 Paste will seal a joint but will not fill up a large gap, which must be done with baking foil as already shown

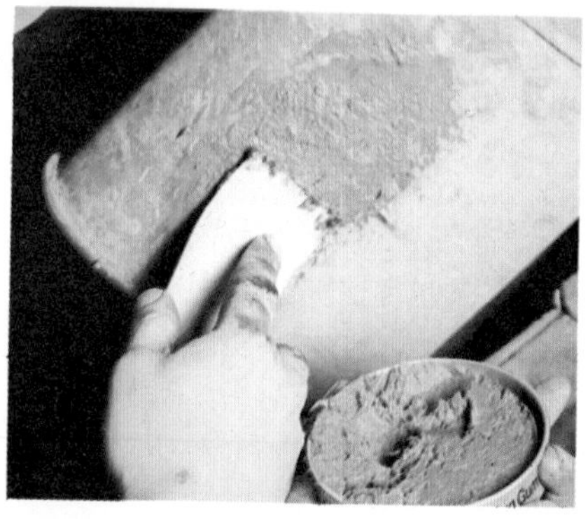

20 Stiff paste, such as Gun Gum, will seal up small holes in an otherwise sound silencer. It hardens with heat

that it can be slipped over the ends of the pipe and secured with heavy-duty clips or 'U' bolt clamps (fig. 23). If the bore of the hose is fractionally too large to offer a snug fit on your exhaust pipe, pack it with foil as described above.

Some manufacturers make an exhaust section which consists of a flexible length of pipe and includes the manifold flange (fig. 25). This can be useful and a money-saver if, for example, this part of the pipe is damaged on a fairly new system—for a relatively small outlay the new section can be inserted, saving the cost of an entire new pipe. The range of models for which this is available is limited, but it is worth checking at motor factors to see if one is made for your car.

If corrosion has not got a firm grip on your exhaust, the exterior can be given a coat of galvanizing paint (fig. 26). This will withstand the high temperatures without burning off. Repainting regularly will give long-term protection on the outside, and although it is impossible to treat the inside effectively, your exhaust will last a little longer.

Replacing the exhaust system

Replacement systems come in varying qualities. The type you buy will depend on what you can afford. At the bottom of the scale is the lowest-priced system, of much the same quality as the original equipment. At the top end is the stainless steel system, which may be anything up to three times as expensive as the standard fitting.

If you intend to keep your car for a long time it is well worth considering stainless steel. Such exhausts are guaranteed for up to five years, and some for life on the condition that the guarantee expires when ownership of the car changes. In between there are many differently-priced types but, whatever you choose, try to buy a guaranteed make.

If you must replace the exhaust yourself, all you need to do is undo the clamps and supports (see above), fit the new component or components, and replace the fittings, making sure they are tight. However, one or two points should be watched:

21 To replace a section of pipe, cut away the damaged part using a hacksaw—a tricky task even under ideal conditions

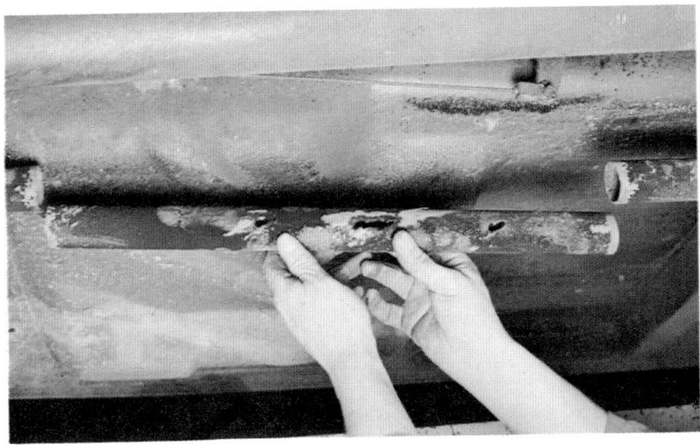

22 Make sure that you replace all the affected pipe—otherwise you might well have wasted all your time and money

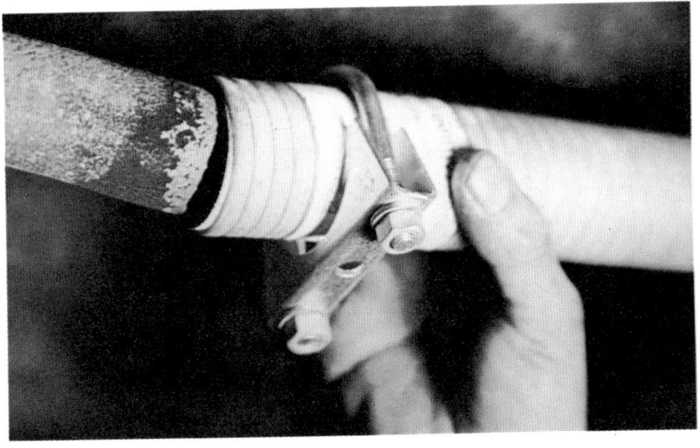

23 Get new 'U' bolts, one for each end of the flexible section. (The white part of the tube is simply the maker's label)

24 The completed repair. The flexible pipe hardens up with engine carbon, and can last as long as the rest of the system

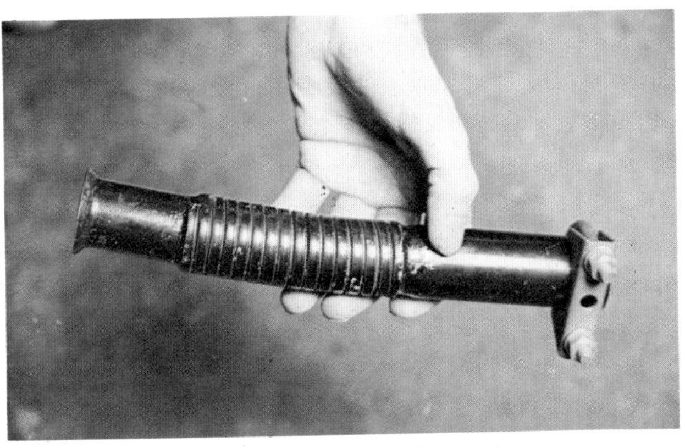

25 If only the manifold end of the pipe is damaged you can replace it with this section—available for a few cars only

George Wright

26 Galvanizing paint can lengthen the life of your exhaust system—if you can do it in good time

As the exhaust is removed from below the car, it may be essential to lift the front of the car at least, so that the vertical section from the manifold can be dropped low enough to get it out. Drive the car on to ramps or lift it with a jack and support it with axle stands. This also provides plenty of space for manoeuvring when you are underneath and faced with removing a difficult or corroded nut or bolt.

Starting with the manifold clamp, loosen, but do not remove, all the mounting bolts down the exhaust line. If you are dealing with mountings that are in good condition, and the exhaust is supported only by a few straps, leave them in place for the time being. When you are sure all the nuts and bolts will come off easily, go back to the manifold clamp and remove it.

When dealing with single-unit systems take off the tail-pipe clamp next. The entire system will now be supported by the mountings right underneath the car body. Remove one clamp or strap at a time, working from each end of the system alternately. The point of this is to stop the exhaust being left suspended from one end only, thus over-straining the last mounting and also hampering its removal. If you leave until last the mounting nearest to the central balancing point of the exhaust, then this problem will be overcome.

If your exhaust can be dismantled in sections, take off the silencer first, then separate the other pieces and remove them as above.

To fit the new exhaust, work in reverse order. But do not tighten any of the clamps or securing attachments until the system is properly in place. When you are satisfied that nothing is pulling against anything else, tighten the bolts, starting this time from the manifold end and working towards the back, where the flexible brackets take up any slight misalignment. Be sure, however, that the manifold joint mates perfectly before you bolt it up—if you use the clamp to pull the pipe and manifold into line the pipe may fracture under the strain.

Fitting a vacuum gauge

Of all the auxiliary gauges fitted to modern cars, perhaps the least common is the vacuum gauge. Yet used correctly it can be a real money-saver, as the gauge will tell you when you are driving most economically. A vacuum gauge can also forecast problems with valves, pistons, gaskets and so on, and may even be used to help tune the whole engine.

Which vacuum gauge you select is largely a matter of personal preference for the working parts of all gauges are basically the same. But there are some important differences to consider. Some, for example, are calibrated in inches or centimetres, while others are marked with coloured sections. The printed information in these coloured sections describes what is happening to the engine with the needle in each particular section. With the calibrated gauges, you have to work out for yourself what is going on.

Almost all gauges are of a standard 50 mm (2in.) diameter, and are purchased as a kit complete with all parts.

Fitting a gauge

Before connecting the pipe at either end, first run it through the bulkhead. In most cases it will be possible to lead it through an existing hole, perhaps the one carrying the main electrical harness (fig. 10), but if none is available in a suitable position a hole will have to be drilled and a grommet fitted.

The pipe should now be fitted to the inlet manifold of the engine (figs. 3-9). Some cars have manifolds already drilled and threaded. The hole will be fitted with a plug which simply has to be removed and the gauge pipe connector fitted. An alternative to drilling a new hole is to check that your car is not already fitted with an accessory such as a brake servo. If so, a tee-piece adaptor will be available which will enable both facilities to be taken from the same outlet.

1 *Above:* Vacuum gauge kit includes gauge unit, tubing adaptor for inlet manifold, unions and necessary nuts and screws for fixing

2 *Right:* Necessary tools for job are hammer, centre punch, hand-drill, drill bit of correct tapping size, tap, wrench and hole saw

3 Mark position for inlet manifold adaptor centrally, where all the mixture will pass, using hammer and centre punch

4 Drill through the manifold using a tapping size drill well greased, to collect all swarf, to save it entering the manifold

If neither of these options is open to you you will have to drill and thread a hole yourself (figs. 3-5). It is sometimes advisable to remove the inlet manifold to carry out the job, but if it is done in situ, grease the drill and tap to remove any swarf (figs. 3-9). With the manifold refitted and the pipe securing fixed,either tape or clip the pipe along its length to prevent chaffing or flapping around.

Decide where you wish to mount your gauge. If there is sufficient space on your dashboard a suitable hole must be drilled to accomodate the gauge. If there is no space or you simply want something different, the instrument may be mounted in a bracket sometimes provided in the kit or in an instrument pod available at most accessory shops. The latter method of mounting has the added advantage of making the gauge easily removable in the event of selling the car without causing any depreciating damage.

If you opt for cutting a hole in the dashboard make sure that there is enough room behind the spot you choose to accommodate not only the gauge but the piping which will lead to it (fig. 11). This piping will not tolerate sudden and violent curves along its length which will cause it to kink.

Having chosen your spot, mark the centre of your chosen area with a punch. Make sure before drilling that there are no pipes or wires in danger. Drill a small pilot hole through the punch mark (fig. 12) and the 50 mm (2in.) hole can then be cut using either a Q-Max type tank cutter or a rotary hacksaw type (figs. 13-15). If neither of these tools is available (they may be purchased quite cheaply), you can of course drill a series of holes around the inner circumference of a carefully scribed circle. Knock out the centre metal and file the jagged edge to shape. This is obviously a more laborious task and requires a certain patience if not skill.

5 Carefully tap the thread in the drilled hole, greasing tap to collect swarf produced. Keep the tap square to the hole

6 After applying a small amount of jointing compound to the threads, screw the adaptor into the tapped hole

7 Tighten the inlet manifold adaptor with a suitable spanner taking care not to overtighten as the manifold is aluminium

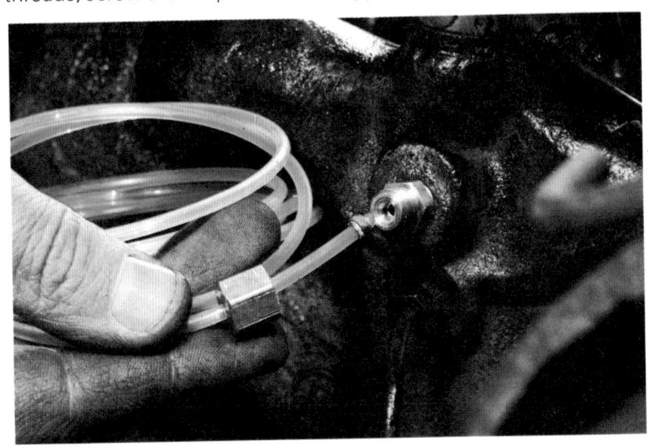

8 Fit union nut over one end of the plastic pipe, followed by the olive, also over pipe end

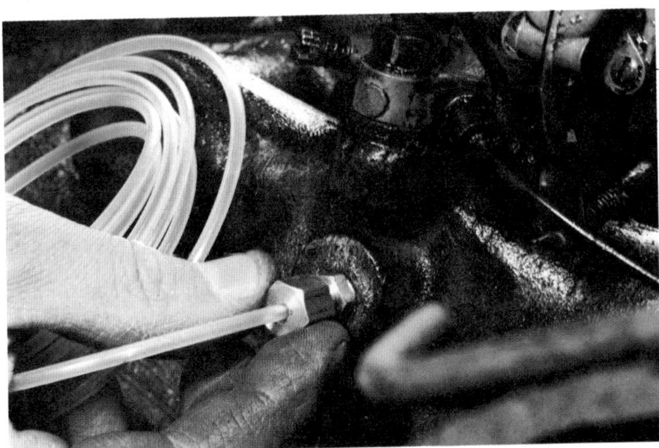

9 Offer up the plastic pipe fitted with union nut and olive to the inlet manifold adaptor and screw up finger tight

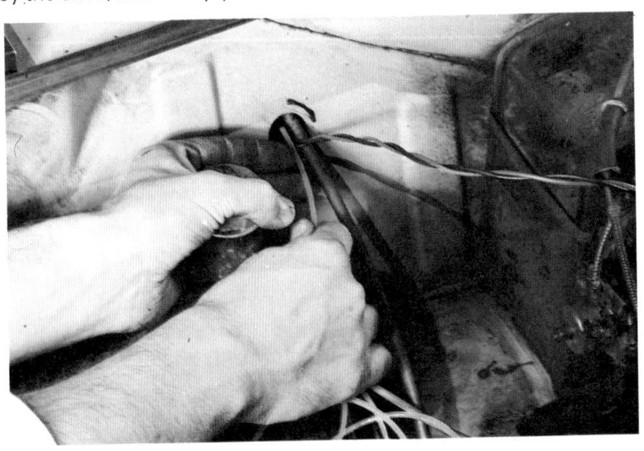

10 After tightening up union with a spanner, uncoil the plastic pipe and feed the free end through the bulkhead

11 After checking for adequate clearance behind the dashboard to accommodate the gauge body, mark round the gauge unit

12 After marking the centre of the circle, fit the hole saw to the hand drill and proceed to drill the centre hole

13 Carefully continue drilling the hole right through the dashboard. Apply gentle pressure and do not rush this process

14 On the completion of the drilling, withdraw the drill saw from the hole taking care not to snag the fascia surface

15 Check that the vacuum gauge unit fits snugly into the hole, easing the hole if necessary with a half-round file

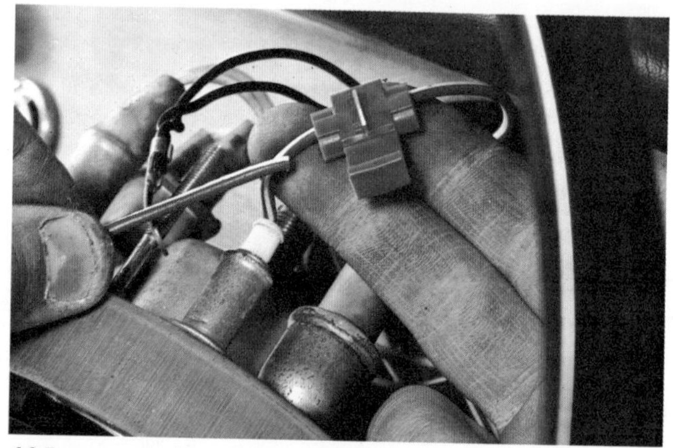
16 For ease of wiring remove instrument cluster and using a connector join gauge lamp wire to panel light wire

17 Next connect the vacuum gauge earth wire to a suitable point on the instrument cluster

18 Replace instrument cluster then pull wires through hole cut for gauge, and trim to a convenient length

19 The red-white lamp feed, the black earth (ground) wire and the plastic vacuum tube are now ready to be connected

20 Insert the lamp feed wire (red-white) into the detached vacuum gauge lamp live terminal and tighten the screw

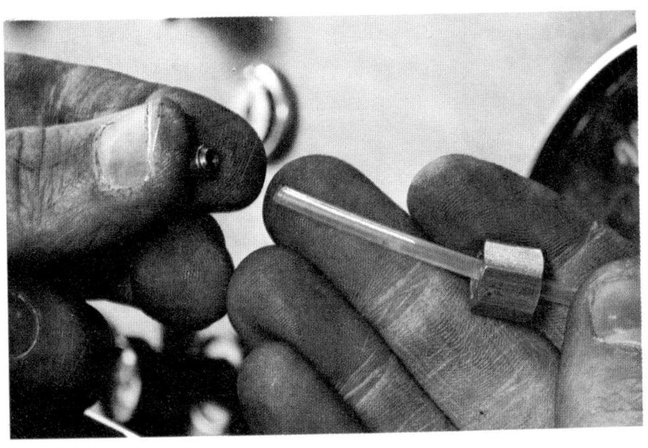

21 After placing the female union nut onto the end of the plastic vacuum pipe follow this with the olive provided

22 Offer up the plastic pipe fitted with union nut and olive to the vacuum gauge boss and screw up finger tight

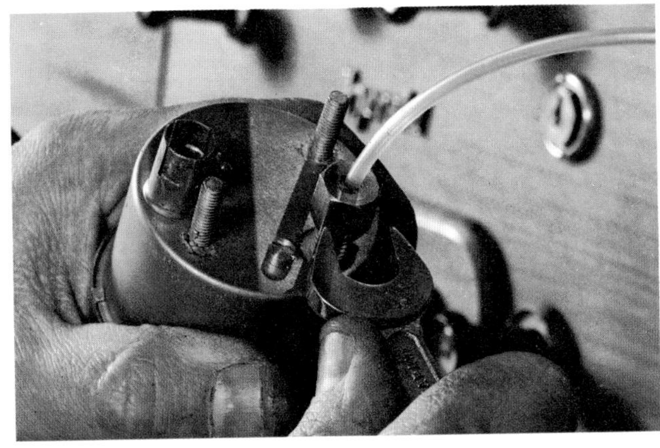

23 Tighten up the gauge-pipe union nut with a suitable spanner taking great care to avoid excessive force

24 Fit the gauge into the hole in the dashboard, couple the earth wire to the gauge fixing yoke, and tighten all nuts

Connecting the gauge

First wire up the bulb wire which should be spliced into an existing instrument feed using a connector (figs. 16-20). Obviously, it will be necessary to wire up to a bulb which will be on at all times the vacuum gauge will need to be illuminated.

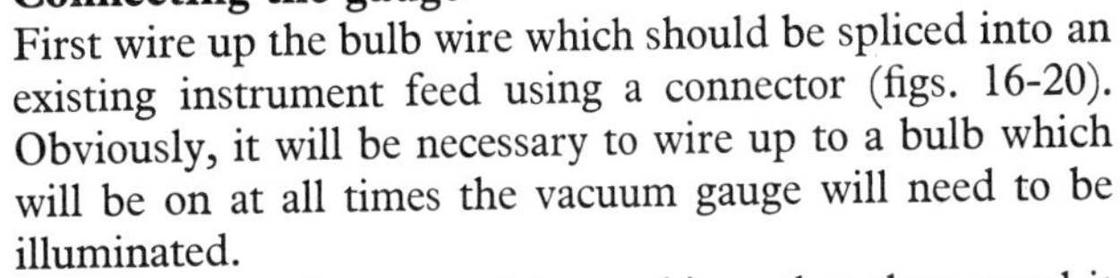

If the gauge is mounted in anything other than metal it will have to be earthed before the lamp will work.

Using the vacuum gauge

For fuel economy drive the car at all times with the aim of getting the highest vacuum reading possible. Clearly this is most easily achieved by light throttle application. Ignition timing can also be set quite accurately by loosening the distributor, and turning it slowly in the opposite direction to that of the rotor arm to obtain the highest reading. When this is reached, turn it back slightly to drop the vacuum reading by one or two divisions.

The carburettor can also be set by turning the mixture screw slowly in either direction until the highest steady reading is obtained.

A mechanically sound engine in a good state of tune should read between 430-530 mm Hg (17-21 in Hg), with the needle holding steady on tickover. If the instrument gives a lower reading but the needle remains steady, any of the following faults might be present: piston or cylinder bore wear, broken piston rings, worn valves or simply incorrect tappet adjustment.

If the gauge reading is reasonably high but the needle fluctuates it could be that the spark plugs need re-setting. Other causes could be a leaking inlet manifold, worn or incorrectly set contact points, uneven cylinder compressions or a worn carburettor.

Fitting an oil cooler

Oil is the lifeblood of a car's engine. It lubricates the numerous moving parts and, by preventing the friction that metal to metal contact would cause, it also helps to keep them cool. Engine oil performs its cooling function by collecting heat from the hottest parts of the engine and transferring it to the sump, which is kept cool by the airflow over and around it. As the oil gives up its heat to the sump casing, it too cools down before returning to the top of the engine. But, if the oil is subjected to loads in excess of those it was designed to cater for, it will tend to overheat and lose efficiency. As the lubricating properties of the oil are reduced, the amount of wear in the engine will increase rapidly.

George Wright

1 This Serck kit contains everything necessary for fitting an oil cooler to your car and provides for either type of oil filter

In the majority of cases engine oil performs quite satisfactorily provided it is renewed at regular intervals. If the engine has a higher than standard state of tune, however, or if the car is used for prolonged towing, it may be necessary to fit an oil radiator, more commonly referred to as an oil cooler. These are in kit form (fig. 1) on the accessory market and fitting one is well within the capabilities of the well-informed DIY mechanic.

When you need an oil cooler

Initially, you may be uncertain whether or not your car needs an oil cooler. Basically the necessity for an oil cooler depends on the state of tune of your engine and the purposes for which you use your car. Under normal use most standard, untuned, production engines do not suffer from the oil overheating as this usually occurs when the engine and, in particular, the oil system, is stressed beyond its designed limits. In most engines, these limits are quite generous. Exceptions to this are some BL front-wheel drive models which feature engine and transmission units lubricated by the same oil supply. On these cars the oil is subjected to greater stress and tends to overheat after prolonged, hard driving. If you have an unmodified engine that exhibits apparent signs of the oil overheating, such as falling oil pressure, excessive noise and a burnt oil smell, the first thing to check is that it does not need a thorough overhaul and re-conditioning.

Virtually all racing and rally engines are fitted with an oil cooler because they are driven at continually high revs, imposing a great strain on the normal oil cooling processes. Naturally, road cars are not usually driven in the same manner, so that the problem of cooling the oil is not so pronounced. However, if you use a modified car for journeys involving sustained cruising at high engine speeds, fitting an oil cooler is a wise precaution.

The strain imposed by towing is less obvious because, unlike a racing or rally car, engine speed is not directly related to road speed. Pulling a heavy load such as a caravan or a trailer, however, calls for a great deal of low gear driving, especially when a car is negotiating a steep incline. Under these circumstances, the engine will be revving hard for prolonged periods without receiving the full benefit of the ram-effect airflow, which is created by the forward motion of the car, around the sump. This airflow helps to cool the sump and plays a part in enabling the oil to dissipate its heat into the atmosphere (see pages 177 to 182). The combination of reduced airflow and high engine speeds can, therefore, cause the oil to overheat over a long and hilly journey.

Towing can also place great stress on the oil in the gearbox, particularly if a car is fitted with automatic transmission. In this case a separate transmission oil cooler may be required. Fitting one of these is covered in the next article in this series.

If you plan to use your car for towing, consult your local dealer who should be able to tell you whether or not an oil cooler is necessary. If you are going to tow in countries where the ambient temperature is consistently high, it is feasible to change your normal oil for special high-temperature oil. These oils are better able to cope with high operating temperatures, but you should bear in mind that such a course of action is not a complete answer to the problem and may bring other problems along with them.

Air-cooled engines, where the cooling function of the oil is even more critical, are inherently prone to oil overheating problems. For this reason most air-cooled cars are fitted with oil coolers as standard.

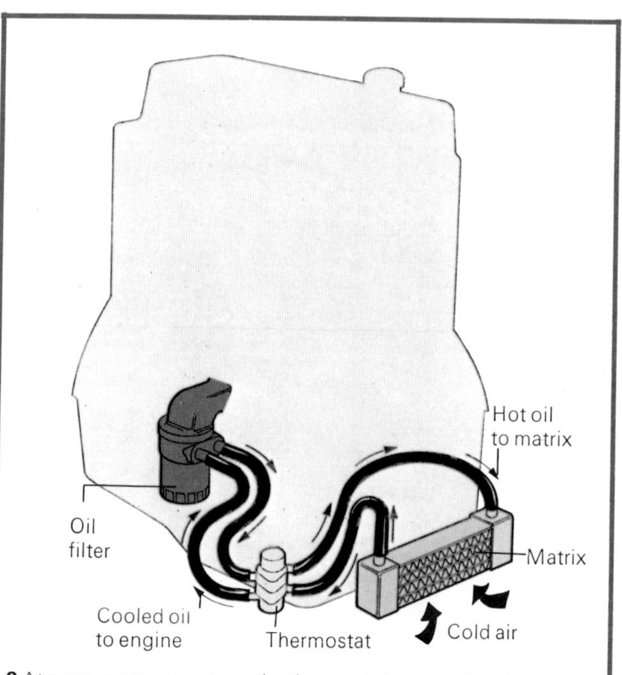

2 At a pre-set temperature, the thermostat opens allowing hot oil to pass through the cooling matrix before returning to the engine

Illustra

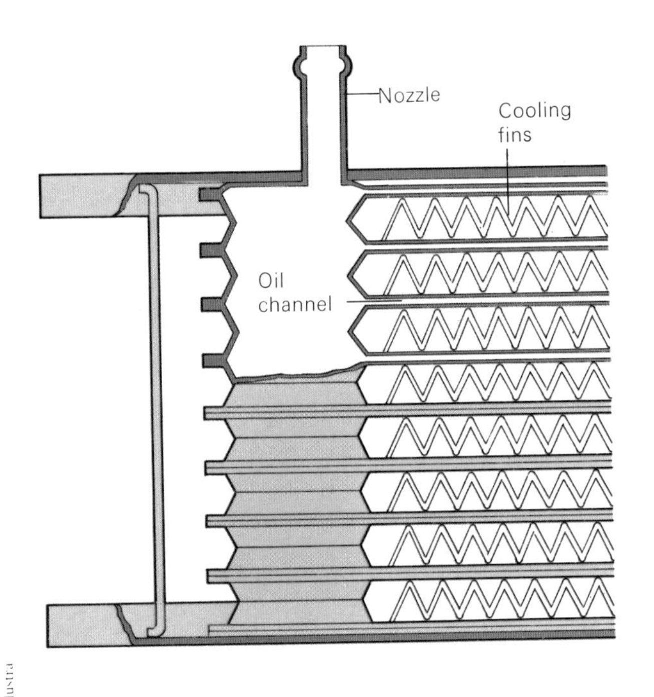

3 The oil is cooled by heat being dissipated by the cooling fins of the matrix which are exposed to the air flow

How an engine oil cooler works

A typical oil cooler, like the Serck unit illustrated, consists of a small matrix, or radiator, which is plumbed into the lubrication system of the car. The matrix is mounted at a point on the car where it will be exposed to as much of the ram-effect airflow as possible. On front-engined cars, this is normally in the engine compartment, just behind the front grille. On water-cooled, rear-engined cars, such as the Chrysler Imp and most Skoda models, the oil cooler must be mounted at the front of the car, even though the water radiator is mounted alongside the engine. The reason for this is that, although the radiator receives only slight ram-effect, it is cooled by a specially-designed, shrouded fan. The oil cooler has no fan, so it relies on the ram-effect to cool it in order to function efficiently.

By means of an adaptor, which is usually fitted at the oil filter head, filtered oil is diverted to the matrix instead of running straight to the top of the engine. The adaptor is usually called a "sandwich block" because, when fitted, it is sandwiched between the filter head and the filter itself. If the cooler kit is fitted with a thermostat, this will be mounted between the adaptor and the matrix (fig. 2) and oil only diverted to the matrix when it reaches a certain temperature. As it passes through the matrix, the oil benefits from the effect of the air flow (fig. 3) and this enables it to disperse heat. This process is almost identical to the one used in water-cooling systems. When it reaches the bottom of the matrix, the cooled oil is pumped back to the sandwich block and then on to the engine where it rejoins the existing lubrication system.

Buying an oil cooler kit

Oil cooler kits are normally available from the tuning divisions of certain manufacturers and from large car accessory shops. Several different makes of kit exist but generally there is little variation in quality. What you should check, however, is that the kit of your choice is complete. This means that it should include all the relevant components of the oil cooler itself together with the correct piping and fitting brackets (see below).

One very important and essential part of any oil cooler kit is the thermostat. This is similar in design and operation to the thermostat in a water-cooling system and diverts oil through the cooler only when necessary—that is to say, when the oil starts overheating. This eliminates any danger of the oil becoming overcooled and not reaching its optimum working temperature.

Some kits include a thermostat, but others do not. They are usually available as an optional extra so check this point on the kit of your choice. If there is not a thermostat included, you would be strongly advised to buy one. Under certain circumstances, overcooled oil can be as harmful to the engine as oil which is too hot (see pages 177 to 182).

To make sure of getting the right kit to match your requirements, start by quoting the make, model and year of your car. Then tell the dealer the conditions under which you intend to use your car and whether the oil cooler is for the engine or for the transmission. Do not be confused by the fact that some kits are supplied for both road-going and racing applications, as the two types are interchangeable.

Fitting the oil cooler matrix

The first stage of fitting an oil cooler kit is to position the matrix. This is the small radiator (fig. 2) which will actually cool the oil. It must be mounted in such a way that a constant airflow is allowed to pass through it whenever the car is moving forward. On front-engined cars this means fitting the matrix somewhere behind or slightly below the front grille; on rear-engined cars, a suitable site near the front of the car must be found.

The instructions with the particular kit that you buy should specify an exact location. This will take into account how much room there is on your car, whether or not you can make use of existing brackets or bolt holes and the length of piping supplied. Make sure you have read the instructions and that you understand them fully before you begin to fit the cooler.

On the Ford Escort Mk I illustrated, the first step is to remove the front grille (fig. 4). This will either be held in place with screws or pop-rivets. If rivets are used you will have to carefully drill them out. On some cars the grille is known to be difficult to remove, as in the case of the Ford Anglia 105E, while on others the securing bolts may have become badly corroded. If you find that your grille is very difficult to remove it may be easier to drain and remove the radiator.

Next, secure the matrix to its mounting bracket using the bolts provided (fig. 5). On the Escort Mk. I there is no need to drill any holes for the assembly, as the nearside top and bottom radiator mounting bolts are used. These should be removed (figs. 6 and 7), but, unless already removed instead of the grille, the radiator itself can be left in position.

George Wright

4 To fit an oil cooler to a Ford Escort you must first remove the front grille. This is usually held in position by screws

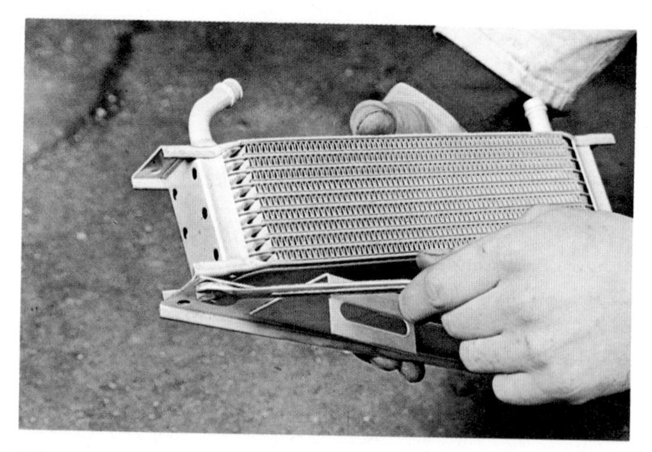

5 Once you have decided which way up the matrix will be fitted, connect it to the mounting bracket with the bolts provided

6 With the battery removed from the car as a safety measure, and to facilitate access, remove the nearside radiator mounting bolts

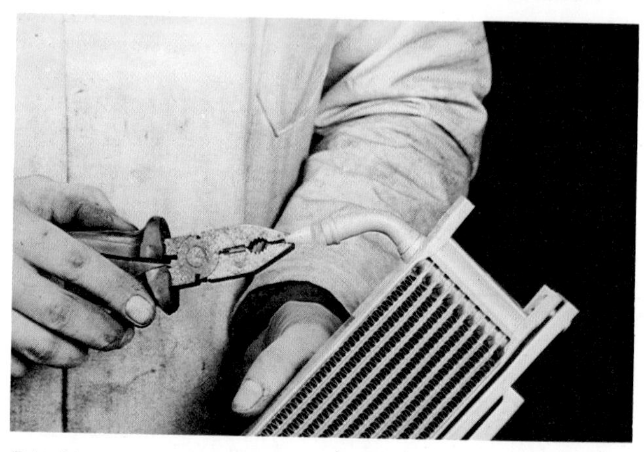

7 At this stage you should remove the plastic dust plugs from the nozzles of the matrix. If they are a tight fit, use a pair of pliers

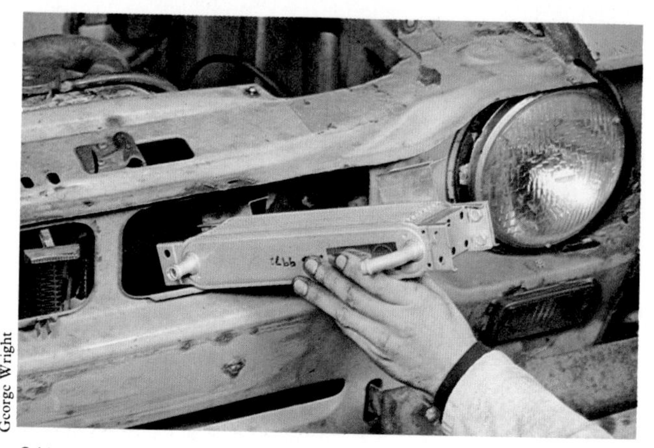

George Wright

8 Now insert the matrix in position. Do this carefully to avoid damaging the water radiator if you have left it in position

Check that the matrix is the right way up (by reference to the instructions) then offer it up to (fig. 8) the assembly so that the matrix bracket is sandwiched between the radiator and its holding brackets, with all of the holes correctly aligned. In the case of the Ford Escort Mk. I the matrix is mounted vertically. Holding the matrix in place with one hand, replace the radiator mounting bolts in their original brackets, making sure that they also pass through the matrix bracket. Tighten the bolts carefully until both the matrix assembly and the radiator are firmly held.

On some cars, such as the BL Mini or the Morris Marina, it is not possible to make use of the existing radiator brackets or bolts to hold the matrix. This is usually due to lack of space but may also be because of the design of the radiator mountings or the oil cooler mounting bracket supplied with the kit. In such cases the kit will specify a part of the bodywork, usually the front valance below the grille, to which the matrix can be bolted. Having secured the matrix to its mounting bracket you can use the assembly as a template to mark and drill the necessary bolt

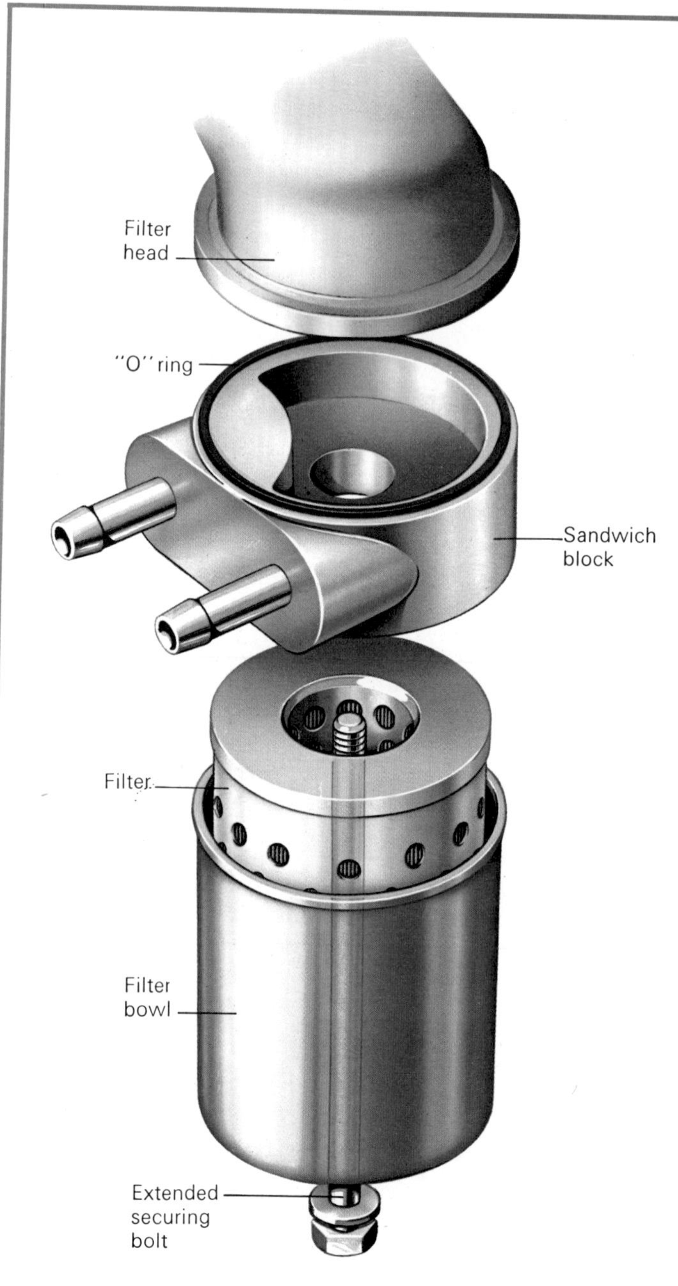

9 On cartridge type oil filters, an extended securing bolt and sandwich block have to be fitted

holes. The bolts to secure the matrix assembly to the bodywork are normally included in the kit. Again, you should check that the matrix is fitted the right way up.

Fitting the sandwich block or adaptor

On most cars, it will not be necessary to fit the sandwich block supplied in the kit to the oil filter assembly, normally the most convenient place to plumb into the oil system. In the Serck oil cooler kits for BL cars fitted with "A" series engines, a sandwich block is not required; the oil is diverted in a slightly different way (see below). Exactly what form the sandwich block takes depends on whether your car has a cartridge type or a disposable, paper-element type of oil filter fitted to it.

If your car has a cartridge type of oil filter, start by placing a suitable container under the filter assembly to catch the dripping oil as you unbolt the filter bowl. Next, remove the filter bowl, taking care not to drop any washers or sealing rings that may be loosened into the oil container. If it does not fall out, use a pin to extract the rubber sealing "O" ring situated in the groove around the filter head. With the filter bowl removed, extract the old securing bolt and replace it with the extended one in the kit (fig. 9). You should also fit a new filter element at this stage.

Following the kit instructions, identify which way up the sandwich block goes. Where specified, fit the new "O" ring which is supplied with the replacement element to the groove around the bottom of the sandwich block and the special sealing ring which is supplied with the kit to the groove in the top. Next, locate the sandwich block in position on the filter head and then offer up the filter bowl below it. Push the new, extended, securing bolt right through the sandwich block and screw it into the filter head as you would when normally replacing the element. Before fully tightening the bolt, make sure that the filter bowl is properly seated. With the bolt tightened, the whole assembly should be firmly held in place.

If your car has the disposable type of oil filter, place a container beneath it, to catch the dripping oil, and then unscrew the canister (fig. 11). Now, remove the "O" ring from the filter head carefully. Refer to the instructions and fit the new sealing ring, which is supplied with a new filter element, to the groove running round the bottom part of the sandwich block assembly. Now fit the special sealing ring, which is also supplied with the kit, to the groove in the top of the sandwich block (fig. 12) and then offer the block up to the filter head. Using the special nut provided, secure the two (fig. 13) and tighten the nut to form an oil-tight seal (fig. 14). Finally, fit a new filter canister by screwing it into the bottom half of the sandwich block (fig. 10).

If you have a BL car that is fitted with an "A" series engine you will notice an external oil feed pipe running across the face of the block to the left of the oil filter head. Do not touch the filter assembly itself. Instead, drain the engine oil into a suitable container and then unscrew the

Filter head
"O" ring
Sandwich block
Union nut
Oil filter canister
Venner

10 With the disposable canister oil filter type a union nut links the canister, sandwich block and filter head

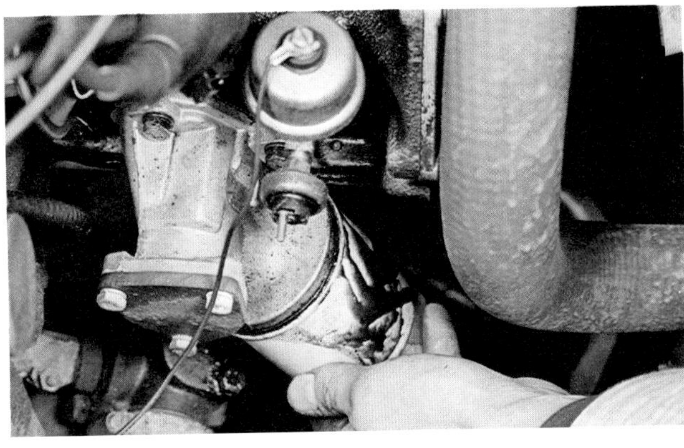

11 With a container placed beneath it to catch the dripping oil, unscrew and remove the oil filter

12 Prior to fitting the sandwich block to the filter head, make sure that the special sealing ring supplied with the kit is in position

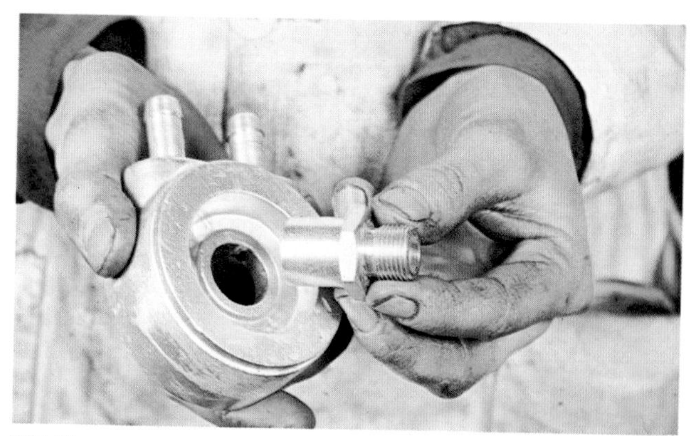
13 When securing the sandwich block in position using a union nut, fit the nut with the non-threaded section uppermost

14 Before fitting the assembly to the car, check that the parts will mate together to form an oil-tight seal

unions at either end of the pipe. Remove the pipe completely. Now screw the two special pipe adaptors into the threads left vacant by the pipe's removal.

Connecting the piping

The next task, even if you are fitting a thermostat into the piping, is to connect the pipes themselves. Fitting the thermostat involves cutting the pipes and by having them in their correct positions before you do this, you can avoid any possibility of making the cuts in the wrong place.

There should be two pipes in the kit; one to take the oil from the sandwich block (or adaptor) to the cooler matrix and one to return it to the engine. In the Serck kits, the pipes are made of flexible material which can withstand the pressure of the oil flowing through them and which can also be easily trimmed to size. Working on one pipe at a time, immerse one end in a cup of boiling water to soften it. Dry the pipe and then slide on a hose clip and a plastic finisher (fig. 15). Connect the pipe to one of the nozzles on the sandwich block (fig. 16), or, in the case of cars with BL "A" series engines, to one of the adaptors on the engine block. Tighten the hose clip and then repeat the process for the second pipe (fig. 17).

Following the route recommended in the fitting instructions, direct the pipes to the matrix. Make sure that the pipes are not stretched or exposed to any hot parts of the engine. Look out for any jagged edges (figs. 18 and 19). If you lose oil due to a leak caused by a chafed pipe, you could suffer a major engine failure. When you are satisfied that the pipes are correctly routed, cut off any excess using a sharp knife. Soften each pipe in water, attach a hose clip and a finisher and then fit the pipes to the matrix. At this stage, either pipe can be attached to either nozzle on the matrix. Tighten the hose clips securely.

Some other oil cooler kits, such as those made by BL Special Tuning, have special screw-threaded collars fitted to the ends of the pipes. These are screwed on to threaded connections on the sandwich block or adaptor and the oil cooler matrix. This method of attachment of the pipes eliminates the possibility of a pipe being blown off by the pressure of the oil, but the pipes, which are pre-cut, are more expensive to produce, so these particular kits usually cost a great deal more.

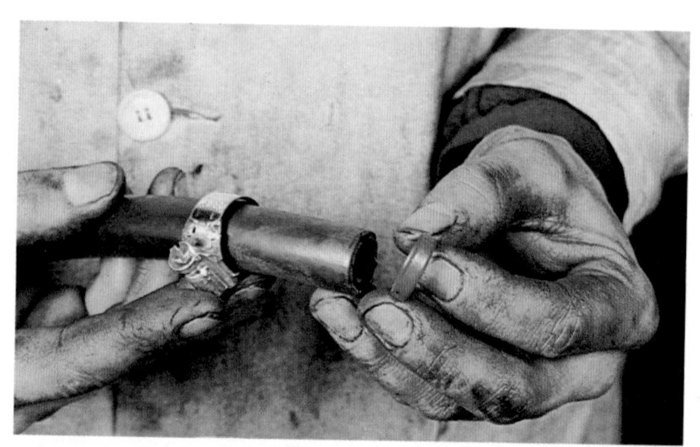
15 Soften the end of the rubber oil pipe using hot water, dry it then slide on a hose clip and one of the red plastic finishers

Fitting the thermostat

You can now commence fitting the thermostat. To do this, find a point where the two pipes leading from the matrix to the engine can be run side by side for a short distance without any danger of them fouling on any components (fig. 20). When you have done this, cut (fig. 21) through both pipes at a point approximately in the middle of the side by side run. Leaving the ends of the pipe hanging, check the engine oil level and top it up if necessary. Now you will have to turn the engine over by hand—best done by pulling on

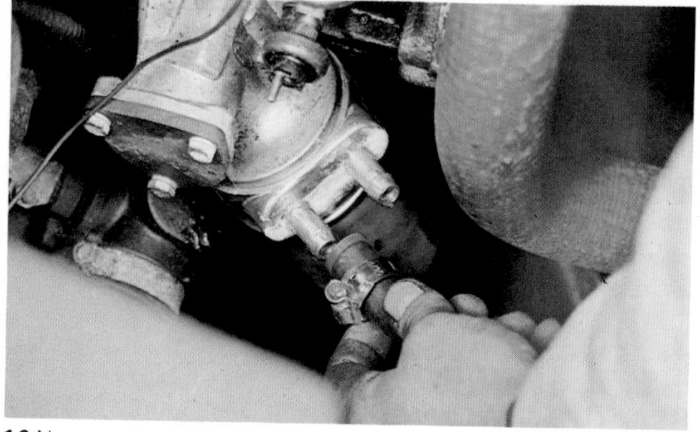
George Wright

16 Next, push the pipe on to one of the nozzles on the sandwich block. Some petroleum jelly smeared on the nozzle will help you

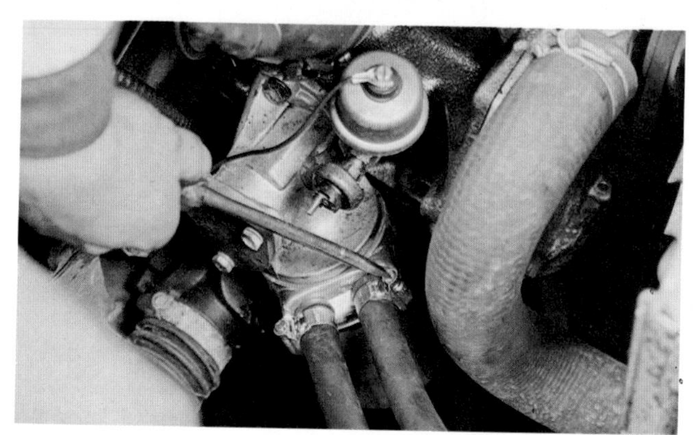
17 When both pipes are attached to the nozzles, tighten the hose clips. Remember, if they leak oil your engine will be ruined

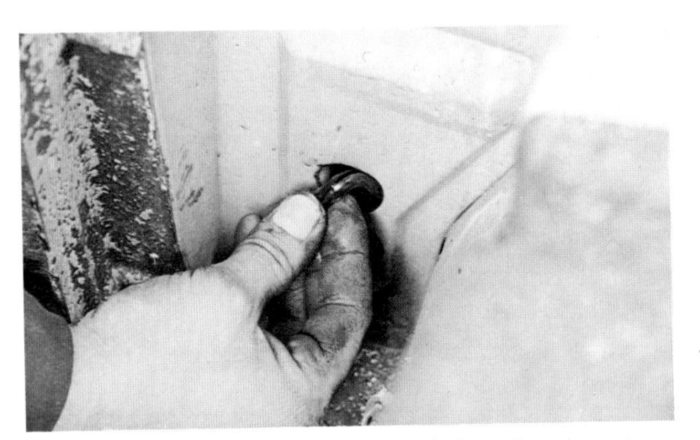

18 If you are going to run the pipes through the car's bodywork, make sure that you fit a grommet to prevent chafing

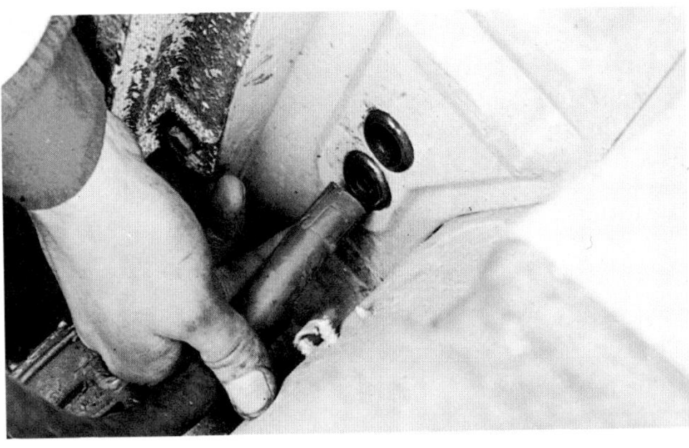

19 Push the pipes through the holes in the bodywork. Re-check that they are not exposed to any hot parts of the engine

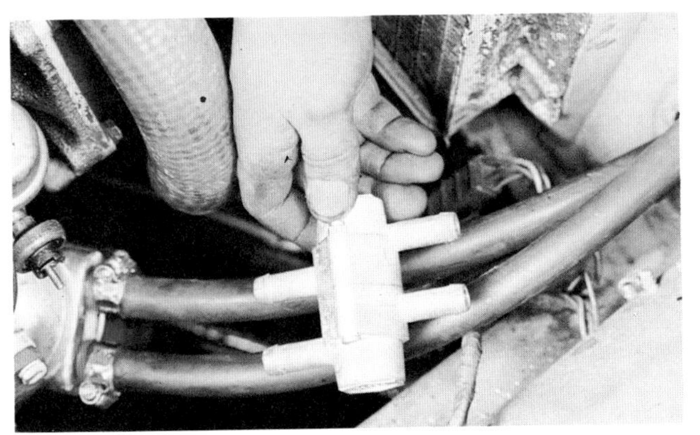

20 To fit the thermostat, first find a point where the two pipes run side by side at about the same distance apart as the nozzles

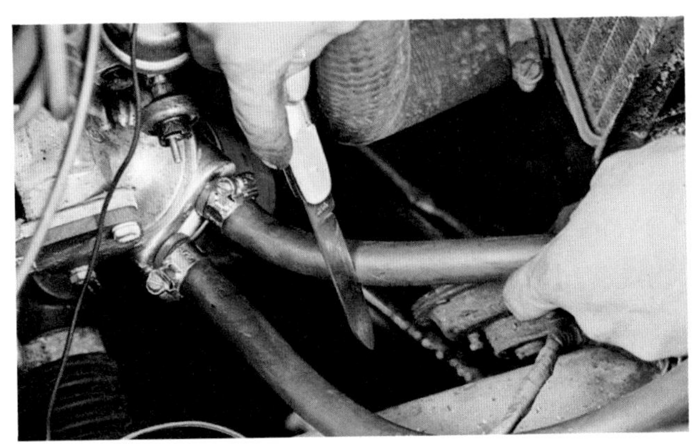

21 Carefully cut through the pipes at a convenient point in the side by side run. A sharp knife should be used

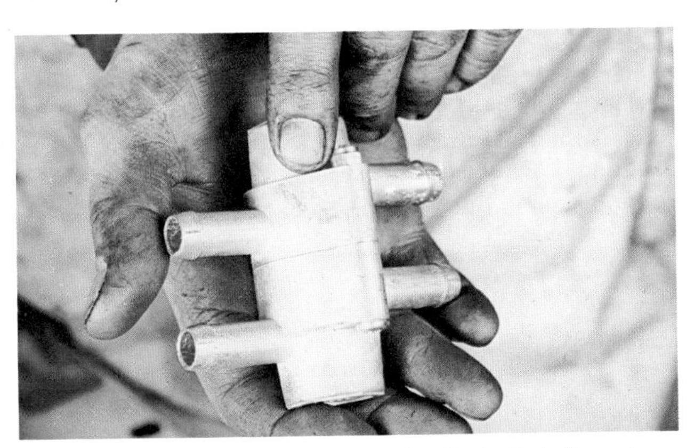

22 Before connecting the thermostat, identify the "inlet" nozzle. If connected wrongly, the thermostat will not work

23 The oil cooler in position. Check the engine oil level, add more if required, run the engine and then re-check and replenish

the fan belt. You may need the help of an assistant during this process and you should disconnect the battery as a safety measure. As the engine turns over, watch the two pipes that are attached to the sandwich block or, on BL "A" series engines, the adaptors. As soon as you identify the pipe from which a trickle of oil appears, you can stop turning the engine immediately.

Take the pipe and soften the end as described earlier, then fit a finisher and a hose clip. Press it on to the nozzle on the thermostat housing that is marked "inlet" (fig. 22). This is most important. If you attach the pipe to the wrong nozzle the thermostat will fail to operate correctly. Take the second pipe connected to the sandwich block or adaptor and connect it to the remaining nozzle on the inlet side of the thermostat housing.

Moving to the two pipes attached to the matrix, soften the ends and connect them to the two nozzles on the outlet side of the thermostat. This is not usually marked. Tighten all the clips and tie the thermostat to one side.

Completing the job

With the oil cooler in place (fig. 23) complete the job by re-fitting any parts that were disturbed during the installation process. If you have had to remove the radiator, do not forget to tighten all of the hose connections and to re-fill it with water. Make a thorough check for any wires that may have become dislodged accidentally and check also that all the connections are secure.

Now start the engine and run it at a fast idle for at least five minutes. Be sure to allow adequate ventilation of the exhaust fumes when you do this. With the engine running at its normal idling speed, check the entire oil cooler system for signs of any leaks, especially round the sandwich block; a leak here will almost certainly be due to badly fitting sealing rings. If this is the case, stop the engine and dismantle the sandwich block and filter assembly. Re-assemble it so that the rings seal correctly and then run through the checks once more. Leaks in the hose connections can usually be cured by further tightening of the securing clips.

Fitting a transmission oil cooler

One of the most common causes of automatic transmission failure is overheating of the gearbox fluid. This happens when an automatic gearbox is subjected to excessive strain, such as those imposed by towing or by driving in hot climates. Not surprisingly, the problem often plagues holidaymakers, for whom a breakdown of this sort can be financially disastrous.

Such failures can be avoided, however, by fitting a transmission oil cooler which will keep the fluid in the gearbox at an efficient working temperature whatever the conditions. Unlike most work on automatic transmissions, fitting a cooler requires no special tools or knowledge. Furthermore, there are several kits on the market, like the Borg-Warner one (fig. 1), which are designed specifically with the DIY mechanic in mind.

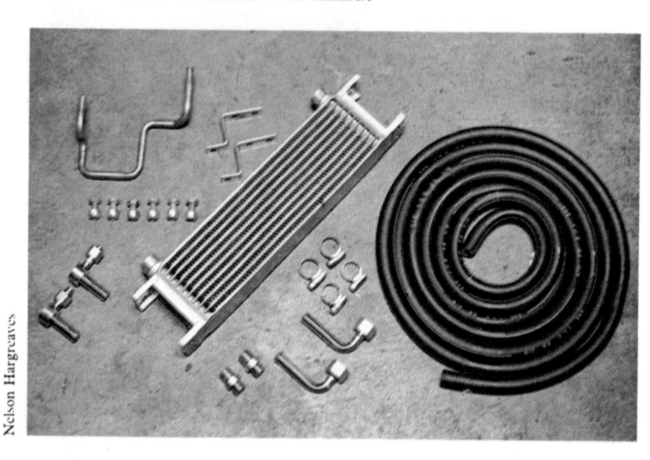

Nelson Hargreaves

1 This cooler kit from Borg-Warner contains everything necessary for fitting a transmission oil cooler to most cars. The matrix and rubber pipe, which must be cut in half, will be used on all cars, though whether you will need parts such as spare unions will depend on the type of transmission fitted

Why gearbox fluid overheats

The fluid in an automatic gearbox will overheat whenever the airflow-exposed sump at the bottom of the unit becomes incapable of absorbing the fluid's excess heat and dissipating it into the atmosphere. During normal driving conditions, the fluid in the gearbox becomes hot as it lubricates and, simultaneously, operates the moving parts. As the fluid is pumped around the gearbox, however, it passes through the sump of the gearbox. The sump, which is cooled by air passing over it as the car moves forward, then absorbs the fluid's heat and dissipates it in the process.

How effectively the fluid is cooled, therefore, depends to some extent on how cool the air is flowing over the sump. In very hot climates, maintaining a cool enough airflow can prove to be an insuperable problem. The solution is to fit a fluid cooler to supplement the existing cooling system.

If you are towing a trailer or a caravan, maintaining the airflow around the sump will again be a problem, especially on gradients. In this case, the car will often be moving too slowly to create much airflow and at the same time the transmission will be working exceptionally hard, transforming high engine speeds into adequate amounts of torque at the wheels. The fluid will, consequently, become hotter than usual but it will not be able to transfer its excess heat to the undercooled sump. The result, unless there is an oil cooler to back up the cooling process, will be overheating and possible transmission failure.

When to buy a transmission fluid cooler

It is certainly not worth buying a transmission oil cooler unless you are quite sure that you need one. If you intend to drive under the sort of conditions described above, contact the manufacturer of your car and ask for advice. The cooling characteristics of automatic gearboxes vary considerably from one type to another and some are designed with deliberately wide margins of tolerance. Automatic versions of the BL transverse-engined, front-wheel drive range of cars almost always need a cooler if they are to be used for towing. But this is because the gearbox and the engine share the same oil, which is therefore subject to a great deal more stress than the fluid in conventional automatic transmissions. Fitting a cooler kit to this type of car is covered in detail in the previous chapter, "Fitting an oil cooler".

Buying an oil cooler kit

Transmission oil cooler kits are obtainable from three sources, depending on the make of car. Some manufacturers market their own kits, usually through race or special tuning dealers. Others leave it to the manufacturers of the gearbox to supply a kit, as is the case with the Borg-Warner one illustrated. The third source, often the most convenient for the DIY mechanic, is the car accessory shop where kits made by specialist manufacturers, such as Serck Services, are available.

When you buy a kit, quote the make, year and model of your particular car. On receipt of the kit check inside to make sure that all the clips, nuts and bolts needed to fit it are included. You should also ensure, unless the kit is for a Borg-Warner 35/65 gearbox, such as the unit illustrated, that a set of instructions is provided to fully cover the details of fitting it to your car. Fitting of the Borg-Warner unit is fully covered in this chapter.

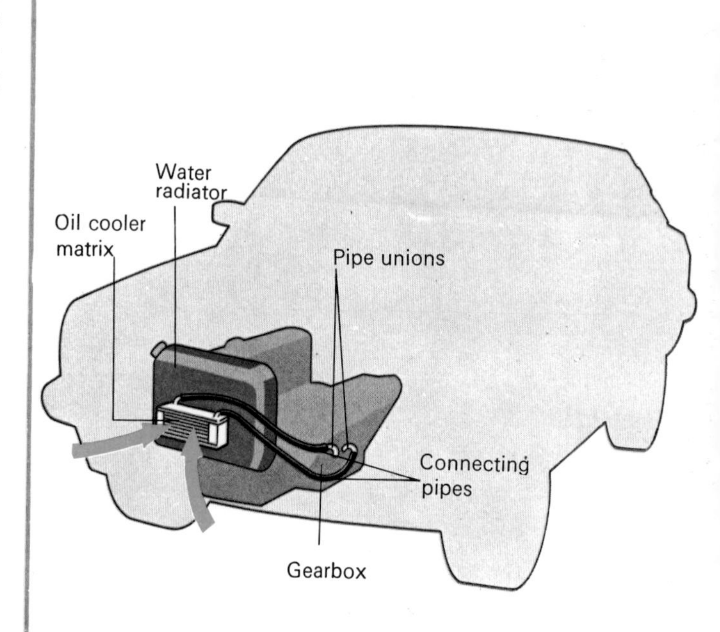

Nigel Osborne

2 A typical layout for a transmission oil cooler kit when in place on a conventional front-engined car

Do not, however, be concerned if there is no thermostat included in the kit as automatic transmissions do not suffer the same harmful effects as those which occur when engine oil is overcooled (see pages 177 to 182). Do not be misled by the use of the term "fluid" either as your specific kit will have been tested for its suitability on the type of gearbox to which it will be fitted.

How a transmission fluid cooler works

The chief component of a transmission fluid cooler is the matrix, which is a type of radiator similar to those employed in water cooling systems. The matrix is mounted at a point on the car where it will be exposed to as much ram-effect from the airflow as possible. Clearly this is usually at the front of the car (fig. 2).

A feed pipe and a return pipe, plumbed into the gearbox fluid flow, connect the matrix to the gearbox. Fluid leaves the gearbox sump by means of the feed pipe, flows to the matrix to be cooled by the airflow and then flows back to the gearbox along the return pipe.

Most automatic gearboxes have provision for connecting the two pipes in the form of blanking plugs or a by-pass pipe on the casing. Where no such provisions exist, it may be possible to drill and tap the casing but this is something which should only be done when specified.

On some gearboxes it is also necessary to divert or replace some of the internal piping made accessible by removing the sump casing. The fluid will then be directed to the cooler via the blanking plug connections instead of flowing directly back to the sump. This chapter describes the procedure for modifying the pipework on the well-known Borg-Warner 35 model automatic transmission but the general principles apply to most automatic gearboxes. The instructions provided with individual cooler kits will give more detailed instructions for the transmission fitted to your particular model of car.

Initial inspection and preparations

Before you start to fit the fluid cooler, an initial inspection must be made to determine whether or not your gearbox has

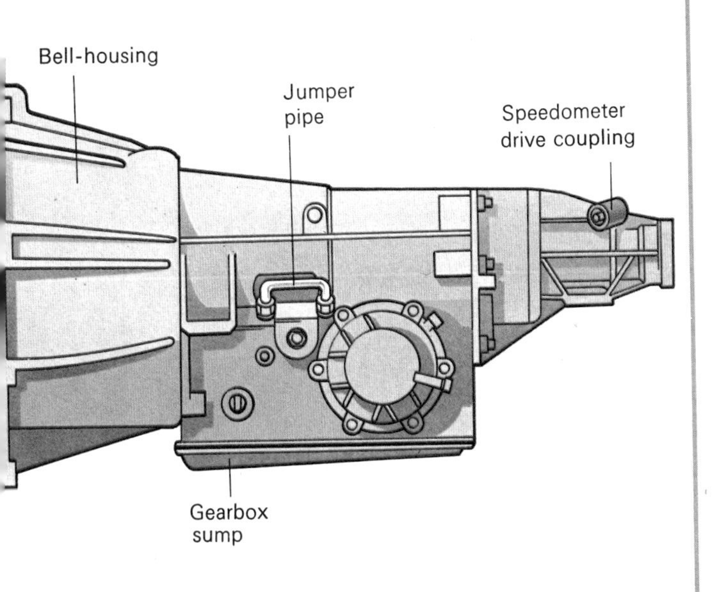

3 If fitted, you will find the jumper pipe mounted on the side of the transmission in front of the identification plate

4 With the car jacked up and securely supported on ramps or axle stands, disconnect the battery as a safety precaution

provision for connecting the piping. Jack up the car and support it on axle stands, disconnecting the battery (fig. 4) as a safety precaution. On the Borg-Warner gearboxes there will usually be two blanking plugs at points A and B as shown in fig. 20 or a pipe, known as a "jumper" pipe (fig. 3), connecting them. If you cannot find either the plugs or a pipe, the casing will have to be drilled and tapped. For this you will require a hand drill together with an 11 mm (7/16ins) bit and a $\frac{1}{4}$ x 18 NPS or NPSF tap.

When you actually come to fit the cooler kit, the car must be kept supported on the ramps or axle stands, with the battery still disconnected. If the blanking plugs or the jumper pipe are readily accessible from underneath, make sure that you give yourself ample working room below the car. Where they are obstructed by the floor pan, remove the carpet from the transmission tunnel inside the car. Next, unbolt the cover plate which gives access to the fluid filler pipe. The blanking plugs or the jumper pipe should now be readily accessible to you and work can proceed but remember that patience and cleanliness are essential.

Because you will be working inside the gearbox, it is absolutely essential to have clean working surroundings, free from dust or grime. Make sure that you also have a supply of fluff-free rags close to hand to cope with any unexpected dirt or fluid spillage and several sheets of clean paper on which to lay temporarily removed components.

One final precaution, well worth taking to avoid accidentally contaminating the gearbox at a later stage, is to blow through the cooler matrix and the rubber connecting pipes with compressed air. This job is best done using a garage air line and it will ensure that any foreign matter left in the kit components is expelled. Always ask for permission before you do this.

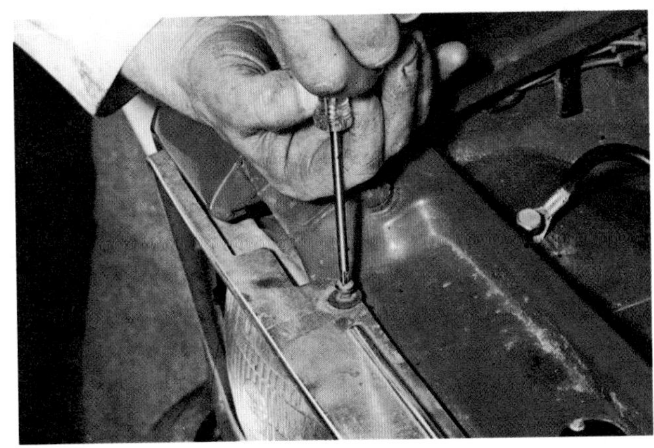

5 If you are going to fit the cooler matrix between the grille and the radiator, undo the fixing screws and then remove the grille

6 Before drilling any holes or disconnecting anything else, check that the matrix will fit neatly into position

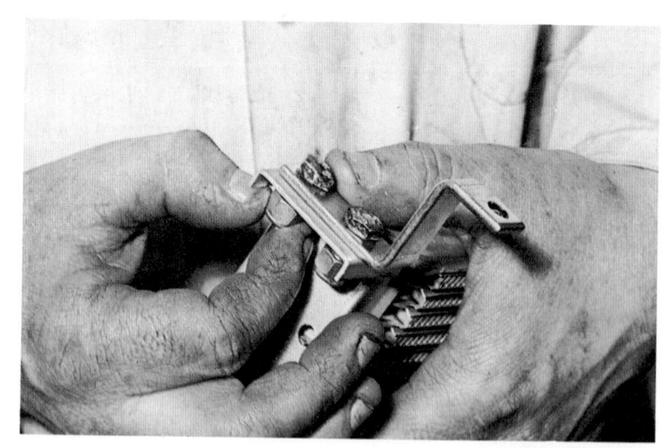

7 Connect the matrix to the brackets supplied with the kit. On some cars, you may be able to use existing radiator brackets

8 Once you know where you are going to drill, mark the position of the holes using a centrepunch and hammer

9 After checking that the drill bit is large enough, drill the holes for the mounting bracket bolts

10 On cars where you need to remove the transmission sump, first take out the drain plug. This particular unit is on a bench

Mounting the cooler matrix

The cooler matrix must be mounted where it can receive as much ram-effect airflow as possible. Some kit manufacturers will specify a certain position for a particular car in order to take advantage of existing brackets, such as those for the radiator. Where no such instructions are given, it will be left to your discretion.

In this case, choose a site near the front of the car, well exposed to the airflow, where the matrix can be bolted directly to the bodywork. On front-engined cars, the panel between the radiator and the grille (figs. 5 to 8) is a suitable place, but if there is not enough room, below the front valance is a good alternative. If you are in any doubt at all about where to position the matrix, contact the kit manufacturer for advice.

Once you have chosen a site, bolt the matrix to its

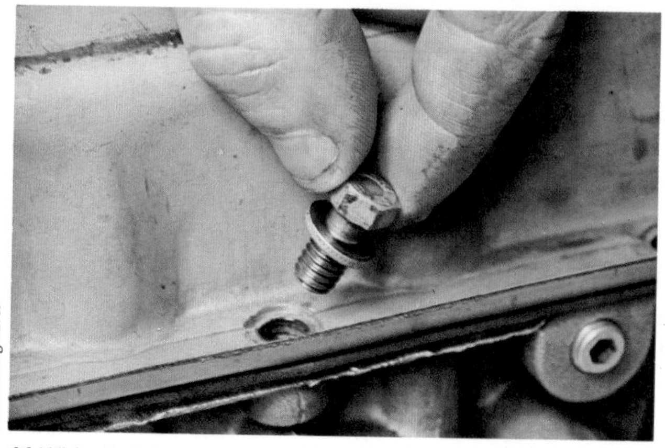

11 With all of the transmission oil drained, remove the bolts around the rim of the sump which secure it in position

Nelson Hargreaves

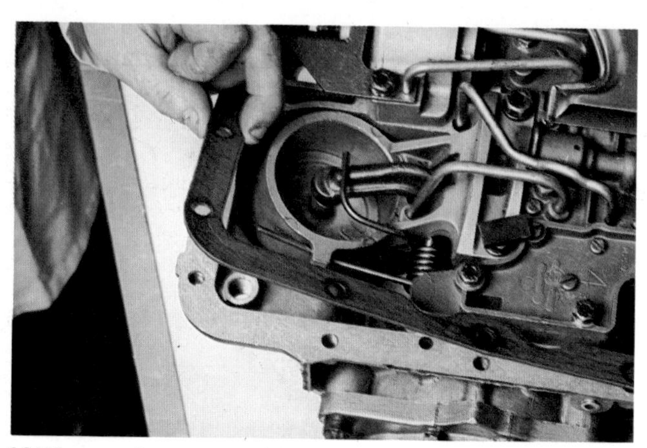

12 When you have removed the sump, peel off the old gasket. Fit a new gasket when you re-fit the sump to the transmission

brackets and then use the assembly as a template to mark the drill holes. Carefully drill the holes large enough to accomodate the mounting bolts supplied with the kit (fig. 9) and then bolt the unit in position. At the same time ensure that the route of the pipe connections will not be obstructed in any way whatsoever.

Where the kit instructions specify the use of existing brackets, mount the matrix accordingly. Do not forget to re-tighten any loosened bolts or screws.

Removing the gearbox sump and internal piping

The next stage, where this is necessary, is to remove the gearbox sump and re-arrange the internal pipework. This will divert the fluid flow to the cooler pipe connections. Start by cleaning around the area of the gearbox drain plug. Now place a suitable container (not food) underneath the gearbox, remove the plug (fig. 10) and allow all the fluid to drain out. With the gearbox completely drained, undo the bolts securing the sump (fig. 11) and remove it. Follow this by thoroughly and carefully cleaning the whole area around the exposed part of the gearbox to guard against the entry of any potentially harmful dirt and remove and discard the old gasket (fig. 12).

Before you go any further, study the diagram shown in fig. 13 and familiarize yourself with the various parts of the gearbox. Identify the front servo apply pipe, the front servo release pipe, the rear servo pipe and the rear clutch pipe. These simply push-fit into their respective locations and all of them must be removed. Carefully pull them out, lay all of them on a sheet of clean paper, cover them with more paper and put them in a safe place.

Refer again to the diagram in fig. 13, identify the magnet fitted to the bolt head at the rear of the exposed area. Pull it off and thoroughly clean away any metal particles that may have adhered to it. Put the magnet to one side of the previously removed pipes.

Still using fig. 13, identify the cable cam located in the front off-side corner of the exposed area. Now release the cable from the cam by carefully freeing the retaining nipple that holds it in place. You are now ready to remove the valve block (fig. 13), which is a complete assembly bolted to the fluid pump above it.

Referring to fig. 13, undo the three fixing bolts which hold the valve block and then gently lower it away from the gearbox. Put the valve block assembly with the other dismantled components, between clean sheets of paper.

Now refer to the diagram in fig. 14, which shows how the exposed area of the gearbox should look with the valve block removed. Identify the four pipes protruding from the engine end of the gearbox fluid pump. It may be that one or more of the pipes has already been pulled out with the valve block in which case you should retrieve the assembly and note which pipe this is.

The reason why all four pipes have to be removed may not be immediately apparent, especially as only the converter outlet pipe is actually replaced (even this is not necessary if a "dog-leg" type of outlet pipe is already fitted). In fact, because the pipes can become slightly displaced as you remove the valve block, removing them is the best way of ensuring that they are re-fitted correctly.

Starting on the nearside, pull out the front pump outlet pipe; label it and then lay the pipe down on clean paper. Moving across, repeat this operation for the next pipe, which is the converter fluid inlet. The next pipe in line is the converter fluid outlet. If your gearbox has an external jumper pipe (fig. 3), the converter outlet pipe will be

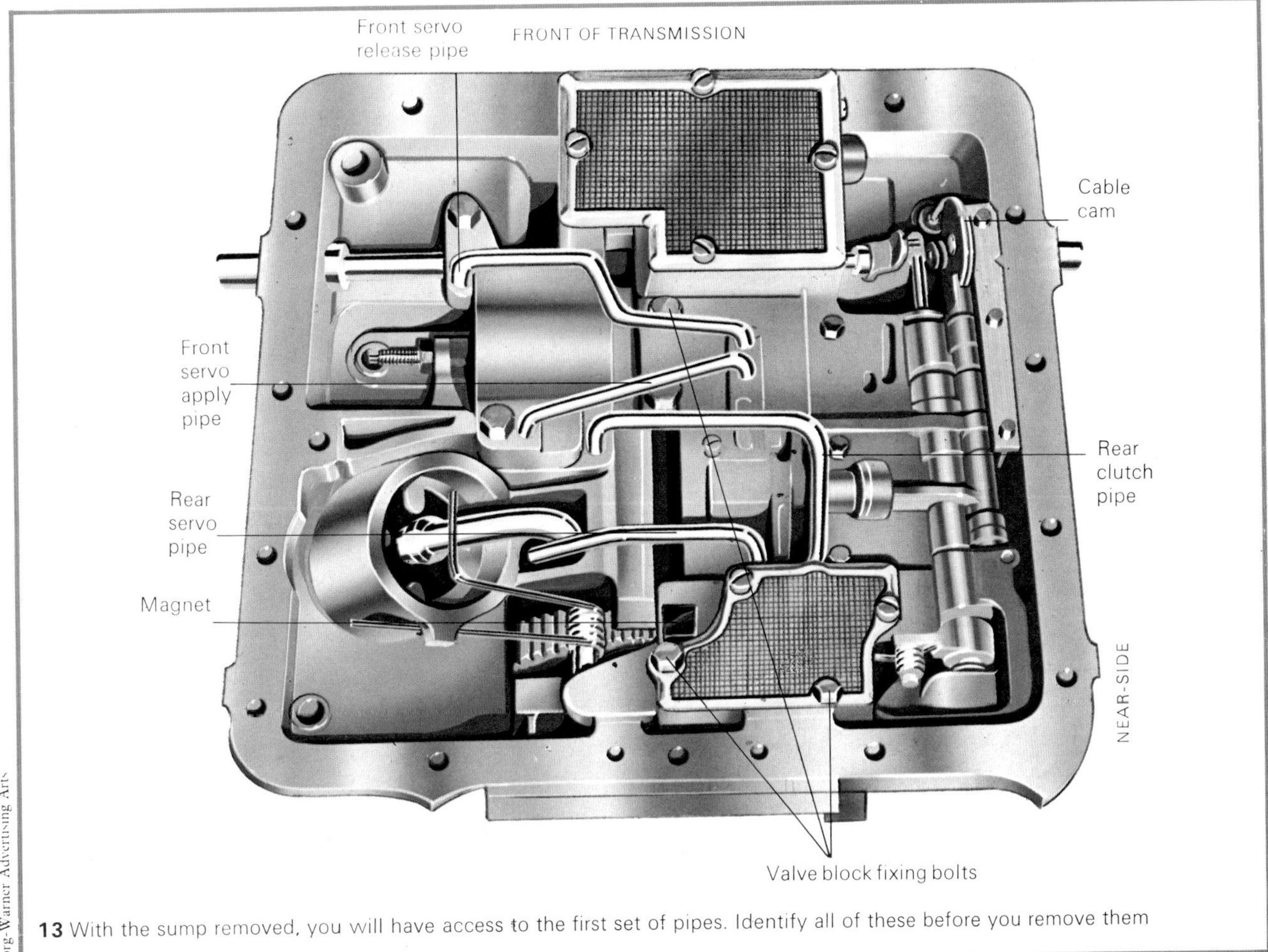

13 With the sump removed, you will have access to the first set of pipes. Identify all of these before you remove them

FRONT OF TRANSMISSION

Front pump inlet

Converter fluid outlet

Cable

Converter fluid inlet

Front pump outlet

NEAR-SIDE

Borg-Warner Advertising Arts

14 Access to the second set of pipes is gained by removing the valve block. This may pull the pipes from their locations

15 Unscrew the dust plug from the inlet and outlet necks of the matrix. Do not do this earlier in case dirt enters the necks

16 Next, screw the metal connecting pieces into position making sure that you will be able to connect the pipes to them

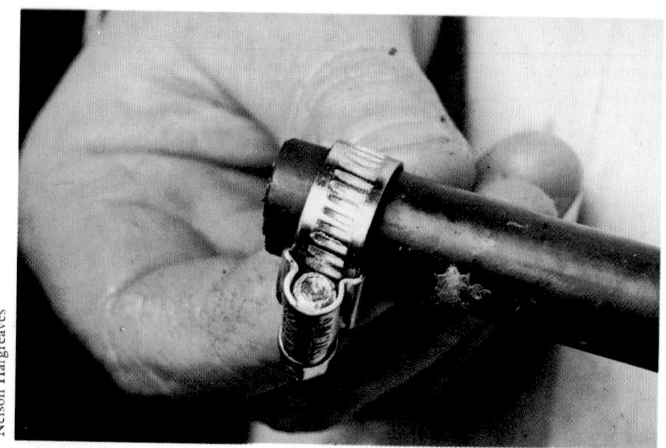

17 After cutting the pipe supplied with the kit in half, slip a hose clip loosely over one of the ends

18 Push both hoses on to the metal connecting pieces and secure them in position by tightening the hose clips

Nelson Hargreaves

"dog-legged" in shape and will run to a boss at the nearside front (engined) corner of the exposed area. In this case, pull out both ends of the pipe and put it with the others. On gearboxes with no jumper pipe, the converter outlet will be a straight pipe similar to the two described above. Where this is so, pull it out, label it and place it with the others.

The last of the four pipes to be pulled out is the front pump inlet pipe. As you are pulling it out, however, take care not to lose its "O" ring seal, which is shown in detail in fig. 27. Once removed, label the pipe and place it to one side with the others.

If you experience problems with fluid dripping down through the converter outlet pipe hole, which is the third from the near-side, block the lower end of the pipe and temporarily re-fit it to stem the flow.

Connecting the matrix

At this stage, the matrix can be connected up. If metal connecting pieces are provided, start by screwing these on to the inlet and outlet necks (figs. 15 and 16). Slip a hose clip over one end of both rubber pipes (fig. 17), press the pipes on to the connecting pieces (fig. 18) and tighten the clips securely. In some kits, there are no metal connections and the pipes clip directly to the matrix.

Moving to the outside of the gearbox, refer to fig. 20 and then unscrew the blanking plugs if fitted. If a jumper pipe is fitted between the two points, remove this by unscrewing the unions (figs. 19 and 20). Screw the two new unions supplied with the kit into the threads exposed by the removal of the plugs or the jumper pipe. Follow this by screwing the two right-angled connections also provided on to the other end of the unions (fig. 21).

Run the rubber connecting pipes from the matrix to the gearbox, making sure that they are nowhere near the engine exhaust manifold or pipe. If there is a possibility of them fouling moving parts, tie the pipes back at suitable points using wire. At the gearbox connections, cut the pipes to length with a sharp knife. Fit two more hose clips on the end of each pipe, press them on to the metal connections and tighten (figs. 22 and 23); it does not matter which way round they go. As with the matrix connections, the gearbox connections (fig. 24) in some kits vary from those described above. The fitting procedure, however, remains similar.

Gearboxes without blanking plugs or a jumper pipe

Some of the Borg-Warner 35 gearboxes do not have blanking plugs or a jumper pipe. In this case, follow the

19 If your gearbox is fitted with a jumper pipe, such as this B-W 65 model, remove it by undoing the two brass unions

20 Lift the jumper pipe away from the gearbox. On cars without a jumper pipe, you may find two blanking plugs here instead

21 Screw the two right-angled connections into position. Ensure that you point them in the right direction

22 If you smear some petroleum jelly on to the connections it will facilitate pushing the pipes into position

23 After fitting a hose clip over the pipes, push them on to the connections. Remember to tighten the hose clips

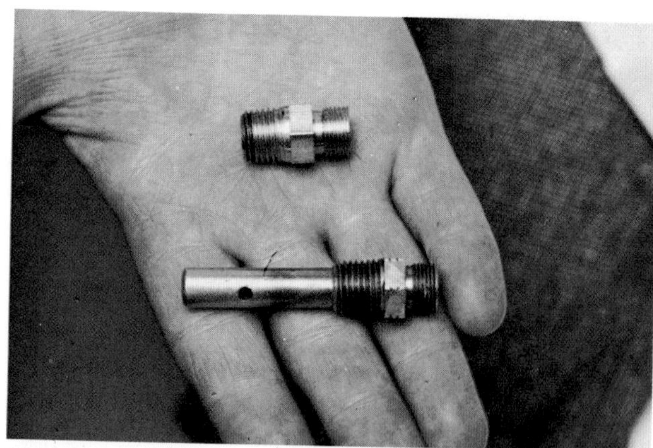

24 If you cannot fit the matrix above crankshaft level, you will need a check valve, shown here, for the transmission

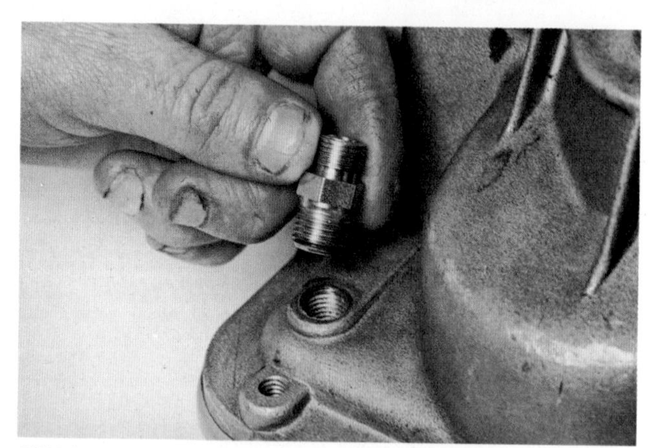

25 If there is no provision for connecting the piping, you will have to drill and tap the casing and fit a union sold with the kit

26 To fit the "dog-leg" pipe supplied with the kit in place of the converter outlet pipe, place it in position and tap it gently

Nelson Hargreaves

27 When re-fitting the front pump inlet pipe, make sure that you also re-fit the "O" ring seal around its base

connecting procedure up to the point where the gearbox connections are screwed in. Looking into the exposed part of the gearbox, you will see two bosses in place of the blanking plug or union threads. Carefully drill through the bosses from underneath, using a manual drill and the recommended size of drill bit, until you break through the outer casing. This may take some time. Next, still using a manual drill, tap the holes to the recommended size. Clean away all swarf and dirt with a rag and check that no other internal parts have become contaminated. With the holes carefully drilled and tapped, you can proceed to connect up the pipes (fig. 25).

Modifying and re-fitting the internal piping

The internal piping will only have to be modified if your gearbox has no external jumper pipe. Where this is the case, discard the original converter outlet pipe (fig. 14) and take the replacement "dog-leg" pipe from the kit. Fit one end of this new pipe into the outlet pipe hole in the oil pump body and push the other end into the boss holding the matrix feed pipe adaptor, as shown in fig. 26. The pipe will locate inside the adaptor to form a fluid-tight seal but you may need to tap it gently into position.

If your gearbox has an external jumper pipe you need only to re-fit the dog-leg converter outlet pipe previously removed. Again, you may need to tap it gently home.

On all of the Borg-Warner 35 model gearboxes, the next step is to re-fit the front pump inlet pipe into its location on the pump (fig. 27). Make sure in this case that the "O" ring seal is still in its correct position. Follow this by re-fitting the remaining converter inlet and pump outlet pipes in their respective holes. Make a final check to ensure that the piping is securely in position and then refer back to fig. 14.

Following the diagram, re-locate the valve block assembly (fig. 13), making absolutely sure that the three straight pipes locate in their respective holes on the upper side. Screw in the three retaining bolts and, using a torque wrench, tighten them down to a torque of 0.3 kg/m (5ft/lb).

With the valve block in position, re-fit the cable mentioned above into its cam by once more sliding back the slide valve. Next, reposition the cleaned magnet on the bolt head (fig. 13). The front servo apply and release pipes, the rear servo pipe and the rear clutch pipe can now be re-fitted into their locations.

Finally, clean the sump casing and, taking a new gasket, re-fit the casing, tighten the bolts enough to seal it.

Completion and checking

To complete the job, re-fill the transmission with the correct amount and grade of fluid. Both this and the position of the filler plug should be specified in the driver's handbook but if in doubt ask your local dealer.

Next, lower the car to the ground, re-connect the battery pull the handbrake on as hard as possible and chock the front wheels. Select "N" on the gearbox and start the engine, running it for about five minutes at normal idling speed and select "P". Increase the idling speed fractionally and run the engine for a further three minutes. While you are doing this, make a thorough examination of all the unions and hose connections to check for fluid leaks. If the rubber pipes to the matrix feel warm when touched, it will prove that fluid is flowing satisfactorily through the matrix itself and that the job has been done properly.

Once you have finished checking for leaks, retain "P" and keep the engine running. Now re-check the gearbox fluid level and top up as required, taking care not to over-fill it. Replace the transmission tunnel cover and the carpets.

Improving the engine fan

The standard cooling fan, driven by the engine via a fan belt, has long been regarded as the simplest and most reliable way of preventing the engine coolant from boiling. In fact it is noisy, rather crude, often unreliable, and runs whenever the engine is going, even though it is rarely needed. A modern and far more efficient alternative is the thermostatically-controlled electric fan, which can be fitted as an accessory to most cars. It switches on automatically whenever it is needed, is quiet and improves the engine's performance in a variety of ways.

Considering its price, it is one of the most useful accessories available to the DIY car owner.

Many motorists are surprised when they learn that for some 90 per cent of the time their engine-driven cooling fan is not needed. During normal motoring the ram effect of air blowing through the radiator is enough to keep the coolant from boiling. Only a lengthy hill-climb or prolonged idling in a traffic jam are likely to raise water temperature to a point where fan cooling is necessary. The rest of the time your fan is an encumbrance, keeping the engine below its optimum working temperature and making it less efficient.

Apart from overcooling your engine, the engine-driven fan absorbs power. It is driven via a belt and pulleys by the crankshaft, and the fan therefore drains away some of the power available at the flywheel. Ironically, this drain becomes greater at higher speeds, when the fan is hardly ever needed. The power loss varies from car to car, but is rarely less than 5 bhp and can be as much as 15 bhp. Every car manufacturer knows that engine-driven fans are inefficient, but they are still fitted to the majority of cars because they are cheap and simple.

Today several manufacturers are fitting fans designed to operate only when they are needed. Peugeot have for many years fitted an engine-driven fan equipped with a magnetic clutch to some of their models. The clutch is controlled by a thermostat which actuates it when the water temperature demands. A more common device is the thermostatically-controlled electric fan, completely separate from the engine. Among the cars which have them fitted as standard are the Leyland Allegro and Princess, Chrysler Sunbeam and Alpine, Citroen CX, Renault 5, Simca 1100, all Ferraris, and the VW front-wheel drive range.

Electric fans offer several proven benefits. Besides releasing more power and keeping the engine at a higher and more efficient temperature, they enable you to use less choke on cold starts as the cold engine is no longer being cooled by a fan which is permanently on. Electric fans therefore save petrol, although exactly how much varies with the type of car and use. It would seem that most cars show savings of around 1.5 km/l. Noise is certainly reduced. Electric fans are quiet when running and the difference is especially noticeable on those cars fitted with notoriously noisy engine-driven fans.

Electric fans as accessories

Thermostatically-controlled electric fan kits are available to fit nearly every car which does not have one fitted as standard. Exceptions are cars with air-cooled engines, such as the VW Beetle and Citroen GS, and cars with rear-mounted engines like the Renault R8/10 and the Hillman Imp. In the UK, there are two firms making fan kits—Kenlowe and Wood & Jeffreys. The Kenlowe fans illustrated

1 The Kenlowe electric fan kit comes complete with brackets, wire and connectors. It should not be necessary to buy any extra parts

2 The first step is to remove your original cooling fan. On this Mk II Jaguar, the fan had to be slid out from underneath the car

3 Because the new fan will be mounted in front of the radiator, the grille must be unscrewed or unbolted for access

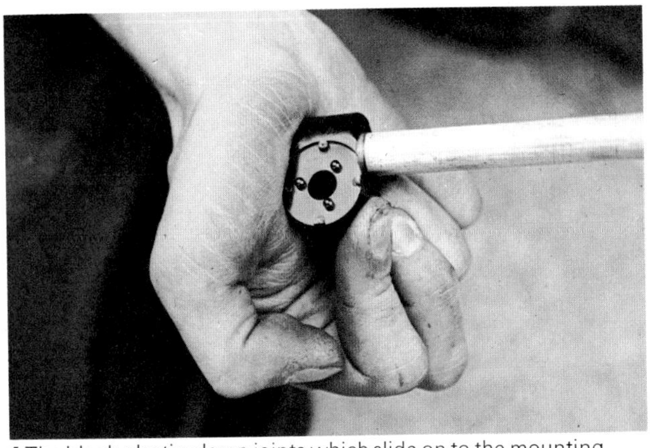

4 The black plastic clamp joints which slide on to the mounting brackets are not tightened until the whole assembly is in place

come complete with fitting brackets, wire and connectors. They are tailored to suit individual cars and for this reason you must give adequate details of your vehicle when ordering. State the make, model and year of your car; whether it has manual or automatic transmission and also whether it is to be used for towing and continental touring. In some cases, where an engine is likely to be under strain, it is recommended that the original fan is retained or twin fans fitted. In Australia, a Melbourne company, Davies Craig Pty., Ltd., and Smiths Industries make similar units to those of Kenlowe and Wood & Jeffreys.

Preparations

Fitting an electric fan is a relatively straightforward job and you will not require any special tools. In a few cases,, however, certain components have to be replaced or substituted, so you should make sure that you buy them before you start the job. On some cars, it will be necessary to remove the radiator in order to fit the fan. This work is covered fully in the next chapter (see page 215). On all cars, it will be necessary to remove the radiator top hose, and it is advisable to check whether yours is in good condition before you start. If it is not, replace it or you may have trouble with leaks. Also check your radiator pressure cap. If it is more than two years old, replace it.

Installing the Kenlowe fan falls into three general stages —fixing the fan unit in place, fitting the thermostat control and setting the thermostat. It is at the first stage that most variations for individual cars are encountered. On the majority of in-line engined cars, the fan goes between the grille and the radiator and is known as a "blower". In some cars there is not enough room to do this and the fan must instead go between the radiator and the engine. In this position, it is referred to as a "suction" fan. Leyland transverse-engined cars, having side-mounted radiators, also require suction fans, but they are fitted between the radiator and the wheel arch/wing valance. Air is then drawn from the engine compartment and over the radiator. Fitting a suction fan is described in detail in the next chapter.

Fitting a blower fan

To fit a Kenlowe blower fan start by removing the old fan. Then bolt the pulley back on to its mounting, using either washers or shorter bolts to take up the space occupied by the fan. On the VW K70 and some Saab 95 and 96 V4 models, the fan and pulley are moulded together as an integral unit. If this is the case, saw the fan blades off the pulley and replace it. On all cars, the next step is to replace and tighten the fan belt.

In order to gain more working space, you should now remove the radiator grille (fig. 3). The fan unit is held in position by two metal brackets and these are attached to the motor backing plate at one end and the car bodywork at the other, by plastic universal joints. This arrangement is designed to give maximum flexibility (fig. 5). Exactly where the brackets bolt on to the bodywork is left to the discretion of the fitter unless otherwise specified, but there are a few points worth bearing in mind. The two brackets should ideally be fixed on different panels to give the unit maximum rigidity. The fan itself must be 6 mm ($\frac{1}{4}$ins.) from the core of the radiator, and unless otherwise stated, it should be central. Remember also that you may have to drill two 8 mm (5/16ins.) diameter holes to accept the bracket fixing bolts and allow sufficient room.

The best procedure for fitting is to slide two of the plastic joints on to the longer ends of the L-shaped brackets and bolt the brackets on to the motor back plate. Slide the other two joints, which will hold the bolts to the bodywork, on to the other end of the brackets and rest the fan loosely on the end of the motor spindle. Offer up the whole assembly to the radiator and take into consideration the following points:

1. The fan must be the correct distance from the radiator and must be free to rotate. Take into account the lip round the core.

2. The fan must not protrude enough to prevent the bonnet closing or the bonnet catch from operating.

3. There must be room to drill the bracket holes.

Note the best position for the bolt holes, marking them if possible. Remove the fan assembly and drill the holes (fig. 6). The next step is to make sure that the fan is securely fixed to the motor spindle and that it is the right way round. There will be a red label on the fan blade and you should follow the instructions on it carefully before tightening up the fan. This is done by tightening the cross-head screw on the fan firmly down on to the flat of the motor shaft. Test it for movement. You should allow a gap of about 1.5 mm (1/16ins) on the spindle between the fan and the motor. Finally, try pulling the fan off the spindle to check whether or not it is tight. Do not remove the metal balancing clips which may be fitted to the fan blades.

Once more offer up the fan/motor assembly to the radiator. Insert the bolts and washers supplied through the plastic joints on the brackets and secure them to the holes you have just drilled. Next, adjust the assembly until the fan is in the correct position and tighten all fixings—the cross-head screws on the four plastic clamps and the four bolts holding them and the brackets to the fan motor and bodywork (figs. 7 and 8).

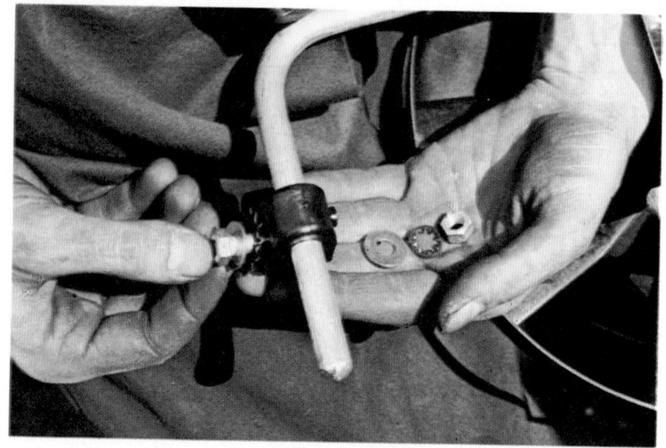

5 The bolts and washers connecting the clamps to the car bodywork and the fan unit must be assembled in the correct order

Nelson Hargreaves

6 You may well find two holes to take the bracket bolts somewhere on the panels behind the grille. If not, drill them at this stage

7 The fan assembly loosely bolted in place. Check the clearance between the fan and the radiator and then tighten the bolts up

8 The final step is to tighten the screws on the bracket clamps. Check the clearance again and that the assembly is quite rigid

Fitting the thermal control unit

The thermal control unit supplied with all Kenlowe fans is the sensor which activates the fan when it is required. The most delicate part of the unit is the copper sensing element and capillary, which should be handled with care. Start by draining off approximately half the water from the radiator and make sure that any heater control valves on the dashboard are turned "on". Next, disconnect the rubber top hose from the radiator, having first loosened its wire or Jubilee clip, and pull it off the radiator neck. Take the copper sensor and pass it into the neck as far as possible without bending it (fig. 11). The sensor should reach the top of the radiator itself, except on the Ford Cortina Mk III. This car has a right-angled neck on the top hose; just leave the sensor in the neck.

At least 25 mm (1ins) from the sensor, bend the capillary back in a U so that it comes back over the radiator neck. Lay the rubber seal on the neck against its end rim (not over it) as in fig. 9. Seat the copper capillary in the groove on the seal and, holding them both in place with your thumb, carefully slide the top hose back on to the neck (fig. 12). Note that if the top hose is in poor condition you must replace it if you are to avoid future leakages. Do not tighten any clips at this stage.

The control box must now be mounted. This should be done on a side panel as near to the top hose as is practicable, and certainly not on the engine. Use the bracket provided and if there are no convenient bolts to hand, drill a fresh hole and bolt it on (fig. 13), or use the self-tapping screws supplied which require a 3 mm ($\frac{1}{8}$ins) drill bit. The bracket is best mounted vertically. Push the spindle of the control unit up through the bracket, with the capillary at the back facing the bracket, and secure it with the washer and screw collar provided (fig. 14). Follow this by pushing the plastic knob on to the D-shaped spindle shaft. The thermal control unit is mounted near to the top hose so that the copper capillary may be kept coiled as much as possible. In this form it is resistant to vibration.

Next, return to the top hose on the radiator neck, which should still be loose. If it has a wire-type clip fitted, you would be advised to replace it with a Jubilee clip which is far more efficient. Turn the clip round until the worm-drive part is exactly underneath and opposite the rubber seal and the capillary (fig. 15). Tighten it up completely. Top up the radiator and run the engine for a few minutes and check for leaks, tightening the clip further if necessary.

Wiring up and fixing the over-ride switch

An over-ride switch with warning light is provided in all Kenlowe fan kits. This enables you to control the fan manually if required and can be mounted at any convenient point below the dashboard. Use it as a template for the two drill holes. Secure with two self-tapping screws—3 mm ($\frac{1}{8}$ins) drill bit. The wiring diagram (fig. 17) can now be followed and the wires connected up between the switch, control unit and fan motor. Use pliers to crimp the terminal connectors provided in the kit on to the bare ends of the wire. Make sure that the switch is earthed correctly; a dashboard fixing screw is usually the best place. Check also that the control unit is earthed as shown, via the metal bracket. If this is not earthed itself you will have to connect the earth wire to some other point that is.

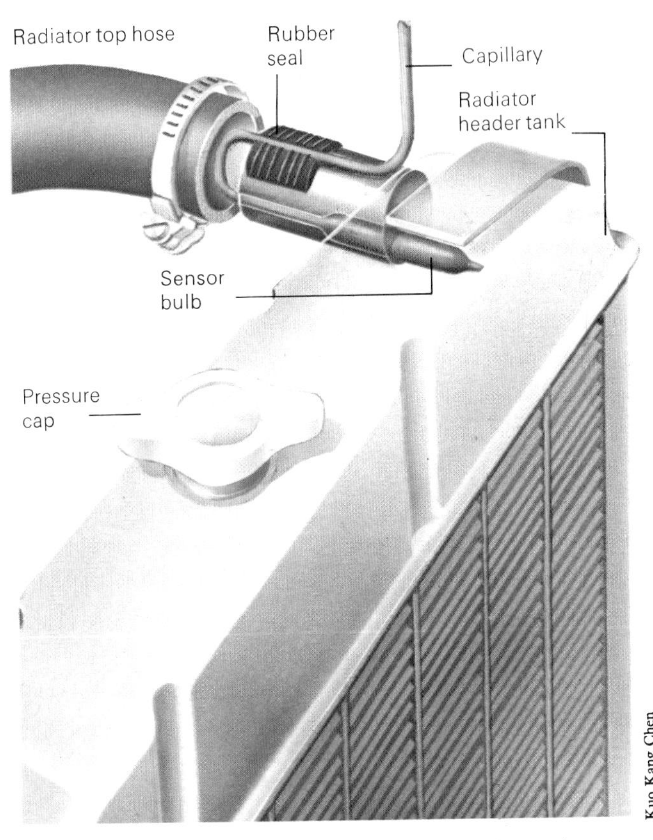

9 The sensor bulb assembly is the most delicate section on the majority of thermo-coupled fan systems and it is advisable that patience is exercised when incorporating it into the cooling system of the car. In particular, the capillary tube and the copper sensing element should be handled with great care during the installation process. The positioning of the rubber seal, capillary connector and the hose clip are crucial if subsequent water leaks are to be avoided and the sensor must be secured in such a position, on the majority of cars, that it is sited with the top section of the radiator header tank.

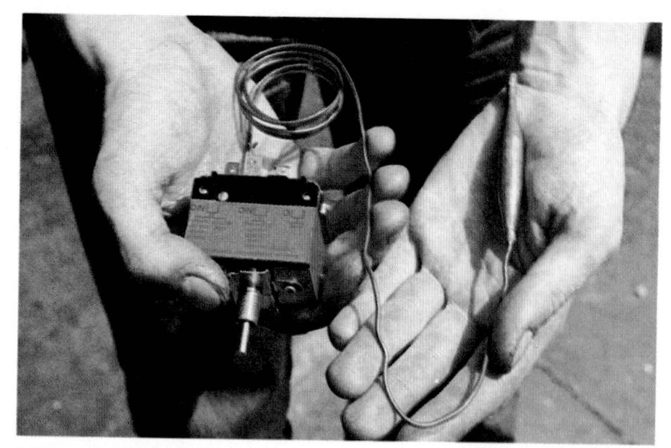

10 The thermal control unit, copper sensing bulb and capillary. The capillary should be left coiled to absorb engine vibration

The wire marked "live supply" must be connected to either a spare terminal or to the spare accessory terminal on the ignition switch. The ignition switch side of the fusebox is sometimes easier to reach. Make sure, by inspecting the fusebox carefully, that the circuit you connect into is a 35amp one (16amp on Ford and European cars). Make sure that you use the correct terminal shrouds as shown in figs. 20 to 24 and that the two special ones for the motor are pushed on properly to guard against water entry.

If you have not already done so, check that the fan is rotating in the right direction by switching it on when everything is connected. Looking from behind the fan motor, blower fans should rotate anti-clockwise, suction fans should go clockwise. Change the wires over on the motor terminals if the fan is found to be going the wrong way (fig. 25).

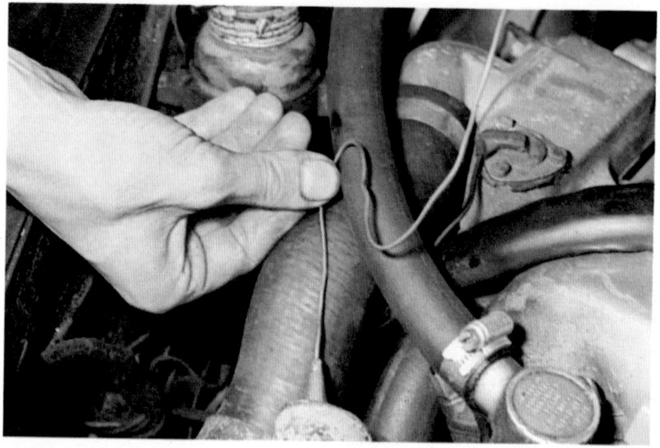

11 Having removed the radiator top hose, insert the sensing bulb into the header tank pipe as far as it will go without bending

12 Next, lay the rubber seal on the pipe, run the capillary along the groove in it and then carefully slide the top hose back on

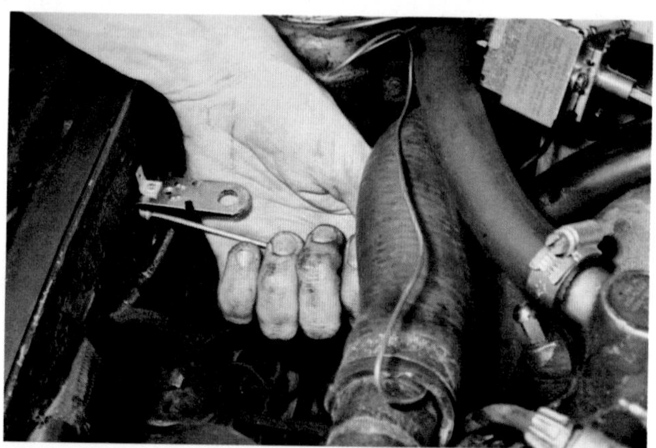

13 Secure the control unit bracket to an earthed part of the car bodywork, as near to the radiator header tank as possible

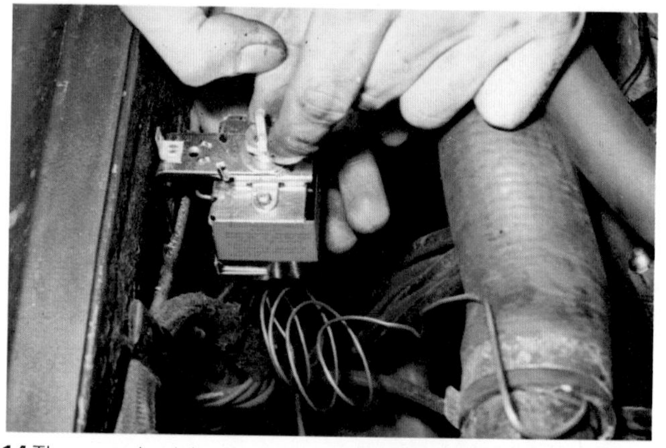

14 The control unit itself can then be fixed to the bracket. Do not forget the plastic knob which presses on to the spindle

15 With the control unit secured, align the top hose clip so that the worm drive is exactly opposite the rubber seal and tighten

Nelson Hargreaves

16 The manual over-ride switch is screwed into the dash panel; if it is insulated, a separate earth connection will be required

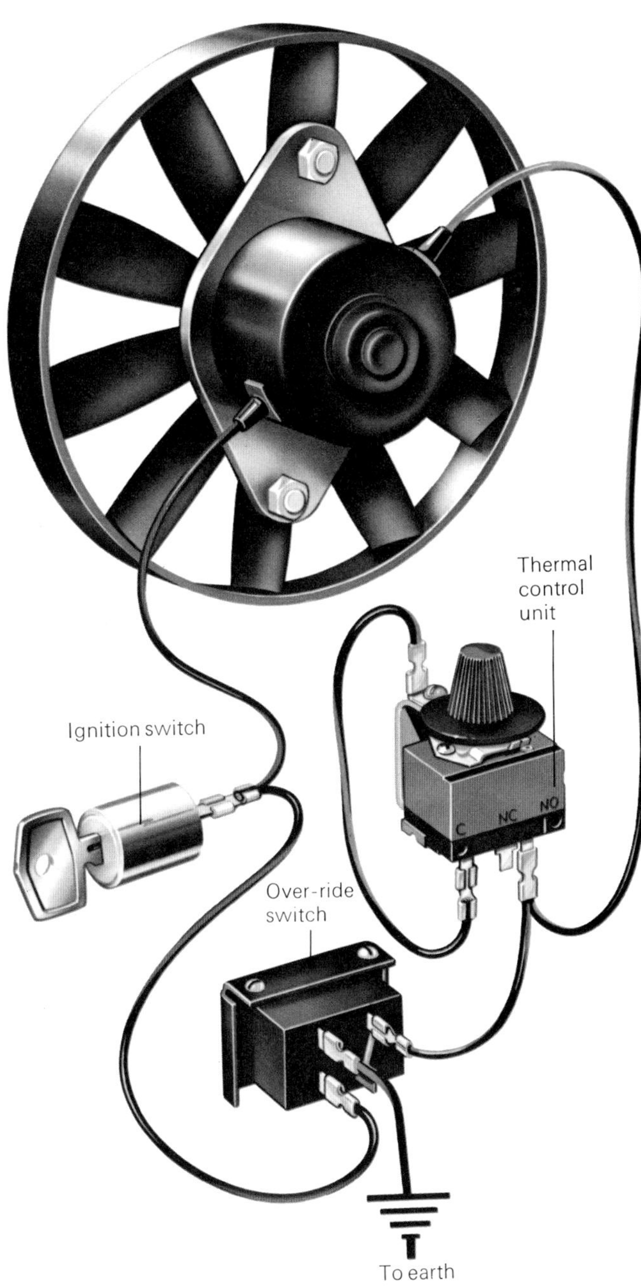

17 A complete Kenlowe fan system, showing how the component parts wire up. The ignition switch has been taken as the live supply

Setting the fan

When you have made absolutely sure that everything is working correctly, that there are no leaks, that the fan is firmly fixed in place and that the manual switch is off, the thermal control can be set. Start by turning the knob on the control fully clockwise, to the "H" position. Now start the engine and watch the temperature gauge rise. In terms of degrees of temperature, the movement of the needle from "cold" to "normal" on the gauge is not in proportion to its movement from "normal" to "hot". In fact, letting the needle run past "normal" setting on the gauge will only raise the water temperature a few degrees, which is quite safe and highly desirable. The engine will be operating slightly hotter. When the needle has reached the point in fig. 19 and not before, turn the control knob slowly anti-clockwise until the fan comes on. Watch the fan, and if it stays on for longer than four minutes, turn the knob one graduation clockwise again. When the knob is set in the correct position, lock it using the large-head Phillips screw provided (fig. 27).

If your car has no temperature gauge, a slightly different setting procedure is used. Turn the knob to "N" and then a further $1\frac{1}{2}$ graduations towards "H". Now take the car for a reasonable drive and watch for the over-ride switch to light. If it does, stop and set the knob a further graduation towards "H", thus increasing the cut-in temperature. Lock the knob using the screw provided.

Using your fan

The Kenlowe electric fan is a reliable unit, and when you have installed and set it correctly there should be few problems. Sometimes the fan motor is rather tight and will blow a fuse when it is first started up. If this happens, simply replace the fuse with one of the maximum rating—35amp. The only other points to watch out for are deterioration in the condition of the radiator hoses and pressure cap. Both of these components become suspect after about twelve months' use, and should be watched carefully or replaced at this time. Hoses which look sound from the outside may well have rotted away internally and can fail when you least expect them to. Worn out pressure caps reduce pressure in the cooling system and thus allow the coolant to boil at lower temperatures.

Finally, remember not to clutter up your radiator grille with badges and spotlamps. These will restrict ram-effect airflow over your radiator and oblige the electric fan to operate more frequently than necessary.

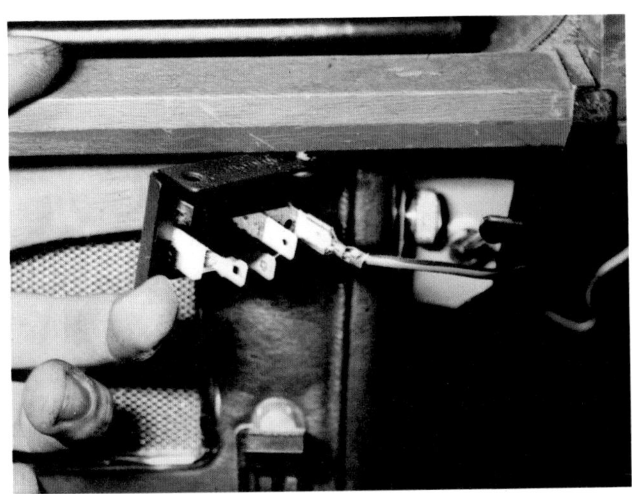

18 In order to gain access to the back of the over-ride switch, it is a good idea to temporarily remove one screw and turn it round

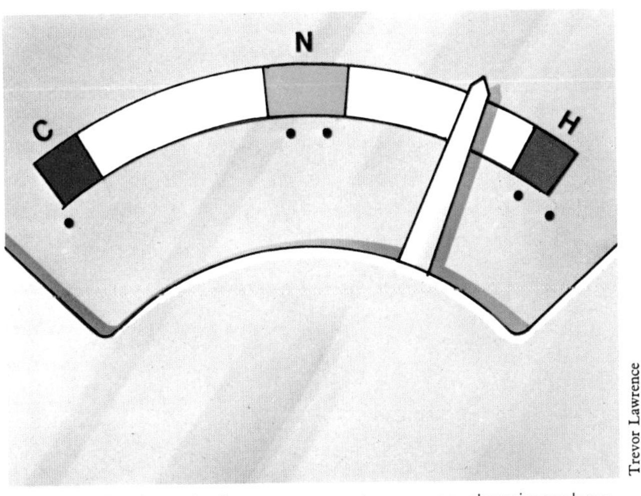

19 The scale of a typical water temperature gauge, showing where the needle should be when the fan control is set to cut in

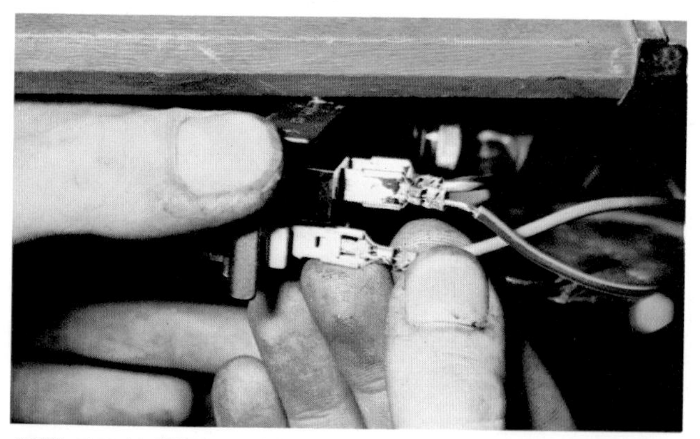

20 The back of the over-ride switch showing the earth wire being connected. The spade connectors are supplied with the kit

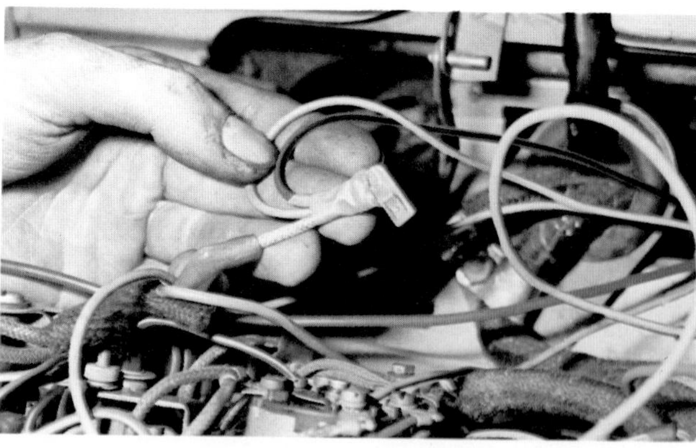

21 If the ignition switch is inaccessible, the live wire can be spliced into an existing one between the switch and the fusebox

22 The small earth lead on the thermal control unit is connected to the tab on the bracket which should itself make a good earth

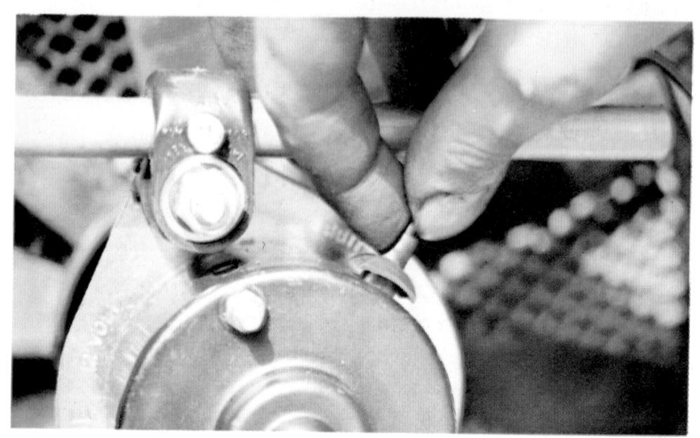

23 Make sure that you use the special terminal shrouds when you connect up the motor. These will help to waterproof the unit

24 Connecting the wire from the control unit to the motor. With everything conected, check which way the fan is rotating

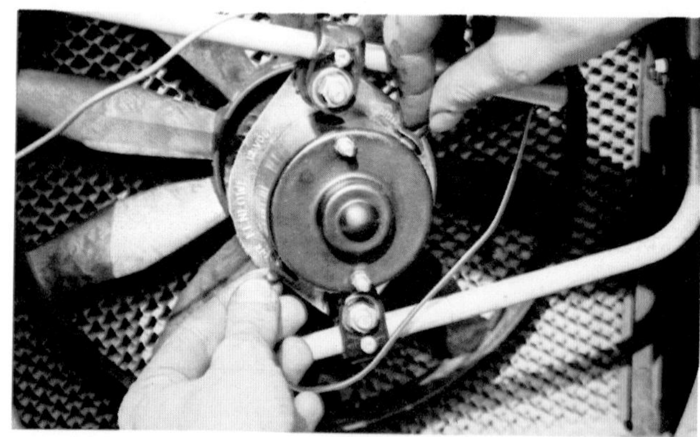

25 If it is going the wrong way, you can change the direction by swapping the wires over, reversing the polarity of the motor

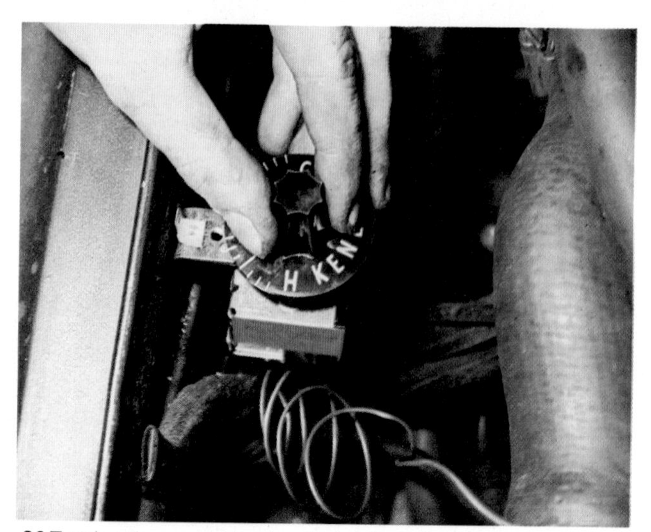

26 Turning the control knob, which will set the fan to cut in at the desired temperature. For clarity, the earth has been removed

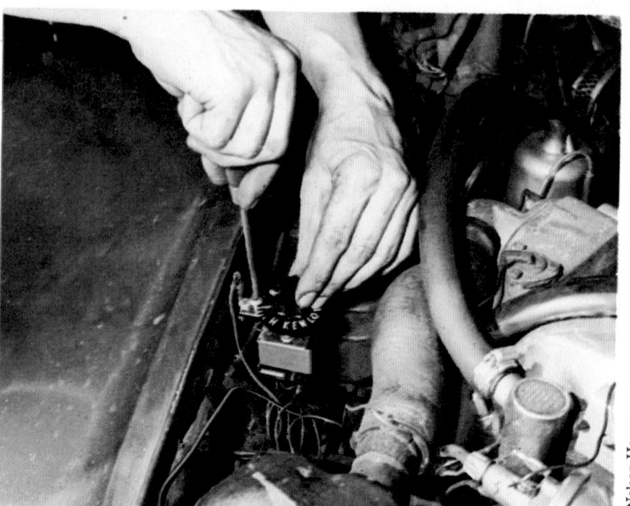

Nelson Hargreaves

27 When the correct setting has been achieved, you can prevent the knob turning accidentally by screwing it down as shown

Non-standard electric fans

On most cars with in-line engines, fitting an electric cooling fan is a simple task. But there are a few models where the work is considerably more involved. Some cars will not accept an electric fan mounted in the conventional position between the radiator and the front grille. Others will do so only after extensive modification. Fitting also calls for extra work on Leyland front-wheel drive cars fitted with side-mounted radiators, where lack of space is the main problem.

The difficulties always arise at the stage where the fan unit itself is being mounted in position. Fitting the thermal control, wiring up and setting the thermostat are basically as described in the previous chapter.

The conventional electric fan works by blowing air over the radiator, rather than sucking it through like an engine-driven fan. On some in-line engined cars, usually because of lack of space between radiator and grille, the electric fan has to work by suction and goes in place of the original fan behind the radiator. A suction fan is also employed on Leyland transverse-engined cars, but is mounted in the nearside wheel arch and sucks air over the radiator from the engine compartment.

With all of the special cases below, it is important to follow the individual instructions given for each car, especially in locating the mounting brackets. The manufacturers have carried out extensive tests to determine the simplest way of fitting their fans and, unfortunately, there are no short cuts.

Special instructions—cars with blower fans

Ford Cortina Mk III: on this car, the radiator has to be loosened to allow the cowl around it to be removed. This in turn provides enough room for a fan to be fitted in the normal way. When removing the radiator, the first step is to drain the cooling system. Disconnect the top and bottom hoses and unscrew the two mounting bolts on either side of the radiator. The plastic cowl for the old fan is also held by these bolts and should be discarded. You can now fit the blower fan by bolting both of its adjustable mounting arms to the lower pressing. This is a panel running across the engine compartment and joining the two front wings. It will already have holes in it to accommodate the bolts. Once the fan has been positioned, you can proceed to re-fit the radiator.

Moskvich: This car has a shutter round the radiator, secured by studs. This should be removed. You must then bolt the two mounting brackets to the two "L"-shaped adaptor brackets provided with the fan kit. These are bolted on each side of the radiator, about two thirds of the way down, using two of the shutter studs and holes.

Morris Marina: The radiator on this car is held on four mountings and has to be moved back slightly to allow a blower fan to fit in front of it. Start by removing the radiator, then take the two rubber grommets found on the lower mounting feet and press them into the centre holes of the "A"-brackets supplied in the kit. Next, bolt the brackets to the mounting feet locations in the car to form two new radiator mountings 25.4 mm (1ins) further back towards the engine. Replace the radiator, fitting the dowels on the

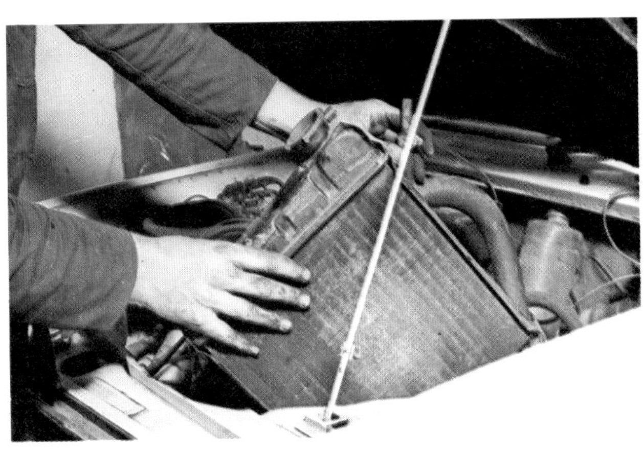

1 Unfortunately, you have to remove the radiator when fitting an electric fan to one of the Leyland transverse-engined models

2 With the radiator and the original fan removed, there is plenty of room to replace the fan pulley and re-tighten the fan belt

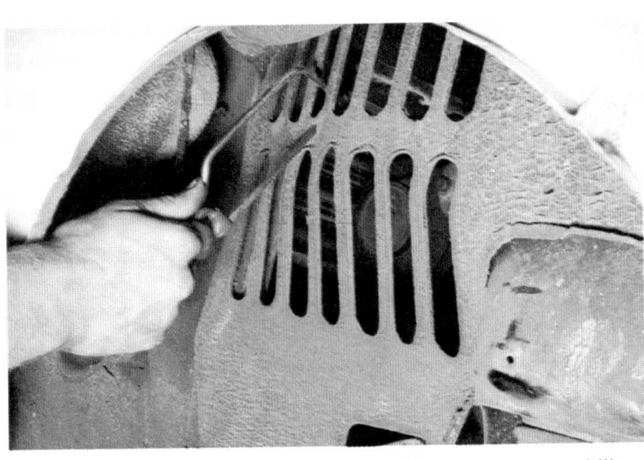

3 When sawing through the wheel arch grille, you can use a drill or padsaw on the thin slats and a hacksaw on the thicker ones

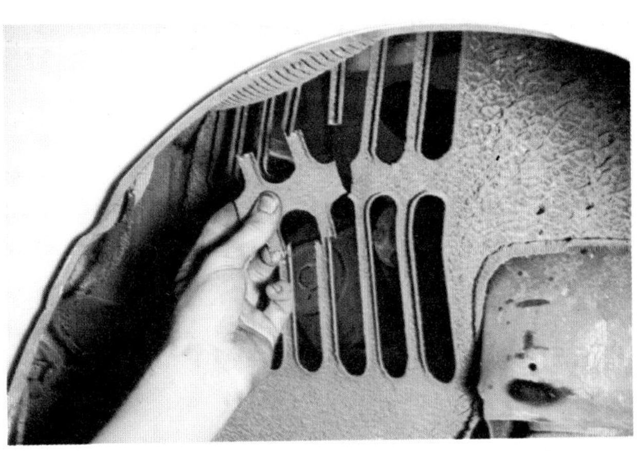

4 Carefully remove the sawn-out section and discard it. It is a good idea to file down any jagged edges left around the hole

Nelson Hargreaves

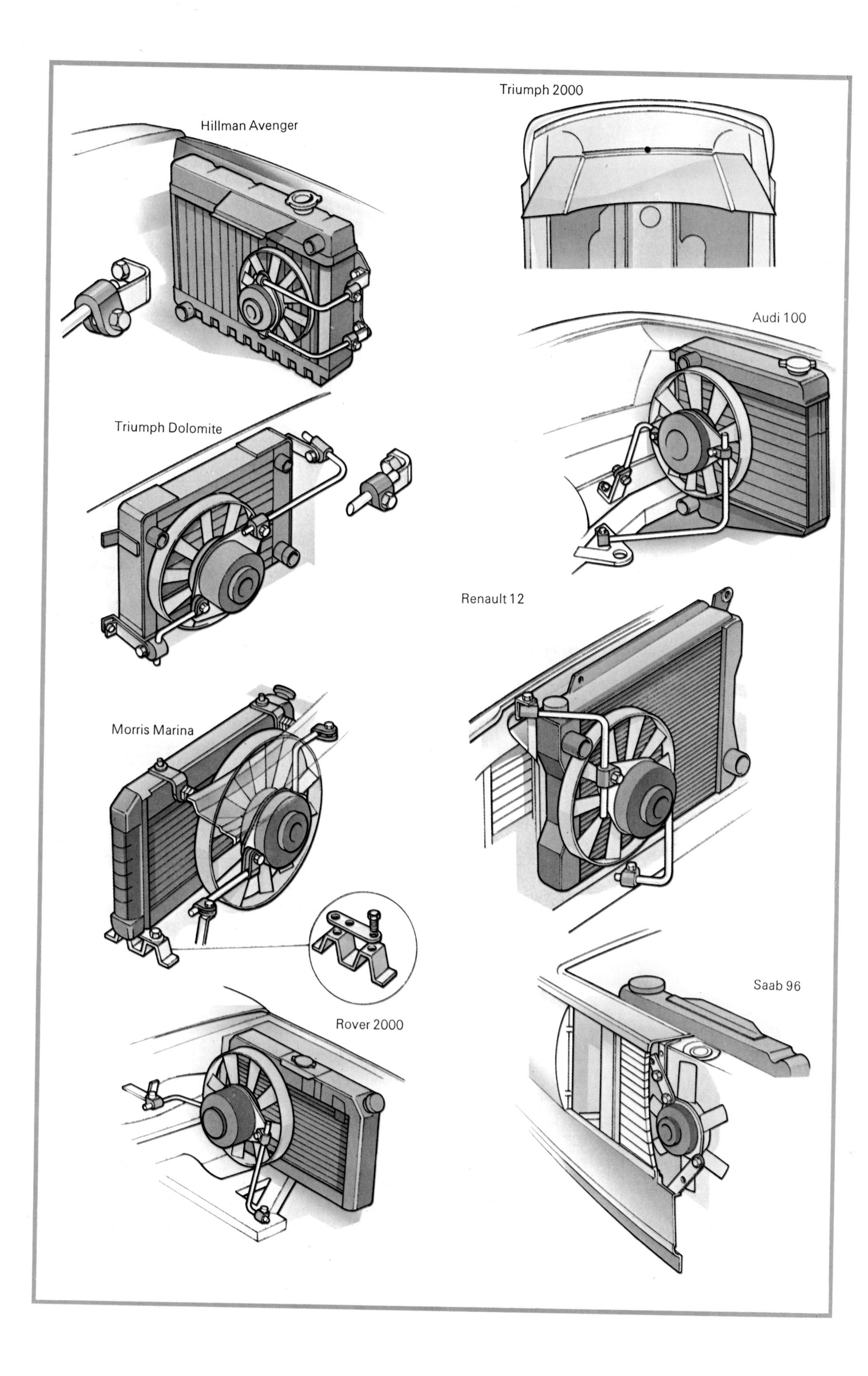
Hillman Avenger
Triumph 2000
Audi 100
Triumph Dolomite
Renault 12
Morris Marina
Rover 2000
Saab 96

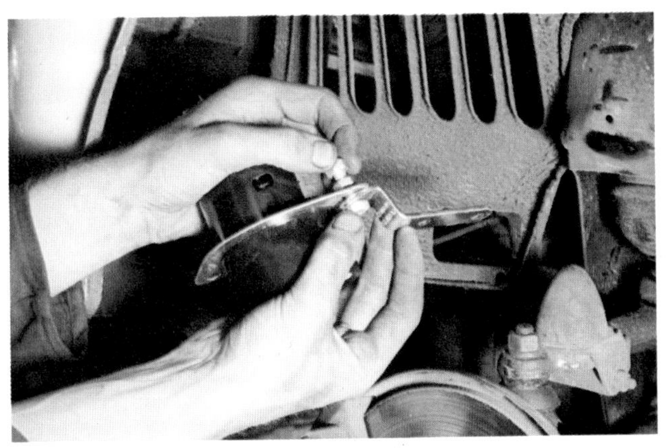

6 On this Mini 1275GT, there is only one mounting bracket. This is bolted to the motor loosely, leaving some room for adjustment

7 The other side of the motor bolts directly to the arch. Locate the fan assembly and mark the positions of the bolt holes

8 Drilling the bolt holes. You will have to drill the two nearest the front of the car from inside the engine compartment

9 When connecting the motor wires, feed them through the plastic cover and the shrouds before crimping on the spade connectors

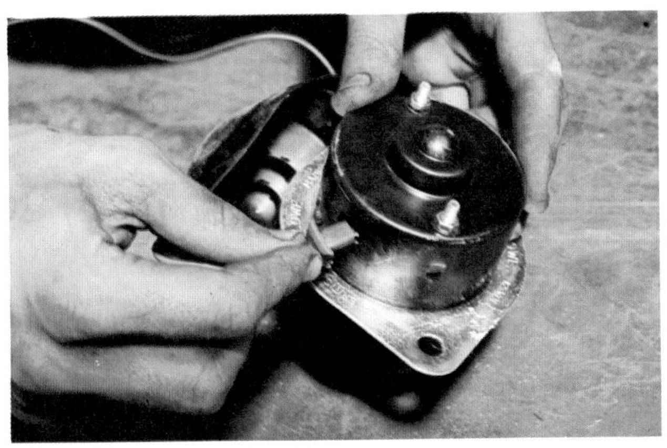

10 The shroud terminals must fully cover the connectors before you join them to the motor to form an extra waterproof seal

11 Before you test that the fan is rotating the right way, make sure that the blade is securely screwed on to the motor spindle

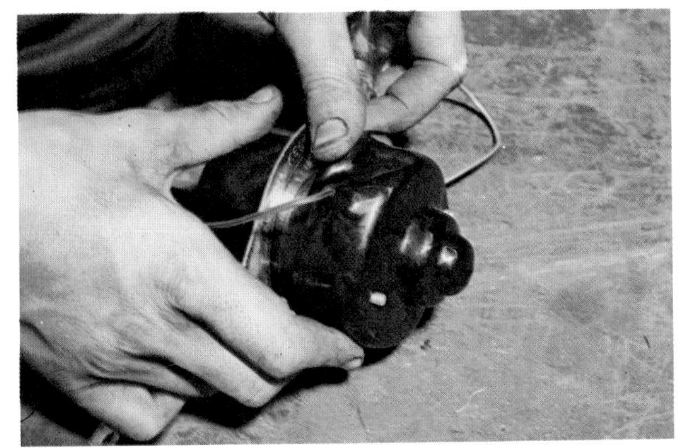

12 Having completed the test and changed the wires if necessary slide the plastic waterproof cover right over the motor body

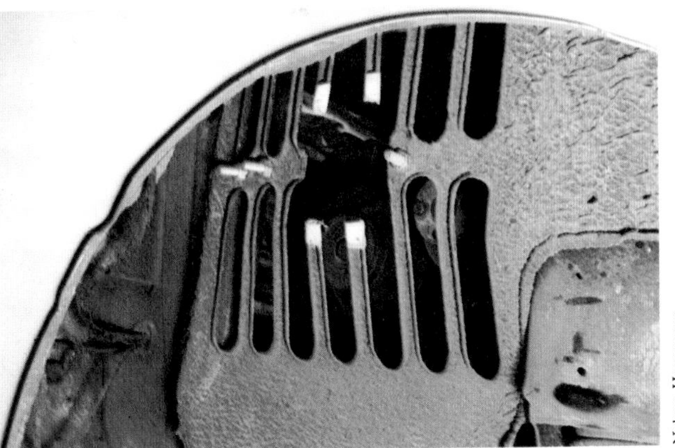

Nelson Hargreaves

13 The motor bolts in position on the wheel arch. The first set of nuts have been screwed down, turning the bolts into studs

bottom fitting into the grommets in the "A"-brackets. The top of the radiator is secured with two long bolts which are provided and these have four nuts each on the shafts to act as spacers between the radiator and the front panel (fig. 5). On the Marina, it is also important to mount the fan mounting brackets as shown in fig. 5.

Saab 95 *and* 96 *V*-4: Some earlier Saab models have rubber radiator securing straps which may have to be lengthened to give sufficient clearance for the fan unit. To do this, obtain a small metal plate for each strap about 25 mm (1ins) square. Drill two holes in each plate, bolt the plates to the straps and then bolt the new assemblies to the original strap fixing points (fig. 5).

Bolt the fan mounting brackets as shown in fig. 5, and pay special attention to the clearance between the fan blades and the bonnet catch with the bonnet down. If your car has a headlamp wiper unit installed behind the grille, you will have to dispense with it to make way for the fan.

Triumph 2000/2500, *Stag*, *Dolomite and Toledo* 1300/1500. There is a small drain hole on these cars in the middle of the front panel under the bonnet fig. 5). This must be blocked, by sticking the two adhesive discs provided, to either side. Otherwise drained water will drip on to the fan motor.

Special instructions—cars with suction fans

The following cars are all designed to take Kenlowe suction fans, which are mounted between the radiator and the engine. The differences between fitting a blower fan and fitting a suction fan are confined solely to the mounting of the unit itself. Installation of the thermal control, wiring up and setting are the same.

Initial preparations for mounting the fan unit are also identical to those for the blower units. The radiator must be part-drained and the top-hose removed. The next step is to unbolt the original fan from its pulley and then to replace the bolts to hold the pulley in place. Use washers to take up the space left by the fan blade. The electric fan unit is assembled in the normal way, by bolting the two mounting brackets to the motor backing plate with the black plastic clamps provided. You should then follow the instructions for your particular car as outlined below.

Unless otherwise stated, there will be no need to drill any holes for the mounting brackets—suitable ones will be found on the car.

Audi 100 *coupe:* On this car the original engine-driven fan is mounted in front of the radiator. It must be removed, together with its pulley and casting, to give maximum air-flow to the new fan behind. It is also particularly important not to clutter up the grille with spotlights or badges which restrict airflow. The Kenlowe suction fan is mounted behind the radiator, alongside the engine. One mounting bracket is attached to the cross-member behind and one fixed to the side panel, using the adaptor bracket provided in the kit (fig. 5). In this case, holes for the mounting brackets will have to be drilled. If your car has disc brake air-intake trumpets behind the radiator which stop the fan being mounted in this position, you must apply direct to the manufacturer for specific fitting instructions.

Chrysler Avenger/Centura: The suction fan is mounted to the left of the water pump (looking from the front of the car) off-set from the middle of the radiator. The mounting brackets have adaptors enabling them to be secured beneath two of the radiator mounting bolts as in fig. 5. Automatic Avengers have a transmission oil-cooler mounted to the right of the water pump. In this particular model the fan can

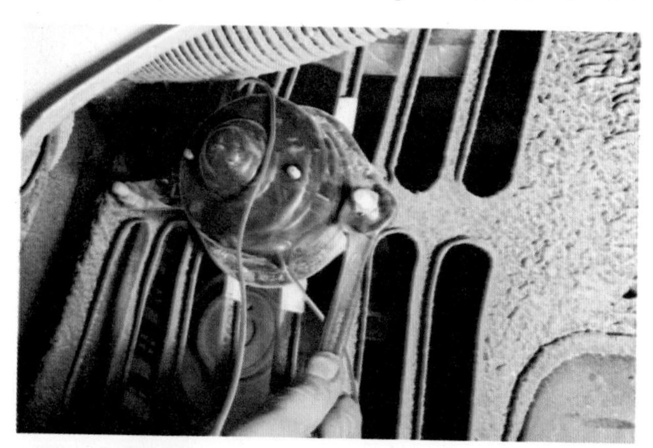

14 Locate the motor and its brackets on to the bolts and tighten down the remaining nuts. The unit should now be firmly held

15 If there are red caps provided in your kit, press them on to the protruding motor shafts to complete the waterproofing

16 Fix on the fan blade from inside the engine compartment. Screw down the fixing screw tightly and then check for fouling

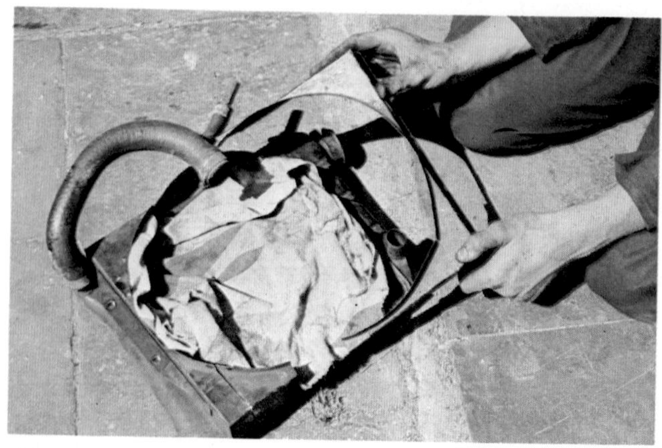

17 To cut down the radiator cowling, start by removing the upper part, held by four bolts. It can then be worked on on the bench

be mounted on the opposite side of the pump.

MGB/C: Mounting the fan on this car is similar to mounting the Avenger fan, except that it is offset to the side of the radiator opposite the generator. The mounting brackets are fixed to the top and bottom radiator mounting bolts on this side. Owing to the lack of space, it is permissible for the fan to extend beyond the radiator by as much as 25 mm (1ins).

Morris Minor/Traveller: Follow the instructions for the MGC but note that the fan is mounted to the right of the water pump as viewed from the front of the car.

Renault 12 *range/R.*15 *TL:* On these cars, the fan is positioned off-centre towards the nearside with the mounting brackets positioned as in fig. 5.

Renault 17 *TL/*15 *TS:* Unfortunately, fitting a fan to these cars is a rather more difficult job and the manufacturer's specialized instructions will be required. Briefly, the radiator must be removed together with the fan cowl if fitted. The timing chain cover must then be replaced by an R.17 TS cover (part no. 7700503974) and gasket, allowing room for the fan to be mounted in the normal way.

Rover $3\frac{1}{2}$ *litre/coupé:* Like the Morris Minor 1000, the suction fan on this car is positioned off-centre, to the right of the water pump. The mounting brackets are also bolted on that side with special adaptor brackets. The top one goes to the panel surrounding the radiator and the bottom bracket to the cross-member underneath it.

Rover 2000/3500 (*old style*): With these cars it is important to mount the fan according to the manufacturer's instructions (shown in fig. 5 for the 2000), otherwise there may be a great deal of vibration. As with other suction fans, the fan is mounted off-set from the centre of the radiator. You should ensure that the motor is not close enough to the water pump to knock against it with the engine running.

Triumph Dolomite 1850/*Sprint:* On this car you must remove the fan and pulley complete by unbolting the casting that holds them on to the cylinder head. Next, drain the radiator and remove all the hoses attached to it except the one at the bottom near the battery. Follow this by undoing the lower radiator mounting bolt, near the horn, and the top one diagonally opposite above the battery. Replace these with the two adaptor brackets supplied and mount the fan as in fig. 5. Replace all the hoses and coolant and finish by fitting the special shortened fan belt provided between the crankshaft pulley and the generator.

Transverse-engined cars

Many transverse-engined cars on the road today have electric fans fitted as standard. Notable exceptions are the Leyland Mini, Maxi, 1100, 1300 and 1800. These cars all have side-mounted radiators, facing the transverse, engine-driven fan on the nearside of the car. The Kenlowe fan fits between the radiator and the wing valance on that side. The original fan is removed and the fan pulley replaced, as with in-line engined cars.

Disconnect the battery, jack up the front of the car and remove the nearside front wheel. The next step is to remove the radiator, the fan belt, fan and pulley (fig. 1). You must then replace the fan pulley (fig. 2). Now turn your attention to the wheel arch and identify the small, slotted grille in it which allows air to flow over the radiator. This must be cut away with a padsaw or hacksaw to allow the fan motor to protrude through towards the radiator (figs. 3 and 4). On the 1800 and Maxi, remove the whole grille. On the Mini and 1100/1300, cut away only the area shown in fig. 22. Next, bolt the two mounting brackets (only one on the Mini Clubman) to the motor backplate as shown in fig. 6.

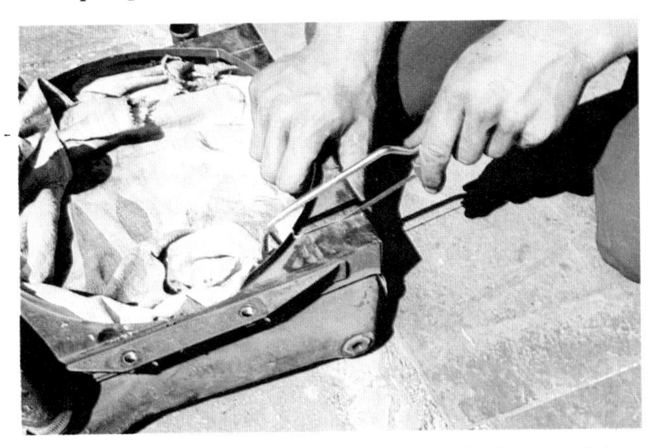

18 You will need to replace it before making the final cuts, which call for the cowling to be rigid. Use rags to protect the core

19 The radiator cowling is made of quite soft metal and it is not difficult to cut through it with a padsaw and hacksaw

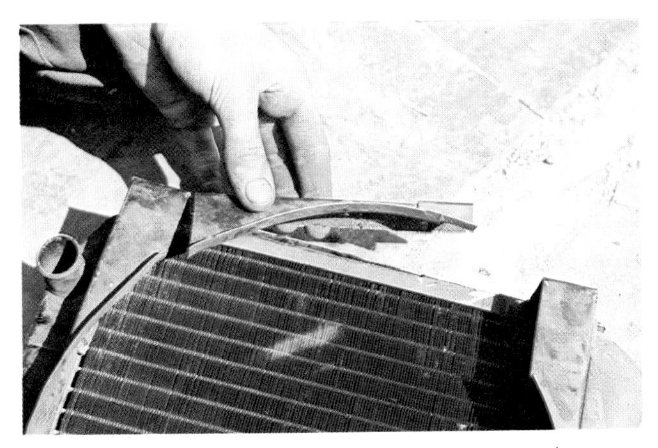

20 The finished job. Before you re-fit the radiator, ensure that the core is free of metal filings, rags and any other debris

Nelson Hargreaves

21 Tightening up the radiator bottom bracket. Make sure you check that the fan blade is not interfering with the core first

Offer up the assembly to the hole in the wheel arch and line up the brackets to suit your particular car. Estimate and then mark (fig. 7) the positions of the bracket or clamp bolts, using fig. 22 as a guide, and drill four (only three on the Mini Clubman) 8 mm (5/16ins) holes in the wheel arch at the appropriate points (fig. 8).

At this stage, the motor must be wired up. Connect two of the shroud terminals provided in the kit to the ends of the two motor wires also supplied and connect them to the motor (figs. 9 and 10). Connect the other ends to the battery terminals and check that the motor is rotating the right way round (fig. 11). If it is not, change over the wires on it. Make sure that the shroud terminals are pushed firmly home, then thread the other ends of the wire through the waterproof cover provided. Push the cover over the motor (fig. 12) and slide the two red caps provided over the protruding motor shafts where they emerge from the now waterproofed motor. The wires can now be left until the final wiring up.

Next, on the Mini, 1100 and 1300, push the bracket bolts through the holes in the wheel arch. Tighten down the first set of nuts to make the bolts into studs (fig. 13). Take up the fan assembly once more and locate it on the studs (fig. 14). Screw down the remaining nuts and washers as shown in fig. 22.

On the 1800, slide the plastic clamps provided on to the metal mounting arms to form adjustable brackets. Bolt one

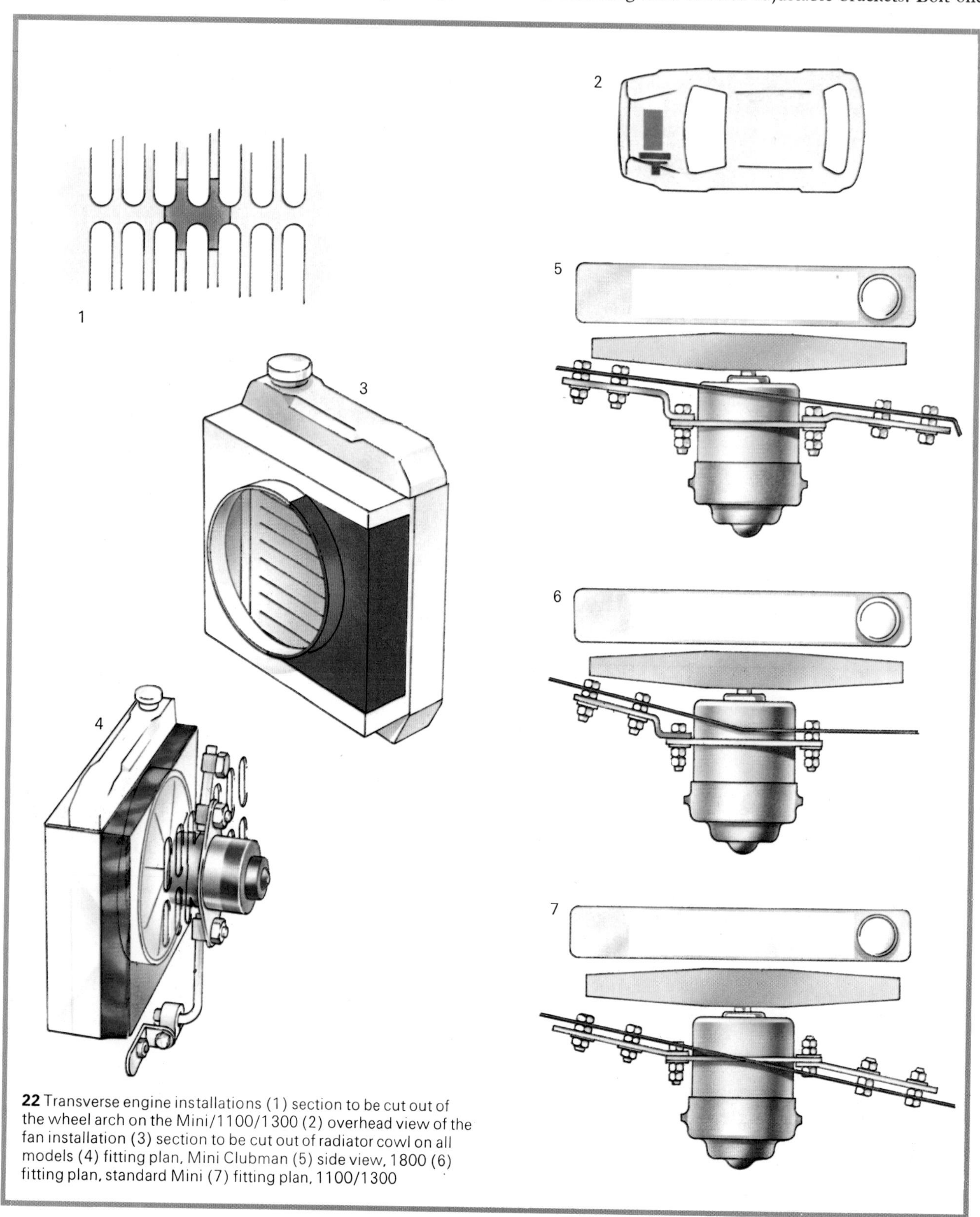

22 Transverse engine installations (1) section to be cut out of the wheel arch on the Mini/1100/1300 (2) overhead view of the fan installation (3) section to be cut out of radiator cowl on all models (4) fitting plan, Mini Clubman (5) side view, 1800 (6) fitting plan, standard Mini (7) fitting plan, 1100/1300

Chris Gillings

end of each bracket to the fan motor, offer up the whole assembly to the wheel arch and bolt it in place (see pages 209 to 214 for complete instructions).

On all cars, small adjustments can be made before fully tightening the bolts or clamps and you should also fit the fan itself at this stage. Make sure that it is the right way round by referring to the instructions on the red label attached to one of the blades. Remember also to allow 1.5 mm (1/16ins) between the blade and the end of the spindle on the motor. After you have checked that the assembled fan is not crooked (refer to fig. 22) tighten the fan locking screw on the spindle (fig. 16) and all the bracket or clamp bolts.

Before re-fitting the radiator, cut away the side cowling as shown in figs. 17 to 20. This is important because it will provide a greater air flow from the front of the car over the radiator and so lessen the need to use the fan.

Twin-fan installations

Several cars with large engines require twin-fan installations. These are mounted in exactly the same way as single fans, using the extra brackets provided in the kits. The most important aspect of twin-fans is their positioning. The fans should go side by side with a gap of 12 mm ($\frac{1}{2}$ins) between them. On no account must they overlap each other. If they extend beyond the area of the radiator core in this position, they must be mounted diagonally across the radiator, still

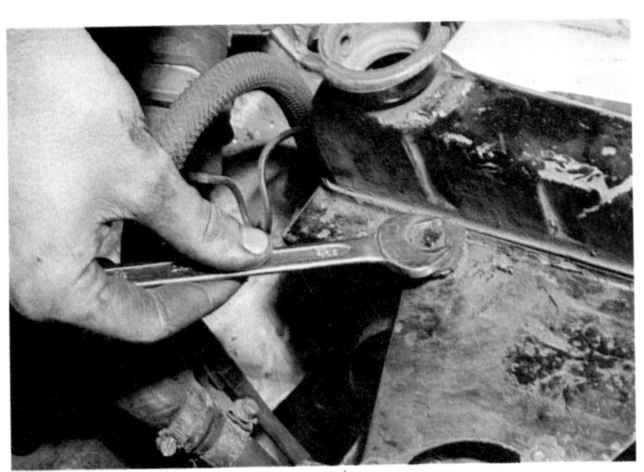

23 Fixing the top bracket. Bits of rubber hose with holes drilled in them are used instead of the old grommets to stop vibration

24 The engine side of the bracket is fixed with two of the bolts on the thermostat housing. Take care not to overtighten them

25 Tighten the Jubilee clip on the bottom hose where it leaves the engine. The radiator end of the hose is hard to reach

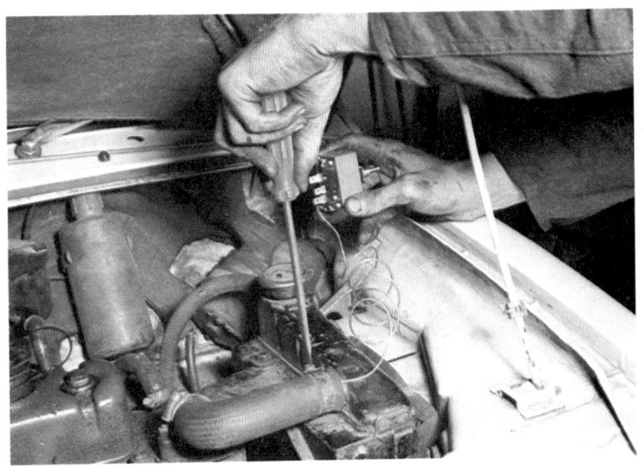

26 With the thermal control sensor inserted into the radiator and the rubber seal in position, tighten the clip on the top hose

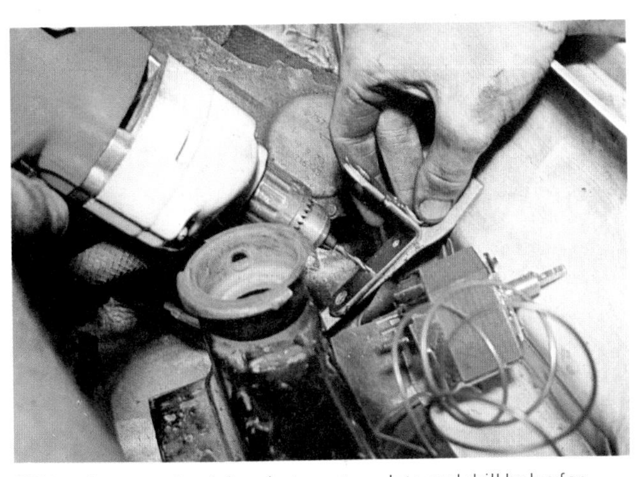

27 Use the control unit bracket as a template and drill holes for the fixing screws. Try to choose a site near the radiator

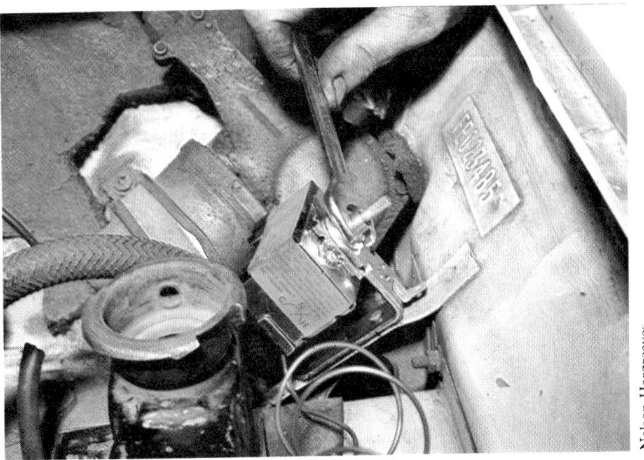

28 Fix the control unit on to the bracket, screwing the half-nut on to the spindle. The copper capillary must run down behind

Nelson Hargreaves

29 To complete the installation, press on the indicator dial and arrange the capillary so that it is coiled and cannot vibrate

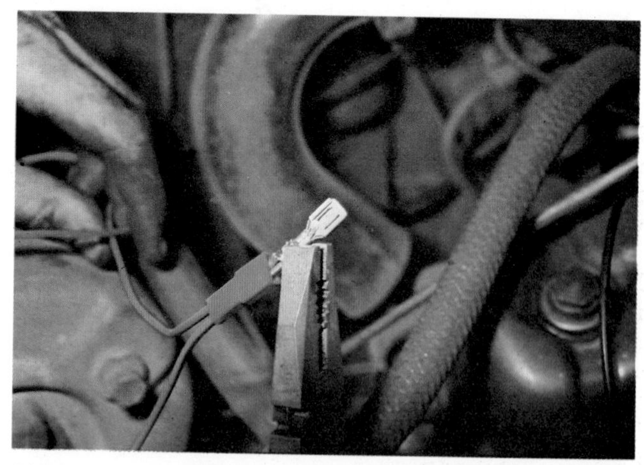

30 Where two wires are crimped to the same connector, remember to feed them through one of the large red shrouds first

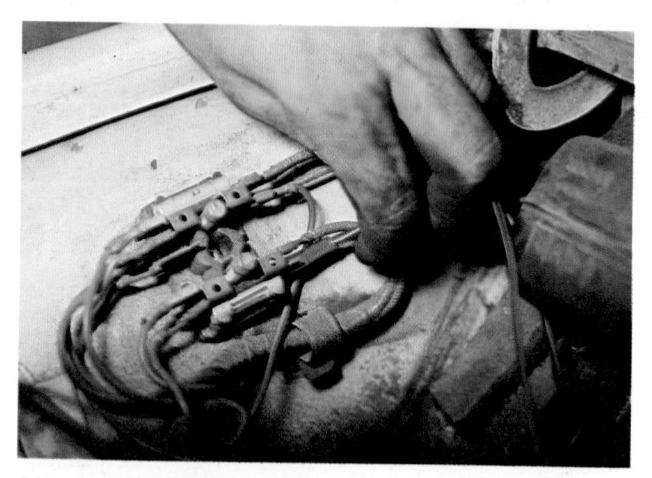

31 Take the live supply to a spare terminal on the switch side of the fuse box. After connecting, tape the wires back to hold them

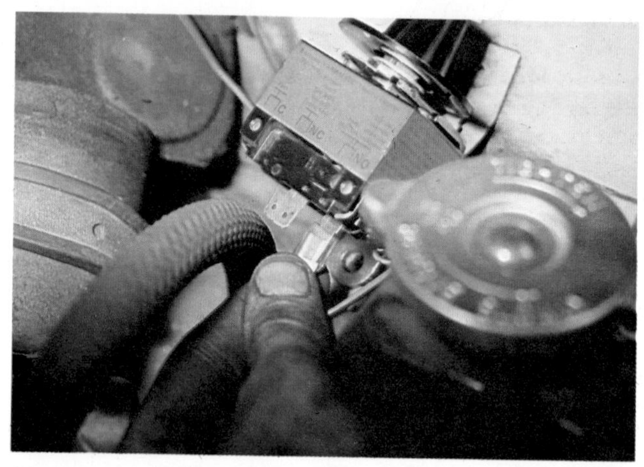

32 The connections at the thermal control unit are made in just the same way. Do not forget the earth wire from the bracket

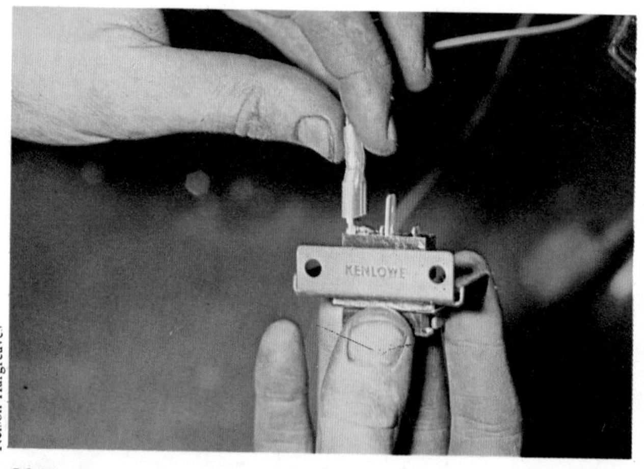

Nelson Hargreaves

33 Finally, connect up the manual over-ride switch. Feed the wire through any convenient hole in the engine bulkhead

34 The switch in place on the fascia. Whenever the fan starts up the warning light comes on, whether the switch is on or off

with the correct gap between them. The higher of the two should be at the same side of the radiator as the top-hose.

Towing and touring

Towing a caravan or trailer, towing in hot climates, and driving in mountainous country all impose a great strain on any car's cooling system. This is further increased if the car has automatic transmission. If your car has a blower-type Kenlowe fan, mounted in front of the radiator, you can put back your original engine-driven fan for this kind of driving. The engine-driven fan will cool the engine under normal conditions, but if it cannot cope at any time, the electric fan is available as a booster. When your towing trip or tour has ended, the engine fan can come off again and you will regain all the advantages of a hotter running engine.

Cars with air-conditioning

Under extremely hot conditions, when a car's air conditioning system is working to full capacity, the condenser located by the radiator will dissipate a lot of heat into the cooling system, so overloading it. The Kenlowe fan should be used in conjunction with the standard engine-driven fan whenever these conditions arise, as it is slim enough to be fitted in front of the condenser.

During the cooler winter months the engine driven fan can be removed as the air conditioner is not in use.

Choosing a basic tool kit

Buying tools can be an expensive business, so it is unwise to go out and buy a large number of expensive tools right at the beginning. Instead, buy only the tools you need immediately, and add to them as you go along.

Never buy really cheap tools. With spanners, for example, the jaws will begin to distort and open out within a reasonably short time—leaving you, in effect, paying for two spanners instead of one. Cheap crosshead screwdrivers imitating the Philips or Pozidriv type will soon have worn heads which damage the ends of the screws. Other cheap tools are liable to snap, bend or rust.

Top quality tools, on the other hand, are fine for professional mechanics, but often unnecessarily expensive for the d-i-y man.

For most jobs, medium-priced tools will prove perfectly adequate, and it is worth looking at Japanese as well as British, American, German or French tools.

At one end of the scale, spanners should be of good quality and in drop-forged chrome vanadium. At the other, the quality of a hammer or a pair of pliers is not so important, so that medium or reasonably low-priced tools will serve quite well.

Spanners

The first thing in buying spanners is to find out what type of nuts and bolts the manufacturer of your car used. This information is unlikely to be given in your car's handbook. So note the make, model, year and chassis number of your car and consult either the manufacturer or a main dealer.

If your car is of British or American design then it is probably assembled with Unified Fine (UNF) or Unified Coarse (UNC) nuts and bolts, for which A/F (across the flats) spanners are required. If it is Japanese or Continental the fittings will almost certainly be in metric sizes.

On some older British cars the nuts and bolts are British Standard Fine (BSF) or British Standard Whitworth (BSW). The same spanners can be used for both types, but two bolts with the same thread diameter will have different-sized hexagonal heads and nuts. So both sizes are usually marked on the spanner—for example $\frac{7}{16}$in. BSF/$\frac{3}{8}$in. Whitworth. Some cars which use mainly A/F sizes still have a few relics in BSF or BSW sizes.

Some modern cars have mixed thread types. Since different parts of the car can be assembled in various countries, it means that a mainly British-made car could have a German gearbox (like some Fords, for instance). In a situation like this A/F spanners will be needed for most of the car but metric should you want to take the gearbox apart.

On some smaller nuts and bolts—particularly those used on electrical units—the threads are likely to be British Association (BA). So, if yours is a British car you will need a spanner to fit these as well.

Open-ended spanners

Open-ended spanners (fig. 1) are probably the most popular and the most versatile spanners, though not always the most efficient. Each spanner has two openings, one at each end of a different size. The sizes usually go up in steps of $\frac{1}{16}$in. or 1 mm and, in most cases, the larger end of one spanner is

1 Open-ended spanners (left) ring spanners (right) a ratchet handle (far left) and a tommy bar, extension and sockets (top)

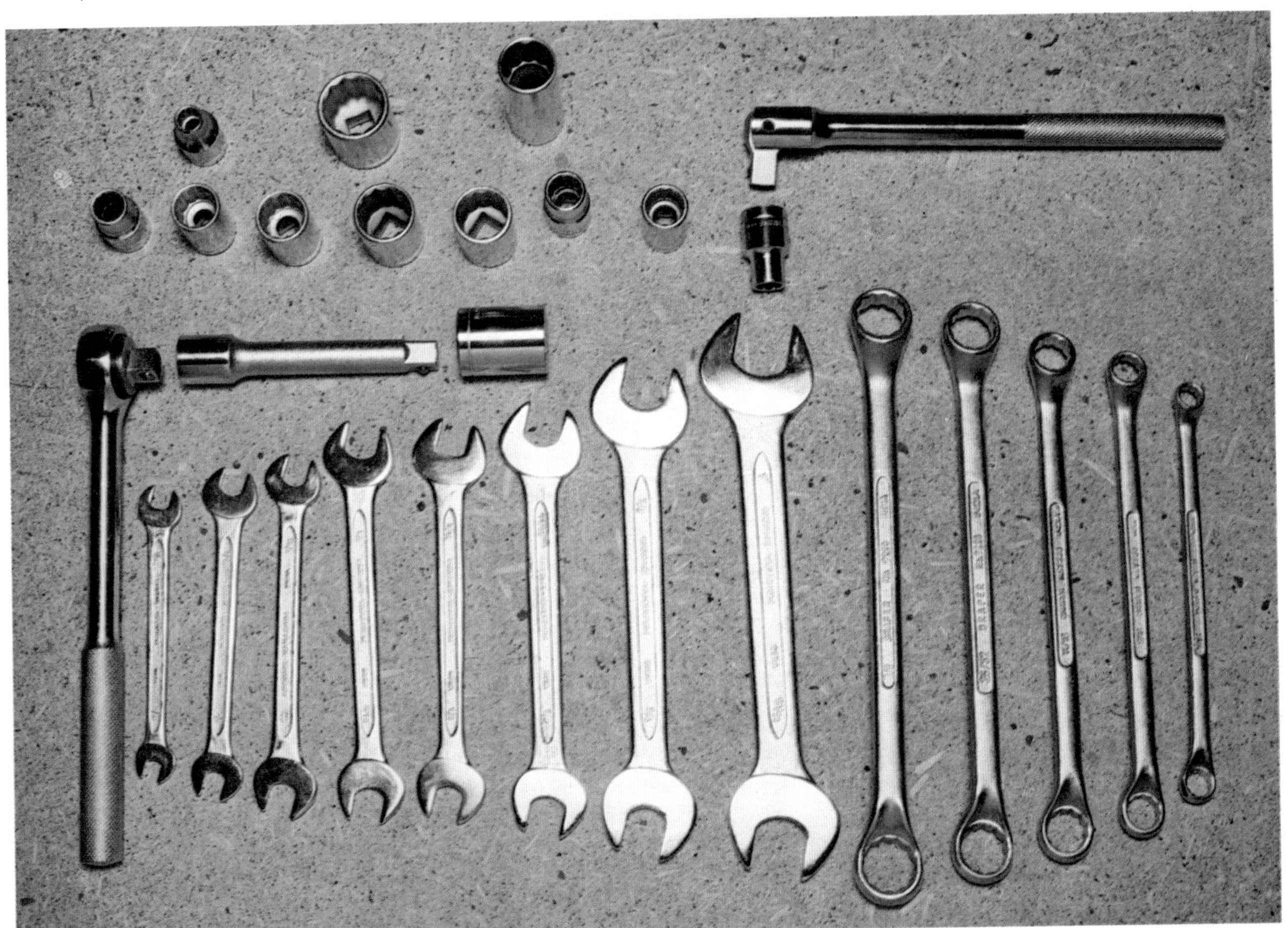

George Wright

the same as the smaller end of the next size up—for instance, a $\frac{7}{16}$in. x $\frac{1}{2}$in. A/F spanner would be followed by a $\frac{1}{2}$in. x $\frac{9}{16}$in. A/F. Similarly, a 10 mm x 11 mm spanner would be followed by an 11 mm x 12 mm spanner.

The length of the spanners in a set usually increases as the jaw size gets bigger, because more leverage is needed on the larger sizes. But if you are offered a choice between short spanners and long ones, it is generally better to opt for the shorter ones. A short spanner can always be made longer to achieve greater leverage by slipping a tube over the end, but a longer spanner cannot be shortened to be used in a confined space.

The jaws of an open-ended spanner are normally at an angle of 15° to the shaft. This makes it much more versatile when used in a restricted space.

It is a good idea to buy only a few spanners to begin with. If your car has A/F nuts and bolts, then the best sizes will probably be from $\frac{7}{16}$in. to $\frac{9}{16}$in.—that is, just two spanners. With metric spanners it is not quite so easy, as there is likely to be a wider variation in the necessary sizes. If you buy spanners covering 10 mm, 11 mm, 13 mm and 17 mm, however, you will have a good start.

Ring spanners

On many occasions the ring spanner (fig. 1) is better than the open-ender. It is stronger, lighter, safer and gives a more positive grip. Because its gripping area has twelve sides instead of the two parallel faces of the open-ender, it can turn a nut more easily. But it cannot entirely replace the open-ender because there are places—a junction in a fuel line, for example—for which it cannot be used.

With ring spanners, the same system of sizing is used as with open-enders; that is, they go up $\frac{1}{16}$in. or 1 mm at a time, with one end of the previous size usually duplicated.

Ring spanners are usually cranked into a swan neck, but they are also available 'flat'. As with the open-ended sort, ring spanners are made in different lengths, so it is a good idea to buy the shorter type if possible.

Combination spanners

To cover the A/F sizes $\frac{7}{16}$in., $\frac{1}{2}$in. and $\frac{9}{16}$in. in both ring spanners and open-enders, a total of four spanners are necessary—two of each type. Somewhat less expensive, since only three spanners are necessary, are the same sizes in combination spanners (fig. 3).

As the name suggests, these spanners have a ring at one end and an open-ender at the other. Both ends are usually the same size (whether A/F or metric).

There is a problem, however, when you want to undo a lock-nut, or hold the bolt-head in one spanner while you turn the nut with another. Where one ring spanner and one open-ender can usually cope in this situation, the combination spanner cannot.

Socket spanners

Socket spanners (fig. 1), which can be bought either singly or in sets, are usually available in A/F, metric and Whitworth sizes in $\frac{1}{4}$in., $\frac{3}{8}$in., $\frac{1}{2}$in. and $\frac{3}{4}$in. drive (that is, the width of the square hole at one end of the socket into which the drive bar fits). They also come in different lengths and depths.

The size, quality and content of a socket set can vary quite considerably but many smaller sets, consisting of six or eight popular-sized sockets, an extension and a tommy bar, are well suited to the d-i-y mechanic. (The more expensive sets include a reversible ratchet, universal joint and a speed brace, in addition to all the possible sizes in A/F, metric and Whitworth.)

Alternatively, if you do not want to buy a full set of sockets straight away, you can start with the four or five sockets you need, adding to these a simple extension and T-handle. Then you buy more sockets and other accessories as you need them, one at a time. For a basic socket set,

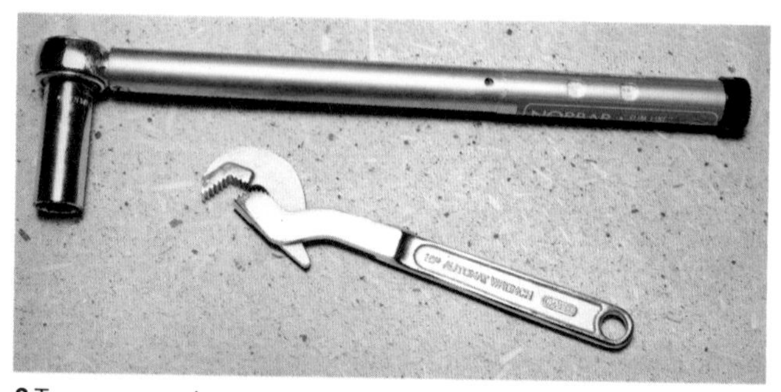

2 Torque wrenches are available in two types. This one (top) is the pre-set type. (Below) A 10in. one-handed pipe wrench

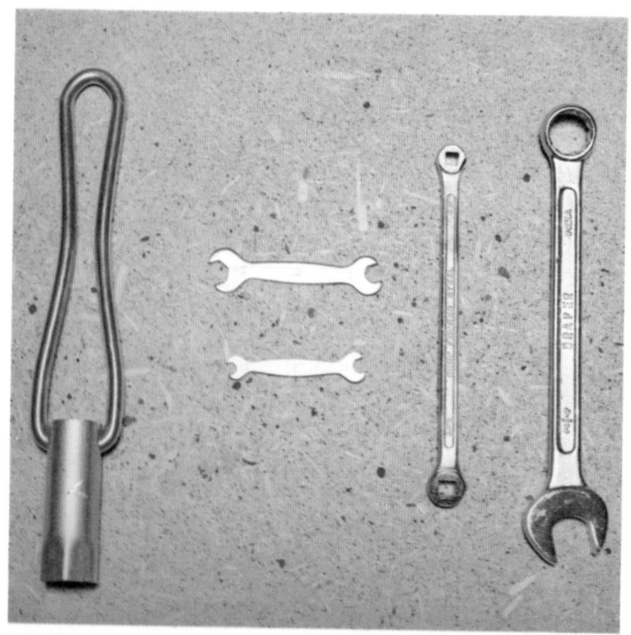

3 (Left to right) A typical spark-plug spanner, two BA spanners, a fixed-head brake-adjusting tool and a combination spanner

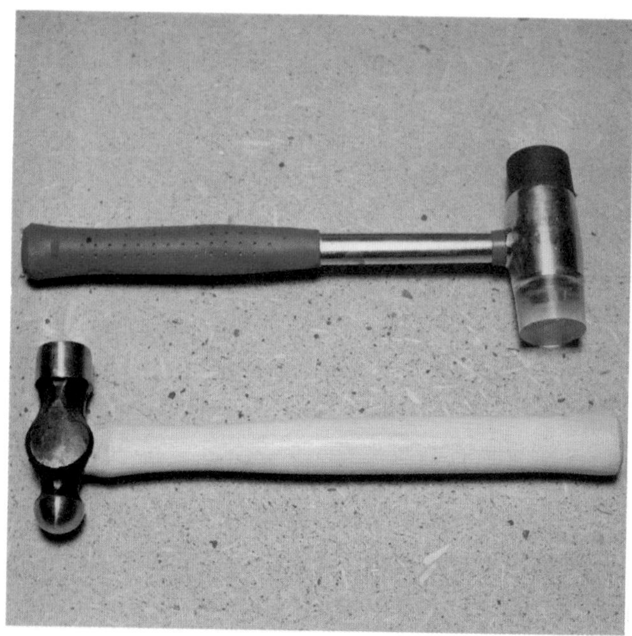

4 (Top) This soft faced hammer has replaceable inserts. A good quality engineers' ball-peen hammer (below) is important

$\frac{1}{2}$in. drive is a good choice.

Some Japanese socket sets, in particular, can be extremely good value for money, offering many more tools and sometimes selling for as little as half the price of rival European sets. They tend not to last as long nor to be finished as well as their competitors, but have ample life for the non-professional mechanic.

Special spanners

If you do not have one already, the first 'special' spanner you will need is a spark-plug spanner (fig. 3). Be careful here, because there are many different types of spark-plug spanner and not all are suitable for every engine.

First you will need to know what type of spark-plug your car uses. In most British and Continental cars the nut size is 14 mm, but some Vauxhalls (for example) use the smaller 10 mm size. Also you need to ensure that the spanner will reach the hexagon of the spark-plug, and that the handle will turn when the unit is fitted to each of your four, six or eight plugs. So buy from a store where you can exchange an unsuitable spanner if necessary.

If you have a socket set, it is possible to buy a special spark-plug socket which comes complete with a rubber insert. The insert grips the spark-plug firmly and prevents it from falling out of the socket. Often, however, the spark-plugs are recessed inside the heat-shields or into the cylinder head itself, in which case a special long socket will be required.

The ignition may also use a special spanner—on British cars, usually a No.2 BA x 4 BA spanner (fig. 3). This spanner also comes in handy for fixing radio bolts and other electrical odds and ends.

Depending on what type of adjusters your brakes have, a proper brake-adjusting spanner or wrench (fig. 3) may be a good buy, since this is one job that should be done with the proper tools. On a Leyland Mini, for instance, a small square adjuster has to turn a large-diameter thread adjuster, which might well be rusted solid. So the correct brake-adjusting wrench is vital; an open-ended spanner will just round off the corners of the adjuster.

As you go along, you may find you need a few box spanners. Although they have largely been superseded by the socket set, they still occasionally come in handy for a specific application like tightening a nut in a confined space. Generally they are used with a tommy bar.

Wrenches

Depending on your car, you may need a special wrench to remove the sump plug or the gearbox filler/level plug. You should be able to get the tool you need from your local franchise holder, but there are general and combination drain plug wrenches available at accessory stores. Do not be tempted to improvise because you do not possess the correct tool. If you 'butcher' the sump plug socket, you will have trouble every time you remove it afterwards.

Adjustable wrenches are regarded with horror by the good engineer. They are certainly not as efficient as the correct spanner for the job, but there are occasions where nothing else can be used. So it is as well to have a good 10in. adjustable wrench in your tool kit. Again, buy a good

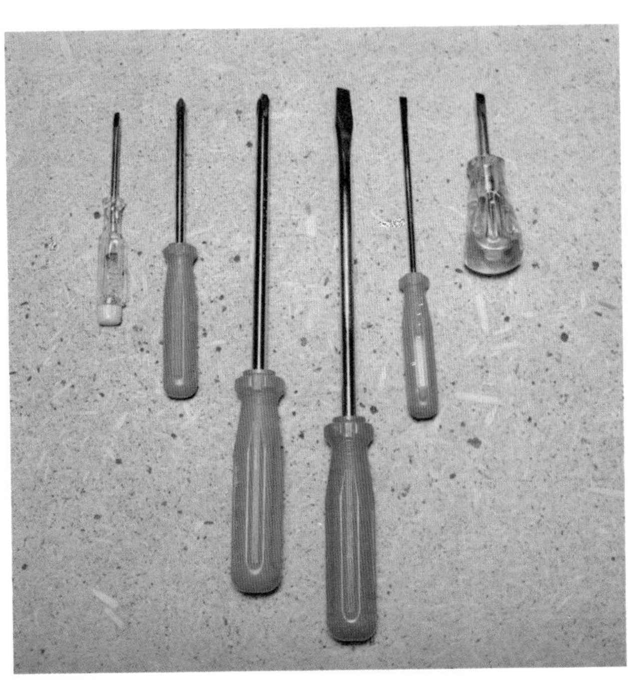

6 Six screwdrivers—an electrical, two cross-heads, two slotted-heads and a chubby—will cope with most jobs about the car

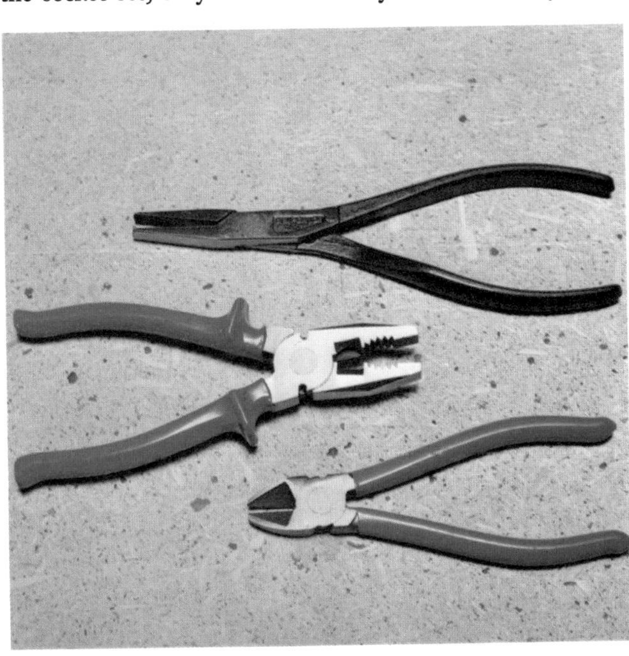

5 Three pairs of pliers that are often needed. (Top to bottom) long-nose pliers, combination pliers and side-cutting pliers

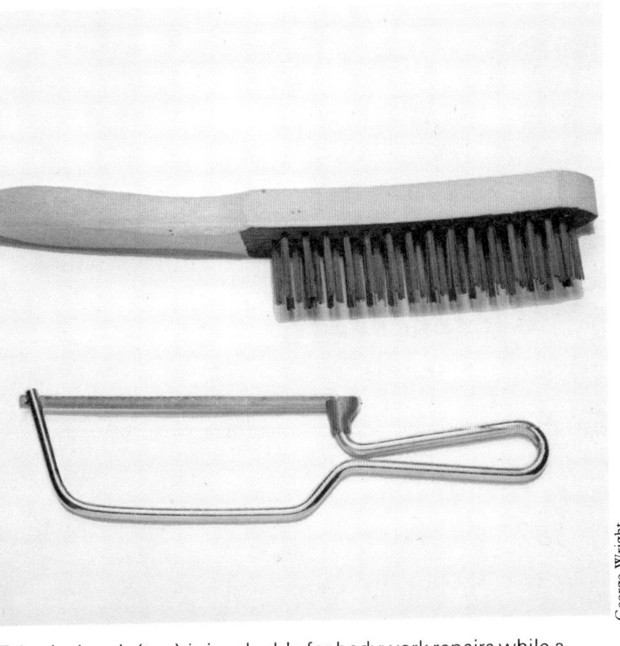

7 A wire brush (top) is invaluable for bodywork repairs while a junior hacksaw (below) can be used in many awkward places

George Wright

quality wrench with fine thread and parallel jaws, and use it only as a last resort and then with care.

Another wrench which may be useful is the lock-on type, for example a Mole wrench. This tool can be used to hold a nut or bolt-head while leaving the user's hands free for something else.

Screwdrivers

One screwdriver is not enough. You will eventually need at least six, and they should all be of first-class quality. For slotted-type screws where the blade of the screwdriver must be a good fit, your tool kit should contain one large, one medium and one small engineers' screwdriver, in addition to a small electrical screwdriver. Particularly useful on the car is a short 'chubby' screwdriver, for places where there is not room for the longer type.

Some kits contain a single handle and a selection of screwdriver bits. They are seldom as strong as an individual screwdriver, however.

You will also need a set of engineers' screwdrivers to cope with cross-head screws, of either the Philips or Pozidriv type. Use the correct one for the size of screw being tackled—they do not interchange very satisfactorily and the result of using the wrong size is usually a chewed-up screw head.

When buying engineers' screwdrivers, always choose the type where the steel shaft is keyed into a tough moulded handle. The better versions have 'flats' moulded in to the handle so that a spanner can be used to apply more turning force.

Pliers

For most of the time you can manage with just one pair of pliers providing they are of the right type. Start off with a pair of engineers' combination pliers (fig. 5), as these will handle most jobs. Next in priority might be a good pair of radio or long-nosed pliers for more delicate work. Finally, side-cutting pliers can be useful, especially for removing old split-pins.

Hammers

You will need at least two hammers in a full tool kit. First buy an engineers' ball-peen hammer (fig. 4) weighing about 0.45 kg or 1lb. Next buy a soft-headed hammer

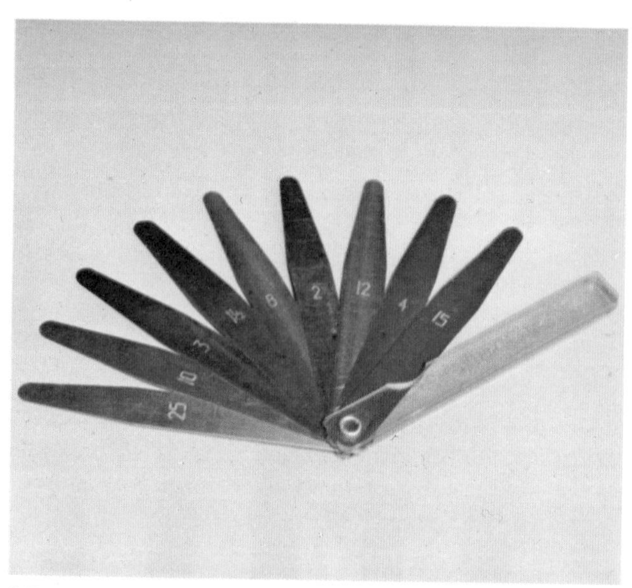

8 Feeler gauges are necessary to check the electrode gap of a spark-plug or the clearance between the contact-breaker points

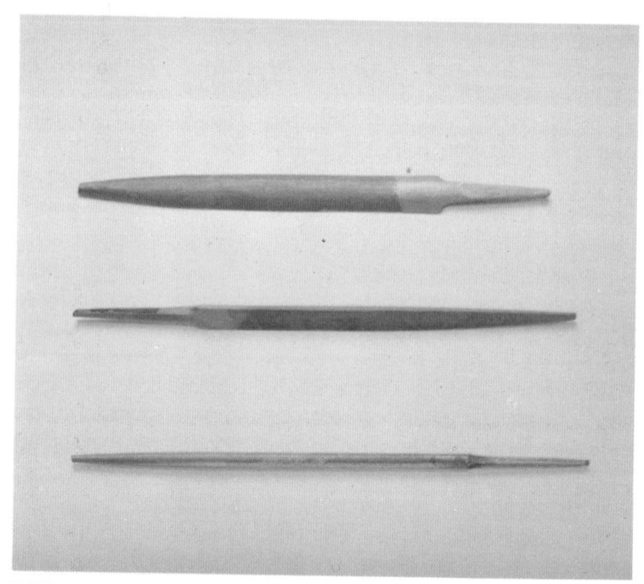

9 When buying files, it is a good idea to start off with (top to bottom) a half round file, a triangular file and a round file

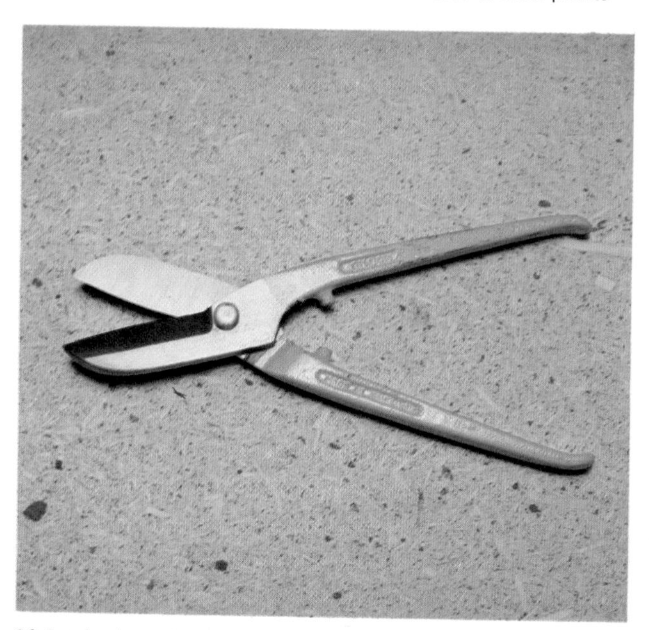

10 A pair of metal-cutting shears—or 'tinsnips' as they are sometimes called—are useful when working with light-gauge metal

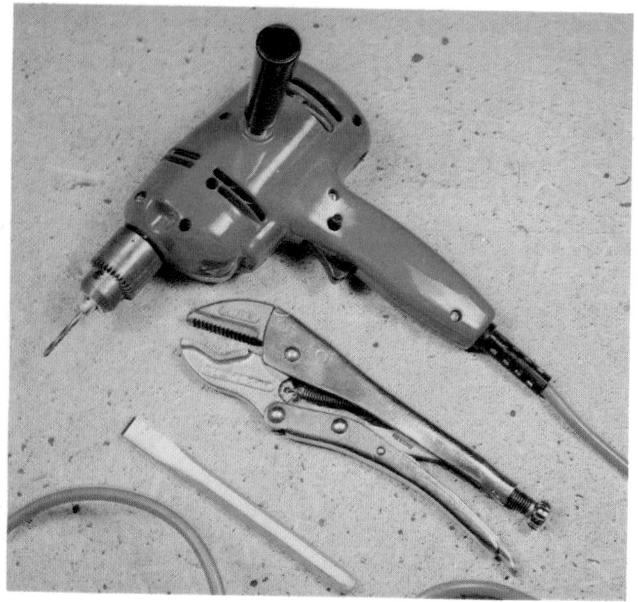

11 A two-speed electric drill, a lock-on or 'Mole' wrench and a cold chisel are all essential tools for the d-i-y handyman

(fig. 4) for situations where a conventional hammer would damage a particular surface—knocking out dents, say.

Feeler gauges

To check the electrode gap on a spark-plug or the contact-breaker gap in the distributor, you will need a set of feeler gauges (fig. 8). Although sometimes sold singly, feeler gauges are nearly always available in inexpensive sets, measured either in thousandths of an inch or hundredths of a millimetre.

Other tools

A number of other tools that you will need for a complete tool kit can be bought gradually, one at a time.

Eventually you will want a *hacksaw*. This tool will cut all sorts of metal, plastic and even rubber and is available in two forms, a large hacksaw and a junior hacksaw. The junior hacksaw, because of its size, is particularly useful since it can be used in all sorts of awkward and confined places.

For fitting accessories, holes need to be drilled in the car, so a *hand drill*—or even better, an electric drill—is essential (fig. 11). With electric drills, it is best to buy a two-speed model with a 12 mm or ½in. chuck. A good set of twist drills and an engineers' impact punch (as an aid to accurate drilling) will also be needed.

Should you decide to do any bodywork repairs you will require a *wire brush* and a *sanding disc*. Wire brushes are useful for clearing rust and dirt, especially from underneath the car, while a sanding disc used with an electric drill is invaluable for removing paint.

Files are available in several shapes and sizes, a combined flat and half-round file being a good first choice for the d-i-y mechanic. Buy one in the medium range, for example 'second cut' (this refers to the number of teeth per inch the file has). A couple of round files are ideal for enlarging holes, and a triangular file will often get into places that a flat or half-round cannot. A *cold chisel* is needed to shift seized nuts and bolts.

On some cars the manufacturers recommend that the ignition timing be checked and adjusted dynamically, and for this you will need a *strobe light*. A good strobe light costs a few pounds, but enables the ignition timing to be set up accurately.

Finally, many of the nuts and bolts on the major components of the car such as the cylinder head have a particular torque setting. This means that, for safety's sake, they should be tightened to a certain limit—and no more. For this, a *torque wrench* is necessary. There are two main types of torque wrench, one that shows how much force you are actually exerting, and the other which can be pre-set to stop tightening when the desired torque is reached. The second is much the better.

Basic tool kit

Although most tools can be bought as you need them, there are some basic items without which you cannot even begin doing your own maintenance or repairs. These basic requirements are:

Set of open-ended spanners (or main sizes only in a higher quality)
Set of ring spanners (or main sizes only in a higher quality)
Spark-plug spanner
Medium screwdriver for slotted-head screws
Medium screwdriver for Philips or Pozidriv screws
Hammer
Pliers
Feeler gauges
Sump/gearbox drain plug spanner
Tool box

Although not strictly part of the tool kit, there are nine other items that you should try to carry in your car at all times. These are a first-aid kit, a fire extinguisher, a tow-rope, a jack, a set of battery jumper leads, a spare gallon of petrol, a torch, a breakdown warning triangle and a spare emergency windscreen.

12 A cantilever tool box, like this one, can house all of your tools. Keep it in the boot of your car in case of an emergency

George Wright

Jacks, ramps and hoists

Car lifting equipment is essential if you are going to work underneath the car. And lifting it up (and keeping it up) provides the access that, on many maintenance jobs, is a pleasant alternative to scraping along on your back in a puddle of oil.

On some jobs, it may well produce more thorough workmanship because you can do the job with less discomfort. On others, it is essential to doing the job at all.

Many d-i-y mechanics try to get by with just the jacks supplied with their cars as original equipment. This is fine for tyre-changing and the like, but downright dangerous if you have to get under the car.

The type of lifting equipment you need—ramp, jack or hoist—obviously depends on the jobs you intend to do. But the quality you need remains the same. Whether you buy new or good second-hand gear, you will want the best, since your life could depend on it—literally.

Ramps

Ramps are wedge-shaped, fixed-height structures, usually made of steel, which allow the car to be driven up their sloping fronts on to a wheel-sized platform. They are ideal for lifting just the front or rear of a car for inspection purposes, or even to remove a large component from underneath.

Their design, however, means that you cannot carry out any assembly work on the wheels, brakes or suspension systems. Some ramps are made in sections so that the sloping pieces can be removed and used as wheel chocks.

Ramps are relatively cheap and, though a useful aid to the serious home mechanic, are really designed for those concerned only with convenient, but limited, routine maintenance (figs. 1, 2 and 3).

Jacks

There are several kinds of jack, of varying degrees of usefulness.

New cars usually come equipped with either *side jacks* or *scissors jacks*. The side jack fits in a hole at the side of, or just underneath, the car, and lifts the car only one side at a time. The scissors jack consists of a threaded bar which, when turned, draws together or moves apart two hinged arms and so raises or lowers a lifting platform. On some types of scissors jack, the platform has a peg which locates in a hole beneath the car body, thus limiting the jack to a single lifting point on each side of the car.

Both side jacks and scissors jacks are suitable only for changing wheels and are not designed to support the car for long periods (figs. 4 and 5).

Bottle jacks, either the hydraulically-operated or screw type, consist of a squat bottle-shaped casting from which a piston, topped with a lifting pad, emerges when the jack is in use. *Trolley jacks* work on a similar principle, but are mounted on a mobile frame. This is convenient when trying to locate a difficult lifting point, as the jack can be moved quickly and easily (figs. 6, 7, 8 and 12).

Both bottle jacks and trolley jacks are ideal for lifting cars on which the built-in jacking points have perished. Both types are expensive, but bottle jacks may be justified if you plan to carry out your own maintenance regularly, especially if this includes major overhauls or repairs.

1 Driving on to ramps is a quick and easy way of lifting the car. Remember to put the handbrake on and chock the wheels left on the ground. You can make these ramps yourself (see page 231)

George Wright

2 Conventional steel ramp

3 (right) Two-piece ramps can be folded for easy storage

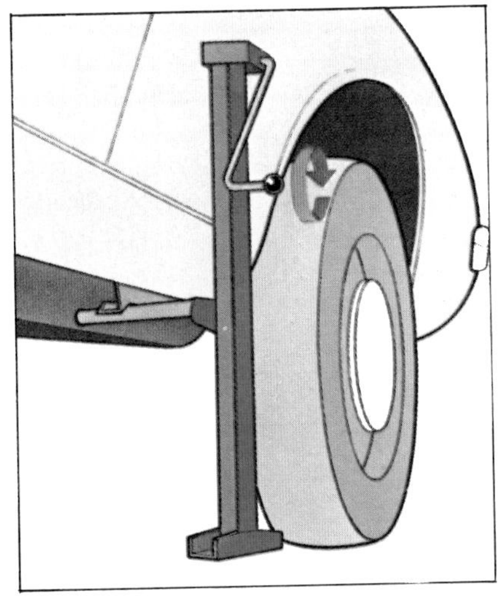

4 Side jacks locate in an access hole and lift only one side of the car at a time

5 The scissors jack lifts the car at any suitable jacking point

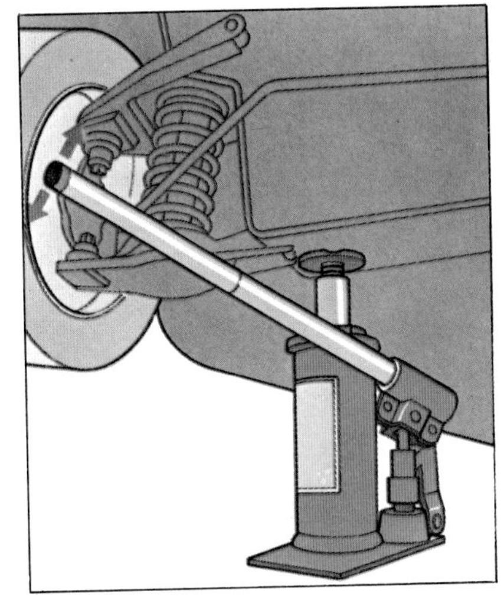

6 Bottle jacks, such as this hydraulic model, are powerful for their small size

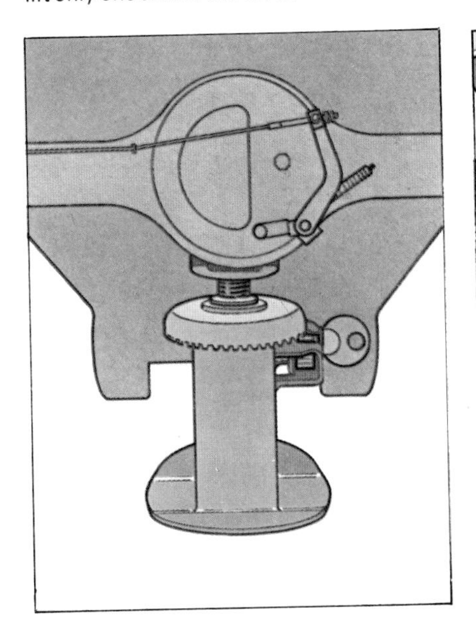

7 The screw bottle jack gets its lift from a threaded piston

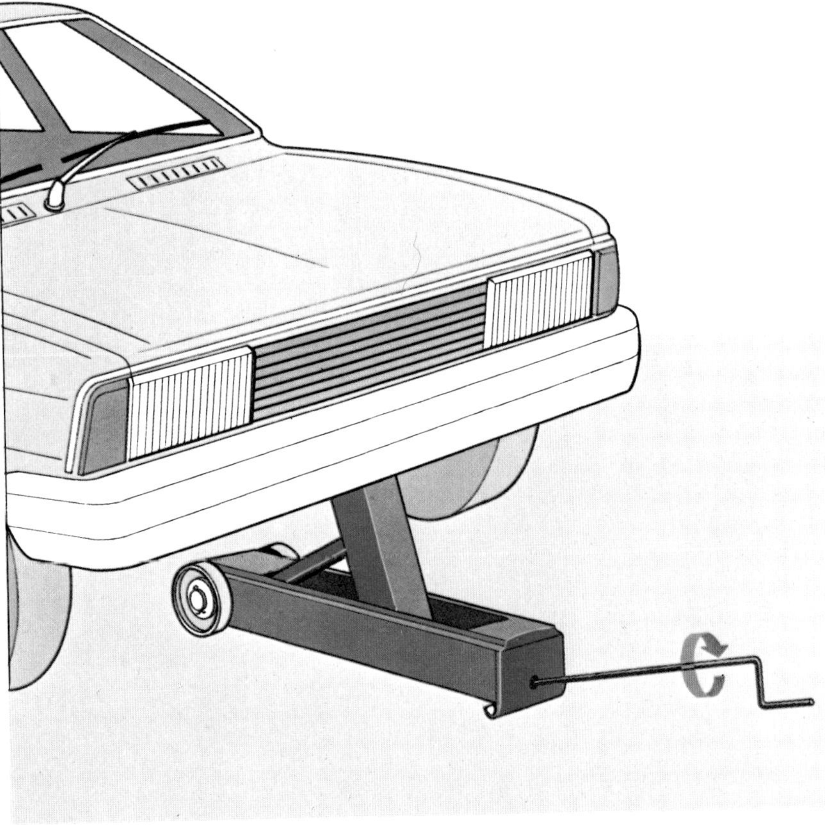

8 The length and width of a screw trolley jack give it great stability even when extended to maximum height. The wheels allow the jack to be moved about easily under the car—useful when trying to locate an awkward jacking point

Terry Allen Designs

Axle stands

Whichever kind of jack you have, axle stands are necessary for complete security against jack failure.

Axle stands are strongly-made steel tripods with a centre pillar that can be adjusted to different heights. They provide a rigid, secure structure that will support a car safely after it has been lifted to the required height with a jack (fig. 11).

The height range varies from 25 cm (10in.) to 60 cm (24in.), according to the weight that the stand is capable of supporting. Stands with a safe working load of 4 tonnes per pair are a popular size, easily supporting most cars.

A pair of axle stands is reasonably inexpensive, and the only safe means of carrying out those jobs which cannot be done with a ramp.

Hoists

Hoists, the only practical means of removing an engine from a car, come in two basic types: those which are self-supporting and fitted with wheels, and those for which some outside support must be provided.

Self-supporting mobile hoists are expensive, and usually found only in commercial garages.

If you have no garage, a hoist of the other type can be suspended from a gantry—a four-legged tubular frame with a connecting bar across the top. The gantry's legs are wide enough apart to allow a car to be driven between them so that the engine can be lifted out. Gantries are often made to be folded up for easy storage when not in use (fig. 13).

A hoist suspended from a joist (beam) across the garage is a cheaper alternative (figs. 9 and 10).

Before buying a hoist, you must be sure that both the hoist and its supporting joist will carry the weight of your car's engine—plus the extra load you put on it by pulling downwards to lift the engine. A reputable dealer will advise you on the lifting capacity of the hoists he sells. Joist sizes and installation details are in the accompanying panel.

Buying equipment

Since safety is the prime consideration—a failure could drop a car on your head—buy equipment only from sources, whether firms or friends, in whom you have absolute confidence.

Stock from bankrupt dealers (which will not have been used before) or from bankrupt garage businesses (which will have been used) is sometimes advertised in the classified columns, and is worth considering. But common sense says that used equipment of this sort will not normally be discarded unless it is old or defective. So buy only from sources you would 'bet your life on'.

When examining equipment, see that all welds are complete and firm; that there are no cracks on cast casings (on bottle jacks, for example); and no signs of poor oil seals or leaked fluid on hydraulic equipment.

How to support your car hoist

Joists used to suspend car-engine hoists in a garage or workshop must carry a double load—both the weight of the engine and the downward thrust you apply in lifting it. But a timber joist of the right size will do the job, and be much cheaper than rolled steel.

Timber joists should be knot-free, set on edge and well supported at both ends (fig. 9). Larger sizes (200 mm and above) should also be braced to avoid twisting (fig. 10).

Do not use an existing tie-beam in the garage ceiling as a hoist support. It is already carrying its design load.

The size of joist needed depends on the weight of your car's engine and the distance the joist must span. For single garages up to 3 m or 10ft wide, the following table gives some sample engine weights and joist sizes:—

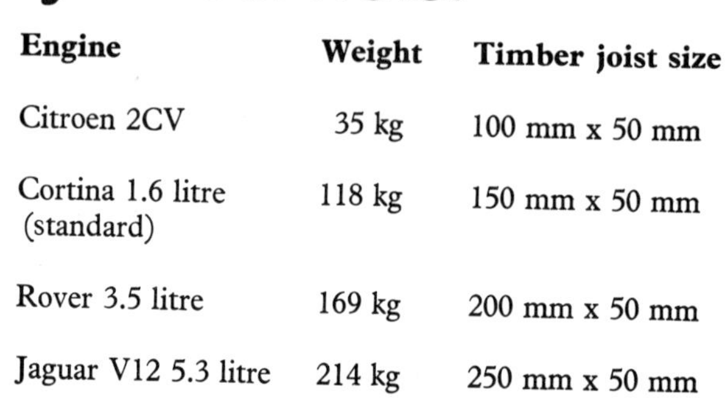

Engine	Weight	Timber joist size
Citroen 2CV	35 kg	100 mm x 50 mm
Cortina 1.6 litre (standard)	118 kg	150 mm x 50 mm
Rover 3.5 litre	169 kg	200 mm x 50 mm
Jaguar V12 5.3 litre	214 kg	250 mm x 50 mm

Tri-Art

9 Set the joist securely on edge and prevent it from tipping

10 A wide-span joist should be braced so that it will not twist

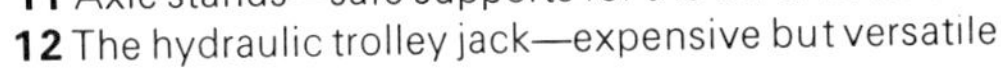

11 Axle stands—safe supports for the car after it has been lifted
12 The hydraulic trolley jack—expensive but versatile

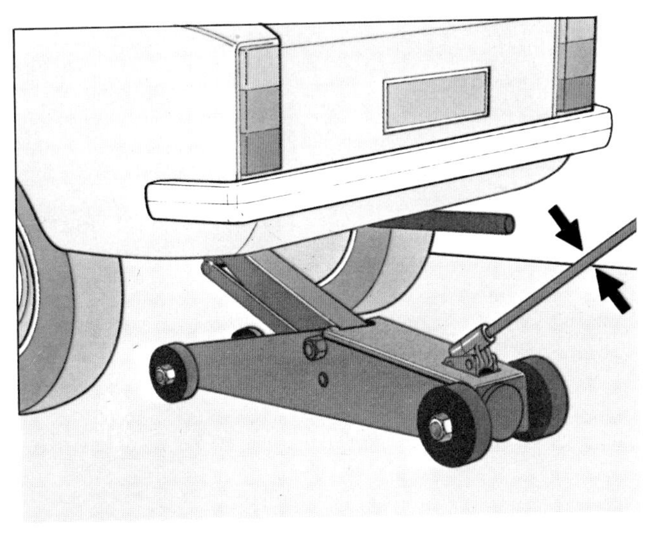

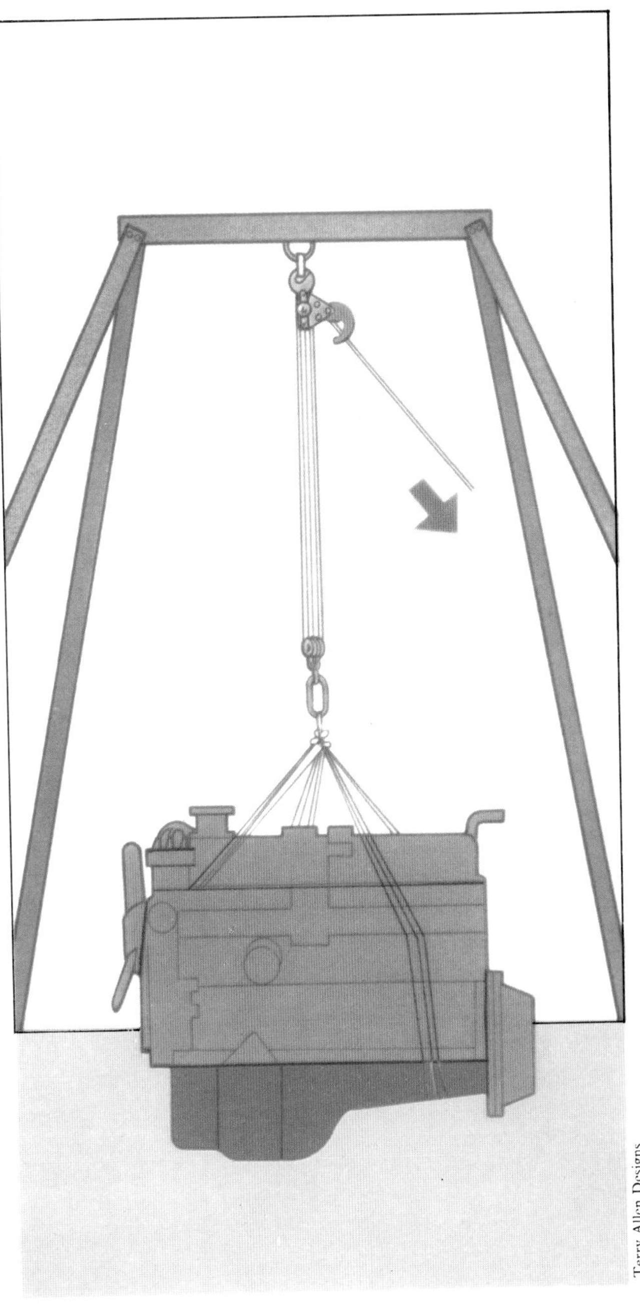

Terry Allen Designs

13 A hoist is essential for lifting an engine from a car. The gantry gives support and allows removal to be done in the open

Check that a jack can be lowered enough to go under your car, and extended to a raised height of at least 40 cm (15½in.). It should also have a dished lifting pad to give you a secure location on the car.

Car ramps should be made of angle-iron at least 2.5 cm (1in.) wide, and have a minimum height of 22.5 cm (9in.). Ramps whose sloping sections can be detached from the wheel platforms make access easier.

Hoists should be tried out to see that they run smoothly, without twisting and snagging, and that the locking mechanism functions smoothly.

Finally, with all such equipment, look at the finish. If it is good, the chances are that the rest of the work has been carried out with the same care.

Making your own ramp

Timber ramps are a satisfactory—and often cheaper—alternative to the steel ramps sold by motor accessory shops.

The type shown here has an advantage over most proprietary ramps in that it has a removable sloping section, giving better access to the underside of the car.

It can be made by any experienced d-i-y carpenter and, if well made, will last a long time.

Materials

The timber used is 19 mm (¾in.) plywood, and all the components will come out of just over half a standard-sized 2,440 mm by 1,220 mm sheet. To save money, second-hand solid timber can be used instead. But in this case the direction of the grain (arrowed in fig. 14) must be correct or the wood could split.

Do not use second-hand plywood which has been lying about in the open, as the plies might shear.

Fencing arris rail is used for the stops on top of the wheel platforms, and 19 mm by 12 mm strip for the tyre grips on the ramps.

No. 8 gauge Pozidriv Twinfast (double-threaded) screws, 45 mm long, are used to fasten the plywood components together, all joints being further strengthened by a waterproof woodworking adhesive such as Aerolite or Cascamite. The stops and tyre grips are glued and nailed.

To link together the ramps and platforms, eight heavy-duty screw-eyes and two lengths of steel bar are needed.

Assembly

The wheel platforms are assembled simply as box sections, but each of the ramps contains a bulkhead for extra strength. The bulkheads are set squarely and vertically about midway along the sides of the ramp, (fig. 15) and their top edges must be planed to the same angle as the slope of the ramp. This allows them to act as load-bearing members.

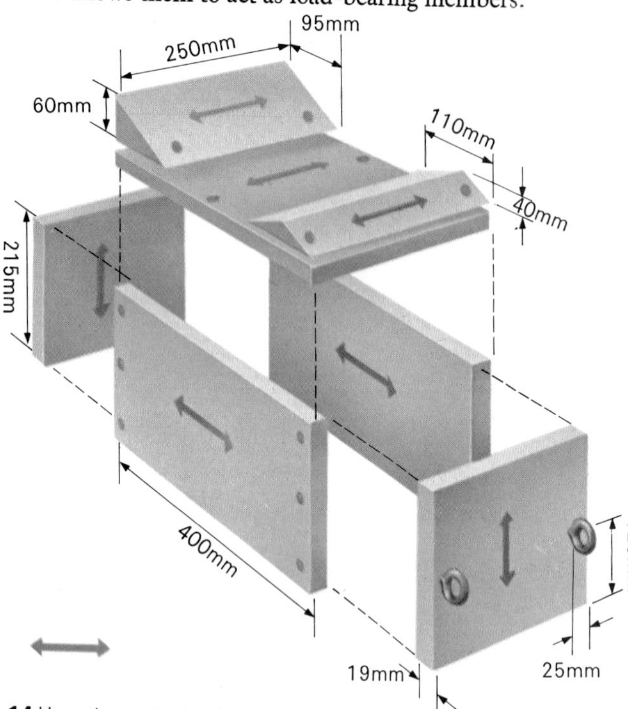

14 How the grain should run in a ramp made of solid timber

Begin by marking-out and cutting out all the plywood components, making sure that all edges are square. (Remember when planing plywood to work from both ends towards the middle so that the ends do not split). Then glue and assemble all components as in fig. 15.

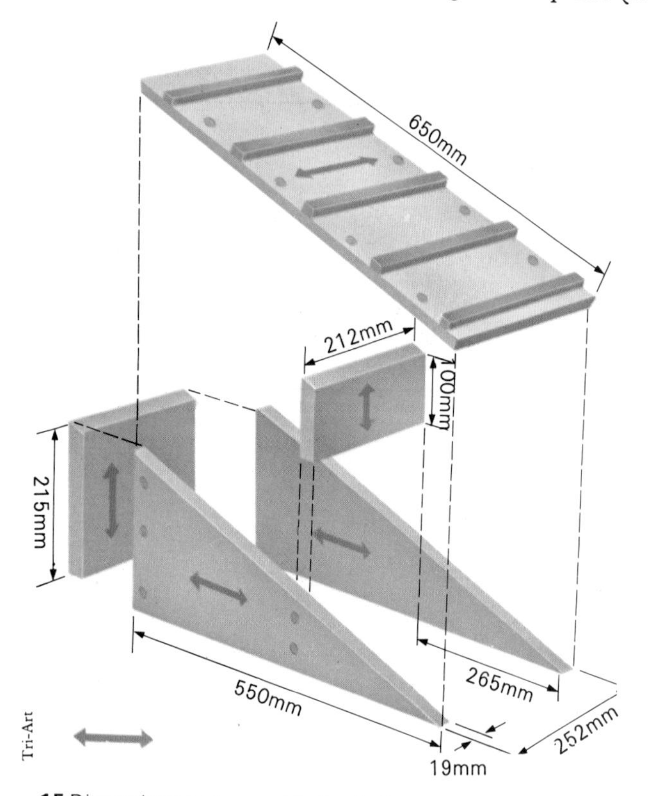

15 Dimensions and assembly details for a plywood ramp

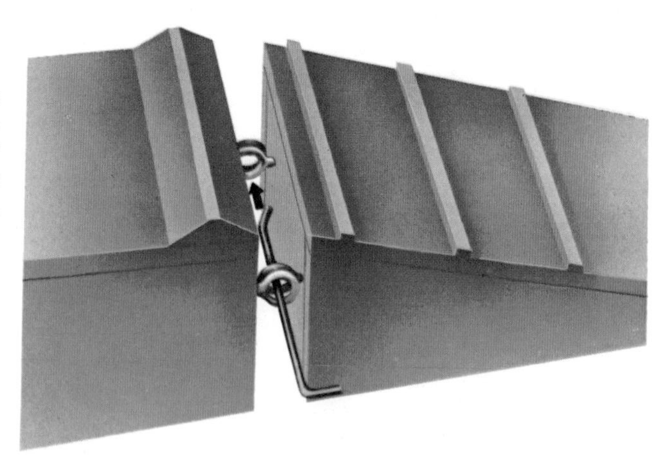

16 A steel bar through the eyes stops the sections separating

The two sections that make up each side must be linked together or they may move apart when the car is driven on to them. To do this, two screw-eyes are screwed in to each section at the same height, but spaced so that those on the ramp fit inside those on the wheel platform (fig. 16). A loosely-fitting steel bar passed through the eyes stops the sections from moving apart.

When finished, the units should be given several coats of exterior-grade paint or varnish to improve their durability.

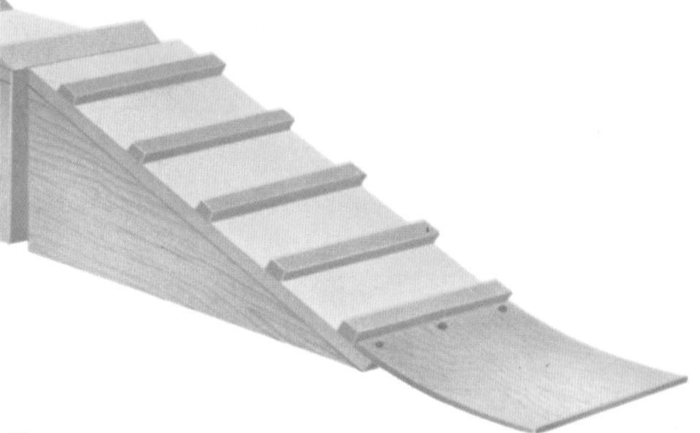

17 A run-on will stop the ramps skidding under the car wheels

Should the ramps show a tendency to skid when the car wheels hit them, a short length of plywood or sheet metal fixed to extend from the bottom of the ramp (fig. 17) will prevent this.

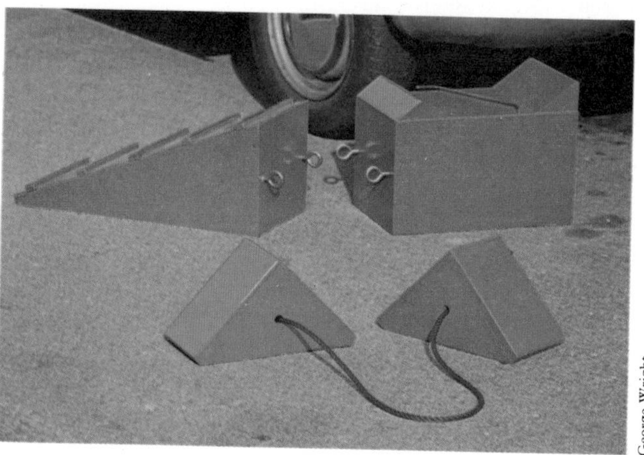

18 The finished ramps, with wheel chocks made in a similar way

Tri-Art

George Wright

Secondhand spare parts

Jake Wynter

1 In a breaker's yard like this one, safety is the most important consideration—never try to work on or near a precariously balanced car

Motoring costs are constantly rising, so many drivers are seeking new ways of saving money. Spare parts can form a large proportion of costs, but the car owner need not despair. A trip to a breaker's yard—albeit a harrowing experience—can provide many useful economies if you go about it the right way. The secret is to know what is worth buying and what is not.

Before you go to your local breakers, you should bear several points clearly in mind. You rarely get something for nothing, especially from a breaker. The prices asked may be much lower than those you would pay for new parts, but you are buying second-hand components and there is no guarantee that they will work satisfactorily. The art of getting a good deal is to be able to judge which items are likely to give good service for a reasonable price and thereby save you money on the cost of a new part, and which are beyond the point of salvage. To make buying second-hand worthwhile, the saving over the cost of a new part should be appreciable. It is not worth taking any risk in order to save a money on a badly needed part.

If you have a relatively new car, buying from a breaker is not good policy, but older models can benefit. In some cases a breaker may be the only source of parts for rarer cars.

When a part on your car requires replacement, you should first find out the price of a new unit. You can then decide whether it is worth buying new or second-hand. Generally, you should buy second-hand parts to replace damaged components. When parts come due for replacement because they have worn, you are better off buying new. You should consider carefully the function of the unit you are replacing. For example, if your car burns a hole in a piston, it is unwise to buy a second-hand replacement. Pistons vary in size and some may be up to 0.762 mm (.030ins) oversize. In addition, you cannot tell at a glance how worn they might be. On the other hand if a connecting rod has broken in your engine and made a hole in the side of the cylinder block, you could usefully buy a second-hand block. You can then use such a block as a basis for re-building the engine, saving a good deal on the price of a new unit.

You should always remember that units bought from a breaker are always unknown quantities, so when buying engine parts go for components that can be reclaimed—for example, crankshafts that can be reground to take oversize bearings, cylinder heads that can be skimmed, or valves on which the seats can be re-cut.

Equipment and safety

Breakers' yards are dirty places, so take along suitable clothing for the task, such as overalls and old shoes. You will probably have to remove any parts you want yourself, so make sure you take a comprehensive tool kit. Some lengths of piping, slipped over the end of a socket drive so that you can exert more torque, will help shift stubborn bolts. A wire brush and penetrating oil may also prove helpful. Bear in mind that the cars you will be removing parts from will almost certainly have been standing outdoors and idle for several months—possibly years—so stubborn bolts will be quite common. Take plenty of old rags with you to clean parts for inspection.

The most important point you should consider in a breaker's yard is safety. Rows of cars may be stacked three high and can be extremely dangerous if you disturb the balance. In some yards you will only be allowed to point out the car you are interested in and the proprietor's staff will remove the part you want. In most yards, however, you have to do your own work. Avoid sudden, violent movements when trying to remove a part and keep alert for the slightest sign of movement of any of the cars in the stack you are working on. Remember also that other people may be working nearby and you should bear in mind that they may not be particularly safety conscious.

If you want to jack up a car, make sure you locate the jack on a chassis-member or solid part of the vehicle that will bear the load. Do not lie underneath. Most breakers will roll a car on its side for you, or will not object to you turning it over, providing you check with them first. Never be tempted to try jacking up a car that has one or two other cars stacked on top as they could become unbalanced and topple over causing personal injury and damage.

2 When buying an engine, turn it over with the flywheel. Listen for grating noises and try to feel how much compression there is

Choosing parts

Breaker's yards are not as straight-forward a market place as the spare parts counter. Most people who go to a breaker are either using it as a last resort or are hoping to save money and the demand for parts is high. The proprietor, therefore, may feel obliged to put himself out to help his customers. If you go to a breaker's expecting individual attention and full after-sales service, the chances are you will be disappointed. Be sure that the item you buy is exactly what you want and is in satisfactory condition (so far as you can tell) because the proprietor is unlikely to change it later or refund any money.

There will probably be hundreds of cars if the breaker's business is of any size. Do not rush to the first model that you see similar to your own car, but walk around the yard and make a mental note of all the relevant models in which you might be interested, along with their condition.

Cars end up in scrapyards for a variety of reasons. If there is evidence of heavy accident damage, but the car is otherwise in good condition, it is likely to be an insurance write-off. Such cars can be a source of good parts, but remember that suspension members and other components may have been damaged or stressed by the accident.

Other cars will be there because they have failed the roadworthiness test and excess corrosion will be clearly evident. It is extremely rare that cars will have been scrapped simply because of mechanical failure, but it is possible that an already rusty car may have been abandoned because a mechanical component finally broke. Check parts from this sort of car with extreme care.

In some yards, engines, gearboxes, rear axles and other major components will have been removed from the cars. Some specialist parts dealers clean and label all units, but these are not true breakers. Removal of major items in the scrapyard tends to be carried out on a random basis whenever the proprietor has time. Some label units—most do not. You can identify engines when they are out of the car,

3 Always look for the engine number. You can use this to discover whether or not the engine will fit your particular vehicle

4 If you are dismantling an engine, make sure that you have got enough space to work in. Try to keep everything clean and orderly

5 When you have removed the desired components, inspect them for excessive wear. If sound, they can be bought for reconditioning

6 Occasionally, quite unusual components turn up in the yard and can save you a lot of money. This is a Fiat 124 cylinder head

Jake Wynter

but to be sure of what your own engine looks like, study it carefully before you go to the breaker's. Buy the unit only if it is exactly the same as your original engine. Gearboxes and axles can be difficult to identify, so if you are in doubt do not buy until you know, by studying your own car, just what the component looks like. Any type numbers stamped on the particular component will help you identify the unit.

It is a good idea before you go to the breaker's to check in your handbook or with your local dealer to see if any specification changes were made during the life of the model. Changes of this sort often result in parts from later models not being interchangeable with parts from earlier machines. For example, certain Jaguars were fitted with an all-synchromesh gearbox part of the way through the production run, but the new units were not interchangeable with the earlier gearboxes which had synchromesh on only three of the four forward gears. Similarly, the internal diameter of the Triumph TR4A gearbox prevents it from being fitted to the TR4 without modifications. These are points you should be wary of, otherwise you could find you have bought an item that is useless to you. Re-selling it privately is time-consuming and you will probably lose money on the deal. Keeping a note of your chassis, engine and gearbox numbers can help you to avoid these pitfalls.

Breaker's yards do not normally have standard prices for parts. In many cases, one member of staff may quote you one price and another member will give you a different figure. By juggling between the two, you may be able to obtain a part at a lower price than that originally quoted.

Engines

Reconditioned exchange engines can be expensive, particularly as many of them are supplied with only the minimum of equipment. Short engines—the "bottom half" of the engine usually comprising the block, crankshaft, connecting rods and pistons and (where relevant) the camshaft—are often supplied without basic parts like cylinder head studs, timing case covers etc. Therefore, you may consider buying a second-hand engine from a breaker's yard a better proposition.

The immediate problem is that, except in rare cases, you cannot hear the engine running. This means you can only buy the unit "as seen" rather than "as seen and heard". It is quite possible to buy a complete second-hand engine and install it directly into your car without inspecting it internally in any way. But this approach to buying can be a gamble and you may find you have acquired a useless engine.

A better policy is to buy second-hand only when reclaimable parts of your present engine have broken. In this case you can buy another engine, strip it and have the required

7 Some components, like these distributors, may be found thrown together. In such a case, you must know exactly what to look for

8 Components like these, which are non-mechanical and not subject to wear, are a safe buy and generally represent good value

9 When buying a radiator from a breaker's, always remember to test for leaks. There should always be water and a container available

10 Next, inspect the condition of the core. Corrosion is the most obvious thing to watch out for but beware also of damaged vanes

11 Carburettors are some of the hardest components to check for wear. You should, however, be able to test the butterfly spindles

12 Do not forget to buy the correct manifold as well. If this is not with the carburettor, the parts will need careful matching

13 It often pays to look around at the breaker's. These two fuel tanks are very different in quality but came from the same pile

14 Water pumps are not normally worth buying from a breaker's, but large or rare ones like this Humber pump are an exception

Jake Wynter

15 Although clutch parts are never worth buying from a breaker's, a sound second-hand fly-wheel can save you a great deal of money

parts reconditioned before you re-build your original engine using the refurbished second-hand items.

If you decide to buy a second-hand engine, carefully examine the unit you have selected before purchase. Try to find the engine number plate to check it with that of your original engine. By reference to your notes on specification changes, you can determine whether the units are interchangeable. The external condition is not too important, but the internal components should turn freely. Check this by turning over the engine with a socket on the crankshaft pulley nut. If the unit is stiff, refuses to turn over, or makes grumbling noises, find another engine.

Examine sumps, timing chain covers, manifolds and similar items for cracks, after first wiping off as much external grime or corrosion as possible. Connecting rods can be purchased, providing you fit new small end bearings, but timing chains should be bought new as wear is difficult to measure and failure can lead to expensive damage.

Crankshafts can be purchased second-hand, but they must be re-ground and have the oilways thoroughly cleaned before use. The manufacturer's measurements in your manual specify the minimum and maximum diameter of the journals for both the big-end and main bearings. To be quite sure that the crankshaft has not been ground by more than the maximum amount, you should take the trouble to remove it from the engine and carefully measure the journals with a micrometer.

Ancillary components

Quite a large number of ancillary components can be purchased second-hand, providing you check them carefully.

Radiators can be checked visually, by first removing the cap. If there is no visible water level, fill the radiator yourself. The yard office will probably provide a bucket of water. Look for signs of external leaks, especially round the neck of the filler and the inlet and outlet points. Examine the core and vanes for accident damage or corrosion. Remember that even though the radiator may not leak, flattened vanes may cause overheating when the radiator is installed in a car.

Never buy hoses from a breaker; it is false economy. A hose failure could strand you and result in a repair bill far in excess of the cost of a set of new hoses.

Breakers are a popular source of carburettors, but be careful. As you cannot listen to the engine, you will not be able to check that it idles properly and the idle of an engine can sometimes pinpoint whether the carburettor is worn. Instead, examine the linkage and see that it seats correctly. On variable jet carburettors you should fit a new jet and needle and seat and on all carburettors you should carefully strip and refurbish them before fitting them to your car. If the carburettor has been standing in the breaker's yard for any length of time it will need cleaning internally and externally, otherwise you may experience fuel flow problems.

It is not worth buying fuel lines or pumps from a breaker, as new units are not expensive. Fuel tanks can be extremely expensive and, as they take up a lot of storage space, spare parts dealers tend not to stock tanks for older cars. Providing there is no corrosion, a second-hand tank can prove a good deal less expensive than a new one. Be very careful when you remove or handle a fuel tank, as any petrol vapour inside can make it dangerous. Never smoke or allow a naked flame to come anywhere near a tank when you are working on it.

It is not worth buying second-hand fuel pumps, either mechanical or electric, as new units are not expensive. Mechanical pumps may be worn or leaking and any gaskets

16 When buying a gearbox, rattle the input shaft. Any undue movement or unusual noises will indicate worn shaft bearings

17 While you are examining the outside, watch for oil leaks and check that the gearbox mountings match the locations on your car

18 Next, unscrew the inspection cover. You will then be able to see the selector forks. Check these and the gears below for wear

19 Leyland transverse-engine gearboxes are more easily checked. In this Mini one, the teeth and synchromesh are very badly worn

may have perished through standing idle. The points on an electric pump often fail through corrosion or may simply stick together through lack of use.

Water pumps on small-engined cars are usually inexpensive to replace. On larger-engined cars they may cost more and providing you can obtain an overhaul kit a second-hand pump may be worth buying. When you have the impeller removed to fit the new parts, clean the pump very thoroughly to get rid of any deposits of scale.

The car component that is most prone to corrosion is the exhaust system. For this reason it is not worth buying second-hand unless you are lucky enough to come across a damaged car that has only recently come into the breaker's and is fitted with a relatively new exhaust system.

Clutches

Clutches are subjected to a great deal of strain and wear. Buying second-hand is completely inadvisable. As the driven plate becomes worn through use, the pressure plate also wears to compensate. The release bearing deteriorates in turn, so the chances are that if you buy a used unit you will be replacing one worn clutch with another. New parts are not expensive and fitting them is a far easier task than replacing the whole clutch asembly.

It is not worth buying second-hand hydraulic components either, even if you replace rubbers, because the cylinder bores also may be worn. On cable-operated systems, the low price of a new cable makes buying second-hand pointless.

If you need a replacement fly-wheel, however, you can buy from a breaker's yard. Make sure that the bolt holes and dowels line up with your clutch pressure plate. Either take this along with you, or make a cardboard template. Check the fixing to the crankshaft is the same and examine the condition of the fly-wheel ring gear. The teeth should be square edged, without any chips or burrs. The face of the fly-wheel should be smooth and free of any deep scores. Always use a new tab washer, an inexpensive item, when you fit the fly-wheel to your crankshaft.

If for any reason you need a new bell housing, check that your gearbox has one that is detachable. Some are integral with the gearbox casing and cannot be replaced individually. On alloy housings look for fatigue cracks round the flange which mounts the unit to the engine. If any are present, the housing is too weak for service.

Gearboxes

Gearboxes are usually reliable components that give long service. Most wear problems centre on the bearings and the synchromesh rings. Turn the gearbox by hand by twisting the flange that connects it to the propeller shaft or the primary shaft. Listen for any grinding sounds. Remove the top cover by undoing the surrounding bolts taking care not to get dirt into the unit. This will enable you to examine the gears themselves. If the box has any signs of grit or dirt inside the casing, look for another unit. The gears should have no signs of uneven wear or chips on the teeth. If any of the mainshaft gears are suspect, it is likely that the corresponding gear on the layshaft is also going to be worn.

The gears should fit on the shafts with no detectable rock and the synchromesh hubs should be a firm fit on the splines, with no signs of sloppiness. Examine the selector forks, which are usually in the top cover, for signs of wear or any ridges on the working faces.

On some front-engined, rear wheel drive cars it is possible to remove and replace the gearbox without removing the engine from the car. The gearbox can be removed either by lowering it away from underneath the car or by raising it through the floor into the passenger compartment.

However, removing the gearbox from the car yourself can be a difficult job, so while you are making the changeover it is worth considering renewing at least the gaskets on the secondhand unit to save having to remove the box for further attention in the near future.

Secondhand running gear

1 In most large breaker's yards, bulky components like these door panels are removed from the wrecked cars and stored under cover

As described in the previous chapter, breakers' yards are full of useless car parts but there are also many components that can safely be used again. By buying carefully, it is possible for the car owner to reduce his running costs but care and know-how are needed if an expensive mistake is to be avoided.

On many older cars, the cost of new parts is so high that it exceeds the market value of the vehicle. In these cases, the breaker's yard may be the last resort and can save the owner having to scrap his own car and go to the expense of buying a new one.

Drive shafts and final drives

If your car has worn universal joints, it is not worth buying a second-hand unit from a breakers, as new parts are not expensive. But if the replacement is needed because of damage to a part that is not normally subject to wear, buying second-hand can make a useful saving. For example, the flange, housing or shaft may have snapped and a breaker's part will be as good as a new one, also cheaper. To check the condition of a shaft, hold the flange of the shaft with one hand and the flange to which it is connected with the other. Try to twist the flanges in opposite directions (fig. 3). They should not have any detectable movement. Try lifting the shaft as well, as this may show up wear.

Some propeller shafts have a universal joint at one end and a splined connection at the other. Make sure that the splines are not burred or damaged in any way and that there are no dents on the shaft itself.

In general, it is not worth buying constant velocity joints or rubber doughnuts from a breaker as it is difficult for a motorist to assess how much wear is present.

When you consider buying a final drive, you must be able to raise the rear of the car so that you can turn the rear wheels. Check that the car is in neutral. If it is in gear and the gear lever has been removed, disconnect the propeller shaft. Turn the rear wheels or the rear hubs if the wheels have been removed and listen for grinding noises. These may indicate wear or a broken halfshaft. Some cars, particularly the Riley 1.5/Wolseley 1500, are prone to broken halfshafts, so if you are buying a rear axle check this point carefully. If the shaft is broken, there should be no resistance when you try to turn the hub or wheel. If the

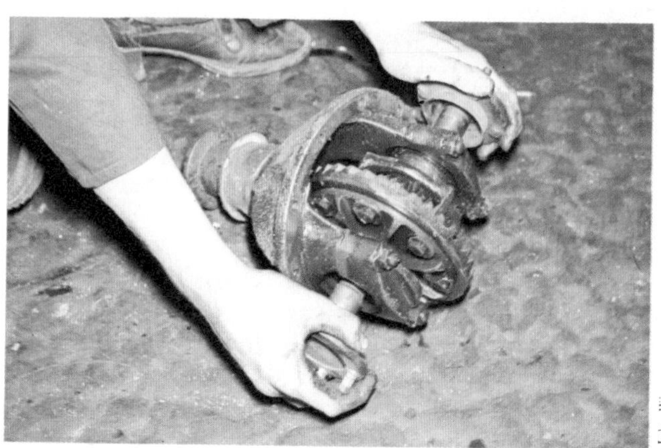

Jake Wynter

2 The best way of checking for wear on a differential. Turn the flanges in opposite directions and feel for play in the gears

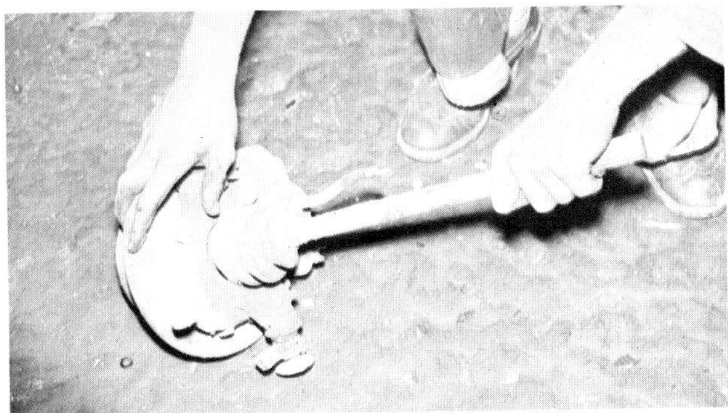

3 Checking a drive shaft like this is best done by "wiggling" the shaft and feeling for play at the point where it joins the hub

4 A complete steering box unit, removed for inspection. Wear in the box itself can be detected by turning the wheel as shown

5 Wear in a steering rack can be checked by removing the unit and then twisting the steering arms. Too much play means it is faulty

shaft is intact, there will be some resistance to rotation. In some types of car, the hub can be pulled straight out if the shaft is broken.

On live rear axles, examine the bearing seals by the hubs for signs of leakage. On all rear axles examine the differential carefully. There should be no signs of fluid seepage around the nose bearing. On cars with independent rear suspension, there should be no leaks around the inner flanges connecting the drive shafts to the casing. Check that the gasket round the rear cover is not leaking, then remove the cover to examine the inside of the differential. The teeth of the gears should have no chips or burrs and the casing should be relatively clean, unmarked and free from grit and dirt (fig. 2).

Before you finally decide to buy a unit, check the condition of any visible threads. If the hubs are still on the axle, examine the wheel studs where disc wheels are fitted or the splines and threads in the case of centre-lock hubs. If the hubs have been removed, examine the condition of the threads on the halfshafts. If the threads are burred you will have trouble fitting the hubs and you may find that your purchase is useless.

Finally, use your notes on specification changes or differences. Some more expensive versions of one particular model may have a limited slip differential. While this might fit a cheaper specification model, you should not fit a standard axle to cars which had a limited slip differential as part of their original specification.

Steering parts

The steering mechanism is one of the most important parts of your car, so do not take chances when buying second-hand. There are parts that you should not buy, not only because they give no saving over buying new, but also because buying them second-hand can be dangerous.

Never be tempted to buy second-hand ball joints or swivel joints. If those on your car have worn, buy new parts. It is quite impossible to gauge the wear on second-hand parts of this type and they can break up when being removed from the car.

There is no reason why you should not buy a second-hand steering rack or box but only after careful examination. It is likely that the components will still be on the car, so test the amount of play present. With an assistant turning the wheel slowly, try to detect any movement in the shaft that runs through the casing on a steering box (fig. 4). On a rack and pinion system hold the steering arms that project from each end of a steering rack and feel for any looseness (fig. 5). Look for any signs of leakage on boxes and racks and check rack gaiters for splits. Split gaiters can be replaced but bear in mind that the internal mechanism may have been damaged by grit.

Some cars are fitted with steering dampers but, as with shock absorbers, it is not worth buying them second-hand. They may not be worn but as you will probably be renewing the damper because the original has worn out, the risk in buying a damper from a breaker is that it may be in the same state. Avoid doing so.

If you want to buy a steering wheel, make sure there are no cracks around the spokes where they join the boss. This is a common failing on many cars which are fitted with plastic wheels and may also be the case with some alloy wheels. If you are after a steering column, rock the wheel up and down to see if the steering column bushes are worn. If there is wear, the bushes will also have to be renewed eventually.

Power-assisted steering mechanisms can be purchased. If you plan to convert your car from manual to power steering, remember that the steering ratio often differs so you will need to buy the steering box as well. If you buy a pump, you will probably have to buy a dynamo with it, as on older models the two are combined. On later cars the pump is often mounted on the steering rack, so make sure you have plenty of tools for removal. The fluid reservoirs for power-assisted steering can also be purchased, providing they have no sign of corrosion or dirt inside. Do not buy second-hand pipes or hoses. If the hydraulic system on power-assisted steering fails, you can still steer the car but the sudden increase in steering effort that may be required can be dangerous, especially if you are travelling at speed through a corner.

It is wise to avoid buying any steering components from a car that has heavy accident damage, particularly if it is at the front end.

Suspension

Buying suspension parts can be one of the more hazardous undertakings in breakers' yards. In many cases it will involve working under precariously poised vehicles and

6 A crashed car like this can often be a useful source of barely-worn parts, but avoid any components around the damage itself

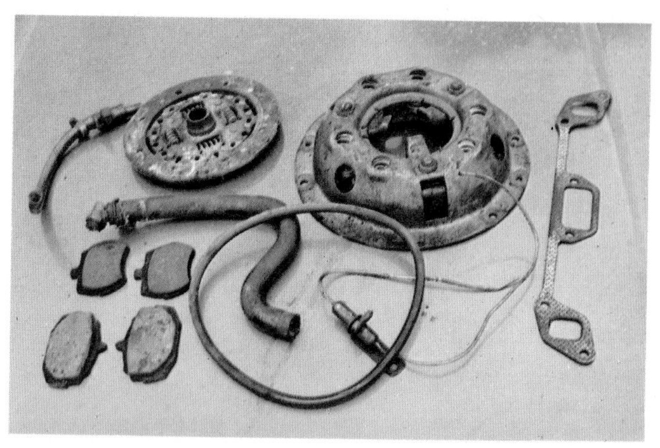

7 Do not buy pipes, hoses, brake pads, clutch plates and gaskets as these are parts which wear naturally

8 As with other suspension components, MacPherson-type struts are best removed for checking. Always renew the damper insert

9 When working on a stacked car, start by making sure that it is absolutely safe. Try to choose one that is readily accessible

removing coil springs, so take great care. The warning given for steering parts with regard to accident damage should also be applied to the suspension. Breakage of such parts in normal usage is rare but it is pointless to take chances for the money being saved.

Many suspension components can be purchased but there are a few that you should avoid. Do not buy rubbers such as suspension bump stops or roll bar bushes, as brand new replacements are inexpensive and a "known quantity". Second-hand shock absorbers "or dampers" are also a false economy. If you want to buy a MacPherson strut assembly (fig. 8), you should renew the damper insert before fitting it to your car.

Providing they are not damaged, you can buy wishbones, trailing arms, radius rods, Panhard rods, uprights and stub-axle housings. Any part of these components that is subject to wear should be replaced before fitting the part to your car. Bushes can be pressed out and new ones fitted and this should give you the added bonus of improved handling and steering response. With uprights and stub-axle housings, check the threads of the stub-axle carefully.

If you are working on a coil spring system, you will probably have to remove the coil spring itself. The procedure involves using special spring-retaining rods. It may be worth checking with your main dealer before buying a coil spring in case different versions of the same model were fitted with springs of different rates. This is particularly relevant where the same bodyshell is used with a variety of engine sizes. Almost invariably, the heavier the engine, the heavier the spring rate.

When buying leaf springs, look for broken leaves or clamps and renew any bushes before fitting the springs to your car. The splines on torsion bars should show no signs of wear. It is best to avoid Hydrolastic suspension units as checking for wear is impractical.

If you buy wheel hubs, check wheel stud threads or the

10 Brake discs are some of the more risky buys at a breaker's. Scoring like this is easily spotted but be beware of warping as well

Jake Wynter

11 The same checks apply for brake calipers and drums like these. Remember to check the inside of a drum for scores and heavy rust

12 This Ford door is typical of the bargains which you may be lucky enough to find when a brand new crashed car is dismantled

13 If you are buying wheels from a breaker, inspect them well before committing yourself because they may be slightly warped

splines on centre-lock hubs. Always renew the wheel bearings. If you want to change your car from disc to wire wheels, careful buying from a breaker can provide you with all the parts you need.

Check that anti-roll bars are not bent through damage and renew any rubber bushes before installing them.

In all cases, where the car is resting off the ground, it can be impossible to check the level of the car and so detect any droop in the suspension. In this circumstance, examine all components very closely.

Braking systems

More than with any other part of the car, you should exercise extreme care if you buy second-hand brake parts. Brake failure can be unnerving at the least and possibly fatal. For this reason, you should never buy second-hand master or wheel cylinders, brake shoes or pads.

Hydraulic cylinders are a completely unknown quantity. On your own car, you know how well they are working and it is possible to replace the rubbers as they wear out. With a second-hand cylinder, however, you cannot tell at a glance how worn the bore is and even renewing the rubbers might not make the unit totally safe to use.

New brake shoes or pads are inexpensive and will last many times longer than used items. It is a dangerous practice to penny-pinch where such important components are concerned. Similarly, you should never buy used brake pipes or hoses. The pipes may be excessively corroded while worn hydraulic hoses might well burst in use. You could buy a brake pipe union, as these are made of brass and are not subject to wear.

It is possible to buy brake drums or discs, but you should carefully check for any scoring (figs. 10 and 11). Further, these components can be out of "true"—something you cannot accurately judge in a breaker's yard.

If you decide to buy a caliper, you should renew the piston seals. While the pistons are removed, make sure the bores are not pitted and that the faces of the pistons are smooth and free from surface corrosion. Before actually removing the caliper, it is a good idea to see that you can undo the bleed nipple. These can become so tight that they break off when you try to undo them and cannot be removed even with an extractor tool. As the brakes will have to be bled once the caliper is fitted, you could end up wasting money.

Brake pedals and handbrake levers can be purchased, as can separate handbrake calipers of the kind fitted to some Jaguars. Be prepared to re-build these before fitting.

Handbrake cables will probably have become stretched, so buying these from a breaker is not worthwhile. Brake shoe return springs are also false economy, so you should buy these items new. You could renew the moving parts of a vacuum servo unit but, like hydraulic cylinders, the condition of the unit is not known and this can lead to problems eventually.

Wheels and tyres

Breakers do not usually charge much for wheels and tyres and to some people this is sufficient incentive to buy these items second-hand.

If you buy wheels, removing them from a car is less of a gamble than selecting them from a pile. Look for any damage to the rims, such as sharp edges or deformations (fig. 13). Check that the bolt holes have not become elongated. You can do this by searching the yard for a car with suitable hubs and trying the wheel in position. Use the wheel stud as a guide to the concentricity of the stud hole.

Check the spokes on wire wheels to see if any are loose or buckled, then examine the splines for signs of wear or damage. If a breaker obtains a car fitted with alloy wheels, they will usually be sold quickly. If you are lucky enough to be there when they come in, examine them carefully for fatigue cracks round the spokes and the centre before you snap them up.

If you do get the chance to buy wheels that are still attached to the car, make sure the car has no accident damage. If it has, it is possible that the car may have struck a kerb, deforming the wheel. When you have bought the wheels, have them correctly balanced before fitting them on your car.

It is possible to buy tyres from breakers' yards, but you should consider the implications of using second-hand equipment, as well as the sort of driving you use your car for. If you generally drive fast, buying second-hand tyres can be suicidal. Even under normal town driving you should avoid striking kerbs with your tyres and running over debris. When you buy used tyres, you have no way of telling if the car has been subjected to this kind of maltreatment, so you are immediately taking a risk.

Body parts

Body parts are in many respects safer and easier to buy from a breaker than any other part of the car because you can see at a glance whether the component is worth buying. Breakers' yards are a haven for body parts and prices asked for them are usually reasonable.

If you want replacement glass, check for any scratches or stone chips. Check the chromium plate on bumpers, radiator grilles and any other brightwork. Make sure that the parts you buy will fit your model, for many manufacturers

14 With older panels, rust is likely to be a problem. A tap with a chisel should reveal just how bad the corrosion has become

differentiate between models by adding more trim. Buying trim from a breaker can give your car the appearance of a more expensive model.

Welded wings can be difficult to remove from the old car, but represent a considerable saving over new panels.

16 Heaters are often good value at the breaker's. Having removed one from a car, check the core of the matrix for blockages

17 Wiper motors and starter motors can also be a good buy. Where possible, have your choice tested on a battery to ensure it works

18 The condition of coils, dynamos and alternators is often more difficult to assess. Do not be fooled by clean exterior surfaces

15 In many larger breaker's yards you will find that ancillary components have been removed and stored separately

A sharp chisel can be useful to break the spot welds. If you remove glass-fibre wings from a car, they will probably be held in place by nuts and bolts. Before you take the panel off, examine it carefully for cracks and bear in mind that many glass-fibre panels are a poor fit, leaving large gaps at each edge where they butt up to other panels.

Before you decide to buy a door remove the door trim and check the inside for any signs of rust. This frequently occurs because the drain taps at the bottom of the door become blocked (fig. 14). Check, too, that the door is a snug fit and has not become warped. Most external body panels can be purchased but some may prove difficult to remove.

Inside the car, most parts can be useful, but again the condition is the critical factor. Before buying window winder mechanisms, check that they work properly. Do the same for seat mechanisms such as recliners and adjusters. Check carpets and trim for mildew and the seats for broken springs or damaged frames.

On no account should you buy second-hand seat belts, whether the car has been in an accident or not. As with tyres, it is not worth taking the chance.

Electrical parts

Most electrical components can be exchanged for reconditioned units quite cheaply in which case buying from a breaker is a waste of time and money. Lamp lenses can be purchased, though, and warning lights can be useful.

Instruments can also be purchased but there is no guarantee that they will work. Breakers' yards can be a useful source of extra dials if you can find a late model car that is in good condition.

Finally, always remember that steering, suspension or braking systems that have been re-built with second-hand parts may injure yourself, your passengers and other road users should any part fail.

Jake Wynter

19 If you can find units to fit your car, light clusters are good value as they are easily checked. Beware of buying gauges though

Learning to weld

1 Making this crawler trolley is a simple welding job. It is one of the many things that can be made to aid car maintenance

Welding adds a new dimension to the home workshop and, when done on a small scale with the basic equipment described here, can open up a whole new field of activity for the d-i-y mechanic.

Welding offers the neatest means of joining ferrous metals like iron and steel, although special electrodes are available for joining a number of dissimilar metals. The two pieces of metal are united by partially melting the substance of one piece into that of the other. A welded joint requires no large area of overlap under normal circumstances and can be much smaller in area than a rivetted one.

There are two basic types of fusion welding. One is gas welding, which from the amateur's point of view needs expensive equipment, a great deal of practice to achieve the correct type of flame, and cumbersome gas cylinders. In unskilled hands, gas welding can be dangerous. The other type is electrical or arc welding and calls for much simpler apparatus which can easily be bought or hired. Above all, relatively little practice is needed to produce a first-class job. Because of the low current consumption, there is no danger of electrocution, and with proper elementary safety precautions, the equipment is perfectly safe to use.

Home welding sets can be bought relatively cheaply but are not really satisfactory in the hands of unskilled operators. For the casual d-i-y welder it is far cheaper to hire the apparatus for as long as he needs it. The cost of running the equipment is very low and the only other expense is the electrode rods which can be bought quite cheaply in a variety of thicknesses in packs.

The equipment comprises a transformer which runs off the normal household power supply, the holder into which the electrode fits, a protective head shield containing a dark vision glass, a stiff wire brush and a cross-pane hammer, preferably with one pointed end.

The transformer changes the domestic power supply to a safe voltage and passes it through an electrode, called a welding rod. This is a pencil-like object with a metallic core and a flux coating. At one end, as with a pencil, a 'dot' of metal in the middle of the rod is exposed. At the other, a short length of the rod is left bare of flux so that it will make an electrical connection with the electrode holder. When a low voltage, high amperage current is passed through the electrode it jumps a fraction of an inch to the article being welded. This creates the welding arc—in effect, a continuous spark—which produces a heat in excess of 3,600°C (6,500°F), liquefying both the tip of the electrode and the edge of the workpiece. Thus the joint is heated to a molten state and the extra metal from the rod fuses it together.

Leading from the transformer are two heavy-duty cables—they are thick to allow for the high amperage which has to be carried and they must not be replaced or extended with ordinary domestic cable. One of these cables, called the welding return lead, normally terminates in a clip or clamp. This is fixed to the article being welded. The other cable is joined to the electrode holder into which is clamped the welding rod. It is always wise to use an earthing cable to guard against any failure of the system. This cable should be attached to the work at one end and to a suitable earthing point at the other. Should you accidentally complete the circuit by touching both electrode and workpiece, a comparatively small current will flow giving you nothing more serious than a slight tingling sensation. At no time can this output rise to a dangerous level.

Safety precautions

Welding constitutes a fire hazard and, because sparks and particles of molten metal may fly some distance, you should ensure that there are no flammable materials anywhere near where you want to work. Oil-soaked rags, petrol, paraffin, white spirits, open cans of paint and plastics should be kept well out of the way. Keep a small fire extinguisher on hand, or, at the very least, a bucket of water.

The welding screen is for the protection of your eyes and your face. It not only reduces the dangerous ultra-violet rays released during welding, which can blind you, but it allows you to watch exactly what you are doing. Dark goggles of the type used in gas welding are not suitable because they offer no protection for the rest of the face and with electrical welding extremely hot sparks fly. Because of this, never weld in shirt sleeves or with light clothing on. Ideally you should wear a leather apron but failing that wear an old jacket buttoned up or a full overall, and wear leather or asbestos gloves. Where possible always try to keep your work horizontal, as the dangers, for example of welding above your head, are obvious.

Welding produces heat; the end of the electrode and the weld line both become molten. Therefore do not handle either without first letting them cool, unless you wear heavy industrial gloves. Do not lay the electrode on the bench where you may inadvertently touch the hot end. A pair of pliers or tongs are ideal for handling the hot workpiece.

Although the welding current is low, do not stand on a damp floor and do not weld out of doors unless it is a dry day.

Choosing electrodes

There is no hard and fast rule by which a particular gauge is selected. This is determined by the type of weld in relation to the thickness of the workpiece. A butt weld in 1.6 mm (16 gauge) steel sheet can be made by using either a 2 mm (14 gauge) or 1.6 mm electrode, the only real difference being that the thicker 2 mm electrode will do the job more quickly.

The degree to which the surface of the workpiece will be melted and re-cast by the intensity of the electrical arc is termed penetration and the greatest penetration results from the use of the larger gauge size electrodes. However, over-penetration may result if too thick a gauge is used and this means that the puddle of liquid metal will extend through to the other side and then drop out. This is called blow-through (fig. 2).

As a general guide a 1.6 mm electrode should be used for welding 1.0 to 1.6 mm material, 2 mm electrode for 1.6 to 2.5 mm material and a 2.5 mm electrode for 2.5 to 6 mm thick plate. For metal thicker than this a 3.25 mm electrode can be used, using what is called the multiple-run technique (fig. 3) to build up a large weld deposit.

It can be difficult to effectively arc weld material thinner than 1.2 mm. The thickness of the metal used on the great majority of car bodies produced today is rarely more than 1 mm (about 20 gauge). To work on such thin metal really requires more specialized equipment than conventional welding gear.

Selecting amperage

All that remains to be done is to decide on the amperage output of the transformer, using the selector switch provided. Each different sized electrode has a recommended current setting and generally four settings are available: 60amps, 75amps, 90amps and 100amps which are suitable for 1.6, 2.0, 2.5 and 3.25 mm electrodes respectively.

The selection of the current setting is largely a question of experience and, as with all things, there is a right way of welding and a wrong way. The correct current, the proper electrode and the right speed of the weld will produce a clean joint without spatter as shown in fig. 5. If the speed at which the electrode is moved is too slow, there will be a broad build-up of metal and lack of fusion at the edge due to the inclusion of the slag which forms on the molten metal. Too slow a speed on thin metal will result in over-penetration with a risk of burning through.

If the current is too low again the build-up is high. With too high a current, the weld is very shallow with excessive spatter—this means that particles of molten metal are thrown out and stick to the surface on either side of the joint. With correct current and proper electrode gap, too fast a speed of weld will be characterized by a very narrow and hence weak weld line (fig. 5).

It is worth spending half an hour with some offcuts of scrap metal and deliberately varying current, electrode gap and speed so as to gain experience. A good weld should be clean, uniform in appearance and should (in the case of a butt joint) protrude slightly above the surface of the metal.

Types of joint

There are basically only three types of joint encountered in welding: end-to-end joining, overlapped, and end-to surface joins. Three different welding techniques are used depending on the particular job. These are the fillet, the butt, and the edge weld.

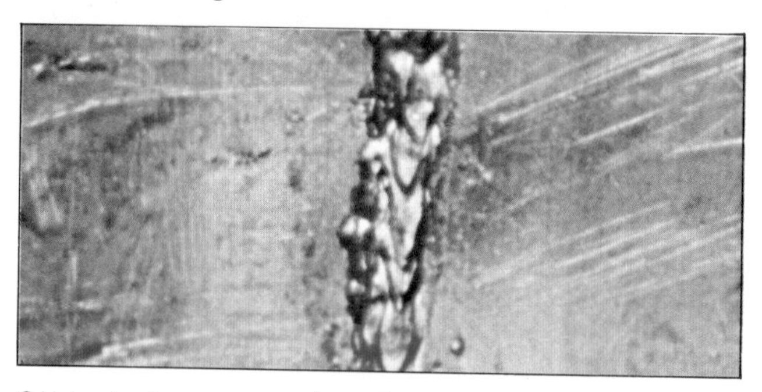

2 Using too large a gauge electrode causes molten metal to burn right through the workpiece. This is called blow-through

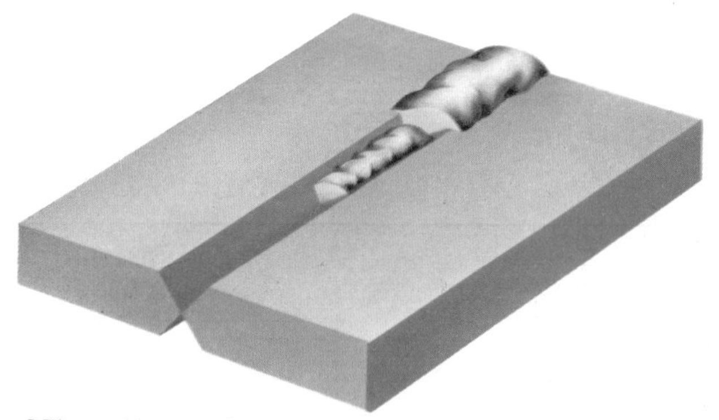

3 The multi-run technique involves laying several runs of weld deposit on top of one another to build up the joint

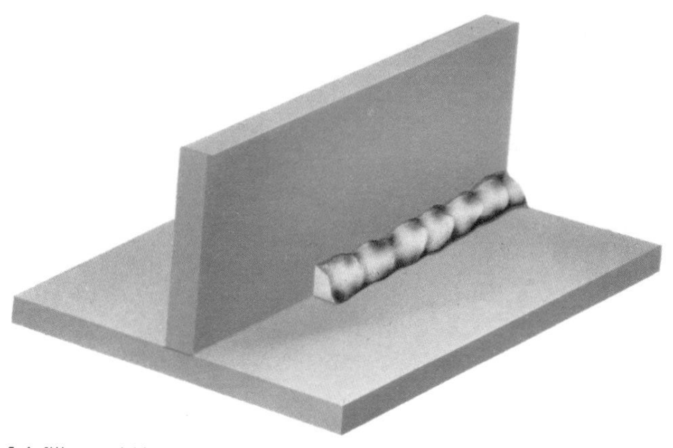

4 A fillet weld is used where two pieces of metal meet at a right angle. It consists of a deposit of weld along the join

The fillet is used where two pieces meet at a right angle and consists of a deposit of weld material along the join. No chamfering of the metal is needed under most conditions (fig. 4).

With a butt weld, where two pieces of metal are joined in the same plane, some preparation is necessary in order to offer the best conditions for fusion. If, for example, the pieces were welded in the 'as cut' state (just as hacksawed), it would be very difficult to achieve any penetration and the major portion of the weld would be on the surface. This would mean a weak and unsightly joint. The proper treatment is to chamfer the two edges with a file so as to produce a V-shaped trough. This not only makes it easier to contain a neat weld but it actually increases the surface area of the joint (fig. 6).

Edge welding is encountered where, as an example, two pieces of bar cross each other. In some instances, this will take the form of a fillet weld, but in other cases, as when two ends come together in the same plane (fig. 7 where one piece is welded on top of another), it calls for the fusing together of a double edge. With metal up to, say 2.5 mm in thickness, no preparation is needed and the weld is just made along the joint. With thicker pieces, though, the edge weld is replaced by the butt weld technique, calling for the chamfering of both pieces.

Because a weld may start wherever the electrode touches the workpiece, it is very difficult to weld into a corner, particularly if it forms an angle of less than about 60°. Sometimes working in corners can be avoided by welding the outside edges of the two pieces.

Learning to weld

If you propose to work on a motor vehicle with welding equipment it is essential to disconnect both terminals of the battery. Failure to do so may result in severe damage to the vehicle's electrical system.

If working in a workshop, first firmly secure the pieces to be welded on the bench using clamps. Soft iron wire (an old coathanger for instance) can be used to hold pieces tightly together. Connect the earth lead to part of it using the clamp provided. Never let anybody hold the workpiece during welding.

The initial arc is 'struck' by bringing the electrode into contact with the metal, using a light tapping action. Any initial difficulty in striking the arc will be due either to dirt on the workpiece or to the flux shield of the electrode preventing metal-to-metal contact. Once the arc is started, withdraw the electrode slightly, or tilt it, to create a slight gap—it is this gap which creates the extreme heat of the arc, melting the electrode core wire and protective flux and the areas of base metal directly underneath the electric arc.

To maintain the arc, the electrode is moved steadily in one direction, either maintaining the gap by visual control or by tilting the electrode so that it rests lightly on the workpiece. If you hold the electrode too close to the work, the arc will break and the electrode will stick. A quick twist of the wrist usually frees it. Otherwise you will have to switch off and chisel off the rod.

To stop welding, all you have to do is withdraw the electrode to break the arc.

One drawback of gas welding is that so much heat is put into the job that distortion may easily occur during cooling, and this often means cracking. With electrical welding, the amount of heat is extremely localized, so the problem does not arise. However, if you are attempting a long butt weld of, say, more than 100 mm (4in.), it is advisable to tack-weld each end first to prevent creep or loss of alignment. Tack-welds are small runs of weld approximately 15 mm (½in.) long which will hold the components in an assembled position prior to final welding.

Unlike gas welding, electrical welding produces a deposit of slag over the molten metal and when cooled this forms a very hard crust. Before you can truly assess the quality of your welding this must be chipped off with a hammer and scrubbed with a wire brush. All the slag must be removed before painting your finished handiwork or rust may set in.

When removing slag from welds, it is advisable to wear a pair of clear glass safety goggles or a clear plastic face shield.

5 A perfect single and multiple-run weld (right). Spatter from too high a current (centre). Weld made too quickly (left)

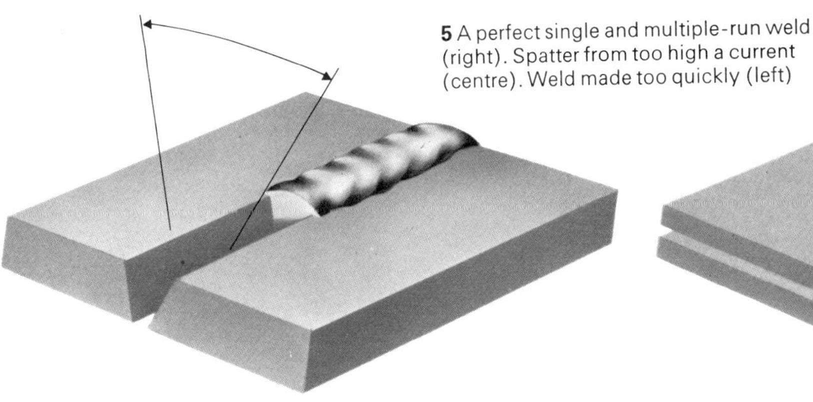

6 Chamfering the ends of a butt joint to a V-shaped angle makes a trough for the weld deposit and gives a strong joint

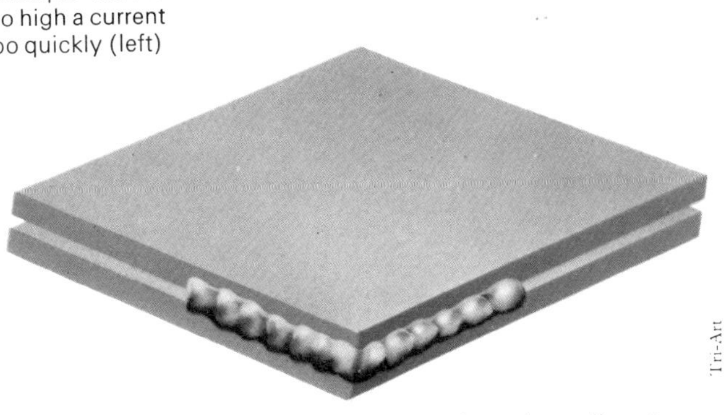

7 An edge weld is made where two pieces of metal, usually not thicker than 2.5 mm each, are joined on top of each other

Where to buy it

Most of the components and accessories referred to in this book are available from major accessory stores. In case of difficulty, we recommend contacting the following manufacturers and suppliers:

Car radios, pages 9-12:
Audioline from Harry Moss International Ltd., 424, Kingston Road, London SW20 8LT
Binatone from Binatone International, Parkar House, Beresford Avenue, Wembley, Middlesex HA0 1YX
Bird from Sydney S. Bird & Sons Ltd., Fleets Lane, Poole, Dorset BH15 3BW
Blaupunkt from Robert Bosch Ltd., P.O. Box 166, Rhodes Way, Radlett Road, Watford WD2 4LB
Clarion from Norse Audio Systems Ltd., 9, Hawksworth Trading Estate, Swindon SN2 1DZ
Hitachi from Hitachi Sales (UK) Ltd., Hitachi House, Station Road, Hayes, Middlesex UB3 4DR
Lucas from Lucas Electrical Ltd., Parts and Service Division, Great Hampton Street, Birmingham B18 6AU
Motoradio from Motoradio Ltd., Sett End Road, Shadworth Industrial Estate, Blackburn, Lancashire BB1 2PT
Motorola from Motorola Ltd., Automotive Products Division, Taylors Road, Stotfold, Hitchin, Hertfordshire SG5 4AY
National Panasonic from National Panasonic (UK) Ltd., 308, Bath Road, Slough, Berkshire SL3 6JB
Pioneer from Pioneer High Fidelity (GB) Ltd., Pioneer House, The Ridgeway, Iver, Buckinghamshire SL0 9JL
Philips from Philips Electrical Ltd., Century House, Shaftesbury Avenue, London WC2
Radiomobile from Radiomobile Ltd., Goodwood Works, Cricklewood, London NW2

Tape players, pages 13-17:
Academy from Kohli & Co. Ltd., Preston Street, Bradford, W. Yorks BD7 1LU
Aiwa from Aiwa Sales & Service UK Ltd., 30-32, Concord Road, Westwood Park Trading Estate, Acton, London W3 0TH
Amstrad from A.M.S. Trading (Amstrad) Ltd., 89, Ridley Road, Dalston, London E8
Astor from Mitchell Overseas Co. Ltd., 79, Uxbridge Road, London W7 3ST
Audioline from Harry Moss International Ltd., 424, Kingston Road, London SW20 8LT
Blaupunkt from Robert Bosch Ltd., Rhodes Way, Watford WD2 4LB
Clarion from Norse Audio Systems Ltd., 9, Hawksworth Trading Estate, Swindon SN2 1DZ, Wiltshire
Eagle from Eagle International, Precision Centre, Heather Park Drive, Wembley, Middx HA0 1SU
Hanimex from Hanimex (UK) Ltd., Dorcan Industrial Estate, Swindon, Wiltshire
Hitachi from Hitachi Sales (UK) Ltd., Hitachi House, Station Road, Hayes, Middx UB3 4DR
Lucas Audio from Lucas Electrical Ltd., Parts and Service Division, Great Hampton Street, Birmingham B18 6AU
Motoradio from Motoradio Ltd., Sett End Road, Shadworth Industrial Estate, Blackburn BB1 2PT
Motorola from Motorola Ltd., Automotive Products Division, Taylors Road, Stotfold, Hitchin, Herts
National Panasonic from National Panasonic (UK) Ltd., 308, Bath Road, Slough, Berks
Philips from Philips Electrical Ltd., City House, 420-430 London Road, Croydon CR9 3QR
Pioneer from Autocar Electrical Equipment Ltd., Chantry Road Industrial Estate, Kempston, Bedford
Pye from Pye Ltd., Car Radio Division, P.O. Box 49, Cambridge CB4 1DS
Radiomobile from Radiomobile Ltd., Goodwood Works, North Circular Road, Cricklewood, London NW2 7JS
Roadstar from Javelin Electronics (Sales) Ltd., Second Way, Exhibition Grounds, Wembley, Middx HA9 0UA
Sanyo from Sanyo Marubeni (UK) Ltd., Sanyo House, Greycaine Road, Watford, Herts
Sharp from Sharp Electronics (UK) Ltd., 107, Hulme Hall Lane, Manchester M10 8HL

Buying aerials, pages 18-22:
Sprint from Sprint Motor Accessory Ltd., 20, Martlesham Heath, Ipswich IP1 1LJ
Maystar from M. A. Distributors Ltd., Industrial House, Conway Street, Hove, Sussex BN3 3LV
Radiomobile from Radiomobile Ltd., Goodwood Works, North Circular Road, Cricklewood, London NW2 7JS
Paddy Hopkirk from Mill Accessory Group Ltd., Two Counties Mill, Eaton Bray, Dunstable, Beds
Binatone from J. Parkar and Co. (London) Ltd., Parkar House, Beresford Avenue, Wembley, Middlesex HA0 1YX
Tragonic from Tragonic Ltd., Apex House, 23-25 Hythe Road, London NW10 6RT
K & K from K & K Ltd., Unit 5, Melinite Industrial Estate, Watford WD2 4DB
Bosch from Robert Bosch Ltd., Rhodes Way, Radlett Road, Watford

Fitting a console, pages 35-41:
Sprint console from Sprint Motor Accessory Service Ltd., Distribution House, Martlesham Heath, Ipswich, Suffolk

Custom fascias, pages 42-48:
Autoplas from Autoplas, 90, Main Road, Hawkwell, Essex SS5 4JH
Rokee from Rokee Ltd., 26, Queen's Road, Coventry CV1 3DQ

Soundproofing, pages 49-54:
Sound Service kit from Sound Service (Oxford) Ltd., 55, West End, Witney, Oxon

Steering wheels, pages 55-58:
Alexander from Alexander Engineering Co., Ltd., Thame Road, Haddenham, Aylesbury, Buckinghamshire HP17 8BZ
Astrali from Astrali Accessories (Midlands) Ltd., Anglian Road, Redhouse Industrial Estate, Aldridge, Staffordshire WS9 8EP
Formula from Formula Steering Wheels (1978) Ltd., Brewhouse Yard, Off Queen Street, Gravesend, Kent DA12 1AU
Intersport from Intersport Motor Products, 14-20 Brunswick Street, Hanley, Stoke-on-Trent, Staffordshire ST1 1DR
Momo from John Brown Wheels Ltd., Wedgnock Lane, Wedgnock Industrial Estate, Warwickshire CV34 5YA
Motec from Brown and Geeson Ltd, Selinas Lane, Dagenham, Essex RM8 1EA

Car horns, pages 59-63:
Alexander Engineering Co. Ltd., Thame Road, Haddenham, Aylesbury, Buckinghamshire HP17 8BZ
Autocar Marine and Diesel Co. Ltd., Cranbourne Industrial Estate, Gosport, Hampshire
Robert Bosch Ltd., P.O. Box 166, Rhodes Way, Radlett Road, Watford, Herts WD2 4LB
Hella Automobile Equipment Ltd., Daventry Road Industrial Estate, Banbury, Oxon
Klamix Marketing Services Ltd., Arrow Road, Redditch, Worcestershire
Lucas (Sales and Service) Ltd., Great Hampton Street, Birmingham B18 6AH
Lyall Lusted Ltd., Vincent Works, Vincent Lane, Dorking, Surrey
Mill Accessory Group, Two Counties Mill, Eaton Bray, Bedfordshire
Harry Moss Ltd., 424, Kingston Road, London SW20 8LJ
Spring Motor Accessory Service Ltd., Distribution House, 20, Martlesham Heath, Ipswich IP1 1LT
Wipac Group Sales Ltd., London Road Buckingham MK18 1BH

Buying seats, pages 65-68:
ASS from Big J Auto Parts/Claritypart Ltd., Jayembee House, 46, Camden High Street, London NW1
Cobra from Cobra Automotive Products Ltd., Heslop, Halesfield 23, Telford, Salop TF7 4EW
Corbeau from Corbeau Equipe Ltd., Ivyhouse Lane, The Ridge, Hastings, Sussex TN35 2UN
Huntmaster from Stylex Motor Products Ltd., Hollands Road, Haverhill, Suffolk
Karobes from Karobes Ltd., Queensway, Royal Leamington Spa, Warwickshire CV31 3JR
Paddy Hopkirk from Mill Accessory Group Ltd., Two Counties Mill, Eaton Bray, Nr Dunstable, Bedfordshire LU6 2JH
Recaro from Wood and Pickett Ltd., Abbey Road, Park Royal, London NW10 7SA
Restall from Restall Bros. Ltd., Anne Road, Smethwick, Warley, West Midlands B66 2NZ

Anti-theft devices, pages 69-72:
Freeline Autoguard from Freeline Ltd., 11, Brook Gate, South Liberty Lane, Bristol BS3 2UN
Krooklok from Brown Bros. Engineering, 1A Manorgate Road, Kingston-upon-Thames
BMS Immobiliser from The Lunken Co. Ltd., BMS Division, 299, Gander Green Lane, Sutton, Surrey
Petromag from Ross Courtney & Co. Ltd., Terminal House, Elthorne Road, London N19
Autosafe from Autosafe Ltd., Trinity Road, Richmond, Surrey
Watchdog ESM/12 and VDL from Watchdog Products Ltd., P.O. Box 27, London N3
Tragonic Tiger from Tragonic Sales Ltd., Apex House, 23/25, Hythe Road, London NW10 6RT
Simba Intertialarm and mortise dead-lock unit from Simba Car Alarms Ltd., Security House, Occupation Road, London SE17
Gnomist from Gnomist International Ltd., Brigitta Maria House, Grove Road, Waltham Forest, London E17
Lander Universal Mini Lock from Lander Alarm Co. Ltd. (Scotland), Rosyth Road, Glasgow G5 0YA

Flared wheel arches, pages 81-85:
Pit Stop car accessories, Beckenham, Kent

Vinylizing, pages 86-89:
Kits from Karobes Ltd., Queensway, Leamington Spa, Warwicks., or Kumficar Products Ltd., Albert Mills, Brighouse, Yorks

Fitting a spoiler, pages 97-101:
Spoilers from Richard Grant Motor Accessories Ltd., The Pines Garage, Tring Road, Edlesborough, Dunstable, Beds
Isopon from W David and Sons Ltd., Northway House, High Road, Whetstone, London, N20 9LR
Holts Cataloy from Holts Products Ltd., Vulcan Way, New Addington, Surrey
Dupli-color aerosol paint from Lloyds Industries, Lloyds House, Handfords, Wilmslow, Cheshire

Personalized wheels, pages 102-105:
Weller Racing Wheels Ltd., Portland House, Lamberts Road, North Farm Industrial Estate, Tunbridge Wells
Dunlop Wheel Division, Foleshill, Coventry
Cobra Automotive Products Ltd., Heslop, Halesfield 23, Telford, Salop TF7 4EW
Custom Accessories, 57, London Road, Romford, Essex
100+ International Ltd., Hainge Road, Tividale, Warley, West Midlands B69 2NY
Revolution Wheels, Chroma House, Restmor Way, Wallington, Surrey SM6 7AG
Tech Del Ltd., 32/36, Telford Way, Brunel Road, Acton, London W3 7SXD
Americar, 27, Bridge Street, Newport, Gwent
Midland Metallic, Rowleys Green Lane, Longford, Coventry CV6 6AN
Cosmic G.T. International Ltd., Mount Street, Walsall WS1 3PG, West Midlands
John Brown Wheels Ltd., Wedgnock Lane, Warwick
Mamba Wheels Ltd., Washer Lane Works, Kings Cross, Halifax HX2 7DX
Wolfrace Wheels, Elms Industrial Estate, Shuttleworth Road, Goldington, Bedford
Ripspeed International, 424/426, Hertford Road, Edmonton, London N9
Tyres & Wheels, 257/259, Portland Road, South Norwood, London SE25

Door and wing mirrors, pages 106-111:
Desmo Ltd., Pensnett, Brierley Hill, West Midlands DY6 7NR
Autosafe, Trinity Road, Richmond, Surrey TW9 2LG
London Bankside Products, Winchmore Hill, Amersham, Bucks HP7 0NZ
Polco Products Ltd., Brent Works, Catherine Wheel Road, Brentford, Middx TW8 8BB
Magnatex Ltd., Bath Road, Heathrow, Hounslow, Middx
F. Claudet Ltd., Ivel Road, Shefford, Beds
Hella Automotive Equipment Ltd., Daventry Road Industrial Estate, Banbury, Oxon
Raydyot Ltd., Waterfall Lane, Cradley Heath, Warley, W. Midlands B64 6QB
Harry Moss International Ltd., 424, Kingston Road, SW20 8LJ
Alexander Engineering Co. Ltd., Thame Road, Haddenham, Aylesbury, Bucks HP17 8BZ
Barnet Plastics, Viaduct Works, Walnut Tree Close, Guildford, Surrey
Mill Accessory Group Ltd., (Paddy Hopkirk), Eaton Bray, Beds
Britax (Wingard) Ltd., Chertsey Road, Byfleet, Surrey

Auxiliary lamps, pages 112-115:
Cibié from Cibié-Britover (Continental) Ltd., Stewkley Road, Soulbury, Leighton Buzzard, Beds, LU7 0EQ
Marchal from Marchal Distributors Ltd., Great West Road, Brentford, Middx
Hella from Hella Automobile Equipment Ltd., Daventry Road Industrial Estate, Banbury, Oxon, OX16 7JU
Bosch from Robert Bosch Ltd., Rhodes Way, Radlett Road, Watford, Herts, WD2 4LB
Carello from Lyall Lusted Ltd., Vincent Works, Vincent Lane, Dorking, Surrey, RH4 3HJ
Lucas from Lucas Electrical Ltd., Parts and Service Division, Great Hampton Street, Birmingham, B18
Raydyot from Raydyot Ltd., Waterfall Lane, Cradley Heath, Warley, West Midlands, B64 6QB
Wipac from Wipac Group Sales Ltd., London Road, Buckingham, MK18 1BH
Lumax from Ceag Ltd., Langdale Road, Barnsley, Yorks, S71 1AX
Stadium from Stadium Ltd., Queensway, Enfield, Middx, EN3 4SD

Washers and gauges, pages 122-136:
Trico-Folberth Ltd., Great West Road, Brentford, Middlesex, TW8 9HP

Meters and gauges, pages 162-182:
Smiths from Smiths Industries Ltd., Cricklewood Works, London NW2 6NN
Jaeger from British Jaeger Instruments Ltd., Edgware Road, London NW2
Time from Time Instrument Manufacturers Ltd., 928, High Road, Finchley, London N12
Speedwell from Speedwell of Chesham Ltd., 260/300, Berkhamstead Road, Chesham, Bucks
Tayaki and Veglia Borletti from Harry Moss (International) Ltd., 424, Kingston Road, London SW20 8LJ
Hella accessories kit from Hella Automobile Equipment Ltd., Daventry Road, Industrial Estate, Banbury, Oxon
Sanpet from Jamex (UK) Ltd., Albion Industrial Estate, Kingfield Road, Coventry CV6 5PZ

Exhausts, pages 183-186:
Bosal (UK) Ltd., 330, Walton Summit Road, Bamber Bridge, Preston, Lancashire PR5 8AL
Peco Silencers Ltd., Sandford Street, Birkenhead, Merseyside L41 1AZ
Grundy Auto Products Ltd., Tafarnaubach Industrial Estate, Tredegar, Gwent, Wales NP2 3XY
Janspeed Engineering Ltd., Southampton Road, Salisbury, Wiltshire SP1 2LN
Howe Exhausts, Main Road, West Kingsdown, nr Brands Hatch, Kent
T. I. Bainbridge Silencers Ltd., Bolton Road, Atherton, nr Manchester M29 9DU

Jacks, ramps and hoists, pages 228-232:
Metallifacture Johnson Sales Ltd., 240-6, Huntingdon Street, Nottingham NG1 3ND
Lake and Elliot Jacks and Equipment Ltd., Chapel Hill, Braintree, Essex
Haltrac Ltd., 119-123 Sandycombe Lane, Richmond, Surrey
GLT Motor Accessories, Spring Vale Industrial Estate, Cwmbran, Gwent

Index

Numerals in *italics* refer to illustrations